KRLA ARCHIVES

KRLA
Chronological Archives
Volume 4
February 12, 1966, to MaY 21, 1966

KRLA ARCHIVES

The KRLA Beat maintained its regular printing schedule during the months covered in this reprint volume.

The Beatles and the Rolling Stones continued to command a strong presence. It was clear that other bands would have a strong impact on the teen scene, including The Mamas and the Papas, The Turtles, The Kinks, The Hollies, The Byrds and The Who. Sonny & Cher continued to get a lot of coverage. Plus they covered other bands that didn't end up having as much staying power, like Sam Shamm and the Pharaohs, Barry Sadler, Herman's Hermits, Freddie and the Dreamers, Nancy Sinatra... the list goes on and on.

Despite being anything but rock and roll, even Barbara Streisand made an appearance or two, as did the Batman TV Show actors and others.

The Adventures of Robin Boyd, originally conceived as a short series of articles, continued to make a presence in most issues, as did a movie feature. There were articles on what to do if you met a star And The back cover featured ads including those for Hullabaloo. Everything you could want on a weekly basis.

In presenting these original issues, we've moved a few of the pages around to ensure that the spreads still lined up. Not a big deal to most people unless you are severly OCD and have access to the original issues.

Copyright © 2016 White Lightning Publishing

KRLA ARCHIVES

America's Largest Teen NEWSpaper

KRLA *Edition* BEAT

Brian Jones: Two Girls in Every Town and a Riot With Every Concert

KRLA ARCHIVES

KRLA BEAT

Volume 1, Number 49   February 19, 1966

BRIAN EPSTEIN or "Eppy" as the Beatles affectionately call him, made an announcement recently which stands to make him considerably rich—if that's possible! And it is, believe us, it definitely is!!

Epstein Pulls Pop Coup Of The Year

LONDON—The man who set pop on its ear roughly two years ago when he succeeded in capturing the world's attention by introducing John, Paul, George and Ringo has evoked the show business coup of all time by merging his fantastically successful Nems Enterprises with the Vic Lewis Agency.

Brian Epstein has always had money—only now he has more. As you know, Nems Enterprises handles 16 top folk and pop groups, among whom are the Beatles, Gerry & the Pacemakers, Billy J. Kramer, Cilla Black, the Moody Blues, the Silkie and the Fourmost.

But apparently 16 acts and several million dollars were not nearly enough to keep the ambitious Epstein busy so he decided to merge with Vic Lewis thus bringing a combination of 500 British and American artists under their protective wing. Lewis' clients include Donovan as well as orchestra leaders Henry Mancini and David "The Stripper" Rose.

The Lewis-Nems merger was only the first of Epstein's two announcements. And his second was even more amazing than his first. By a separate agreement Nems will control the British appearances of Americans who are represented by the General Artists Corporation of America.

Would you believe that GAC's client list includes the Supremes, the Turtles, the Lovin' Spoonful, the Tijuana Brass, Roger Miller, Tony Bennett, the Everly Brothers, Eydie Gorme, Steve Lawrence, Johnny Mathis and Johnny Tillotson just to mention a few? Well, you'd better believe it because it's absolutely true!

And it means that Epstein now has a rather large share in the pop pie of both the U.S. and England. In plain language it means that a million dollar Nems Enterprises stands to be a few million dollars richer and that Epstein has some control over practically every top act in the business!

He's come quite a long way from managing that store in Whitechappel, Liverpool, hasn't he? Wonder where he can possibly go from here—to managing Elvis maybe?

'Darling Charlie' Coming Our Way?

By Louise Criscione

If we're lucky, and I hope we are, we will soon be blessed with "Charlie Is My Darling." And exactly *what* is "Charlie Is My Darling" and why should *we* be blessed with it, you ask?

For openers, "Charlie" is a maze of riots, send-ups, half-finished sentences and wild shots. It's a Rolling Stones' special which conceivably will be aired on American television sometime this Spring.

The film is, of course, an Andrew Oldham brainchild and was actually shot many months ago when the Stones ventured out on a hysteria-producing tour of Ireland.

Oldham thought it would be a marvelous idea to have a cameraman, Peter Whitehead, follow the boys around as they played concert after concert and evoked riot after riot.

Suits Them

And what Whitehead came up with is a personal insight into what life on the road with a pop group is really like. It's not nearly as glamorous as perhaps you'd think it is—in fact, it's not glamorous at all. But it *is* interesting and enlightening and it suits the Stones perfectly.

Inside the BEAT

Inside Ringo's Nose 2
Chris Once Topped Beatles 4
On The Beat 5
An Open Letter To George 6
Want To Be An Animal? 7
The Only Real Fifth Beatle 10
British Top 10 11
Yeah Well, Beatles 12
A Visit With Jeremy 13
Adventures of Robin Boyd 14
The BEAT Goes to the Movies ... 15

The BEAT is published weekly by BEAT Publications, Inc., editorial and advertising offices at 6290 Sunset Blvd., Suite 504, Hollywood, California 90028. U.S. bureaus in Hollywood, San Francisco, New York, Chicago and Nashville, overseas correspondents in London, Liverpool and Manchester, England. Sale price, 15 cents. Subscription price: U.S. and possessions, $5 per year, Canada and foreign rates, $9 per year. Application to mail at second class postage rates is pending at Los Angeles, California.

Besides the riot scenes there are interviews with the Stones, a Jagger imitation of Elvis Presley and an interpretation of George Harrison's guitar work.

Oldham announced that "Charlie Is My Darling" will definitely be shown on British television but there has, to date, been no confirmation of its American airing, or if it will be aired at all.

However, *The BEAT* learned from a spokesman for the Stones that negotiations are currently underway to sell "Charlie" to one of the American networks. With the Stones as hot as they currently are, it seems more than likely that "Charlie" will be picked up and if so it is safe to say that its TV ratings will be sky-high. The thousands of Stone fans will *see* to that!

Speculation around the town is that another of the Stones should take that trip up the altar. After all, there are now three married Beatles but only two married Stones.

So, if the Stones want to keep up with the Beatles, they've got to marry off another member. And the likeliest candidate would have to be Mick.

Why Mick? Because he's been going with the same girl, Chrissie Shrimpton, for ages now while Keith has a girl in every port and Brian has two (at least) girls in every city in the world!

Wedding Plans

Don't get too excited, though. Mick still denies any wedding plans. And who knows, maybe the Stones don't want to keep up with the Beatles in the marriage department anyway!

The Stones are about due for another album and a single. Their record company is still fighting the idea of titling the Stones' next LP effort, "Could You Walk On The Water?" Regardless of what it's titled, the album will feature tracks cut in December at RCA in Hollywood. Ditto for their next single.

Keith has kept himself occupied lately by directing an instrumental LP which features two Jagger-Richard compositions, "Mother's Little Helper" and "Sittin' On A Fence" both of which are possibilities for "Could You Walk On The Water" or whatever they finally decide to call it.

Of course, you know the Stones will pay RCA another visit next month to cut the soundtrack for their first movie, "Back, Behind And In Front." And in between they'll sandwich in an appearance on "Ed Sullivan" and a tour of the Far East.

Keepin' busy, these five Rolling Stones.

... Next One Married?

KRLA ARCHIVES

Inside Ringo's Nose

By Gil McDougall

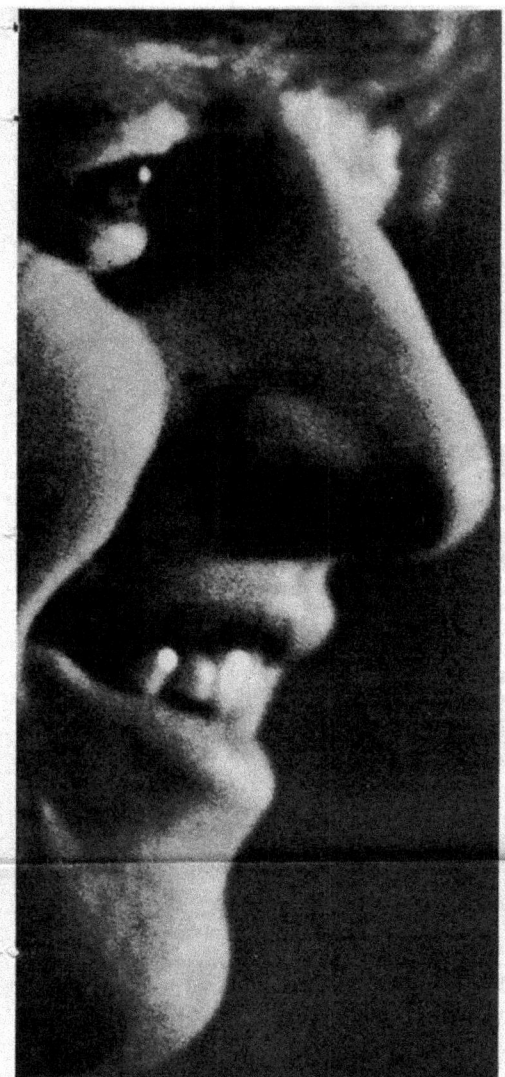

It is clearly one of man's finest super-structures. It is clearly the biggest talking point since the Russians invented Elvis Presley. It is, to coin a phrase of a much wiser man than I, clearly eighteen per cent of his entire body. It is Ringo's nose.

Before all of you Beatle fans take up your pens to let loose a literary onslaught on this writer, let me state quite plainly that I am the world's most fanatical Beatle supporter. I am not knocking Ringo's nose, but merely making observations on it, or rather of it.

Actually the Beatles themselves are right in front when it comes to Ringo nose knocking. They carried on quite a discussion about it in "A Hard Day's Night," and on another occasion when Ringo was asked why he carried so many rings on his fingers he replied, "Because I can't get them all through my nose."

When one considers the many and varied talents that all four Beatles have, it is easy to understand why Beatlemania has been with us so long. But it is also worth a moment of your consideration to ponder as to how the Beatlemania ball first began to roll.

Nose Credit

The place, of course, was England and the causes of the beginning of Beatlemania are numberless, but a large chunk of the credit should be given to Ringo's nose. The Beatles had had a record on the British charts for some time when suddenly the British Press, who love a good story, discovered Ringo's nose. Immediately the Beatles and the nose became the objects of the nation's, and finally the world's, curiosity. The flash bulbs were going so fast that Ringo looked like Blackpool Tower at the height of the season. By October of 1963 you couldn't pick up a paper without staring the Beatles straight in the nose. Marlene Dietrich played on the same bill with them and she said: "It was a joy to be with them. I adore these Beatles." And John said: "It was a joy to be with her. I adore Marlene," in a shrill voice.

Ringo's nose was not the only thing that was subjected to a very close scrutiny. His hair also came under attack. At a British Embassy reception a young man attempted to grab Ringo's hair and received instead a sharp prod in the ribs. The fellow afterwards claimed that he had been attacked. Actually hair is probably the answer to Ringo's problem, if he wants to consider it as a problem.

Beard Goes

Everybody noticed that in "A Hard Day's Night," Ringo looked great with a beard and his hair swept back. When he joined the group John Lennon told him in a phone call, "You can keep your sideburns but the beard has to go." Also his hair had to be combed down in Beatle fashion. If his nose really did start the ball rolling then I guess that it was all for the best. Ringo, I suspect, still prefers the beard. When he, John, Cynthia and Maureen departed London for a vacation this January he was sporting a beard.

Before Ringo joined the Beatles nobody wanted to photograph Ringo's nose very much at all. Working as drummer with the Rory Storm Rock 'n' Roll group Ringo was almost as popular with the girls as he is now. Mrs. Vi Caldwell, who is Rory Storm's mum and a good friend of all the Beatles, had this to say of Ringo: "People are always pointing out his big nose nowadays, but you didn't notice it so much then because he had his hair swept back."

It's only since it's been combed forward that his nose has stood out. Paul, John, George and Ringo spent many nights with Rory at his mother's house, drinking tea and talking well into the morning. Mrs. Caldwell remembers Ringo as: "A bit quiet sometimes and could be depressing. But then when John and Paul get started it's a bit hard for anyone to get a word in. Ringo looked a bit small, but he was always my favorite. One day he bought a car, but before he could drive it he had to put a cushion on the driver's seat."

The replacement of Peter Best by Ringo Starr was an unpopular move in just about every possible way. The fans were annoyed and showed it with threats and even violence.

Best Out

Paul and George talked John around to their point of view and then the three of them went to Brian and demanded Best out and Starr in. Despite all this opposition to Ringo he very quickly became as popular as the rest of the Beatles, and Brian Epstein was later to describe him as: "Very uncomplicated and a very good drummer. He is one of the most lovable men in beat music."

It has been said that Ringo Starr is the classic example of how to succeed without really trying. It has also been said that no man ever deserved success more. He doesn't have the drive of Lennon or the charm of McCartney, but he does have a dry wit and a warm friendliness that is guaranteed to defrost solid ice. In his childhood Ringo had more than one illness but he was helped through this period with "the best mum and dad that anyone could wish for." Ringo has expressed his appreciation many times over to his mother and step-father. It took some talking but he finally persuaded them to move into a luxurious home in Liverpool that he had bought for them.

Who Cares?

Still in his mid-twenties the little man from Dingle is a millionaire and about as successful as any man could wish to be. Maybe it was Ringo's nose that started the Beatlemania ball rolling, but who cares! It is his own personality and his value as a performer that keeps him where he is—right on top.

Well, that's it. The two of us, and a couple of million other readers, have been "Inside Ringo's Nose." I doubt if he felt a thing.

Bits And Pieces Of The Beatles

GEORGE HARRISON'S discotheque is not going as well as expected. Actually if there was one thing that the BIG L scene didn't need it was another discotheque. Pretty soon the clubs and the pubs will outnumber the people. Even so, with his name you'd have thought . . . Oh well, maybe if he books the ROLLING STONES!

This writer does try to avoid such epic columnist comments as: RINGO STARR uses pink toothpaste, or JOHN LENNON wears socks, etc., etc. I haven't even revealed that PAUL McCARTNEY likes to sleep in the nude. After all, if I were sued how could I prove something like that. Despite this I would like all America to know that PAUL answered a BBC query on his sleeping attire with: "I wear red, blue and yellow stripes. GEORGE comes round every night and paints them on me." It's an old LENNON retort, but the BBC type just didn't dig the humor.

To build a Go-Cart track in your backyard you've got to have plenty of enthusiasm for that sport. You also have to have as much money as RINGO STARR. I can just see RINGO in about ten years telling young ZAK . . . come on son, I'll race you to the bank . . . and if they wanted to make an obstacle course they could put sacks of two-bob bits at various points along the track.

After observing PAUL McCARTNEY'S father I had to agree with everybody else, he really is a great bloke. It isn't hard to see where PAUL picked up his well-mannered charm. Mr. McCARTNEY senior was a professional musician himself once. If he had met BRIAN EPSTEIN'S father twenty years ago, who knows what might have happened!

No matter how small a comment the BEATLES might make, it is always blown up into something approaching an oration. If one of them happened to mention a partiality for fried onions, many of the fan magazines would build this up into a two or three page story. This really irritates LENNON. When in the Bahamas JOHN said: "People keep asking you who you like and then when you tell them what records you buy, that's it." JOHN went on to say that he had only to casually mention DYLAN once during an interview and in all probability it would be written up as a "big DYLAN thing."

Talking about fan magazines, one of them stated in its February 1966 edition that when the BEATLES played at Hamburg's Star Club, "It was so cold they often had to wear overcoats while performing." I'm afraid that I will have to see photographic proof before I believe that one. A lot of water has flushed through the radiator since 1945. Today the Germans are one of the most prosperous nations on earth, and can well afford heating in their clubs.

It is not true that the BEATLES now own most of BIG L. It's not true at this particular time, but at the rate that they are investing their money in real estate, GEORGE may yet become the Lord Mayor of London. HARRISON especially is concerned with ensuring his financial future. When you think of the many stars who ended up broke, GEORGE'S wisdom certainly shines through.

It is unlikely the BEATLES will ever live permanently any place outside England. It is possible that they may set up "secondary" homes perhaps in Spain. PAUL & JANE already spend plenty of time in Portugal. JOHN is building a home on the Costa Brava coast. LENNON also wants his children to be educated in England. RINGO wants this also but he has said that Spain is a good place to bring up children. GEORGE HARRISON has said very little on the subject, but he does have a sister living in the U.S. Even so it is unlikely that GEORGE will ever call any place outside the U.K. his home.

PETER BEST may not win his libel suit against the BEATLES, but he will surely become the world's best-known loser.

Sam Returning

Those Wooly Bully men, Sam the Sham and the Pharaohs, have just completed trying out their new image on their first European tour.

The group started the tour in West Germany, where their record sales have been fantastic. They then went onto Vienna, Paris and Amsterdam before flying off to London for several television appearances.

The group, who have just shaved off their beards, let their hair grow and changed stage costumes, had one of the top selling records in the world in 1965 with "Wooly Bully."

KRLA ARCHIVES

NOW! YOU CAN PLAY GUITAR WITH THE VENTURES

...with these unusual albums

BLP-16501

BLP-16502

LEARN TO PLAY THE VENTURES' BIGGEST HITS
BY THE GUITAR PHONICS SYSTEM

Each album contains:

- Complete verbal instructions
- Examples, played by the Ventures, of each guitar part (Lead, Bass and Rhythm), plus complete selections with your part missing
- Illustrated booklet, with easy-to-follow diagrams of each guitar part for each song

Available wherever records are sold

Write for free illustrated Liberty/Dolton catalog:
Liberty Records
Dept. K-1
6920 Sunset Blvd. | Los Angeles, Calif. 90028

Please send me a free copy of the Liberty/Dolton catalog.

NAME_____
(Please Print)
ADDRESS_____
CITY_____ ZIP CODE_____
AGE_____ SCHOOL_____

KRLA ARCHIVES

Chris Montez Back
Once Topped Bill Over The Beatles

By Louise Criscione

First record hits are not too unusual but comebacks are almost unheard of in the funny world of show business. But every once in a while both things happen as they did to Chris Montez.

In 1961, Chris graduated from Hawthorne High School and immediately ran into Jim Lee who just happened to be looking for some hot new talent to launch his infant record company.

He spotted that hot new talent in Chris and it was not long before he had Chris under contract and recording a hit in the form of "All You Had To Do Was Tell Me."

Chris followed up his first hit with a second and much more successful disc, "Let's Dance." The record was not only a hit in the U.S. but all over the world as well and it brought Chris to headline a tour of England. Which is again not too unusual until you find out who played *under* him on that tour. It was none other than the Beatles! The year was 1963 and although the Beatles were just beginning to break in England they still had a long way to go before they were to hit the top.

Just All Right

"They were just getting started," recalled Chris. "They had played in Germany and had been booked for the tour. In some places they went over big and in other places they just did all right.

"I thought they were nice, funny guys, especially Paul. We were on a bus together for seven or eight weeks, we ate together and goofed off.

"When they first came to L.A. I went to Bel Air to visit them. They were really glad to see me. Nothing had really changed. They told me that they'd be looking for me if I ever came to England again.

"If I ever become as rich and famous as they are I hope I stay the same. There's no need to let all this stuff go to your head. You don't get anything out of it," said Chris.

Certain people who claim to have met the Beatles seem to delight in revealing that Paul is very conceited. I wondered what Chris thought—after all, he had known them before they were the international stars which they are today.

Paul Not Stuck

"They have more fun just being themselves rather than in trying to impress people. I think Paul is the best looking one of the group. I don't think he's stuck on himself but I think he knows that he's a pretty good-looking man. He's got all he needs but he never brings it up. He *knows* but he's not conceited," replied Chris.

Chris' visit to the Beatles Bel Air hideaway was ironic if nothing else. The last time he saw the Beatles he was the top bill on his own tour and the Beatles were just a group added on to fill the show. But when he met them in Bel Air *they* were not only the headliners of their own tour but they were also the show business phenomenon of the decade. And Chris? He hadn't had a record out in two years.

"There was a long complication with my recording company," revealed Chris. "I sort of had to buy my way out of it. It's frustrating not to be able to follow-up a hit record but if it wasn't your fault then there's not much you can do about it.

Lost

"I was new in this kind of game and I sort of got lost," Chris continued. "Most of the time I was just trying to settle this agreement and get it out of my hair."

It took a full two years for Chris to get the "agreement" out of his hair, so he took the opportunity to go back to school. And he's still there as a music major. Is schooling really that important to a singer?

Chris thinks that it is. For one thing it gives him a wide background in music and for another he feels more at ease in a recording session because he knows what they're talking about. "They respect you more and it helps in phrasing and in your vocal and it makes you seem kind of intelligent," Chris laughed.

Chris wanted to get into the business for as long as he can remember. "I always liked the field of music but really I want to be an actor. As I'm getting older, I don't let it get me down like I used to. Sooner or later it will happen."

Would he grab any role which came along? "I'd have to sit down and have a conference with my lawyers. I don't have a manager so they're the ones who advise me.

Rather Serious

"If it was just a flash thing I wouldn't take it. I don't especially care for those beach party movies. I'd rather have three or four minutes in a serious movie than ten minutes in one of those beach party things," said Chris.

I asked Chris if he felt that the excitement which the Beatles had brought into our fading pop scene of two years ago was as strong today as it was then.

"I think it's dying down. There was an Elvis at one time and I think the Beatles are the ones today. I don't think anyone can even give them any competition. They'll just go down in history and then there will be someone else and someone else after that."

Having a number one hit under his belt, I thought Chris would be a good person to ask just how important a chart topping record is to an entertainer.

Don't Know

"I don't think it's that important," Chris replied. "I think getting a good sized hit is just as important because a lot of people don't even know how the chart ratings are going anyway. If you're noted as an artist then you're successful in your field."

As his latest record, "Call Me," bounds up the nation's charts it looks like Chris' comeback is complete. I hope so anyway. And you want to know something? The Beatles hope so too—Chris is a friend of theirs, they remember that tour in 1963.

...CHRIS MONTEZ

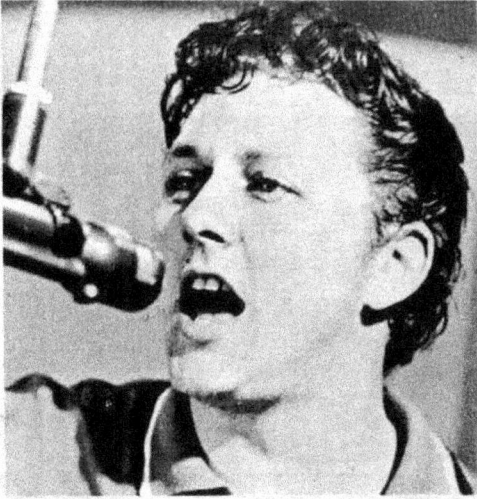

...BOB LIND

Bob Lind Wants No Special 'Bag'

When was the last time you met a really honest human being? Probably a very long time ago, huh? A certain Greek fellow named Demosthenes spent his entire lifetime several hundred years ago trying to find a truly honest man, but unfortunately—he sort of lost out.

At the risk of causing dear old Demosthenes a rather uneasy rest, I'm now going to make a startling announcement: I have found a very honest and sincere human being. His name—Bob Lind.

He sings of the "Elusive Butterfly," and when you meet him you begin to understand just why. His own world is one of fragile butterfly wings, ever ready to take off in flight of whim and fantasy.

Born November 25, 1942 in Baltimore, Maryland, Bob grew up in Chicago. He spent three full years in college—and then flunked out. He failed not because of an inability to understand and keep up with the work assigned, but because he was busy creating his own literature—writing songs, which were far more like poetry than most songs which you will ever hear.

When Bob first turned seriously to the world of music, he would sing the songs he wrote to people he knew. At that time, he also performed some songs by other composers. Now, he will sing only those songs which he has written, the songs which have meaning for him—and hopefully, for his audience, as well.

Bob actually began playing the guitar at the age of eleven, when he had four brief lessons from a teacher who soon vanished. Flashing his quiet smile, Bob explains that "I kind of learned from pestering people." Well, whoever it was that Bob pestered, ought to be mighty proud of him now.

He is a very sincere, almost shy individual; and when he explains to you that, "When I'm by myself I like to write songs; I don't like to be alone" you can't avoid the urge to reach out and reassure him that he needn't be alone again. And yet, you know somehow that he will be. For Bob Lind is a loner, almost of necessity—for few people can communicate on the same plane of genuine feeling with him.

One of the first things you will notice about Bob, are his clear, blue eyes. They look straight at you—no reservations about it, he isn't going to hide—and they make you believe in whatever he wants to say.

Bob will fix those blue eyes of his on you, and then firmly insist: "I would not like to be categorized—you know, that I'm in such-and-such a 'bag'—I would like to be just listened to with an open mind."

What about the songs which Bob writes and sings? His managers—Charlie Greene and Brian Stone—explain that they are poetic songs. "He has a personalized thing he does to a song—and he does it beautifully, honestly, and simply."

Of his own work, Bob says that: "The songs I write are songs that have come out of my experience—I can't manufacture them." And this is probably the key word in Bob's life: manufacture; he simply doesn't manufacture anything. Everything he is and does is very much for real.

If you put this idea to Bob, he will think about it for a few moments, and then with a sigh almost of resignation, he will concede: "I don't know if my songs are good or bad—because I don't know good or bad—but yes, they *are* honest."

If you suggest to Bob the idea of infinity, he will relate that thought to stars. Pronounce the word "loneliness," and Bob returns the one word, "dark." He is not a complex individual, purposely trying to perpetrate an attitude of mystery. He is just a very honest, uncomplicated, pleasant, exceptionally talented young man.

And when you get right down to it—that's really saying an awful lot, isn't it?

KRLA ARCHIVES

No Second Hand Roses

...BARBRA STREISAND

By Carol Deck

A lot of words have been used to describe Barbra Streisand but the one that pops up most often is *unique*.

From the spelling of her first name to her kooky clothes to her amazing performances she projects that thing known as star quality.

When Barbra sings, the audience doesn't just sit and listen. They are drawn up into her magic and they participate in her performance.

She was first heard on the original Broadway cast recordings of "I Can Get It For You Wholesale" a mere three years ago and is now one of the top selling female vocalists in the country.

In her first year as a recording artist she became the only female vocalist in recent history to place two albums among the nation's top ten best sellers in one year with "The Barbra Streisand Album" and "The Second Barbra Streisand Album."

All Gold

She's also the only current star who's won a gold record for sales of over $1 million for every album she's recorded.

She was born in Brooklyn but left as soon as possible. "I had these dreams of being a star, of being in the movies, but in Brooklyn I always felt like a character out of Paddy Chayefsky."

She took acting lessons in Manhattan and did a bit of summer stock, all the while attending as many Broadway auditions as she could looking for parts as either an actress or singer.

She used "Allegheny Moon" as her first audition song. "They don't write songs like that any more," she says, "at least I hope not."

In The Village

After winning a talent contest at a Greenwich Village nightclub she began to get bookings around the Village.

She was spotted at the Blue Angel by David Merrick, the producer of "I Can Get It For You Wholesale," and signed for her first major role.

Shortly after the show opened she married Elliot Gould, who had played the starring role in the musical.

Since that time she's appeared on practically every major television variety show, starred in "Funny Girl" on Broadway, made public appearances from New York to California and released several hit singles and albums, each with the originality and uniqueness of "People."

Looking In?

Many people see Barbra as an outsider looking in, but if she's an outsider, she's an outsider by choice. She refuses to accept one set of values as right above all others and is willing to pay the price of being labeled a beatnik.

She's an individual in a generation of conformists, but she speaks for that generation, a generation that may not be sure of what it wants, but has a fair idea of what it doesn't want.

Her latest single is "Second Hand Rose," but this girl is definitely a first.

On the BEAT

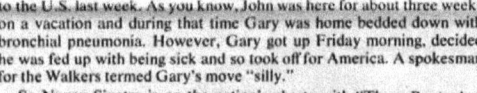

By Louise Criscione

You are probably under the impression that George and Patti had their wedding date planned for months in advance, right? Well, so did I but Walter Shenson, Beatles' movie producer, says it isn't so. Walter flew to America last week for a few days and George was all set to go with him.

But at the very last minute George changed his mind. He didn't tell Walter why—just said that he had decided against going. So, Walter was even more surprised than most people when he picked up the papers and discovered that George and Patti had gotten married.

Wonder when the Righteous Brothers will start recording together again. "Ebb Tide" was a great record but it kind of left Bill out. "Georgia" is a good record, though it sounds a lot like Ray Charles, which is okay except that it isn't Ray, but it leaves Bobby out. Maybe they'll change their name to the Righteous Brother?

The mind of Andrew Oldham has been hard at work again. He would like the Stones' next album to have a picture of the Stones standing by a reservoir with the title, "Could You Walk Over The Water?" However, their record company declares that there "ain't no way" that's ever going to happen! We'll see—but I wouldn't put *anything* past Oldham.

The Kinks are coming back to the U.S. for a six-week tour in April. They are also set to appear in seven Eruopean countries during the up-coming months.

Silly Move?

Gary Leeds of the Walker Brothers made an unexpected trip to the U.S. last week. As you know, John was here for about three weeks on a vacation and during that time Gary was home bedded down with bronchial pneumonia. However, Gary got up Friday morning, decided he was fed up with being sick and so took off for America. A spokesman for the Walkers termed Gary's move "silly."

...BOBBY HATFIELD

So Nancy Sinatra is on the nation's charts with "These Boots Are Made For Walkin'". Figures, doesn't it? I mean, with her father's name, money and power how could she fail?

I don't know about you but this sort of thing makes me wonder. There are so many talented people around who aren't making it simply because they don't have a million dollars behind them. It seems kind of unfair to give people breaks because they have money, doesn't it?

Of course, just because I'm mentioning it in my column won't change things at all but it might move some of you into action. And maybe the next time you find a talented group who isn't making it because they don't have money and power behind them you'll pitch in and help. It's really worth it and besides, our record scene needs a good shot in the arm.

Ed "Pop" Sullivan

Looks like Ed Sullivan is going to take honors for the best pop show on television. He's set to have the Stones and Tom Jones co-starring on one show which will be followed shortly by Dave Clark. Also scheduled for appearances are the Animals and Paul and Barry Ryan.

Ever wonder what became of Barry McGuire? Well, he's still hanging around but minus a hit record. Barry's in New York appearing at the Phone Booth and reports say that the hippies love him but that the rest of the population is avoiding the spot like some sort of plague.

The San Remo Song Festival is currently rolling with such artists as the Yardbirds, Bobby Vinton, Chad & Jeremy, Gene Pitney, P. J. Proby, Pat Boone, Francoise Hardy and the Christy Minstrels taking part.

It's quite an honor to perform at the Festival but it's also a lot of work because the entries are sung in Italian. Funniest thing about this year's Festival is the fact that Chad & Jeremy are listed as a *United States* entry!

...JEREMY CLYDE

Speaking of Chad & Jeremy, weren't they great on "Laredo?" They certainly proved that they can hold a show together all by themselves. Maybe now they'll get the series they've wanted for so long.

KRLA ARCHIVES

An Open Letter To George

Dear George:

Have you ever sat and stared at a blank sheet of paper, hoping the words you're about to write will matter to someone besides yourself?

That's the way I feel right now. For the past year, I've been writing about you. But this is the first time I've ever written to you.

I imagine it will also be the last.

I wonder about a lot of things. I guess everyone does. Especially young people. We're new. Doing everything for the first time.

One of the things I used to wonder about was how marriage could possibly ruin a star's career.

It just didn't make any sense. To me, marriage couldn't really change anything between a fan and a favorite.

It couldn't destroy your communication with him. You never had any in the first place.

Still The Same

It couldn't alter the things you like about him. He'd still look the same. Act the same. Sing the same.

His marriage wouldn't make him any less available to you because he never really was.

All it could change was his personal life. Something you were never part of anyway.

You'd still have just as much of him as you ever did. So why would you lose interest?

And how about the stars who were very much married when they *became* famous? John Lennon. David McCallum. Sonny and Cher. Marriage certainly hasn't hampered *their* success.

Still, it happens. It always has. Many stars, well on their way up the ladder, have lost their footing after a march down the aisle. And it's happened far too often for the sudden drop in popularity to just be coincidence.

Marriage Question

So, I just kept wondering. I didn't stay up nights or anything. But I was curious about the marriage question. Because there didn't seem to be any answer.

It's funny how just living can answer a lot of questions for you. Without your ever really having to ask.

Just being alive on January 21, 1966, answered this one for me.

I could say I'll forget all about that morning someday, but I'd only be kidding myself.

Life is a handful of time fragments. Millions of moments. Good ones, bad ones. Little ones, big ones. You can't remember them all, so your mind collects the important moments and presses them between your pages.

I'll remember. January 21 was important.

I could also come up with the old adage that ten years from now, I'll look back on all this and be amused.

But that wouldn't be true either.

I'll never let myself become the kind of person who could laugh at the first time I ever really cried.

I'm not going to tell you about that. There aren't any words. But I do want you to know the answer to that question.

I heard the news. Then I understood. How it happens. Why it happens.

You love a star. He gets married. True, it doesn't change him. It changes you.

You don't lose interest in him. You lose a part of yourself.

You still have just as much of him as you ever had. You just don't have quite as much of you.

Something's Gone

Something's gone. The warm things that used to happen when you thought of him don't happen any more. And you had thought about him so often, that warmth had become a portion of your being.

Suddenly, that part of you is empty. Vacant. Because when you think of him now, the warmth is destroyed by the memory of the cold, numb moment when she won and you lost.

And the explanation about the already-married stars . . . it's so simple.

Their fans keep warm. They hurt sometimes because it's already too late to even hope, but they never have to experience that moment of shock that freezes you over inside. They can keep dreaming because they know they'll never be forced to wake up.

Career Ruined?

That's how it happens. And why. But there's more. I understand why marriage can ruin a career. But I also understand why it doesn't always.

The personalities who do fade for this reason are shooting stars. They grow dim because their own fire isn't strong enough to melt the ice in you. They can't provide anything to fill up the empty spaces they've created. They're all used up. And as their glow loses its strength, they stop being your weakness.

I'm not writing this letter to assure you that marriage won't ruin your career. You already know that.

I don't really know why I *am* writing it. It doesn't make much sense. Nothing I write ever does. But I guess I just had to talk to you and this was the only way I knew how.

I guess I also want you to know why your marriage hasn't ruined you for me.

I don't feel the same way about you. I couldn't possibly. There's more than enough of you to replace that special warmth. But it will take awhile. And even then, I won't feel the same.

Already, you're less a boy to me and more a man. I don't mean I care less. I think I mean I care more. In a different way.

That's because I'm the one who's changed, not you. And in spite of the ache I feel every time I think of what has happened, the change is for the better.

Because I'm less a girl and more a woman now.

That's everything I wanted to tell you, except one.

When I talk about you and write about you from now on, I won't say the old things. You belong to someone and I can't really rave on the way I used to. Not as much, anyway.

I Love You

But there is one thing I never did say, because I was embarrassed to. Everyone probably knew anyway, but I would still have felt silly.

I have to say it now. Right now. Whether I feel silly or not. Because I have to tell you, just one time, and I'll never have another chance.

I have to say the words and taste them and write them on a paper so I can touch them years from now and remember both of us.

I love you, George Harrison.

Shirley Poston

MR. DYNAMITE GETS AROUND — On a recent trip to the West Coast to discuss plans for a movie about his fabulous career, James Brown appeared on numerous national television shows with his latest best seller, "I Got You," and premiered his next, "Ain't That A Groove."

KRLA ARCHIVES

A Jazzman Speaks Out On The Beatles

By Carol Deck

Jazz.

If that word didn't scare you away and you're still reading, congratulations, you're among a maturing generation of pop fans whose world expands daily.

The BEAT, in our constant effort to bring you what *you* want, is starting a new policy of bringing you artists who may not be exactly in the middle of the pop scene but are big in other fields.

We'd like to start by introducing you to one of the greats of the jazz world who's just recorded a Lennon-McCartney song and has some definite ideas about the Beatles' success.

Bud Shank is well known in the jazz world for his masterful playing of saxophone, clarinet and flute and he's now breaking into the pop world with his version of "Michelle," released first as a single and now in an album.

Why "Michelle"?

"Michelle" was the first Beatle song he'd ever recorded and he says he chose it because "it's more sophisticated, more involved musically than most of their music."

But it isn't the involvement that Bud feels is responsible for the Beatles' fantastic success, it's their mistakes!

"A lot of the Beatles' success is that they don't know what they are doing," he explains.

"A person that has no technical knowledge of a subject can often get into it deeper than someone who has."

Bud feels that if the Beatles had had much formal music training they wouldn't write or sound the way they do.

"A well schooled musician just wouldn't have written like that. It's all wrong, but it's right."

After some indication from various parts of the country that Bud's "Michelle" was going well, he decided to cut an album around it, which is sort of the backwards way to do things. And on the album he included another Lennon-McCartney composition, "Yesterday," which he also finds wrong.

All Wrong

"It's all wrong musically. It's written in seven bars. It won't fit eight bars, we tried.

"We figured we were doing a jazz musician's interpretation so we should make it comfortable, but it was all wrong."

The Beatles' songs may be wrong but if you make them right you destroy them.

Bud has similar feelings about John Lennon's writings. He thinks Lennon's books are brilliant because John "doesn't know what he's doing." And he warns that John "may be learning and if he does it may destroy him."

Jazz and pop used to be two separate worlds but they're merging more now, just as folk used to be independent but now is an integral part of rock and roll. Bud feels that this merging of jazz and pop is largely on the part of jazz artists.

"As jazz artists all we've ever asked is that people take back the cover and look in and not just judge us by our looks," he explains.

"Now *we're* taking back the cover and looking into other fields. We're doing what we've been asking other people to do but weren't doing ourselves."

And he feels that teenagers are ready for the merger.

"I think teenagers are becoming more mature in their taste. They're becoming more aware of things in general and you don't have to hit them between the eyes with everything. They're more sophisticated."

This venture into pop with "Michelle" is not Bud's first. You've probably heard him many times, although you undoubtedly didn't know it. He did the music for two of the Bruce Brown surf movies — "Barefoot Adventure" and "Slippery When Wet."

California Dreaming

He plays regularly as a session musician for things like the David Rose Orchestra on The Red Skelton Show and he's played on many top pop hits including the Mamas and Papas first record, "California Dreaming," which he does the flute solo on.

He's done jingles for commercials and he's delved into the classical field in his work with Laurindo Almeida, one of the world's top classical guitarists.

So pop fans, we'd like you to meet Bud Shank, a many talented man who's coming your way with a soft and easy version of a song by your two favorite composers.

...BUD SHANK

Want To Be An Animal?

By Doug Gilbert

That question may not be as far out as you think. Today's beat is constantly changing and to keep up with it the groups often have personality changes. Performers are leaving, joining, or just simply switching groups at an amazing rate. It is a fact that not all of the new arrivals are established stars. On the contrary many of them are virtual unknowns. This does not have to mean that they are inexperienced however. Obviously no established group is going to take on anyone who would be detrimental to their over-all sound.

Young musicians in the U.K., who might have been playing locally for years, have been amazed to find themselves invited to join a group with a record high in the charts. Though Liverpool has the best reputation as a city of talent, London, being that much bigger, is swarming with groups. In London's East Side you will find Rock 'n' Roll in almost every Pub, and there is a Pub on every other corner. The talent is there to choose from, and every so often some young bloke will get lucky and be discovered by a "name." Manfred Mann is a case in point. He added two musicians, to an already impressive line-up, just before Christmas and they are still with him.

In 1965 even the fabulous Animals took on new talent. This happened when organist Alan Price (remember his great playing on "House Of The Rising Sun") decided to leave the group, even though they were doing so well. He eventually formed The Alan Price Set, which is doing well but still has a long way to go. Alan was replaced by completely unknown, as far as the pop fans knew, Dave Rowberry. The Animals chose well.

Prior to joining the group, Dave had been playing jazz in and around Newcastle for some years. He had been featured at the "Downbeat Club" on many occasions, and had played with Ronnie Stephensen and Gary Cox, the latter played a fantastic tenor sax. Dave had had plenty of experience before he hit it big with the Animals. Nevertheless he was a pretty young fellow and a complete stranger to the charts.

Dave Rowberry later recalled that the only time he had met any of the Animals, before joining the group, was in Newcastle where he exchanged greetings and a drink with Eric Burdon. Then suddenly he was in. Dave Rowberry first appeared, without any rehearsal, with the Animals on Ed Sullivan's show. This was immediately followed by a tour of Japan, where they did a forty-minute show every night. This was Dave's proving ground and that is exactly what he did. If Dave didn't know any of the Animals before joining the group, he knew them all by heart at the conclusion of the Japanese tour.

During the past seven months the Animals have toured Spain, Belgium, Germany, Japan, the USA twice and finally Poland. The Polish tour had been long awaited by their fans in Warsaw, and the fans there made Dave just as welcome as they would have made Alan Price. The Animals were surprised to find that in Poland their "Animal Tracks" LP was selling on the "black market" for $48.60, and the Rolling Stones album, "Out Of Our Heads" was going for $51.30. This is pretty fantastic but then the only contact that Poland has with Rock 'n' Roll is by listening to British radio stations.

Being an ex-jazzman Dave Rowberry enjoys working with the Animals because they are always looking for new sounds and trying to develop musically. They have recently been experimenting with a big band sound. We can expect great sounds from that, and we can continue to expect great sounds from the organ of Dave Rowberry — The man who became an ANIMAL.

...DAVE ROWBERRY

KRLA ARCHIVES

KRLA Tunedex

This Week	Last Week	Title	Artist
1	2	JUST LIKE ME	Paul Revere & The Raiders
2	1	WE CAN WORK IT OUT/DAY TRIPPER	The Beatles
3	4	ZORBA THE GREEK	Herb Alpert & The Tijuana Brass
4	5	CRYIN' TIME	Ray Charles
5	6	NO MATTER WHAT SHAPE	The T-Bones
6	8	MY LOVE	Petula Clark
7	12	A WELL RESPECTED MAN	The Kinks
8	14	ELUSIVE BUTTERFLY	Bob Lind
9	3	LIGHTNIN' STRIKES	Lou Christy
10	7	SOUNDS OF SILENCE	Simon & Garfunkel
11	19	FIVE O'CLOCK WORLD	The Vogues
12	20	LOVE MAKES ME DO 'FOOLISH THINGS	Martha & The Vandellas
13	23	YOU BABY	The Turtles
14	11	MY WORLD IS EMPTY WITHOUT YOU	The Supremes
15	10	ARE YOU THERE?	Dionne Warwick
16	9	UP TIGHT	Stevie Wonder
17	15	GOING TO A-GO-GO	The Miracles
18	13	THE MEN IN MY LITTLE GIRL'S LIFE	Mike Douglas
19	4	TIJUANA TAXI	Herb Alpert & The Tijuana Brass
20	29	MY BABY LOVES ME	Martha & The Vandellas
21	27	I AIN'T GONNA EAT MY HEART OUT ANYMORE	Young Rascals
22	28	SET YOU FREE THIS TIME	The Byrds
23	33	TIME	The Pozo-Seco Singers
24	17	A MUST TO AVOID	Herman's Hermits
25	—	THESE BOOTS ARE MADE FOR WALKIN'	Nancy Sinatra
26	22	IT WAS A VERY GOOD YEAR	Frank Sinatra
27	34	WHAT NOW MY LOVE	Sonny & Cher
28	25	SANDY	Ronnie & The Daytonas
29	38	WORKING MY WAY BACK TO YOU	Four Seasons
30	24	SPANISH EYES	Al Martino
31	31	BARBARA ANN	The Beach Boys
32	—	DON'T MESS WITH BILL	The Marvellettes
33	—	BATMAN	Neil Hefti
34	—	AT THE SCENE	The Dave Clark Five
35	35	A HARD DAY'S NIGHT	Ramsey Lewis Trio
36	—	THE CHEATER	Bob Kuban
37	—	THE BALLAD OF THE GREEN BERET	Sgt. Barry Sadler
38	—	ANDREA	The Sunrays
39	—	LOOK THROUGH ANY WINDOW	The Hollies
40	—	THE DEDICATION SONG	Freddie Cannon

DAVE HULL

BOB EUBANKS

DICK BIONDI

JOHNNY HAYES

EMPEROR HUDSON

CASEY KASEM

CHARLIE O'DONNELL

BILL SLATER

BOB EUBANKS wanted us to prove to you that he doesn't spend all of his free time on the back of a horse. He's shown here being honored by L.A. Mayor Samuel Yorty for his work during a recent youth project.

Inside KRLA

Zowie, gosh, bamm, zok!! Batman has come to KRLA!! And KRLA has gone *Bat*ty!!! Just about everyone in the whole wide, Bat-filled world seems to have gone *Bat*ty right along with us, 'cause the response to the Batman contest has been absolutely phenomenal.

If you haven't sent in for your Bat Kit as yet, you'd better hurry up and do so before you miss out. Just send in your name and address, and you will receive by return mail your official Bat Kit — including the Bat emblem, a flash light adapter, your Bat Club membership card, the official Bat code, a picture of Bat Man, and some sticky little Bat dealies!

Well, that's what Dave Hull calls them — but then, you know the Hullabalooer! Anyway, what they *really* are — sort of — is Bat stamps. You know — like, "Bat Man does," and "Robin doesn't."

So whatever else you do — be sure you send in for your Bat Kit and join all of us here at KRLA as we all go positively *Bat*ty!!!

"Hearty" Entries

Once again, the annual Valentine Art Contest here at KRLA has been a whopping success. Last year we were inundated with over 47,000 "hearty" entries, and I just *know* that we have surpassed that mark by far this year, and *weeks* before the contest was officially over.

How do I know that? Well, you see — it's only that everyone here at KRLA has been sort of moved out due to the excess of valentines which are to be found everywhere — and I do mean *everywhere!!*

Poor Casey! He just hasn't had too much luck *ducking* from trouble lately. Oh — I guess I'd better explain that. You see, about a week and a half ago, Lynn Carey — the 19-year-old daughter of actor MacDonald Carey — visited the studios of KRLA. Now, ordinarily that wouldn't have caused any great amount of difficulty — KRLA is constantly receiving visitors — however, Miss Carey didn't visit alone.

It all actually started back when Lynn agreed to appear in the funny new film, "Lord Love A Duck." Everything was going along just ducky (sorry 'bout that!) until the California Duck Processors Association selected Lynn to arouse public interest in Duck Week.

So it was that the aspiring young actress appeared one bright and sunny day at the studios of KRLA — complete with a little duckling in tow. Before you could turn around twice and quack softly in the key of C — Lynn had presented her little feathered friend to our own fine-feathered disc jockey — Casey Kasem.

Needless to say, the Caser has been going somewhat *quacky* lately trying to care for his newly-acquired companion and any suggestions you might have would be appreciated and carefully considered.

Oh, by the way — Casey is now receiving applications — in care of KRLA — for the adoption of one small duck!

Club Date

Hey — have you all gone down to Dave Hull's fantabulous new club, the Hullabaloo yet? If you haven't, you're missing out on a whole lot of fun. There are great guests at the club every single week-end — Friday and Saturday evenings, with special matinees on Sunday afternoon.

The Yardbirds, the Everly Brothers, the Liverpool Five, Chad and Jeremy, and the Turtles are just a few of the many great artists who have already appeared at the club, and coming in the future will be many more great groups and artists.

And you can always see the club regulars — The Palace Guard — at the club, playing all of the top tunes for your dancing enjoyment. So be sure to stop by this weekend and get in on all of the fun going on at Dave Hull's Hullabaloo.

Three Weeks Only! February 8-27

THE ASSOCIATION

with their hit "One Too Many Mornings"

and comics **George McKelvey** until February 13

and **Pat Paulsen** February 15-27

The ICE HOUSE GLENDALE
folk music in concert

phone 245-5043 for reservations

KRLA BEAT Subscription

SAVE 33% Of Regular Price

☐ 1 YEAR — 52 Issues — $5.00   ☐ 2 YEARS — $8.00
☐ 6 MONTHS — $3.00

Enclosed is _____   ☐ CASH   ☐ CHECK

PLEASE PRINT

Send to: .... Age ....

Address: ....

City .... State .... Zip ....

MAIL YOUR ORDER TO: KRLA BEAT
6290 Sunset, Suite 504
Hollywood, Calif. 90028

Foreign Rate: $9.00 — 52 Issues

KRLA ARCHIVES

HOLY HIT RECORDS!!! — There's a crime wave going on at KRLA and both Casey Kasem and the Hullabalooer have been threatened — but never fear, Batman will save them!!

IN SEARCH OF FOLK
Speaking of Sparks

By Shannon Leigh

We sat in the brick-walled, darkened room with the light dimly streaming through the stained-glass windows in the late afternoon. In the background, somewhere behind the heavy Spanish doors we could hear what sounded like church music.

It wasn't church music, nor were we in a house of worship. This week, our search for folk had taken us to the far reaches of Los Angeles — Westwood, to be exact — and we were sitting in one of Randy Spark's two offices.

Randy Sparks, the 32-year old performer who has become one of the most successful young men in the music industry, is the owner of Ledbetter's in Westwood. The club has seen the beginnings of several successful groups and Randy spent a few moments telling *The BEAT* about a few of them.

"The club is an unusual kind of an entity. It is *strictly* for the purpose of rehearsing with a live audience for the purposes of breaking in an act; getting the feeling of being on stage — which is a very important thing.

"We also have a full recording studio set-up. We have great live recording sessions on occasion.

"The club is an integral part of our operation in as much as we use it as a home-base for *finding* talent, for *developing* talent, and for *showcasing* the same talent.

"The club was started a little over two years ago strictly as a place where we could build a farm team for the New Christy Minstrels."

Randy made some rather interesting observations on the nature of his club, Ledbetters. Contrary to what might be popular belief, Randy maintains that, "the club was started as an experiment — it was never meant to be a profit-making organization, though on occasion we have made profit."

After a thoughtful pause, Randy went on to explain: "We're very much in the talent business — we're not agents, we're not managers, we just like to help young people. If we win — we all win together. It's very much like a family."

In order to give more and more young people an opportunity to break into show business, Randy has a very interesting set-up at the club. "We have a normal function on Sunday at our club — which most people call a "hoot" — probably a better word for it would be, 'A-Helping-Hand-Concert!!'

"Young people from out of town or young people who live in town who want to try their hand at entertaining and who feel they are reasonably rehearsed, come in and sing for the audience.

"If they do really well, they are very often given a chance to be a part of our organization or they are invited to come and do some test pressings, or they are invited to come in and rehearse and find out the extent of their talent."

Randy was very earnest as he leaned forward to explain to *The BEAT*, "Some of the people we've started have gone nowhere — and I'm not ashamed of these people, because they've had their chance. Maybe they *should* be doing something else. We have started, over the past couple of years, approximately a hundred people.

"The successful ones are the Backporch Majority. They do very well in concert and they are going to be an important act; they *are* an important act right now.

"There's another group called the Texas Twosome. They're in the Country field and they're a little different — they're kind of a young, modern answer to the needs of country music."

Tell your friends about
DIAL-A-DISC
HO 1-2220

BOBBY FULLER AND FRIENDS — The Bobby Fuller Four recently recorded the fast selling "KRLA — King of the Wheels" album.

BOB LIND catches up on the elusive goings on in the pop world.

OUR HERRINGBONE IS WAY IN

SUEDES AND CORDS TOO

LENNY'S BOOT PARLOR
1448 GOWER STREET
JUST SOUTH OF SUNSET
HOLLYWOOD ★ 466-7092
FREE PARKING

KRLA ARCHIVES

Mamas And Papas Pop A Few Words

By Ollie Tooms

All right world—are you really sure you're ready for this now? Okay, here they come—The Mamas and the Papas. That's about all that we have to say about them—I mean, how could you possibly describe them, anyway?

That's exactly the question I kept asking myself after they left The BEAT offices the other day—and I still haven't found the answer! But—ingenious BEAT reporter that I am, I think I have at least come up with a partial solution. Instead of trying to describe them, I'm just gonna let them describe themselves! I'll throw some words at them, and then they can throw a few verbally fiendish thingies right back at us.

Only three members of the group managed to find The BEAT offices—Michelle, John, and Cass, so you will find their names in parentheses after the question which they have replied to.

folk-rock: "going" (Michelle)
Dylan: "Bob" (John)
P.F. Sloan: "precocious" (Cass)
red: "Mrs. Harrison" (Michelle)
author: "Lennon" (John)
music: "fruit of love" (Cass)
money: "Take 22—that's always the money take." (Michelle)
hobby: "music" (John)
ambition: "To become at one with the Cosmos!" (Cass)
hate: "Ava soup" (Michelle)
protest: "Methinks she doth protest too much!" (John)
goal: "Six points" (Cass)
car: "15 liter Maserati" (Michelle)
people: "Lots of them" (John)
Beatles: "John, John, John, John..." (Cass) (Ed. note: Cass is somewhat enamored of the celebrated Mr. Lennon, MBE!")
long hair: "guinea pigs" (Michelle)
guitar: "me" (John)
food: "none" (Cass) (Ed. note: Cass is also somewhat imprisoned within the confines of the latest carbohydrate diet.)
Batman: "doesn't fly" (Michelle)
England: "Swings!" (John)
love: "'deed I do!!" (Cass)
jazz: "I just don't relate to jazz at all." (Michelle)
Lou Adler: "Basketball" (John)
names: "Necessary" (Cass)
question: "Adventure" (Michelle)
milk: "Tarzan" (John)
harmony: "Gretsch!" (Cass)
fights: "The Monster!" (Michelle)
Donald Duck: "Right wing!" (John)
suede: "Everything" (Cass)
The one thing I like the least: "Bad harmony." (Michelle)
I am happiest when: "I'm working." (John)
I am most sad when: "We're flat!" (Cass)
When I see the sun: "I think of Akhnaton." (John)
It discourages me to: "Find out how many carbohydrates there are in vinegar!!" (Cass)
I am emotionally affected by: "Mexican landscaping." (Michelle)

See what I mean? It's sort of impossible to describe all that to you! But that's nothing—listen to what Cass had to say when I asked her how the group had been formed: "It seems that there was this explosion and four pieces of it landed together on an old Fender amplifier. Well, sitting under the counter at Schwabs' drug store one day we were discovered."

John interrupted her here to explain that actually, it was only that Cass had followed the three original members of the group around the world for eight months until, finally—in desperation—they took her in as a member.

"We actually needed a voice like Cass' in the group, but she didn't have the range. Well, she followed us down to the Virgin Islands where we were working in a club, and one day at a construction site a lead pipe fell on her head. After she came out of the hospital, she had three more notes in her range—so we took her in."

The three Mamas and Papas had one thing to say before making their departure, and they addressed it to their fourth—and very absent—member: "Dennis—wherever you are—please come home; all is forgiven! Love, Cass."

The Only Real Fifth Beatle

Dear Readers,

I wasn't sure whether I wanted to write this or not. Now that I've completed it I still don't know. It is a bit sad and rather reflective. It is also a part of the Beatles' life that is often omitted for those very reasons. But Stu Sutcliffe was a part of the Beatles' life and I don't think that they would want him to be glossed over.

Gil McDougall

One of the things that fans like the Beatles for is the fact that their climb to the top, and indeed their lives, has been far from the proverbial bed of roses. At one time or another they have all been hit with unhappiness or tragedy. The greatest tragedy of all fell upon a young man named Stu Stucliffe. Stu, perhaps more than anyone else, would today have the right to call himself "the fifth Beatle."

John and Stu were both attending the Liverpool Institute of Art when they decided that it was time to get out and make their own way in the world. This was very premature as their income was practically negligable. Despite this they moved to a bed-sitter in down-town Liverpool. For some time they had a ball, throwing party after party. Eventually though, starvation got the better of them and they all decided to go home.

John, Stu, Paul and George continued to play all of the bookings that they could get. After a while they got something of a break when they were booked to back singer Johnny Gentle on a tour of Scotland. Great things were hoped for from the tour but absolutely nothing was to come of it. Drummer Peter Best, who's mother owned the Club Casbah in Liverpool, persuaded her to book the Beatles, and this was some encouragement to them. One of their biggest breaks came when they were booked for the Kaiserkeller and the Star Club in Hamburg. Paul was especially pleased about it, and as they had no drummer he talked Peter Best into going with them.

It was in Hamburg where they began to develop the style that was to take the world by storm. Had you told them this at the time you would have probably gotten a very sour retort. They were earning forty-five dollars a week, and were forced to live in two rooms over a cinema. John, Stu, and George shared one room and Paul, Pete and singer Tony Sheridan shared the other room. Tony Sheridan was later to cut, "My Bonny," with the Beatles.

Their home was furnished by six army cots and a single light bulb. Ventilation of the flat was by a fan-light, and there was no heating at all. The flat, with wall-to-wall wood, was threadbare by any comparison. Washing was a problem also, as there was no running water. Just a wash-basin, a stand and a jug. Their diet of cornflakes, bread, and beer probably made John and Stu wish for the old Liverpool bed-sitter days.

Despite the privation that they endured this was really a very lucrative period for the boys for this was where they began to form the Beatle-Style. In those early days they all took turns to vocalize. Stu liked to specialize in the soft slow ballads, and really had the frauliens rolling in the aisle. Not that there was much of an aisle to roll in. The clubs in Germany are invariably crammed as full as possible with tables, leaving only a few feet for dancing.

The Star Club and the Kaiserkeller were no exception to the rule, in fact they might well have been ahead of every other club in that parricular sphere. In the vocalizing Pete Best had a couple of comedy numbers which were very well received. When Paul or John played piano, Stu would take up bass or rhythm guitar. He also played some lead.

With all of the frauliens flocking to where they played, the boys were at no loss for dates. Though by this time John had made up his mind to marry Cynthia, and so he took it pretty easy. Stu, on the other hand, met a fraulien named Astrid Kirschner and they went steady from there on in.

The Beatles would proabably have stayed in Germany much longer, but the German Police discovered that George was only seventeen and John had no work-permit. There was nothing for it but to return to England. Stu, being hooked on Astrid, decided to remain in Germany. He then enrolled at the Hamburg College of Art, but had the boys returned he would have probably rejoined the group immediately. Fate however, was not to have it so.

Eventually the Beatles were able to remove the legal restrictions which prevented them from playing in Germany. So, with a string of engagements at Liverpool's Cavern Club having re-inforced their ego, they once again set off for Deutschland. They were looking forward to seeing Stu, all of their friends and even their rooms over the cinema, crummy as they were. A tear-stained Astrid met the Beatles and told them that Stu was dead. Dead of a brain tumor that neither Astrid or the Beatles had known about. They were all stunned, it was too unbelievable. Lennon said hardly a word, there was nothing he could say. Stu was dead and that was that. But John was close to Stu, having known him longer than the others, and he was completely shattered by the news. He said nothing but it was there on his face for all to see. For the remainder of their time in Germany John often went to see Astrid and after leaving he wrote her several times.

Sutcliffe's personality is perhaps still a part of the Beatles, because out of all the musicians that have played with John, Paul and George, he like Ringo Starr is of the same mould. Stu died a painful death. The fact that he lived will be remembered.

KRLA ARCHIVES

WHAT ARE ALL THE TURTLES POINTING AT? Hmmm — wonder if they are trying to tell us something. Could they be saying that it's "You Baby?" Or perhaps they are simply pointing at a speedy rabbit who was just passing on down the road. Or maybe they discovered all of us hiding under this huge tortoise shell!!

How The Turtle Music Is Made
By Jamie McCluskey III

There just ain't *nothin'* slow about them Turtles, baby! I mean, like — they went and broke *all kinds* of attendance records recently when they drew over 4,000 screaming fans to a recent two-day personal appearance.

And that isn't even *mentioning* the phenomenal success which they have had with their disc sales. They have released only three records so far — and all three of them have been Top Ten hits. Their latest, "You Baby," is certainly no exception to the Turtle's fast-moving rule.

Individually, there are six Turtles. Howard Kaylan, who was born in New York, plays saxophone, clarinet, tambourine, and harmonica. He is also one of the lead vocalists for the group.

Before joining the ranks of the Shelled Ones, Howard worked for three years as a member of a rock 'n' roll band and went on to become a disc jockey on a Los Angeles radio station — Top 40, of course.

He attended the University of California for a year, but then finally gave in to his overwhelming urge to become a performer. In one of his more candid moments, Howard admitted that, "I couldn't fight it any more; I'm basically a ham at heart!"

Turtle Number Two is Jim Tucker, who boasts total proficiency with both the harmonica and the guitar. Jim had also performed with other groups before joining the Turtles and established a fine reputation for himself as an accomplished guitarist.

He enjoys jazz and rock 'n' roll, and one is quite likely to discover him clad in typically English gear. (literal translation: English-style clothing.)

Climbing into position Number Three is Turtle Al Nichol, who hails from North Carolina. Al swears that he cannot remember a time in his Turtled life when he didn't want to be a singer, although it was a full two years in college before he finally gave himself up to a life-time of music.

It was a decision worth making though, as Al is a talented musician, able to leap tall mushrooms at a single bound — as well as being able to create wonderful things on the guitar, piano, organ, bass trumpet, and the harpsichord.

Mark Volman hops in on the fourth Turtle Spot of the evening, as the most talented clarinet, saxaphone, drum, and harmonica player in Never-Never-Land. He also claims that he had at one time seriously considered devoting his life to the pursuit of fires — in other words, he wanted to be a fireman. *Howsomever* — music rushed in and saved the day by converting Mark and making him into a total rock 'n' roll addict. He is now — we are happy to report — a hopeless case. Hopelessly addicted to making great Turtle music.

Leave it to Charley. Yep, Charles Portz just had to drop in and round out the figure to an even Turtle Quintet. Oh well — some days you just can't lose for winning!

Charles is another vocalist-type with our boys, the Turtles. *But* — he also specializes in the creation of unbelievably keen sounds on the guitar, bass, and harmonica.

While still in high school, he was the California State Diving finalist, at which time he "fooled around with music just for kicks."

He then "kicked" along in college for about a year, and finally took the real "plunge" into the field of music, where he soon found himself splashing around with the likes of the Turtles in a great big pond of success.

After Charley, we find a sixth Turtle ambling along, and just arbitrarily we shall refer to him as Don Murray. Don is the man who makes with the drum beats in the back of the group. He is also quite hooked on Spanish food, suits with vests, and polka dot shirts.

Not only that, but Don just happens to be about the most "camp" individual of the lot. Know why? 'Cause he digs collecting "collector's comic books; predominantly early Walt Disney!!!"

Hmmmm — methinks I detect some foul shades of Batman lurking hereabouts! Well, nevertheless — if you add them all together, you will undoubtedly arrive at the sum of six Turtles. Which generally adds up to being nothing more or less than simply great — *times six!!!*

It's In The Bag
By Eden

A little belated perhaps, but nonetheless I would like to extend my very best wishes to Patti and George Harrison. Have to admit that this latest Beatle marriage took us all by surprise at *The BEAT* — even though George *has* been telling us that he would marry Patti for some time now. Poor Shirley Poston — I'm not sure if she'll *ever* get over the shock!!

Speaking of George — hang on, now, Shirl! — I thought you might be interested in hearing a few of the replies George gave recently when a national music paper in England threw a few words at our Man From MBE. So if you're ready, here we go:

Christmas: "Fun and twinkling lights. Nothing religious for me, really."
Jagger: "Mick. The singer with the Stones."
Pop Art: "I haven't seen enough to form an opinion."
Hamburg: "Yeah, yeah, yeah."
Folk: "Good folk is great, but there's too much bad folk which people say is great."
James Bond: "Over-done."
Elvis: "Well done."
P. J. Proby: "A bit foolish, but great to have around."
Policemen: "A bit simple and not understanding."
A Talent For Loving: "A good book. A western, but different to others."
Middle-aged autograph hunters: "Depends on their attitude. They are not bad on their own."
Communism: "It's terrible. I only know a little bit about it, but what I know is off."
Eppy: "An amazing businessman and our pal."

A few Animal tracks here and there lead us to some rather interesting findings. The boys have switched labels in England and are now on Decca. Their first record on the new label was released in England on the 12th, and is entitled "Inside Looking Out."

Interesting note on this disc is that it is the first to be penned for the group by lead singer Eric Burdon and fellow Animal, Chas. Chandler.

I am certain that you have all heard of the brilliant composer Richard Rodgers. But believe it or not — Mr. Rodgers has also heard of *us* — forgotten breed of teen-agers that we are!!

Just recently, the distinguished musician-composer went on record saying: "I couldn't write for the Beatles. I don't know how. If I tried, I think I'd fall flat on my face because it's something I'm not equipped to do."

Mr. Rodgers also explained that he doesn't feel that he really understands the so-called "rock and roll," but was quick to add: "Who am I to say that it isn't any good?"

Hear, hear!! Now that's what we like to hear. A little honest humility from someone like you. Thank you, Mr. R.

Awwwww — poor baby! Y'know what happened to Brian Jones? Had an autoharp flown all the way to England from the Colonies — and then it was smashed in transit.

I believe that that is what our British friends call simply *smashing*.

Just a few weekends back, Herman's Hermits' recording manager, Mickie Most, rounded up the boys and recorded them — this time in *French!* Hmmmm — Parlez vous francais, Herman-luv???

Spencer Davis of the Spencer Davis Group — a fab new bunch of singers from over the foam — looks like a cross between Paul McCartney of the Beatles, and Jim McCarty of the Yardbirds — and that ain't bad!!!

The Rock 'n' Roll Days of Bill Haley

If the late disc jockey Allen Freed invented the term, Rock 'n' Roll, he did it to describe the music of Bill Haley. Bill Haley, whose record, "Rock Around The Clock," was sweeping the world.

The Beatles alone are the only musical act that has ever surpassed the frenzy that a concert by Haley aroused. When the Haley band started to beat the fans acted as though possessed. They danced in the aisle, they cheered, they clapped, they stamped, they tore their own seats from the floor and the draperies from the walls.

Bill Haley wore his kiss-curl, the band jumped up and down and the fans shrieked. The records rolled off the press, the money rolled in, and the promoters rolled on the floor — in agony. The cost of re-decorating a concert hall, after a Bill Haley concert, sometimes surpassed the actual take.

The Comets were the most fantastic musical event in the history of popular music. They played the music that youth wanted to hear, it was Country & Western, it was Rhythm & Blues, it was the greatest new dance beat since the age of swing, it was Rock 'n' Roll.

The "King" made a movie, it was a success, it was Bill Haley, it was "Rock Around The Clock." The fans loved the movie, but it was too much for them, the motion picture's music made them exhuberent, it made them feel destructive, so they tore up their seats from the floor, and they tore the draperies. So it was banned in some towns, and then some cities, and then some countries.

But Rock 'n' Roll could not die, so it had to progress. New artists had new idea's, they had new rhythm's, they had new drumbeats, and Bill Haley had Rock Around The Clock. But the new rhythm's and the new drumbeats affected the fans, the music made them dance as Rock Around The Clock no longer did.

British Top 10

1. KEEP ON RUNNING...Spencer Davis Group
2. MICHELLE...The Overlanders
3. SPANISH FLEA...Herb Alpert
4. LETS HANG ON...Four Seasons
5. LOVE IS JUST A BROKEN HEART...Cilla Black
6. DAYTRIPPER/ WE CAN WORK IT OUT...The Beatles
7. A MUST TO AVOID...Herman's Hermits
8. MY GIRL...Otis Redding
9. TILL THE END OF THE DAY...The Kinks
10. YOU WERE ON MY MIND...Crispian St. Peters

KRLA ARCHIVES

Yeah, Well Beatles
A Touch of Traffic—A Bit Of Cold

By Tammy Hitchcock

Since George went off and got married (on our deadline day yet—which was most inconsiderate of him really) I thought I should, in all decency, put the Beatles on our "Yeah, Well Hot Seat."

'Course, I'm not too happy with George at the moment. Not because he married Patti. I think that's great! I mean, if he couldn't have *me* he might as well take *her*. What I am upset about is that he got married on *Friday*. I've already explained that Friday is our deadline day but unless you've worked on a paper I don't suppose you really understand what that means.

In this particular case it meant that we had the paper all finished (well, *almost* finished) and George had to go and get married. It tore up the whole office, and I kid you not!

In order to capture the two fab pictures of George and Patti we had to travel all the way downtown to the offices of UPI and AP. Which wouldn't have been too bad except that it was Friday afternoon during the rush hour.

Which isn't funny—honest! Usually the boss and I would have gone over in her Stingray but we didn't have enough time to get lost so "Dear Susan" and I had to go alone.

I drove and Susan ran—literally. You know how hard it is to find a parking space downtown during *any* hour but this Friday everyone outdid themselves. So, I dropped Susan off on the corner in a *No Stopping Zone* and while she jumped out I explained to the policeman how my car just happened to have stopped cold right there at that particular spot.

I don't think he really believed me, but since all the traffic behind me was stopped and everyone was honking he didn't give me a ticket.

Yeah, well that was great but it meant that I had to drive around the block and pick Susan back up. Which was one big mistake. Driving around the block, I mean.

You see, it took approximately one half hour to get around that darn block. When I finally made it I was on the wrong side of the street and that same policeman was eyeing me suspiciously so I decided to make the tour again and pick Susan up on the right side.

The Shivers

Yeah, well it was a little better the second time around (they always say it is, you know). It only took me *fifteen* minutes. That meant that poor Susan had been standing on the corner for a total of 45 minutes—shivering and deciding that I had surely forgotten her but still clutching the precious pictures of George and Patti.

I looked at the policeman, he looked at me—and Susan started walking the *other* way! You see, she wasn't wearing her glasses. She had seen a Mustang pull up but she wasn't sure that it was me and she didn't want to get into a stranger's car. So, she just kept walking.

Yeah, well along about this time the policeman wasn't just *looking*, he was coming over. I figured I'd had it and the next phone call I made would be from jail. I screamed frantically at Susan to for heaven's sakes get in the car and she squinted at the car unable to see for sure if it was me, all traffic came to a halt but all horns were in perfect working order and the policeman was *almost to the car*.

Would you believe total, absolute panic? I'm not exactly sure what happened next but somewhere in the space of a minute, Susan put her ESP into practice, decided it was me after all, hopped into the car just as the policeman reached my window.

Logical Lie

We both explained how George had gotten married and how it had just *ruined* everything and that's why we were holding up five miles of traffic and parked in a No Stopping Zone. Which was really very logical.

Yeah, well that did it. I don't know if it was the sight of a slightly blue "Dear Susan" or the sight of a crazy Tammy (and a woman driver to boot) which did it but something told that policeman not to mess with us. So, he just ordered us to "Get that vehicle moving—at once!"

Anyway, we made it back to the office all in one piece and without making a stop at the local jailhouse. And as a bonus we had two pictures of George and Patti which had come directly from England via Telstar, though I must admit they were almost frozen too.

Yeah, well that doesn't have a heck of a lot to do with the Beatles, does it? And I did start out by saying that I was going to put John, Paul, George and Ringo on the "Hot Seat," didn't I? Would you believe that I tell lies?

You wouldn't? Then I guess I'm forced into talking about the Beatles. The thing I like best about the Liverpool Four is their wild sense of humor. It's gear, fab, groovy and all that other.

Press Agent

You remember the time the Beatles held their New York press conference and someone asked John how he would account for the Beatles' success. "We have a press agent," John replied strictly deadpan.

And then there was the time the Beatles were on their way to the British Embassy in Washington to meet Sir David Ormsby Gore. George turned to their press agent and asked, "Who is this Ormsby Gore anyway?"

"Ormsby Gore," answered the agent. "Don't be soft," snapped George, "I know that but is his name Ormsby or Gore?"

"It's Sir David Ormsby Gore."

"Is he a Lord?" inquired Goerge.

"No, he's a Knight."

"Was he gored when he was knighted?" George asked.

Yeah, well I don't think the press agent ever answered George. And to tell you the truth, I don't know if he was knighted in the gorge or if he was gored when he was knighted.

I think the funniest Beatle quote I ever heard was when George and John were vacationing in Tahiti. They chartered a boat and became regular sea dogs.

Dirty Big Fish

Only John forgot to wear his glasses, so this one day he was peering over the boat's railing when he shouted to George: "Hurry, George, I see a dirty big fish and he's wearing sun glasses."

Being a good friend, George dutifully rushed over and looked down at the water. "John, me lad," George said seriously, "that ugly fish is *you*."

Yeah, well it was too. John can't see much without his glasses (he suffers from "Dear Susan's affliction) and that "dirty big fish" was indeed John's own reflection.

Yeah, well that's the Beatles for you! I wonder how we ever managed to live without 'em.

A Road Tour For Joe Tex

Joe Tex, who first hit the charts with "You've Got to Hang on to What You've Got," is a very busy man nowadays.

He's in the midst of five solid months of one night stands that started in Denver in January and will end in Hollywood.

That's hangin' on to what you've got, Tex.

KRLA ARCHIVES

The Beat Visits Jeremy

Ever wonder how a popular bachelor pop star spends his off days? We did, so our *BEAT* photographer followed Jeremy Clyde around his London flat as he sleepily cooked up some breakfast and then headed upstairs to the rooftop to catch a bird's-eye view of London.

Luckily for us, it was a clear day and the view from Jeremy's rooftop is *out of sight!* Next Jeremy led our photographer back down the stairs where he rounded up some old swords. Fancies himself a swashbuckling hero maybe?

As our weary photographer made his way to the door Jeremy waved a cheery goodbye over the kitchen door. So now you know what Jeremy Clyde does with his days off—fools around just like the rest of us!

... IT'S A SAD LIFE WHEN ONE HAS TO COOK ONE'S OWN BREAKFAST.

... ALL THAT COOKING TIRED JEREMY OUT SO HE TAKES A FEW MINUTES REST.

... AND THEN IT'S ON TO FUN AND GAMES.

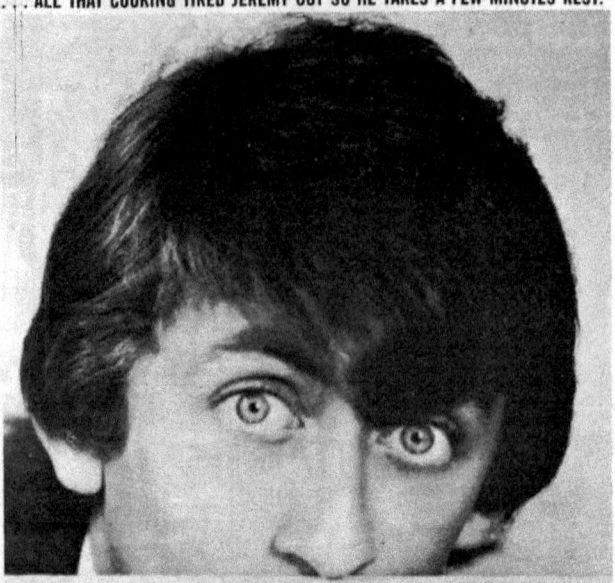

... WOULD YOU BELIEVE PEEKING OVER THE KITCHEN DOOR?

KRLA ARCHIVES

The Adventures of Robin Boyd...
By Shirley Poston

CHAPTER FIFTEEN

Monday was forever in arriving, and when it finally got there, it was blue. And so was Robin Boyd.

She had spent all day Sunday hugging Mick Jagger's jacket, but a lot of good it had done her. The jacket absolutely refused to hug back the way it had the night she was sent home from England.

George was *gone*. It was as simple as that. And, if she didn't rectify her latest smooth move within the next two weeks, George was going to *stay* that way. And so were her magic powers.

Shivering inside the jacket (which she had worn because it looked rather good on her if she did say so herself) (and, she did), Robin jammed her books under her arm and stalked off into the sunrise.

Ordinarily, she nagged her father into dropping her off at school on his way to the office, but on this particular morning, she preferred to walk.

Way Out

Not only because it was difficult to stalk when riding in a car. Also because it would take her one-half hour to make the trip on foot, which is exactly how long she had given herself to think of a way out of this mess. Or else.

And a mess it was.

It wasn't bad enough having to remember the events of Saturday last. The a.m. newspaper had served as a painful reminder.

"Rock Concert Ends In Riot." So said the story on page twelve.

The Rolling Stones, it seems, had added something new to their act. The lead singer's jacket, it seems, had flapped out of the auditorium at the close of the evening.

And the British teens in attendance, it seems, had mobbed the group twice as hysterically. Proclaiming them not only a fab and gear group, but he greatest wizards of our time as well.

Well and good, thought Robin dourly. For the British teens in attendance, that is. But what about the poor Stones? The fivesome who knew *better*? Who knew that where they *were* fab musicians, they were *not* gear musicians? Who, as a result, were cowering somewhere at this very moment, fearing for their sanity?

Further continuing to stalk, Robin began to fear for her own.

What if she *didn't* come up with a solution? She would never again get to be a bird in both senses of the word. She would never get to terrorize -er- visit the Beatles or the Stones again, to say nothing of the groups she had yet to terrorize -er- visit.

And Then What?

And what's more, she would *never ever* get to find out what happened next after George, that very special Liverpudlian of genie fame, said "Shurrup and give us a kiss."

Shivering again, Robin further burrowed into Mick's jacket and thought violently. And got nowhere. Except to school without a plan.

Her first two classes dragged miserably. (How else could they drag when one was a sixteen-year-old failure? And she was just on her way to third-hour English when it happened.

Reaching into the pocket of Mick's jacket in search of the bubble gum she'd stashed there earlier, Robin gasped and stopped dead still.

Unmindful of the fact that approximately one thousand fellow students immediately collided with her, Robin drew her hand out of the aforementioned pocket and re-gasped.

For, winking and shining in the palm of her aforementioned hand, was a diamond ring.

Her knees knocking loudly, Robin scurried to her desk and sat down with a clunk.

What was a *diamond ring* doing in her (that is, Mick's) pocket? It hadn't been there before! She'd combed the coat with a fine-tooth (which is hard on tweed) and found nothing!

Then, suddenly, the significance of the ring rang (can you tell me what's a ring-rang?) true. It was a clue! George was trying to tell her something.

"George," she breathed aloud, causing approximately thirty-five fellow students to fear for her sanity. "You aren't *completely* gone," she further breathed, causing the aforementioned number of students to be firmly convinced that she, however, was.

Robin smiled rejoicefully (if there is such a word) (there is now), in spite of the fact that she didn't have the foggiest notion what the clue meant.

Fifteen minutes later, she knew what she must do.

She knew it the moment her teacher said: "We will now write a letter to our pen pals overseas."

"*Wow!*" Robin exclaimed happily, causing her teacher (Miss Agnes Mard, from one of South Dakota's smaller towns) to smile toothily at this unexpected response.

Dear Michael

"If you do not have a pen pal overseas," Miss Mard continued, "you may select one from our overseas pen pal list." (Which somehow figured.)

But Robin scarcely heard her. She was too busy addressing an envelope to an overseas pen pal by the name of Michael P. Jagger.

Shortly thereafter, she composed the following letter.

Dear Michael:

How are you? I am fine. I certainly hope you are fine also. The weather here is good. Is the weather good there? I certainly hope so.

I will write and tell you all the latest news again soon.

Your friend,
Robin Boyd

P.S. I still have your jacket, and your ring. I'll keep them for you until I hear otherwise.

Robin Boyd then sat back in her desk and smiled fiendishly.

If her assumptions were correct, the mysterious ring actually did belong to Mick. And Mick, thanks to George, was now firmly convinced he had left the aforementioned ring in the pocket of the aforementioned jacket.

He'd Know

Which meant, of course, that when he read her letter, he would know that it's writer was somehow involved in the flapping incident which was now causing him to fear for his sanity.

What would happen next, Robin could scarcely imagine. But, she was certain, *something* would.

Robin's certainty did experience one anxious moment on the way out of class, when Miss Mard peered curiously at the address on Robin's overseas pen pal letter, but her panic was short-lived.

Mick's famous name failed to ring a bell because Miss Mard did not know a Rolling Stone from a doorknob. Which Robin felt was fair enough since she herself did not know a verb from a vacuum cleaner.

However, as the days slowly passed, Robin's panic returned. Tuesday crept by. Wednesday lagged. Thursday seemed endless. Friday was an utter eternity. And Saturday was sheer terror. Until the telephone rang.

And, as she nervously picked up the receiver, Robin knew that the *something* she'd been expecting to happen was about to.

(To Be Continued Next Week)

...BUFFY SAINTE-MARIE

Buffy—Popular And Influential

By George Lincoln Culver

She is only 22 years of age, but she writes her songs with a pen of maturity and thought. She has been performing professionally for only about three years now, and yet she has already achieved the status of being one of the most popular and influential folk artists in America.

Her name sounds almost French yet she is an American Indian, of the Cree tribe, and an alumna of the University of Massachusetts where she received her degree in education and Oriental Philosophy. She was also named as one of the ten most outstanding seniors in her graduating class, and she attended Smith, Mount Holyoke, and Amherst on a special program which was sponsored by the four colleges.

She is, to say the least, a most unusual and talented young woman. Her name—Buffy Sainte-Marie.

Buffy has been writing and composing songs since she was a child growing up in Maine, but it wasn't until she was in her last year at college that she first sang them publicly.

She was received with exclamatory ravings, and encouraged to pursue a professional career as a singer, and a writer-composer after she completed her stay at the University.

Since then, Buffy has appeared in most of the folk clubs all across the United States and Canada, including the Gaslight Cafe in New York; the Ash Grove in Los Angeles; and the Purple Onion in Toronto, Canada.

Buffy's songs are passionate, emotional, and sung with the personal feeling and conviction which only she can give them. Her first album on Vanguard was entitled "Buffy Sainte-Marie: It's My Way!" and has rapidly become one of the most popular of folk albums on the market.

Buffy was recently featured on a Canadian TV network special, and is currently completing work on her second album for Vanguard — "Many A Mile" which is scheduled for release shortly.

KRLA ARCHIVES

THE BEAT GOES TO THE MOVIES

"That Darn Cat"

By Carol Deck

Walt Disney has done it again and produced another rollicking family type fun picture, this one titled "That Darn Cat."

That Darn Cat, known as D.C. to his friends, is a large Siamese feline whose hunger is exceeded only by his quick temper and contempt for stupid people.

D.C. runs into a federal kidnapping case by simply following his nose, which has become interested in a hunk of salmon being carried home by one of the kidnappers. D.C. follows the salmon into the kidnappers hideout where the victim of the kidnapping, a bank teller named Margaret Miller, fastens her wrist watch around his neck in a silent bid for rescue.

She manages to scratch part of the word "Help" on the watch and that's what leads D.C. into the mess. D.C.'s owners, two young single girls whose parents are away, take opposing views of the meaning of the watch around the cat's neck.

Patti, the younger girl, played by Haley Mills, immediately surmises the meaning of the watch and plots to get the FBI to do something about it. But Ingrid, the older sister played by Dorothy Provine, figures the whole thing is absurd and maybe D.C. just likes to wear a watch.

But Patti persuades one FBI agent, who just happens to be allergic to cats, to take the case. She figures D.C. can lead them to the kidnappers and all the agent has to do is follow D.C. to them.

The agent's only problem is how to track a cat, particularly a clever cat who doesn't like to be followed on his nightly prowlings around town.

The whole thing leads to some hilarious scenes with electric beeping systems to track the cat, a rather silly car pool and any number of mixed up romances.

"That Darn Cat" is an alarmingly realistic movie if you've ever been owned by a cat, and even if you haven't you'll realize that maybe animals are smarter than people sometimes.

DEAN JONES, as the FBI agent, and Hayley Mills attempt to get paw prints of D.C. to aid in the search.

SUCCESS??? Well, they got a lot of paw prints. Let's hope at least one of them is on that sheet of paper.

... RODDY McDOWALL AND D.C.

... HAYLEY MILLS

... DOROTHY PROVINE

KRLA ARCHIVES

America's Largest Teen NEWSpaper 15¢

KRLA Edition BEAT
MFP

FEBRUARY 26, 1966

Nancy Sinatra: What Next For Newest Star?

KRLA BEAT

Volume 1, Number 50   February 26, 1966

Detroit Council Honors Supremes

The Supremes who have undoubtedly received more honors than any female pop group living (or otherwise) have tucked yet another one under their belts.

The Detroit Common Council recently paid Diana, Mary and Florence one of the highest honors any city can bestow upon a resident when they passed a resolution commending the Supremes for the high moral standard which they are setting for Detroit's, as well as America's, teenagers.

It was only last month that the Supremes were chosen to perform at the Inaugural Ball of Detroit's Mayor, Jerome P. Cavanaugh. And then it was off to Puerto Rico for a stint at San Juan's El San Juan Hotel.

The busy Supremes also managed to appear on "The Red Skelton Show" where they showed the world that not only can they sing but they can maneuver some pretty tricky dance steps as well.

February 17 stands to be one of the biggest nights in the already precedent-setting career of the Supremes because this is the night that they make their triumphant return to the Copacabana.

When Jules Podell announced months ago that he was booking the Supremes at New York's famed Copa many scoffed at the idea declaring that the crowd which the Copa draws would not be the least bit interested in a pop group, especially a *female* pop group.

But these doubters were forced to eat their words as the Supremes drew capacity crowds every single night during their engagement. In fact, they impressed the Copa's management so much that they lost no time in booking the Supremes for a return engagement.

It all goes to show that you just can't keep a fantastic group like the Supremes down. No matter where they play they win the audience everytime—talent is talent no matter where it appears.

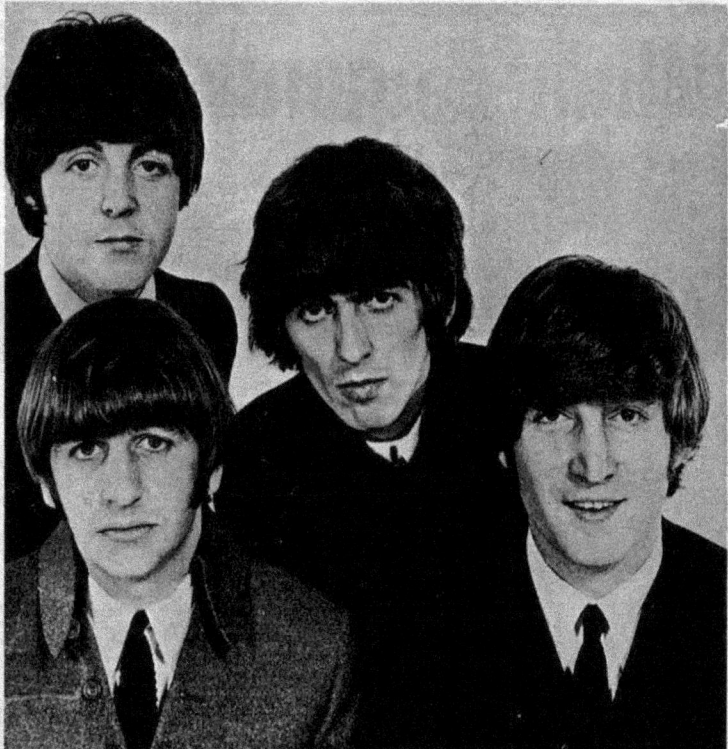

THE BEATLES' first concert date of '66 has been announced by their press agent and **BEAT** writer Tony Barrow. It will be played on May 1 at the Wembley Empire Pool just outside of London. On the show with them will be the Stones, Herman's Hermits, Tom Jones, the Fortunes, Dusty Springfield and at least 10 other acts.

'Batman' Is High Camp

Every now and again there is a revolution in the television industry. Everything is running along smoothly, we have an equal amount of cowboys, private eyes, comedians and singers. Then all of a sudden someone invades the airways with a new and fresh idea.

Think back. "Bonanza" came on and snatched the ratings pronto. And almost immediately our television screens were saturated with "Bonanza" imitations. Ditto when Doctors Casey and Kildare descended upon us. And now, of course, it's "Batman."

Never in the entire history of television has a new show polevaulted to the very top of the ratings in a period of only three weeks. But then Batman can do just about anything. He is currently perched at the pinnacle of television success and from all indications looks as if he'll reside there for quite sometime.

"Batman's" unprecedented rise to the top of the ratings has had a rather mixed reaction from the cast and crew. Naturally, they're pleased and excited on one hand but on the other the whole thing spells nothing but plenty of hard work.

Two At Once

Twentieth Century Fox produces "Batman" but, unfortunately, there isn't room on the studio lot to film the show so Twentieth has been forced to rent space at the Desilu Studios. And because "Batman" was a late season starter, airing only last month, they are filming two shows simultaneously.

The feverish crew members toil from 7 a.m. until ten in the evening and it is not unusual to find the cast and crew still performing before as well as behind the cameras as late as midnight.

A television show in production has always been strictly off limits for kids. In fact, most shows are closed to *everyone*. But again "Batman" finds itself an exception to the rule. Officially it has a closed set but unofficially it is often visited by the children of various television higher-ups.

It's hard to explain the success of "Batman." Some attribute it to the show's new and fresh approach but most credit it to the fact that "Batman" is high camp. And being so high camp has led the series to be adopted by the chic, hippy "in" group, otherwise known as the Jet Set.

Huge Budget

The ABC Network has agreed to allot $65,000 per segment for "Batman." Much of the budget is used for all the special effects and gimmicks, such as the Bat Mobile et al., which has helped to increase Batman's amazing ability to handle all "bad guys" as well as boost his already high ratings.

Adam West, Batman in disguise, is a serious and intensive young man and in large part the success of the series is due to West. His friend and cohort, Burt Ward, but probably better known to you as Robin is something else again.

He fell into the Robin bag almost completely by accident. Burt was a student at UCLA when his real estate father sold a house to a producer and casually mentioned that his son, Burt, was looking for a show business break.

The producer helpfully suggested the name of an agent. And here Burt himself takes up the story, "I was just looking for a role as an extra. I didn't even know what part I was reading for! I'd never even acted in high school," grinned the boyish looking Burt, "so it's good that the part doesn't require any acting."

Well, whether the part requires any acting or not the series is a smashing success. So, watch for the carbon copies to begin burning our television screens next season. They'll probably all be there—the Green Hornet, Wonder Woman, the Plastic Man — the whole crowd. We can't escape them—they're tired of being comic book heroes, they want to be high camp too!

. . . THE SUPREMES

Inside the BEAT

Lennon Speaks of Dylan	2
Hotline London	3
Kinks Vs. Rolling Stones	4
When You Meet A Star	5
The Sinatras' Good Year	6-7
Sam The Sham—Minus Beard	10
Pop Is Comin' Up Hollies	11
War Without Protest	12
Londoners Look At Beatles	13
The Nurk Twins—Now	14
The BEAT Goes to the Movies	15

The BEAT is published weekly by BEAT Publications, Inc., editorial and advertising offices at 6290 Sunset Blvd., Suite 504, Hollywood, California 90028. U. S. bureaus in Hollywood, San Francisco, New York, Chicago and Nashville, overseas correspondents in London, Liverpool and Manchester, England. Sale price, 15 cents. Subscription price: U.S. and possessions, $5 per year; Canada and foreign rates, $9 per year. Application to mail at second class postage rates is pending at Los Angeles, California.

KRLA ARCHIVES

When Legends Speak of Legends

By Doug Gilbert

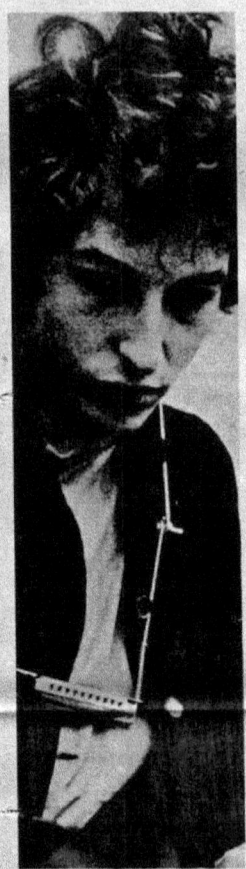

When an established performer gives his opinion on the ability of another star, the result is often a gain or loss of status for the person being discussed. Of course, this is sometimes reversed. As when Tom Jones was recently critical of the Beatles. A majority of Tom's fans considered his words to be both unwarranted and unfair. Whatever your reaction, the fact is that Tom's prestige did suffer. Though obviously it can only be a temporary loss. After all, Tom is a singer of tremendous ability, and this ability will certainly make up for anything that he might have said in the heat of the moment.

Normally stars are not too critical of other stars as it is considered unprofessional. Personally I don't agree with this idea. The Beatles are among the most outspoken of people, regardless of whether their words are courteous or not, so they can't complain about anybody else speaking his mind—and they don't.

Thanks To John

John Lennon can be both generous and ungenerous in his choice of words, but he usually makes a good point. As when he once spoke of Donovan: "I bought Donovan's 'Catch The Wind' so that I could listen to it, without having to look at him." However, when he likes something or somebody John tells the world about it. His praise of Bob Dylan was a deciding factor as to the success of Dylan's first trip to England.

When a Beatle gives an opinion it gets around faster than a declaration from the House of Windsor, so after John praised Dylan, English fans went out and bought up all the available seats for Bob's string of concerts. Before embarking on his U.K. tour Bob Dylan was comparatively unknown in the world of popular music. It is true that he was already accepted in the folk circles as a sort of demi-God, but either there are not many folk fans or else they don't buy as many records as their Rock 'n' Rolling cousins. After Bob added a beat to his music he was gradually becoming more popular but it was the U.K. trip that finally started the ball rolling.

Dylan for Dinner

John Lennon has said that he first heard of Dylan in France where Paul picked up an album by Bob, and they both spent the rest of the day running the grooves off it. Later in 1964 he met him in New York, during a Beatle tour, and they became pretty good friends. When Dylan reached England he was invited by John to stay at his Tudor Mansion in Weybridge. Dylan accepted, at least for dinner, and so he got to know Cynthia.

Neither the Mods or the Rockers are prone to believing everything that they hear, but in England John Lennon is fast becoming something of a folk leader, so the kids hear what he has to say and then test his words by checking the facts for themselves. They checked out Bob Dylan and they liked what they heard.

Even if the concerts had not been sell-outs, the people who did attend would have recognized Dylan's brilliance and put the credit where it belong. But that kind of acclamation travels much slower than the voice of Lennon.

When Dylan returned to America he found that he was the leader of a new Folk-Rock revolution that was sweeping the U.S. from a point somewhere along Madison Avenue. Months later Lennon was asked how he felt about being something of an unpaid publicity man for Bob. John replied: "If I was, I don't mind—Dylan is a great talent. Donovan has done more to promote Dylan anyway." Donovan and Dylan fans in the U.K. are still arguing as to whether Donovan is an original artist in his own right, or simply a carbon copy of Dylan.

One thing that I do feel confident in saying is that Robert Zimmerman's talent, in his particular musical sphere, is almost beyond comparison. Had he never left Hibbing for a fourth time; had he never spent his summers treading and devouring the dirt of this continent, or his winters freezing to the bone in the City of New York; had he never heard the wail of a mouth-organ or the rhythm of a guitar, he would still have emerged from the mass of talent that is America and made his presence felt.

Dylan's Success

Dylan's success has also brought problems. His major one seems to be the fanaticism of some of his fans. Donovan recalled a Dylan concert that he attended: "This fellow came up to Dylan and said that he would kill for him. He kept asking Dylan who he wanted him to kill." People like this are too far gone for persuasion, but ordinary fans should keep in mind that Dylan is a man—not a God. Indeed he is a small and seemingly frail man, but a man who has displayed a brilliant comprehension of the very soul of rhythmic music.

For Girls Only

By Shirley Poston

SPEAKING OF GEORGE...! I couldn't say that last week... I just couldn't. But thanks to all of you, I'm almost my normal, retarded self again!

I don't mean to be soft, (except in the head, and that happened years ago), but I just had to sit down and *blither* when the mail started roaring in.

George's Marriage

The rush of cards and letters about George's marriage began on January 22, and it still hasn't stopped. And you'll just never know what you've done for my morale.

I never *dreamed* that so many of you would stand by me (there, poised on that cliff overlooking the city) (well, I *felt* like it.)

Wow, have you taught me a lesson. Two of them. From now on, I'm going to appreciate my friends more. And I'm going to stop feeling so sorry for myself.

If you don't mind, I'd like to make this whole column one big thank-you letter. I can't possibly mention all of you by name, because that would take *ten* columns, but I'll cram in as many mucho-gracias as I possibly can.

First of all, a million thanks for the sympathy cards from Toni Holiday and Marianne Curson (co-presidents of the Phoenix, Arizona Branch of the Official Rolling Stones Fan Club)... from Cynthia Brunham of Los Angeles (who said in a P.S.—"There's still Mick Jagger if that's any consolation")... from Barbara Salkeld of La Mirada (a hand-made card yet, mit flowers!)... from Mary Louise Winters of Encino (another hand-made masterpiece, complete with "tear-stains" and four aspirins)... from Sally Mitchell of San Carlos (this card had a sad-looking horse on the front, and on the inside it said "heard you got hitched" Sally crossed out the "you" and wrote in "George And Patti"—under the part where the card read "Congratulations," she penned "You ran second." (Gave me shivers!)... from Katie Henderson and Ellen Love of Ventura... from Susan Lopez of Los Angeles... and too many more to mention. Make that *two* million thanks!

Just a few personal thanks for the many wonderful letters. To Leora Thyrring of Livermore who took my mind off myself (and it was about time) by telling me all about the time she gave George a great big smack (as in kiss) at the San Francisco concert. Only problem was, it turned out to be a total stranger instead!

To Suzy Beckenbach of Pacific Palisades who told me to sit down and have a cuppa tea (I did, too)... To Kathy Lear of Santa Monica who said she was sorry my plans to trap George were smashed (*she's* sorry???)... To Linda Wetzel of Garden Grove who said "I think you would be a better wife to George" (for which I shall luv her forever) (unfortnately, George doesn't agree.)

To War?

To Debbie Burns who said she hoped I'd continue to rave about George in my column (I wasn't going to, but you can see about how long *that* lasted)... To Jayne Hand of El Cajon who sent me a copy of a George poem written by her friend, Jeannine La Plant... To Gloria Hamblin from Upland who sent me a copy of a beautiful Beatle poem called "When England Went To War." If all of you haven't heard this poem, please let me know and I'll print it here. It's desperately sad, but it really makes you appreciate your own special Beatle, and the other three as well... To Leslie Boom of Santa Rosa for sending me this same poem.

Last but not least of those there is room to mention this week, thanks to Sheryl Cord of Los Angeles for her letter, and one line in particular..."I'm not a George fan, but I'm wearing black to school like the rest of my friends, in your honor."

That made me *double*-blither. So did all the letters that began "you were the first person I thought of when I heard the news about Patti and George." Because I did the same thing. Thought of myself first. Not of his happiness, or the sadness his marriage was causing so many others.

I hope I'll never be that selfish again. I wish I could write to every Harrisonite in the world and reassure them that they aren't alone either.

Whoops! I'm forgetting something! And that is to say *three* million thanks to all of you who called *The BEAT* to see how I was taking the news. Sorry I wasn't there to take the calls. I suppose you think I was off somewhere, having a tantrum. I also suppose you're *right!*

If something really disastrous happens to you, why not write and tell me about it? Then I'll have the readers of "For Girls Only" write to *you!* Not by name, of course. I would forward the letters, like with "Bev" and the Lennon girl from England.

The Miracle

Think about it. Maybe we could make it into a club or something. Maybe I'm also out of my mind (the rumor to this effect continues to persist), but your letters sure came to my rescue, and I don't see why the same miracle couldn't be worked for others.

I'm still sad about George (and am certainly never going to *speak* to him again) (lies, all lies), but if this makes any sense, I'm sad in a different way. Like I love him in sort of a different way now.

Oh, shut up, Shirl. Why are you being so maudlin when for the last three nights you stayed awake plotting how you're going to "borrow" George from Patti? (P.S. to Patti—I'll give him back, I promise.) (I think.) (But not very often.)

Now, if you'll excuse me, I have to get back to that plot. Poor, dear George. Thought you were safe, didn't ya?

KRLA ARCHIVES

HOTLINE LONDON
Pop Music World Turns To Spring
By Tony Barrow

In the Spring, they say, a young man's fancy turns to what the birds have been contemplating all winter. They say something like that. Anyway, the point I want to make is that Spring has come to England a little early this year if the first '66 crop of pop business romances is anything to go by.

The day after Patti Boyd married George Harrison, one of The Seekers tied the knot. He's Keith Potger and he married a pretty bank clerk, Pamela Powley, down in Bournemouth, the South Coast seaside resort where John Lennon's Aunt Mimi lives. True to their chosen group name, this Seeker sought plenty of wedding day publicity but the papers were so loaded with pix of Patti and George that Pam and Keith scarcely got a look in despite the fact that six hundred fans blocked the street outside the church to cheer them.

Silkie Merger

One other couple was less anxious to draw attention to their wedding. "You've Got To Hide Your Love Away" was the title of the Beatle-penned ballad which took The Silkie into America's Top Ten a few months back. Now that title takes on a new significance for I can reveal that two of The Silkie—dark-haired songstress Silvie Tatler (21) and fair-haired vocalist/guitarist Mike Ramsden (22)—married one another in almost total secrecy at the beginning of January. Indeed, as I type these words, no more than a handful of the couple's closest friends know about the marriage!

... Silvie Tatler

The Silkie were due to fly into New York to promote their latest self-composed Fontana single, "Keys To My Soul," via an Ed Sullivan appearance just after New Year. The trip was postponed and a few days later Silvie and Mike went through their short, quiet marriage ceremony at a registry office in New Brighton, just across the River Mersey from the Liverpool docks. Their stay-at-home honeymoon lasted less than one weekend.

In the meantime several other big chart personalities have been hotly denying reports of romance. Mike Smith of the DC5 has been seeing plenty of Jill Claydon but he refuses to admit they're more than good friends. Equally firm about the 'no-wedding-plans' bit is Tony Hicks of The Hollies. For the past few months he's been going steady with Samantha (Sammy) Juste, attractive young deejay from BBC Television's "Top Of The Pops" show. And R & B artist Georgie Fame strongly denies rumours that he's about to marry a mysterious young lady called Carmen.

Cilla, Too

Not all the week's kiss 'n' cuddle news is restricted to our male chart stars. Cilla Black, currently at the pop peak of the best-sellers with her single "Love's Just A Broken Heart," admits that her blond 24-year-old Liverpool road manager, Bobby Willis, is a "steady boyfriend."

"He's rather smashing" she says. "We're certainly not engaged and there are no plans to marry. We've been going steady for some time. I've known him for four years." Adds Bobby: "Cilla is a marvelous girl to be with."

As you know, the new single from The Rolling Stones is titled "19th Nervous Breakdown," another original composition by Mick Jagger and Keith Richards.

Although this track was recorded at studios in Hollywood, The Stones made additions to the original tapes at a special session in London a few days ago. "19th Nervous Breakdown" was rush-released in America during the second week of February when The Stones will be back on your side of the Atlantic prior to their Australian concert tour.

In Britain the single was issued one week earlier and over here we shall have Mick Jagger's answer to Paul's "Yesterday," the ballad recording of "As Tears Go By," on the lower deck of the disc.

NEWS BRIEFS . . . Balladeer Vince Hill has been on the British pop scene for a long time but has only just entered our Top Twenty with his latest deck, "Take Me To Your Heart Again." The title is to be released in the U.S. by Capitol on February 14. Vince will be heard on the soundtrack of the upcoming Frank Sinatra/Kirk Douglas/John Wayne movie "Cast A Giant Shadow" for which he has recorded "Love Me True" under the supervision of Elmer Bernstein . . . Nancy Sinatra has her first major disc hit in the United Kingdom with her latest Reprise release, "These Boots Are Made For Walkin'." Love those kinky lyrics! Nancy is at No. 1 this week.

New singles due in our shops include "I Can't Let Go" by The Hollies, "La-La-La" from Gerry and The Pacemakers, "Woman" by Peter and Gordon, "If You've Got A Minute Baby" by Freddie and The Dreamers (just available in America) and P.J. Proby with "You've Come Back" . . . Herman's Hermits now due into San Francisco on July 2 for start of concert tour. Their newest recording is, of course, "Listen People."

Knickerbockers Keeping Active

The BEAT introduced you to the great Knickerbockers way back in November before their smash disc, "Lies," had even been released. Without hearing the record we predicted fabulous things for the Knickerbockers—and we were right!

Since we last spoke with the four boys they've been busily making a name for themselves. They have appeared on practically all of the pop television shows, played clubs, released a hit record, an equally successful album and are soon to begin work on their first movie, "Out Of Sight," a pop film out of Universal.

Knickerbocker activity is not going to cease either—at least, not in the near future. They're set to start a series of appearances on "Where The Action Is" to be followed up shortly by a cross-country tour with the Dick Clark Caravan of Stars. There is also a possible European tour in the offing but it probably won't come about until next Fall.

Amid all their appearances the Knickerbockers have managed to get themselves involved in somewhat of a controversy surrounding their excellent imitations of the different pop groups.

Many have said that although the Knickerbockers can mimic just about everyone in the business better than anybody else they come out without a really original sound of their own.

But the Knickerbockers don't see it that way at all. Jimmy Walker, skin-pounder for the group, says: "Our material consists of almost everything that you hear on the radio. We enjoy playing every type of music that we hear on the radio because we usually wind up working at it very hard and it comes out pretty well."

"We always feel that people love to go to a night club or a show and hear a group that can imitate, or come close to, the sound that they hear on the radio everyday because this way they can judge how good or bad you are."

When you come right down to it a little bit of controversy never hurt anyone and, in fact, it tends to help. Whether or not you like the Knickerbockers' imitations, at least you pay attention when you hear them on the radio. You form an opinion and in order to do it you *have* to listen—maybe you'll even go to see them perform "live."

So, anyway you look at it the Knickerbockers are coming out ahead. And how much do you want to bet that they'll stay out there in front a long, long time because Buddy, Jimmy, Beau and Johnny have talent, determination and a hit record going for them. And with all that they just *can't* lose.

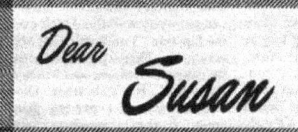

Dear Susan

Where's the best place to write to Bob Dylan? —Lorri Ungaretti
In care of Colombia Records, Sunset Blvd., Hollywood, Calif.

Which of the Stones are heard on "As Tears Go By?" —A George Fan
Mick sings lead, though Keith is the only Stone playing on it.

How old is Dave Burgess, Liverpool Five, and when is his birthday? —Carmen Perez
He was 21 last August 7.

Did Bob Dylan write "Turn, Turn, Turn?" —Robin
No, Pete Seeger did.

What's the difference between a Mod and a Rocker? —Joyce Walker
A Mod stands for 'modern.' A rocker is usually one who wears leather jackets, boots, rides motorcycles, etc.

What ever happened to the Sir Douglas Quintet? —Bob Ramey
They're still around, but are having difficulties trying to get another nation-wide hit.

Is Phil Spector married? —Micki Hartizien
Yes.

What is Cher's real name? —Joan McCaffertey
Cherilyn LaPierre Bono.

Does Cher have any brothers or sisters? —Joan Hackett
She has a sister, Georganne, who's 15.

Can you tell me something about "Alfie" on "Never Too Young?" —Cherly Bidder
Alfie, or David Watson, was born 22 years ago in London. He stands at 5'11" and has dark brown hair and eyes.

Does Joan Baez have any brothers or sisters? —Mike Love
She has a sister named Mimi, who is also a folk singer.

What is Keith Allison's real name and what are his favorite foods and colors? —Kathy Rose
Sidney Keith Allison likes the color black, and is mad about chicken, cornbread, and iced tea.

KRLA ARCHIVES

Are The Kinks A Threat To The Rolling Stones?

If there is one thing that we can be sure of in popular music, it is that the Beatles are the number one favorites. Nobody, but nobody, beats the Beatles! But who is number two?

The Rolling Stones have more or less been considered of late as the number two group in the world. It is true that they have had considerable opposition from such performers as Herman, the Beach Boys, the Byrds and the Animals but broadly speaking, the Stones have held onto their place as "second in command." This actually is pretty remarkable when you remember the first tour of America that the Stones did. It was an utter failure.

Unlike the Beatles, the Rolling Stones have built up their following over a period of time. And what a following it is now. Only the Rolling Stones could out-draw the Beatles, as they did at their concert in 1965 when they played at Shea Stadium in New York.

One of the biggest challenges, of recent months, to the Stoney Empire has been from the Kinks. The Kinks have been notching up hit after hit in the U.K. and have also had great success in the U.S.A. Their most recent hit "A Well Respected Man" is one of their greatest—in my opinion.

The Kinks are probably one of the most rocking groups around. The first record that they released was a real old-time rocking Little Richard number entitled "Long Tall Sally." This song was not very big for them (Probably because British Rock 'n' Roll fans, usually artists who record original numbers by Little Richard or Chuck Berry—only the Beatles can get away with this.) However, the flip-side "You Really Got Me" was a hit. This song was penned by Ray Davies, as are most of their hits. Ray's brother Dave Davies, who has penned many songs, is also a member of the group. Brothers Ray and Dave do most of the singing for the group. Ray's composing efforts have been recorded by Dave Berry, the Honeycombs and his song "I Go To Sleep" has been done by Peggy Lee and by Cher on her LP "All I Really Want To Do." Ray also has sent a couple of songs to Elvis Presley for possible recording. The other two members of the group are Pete Quaife and Mick Avery, who are as equally talented as the Davies brothers.

Kinkmania is gathering momentum and they are always greeted by huge crowds no matter where they play. During their recent tour of Germany the crowds really got out of hand. Immediately preceding the Kink tour in Germany, the Rolling Stones had almost been mobbed. Because of this the Federal Republic's police force had doubled their patrols at Kink concerts. This didn't make much difference as the crowds still managed to break through the cordons and surge around the stage. All of the crowds were yelling and screaming and as the police tried to move them to their seats there were many fights. Even so the German police action did prevent the Kinks from being mobbed. The whole tour was pretty fantastic and all of the crowds were close to rioting. Despite this the Kinks later reported that they enjoyed every minute of it. They were supported on the tour by some German groups. Among these was Englishman Tony Sheridan, who also used to sing with the Beatles at Hamburg's "Star" Club.

The Kinks are great fans of Lonnie Donegan, Buddy Holly and the Everly Brothers, and much of their work is based on the style of these famous artists. They are not alone in this of course. The Beatles have been greatly influenced by Donegan and some of their songs have a great "Holly" flavour. Ray and Dave try to write new songs as often as is possible, but many of their recent hits were penned years ago. None of the Kinks make any pretensions at being great singers or musicians but as Ray once said, "I give it everything that I have."

It took the Rolling Stones quite a period of time to achieve their present status. Maybe it will take the Kinks just as long, but the fact remains that they are a definite threat to the established order of the "second in command."

On the BEAT

By Louise Criscione

The whole pop world is still talking about George and Patti, and although they set the wedding date only a few days beforehand, George reveals that they decided to get married around Christmas.

"We were in the car and Patti was driving and I said, 'How about getting married, then?' and she said, 'yes, okay,' without taking her eyes off the road!"

At their press conference Patti wore a capri outfit but George let it be known that *he'll* wear the pants in the family. "I know Patti's wearing the trousers now, but I'd like to assure you I'll never be wearing the skirt!"

One other little note and then I'll drop the subject for good. Of Paul, George had this to say: "Actually, I feel sorry for him. He'll be hounded to death now us other three are married." There are no hard feelings, though, and Paul gifted the newlyweds with a Chinaman's head which George pronounced, "great."

Dave Clark Talks

The Dave Clark Five will shortly be paying a visit to Hollywood to discuss their next film. Dave has already had lengthy talks with Howard Koch, head of Paramount, when Mr. Koch flew to London. The movie is set to roll in late July and will be shot in London.

The Fortunes made quite a few fans in America but the whole trip ended up costing them something like $30,000. How did they manage that one? "We had two weeks to hang around with nothing to do," replied Rod Allen, "we just *had* to spend money."

...DAVE CLARK

They were forced to "hang around" because they ran into all sorts of problems with our Musicians Union and work permits and things like that. Anyway, the Fortunes are figuring on bringing the entire work permit problem to the House of Commons. They'd like to get the mess cleared up (and so would everyone else) so that when they return to the U.S. in May they can do so without any more hitches.

Marianne's Back

Marianne Faithfull is back in the thick of things again after the birth of her baby. She has already done several shows in France and at the end of February she will travel to Italy to promote her first Italian release, "This Little Bird," or however you'd say that in Italian!

Len Barry wants to be a movie star. Says: "I'd like to try the movies but no Beach Party types, please. I'd like to try a real dramatic part without the singing bit."

In fact, Len has already turned down a singing part in a pop movie because he felt that it would hurt rather than help his career. I admire Len for his honesty, anyway. He admits to being very much influenced by the late Sam Cooke. "I'm sure I've taken some of Sam's own phrasing and ad libbing ways in my own act." Well, it may not be too great of a thing to do, copying someone else I mean, but at least Len's frank about it.

Hollies Comin'?

The Hollies have been going to tour Stateside for months now—so when are they going to get here? "Look Through Any Window" is really a gas of a record but if they want an assured hit follow-up they'd better get over here in one big hurry.

Did London's Marquee Club ever swing last week! As you know, Paul Jones, lead singer for the Manfred Mann, was injured in an automobile crash but he thought he could come back to work right away.

However, his doctor had other ideas. He ordered Paul to keep his arm in a sling for several weeks to relieve the pressure from his broken collar bone. Paul's vocal ability hasn't been injured at all, but the doctor felt that his collar bone couldn't stand a possible tug from some admiring fan, so Paul is temporarily sidelined.

Despite Paul's absence the Mann decided to go ahead with their scheduled appearance at the Marquee, and friend, Eric Burdon, agreed to substitute for Paul while Eric Clapton, former Yardbird lead guitarist, sat in for another missing Mann. Must have been some show!

...ERIC BURDON

Mick Jagger told a magazine that he hates milk in anything—wonder why he poured about a half a pint of milk into his coffee when the Stones were recording at RCA?

KRLA ARCHIVES

What To Do When You Meet A Star

... DON'T PANIC

... EASY ON THAT HANDSHAKE

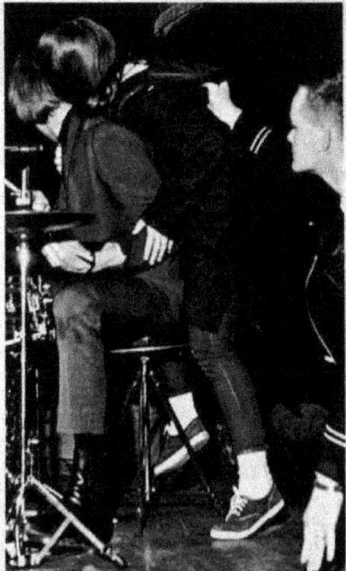

... KEEP CALM

... DON'T CHEW YOUR NAILS

Has this ever happened to you?

Something unusual occurs. Something unusually great on one hand, and unusually *un-great* on the other. And when it's all over, you find yourself wondering whether you should be laughing or crying. The event was that much a mixture of good and bad.

Well, this very sort of thing happened to a *BEAT* reader, who later told us about it in a letter.

She asked us not to print her letter, or her name, so we won't. But the problem she experienced needs talking about, because it happens to many of us.

The problem being what on earth to do when you meet a star. Not an arranged meeting. The you'll-never-guess-who-*I*-saw-today type. Where you suddenly find yourself in The Presence Of, and start praying you won't do the wrong thing. Because if you do, that nice warm feeling can turn into a cold snap and take most of the fun out of your big moment.

Before we continue, a word of warning. If you're thinking you should *be* so lucky to have such problems, don't be so sure you won't one of these days. Your chances of running into a star aren't as slim as they might seem.

On The Ground

Today's personalities are very down to earth. Instead of sticking to fancy restaurants and private parties, they congregate in the same places where we go to have fun.

Besides, for all you know, you and your favorite might even go to the same dentist! (Yech.) Or the same record shop. (That's more like it.)

And when you're suddenly star-gazing at close range, it's going to be very important to you that you do the right thing.

So, as any good Boy Scout could tell you, BE PREPARED!

How? Here's how. Because here's a list of Do's and Don'ts, guaranteed to help keep your big moment from deflating.

DON'T, for gosh sake, *gush!* Most people, stars and otherwise, are incurable hams. But compliments are like candy. Delicious at first. Sickening when overdone. If you can't resist the urge to say "You're great," say it! But say it one time with feeling, not in the form of a production number.

Do say *something!* Many stars literally dread meeting strangers because of the not very refreshing pause that often follows the "introduction." When there's a gap in the conversation, just standing there widens it. The trick of avoiding such situations is for you to keep one fact firmly in mind. You may be a stranger to the star, but he isn't one to you. (You may know more about him than *he* does.) So, if he's mad on music, there's your key. Talk about something you know *he* is interested in.

DON'T let the conversation become an "interview." A star spends so much of his time answering questions, a few moments of small talk would probably be a pleasant relief.

DO ask the star's permission if you would really rather interview than rave. A chance meeting isn't the time or place for an interview, but if you have a legitimate reason for wanting to ask questions, tell him what that reason is and see if he's agreeable before you whip out the old notebook and start jotting.

DON'T let the fact that you're nervous make you twice as nervous. Who *wouldn't* have the twitches at a moment like that? If you fumble around, just pass it off with a laugh. Remember, you're in the company of someone who is used to people fainting and trying to snatch him baldheaded. So a few blushes or stammers aren't going to shake him.

Be Ready

Do *really* be prepared where your *ultra-special* faves are concerned. The ones you'd rather fall down a well than bore or bug. Next time you have nothing to do in the study hall, give the matter some thought. Like, plan what you'd say to you-know-who if you're able to snare five minutes of his time. It's a fun thing to do, and just might come in handy someday. (Hey! *We've* just given this matter a little more thought ourselves and we want in on the fun. More on this subject in a near-future *BEAT*.)

DON'T wear out your welcome. Since the meeting just sort of *happened*, he probably has other plans. If he starts looking uncomfortable or keeps clearing his throat, don't offer him a cough drop. Clear *out!*

DO refrain from falling into a panic if you run into a star you can't place. (This happens frequently because of the vast number of TV stars and singing group members.) If you know it's someone, but can't think of *who*, just say something like "I know your name as well as I know my own, and right now I can't remember either one of them." (Say, that's pretty funny if we do say so ourselves.) (And, we just did, which figures.)

DON'T miss the next issue of The BEAT. If you do, you'll miss our feature on one of today's most popular sports ... autograph hunting!

... WELL, AT LEAST THEY'RE SAYING *SOMETHING*

KRLA ARCHIVES

The Sinatras — A

By Jim Hamblin

Jim Hamblin has got to be the world's most devoted Sinatra fan. He's a personal friend of the entire Sinatra clan, never missing a Sinatra appearance in Vegas, and in fact, never missing a Sinatra appearance anywhere! Jim is also an amateur photographer who once captured a picture of Sinatra Sr. which Frank admitted was the best photograph of himself which he had ever seen!! And since Frank has been the subject of at least a million photos, his approval of Jim's work was quite an honor.

Because the Sinatras are all having such a "Very Good Year" and because Jim probably knows more about them than any living being we asked him to share the Sinatras with all BEAT readers.

There he is. The man that every disc jockey in the country calls "The Chairman of the Board."

Life Magazine described him simply as "The greatest singer of popular music today."

He has been everywhere, done everything. He has won an Academy Award for film acting, been honored by foreign nations for his humanitarian activities for children (France game him The Order of the Public Saint) and been the subject of more vile slander than any man since Joseph Stalin.

He flies around in helicopters and his own private $600,000 jet plane. When little children in Tokyo talk about it, they say they are going to "the Frank Sinatra," referring to a huge community service building in downtown Tokyo, paid for by several Sinatra charity performances.

He is the man who sent $100,000 to a Los Angeles college, with the express condition they not reveal the donor. (They didn't. We found out another way).

Big Tipper

And he's the man who will notice if someone overcharges 50c for lunch, then leave the waiter a huge tip. He's the man who punched a waiter in the mouth when a Negro was refused service in a restaurant.

And when George Raft, the famous film gangster, ran into tax trouble, the first phone call he got was from Sinatra, who said he would give him "anything you need" to get out of the scrape with the Internal Revenue boys.

And Sinatra is the man who years ago used to stop by a restaurant in Redlands on his way to Palm Springs, and pick up the children of the cocktail waitress, for a weekend in the sun and his saltwater swimming pool. And he recently sent a check to cover all the costs of that same waitress' cancer operation ($1,000).

As President of Sinatra Enterprises, he oversees the business of a multi-million dollar corporation that makes movies and records, and finances all kinds of show business ventures.

In A Jar?

He's been accused of slugging photographers, running over reporters with his car, and entertaining up to 6 women in one night. ("If I had as many love affairs as are reported in the press," noted Sinatra recently, "I would now be speaking to you from a jar at the Harvard Medical School. Nobody with that much action would be able to walk around.")

And, he's the man that recently told a nationwide TV audience that he wanted to be remembered most as a man who had good friends, "and loved his family, most of all."

Sinatra's marriage to Nancy Barbato in those long ago years in New Jersey has long since been terminated. By court order she receives one third of his income (a gross of about 4 million dollars a year) but the relationship goes far beyond that. He is a frequent visitor to Nancy Senior's home in Bel-Air, and family gatherings are not uncommon.

Always at his Las Vegas openings and other appearances, Mrs. Sinatra is said to be, by intimates, the only woman that Sinatra might ever really settle down with, in spite of rumors about Mia Farrow, and other lithesome starlets.

Wish Softly

If you were a friend of Frank Sinatra's, you'd soon learn not to wish out loud when he's around. He has been known to lavish expensive gifts on people after overhearing their saying something about wanting a watch, a diamond, or even a shipment of lobster. And at any time you may park your car somewhere, and return to find a new Lear Stereophonic tape music system installed.

Last December 12th, Frank Sinatra was 50 years old. And since his early 20's he has been a star and the idol of one generation or another of yearning females.

Consistently voted the top "jazz" vocalist of the year, Sinatra is popular for a very basic reason. *He's the best.* That's what he set out to be, and that's what he has become.

And Sinatra says he can do it again, for somebody else.

"Singers are made, not born," he says. "They're made by years of study, unbelievable hard work, and exhausting experience in front of tough audiences.

"People think when they see a singer stand up there that he just opens his mouth and out it comes," he explained. "I wanted a certain type of voice phrasing without taking a breath at the end of a line or phrase.

Studied Violin

"I studied the violin playing of Heifetz to see how he moved his bow over the fiddle and back again without seeming to pause. I applied this to my singing.

"I watched how Tommy Dorsey took his breath when he played the trombone. He never seemed to open his mouth to draw breath at all. I learned to control my breath by swimming the length of an Olympic-size pool *under water*. I increased my lung power by pacing myself on a track every day—first walking a lap, then running, then walking again.

"I did exercises and push-ups. It was hard work but the hardest thing, when I finally felt I was ready to sing, was to pick the songs that meant something.

"And even when the words didn't mean much—and most of them didn't, I had to learn how to sing them in such a way that they seemed to be important and true.

"I had to learn to read every song the right way and make a contact with the audience. And all the time I knew the audience was saying: 'How does the guy get the breath to do it?'."

"When I sing now, it is physically arduous. Before I start a singing engagement, I have to go into training. I cut down on smoking and drinking and I play a lot of golf and go back to physical exercises."

To prove that his kind of singing can be taught, Sinatra has made a unique offer. He is willing to take any fledgling boy singer and guarantee to turn him into an international star in two years.

"I would pay him a good salary for himself—and his wife, too, if he were married," Sinatra said. "And without taking anything for myself, I would teach him all I knew—everything I have learned over the years.

He Guarantees It

"*In two years I guarantee he would be a star.* My reward would be to sit out front on his first big night and listen to the applause. If I can find the right boy I know it could be done."

Are there any rewards to singing, besides applause? Well, here's one answer to that:

Reprise Records launched a major sales and promotion campaign in honor of Mr. Sinatra's birthday, and now the figures are in. They sum up all that can ever be said about this man who sings his heart into every song.

From November 25th until December 24, 1965, *just one month*, NINE MILLION DOLLARS of Frank Sinatra's recordings were sold over music counters around the world.

Happy Birthday, Frank, and please don't ever stop.

FRANK SINATRA—Undisputably the best dressed of the stars, shows excellent taste in all clothes he wears and has a special passion for orange. He lounges at home in very bright orange sweaters.

KRLA ARCHIVES

Very Good Year

... NANCY SINATRA

NANCY'S WALKIN' IN!!

Here's the gal who has assigned herself the most difficult job in the whole world — being something besides the daughter of the world's most famous singer.

Her name is Nancy Sinatra, and on June 8th, 1966, she'll be 26 years old. And her desire to develop talents of her own must have started a long time ago, because Nancy has been studying as a performer for as long as she can remember.

Music lessons include 11 years of piano, 8 years of dance and technique, and another 5 years of study as a dramatic actress, under the tutelage of famous instructors. The noted composer, Carlos Menotti, taught her piano.

Nancy is appearing frequently on television shows lately and on any particular night you're liable to find her in nearly any kind of role.

You may have missed those shows, though, and you may have even missed her appearances since 1959 on such shows as Perry Como, The Virginian, and Burke's Law.

But nobody can overlook her now, with the sudden success of her single recording of "These Boots Are Made For Walkin'," already a national hit and headed for the top of the charts.

It is not her first record, and some other songs she's cut have been big in foreign countries, but there has been nothing like the response to her newest. As a singer, she's been working for Reprise Records since 1961, and it looks as if she's "locked onto" the right song.

What to do for an encore? Hard to say, really. Good songs are hard to find, million-sellers practically impossible.

On the personal side, Nancy is a little gal, only 5-foot-3, and weighs in at about 100 pounds. But if you ever meet her you'll find out first of all that she doesn't *look* little, because her dynamic personality blossoms out and covers the room. Brown hair and brown eyes accent a big wide beautiful grin, and a face ready to laugh.

Her publicity men call it "natural warm charm, bright wit, and a razor-sharp mind" . . . and you know somethin'? They're right!

ANOTHER SINATRA — Frank Jr. recently appeared in Las Vegas at the same time as his father. The marquee at the Flamingo Hotel read "FRANK SINATRA JUNIOR" while at the Sands, underneath the name FRANK SINATRA in little teeny letters was the word, "Senior."

STEPPING INTO IMMORTALITY. Frank Sinatra places footprints in the forecourt of Grauman's Chinese Theater, surrounded by his two daughters, Nancy and Tina, and close friend Dean Martin. Martin, who went through the route in early in 1964, quipped, "Watch out, Frank, I think it's a plot. They're going to let that stuff harden and use you for a traffic sign." Yes, it was a very good year.

KRLA ARCHIVES

Inside KRLA

Many of you have written in to ask about some of the people who work behind the microphones — way, *way behind* the microphones — and this week we decided to introduce a couple of these people to you.

First on our list is a charming lady with the almost-unlikely name of Sie Holliday. Her real name is Shirley, but her nickname — oddly spelled though it may be! — is Sie, and she is the one responsible for the delightful children's promotions which you hear on the air.

Her official function at KRLA is to act as Traffic Director. Now we don't mean to insinuate that the lobby of KRLA strongly resembles a race track or anything (although, at times — even *we* have some rather strong suspicions!), but that is her official title.

What is actually involved in that is the programming of the commercials, and the preparation of the station logs and books which the DJ's all must follow. Sie also does various library public service tapes. And, if you recall, she used to portray the part of Daphne in some of Emperor Hudson's merry adventures from six-to-nine every A.M.

Sie majored in radio when she was in college, and has always worked in the fields of radio broadcasting and television. A few years ago, she was the all-night disc jockey on a Top 40 station in San Diego — and at the time, she was the only female to hold such a position on all of the West Coast. She also spent a short time as a disc jockey right here on KRLA.

Our other guest also remains behind the scenes to some extent, although he is generally much closer to the microphone than the other "invisible" members of the KRLA cast and crew. His name is Jim Steck, and he is one of the newsmen in KRLA's fine news department.

Beatle Adventures

Most of you know by this time of Jim's Beatle adventures with Dave Hull about two years ago when the two of them stowed away on the Beatle airliner bound for Denver. Jim tells me that the whole stunt was originally his idea, and that "as a joke, I tried to talk Dave into it." But we never really thought we'd get away with it.

"We were the last ones on the plane and first ones off at Denver. It was really funny — we had just finished saying good-bye and everything to the Beatles in Los Angeles, and then when they got off the plane in Denver — there we were to greet them. They were flabbergasted to see us there."

Jim claims a special affection above all the Beatles for Paul, whom he considers to be about the most charming, but says that: "The greatest thing about the Beatles was the exclusive interview I was able to do with John. He was very relaxed and in a good mood, and we just sat around alone and talked for a couple of hours."

The funny thing is, Jim actually saw the Beatles a little over two years ago at the Palladium when he was in London, and this was before they had ever come over here and become so successful. Jim came back raving — but somehow, people just weren't listening. Well, that'll teach 'em!

Speaking of London, Jim will be going back very soon. In just about two or three weeks now, Jim will be leaving for Europe for a two-month vacation. He has ordered a Porsche which he will pick up there (and later have sent back here to the States.) He will drive all around Europe by himself.

If the column looks slightly green at this point, don't worry — it's all right, it's only my *envy* oozing through the lines!! I've already warned Jim that I may stow away in his baggage or something (all's fair in love, war, and European vacations!), but Jim has threatened to have his baggage guarded at gun point, or something. Oh well!

Pop Scene

At least he did promise me that we will be paying special attention to the pop scene all over Europe, and he will be reporting back to us from time to time. So between the two of us, we will try to keep you posted on all of the latest happenings abroad.

Visitors to the station recently have included Noel Harrison, the Fortunes, Neil Sedaka, Johnny Walker of the Walker Brothers, and about five million KRLAddicts.

Dick Moreland informs us that he has purchased a brand new color TV for the sole purpose of watching "Batman!" And the question of the week is: *Who* put the "Bat Manager" sign on John Barrett's door??? Golly whiz-bang, everyone — I wonder who could have done it?!!

KRLA'S JIM STECK is shown in action as he interviews Jack Warner.

NOPE — The Mardi Gras hasn't quite come to KRLA as yet. It's just KRLA's own female whirlwind, Sie Holliday rejoicing on the balcony over a huge bag of fan mail she received when she was on the air as the only female Deejay in Los Angeles.

CAN WE TRUST OUR EYES? Why, yes — I do believe we can. Well, would you believe five Turtles in front of the Hullabaloo in Hollywood? No? Oh, well — how about a small group of well-trained vocal amphibians?!!

KRLA BEAT Subscription
SAVE 33% OF REGULAR PRICE

☐ 1 YEAR — 52 Issues — $5.00   ☐ 2 YEARS — $8.00   ☐ 6 MONTHS — $3.00

PLEASE PRINT Enclosed is _____   ☐ CASH   ☐ CHECK

Send to .... Age ....
Address ....
City .... State .... Zip ....

MAIL YOUR ORDER TO: KRLA BEAT
6290 Sunset, Suite 504
Hollywood, Calif. 90028

Foreign Rate: $9.00 — 52 Issues

UCLA Obtains Mancini Songs

Henry Mancini has turned over six original manuscripts of his music to the UCLA library for use by cinema and music students.

The manuscripts were presented to the university after a request from the university. The request was unusual, as it is usually reserved for composers in the field of classical music.

The scores include "Experiment in Terror," "Soldier in the Rain," "Charade," "Shot in the Dark," "Pink Panther" and his recently completed "Moment to Moment."

Mancini also presented the university library with the first draft of his book, "Sounds and Scores."

Frankie Avalon In Two Films

Frankie Avalon has stopped all night club appearances temporarily to concentrate on his acting career.

He's now devoting himself strictly to his next two starring films for American International, the makers of the Beach Party movies.

Frankie's next two movies are entitled "Fireball 500" and "Dr. Goldfoot and the 'S' Bomb."

Tell your friends about
DIAL-A-DISC
HO 1-2220

KRLA ARCHIVES

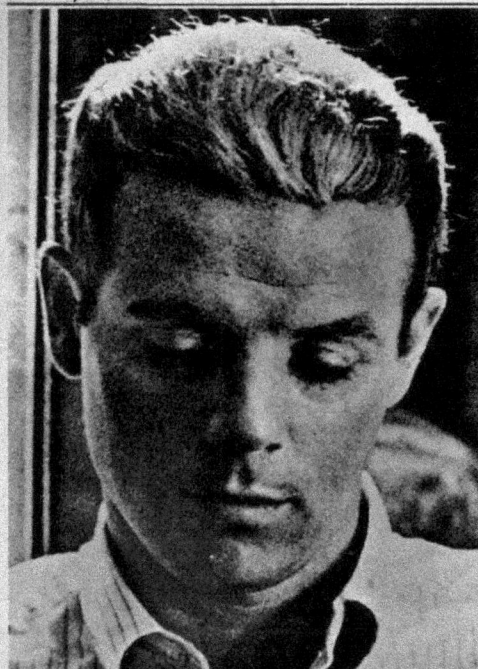

IN SEARCH OF FOLK
Chad Mitchell's World of Song

By Shannon Leigh

On a night, not too long ago, one of The BEAT'S fine reporters —Carol Deck—and I journeyed across town to The Troubador to enjoy the first solo performance by a young man named Chad Mitchell.

I usually use my column space each week telling you of an artist, or group of artists, whom I have "found," and frequently label them "folk." To say that I was overwhelmed by the performance given by Chad that evening would be the supreme understatement, and I could quite easily write several columns commending to you the many talents of this versatile and sensitive young man.

But, for once, I won't. I was not the only one to be very impressed by this phenomenal young singer; my friend, and talented co-worker, Carol, also found herself somewhat "destroyed" by the entire performance.

Therefore, in this week's search for folk, you will have a new "guide" to lead you down the paths of discovery. Her name is Carol Deck, and I think that it will be an interesting and enjoyable experience for all of you.

Every good performer combines numerous qualities of entertainment to achieve his particular style, but there is still usually one quality that stands out in each person, be it a gimmick or looks or a particular talent.

With Chad Mitchell it is sincerity, or perhaps reality.

Each song lives for each member of the audience. This physically slight but vocally powerful young man stands before a mike and sings of war and makes you ashamed, sings of love and makes you glad you're you, sings of loneliness and makes you want to rush on stage and tell him you care.

And you do care. He stands there with his feet together, leaning slightly forward and stretches his arms out to the audience as he sings "Buddy Can You Spare Me A Dime?" and everyone present feels the sincerity of his plea.

No Translation

Or he sings a haunting song by Jacques Brel in French and although many in the audience don't understand French you can read the meaning of every word on Chad's face and in his motions. You know he's singing of lost love.

He stands alone now on the stage. After several years with the highly successful Chad Mitchell Trio he is now trying to make the transition to solo performer.

He left the trio because he felt he could go no farther with them. "I found that the situation was such that I couldn't work artistically with them," he explains.

"I felt I was cheating me and them by staying. The situation was affecting our performance."

And he admits, "I feel much freer without them."

So he's a solo singer now. He's just completed a California engagement, only his second since he left the trio, but he's not rushing into anything.

He was in a Broadway play called "Postmarked Zero" which closed shortly after opening and he's appearing at four colleges this month but he's not rushing into a record release until he's a little more sure of himself.

"I've got to learn more concretely what I'm doing in this field before I try others."

"I'm not in much of a hurry because I don't know what I'm doing. Some of my material is new to me and I have to have more command of it."

In trying to describe his style he discounts the fact that he has a beautiful voice—"That I can sing is a technicality that I was born with."

But he uses a French word, chanteur—it means an entertainer who can present the world of a song to an audience as well as his own personality.

It's The Lyrics

"A number of American performers who move me not at all dwell solely on their personality and fail to present the world of a song and sometimes even subordinate the song to their personality," he says.

"I'm trying to make my material live by virtue of its lyrics and not just my personality."

And yet Chad's personality does come through so well when he performs because it blends naturally with each song that he does.

He's in a period of transition now, feeling his way around, searching for his individual style. If you see him perform now and see him again in a year, he may be different then but he'll still be Chad Mitchell, a very personable, alive, sincere, real man . . . and a very exciting performer.

As he looks at what lies ahead now, he states his goals simply. "I hope I will be able to become what I want to be and that people will want to see it. I know it'll take me some time to achieve that degree of perfection."

He's got a degree of that perfection now, as well as a degree of that overused term, sincerity, and a very large degree of reality.

We'll be hearing much more from this young New Yorker.

KRLA Tunedex

DAVE HULL

BOB EUBANKS

DICK BIONDI

JOHNNY HAYES

EMPEROR HUDSON

CASEY KASEM

CHARLIE O'DONNELL

BILL SLATER

This Week	Last Week	Title	Artist
1	25	THESE BOOTS ARE MADE FOR WALKIN'	Nancy Sinatra
2	1	JUST LIKE ME	Paul Revere & The Raiders
3	3	ZORBA THE GREEK	Herb Alpert & The Tijuana Brass
4	19	TIJUANA TAXI	Herb Alpert & The Tijuana Brass
4	13	YOU BABY	The Turtles
5	4	CRYIN' TIME	Ray Charles
6	7	A WELL RESPECTED MAN	The Kinks
7	8	ELUSIVE BUTTERFLY	Bob Lind
8	11	FIVE O'CLOCK WORLD	The Vogues
9	2	WE CAN WORK IT OUT/DAY TRIPPER	The Beatles
10	5	NO MATTER WHAT SHAPE	The T-Bones
11	9	LIGHTNIN' STRIKES	Lou Christy
12	21	I AIN'T GONNA EAT OUT MY HEART ANY MORE	The Young Rascals
13	6	MY LOVE	Petula Clark
14	14	MY WORLD IS EMPTY WITHOUT YOU	The Supremes
15	27	WHAT NOW MY LOVE	Sonny & Cher
16	22	SET YOU FREE THIS TIME	The Byrds
17	16	UP TIGHT	Stevie Wonder
18	20	MY BABY LOVES ME	Martha & The Vandellas
19	17	GOING TO A-GO-GO	The Miracles
20	23	TIME	The Pozo-Seco Singers
21	33	BATMAN	Neil Hefti
22	26	IT WAS A VERY GOOD YEAR	Frank Sinatra
23	—	CALIFORNIA DREAMIN'	Mamas & The Papas
24	29	WORKING MY WAY BACK TO YOU	The Four Seasons
25	28	SANDY	Ronnie & The Daytonas
26	37	THE BALLAD OF THE GREEN BERET	Sgt. Barry Sadler
27	—	I'M SO LONESOME I COULD CRY	B.J. Thomas & The Triumphs
28	32	DON'T MESS WITH BILL	The Marvellettes
29	30	SPANISH EYES	Al Martino
30	35	A HARD DAY'S NIGHT	Ramsey Lewis Trio
31	—	THE BATMAN THEME	The Markettes
32	—	LISTEN PEOPLE	Herman's Hermits
33	34	AT THE SCENE	The Dave Clark Five
34	39	LOOK THROUGH ANY WINDOW	The Hollies
35	36	THE CHEATER	Bob Kuban
36	—	HUSBANDS & WIVES	Roger Miller
37	38	ANDREA	The Sunrays
38	—	KEEP ON RUNNING	The Spencer Davis Group
39	40	THE DEDICATION SONG	Freddie Cannon
40	—	WOMAN	Peter & Gordon

HELP!

HELP!
I need scraps of yarn that are no longer big enough to benefit you. I will gladly pay for handling cost.
Elizabeth Oldham, 4806 Gaviota Ave., Long Beach, Calif. 90807

HELP!
A 17 year old English girl wants a boy pen pal who is 17 or 18. Boys only. Write to Miss Ceri Rees, The Vicarage, Boncath, Pembrokeshire, England.
L.C.

HELP!
I am starting a band for recording and public appearances. I need a lead guitar, rhythm, bass and organ. Must have own equipment, be 13 to 17, and willing to work hard! Anyone interested must also live in Inglewood area. *Please contact Rick Heltebrake, 1222 S. Inglewood, Inglewood, Calif. 90301.*

HELP!
I am a great fan of that fab group—the Moody Blues, but I am having trouble purchasing a copy of their record "Go Now." If anyone has a copy of this record they wish to sell or knows where I can purchase one, please write me. *Marty Halpern, 1802 Chanticleer Rd., Anaheim, California 92804*

HELP!
I have two L.P.'s that I want to trade for "Marianne Faithfull," "The Kinks" or an album by Georgie Fame. I have "Surfer Girl" (by the Beach Boys) and "The New Christy Minstrels in Person." I also have a huge list of singles which I want to swap. Please send a self-stamped, addressed envelope to *Sammie Cannon, 6523 Belon Street, Long Beach, Calif. 90815.*

HELP!
Music for hire. Four good musicians for private parties, school dances, etc. Contact *Brook Hall, 26641 Westvale Rd., Rolling Hills, Calif.*

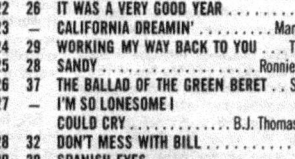

Eve's APPAREL
See if you can BEAT our prices on our new Jr. and missy lines. Samples at wholesale or less.
1800 N. Vermont   NO 3-4456
Hollywood, Calif.

KRLA ARCHIVES

Minus Beard And Turbans
Sam & Pharaohs Host Press

By Louise Criscione

HOLLYWOOD — Press conferences for pop artists are getting to be a welcome habit around here. Of course, press conferences have been going on for ages but it wasn't until the Beatles hit our shores that pop stars began getting into the act in a big way.

Since then, all of the big English groups have held conferences in practically every major city in which they've stopped. And now the American groups are beginning to follow suit.

Yesterday a cleanly-shaven Domingo Samudio, better known as Sam The Sham, and Butch Gibson, David Martin, Jerry Patterson and Ray Stinnett — collectively known as The Pharaohs hosted a breakfast for a few chosen members of the press.

Sam and his Pharaohs went way out for the breakfast which was held in the Hollywood Room of the Knickerbocker Hotel. Hours before Sam et al. showed up red jacketed waiters were busily setting up the two long tables and making at least a hundred cups of coffee while the chiefs were even busier cooking breakfast for the starving reporters.

Arrival Time

About 9 o'clock (middle of the night for me!) the invited guests began arriving, the networks began setting up their cameras and then shortly before 9:30 Sam and the Pharaohs made their entrance. *Early!*

There had been some speculation that Sam would not show up. Reportedly, Sam had had some illness in his family and had flown straight on to Texas instead of coming into Los Angeles from the group's smash European tour.

Famous Beard

However, Sam was very much present and looking a million times better with his beard completely gone. As you read in *The BEAT*, Sam hated his beard and decided to do away with it. However, one slight problem occurred. His German fans were waiting anxiously to see the famous beard so Sam was forced to reluctantly grow it back.

But he swore that before he left Germany he would be beardless once more. And when he walked into the Hollywood Room he was true to his word — beardless!

The Pharaohs felt that if Sam could shave off his beard they ought to be able to throw away their robes and turbans which they had acquired a distinct disliking for. But again the German fans objected so the boys rummaged through their wastebaskets and donned the robes and turbans for the last time.

"Wooly Bully" had been such a monstrous hit all over the world that Sam and the Pharaohs had the distinction of being named the top U.S. rock 'n' roll group in Germany.

And, unfortunately for the group, the only pictures which their German fans had ever seen of them had them all rigged out in their Egyptian attire. But now everything is okay, they've been seen minus robes etc. and they hope that they will never have to wear those outfits again.

Sam told me how the whole thing had actually started as a joke. "We were playing a club," said Sam, "and we put on those things for a joke. But it caught on."

That was an accident but their show business careers were anything but an accident. Sam's brother who is a surgeon opposed his becoming an entertainer. He had even offered to pay Sam's way through law school. It was a tempting offer you may be sure. It would have meant a steady and assured income and the kind of security which is missing in the world of music.

Soft Spoken

But Sam is determined — quiet but determined. He didn't want to be a lawyer — he wanted to be a singer. Naturally, his family was a little upset with Sam's decision. Actually, they were more worried than anything else.

Now, of course, they are quite proud of him but for awhile it was

... SAM THE SHAM AND THE PHARAOHS WITH THEIR NEW LOOK.

tough going. Sam learned the hard way that there are no short cuts in life and only hard work pays off.

If he had one wish in this world it would probably be to sing at the Metropolitan Opera House. It's his biggest ambition in life. Although he has made a large dent in the pop field he admits, "I would still like to sing at the Met."

Sam is ambitious and competitive. It doesn't scare him, in fact, it has helped him. He won't stop at just being a pop entertainer — he'll go on. Not only to the Met, but to motion pictures if he can possibly manage it.

He has already appeared on the movie screen but not in the kind of film which he would like to do. He wants to be a serious actor, preferably in westerns.

Typically Cowboy

He'd be great in westerns, too, they'd suit him. He looks typically cowboy with his black eyes and equally black hair. He speaks slowly and with a definite drawl. He's more of an observer than anything else — he would never be heard above the roar of a large crowd. He states frankly, but with a twinkle in his dark eyes, "I don't have any philosophy, I just enjoy life."

Sam is American born but very Latin in his ways. He has an enormous amount of dignity and takes for granted that when he has something to say people will listen. When he was a young boy he went out and bought himself a copy of "Manners For Millions" which he memorized and never seems to have forgotten. He's been described as a Latin gentleman — and he is.

Paul Gibson, nicknamed Butch, also ran into opposition from his family when he informed them of his decision to go into show business. They wanted their son to be a doctor but like Sam's family they shrugged their shoulders and let him go ahead with his ambition.

He admits to being the slightest bit shy. "If a woman isn't aggressive I'd never have the courage to talk to her," Butch grins.

The Laugher

Dave Martin, another Texan, has the wildest sense of humor in the group and seems to be laughing all the time. Jerry Patterson plays drums for the group and rather typical of Southerners, Jerry speaks very hesitantly but at some length once he gets started.

Jim Stinnett, christened "Ray" by his co-horts, is the smallest member of the group. But his red hair, freckles and blue-green eyes make him stand out. He seems very shy and always thinks before he speaks. His ambition is simply "to keep going."

Breakfast finished, Sam and the Pharaohs broke into a few verses of "In The Still Of The Night" and then raced for a piano which was stationed in the corner and let out with a wild version of "Wooly Bully."

Performance completed, they walked slowly to the door. Behind them lay a tiring but satisfying tour of Europe — ahead of them stretched a ten day stint at a local Hollywood club, a series of television appearances and a tour of the Mid-West.

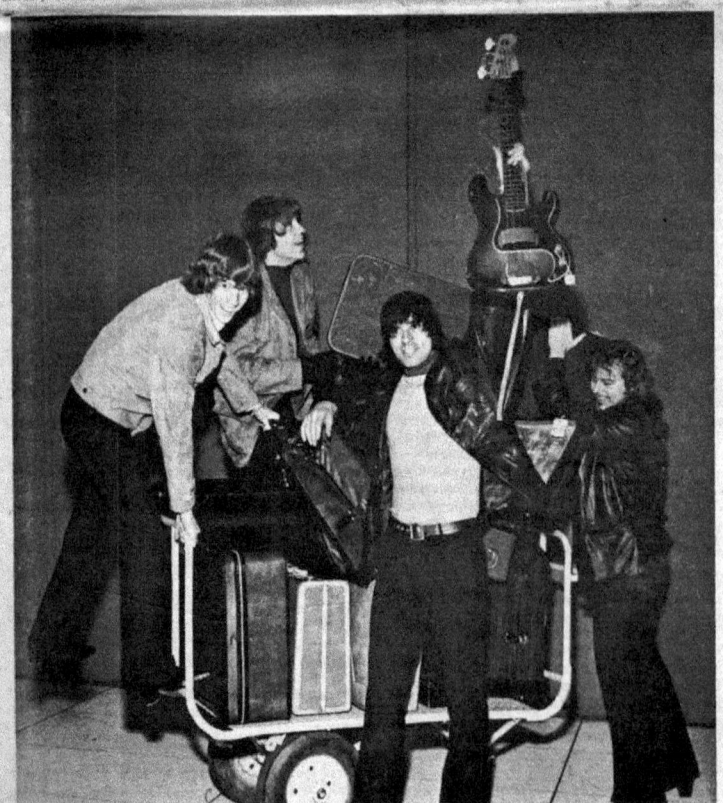

BEAT Photographer, Chuck Boyd, was on hand to greet the Pharaohs as they arrived at Los Angeles International Airport minus Sam who had stopped off in Texas for a quick visit with an ill member of his family.

Pop Is Comin' Up Hollies

By Louise Criscione

If you "Look Through Any Window" you probably won't find a Holly lurking inside but if you try a pop television show, a concert (of the rocking type, of course) or a top club you stand a much better chance of catching Graham Nash, Tony Hicks, Bobby Elliott, Eric Haydock and Allan Clarke playing their kind of music for all they're worth. And today they're worth a lot!

The five Hollies sprouted out of the teen clubs in Manchester, England. Graham, who handles rhythm guitar and aids in the vocals, was a school mate of Allan's, the Hollies' lead singer. In fact, when the two boys were still in grammar school they formed a duo, calling themselves appropriately enough, The Two Teens.

When Graham and Allan reached the ripe old age of 15 they acquired quite a distinction, that of the youngest act to ever have appeared at Manchester's Cabaret Club.

Their schooling finished, the two went into engineering for a short time playing clubs in the evenings as The Guytones, later as Rickey and Dane, and still later as the Four Tones.

Finally Hollies

When the Four Tones decided to call it quits, Graham and Allan joined Eric and Don Rathbone as The Deltas. However, that didn't last long either and in early 1963 The Deltas split. But Graham, Allan, Eric and Don weren't finished with show business just yet, so they formed The Hollies.

They were, however, missing a very important element—a lead guitar. They knew who they wanted—a young man by the name of Tony Hicks. But Tony had other ideas. He was an electrical apprentice, he knew that the Hollies wanted desperately to make it big so he wasn't too interested in joining up with them.

The four Hollies were a little more persuasive than Tony had imagined and they eventually succeeded in talking Tony into at least listening in at one of their sessions. He liked what he heard, liked it so much that he agreed to take time off work to go to London with them for a recording test.

Full-Fledged Holly

The test went so well that Tony quickly changed his mind and by the time the boys returned to Manchester Tony was a full-fledged Holly.

Apparently, Don wasn't too happy with the group so about this time he decided to leave and was replaced by the current Holly skin-pounder, Bobby Elliott. And the Hollies as they are today were officially on their way.

Their first release, "Ain't That Just Like Me," found its way into the English charts and it also found itself being listened to by a movie producer who immediately booked the Hollies for a screen test.

Their second disc, a revival of "Searching'," climbed higher than their first but it wasn't until lucky number three, another revival—

... THE HOLLIES (l. to r.) GRAHAM NASH, ALLAN CLARKE, TONY HICKS, ERIC HAYDOCK and BOBBY ELLIOTT.

Stay," that the Hollies fought their way into the British top ten.

Of course, the Hollies had been a big group in their native Manchester for quite sometime but with the release of "Stay" all of England suddenly discovered the five Hollies in a big way.

And since then they have been turning out hit after hit in Britain. But their American success story has taken quite awhile longer.

"I'm Alive," a gigantic hit in England, made a rather fair-sized dent in our charts but it wasn't until "Look Through Any Window" that Stateside teens really began paying attention to the Manchester-bred group.

Outspoken

They claim to have no particular image, though most people tab them a surprisingly clean-cut group. Image or no image the Hollies are, above all, frank. They say exactly what they feel like saying whenever the mood hits them—and it hits them often.

"When I'm on stage I'm like a machine," admits Graham. "I sing and smile automatically while sometimes my mind is thinking about something else, something completely irrelevant."

Concert riots have always been a subject of conversation with many people convinced that the artists themselves start, or at least encourage, mobbings. Holly, Allan Clarke, numbers himself among these.

"Anyone can get pulled off stage. All you have to do is put your foot over the edge and off you go! You're asking for it," says Allan.

Graham goes along with Allan but puts it much stronger. "All groups who claim to have mass riots every night are fakers. But good luck to them!"

Popular Tony

Tony Hicks often takes the honors as most popular Holly. The girls know why they like Tony and Tony knows exactly what he likes in girls. Which is fair enough, after all.

He appreciates natural girls who wear very little or no make-up if they can "get away with it," adds Tony with a grin.

In pictures or on TV Tony looks very small but actually stands a full six feet. So, he likes girls who are "quite tall, around five feet six inches."

Tony finished up his description of the sort of girl he likes with: "I like to see a girl driving a car, especially if it's an open sports car. Long hair blowing back in the wind and all that. No, I don't mind women drivers a bit—as long as it's not *my* car they're driving!"

The Hollies were the recipients of some rather harsh criticism from the quietest of the Beatles, George Harrison, not too awfully long ago when they recorded George's composition, "If I Needed Someone."

The usually tight-lipped Beatle jumped all over the Hollies' record declaring it "rubbish" and shouting that "they've spoiled it."

The criticism hurt the Hollies deeply and made them a little angry in the process. They probably wouldn't have minded George's criticism of "If I Needed Someone" so much but George didn't leave it at that. Instead he went on to announce that on their records they sound like a bunch of "session men who've just got together in a studio without ever seeing each other before." And that *really* hurt.

George's Knock

Graham took the floor in the Hollies' defense. "The thing that hurt us the most was George Harrison's knock at us as musicians. And I would like to ask this—if we have made such a disgusting mess of his brainchild song, will he give all the royalties from our record to charity?"

I'd like to point out, for whatever it's worth, that *none* of the royalties from that record ever went to charity.

"I'll tell you this much, we did this song against a lot of people's advice," continued Graham. "We just felt that after nine records we could afford to do something like this without being accused of jumping on the Beatles' bandwagon. We thought it a good song and we still do."

Still "Great"

Graham added that his own opinion of the Beatles had not changed at all in spite of George's harsh criticism. He likes their music and, in fact, goes so far as to say, "they're great."

The uproar caused by "If I Needed Someone" was the reason the Hollies decided to use "Look Through Any Window" as a follow-up. They had originally intended to go with "Someone."

But I'm glad they didn't. After all, we have enough American artists recording Beatle songs so it was a welcome relief when the Hollies showed up on our charts with "Window."

Just a warning—watch out for the five Hollies. They're due Stateside within the next month or so. It's taken a long time but I think they're going to make it very big over here. What do you think?

KRLA ARCHIVES

Barry Sadler Sings Of War Without Protest

By Carol Deck

On the pop charts right now are songs by attractive young men and women about love and the loss of it, about silence and stomachs and about butterflies.

And on those same charts is a song by a man, a man apart from the rest, about a thing called courage and another thing called war.

We've heard a lot in the last year or so of protests against war but now we hear from a man who knows what war is, a man who's been actively engaged in it, and a man who's proud of his part in it, a man who's proud to fight for America.

Active Duty

He is Staff Sergeant Barry Sadler, a 25 year old New Mexico soldier who recently returned from active duty in Vietnam.

His song, "Ballad of the Green Berets," is a tribute to the group of highly skilled and trained men within the U.S. Army who wear the Green Berets and who carry out missions beyond the scope of regular troops.

The fact that S/Sgt. Sadler is alive today is an indication of the high quality of man that the Green Berets represent.

Last Spring, while leading a small combat patrol in Vietnam, he fell into a mantrap and his leg was punctured by a poisoned spear made of sharpened bamboo called a pungi stake.

But Sadler is a trained medic who wants eventually to get his M.D. and so he operated on himself in the middle of combat, cleaning his wounds between fainting spells.

He was finally discovered and rescued and sent to the Philipines before being returned to the U.S. for full recuperation.

By the time he returned to America he had written over 10 songs about the war. He contacted a music company about them and the publisher turned out to be a friend of the author of a book called "The Green Berets."

Cover Model

The publisher arranged for Sadler to pose for the cover picture on the paper back book and to publish a full album of his songs.

From that album comes his first single, "Ballad of the Green Berets," a simple but touching ballad in the American tradition of quiet bravery.

He's performed the song on The Ed Sullivan Show and the Jimmy Dean Show, but he's not a full time entertainer. He's still in active service and at the time the album was published was Medical N.C.O. for the Green Berets at Fort Bragg in North Carolina.

No Privileges

We may not see very much of this man for most of his activities are classified information and he gets no special privileges from the Army to get leaves for performances or recording sessions, he just has to fit them in where he can, but his songs may very well join the list of songs of war that are such a part of our heritage.

From "Yankee Doodle" in the Revolutionary War to "The Battle Hymn of the Republic" in the Civil War to "Over There" in World War I men have been inspired by wars to write stirring pieces.

Now we have Staff Sergeant Barry Sadler to record the feelings of the men fighting the dirty little war in Vietnam.

...S/SGT. BARRY SADLER

The Adventures of Robin Boyd

By Shirley Poston

CHAPTER SIXTEEN

Robin Boyd didn't know what was going to happen when she picked up the phone that Saturday morning (which, incidentally, was ringing at the time) (the phone, not the morning), but she had the hot, flushed feeling that something was up besides her blood pressure.

She knew she was right when the voice on the other end of the wire said, in clipped British tones:

London Calling

"London calling Miss Robin Boyd."

Robin turned as white as seven snowbanks.

"Who?" she stammered, never having heard of the party in question. (Robin was a nice enough kid, but did have a tendency to become slightly forgetful at times.) (No one is perfect.)

"It's the wrong Boyd again," the operator said tiredly, and another voice on the end of the wire said something that sounded a lot like "Oh well" but wasn't.

"Wait!" screeched Robin, breaking several eardrums as it all came back to her. "I'm Robin Boyd!!" (And, by some strange coincidence, she was.)

Moaning with relief, the operator clicked off and the other voice said "Hullo?"

Robin gasped. That voice sounded just like ... but no, it just *couldn't* be!

"Hullo?" the voice repeated. "This is Mick."

Robin fell to the floor in a quivering lump. "Mick *Jagger?*" she breathed in disbelief after retrieving the receiver from a nearby wastebasket.

"No," answered the voice, not without a touch of sarcasm. "Mick Schwartz."

"Mick!!" she bellowed, trying to lurch to her feet. "You mean I'm actually *talking* to the *real* Mick Jagger?" she further bellowed, retrieving *herself* from a nearby wastebasket.

"I fear so," the voice said resignedly.

Robin lept about the room (fortunately, the phone had a long cord), but suddenly she came to her senses. Good gravy! She was making an absolute fool of herself!

Pausing gracefully in mid-air to regain her composure (should she ever have nothing to do some afternoon, she really should take up track), Robin changed her tactics.

"Who's This?"

"Hello there," she purred sweetly. "How are you?"

The voice sighed. "Who's this?"

"This is my sister," Robin said nonchalantely. "I mean, you were formerly speaking with my *sister*, Robin. *I'm* the Robin Boyd you want to talk to."

"Huh?" said the voice, not without a touch of stark terror. "Are you the Robin Boyd who has my ring?"

Robin grinned fiendishly. Her letter had worked!

"Of course," she said soothingly.

Robin heard a sharp gasp on the other end of the wire (a habit she must encourage Mick to kick as it gave one gas.)

"Can you tell me how you got it?" Mick quivered fearing for his sanity.

"Of course," Robin said soothingly, falling into the wastebasket again. Of course *not!* Just how *did* she get it? That is, how would she *explain* the mystery without blabbing everything and losing her magic powers forever.

In England

Then, as Mick screeched "WELL?," Robin knew what she must do.

"Mick, dear," she said in her most confidential tone, "I was in England last weekend, and I made your jacket flap out of the concert."

"*How?*" Mick pleaded. "How, how, how," he added hopefully.

"I did it with wires," she replied. "I've been taking magician lessons," she added hopefully.

"Actually?" said Mick, regaining his compusre.

"Eggtually," Robin echoed. "I sneaked back to your dressing room and arranged the entire thing before the concert."

Mick laughed, not without a touch of hysteria. "You're blasted good, y'know," he said after he finished laughing not without a touch of hysteria.

Robin gasped at this compliment from the famous Ringo—sorry about that—Rolling Stone. Then she puffed up with pride, not to mention gas.

"It was nothing," she simpered.

"Oh, but it *was!* I'm almost tempted to add you to the act!"

Robin turned as white as ... as ... well, let's face it, there just *isn't* anything that white. "No, no," she bleated. "I couldn't! I'll send the ring back right away though!"

"How about the jacket?"

Robin re-grinned fiendishly. "How about that?" she chortled.

"It's a deal," Mick chortled. "Not to mention a pleasure ..."

"But you have to hang up now, right?" Robin interrupted, wanting to be several miles from the nearest telephone (and wastebasket) when that I-did-it-with-wires bit sunk in.

"Right!" exclaimed Mick, "but before I do, I have one last question."

Robin quaked. "Yeah? I mean, yes?"

"That nut ... I mean, that girl I was talking to earlier. You know, your sister. Is her name really Robin, too?"

"Of course," Robin said soothingly. "Ta, Mick."

"Ta," Mick echoed, fearing for *her* sanity.

Logical Thing

Robin then hung up the phone (which seemed the logical thing to do since the conversation was over), and prepared to plunge under her bed in panic.

With *wires?* Getinze *serious!* Wait until Mick thought *that* one over. Why, he'd ...

Suddenly, Robin did an about face (which ain't easy in a wastebasket). The strangest feeling had just come over her. Mick *wouldn't* question her story! She knew this as well as she knew her own *name* (no remarks, please!) Because she had told him the *truth!*

She *had* been in England, *had* sneaked into his dressing room, *had* done it with wires! The little wire Byrd spectacles she wore when she was a *real* bird, without which she would have been blind as six bats and would never have seen Mick's jacket in the first place and never would have chosen it as her hiding place in the second place on that fateful night! (You have just visited the world's longest sentence.) (Come back soon.)

"Whew!"

"WHEW!" Robin shouted, causing several neighbors to wonder if even their best friends *weren't* telling them.

She'd won! She had "used her own ingenuity to repair the damages," just like *they* had decreed. Her magic powers would be returned! And so would George, her beautiful Liverpudlian genie! Just as soon as she mailed that ring back to Mick Jagger!

Racing into her room, she bravely flung open the closet door (you don't know what bravely *means* until you've flung open the door of Robin Boyd's closet), and rummaged happily in the pocket of Mick Jagger's pocket.

Shortly thereafter, she plunged under her bed in panic. But the ring wasn't *there* either.

(To Be Continued Next Week)

How London Feels About The Beatles

By Gil McDougall

Who is "in" and who is "out?" What do London's Mods and Rockers really think of the beat scene, and how do they rate the Beatles? If you would like to know the answers to these questions, as I did, then read on.

America is always being told what celebrity after celebrity thinks of the Beatles. So I thought that, for a change, I would compile an article consisting of the opinions of the people who set the style in popular music—the Mods and Rockers. I achieved this by embarking on a pub-crawl of some of London's "in" places. The various discussions were rather intermittent, as you will see, and on some occasions I never did get to hear a complete summation of the scene.

During the tour, I deliberately avoided such places as the Ad Lib, the Scotch Club and the Marquee. The reason: These places, and more, are still very much "in" but they are invariably packed with big names and I did not feel that they would represent a fair sampling of British opinion. Instead I went to these gear clubs and pubs: The Ship in Stepney; the Dragon in Hackney; the Bridge Tavern in Canning; the Rising Sun at Bethnal Green and finally, the Two Puddings. There were many more places, but this was about all I could cope with in one night. All those mentioned had Rock 'n' Roll bands, and they were all frequented by Mods (Rockers seem to be dying out.) English Mods are one up on most of their American cousins as they are allowed to enter the clubs and pubs at the age of eighteen, consequently most start when they are about sixteen.

Okay, now put everything aside, shut yourself in your room, turn up your radio, and come on a rave-up pub-crawl with me to the gear places in Big L.

"The Ship"

Beatles? They've been around too long and are getting stale... Ringo's down to earth and John is definitely a giggle... when I think about how long they've been in now, I begin to feel old... getting a bit too old for that stuff... you've got to take life more seriously when you get to nineteen... Well, yes, they have talent but they are dead now... now take the Blue Beat, it's been around for five years and only just beginning to catch on... it's great music... stiff at knee's, throw arms everywhere and make like a gospel singer... hips to the side four beats at a time and the rhythm is like a locomotive thumping along a track... sound like a drum and the words are really mad... it makes me laugh when people talk about Mersey music... Liverpool's a dead city now... you don't see the Beatles or Epstein living there... now in Manchester you can really have a rave-up...

"The Rising Sun"

The Rolling Stones are better—there's a really exciting sound... some people just can't recognize talent... they are brilliant... of course the Beatles are here to stay... now take my bird—she's dead potty about Paul... a bloke that engaged... Liverpool is a thing of the past now. I was up there a month ago and they're doing things that went out ages ago... the swim... the monkey... the huggy-bug... that stuff went out in Big L. a long time ago... the block and the bang are still "in"... there will always be competition between the cities... I like the Beatles because they make good records but I also like Tchaikovsky... they can't sing a note, it's just the sound... I'm jealous of their money though... that Paul's the one... what a bighead... if you see them in photographs or on Tele he's always in front fooling around and talking... Paul's fab... he's really a nice fellow too... he's a bighead... he needs some-

one like Lennon to tell him where it's at...

I think that the Merseybeats are just as good but I like the Beatles because they don't put on any fancy airs... the grown-ups like them too—just to get in with us... they are a young thing and grown-ups shouldn't try to get in with us through them... I like Lennon because he's pretty cool... did you see him last night when that interviewer asked a really stupid question... John just sort of looked at him once and then the bloke withered away... okay so I'm a Rocker... my boy's a Rocker and I'm proud of him... he's got guts... I'd marry him tomorrow... if he was agreeable... I have seen in some dance halls, a white line painted along one side of the dance floor... Rockers one side and Mods the other... if you ask me that's asking for trouble... it only makes the Rockers more mad and inclined to hate the Mods even more... Mods go to dance halls... discotheques... the Palais... the Rockers are prehistoric with Elvis-type sideburns... Elvis is old-fashioned now only the Rockers keep him up... the Mods are the smartest every time... people talk about them taking

purple hearts but not many of us do... (this fellow liked to illustrate with his hands and for his final gesticulation he sent several glasses flying with his arm.)

Thinking that this was a good time to leave, I got up. As I did so I noticed that Kink Ray Davies was talking to the Rock 'n' Roll group on-stage. I attempted to make my way over there, but the place was packed and by the time that I got there he had disappeared. The lead singer told me that he had been "spirited away," and so I left it at that.

"The Dragon"

My dad thinks that the Beatles set a bad example for us teenagers... he thinks that they shouldn't drink and smoke so heavily but why should they pretend to be doing something that they're not... it's like saying that it is okay to be hyprocritical as long as you don't smoke... well I'm a southerner and I don't like the way all these northerners are taking over... Wilson is taking over the government and the Beatles are taking over everything else... I think that the people of today... the young people I mean... are best represented by Lennon with his mod-to-hip aggressive sort of attitude... but I can't say that I like him very much... I don't know if they are going out or not... they came in on Ringo's nose... Paul's good looks and John's personality... as far as I know they've still got all three things.

"The Iron Bridge"

... there was a time when I liked them quite a bit... I suppose that I still do like them... I buy all their records... they're knocking the stuffing out of the neo-Victorians... in the beginning they were really great, but they seem to have quieted down now... the Stones are the hip one's now... I'd hate to marry a Mod... my boy's a Rocker... his ambition in life is to do a ton down the M.1.... he'll do it too... they say Rockers are scruffy but it's not true... you know what Mod stands for—moderation in all things... what a way to carry on... they can say what they like about us—we know what the score really is... they aren't worth worrying about... I think that Elvis is great...

"The Bridge Tavern"

When they appear on a discussion show George hardly ever has anything to say... he's very quiet all the time... you couldn't say the same for John and Paul... their music is the greatest... there will never be anything like the Beatles... it's sort of like Churchill – that kind of thing only comes once... Rockers are a bunch of scruffs... I buy plenty of clothes... they call it Mod street now, not Carnaby Street.

Mods and Rockers like beat music, but they like different kinds... the Rockers always dig Elvis but the Mods like the groups... the Stones... Kinks... Yardbirds... Unit Four Plus Two... P. J.... and the Beatles... everybody has to say that the Beatles are going out, but they've been saying it for a year and a half now.

"The Two Puddings"

Mods go down to Carnaby Street with their own designs for clothes and John Stephens makes them up... a lot of Mods still model their clothes on the Beatles... trousers have seventeen inch bttoms... boots are made from imitation crocodile or python... shirts are giraffe collar—they are very high and crease up... three buttons on the jackets with narrow lapels and two vents in the bottom... I never watch Tele unless it's "Ready Steady Go" or something like that... I like the Yardbirds, they're really way out... Ringo's so easy-going it makes me wonder if the others take advantage of him.

Do you know how many cars John Lennon has got?... and here's me riding around on a Vespa... well, you bought his records... you've got to admit they have made some great records... yes, I'd buy them again if it came up I suppose... I think that it's John's personality makes them really you know... yes, that's true in a way but look at how cute Paul is... actually they all contribute... they probably wouldn't be so great if they split up... they'll never split, not with a combination like that... I don't think that any of the others can touch them really... not in any field... Time gentlemen, please.

What About Me?

What about me? I listen to Blue Beat music, but I don't dance the Blue Beat way. I dig Mod clothes and wear them, but not all the time. I dig everything a Mod raves over, but I don't hunt with the pack. I dig the Beatles and I do think that they are here to stay. England's Mods also dig the Beatles and though there are a few voices of dissent they all appreciate that rarely is such great talent grouped together in one combination. Not only do the Mods *think* that the Beatles are here to stay but they are determined to make sure that they do just that. The Beatles are Mods and the Mods are Beatles – may their tenure be as long as their talent.

Bob Dylan Touring U.S. and Canada

NEW YORK – Bob Dylan is currently embarked upon one of the most ambitious cross-country tours of the country to date. During the course of the tour, he plans to cover 14 states as well as parts of Canada.

The trip, which began the week of February 5, is one of the longest personal appearance tours of Dylan's career, and states listed on the itinerary include: New York, Tennessee, Virginia, South Carolina, Connecticut, Pennsylvania, Florida, Missouri, Nebraska, Colorado, Oklahoma, New Mexico, Oregon and Washington.

The tour will extend to parts of Canada, including Ottawa, Ontario, and Montreal, Quebec and will wind up about March 27.

Nurk Twins Have Come A Long Way

By Gil McDougall

Who are the "Nurk Twins?" Long before the Beatles, the Silver Beatles, and before many other group-names were even thought of, there descended upon the city of London a musical duo who called themselves the "Nurk Twins." They were, of course, John Lennon and Paul McCartney in theatrical disguise.

John and Paul had gone south to enter a talent competition that was sponsored by the BBC. Their performance was a dud and the BBC scout just didn't want to know. Before you break-up at such an over-sight, let me remind you that this event occured almost four years ago and the boys were not the polished performers that they are today. The Nurk Twins may have thought that they were Britain's answer to the Everly Brothers, but in fact they still had a long way to go.

Talented Composers

Since this early disappointment Lennon and McCartney have emerged as two of the most talented composers that the popular music world has ever seen. When they took that first train trip to London, they were eager but inexperienced and, in fact, had little to offer "Tin Pan Alley." Today their songs are recorded by such talents as Ella Fitzgerald, Peggy Lee, Henry Mancini and many others too numerous to mention. It is interesting to note that success eluded the Beatles until they started singing Lennon and McCartney originals.

John and Paul formed the Nurk Twins through a mutual friendship and desired to become performers in the world of Rock 'n' Roll. It has been said that had Lennon and McCartney never become close friends, had they just remained working associates, then they might never have written such great songs. Evidently as friends they are able to compose on a much better working basis. Their composing sessions are part of their friendship because they enjoy working together.

Of course not all of their songs are great one's, but the few exceptions are never produced. As Paul has said: "The first song that we ever wrote was 'Too Bad About Sorrows.' We never recorded it because it was too crummy. They don't often turn out like that but when they do we just don't do them."

Dislike Covers

Sometimes they release a song later one of them wishes they hadn't done. Remember their version of "You Really Got A Hold On Me," which was originally done by the Miracles. Their recording was a success, but some months later John said: "Oh God, I can't stand that now. I never like any cover that we do, though at the time it was only a vague cover. No-one in England had ever heard of the Miracles then but it has always embarrassed me—it's me trying to do a coloured voice, and I can't do that."

Every composition by John and Paul contain contributions from both, but sometimes one will put in a bit more than the other. One example that quickly comes to mind is "Norwegian Wood." This was at first a poem by Lennon entitled, "This Bird Has Flown" and the melody was added later. When discussing the subject of who writes what, and why one of them sings a particular song Paul answered with: "This is usually decided by whoever gets the first idea for it. John had the original idea for 'I'm A Loser,' and I just helped a bit. I had the original idea for 'She's A Woman' and then John helped a bit with that. Sometimes it happens that we decide John has a better voice for a particular song—there are actually many reasons." The extent that each contributes to each song varies so much that it is difficult to be able to say that one of them wrote a particular composition. However, we do get something of an inkling when Lennon comes out with such things as: "Now,

...THE NURK TWINS

'Ticket To Ride' was three-quarters mine and Paul changed it a bit. He said let's alter the tune. It was not as commercial as most of our singles because it wasn't written as a single, it was intended to be in 'Help.' It was the first time that a song had been brought into a studio that hadn't been written for that purpose."

The amount and the variety of songs that John and Paul produce is quite phenonal. It is conceivable that such an effort would take them all of their waking time, but this just isn't the case. When Lennon and McCartney were asked about this both replies were a little hazy. John put it this way: "I usually write when there is nothing else to do. Most of the time this is at home. I just sort of sit down and do it. It is quite dry at times, but mostly the ideas come thick and fast."

On the same subject Paul said: "We get our ideas from anywhere. Sometimes it's just inspiration and sometimes it's because somebody tells us to sit down and write because we need songs for a new album. When that happens I go out to John's house and we'll just sit down for the day and try to write a couple of songs. I don't know where we get our ideas from exactly. It's a mutual thing we just sort of kick something off in each other."

Some of their composing sessions are a bit tense as they are often being urged to hurry for one thing or another. Sessions like this are interrupted only by Cynthia bringing in some tea for John and coffee for Paul. Lennon and McCartney worked very hard on their songs for the "Rubber Soul" album. So hard in fact that right after that, when they were presented with the M.B.E. from Queen Elizabeth, John told the Queen that they had just come back from a vacation instead of saying that they had been hard at work.

A supposedly wise man once said, that if the kids can't dance to it, they will not buy it. This theory is certainly disproved when you consider the range in variety of Beatle hits. From the beat of "I Wanna Hold Your Hand" they have progressed to the soul of "Norwegian Wood," and the beauty of "Yesterday." I myself have often wondered just what type of songs Lennon and McCartney prefer to write. John cleared this up with: "I prefer writing up-tempo songs I suppose. I don't care about a song having a message—I just write a love song. Most of our hits are cheerful. I like them a bit aggressive too."

Beatle Spectacular

Whatever they may personally like, it is plain to see that popular music fans, and singers alike, enjoy anything that they can turn out. Singers and orchestras from almost every nation in the world have recorded their own versions of Beatle songs. With this thought in mind, British Television recently produced a spectacular of these artists singing their interpretations of music by Lennon and McCartney. The show featured as many artists as possible and among this distinguished gathering was Henry Mancini, who is himself one of our greatest composers.

The boys had a great many things to do and a great many places to appear when the show was in the production stage, but they agreed to participate because the thing was being produced by Johnny Hamp who risked his job by giving them a TV spot when they were still unknown. One special part of the show that Paul enjoyed was the rendition of "And I Love Him" by Ester Phillips. Paul revealed that he thought that Ester's record of the same song was really tremendous. The completed show, which was a tribute to the composing talents of the Nurk Twins, was a great success in the U.K. and will almost certainly be presented in the U.S.A.

Achievement

During the production of the show John mentioned a sense of musical progression in the music of Lennon and McCartney when he said: "We try to find a truth for ourselves, a real feeling. You can never communicate your complete emotion to other people, but if we can convey just a little of what we feel then we have achieved something."

After "Rubber Soul" you may have felt yourself a sense of participation in the feeling that John was referring to. You may even have marvelled at the constant stream of melodic ingenuity stemming from John Lennon and Paul McCartney. If you did, then when John and Paul say "there are only about one hundred people in the world who really "understand our music" you may well feel that you are one of the hundred.

THE BEAT GOES TO THE MOVIES

'The Slender Thread'

By Jim Hamblin
(The BEAT Movie Editor)

AN ACTOR'S FACE IS HIS FORTUNE, so the saying goes, and nowhere is that more true than in this entry by Paramount Pictures. The story: A woman is committing suicide, using pills, and she decides to talk about it while she is dying.

That's it. The whole bit. And the stars of the film must make a gripping drama of that one single phone call.

Selected are Sydney Poitier and Anne Bancroft. Both were good selections. Each turns in the kind of performance reserved only for the very talented kind of movie actor and actress.

The story, from an original report in LIFE Magazine, was scripted by Sterling Silliphant, writer of the Route 66 and Naked City television series.

The sad part of the picture is the fact that somewhere along the line a decision was made, "Well, this is one of those dramas, so let's shoot it in black and white and save a couple of hundred dollars on color film. And oh, yeah, shoot it in square-screen, too, none of that wide jazz. My dog don't like it."

Which we suppose is all just as well, because the movie will undoubtedly be shown on TV within a very short time.

Doesn't anybody know that every movie shown on TV will need to be in color in a few short years? That alone should have convinced the producers to tint the Seattle landscape where this picture was made.

But don't get us wrong, black and white as it may be (is there some symbolism we haven't caught before?) it is a fine film, and makes you happy that people still care enough to create such works of art.

IN ONE OF THE MANY FLASHBACKS in the film, we see the events leading up to the woman's decision to commit suicide. Here they attend a night club-a-go-go for an evening out. There are many great dancing scenes like this in the Paramount flick.

POITIER IS A VOLUNTEER at a "Crisis Clinic," and listens as a deperate woman unfolds her life as they talk. Special equipment hooked to the phone registers her pulse slowing down dangerously . . .

THE SAD BEGINNING . . .   **. . . AND THE HAPPY ENDING.**

KRLA ARCHIVES

Dave Hull's HULLABALOO
The Rock & Roll Showplace of the World
6230 SUNSET (AT VINE) HOLLYWOOD, CALIF.

OPEN EVERY FRIDAY & SATURDAY NIGHT PLUS SUNDAY MATINEE

STARRING THE WORLD'S TOP RECORDING ARTISTS

FEBRUARY 13 — ONE DAY ONLY

THE BYRDS
TWO SHOWS ONLY — 4 P.M. & 8 P.M.
PLUS
THE PALACE GUARD

FEBRUARY 18 AND 19

DICK & DEE DEE
THE SHINDOGS
THE PALACE GUARD

FEBRUARY 25 AND 26

THE NEWBEATS
Doing Their Hit — "Run Baby Run"
THE PALACE GUARD

STARTS FEB. 20th EVERY SUNDAY MATINEE

MOVIES
"DRACULA," PLUS "FLASH GORDON SERIAL"
PLUS LIVE STAGE SHOW WITH THE PALACE GUARD

THIS CHIP WORTH **50¢ OFF** ON A HULLABALOO PIZZA

MAKE RESERVATIONS — HO. 6-8281

KRLA ARCHIVES

America's Largest Teen NEWSpaper 15¢

KRLA Edition BEAT
MARCH 5, 1966

'Listen People!' Herman Has Another Hit

KRLA BEAT

Volume 1, Number 51   March 5, 1966

HOTLINE LONDON
Full-Scale Tours Showing No Profit

By Tony Barrow

Far too many live pop shows in the U.K. seem to be losing money. A great deal of the real action has gone from the concert tour scene. Last winter some of the most reliable promoters in the business lost many pounds by playing packages boasting three or even four major names to houses which were less than half full. The number of stars—British or Americans—who can crowd our theaters and cinemas to capacity and show a tour profit, may be counted without going into double figures.

The Stones and The Beatles still classify as hot box office attractions. Tickets sell out as soon as bookings begin. Numbered amongst the very few U.S. visitors of this calibre are Roy Orbison and Gene Pitney. Gene's latest road show, co-starring Len Barry, opens up this month and fairly satisfactory advance business is reported at the majority of venues.

In the last week of March, Roy Orbison is due in for a series of more than fifty concerts for which he will be joined by The Walker Brothers plus up-and-coming Scottish songstress Lulu. It's too early to predict how that show will fare although the slight decline in Orbison's popularity could be balanced out by the immense fan following accumulated by The Walkers.

Otherwise, there are far fewer full-scale concert tours scheduled this season. Most of our American visitors come in for promotional dates — several TV appearances and, perhaps, the odd ballroom engagement.

Pop Show Future

What is the future for live pop shows here? The answer could lie in the type of lavish, fast-moving production which Brian Epstein put on last autumn. He put together The Everly Brothers, veteran chart favorites who still command a wide U.K. following, Billy J. Kramer with The Dakotas plus Cilla Black. To this array of names he added Lionel Blair and His Kick Dancers, a team of good-looking gals who added colour to the show with their expert dancing and magnificently way-out clothing.

Promotionally, Epstein teamed up with the pop pirate ship Radio London who plugged the tour good and hard at three-hourly intervals every day for a month! This was the first time a radio station had pushed a British concert tour. It was also the first time the fans had seen a team of dancers on this type of show.

The other answer seems to lie in an entirely new entertainment formula now being introduced in key cities up and down the nation. Springing up fast and showing immense crowd-pulling promise is a string of mass-market nightspots.

These places rule out the under-eighteens right away by selling beer and spirits from several different bars. Meanwhile, couples in their late-teens and early twenties are flocking to the new night clubs, which have names like the Stockton Fiesta, The Newcastle Dolce Vita and Mr. Smith's. The amenities include gambling (with low average stakes of around fifty cents), dancing, good-menu dining PLUS top-name cabaret.

The clubs are paying excellent fees for Britain's biggest pop stars who appear for 45 minutes at around midnight six evenings per week. Artists ranging from Dusty Springfield to Gerry and The Pacemakers and from Cilla Black to P.J. Proby are being booked.

If the trend towards this type of presentation continues, the by-product of the whole deal could be an increase in adult pop record collectors which would be a useful shot-in-the-arm for our disc industry.

Stone Bits

Before flying to New York (Friday, February 11) The Rolling Stones undertook only two television appearances to showcase their new single, "19th Nervous Breakdown." One was "Top Of The Pops" and the other was "The Eamonn Andrews Show" which is in the vein of your "Tonight" series. Mick Jagger sat on the programme's panel and talked with Eamonn Andrews but the rest of the Stones performed their one number and departed immediately afterwards.

Mick Jagger has spent the last few weeks working on new album numbers with Keith Richard and choosing furniture and fittings for his new apartment. Last week he spent a whole morning ("morning for me means from two until dusk in the afternoon") painting a chest of drawers he'd just bought.

Incidentally, British trade-paper reviews of "19th Nervous Breakdown" have been very mixed. *Melody Maker* said: "Some monotonous parts and some interesting parts . . . if this hadn't been recorded by The Stones it wouldn't be a hit." *Record Mirror* commented: "Mick's voice
(Turn To Page 15)

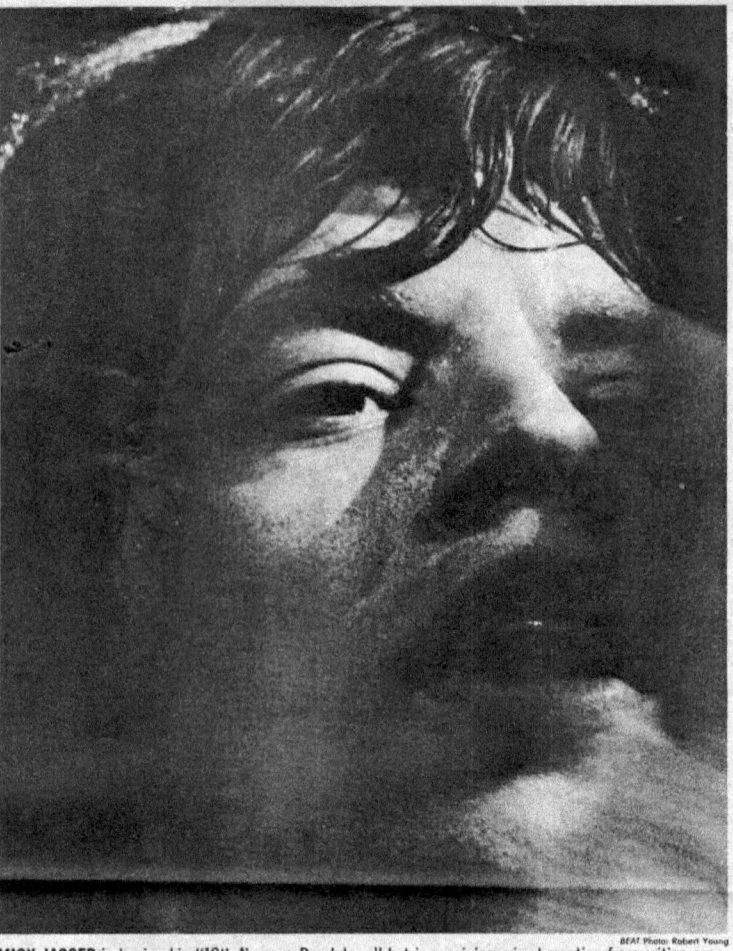

MICK JAGGER is having his "19th Nervous Breakdown" but is receiving mixed reaction from critics says Tony Barrow in his "Hotline London." But the Stone fans love the new single and will send it to the top.

Thanks To BEAT Reporter
People Listen To Herman

Herman has done it again! As you all know, Herman has made a habit of releasing albums which receive enough air play to force MGM to pull off at least one of the tracks for release as a single.

He started the ball rolling with "Mrs. Brown," followed it up with "Henry The VIII," and now, of course, he has "Listen People" flying up the charts. But this time Herman didn't do it alone—he was unwittingly helped by *BEAT* reporter, Susan Frisch.

Way back in September one of the Frisch family's friends, an executive at MGM, sent Susan a dub of "Listen People." It was scheduled for part of the sound track album from the film "When The Boys Meet The Girls."

However, the MGM executive had his doubts about the song's appeal to teens so he sent Susan the dub and asked for her honest opinion as a teenager. Susan was immediately knocked out by "Listen People" and lost no time in telling the MGM executive that it was one of the best songs Herman had ever recorded, a sure-fire hit.

He obviously valued Susan's opinion and decided not to chuck "People" after all. The song was included on the "When The Boys Meet The Girls" LP but was *not* scheduled for single release.

But once the record began getting air play, distributors took for granted that it would be a single and began ordering it. After over 600,000 copies had been ordered MGM took the hint and shortly released "Listen People" as a single.

So, thanks to Herman's Hermits, Susan Frisch and *you*, we have a fab new Herman single. We all did pretty well for ourselves, don't you think?

Susan is so proud of herself that she is currently strutting around here on cloud nine. We all tease her but we figure she does have a right to be proud—after all, if it wasn't for her we might never have heard "Listen People." Of course, Herman and his Hermits had a bit to do with it too!

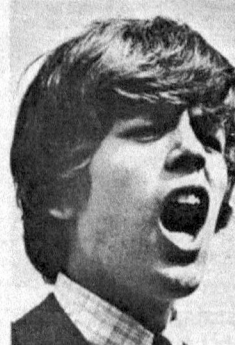

...SPEAKIN' HIS MIND

Inside the BEAT

Yeah, Well Walker Bros. 2
David McCallum Speaks 3
Short Hair for P.J. 6
Reflection on George Chakiris 7
Bill Cosby Hemonself 11
Noted in The U.K. 12
"Way Out"—Way In 13
Adventures of Robin Boyd 14
BEAT Goes To The Movies 15

The BEAT is published weekly by BEAT Publications, Inc., editorial and advertising offices at 6290 Sunset Blvd., Suite 504, Hollywood, California 90028. U.S. bureaus in Hollywood, San Francisco, New York, Chicago and Nashville; overseas correspondents in London, Liverpool and Manchester, England. Sole price, 15 cents. Subscription price: U.S. and possessions, $5 per year; Canada and foreign rates, $9 per year. Application to mail at second class postage rates is pending at Los Angeles, California.

Yeah, Well Walker Bros...
Wanta Buy A Car, Fellas?

By Tammy Hitchcock

I really don't know how I've missed putting the Walker Brothers on our "Yeah, Well Hot Seat." I mean, that is a gross oversight! After all, they are the biggest things to hit the pop scene in ages—just ask them!

I'm just kidding, they really are a nice threesome. Talkative, but nice. You know they all sport relatively long hair (about shoulder-length to be more explicit) and it caused them quite a bit of trouble here in the U.S.

John remembers the problems he used to have when he went out for a hamburger. "They'd whistle and say, 'ain't she sweet' and I used to have to bluff my way out of it by putting on a Liverpool accent and then someone'd say, 'lay off, can't you see the guy's English'?"

Yeah, well that was clever of you, John. Only what do you do now that you're in England—put on an American accent or stop buying hamburgers? "No, you'd drop dead from hunger," admits John. Yeah, well you don't *have* to live on hamburgers—you can always try hot dogs.

Thrown Out

Although they've certainly made a large splash in England, the Walkers have encountered their share of troubles there too. Like Scott and Gary being evicted from their apartment.

Gary tells the story this way. "A little man came around the other day with a big petition signed by about 100 people who claimed to have heard our last party about three blocks away." So, they decided to throw the two "Brothers" out.

Yeah, well you shouldn't feel too badly about being thrown out. At least, the people who heard your second to last party *five* blocks away didn't sign any old petition! Some people are just spoil-sports and others just don't dig all-night parties.

John recently purchased a Bentley which he raved on and on about for what seemed like ages. But of late John has been rather mum on the subject of cars and Gary finally revealed why.

"It fell apart," laughed Gary. "He was driving down the road and the sun roof snapped open forever. Now he gets more snow in the car than there is outside!"

Yeah, well cars are right up my alley. I suppose everyone who reads this column with any amount of regularity knows by now that I am the proud possessor of a beautiful Chevy which I have been trying to palm (oops, I mean sell) off to some pop person. Actually, I'm to the stage where I'd sell it to *anybody!*

Firts I tried Brian Jones but he didn't dig the idea much, just sort of looked at me like I was off my nut (which I admit I usually am), then I heard of Mick Avory's misfortunes with his new car and heroically offered to sell him mine. But he too turned down the chance of a lifetime.

I'm kinda glad Brian and Mick didn't have enough sense to buy my car, though, because I think it would be just perfect for John. You see, he wouldn't have to worry about the sun roof snapping off 'cause it doesn't have one! Doesn't have a right front hubcap either. I guess somebody swiped it or else it fell off and I was playing the radio so loud that I didn't hear it make its departure—which is very likely.

Anyway, I'd be more than happy to sell it to you, John. Real cheap. In fact I'd let you have it for blue chip stamps! But you'd better hurry up—somebody already ran into the side of it and if you don't act immediately somebody will probably steal the muffler. But don't worry, they can't stifle any gas 'cause I have a padlock on it and if you think I'm putting you on about that lock business you're crazy!!

Up It Went

Yeah, well enough about cars—now on to television sets. Apparently, Gary is not the mechanical genius he thought he was, therefore, while attempting to get BBC-2 in, he blew up the set.

Unfortunately, I don't have a television set which I am prepared to part with (even for blue chip stamps) but I sure know somebody who would be ecstatic to part with *his* imitation of a television.

And that is Jimmy May of the Liverpool Five. You see, the Five were renting this TV and it broke down so they sent for a "new" one, they *thought*. But you just should have seen what arrived—it had to be one of the first television sets ever made!

Anyway, the rest of the Five thought it was rather funny—the television, I mean. It had about a two inch screen which refused to focus. We thought we were watching a western but it actually turned out to be "Batman." That's how horrible it was. Jimmy calls it an orange crate with a light bulb in it and he's not far off.

He even threatened to throw the "orange crate" into the swimming pool, thought better of the idea and decided to throw *himself* into the swimming pool but thought better of that too and ended up watching the out-of-focus set just in case it surprised him and came up with a clear picture.

For Free Even

Yeah, well Jimmy never was surprised and the set is still sitting up there so I know that he'd be glad to give it to you, Gary—even cheaper than I'd be willing to part with my car!

Since I found a car for John and a television set for Gary, in all decency I really ought to find something for Scott, don't you think? Well, even if *you* don't I do and I've got just the thing for him—one of those blow-up rubber surfing things for people who like to surf but can't afford a board.

Back in my Gidget days (when Sandra Dee was playing Gidget but I wished desperately that *I* was) I purchased this rubber blow-up thing because I was one of those people who wanted to surf but couldn't afford a board and besides that had dinged enough other people's boards to be forever banned from the beach.

So, I still have the "thing" but I could be persuaded to let you have it for the minimal fee of shipping Jim McCarty of the Yardbirds to me! The reason I'm letting you have it so cheap, Scott, is because it has a small hole in it but it still works fine because I fixed the leak with a piece of over-chewed gum!

If I do say so myself (and I'm the only one who does) I think I missed my calling—I should have been a saleswoman! Okay, stop snickering... I should have been a sales*girl.*

Yeah, well.

On the BEAT
By Louise Criscione

The Turtles, just off a smash Hollywood night club date, have embarked on their third cross country tour as headliners. The tour will wind up in New York on March 2nd where the Turtles will head into the Phone Booth for a ten day engagement.

The Turtles got their start in local L.A. clubs but this Phone Booth date had them a little worried. To begin with they had heard all sorts of horrible things about New York clubs and then some helpful soul informed the boys that the Booth was next to Arthurs, which made the Turtles *really* scared!

But things are cool now. The Turtles had a talk with Joey Paige, who was in New York during the Christmas holidays. They asked Joey to name the three grooviest places to play in New York and without knowing that the Turtles were scheduled to appear there, Joey promptly named the Phone Booth. Hearing that, the Turtles are now ready to tear the place up!

Jerry In Movies

Also heading out on a tour is Jerry Naylor. Jerry is particularly excited about this tour because he will be playing his hometown, Stephenville, Texas. Some exclusive news about Jerry—he is up for a feature role in a Universal film. The studio plans to build Jerry into a young leading star and I hope they do—he's one of the nicest people in the business.

And then there are the Byrds—also on tour. They'll be visiting 20 cities, among which will be New York, Chicago and Washington.

For the first time since they became the Byrds they were forced to play a date minus Gene Clark who was in the hospital suffering from overwork and just plain exhaustion. Gene's fine now, though, and will be along with the rest of the group on their tour.

...HOWARD KALAN

The Righteous Brothers did so well in Vegas with Frank Sinatra that they have been invited back to appear at the Sands from July 20 to August 16. They're set to play Harrah's Club in Lake Tahoe with Jack Benny and New York's Basin Street East. Looks as if the two Brothers Righteous have officially hit the big time, doesn't it? About time too.

Genius Of Jagger

Stones' new single is a groove, isn't it? Mick thought up the title during their last Stateside tour when all five Stones were so tired and worn out that they probably felt as if they *were* on the verge of their "19th Nervous Breakdown."

Keith Richard has joined Brian Jones as a Rolls owner. Brian has a silver-grey Rolls while Keith has just purchased a dark blue Bentley Continental. Mick is still true to his Mini-Cooper and Charlie and Bill are faithful to their feet—they don't own cars at all!

QUICK ONES: Allen Klein, Stones' co-manager, has been charged with tax evasion. Amount involved is said to be over $8,000... John Steel, Animal drummer, says he is not going to leave the group despite rumors to the contrary... Dionne Warwick believes the only possible way to get an authentic colored sound is to be Negro... Nancy Sinatra is naturally thrilled over the worldwide success of "Boots" but admits that her real ambition is to be happily married and the mother of six children... Marvin Gaye is up for the role of the late Nat King Cole in a film to be made on the life of the "King"... Although Frankie Valli has released a record on his own he swears that he isn't even *thinking* of leaving the Four Seasons... The Who are coming.

Paul Revere and his Raiders don't want to be left out of the touring bag so they are off and playing such places as the McCormick in Chicago (with the Righteous Brothers, who incidently are going to release a record with *both* of their voices on it!), Cleveland, Honolulu and the Orient.

On the not so happy side for the Raiders, they've lost Drake to the National Guard. He is currently enjoying a five week period of grace and then he will serve six months active duty. During Drake's absence his place will be taken by one of the members of Don and The Good Times.

...PAUL REVERE

KRLA ARCHIVES

Exclusive BEAT Interview

David McCallum

By Bob Feigel

When you first meet an actor, especially one you watch week after week in a television series, you naturally expect him to be just like the character he plays.

There are two reasons for this:
1. You've probably never seen the actor when he wasn't playing a "role."
2. The role he plays is, very often, more interesting than the actor himself. (It's terribly disappointing to find one of your super heroes to be a mere human.)

In David McCallum's case, I expected an intelligent, articulate individual, complete with accent, upside-down triangular "beep" button, and a cigarette case tuned into "Solo at Elsinore."

Except for the button and the cigarette case, and with the addition of "friendly" and "sincere," David McCallum was exactly as I had pictured him. And, much more interesting than Illya Kuriachin.

THE INTERVIEW

BEAT—*Where and when did you receive your training as an actor?*
DAVID—As an actor, I went into amateur societies when I was about ten or eleven years old. I'm not sure when it was exactly, but I was very young.

Then I worked in the theater in the Church, of all places, for a long time and then at school. Then with the British Broadcasting Corporation as a voice on the radio because I had a Scotch accent. Then I went to drama school, and into stock plays, or what we call repitory.

BEAT—*How did you work your way into motion pictures?*
DAVID—I started out as an electrician. I worked as an electrician in a repitory company because you couldn't get in as an actor. Then I became a stage manager, a carpenter, and worked with the Glinebourne Opera Company in property work. Then I went to the Oxford Playhouse theater and that was the first time I was in a play as an actor.

BEAT—*Wasn't it about now that you got into television?*
DAVID—Actually, I was doing television between plays. One day a photograph of mine just happened to be on a producer's desk when a director wanted a particular type. And I went on contract for TV.

BEAT—*What was your first motion picture?*
DAVID—A thing called "A Secret Place."

BEAT—*And what "particular type" did you play in this?*

DAVID—Well, at the time they said they were looking for a young James Dean type. And, that was the "word" in those days, when they needed something to look a bit that way. They wanted a sort of young, impetuous nut.

BEAT—*David, it sounds as if you've had every job possible in the theater and a lot of hard work to get where you are today.*
DAVID—Well, I've had every job in the theater except wardrobe mistress, and I don't think I'm ever going to get around to that.

But, you know, this whole industry is very fascinating to me. They say, and I'll be a little trite, "variety is the spice of life." Well, I thrive on it.

Of course, there's a colossal amount of boring talk, stupid people, and some *trash*. I don't mean that to be rude to people, but there is an awful lot of people in the entertainment field of a low order and you have to fight like hell to keep your head above water.

BEAT—*Did they have you in mind when they wrote the Man From U.N.C.L.E.?*
DAVID—They had no one in mind. They wrote a part that was almost entirely up to the person that did it. The only thing they did say about it was that he was to be a Russian. That was it.

BEAT—*Why did they make you a Russian?*
DAVID—So there would be no element of the international, or East/West conflict in U.N.C.L.E.

It's the black hats against the white hats or the old Western formula of the good guys and the bad guys. In this way you can get away from the James Bond image of the Reds vs. the United States.

We have quite enough of that in the real world.

BEAT—*You play your part on U.N.C.L.E. so convincingly and yet, it's still difficult to imagine anyone else playing the part of Illia.*
DAVID—That's because it's me doing it. I *am* Illia and therefore there's bound to be a colossal amount of me coming through it.

This is something which I learned very many years ago in stock theater. I used to do many parts which were characters and where I'd be somebody else and do something else. One day an actor said to me, "No matter how much you struggle to make a characterization, never forget it's actually you giving the performance. Know yourself before you start to cover yourself with another personality."

That's very good advice. It was to me.

BEAT—*Robert Vaughn has been spending a lot of his spare time lately in legitimate theater. Do you have any plans along this line?*
DAVID—No! I did many, many years of that, and as far as I'm concerned, my life at the moment is the Man From U.N.C.L.E. (as long as the contract and the show lasts). And, in between shows, I want to do motion pictures.

BEAT—*Do you have any recording plans?*
DAVID—I don't have any recording plans as a singer, or in the conventional sense.

I had an idea that I would love to interpret the modern forty beat tunes by the way. I took the idea to David Axelrod, got together with H.B. Barnum, and got the instruments I wanted to play. I wrote a couple of the tunes and wook eight of what I think, are the best songs that are going around at the moment, like "Satisfaction," "1-2-3," "Taste Of Honey," and "Yesterday." We took these and played them my way, and it's a kind of groovy record. I like it.

BEAT—*Since you've done just about everything else, when do you plan to get into my field?*
DAVID—Literary?

BEAT—*Yes, literary!*
DAVID—I write quite a bit, but you've got to decide what you're going to concentrate on and I'm primarily an actor. Music, as a sideline, and acting are my only interests right now.

BEAT—*Getting back to music, do you think the great variety in popular music today indicates a more sensitive, less arbitrary acceptance of music by the general public?*
DAVID—I think the whole thing goes in a cycle. Every form of music goes in a cycle and the numbers of people who enjoy any particular group of selections change all the time. It's constantly changing, and I think the only thing that will remain the same are the certain songs or tunes that will be written—maybe today, maybe tomorrow—and will last indefinitely. In the last twenty or thirty years there are pieces that will almost go down through history as did the great compositions of Bach, Beethoven, Berlin, etc.

BEAT—*What do you think of the Beatles music?*
DAVID—I love the Beatles and what they come out with. They write wonderful music and lyrics. "Yesterday" is one of my favorite songs. It's beautifully written. A few years ago, if you tried to record that, nobody would have accepted it.

BEAT—*Since Man From U.N.C.L.E. made it's debut, quite a few copies have been introduced to television. What do you think of these copies?*
DAVID—It's very flattering to us to be copied. I must admit, however, that I do not have time to watch a lot of television. I use it mainly, as many people do, for news and those special programs like the Streisand Show, and I haven't seen many of the other shows. So, my opinion on this subject wouldn't be valid.

But, I know how much hard work television is and I know how much hard work a television series is, because I do it. So, all I can say, is that anybody who takes the trouble to sit down and try to write, cast or perform or have anything to do with a series deserves the best possible luck. And, I personally wish everybody the best possible luck, although it doesn't always work out that way.

Just then a pleasant female voice broke in, "Mr. McCallum, sorry to interrupt, but Bobby Webb is looking for you."
DAVID—Looks like they want me back on the set, Bob. Thank you very much.

BEAT—*Thank you! And the best of luck.*

KRLA ARCHIVES

Noel, Noel, Noel

...THE SINGER

...THE POET

...THE SON

By Carol Deck

It was very quiet and very still in the BEAT offices. I was alone and tired, only half alert.

From the back workroom where I sat I heard someone come in the front door. I arose wearily and went out to see who it was.

There in the reception room stood a promoter I knew and a lanky man who looked as tired as I felt.

"Hi, Carol, I'd like you to meet Noel Harrison, who has to catch a plane in ten minutes."

Trying not to look as flustered as I was I invited them both back to the inner office and we had a quick and quiet little chat.

Noel Harrison is to most of us just Rex Harrison's son and a singer with one big hit in this country—"A Young Girl."

But I discovered, as you do with most people, that he's much more than that.

A Quiet Poet

Noel is a poet and a clear thinking man who expressed himself in a quiet dignified way. He was rushed, but you couldn't tell it from his appearance. He had to catch a plane for Puerto Rico where he's been booked at the Hilton hotel, but he sat in our office like he had his whole life to spend just talking about whatever we wanted to talk about.

Although he's British, he's been living in New York for about six months now and for definite reasons.

"I found people would listen to me more here. I'd been working in England for a long time.

"Everyone puts everyone in a bag. They put me in a bag very early. They thought of me as a folk singer working for society people.

"I think I made a lot of mistakes, not so much mistakes as failures. It's difficult to live them down in the same country. I'm starting all over again, with 11 years' experience."

And he knows exactly what he's doing in both his singing and his writing.

Sings Words

"I'm singing words. I'm not groping when I'm writing. I perform words."

Words are very important to Noel and one that he used to describe what's he's trying to do is "diseur"—it's a French term translated loosely as a sayer of songs.

"Diseurs" are people like Bob Dylan and Bob Lind who write poetry and songs where the words are the thing. Noel is a great fan of both Dylan and Lind. He says Lind is in the same league with Dylan and we'll be hearing a lot more from him.

And Noel's newest release here is a Dylan song—"It's All Over Now, Baby Blue." He called "Baby Blue" a parable but refused to specify exactly what it is a parable of, for each person sees a song in a different way. But he did say what the song isn't—"It's not someone saying goodbye to a girl he'll never see again."

No Explanation

Noel won't explain Dylan songs to anyone. He says, "People who ask what Dylan means are missing the point."

During his short visit here Noel also told us how he got started and how one of the Beatles was partially responsible for "A Young Girl."

He started as an actor when he was 17, spent two years in the Army, and then took up the guitar.

"I needed some money and someone suggested singing in a little restaurant. I sang around the tables. I was singing 'A Young Girl' then and Paul McCartney used to come down to hear it. He asked me why I didn't record it."

So he did and it was a huge success in America, but England was another story. Because of his very narrow reputation over there he couldn't get it released. In fact it was just released in England a few days ago.

So it looks like Noel Harrison is ours now. England just doesn't know a good thing when they have it. And after all, they have that other Harrison, they can afford to share one with us.

For Girls Only
'Sore' Not 'Saw'

By Shirley Poston

They are coming for me soon, with a large net.

I know this as surely as I know my own name (which is — umm — drat, it's right on the tip of me tongue.) (Oh well, I can always ask someone.)

Anyway, about them stealthily approaching me, armed with straight jackets. I just know it's going to happen.

For the last couple of hours, I've been reading over some old copies of The BEAT. And I discovered that while the newspaper has been getting better and better, I've been getting worser.

Do you realize that this column actually used to make *sense*? And remember when it was sort of traditional for me to start off the column with some clever (oh, sure, Shirley) (so *there*, I did remember it after all) remark about the boys who were sneakily reading our corner of The BEAT whether we liked it or not?

Well, I've blossomed into such a blooming nut, I now start off this column by saying "speaking of George!" And I don't even care if every boy in the world reads it!

I ask you, what has become of me? I also ask you, what has become of *you*? When I used to write a sensible column, I got lots of nice, calm letters. Now that I've gone off my nut and started acting like a total retard, I get about *ten times* as many letters, and most of them sound almost as wacky as I do!

Do you suppose there's a possibility that they're coming for *all* of us? If so, they'd better get a bigger net.

Something else I noticed while I was paging through back issues.

In a certain chapter of Robin Boyd, I said something I thought was really hilarious (ham that I am.) When Robin flew across the stage to give John the line he'd forgotten (from "Till There Was You") she said:: "And I never *sore* them winging."

But, in *The BEAT*, the line came out—I never *saw* them winging. I'll just bet the printer noticed that word at the last moment and thought it was a mistake. Guess he just doesn't stay up all night playing Beatle albums like some people I might mention.

Did you know that they almost had Paul re-record that line because of the way he pronounced the word *saw*? But they changed their minds and left it in for flavor, and I'm glad they did because it's adorable.

If I can get my mind off the Beatles for about five seconds (which won't be easy) (because I don't have one) (a mind, not a Beatle) (come to think of it, I don't have either) (blast it all) . . .

Do you recall my mentioning the pop singer from Liverpool who is now in the U.S. Army, temporarily stationed at Ford Ord? Well, I don't. Oh, I do so, and I've finally gotten his address so all of us can drop him a line while he's still in sunny California.

Here's where you can write him: Pvt. Peter Sweeney, US56395545, Service Co. USAG, Fort Ord, Calif. And please do. He's twenty, and a real doll, even if those meanies did cut off his luvley long hair.

Speaking of English boys, I about had a nervous breakdown writing the Robin Boyd chapter in this *BEAT*. Because I got to thinking about how different most British lads *are* from most American guys.

Well, I don't know if they're really different. Maybe I'm just different. But everytime I even hear an English accent, I fall into a panic.

Does that happen to you? If it does, have you ever stopped to think about what causes it? I mean, why boys from England are so *irresistable*? I hope I'm the only one who feels this way. If that's the case, I can have them all to myself.

But, with my luck, everyone reading this also points and quakes in the presence of anyone (or anything) from the U.K.

Zowie, gleeps and other expressions stolen from the Batman! I've just had the most gastric idea! It's about time someone wrote a big, long article on how to trap an Englishman! And guess who's going to write it!

If you have any hints or ideas, or have done any personal research (ahem) along these lines, race to the nearest post office and mail this info to me. And, if you have a spare Englishman hanging around, send him along too.

Well, things are certainly up to par today. I'm about out of room, and I haven't said one rational thing yet. But I'm about to.

I've received another of those "thought-provoking" letters. It was from a girl in San Francisco who asked me to please not mention her name, and it was on the subject of "dreams."

The letter said: "The dreams you print in your column are great, and very funny. I make up crazy situations like those a lot of times when I can't sleep, but I sometimes make up very serious dreams, too. I wonder if anyone else ever does that."

Well, wonder no more. I do the same thing. Comments, anyone? (Please? So we won't think we're the only two people in the world who really get carried away?)

Hey! I've just thought of something I've been trying to remember for days! (And it isn't my name.) Remember the "Bev" letters so many of you wrote to the girl who felt she couldn't live without Paul? Well, I've had another of those! This one is from a girl in England, who is 19 and so wild about John Lennon, she can't think of anything else! And this situation is making her so miserable she doesn't know which way to turn.

Would all of you please at least send her a note? Mail them to me, and I'll send them along to her. I won't open them, I promise, but be sure to print U.K. in the lower left hand corner of the envelope so I'll know who the letter is for.

Zipes. I'm *completely* out of room now, so had better dash off. Keep your letters coming and I'll see you next *BEAT*!

Epstein To Buy Elvis?

Apparently, *The BEAT* has more power and influence than even *we* thought we had. Remember in the February 19 issue of *The BEAT* we revealed Brian Epstein's merger with the Vic Lewis Agency?

We casually mentioned at the end of the article that since Epstein owns the Beatles and controls just about everyone else, the only conceivable way up for Epstein would be to manage Elvis. It was pure speculation and logic.

Elvis himself was so upset about the remote possibility of having Epstein as his boss that he immediately placed a long distance phone call to Col. Parker. Well, what about it, asked Elvis—was it true?

The Col. calmed Elvis down considerably and then let the bomb explode. No, assured the Col., he wasn't going to retire *unless*, of course, the Beatles had enough money to buy both him and Elvis out.

You can well imagine what an impact the Colonel's remark had on Elvis. After all, the Beatles are piling up quite a bit of loot, and it is not unlikely that they *will* one day be able to buy both Elvis and the Col.—for cash!

And the Col. had said that if the Beatles *could* afford the purchase he would probably sell. A quick phone call was then made to RCA where a spokesman indignantly stated that the Beatles didn't have *nearly* enough money to buy either Elvis or the Colonel.

On the other side of the Atlantic, Epstein was playing the whole thing cool. For some time he didn't say anything at all. Tony Barrow approached Epstein concerning the possible sell-out and was answered by Epstein with a laugh—which you can take for what it's worth, if it's worth anything.

Pressed on all sides for a statement of some kind, Epstein finally revealed that if he ever did take on an American artist he would most probably pick an unknown. More satisfaction that way, you know.

Still, the rumors persist and if Col. Parker ever does retire we wouldn't be a bit surprised to see his place taken by Epstein. Would you?

Nancy's Walking On Boots Of Gold

By Anna Maria Alonzo

Have you noticed those rather suspicious-looking footsteps which have been appearing all over the nation's pop charts lately? You should have—they belong to a rather important young woman named Nancy Sinatra, and it would seem that Miss Sinatra has been kicking up her "boot" heels quite a bit lately. And the dust she's kicking up with those boots of hers is made of solid gold!

It is never easy for a female singer to top the nation's pop charts, especially when she is not generally associated with the pop field of music. But Nancy seems to have successfully overcome this handicap, and within the short space of seven weeks managed to sell 510,000 discs—a phenomenal number for *any* artist in so short a period of time.

Has the golden name "Sinatra" helped her along, or has it been a hindrance? *The BEAT* put the question to Nancy in an exclusive interview just before her recent trip to New York, and after considering it for a moment, she replied: "I don't think it has been *either* way. Possibly people expect more because of the name "Sinatra;" perhaps they expect me to be as talented and professional as he is, which is a little unfair, but it's understandable."

The record which is responsible for all of the wonderful things now happening to Nancy was originally recorded in November of 1965, but it wasn't the first which she had ever released. There were about ten before that, none of which found success in this country, though she has enjoyed hits in other countries. Nancy has received training from a vocal coach, but says that her father has never attempted to instruct her in her singing career.

If you have listened closely to "These Boots," you know that it is unlike any other hit record of the last few years. It is also unlike anything which Nancy has recorded before, and in speaking of this disc, Nancy has suggested: "I'd describe my voice as a new sound, a calculated sound. It's not the nice little girl, or all-American girl sound."

A hit record will inevitably open doors heretofore closed to an artist, but for Nancy—"Boots" has been the magic word to a whole new career. She seems to like the idea of motion pictures, and when I asked if her chart success would affect her current standing on the Silver Screen, she replied: "I would assume that it will. I guess they figure that if you can sell that many records, you can probably sell that many tickets."

After pausing for a moment to give the subject further thought and analysis, Nancy continued: "I'd begun to think of myself primarily as an actress, but since the record—I've had a change of career and a new image altogether different from the sweet young thing I've been doing in pictures. I can't play teen-age roles anymore or appear in those bikini movies. The record has opened new doors for me. I'm a woman now—not a girl."

Don't think for a moment that Nancy hasn't inherited her own fair share of that wry, Sinatra wit—'cause she has. Considering, briefly, the movies she might make, and the many movie scripts which are continually being submitted to top actors and actresses—she comically assured us: "I don't think that I'll be wearing *boots* in every picture—but if the role calls for it, I'll wear them!!! Courreges boots, cowboy boots, *any* kind of boots!!!"

She is insistent on one point—she doesn't want to be an artist contained in one single field; she wants diversity in her profession in very large doses. As she explains, "The more I can spread out—the more educated I can be in my business, in all aspects of it. That makes you more well-rounded." And that she definitely is. Versatility might well be considered one of Nancy's closest friends.

But this wasn't merely accidental. Her's is a studied talent and versatility. She spent 12 years studying the piano, and eight years taking dancing lessons. She may be only a junior member of the Sinatra clan—and a female member, at that!—but she is, none the less, a professional all the way.

Nancy explained to me that she has no one special type of song which she prefers to sing, although it should be "a song that has something to say. It can be almost any kind of song, but the mood can be different, and that makes it interesting." She admitted to a definite preference to the pop music, and said that she would rather record that sort of song than something with a very large, lavish arrangement.

Her latest album, entitled simply "Boots" contains many of the top pop songs of the day, including "It Ain't Me Babe," by Bob Dylan—one of Nancy's favorite composers—and poets—as well as some Lennon-McCartney compositions and the Rolling Stones' "As Tears Go By." Nancy greatly enjoys singing the songs of the talented team of composers—John Lennon and Paul McCartney—but laughs as she explains that she would prefer "to sing something which they haven't already recorded, 'cause you don't really have a chance then!"

Nancy is an unusually conscientious young woman, and you must feel an increased amount of respect for her as a human being—as well as an artists—when she explains why she will not go out on tour after just one hit record as so many artists do. "I don't like to feel that because I have a hit record, I have to take people's money. I don't want to capitalize on it, and the whole idea is very distasteful to me. I have plenty of money, and *no one* needs *that* much money. I don't want to go on tour until after I've had maybe three or four good records, and I know that the people want to see me."

Once again considering the changes which this smash hit has wrought in Nancy's career, she agrees that "It sort of speeded it up a couple of years." That it did, but it seems quite certain that now it has really begun—Nancy, *and her career*, are going to be around for a lot longer than just "a couple of years." Somehow the name "Sinatra" has a certain ring synonomous with success—and Nancy has a whole lotta ring-a-ding-ding yet to do!!!

KRLA ARCHIVES

Writer Tips, Part 3
A Record Producer Speaks
By Eden

One of the most important men in the record industry today is the record producer. He is the "man behind the scenes" on all of the music you hear when you tune in to your favorite radio station—he is the one responsible for creating those records you buy.

This week, we are going to step behind the scenes briefly and speak with a young man who is the associate producer at Columbia Records. His name is Larry Marks, and he was kind enough to give *The BEAT* this exclusive interview.

Larry explained that he himself is a writer and arranger as well as a producer. Then, "I think producers are becoming somewhat the way a composer for cinema has become. They have to not only *write* the music now, but they have to *orchestrate* it and *conduct* it."

In order to give you a better idea of just what goes into the production of a record, Larry provided *The BEAT* with a step-by-step description of the entire process, beginning with the selection of the material.

"Once the material is decided upon, by both the producer and the artist, the next step is finding the proper arranger, or arrangement, for the material.

"The third thing is to book studio time, which is like impossible to get!! Then the song is run down between the producer, the artist, and the arranger. Instrumentation is decided upon. The date is booked, usually built around a few key musicians—there's always something in arrangement that is imperative.

"The fourth thing is the session itself. After the session is through, there's a mix-down: professional tapes are usually cut in no less than three tracks and up to eight tracks, and you have to have a monaural track in order to produce an acetate (the finished master.)

"Multiple tracking takes place when there are particularly difficult voice tracks to go over it: like more than one voice track—excluding choruses which are usually cut on the date.

"But if you have a lead singer who's going to sing in unison with himself, or do three or four parts, the track is usually cut on three tracks.

"Then the three instrumental tracks are transferred to an eight track tape which gives you five empty available tracks—and then you cut the voices.

"When you have the six or seven tracks, you have to go into a mix-down: you mix them down, level-wise, one track against the other to one track. Most records really *happen*, or, take shape or form, while you're mixing. When you mix from six or seven or eight tracks down to one track, you take each track individually and add equalization and echo as you go along. Most records are probably made or lost in the mixing.

"Material is probably the hardest thing to find. It usually comes from publishers—you rely a great deal on five or six of the best publishers. If you have some kind of individual style or something you're looking for in material to place with a particular artist, or you have a particular direction you want to go into—the best way to do it is to call the best five or six working publishers: tell them what you're looking for, and when you're recording and have them start to bring material in."

There was one point which Larry was quite adamant about making, and it was in an effort to clear up a popularly-held misconception about the Top 40 records of today.

"It's a big misconception that rock 'n' roll records are thrown together. 'Rock 'n' roll' is even a bad term; it doesn't fit. Top 40 is popular music, that's what it is—there are all *kinds* of popular music. It may appeal to different kinds of values, but it's all popular music.

"There is as much time—if not *more*—usually spent on a Top 40 record, than on a Tony Bennett-type of record."

In this first part of our look behind the recording scenes, we have seen much of what goes into making the records we listen to. In the second installment, we will speak with Charlie Green and Brian Stone—along with several other top record producers—about the ways in which they go about producing the Number One hit records which we are listening to.

POOR LOU CHRISTIE. He certainly looks happy in this photo with his two Hawaiian friends but shortly after this picture was taken Lou decided to try his hand at surfing. Unfortunately, his instructor's board pearled, found Lou's nose and proceeded to break it! Lou is okay now though, and ready to head out on a 35 day tour which begins April 15 and winds up on May 18 hitting most of the nation's large cities.

Short Hair And A Tux?

By Carol Deck

A short time back *The BEAT* got a phone call from one Bongo Wolf, who had at one time been P.J. Proby's best friend and had some comments to make on Proby and his recent lack of success.

After printing that interview, we received another phone call, this one from another friend and business associate of Proby who had a few comments to make on Bongo's comments.

Jim DeMarco is a record company executive who was Proby's road manager for a while in Europe. He's known Proby for nine years and states flatly that P.J. Proby is "one of the most talented people to be born into the white race."

He realizes that Proby is a very controversial figure both in America and in England because of his highly suggestive stage antics but he says people only see one side of Proby.

His Talent

"Nobody ever says anything about his talent—as a singer, writer, painter and athlete," Jim complained.

"Nobody ever prints how sensitive he is. He's actually one of the most sensitive people I've ever met and that's why he's such a perfectionist and so hard to get along with."

Bongo, Jim says, was more of a mascot than a friend to Proby. He explained that Proby first met Bongo when Proby was getting nowhere in show business.

"Bongo used to steal food from his house and bring it to Proby on the bus. Bongo always believed in Proby and built him up as a sort of God."

Jim also explained where Bongo, who's real name is Donald Grollman, got his nickname.

"Bongo has a complete library on werewolves and things. He always carries things like fangs around with him so we started calling him the Wolf. When he started with the bongos P.J. started calling him the Bongo Wolf."

No Denial

Jim wouldn't deny Bongo's claims that Proby is hard to get along with. He just said "extremely talented people are always difficult people."

And Jim agreed with Bongo that the pants splitting episode wasn't Proby's fault. "The material was guaranteed by the tailor not to split," Jim said, "but the entire thing was so over written and over done.

"Proby was so big it just made him bigger. When they banned him, he just became more in demand."

However, Jim said that Bongo's coming back to America was not entirely voluntary. "Bongo was deported, kicked out of the country. When he was in Denmark they wouldn't let him back in England, so he had to go home." Jim also added that Proby was very unhappy about Bongo leaving.

Short Hair Now

Jim assured us that Proby has actually cut his hair and now wears a tuxedo on stage.

And the chances of Proby coming back to America? "He's taking out dual citizenship because his own country really hurt him," Jim said, "but there is a possibility that he'll come over in April to do some night club appearances.

"He says if America wants him they'll start buying 'Maria,' his latest single release."

There you are Proby fans, now you know how to get him back to America.

KRLA ARCHIVES

Reflections of a Man

By Eden

There are people who strongly resemble a shimmering piece of cut-glass, sparkling in the lights from this world and reflecting all of the many-colored, many-sided facets of their own spheres of existence. George Chakiris is such a person, and for a few precious hours recently—he shared some of his reflections with me. Now, I'd like to hold them up to the light for a time and share a few with you.

If you look quite closely, you might be able to see the somewhat paling lights of his childhood, still lingering on in the shadows of his memories. George was born in Norwood, Ohio, on September 16, 1934. His was a large family of six children, and they moved about a good deal during those formative years of childhood.

George has many contrasting reflections, especially those lighted by the flickering lamps of time and space. He was dynamic and powerful as the Puerto Rican Shark—the young man they called Bernardo. But, the young boy they called George was different; he was a quiet sort, and as a youngster—he tried to hide the impatient lights of ambition growing within him:

Not "That"

"I never let anyone know about it. In school when they always asked you 'What do you want to be?'—I would never say *that*, because I felt stupid saying it!" "That" was his sincere desire to be an actor, and it took a girl—a very *special* girl—to shut out the glaring light of embarrassment for George.

She was a girl he went with while in high school, and she was a dancer. She encouraged George to join her and before too long, they succeeded in dancing away the entire aura of "stupidity"—so much so that after a year and a half of classes at Glendale City College, George moved to Hollywood where he obtained a job and began to study dancing seriously at night at the American School of Dance.

Bright lights of a big city, the somewhat foreign lights of the English theatre; George portrayed the role of Riff in the successful London engagement of the smash musical, West Side Story. But long before those lights could become permanent fixtures, another crystalline side of George's life—at the time somewhat hazy in a blurring light of confusion—whirled into view.

It was a change from the flooding rainbow-lights of the theatrical world, to the glaring of the sound stage klieg lights; to the neon of the cinema marquee: George had won a starring role in the motion picture adaptation of West Side Story. But no longer could he cling to the security of the familiar role of Riff—he suddenly found himself alone in the glaring spotlight which belonged to Bernardo. It was another rough-edged piece of sparkling glass—but one which brought to him the glittering reflection of success, and the golden light of an Academy Award.

Never Stops

A piece of glass never stops reflecting the lights around it, and even in the absence of some exterior illumination—it has an effervescent glowing all its own glimmering deep within. Look closely with me now, and wonder if George has set that inner-light to traveling on a self-planned path of destiny. What direction will his colorful career take on now?

"I don't think of it in terms of my *career*—I sort of think of it in terms of my *life*. I'm free of my Mirisch contract now, so I don't have to do anything that I don't

want to do. Naturally, I'd like to do something of quality and work with people that I think are good and talented, and that I can enjoy working with. Really, more than anything—I would just like to have more and more independence, so that I'm free to do as much as I can: just free to live my life the way I want to live it and not have to think: 'Oh, well yes—I'd *love* to do that, but I *should* do that because it will help my career, etc.'

"I'd like to do some things on the stage—and then I'd like to spend time *away* from it, too. I don't want to work all the time. I don't mean that I'm lazy, but there's just so much more that's as interesting as films. I love dancing still—in fact, probably more than anything."

More Yet

And there are many things which George has done in the last three years, and many things which he is doing now. Many lights have flickered on the glassy planes of George's life, and though they were of the moment—there are still many moments yet to flame into the light of existence for him.

He is concerned now with developing the sparkling talent he has as a vocalist—not yet exposed in depth to the public ear, but somewhat overshadowed by his other talents only through lack of time. He has a new single about to be released—"Little Girl" b/w "Trying So Hard (To Forget You)"—and thinking about it says, "The sort of vein I'd like to go in is not necessarily just the pop stuff. Stuff more like Tony Bennett, Barbra Streisand—that's what I really *feel*."

What's Real

There is a side of George's personality which finds enjoyment in some of the Beatles' work and thinks them "very clever;" there is another side which cannot appreciate the Rolling Stones, and still another side reflecting thoughts like: "I'd rather listen to Bob Dylan, I think some of his songs are *really* far out. Some of his lyrics really kill me because they're right on the nose!"

There is a very genuine side of George Chakiris trying to reflect the qualities of *others* about him. He enjoys a person who is kind and considerate, one who possesses "just sort of a basic honesty—knowing what's real and what isn't."

There is a little anger gleaming from the side of George which hates the exploitation of youth, and a light of determination shining when he says, "Honesty is very important; I think it takes a lot of guts to be hones but in the end it's better."

George is a very sensitive, "feeling" sort of person—and he reflects this strongly in all of his many sides. Through his acting, dancing, singing, and in his everyday contacts with other human beings.

Man And Boy

To others? George reflects the lights of kindness, of thought *and* thoughtfulness; he is the strength of a man, and the innocent laughter of a small boy. He illuminates the attitude of sincerity with a truth and honesty which are seldom found. Of himself and of his own accomplishment, he reflects this light of honesty and thought: "As far as I'm concerned, in any of the things that I can even do a little bit—singing, dancing, or acting—I haven't gone anywhere near what I'd like to, so I have to feel that I've accomplished something before I go on to something else."

He *has* accomplished much already, and the lights shining far ahead in his future assure him of continued motion—for he will accomplish even more. The only sad reflection is that he *is* moving—almost too fast to follow—and there is a little sadness in your own reflections when you realize that you can't detain him any longer. The many-sided figure who is George Chakiris must move along—rapidly—now, for he has so many more lights which he must shine.

KRLA ARCHIVES

Paul Newman is 'Harper'

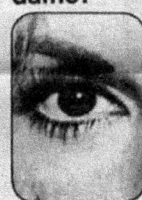

This is a different kind of cat named Lew Harper... and excitement clings to him like a dame!

A GERSHWIN-KASTNER Production
CO-STARRING (IN ALPHABETICAL ORDER)
**LAUREN BACALL · JULIE HARRIS · ARTHUR HILL
JANET LEIGH · PAMELA TIFFIN · ROBERT WAGNER
SHELLEY WINTERS**
Screenplay by WILLIAM GOLDMAN · Produced by JERRY GERSHWIN and ELLIOTT KASTNER · Directed by JACK SMIGHT
TECHNICOLOR® PANAVISION® FROM WARNER BROS.

EXCLUSIVE ENGAGEMENT
NOW PLAYING!
PACIFIC'S **PANTAGES** THEATRE · HOLLYWOOD
HOLLYWOOD BLVD. near VINE · HO. 9-2211

Inside KRLA
By Eden

KRLA has been a very popular place the last few weeks—as it always is—but it has also been a very much visited place, as well. Dropping by our hallowed halls of late have been such notables as Noel Harrison, the Fortunes, Neil Sedaka, John Maus of the Walker Brothers, and there has even been a rumor running rampant 'round the studio that Robin dropped by, sans his Caped Crusader friend.

The KRLA Flying Saucers were a huge success at the Pan Pacific when they flew in for a brief visit at the Car Show held there recently.

Then of course there is the story of Dick Moreland—mild-mannered, affectionate, loyal KRLA DJ; bespectacled leader of the hippy, hippy In Crowd in KRLA-Land who recently took his little money-stocking out of hiding, and after the cloud of moths disappeared—marched directly down to his local Vast Wasteland dealer and purchased a Color Conveyor of same for the sole purpose of watching "Batman" in color. Oh well—they say it takes all kinds!!!

If you are keeping up with our fab KRLApes, then you might be interested in the dates of some of their upcoming games. They will be appearing in Palmdale—another of their famous roadtrip games—on March 9, and at Canoga Park High on March 29.

Then on April 6 the Apes will travel out to Northridge for a game at San Fernando Valley State College, and to Heart High in Newhall for a game on April 20.

You all know Charlie O'Donnell, and you are probably familiar with the name Nino Tempo—the male counterpart of April and Nino. But did'ja know that good ol' Charlie was the producer of the single session when Nino and his group—the Pulaski Highwaymen—recorded "Michelle."

Back to your favorite Valentine and mine—Dick Moreland—oops! That was last month, wasn't it? Oh well, Dick has always been a "hearty" sorta fella, anyway. He now has a new hero—The Mouse. No, really—he does! Not only that, but he has a membership in the Mouse Fan Club of America, and owns a copy of The Mouse's very first record—"A Public Execution."

Now that might just sound odd to you, but in a few months time that record will probably be quite priceless as it will undoubtedly be the only one of its kind in existence anywhere in the civilized world. As it is now, Dick is probably one of the only people who has a record, and probably in a short time he will become the only one who still has a copy of the disc intact!

Did you know that KRLA is the only radio station with an upstairs, fully-furnished, wall-to-wall Bat Cave? It's true; and as things stand now, not even the DJ's here at the station know what is *really* inside of the Bat Cave, 'cause it's always kept locked!

We *do* know that there are quite a number of valentines up there—but that's about all that we can take credit for! There is a theory currently circulating among the DJ's and other various KRLA "In" personalities that the Bat Cave is actually John Barrett's secret, upstairs office-hideout where he conjures up all of the fiendish plots which he springs on the poor, unsuspecting DJ's at the weekly DJ meeting.

Hmmmm—could it be that our own John-John is really "Batman" in disguise???? Tune in next week for further clues.

NOW THRU MARCH 6
JUDY COLLINS
PLUS PATRICK SKY
COMING ATTRACTIONS
MAR. 8-13 EDDIE BROWN OF JOE & EDDIE
MAR. 18-21 BROTHER DAVE GARDNER
AT DOUG WESTON'S
Troubadour
RESERVATIONS: CR. 6-6168
DO YOU KNOW WHO WILL BE AT THE TROUBADOUR MAR. 15-17? TO FIND OUT ♦ CALL CR 6-6168 ♦

KRLA BEAT Subscription
SAVE 33% Of Regular Price
☐ 1 YEAR—52 Issues—$5.00   ☐ 2 YEARS—$8.00
☐ 6 MONTHS—$3.00

Enclosed is _____   ☐ CASH   ☐ CHECK
PLEASE PRINT

Send to: _____ Age _____
Address: _____
City _____ State _____ Zip _____

MAIL YOUR ORDER TO: KRLA BEAT
6290 Sunset, Suite 504
Hollywood, Calif. 90028
Foreign Rate: $9.00—52 Issues

KRLA ARCHIVES

March 5, 1966 — THE BEAT — Page 9

SPECIAL REPORT
In Draft You Can Catch Your Death

By George Lincoln Culver

The people at KRLA are very much concerned with the feelings and opinions of their audience and constantly endeavor to bring them the finest in musical entertainment and news programming.

Aware that we have a large draft-age audience at the station, Lou Erwin—one of the fine newsmen at KRLA—decided to bring to them a discussion, on an adult level, of a problem which is currently in the uppermost thought on the minds of many of our listeners. That is, of course, the draft.

The entire project—which ran for approximately three weeks, concluding with the special documentary presented on Sunday, February 13—involved countless hours of intensive research and interviews with college students, as well as many other persons directly involved. At the conclusion of the project, complete tapes and transcrips of the entire project were sent immediately to Senator Kuchel in Washington.

Lew found that there was actually no predominance of one single opinion on the issue among all of the people with whom he spoke, although one general comment he did find was the disdain for the new policies concerning the student grades.

In his discussions with college students, Lew found some believing that the draft is wasteful and inefficient—although they said they would support the war in Viet Nam—simply feeling that the draft and the Selective Service Administration should be altogether abolished.

To paraphrase Lew Erwin in one of his special reports on this project, KRLA has presented the voices of young men who are opposed to the government's draft policies. There were some young Conservative intellectuals who saw that these policies were wasteful, inefficient, and destructive of human freedom.

Some leftists spoke out in opposition to our policies in Viet Nam, and there were still many bitter denunciations of all of these various ideas.

The only question left is what do *you* think? Where do you stand on the question of the draft? The problem is one of *all* the American people—and one which hasn't received anywhere near the amount of discussion or attention which it rightfully deserves.

UNLIKE ANYTHING YOU'VE EVER SEEN!
BATTLE OF THE BULGE
WARNER BROS. SUPER CINERAMA PRODUCTION

WARNER BROS. PICTURES PRESENTS A CINERAMA, INC. PRODUCTION "BATTLE OF THE BULGE" Starring HENRY FONDA · ROBERT SHAW · ROBERT RYAN · DANA ANDREWS · PIER ANGELI · BARBARA WERLE · GEORGE MONTGOMERY · TY HARDIN · CHARLES BRONSON · HANS CHRISTIAN BLECH · WERNER PETERS · JAMES MacARTHUR and TELLY SAVALAS · Written by Philip Yordan, Milton Sperling, John Melson · Produced by Milton Sperling, Philip Yordan · Directed by Ken Annakin · A SIDNEY HARMON IN ASSOCIATION WITH UNITED STATES PICTURES, INC. PRODUCTION · TECHNICOLOR® · ULTRA-PANAVISION®

PACIFIC'S CINERAMA DOME Theatre — SUNSET AT VINE · HOLLYWOOD — NOW PLAYING!
For Reserved Seats Information Please Call HO. 6-3401 — For Theatre Parties & Group Sales Call TR. 6-2935

KRLA Tunedex

This Week	Last Week	Title	Artist
1	1	THESE BOOTS ARE MADE FOR WALKIN'	Nancy Sinatra
2	4	YOU BABY	The Turtles
3	23	CALIFORNIA DREAMIN'	Mamas & The Papas
4	3	ZORBA THE GREEK	Herb Alpert & The Tijuana Brass
5	6	A WELL RESPECTED MAN	The Kinks
6	8	FIVE O'CLOCK WORLD	The Vogues
7	12	I AIN'T GONNA EAT OUT MY HEART ANYMORE	The Young Rascals
8	32	LISTEN PEOPLE	Herman's Hermits
9	9	WE CAN WORK IT OUT/DAY TRIPPER	The Beatles
10	9	LOVE MAKES ME DO FOOLISH THINGS	Martha & The Vandellas
11	7	ELUSIVE BUTTERFLY	Bob Lind
12	5	CRYIN' TIME	Ray Charles
13	20	TIME	Pozo-Seco Singers
14	18	MY BABY LOVES ME	Martha & The Vandellas
15	—	HOMEWARD BOUND	Simon & Garfunkle
16	13	MY LOVE	Petula Clark
17	26	THE BALLAD OF THE GREEN BERET	Sgt. Barry Sadler
18	21	BATMAN	Neil Hefti
19	15	WHAT NOW MY LOVE	Sonny & Cher
20	27	I'M SO LONESOME I COULD CRY	B. J. Thomas
21	16	SET YOU FREE THIS TIME	The Byrds
21	28	DON'T MESS WITH BILL	The Marvellettes
22	24	WORKING MY WAY BACK TO YOU	The Four Seasons
22	25	SANDY	Ronnie & The Daytonas
23	38	KEEP ON RUNNING	The Spencer Davis Group
24	37	ANDREA	The Sunrays
25	34	LOOK THROUGH ANY WINDOW	The Hollies
26	33	AT THE SCENE	The Dave Clark Five
27	—	DARLING BABY	Elegants
28	35	THE CHEATER	Bob Kuban
29	40	WOMAN	Peter & Gordon
30	—	LOVE IS ALL WE NEED	Mel Carter
31	—	SHAKE ME, WAKE ME	The Four Tops
32	36	HUSBANDS AND WIVES	Roger Miller
33	39	DEDICATION SONG	Freddie Cannon
34	—	BABY SCRATCH MY BACK	Slim Harpo
35	—	IT'S TOO LATE	Bobby Goldsboro
36	—	PROMISE HER ANYTHING	Bob Jones
37	—	THE ONE ON THE RIGHT IS ON THE LEFT	Johnny Cash
38	—	19TH NERVOUS BREAKDOWN	The Rolling Stones
39	—	DAYDREAMIN'	The Lovin' Spoonful
40	—	CALL ME	Chris Montez

DAVE HULL

BOB EUBANKS

DICK BIONDI

JOHNNY HAYES

EMPEROR HUDSON

CASEY KASEM

CHARLIE O'DONNELL

BILL SLATER

MORE ADVENTURES OF... EMPEROR BY... MIKE McGUCKIN

Miss Teen Applications

Would you like to be "Miss Teen International," and win a bounty of prizes including a 1966 automobile?

If you are between the ages of 14 and 18 years of age and interested in participating in the pageant call Mrs. Bush at (213) 462-6464 or write to Teen-Age Fair, 6290 Sunset Boulevard, Hollywood, California. Deadline for application is March 4.

The "Miss Teen International Pageant" will be one of the major highlights of the 1966 Teen-Age Fair, which will be held April 1-10 at the Hollywood Palladium.

For the first time, teen beauties from foreign lands will be flown to Hollywood to compete against the best of American teen-agers. A one-hour special covering the final judging and crowning of "Miss Teen Internatin," will be televised nationally, April 6, on the ABC-TV network.

Eve's APPAREL

See if you can BEAT our prices on our new Jr. and missy lines. Samples at wholesale or less.

1800 N. Vermont — NO 3-4456
Hollywood, Calif.

KRLA ARCHIVES

The First Lady Of Pop

By Judy Felice

... PETULA CLARK

Petite, "cute as a button" Petula (Pet) Clark has probably done more, seen more, and received more awards than any other female vocalist on the pop scene.

Although she has sold over 20,000,000 records in Europe she didn't have a hit in the U.S. until 1964 when Warner Brothers Records obtained the releasing rights to all of her hits for the United States and released "Downtown." The release immediately became a hit in America and won for her a NARAS "Grammy."

The "Grammy" made Pet even more of an international singing star. Up to this time she had the No. 1 hit record (with different songs) in Denmark, Germany, Switzerland, Holland, England, France and Italy.

Born in Epsom (in Surrey, England) Pet began her career at the age of nine on the BBC, singing and reciting poems for the families of British soldiers during the Second World War. By the time she was twelve, Pet had made over 500 appearances.

As an actress, Pet has starred in over twenty-five films but has always placed her cinema career second and concentrated on her recording career. She recorded her first single at the age of seventeen and now cuts 20 singles per year.

Pet received the Grand Prix National de Disque Francais with her single "Ya Ya Twist" during the Twist era in France. She has traveled throughout Europe starring on radio, TV, and making numerous personal appearances. Pet set new marks in the recording business as the first vocalist to have a bi-lingual hit with her first English hit record, "Gondolier" when it was released on the Gallic label in French.

In addition to awards already mentioned, Pet received the Golden Rose, twice—a continental award for outstanding show business personality and the "Most Outstanding TV Artist of 1950" award. Asked what the biggest influence on her career was, Pet answered, "My father while in England and my husband in France."

DISCussion

By Eden

The day has come! Yes, it's true folks. I have once again become addicted to my habit of olden days—I am again a confirmed channel changer—forever turning that blessed knob!

And it's all because of a brand new song by a brand new group—they are The Spencer Davis Group from England, their record is called "Keep On Running," and it is for absolutely certain that they have a smash on their hot little British hands.

This record has to go straight to the Number One position on the American charts, and I predict very big things in the near future for this group.

They might remind you somewhat of the Yardbirds instrumentally, but they are most certainly unique and individual in their over-all sounds and stylings.

They held down the Number One position on the British Pop Charts for several weeks, and have only just fallen to Number Two—so watch out for them, 'cause they may just be taking over.

* * *

Whewww!! Stones have a new one out, called "Nineteenth Nervous Breakdown." All right gang—I'll buy that. I'll also be willing to bet that there will be a rather large number of Stones' fans buying this new disc.

It doesn't really have the solid, driving sound of "Satisfaction," but it does have some good instrumental work and a catchy tune-and-beat. The tracks do sound almost as though they had been Spectorized—somewhat clouded and not as clear as some of the other Stone sounds, but it is undoubtedly going to be another large chart item for the boys.

Somebody somewhere is having ulcer-type stomach unhappiness 'cause many American disc jockeys began playing four previously-unheard (in America) Beatle records. The tunes are "Drive My Car," "If I Needed Someone," "Nowhere Man," and "What Goes On."

All four were included on the 14-track British "Rubber Soul" LP, but were scheduled for single release in this country by Capitol Records. If you will check some back issues, you will see that *The BEAT* told you all 'bout them when they were first released, but somehow it was supposed to have been some sort of deep, dark secret.

Who of The Who Can't Stand Who

The Who may well turn out to be the angriest young men of the century. An opinion from a member of The Who often comes out as forcefully as a twenty-one-gun salute. However their comments are not usually a salute. The group is very critical of other performers. The Yardbirds, Ken Dodd and the Bachelors have all been in the firing line recently. The Who do not reserve their "angry young man" attacks only for other artists however. They were bitterly critical of their own first LP. Their total opinion of the album was that they could have done much better indeed. Of one track "My Generation," which was already a single hit, Pete Townsend said: "Rubbish! Any record that can't get to number one is rubbish." Talking about another track, "It's Not True" Pete said: "This is everyone else's favorite track. I hate it. Yes, I'm thinking of giving this one to a country and western group actually. They're called the Small Faces."

Perhaps because of the continuous earthquakes emitting from The Who, there are often rumors pertaining to splits in the group. It has been said that Roger Daltrey and drummer Keith Moon would both be leaving, but all rumors are denied by manager Chris Stamp. Even so things do not appear to be very peaceful within The Who. Manager Chris has been quoted as saying: "Everybody knows there is conflict within the group, and there have been some hefty rows lately, but this doesn't mean that the group will bust up." He went on to say: "They just argue about their 'sound' and talk about the things that they want to achieve sound-wise."

Apparently these arguments are sometimes very lively because group-member Roger Daltrey reported that there was a near "punch-up" during a discussion over the treatment that should be given to "My Generation." According to remarks that Roger frequently makes some members of the group just can't stand each other. Despite this, Daltrey is convinced that "The Who" will never split up. He has said: "Don't believe whatever you've seen before. We have arguments all the time, but that is what gives us that extra spark. 'The Who' thrives on friction."

It is possible that The Who are able to get rid of some of their excess energy on-stage. So wild is their music that the effect on their instruments is shattering. They report that because of the punishment the instruments take they have to buy new guitars and drums every other month. Let us hope that some of this expensive burden will be relieved by the fair amount of success that their record "My Generation" has had throughout the world. Apparently the stuttering gimmick on that record was practically an accident, because after it's climb up the English charts Daltrey said: "It was freezing in the studios when we recorded it. That's why I stutter on the lyrics."

KRLA ARCHIVES

Bill Cosby Hemonself

...BILL COSBY

Now, then—you say you want to be a spy, huh? Okay—let's begin from the start with a super-snoop and play like we are mild-mannered sleuths—able to beat Batman at a single bounce. No? Well, would you believe a year's subscription to the James Bond Fan Club in honor of the men from U.N.C.L.E. from the 341st Icelandic Branch? Oh!... well, see how *this* grabs you: one whole hour with Bill Cosby.

Right!!! That's just what I thought you'd say. So, let's go.

If you are quick of wits (if not, please employ special Quick-Wit Zap Gun), you will readily determine that we are presently seated in the dressing room of one Mr. Bill Cosby—seated directly across from us in a moderately-flowered, understuffed chair—on the set of "I Spy."

A little spying into his insidious past renders us some rather relevant information—irrelevantly speaking—and we find that he was born in Philadelphia, Pennsylvania July 12, 1937. With that rather solid beginning behind him, he went on to high school, then in 1956 was inducted (that's "Spy" for *drafted*, men) into the service, and was admitted to Temple University in 1960 as a Physical Education major in the teacher's college.

And now we come to the moment of accusation; the confrontation of Criminal Comic Cosby with the evidence: you *always* wanted to be a comedian, didn't you? "Well, I *think* I did; I always enjoyed being funny—for euphoric reasons, I guess, 'cause I believed that as long as people were laughing at me, they loved me—which is not necessarily true. Other reasons, such as *conmanship*; I learned to con people to get my way! And I always loved sports, so the two sort of lasted for a long, long time with me.

"Sports, making jokes—keeping people laughing, was a sign of acceptance. It was great for me."

Really Off

I guess the secret is out now—you all (all of you being expert spy-types) have undoubtedly figured it out for yourselves by now. We can't hide the truth from you any longer. Off-stage Bill Cosby really *is* off-stage. He isn't always "on," as are many comedians and entertainers. And when he isn't supposed to be entertaining someone, he can be very serious and thoughtful.

It all sort of revolves around a little something called "intelligence" which Bill seems to possess in great, heaping quantities. So, we'll wait a minute while you put away your Secret Super Spy Stuff for awhile, and then we'll find out a little bit about a very complex, intelligent, warm, interesting, attractive young man named Bill Cosby.

Where do comedy routines come from? Do you find them in your own experiences past? "Yes, they're based on my own experiences in life. I never sit down and write anything. Everything I do, every piece of comedy I have ever recorded, anything you have ever seen me do—always happens, at one time or another, on somebody's stage or while I'm talking to someone. It never happens while I have pen-in-hand—I cannot work this way.

"My childhood experiences *are* true, and of course, you have to embellish certain things. Sometimes I embellish with the attitude, rather than blowing up a line into a world of fantasy or feeling. I may project a kid's reaction, a reaction that we had to something —enlarged—therefore causing you to laugh. Right now I'm working with my childhood, so you may see a lot of things which have happened to you."

First Time

When Bill accepted a co-starring role in a television series and began filming "I Spy," he entered the world of the dramatic actor for the first time. He suddenly found himself clothed in garments other than just those of the comedian. Nearing the end of his first successful season on TV as an actor, Bill looks back—and ahead—in reflection: "Yes, I am pleased with what I've done, and I think to this day—I've come as far as I can being as natural as I can. I made the decision today to study a little more—to study what I'm doing, to study the scripts a little deeper, know what is going to happen a little more. Now I think it's time to broaden my scope—to broaden my talent, my attitude, my ability, or whatever it is—as far as acting is concerned."

It takes a lot of concentration and intensive self-analysis to tear a role you are playing—as well as yourself—apart and determine just what is needed to build it into a solid, believable, successful structure. Bill is always conscientiously studying his performance, tearing it down, and building it up again. "I try to get something going within myself—something that I've experienced, so that I can put it on the screen—which is what the critics call *playing yourself*. What I'm trying to get away from now is that—I'm trying to become an Alexander Scott more than a Bill Cosby, but I still want him to have the same attitude that Bill Cosby has, but just do different things and still be 'lovable' — *quote, unquote*!!"

Bill is responsible for the introduction of several "Cosbyisms" into the everyday, colloquial language spoken by people *off* the set of "I Spy," from coast to coast. I asked him about the expression "the wonderfulness of ..." and he explained just how it came about.

"At the time, we were working with a delightful director by the name of Mark Rydell, and we used to have a little sing-songy thing whenever we greeted each other: 'Well, now—how's yourself, and the joy of your eyes, and the smell of your face, and the sorryness of yourself, and the wonderfulness of yourself' and so forth, and this is how it developed."

"Hemonself"

Bill then went on to explain that he and Bob Culp have already gone far beyond this now outdated Cosbyism, to bigger and better ones! I asked what the newest expression that we would all soon be using thanks to the "Wonderfulness Brothers" would be and he laughed and told me: "It's a phrase called 'Hemonself,' which is taken from my father's wonderful vocabulary. It's a combination of a man saying *himself* and *he* and *own self*; *he* and *own self* equal 'hemownself.'"

A talented comedian and man of humor, Bill admits an interest in dramatic roles. "I'd be very much interested in a straight, dramatic role—although I would like to do comedy. I love comedy, and I think—if given the proper script, something that is genuinely funny —I could probably bring *some new* things to the screen and also some *very funny* things to the screen."

Music? Oh yes—Bill does dig music, and he digs it "soulful, rocking, and twangy." He listens to pop music and is very definite in his very considered opinion of it: "I dig some of it. I don't like *all* of it. As I said, there are some groups that just don't sound good to me. I like the *bluesier* sound —in other words, the more Negro sound. This is a sound that I grew up with, and this is a sound that—to *me*—has more inherent rhythm. The Beatles write very, very beautiful stuff that hangs in my mind and I can whistle and hum. I love Smokey Robinson and the Miracles, James Brown, Ray Charles—I *dig* the Rolling Stones, I dug them before anybody ever found them, I was in love with the Stones!"

Likes Dylan

Then came a revelation from one Mr. Cosby about a certain Mr. Dylan: "I like Bob Dylan. I met Bob before he went into the folk-rock bag, when Bobby was working in Greenwich Village. We all come from a place called the 'Gaslight Club.' I remember a folk singer named Len Chandler who said to me, 'This cat is one of the greatest writers you'll ever meet. You should hear some of his stuff.' This was *four* years ago."

Bill has a very deep and warm friendship with his co-star, Bob Culp, and together the two of them have come up with a sort of language all their own. It's composed of English, but it is, nonetheless, incomprehensible to anyone else but them. Not only that, but Bill says that they are always changing the code—so if either of their wives should come too close to detection, they are assured of keeping their secret. Bob's wife did succeed in breaking the code just once—but that will *never* happen again!

An ambition for the future does not mean an infinite career in the field of entertainment for Bill. Although it will probably come as quite a surprise to most of his fans, Bill has quite another set of plans in mind for himself: "If what's happening now promises to grow —and it does—then I'll be out of here in five or six years, and I'll go back to school and teach. I want to teach junior high school, very lower, lower class level, because these kids need help. The teachers who teach in that area need a boost, and I think that an entertainer giving up the stagelights, and so on, to come in and teach, without really wanting to wield a giant stick—a guy who just wants to come in there and do his job, do it quietly without sounding on everybody—I think it would give them a boost, give the students a boost, and perhaps lend an answer to some of the problems that exist in that area."

A funny man? Yes, he is a brilliant humorist and observer of human actions and emotions. An actor? Yes, a very *good* actor, and one who is still developing. A devoted father, a loving husband, and a warm friend; sincere, honest, and very genuine. All of these words could be used to describe him.

But as far as the *wonderfulness* of *hemownself* is concerned: he's a pretty fantastic person, this Bill Cosby.

THE "WONDERFULNESS BROTHERS:" Bobby and Billy Wonderful.

DRUMMERS

YOU HIP TO METAL DRUMSTICKS?

Experts agree... Practicing with these weapons will do these important things for YOUR BEAT!

- Give you more **power**—to make yourself heard above amplified instruments.
- Give you new **stick control**—to play today's beat rhythms with more precision and fire.
- Give you more **endurance**—to keep excitement at its peak all nite long.

Try 'em and see for yourself what fantastic results will follow. ORDER YOUR PAIR NOW!

$5.95

Harriman's
1884 Pandora Avenue
Los Angeles, Calif. 90025
(Sorry, no C.O.D.'s)

KRLA ARCHIVES

Bobby Goldsboro Turns Out Stream of Hit Songs

Every Spring everyone in the country re-arranges their schedules so they can attend or at least watch on television the World Series and singer Bobby Goldsboro is no exception.

Bobby is such a baseball nut that his contract includes a clause that says he never has to record while the Series is being played.

Bobby's only been in the business for a few years but he's already turned out hit after hit.

He was born Jan. 15, 1941 in Maryanna, Florida and attended school there until he was in the ninth grade. Then his family moved to Dothan, Alabama, where he completed high school and went on to Auburn University.

He stayed at the university for two years before giving in to the one thing he really wanted to do—sing and play guitar.

After a short period of free lancing he joined Roy Orbison as a guitar player in January of 1962. He learned a great deal from Roy during his two years with him and they formed a lasting friendship.

Early in 1964 a friend of Bobby's played some tapes Bobby had made for an executive of United Artists Records, who immediately flew to Dothan and signed Bobby to an exclusive contract.

His first release under the contract was "See The Funny Little Clown," a smashing success that he had written himself.

In the Spring of that year another happy event took place for Bobby. He married his high school sweetheart, Mary Alice, another

... BOBBY GOLDSBORO

baseball nut. Both of them are also great swimmers.

Since then Bobby's had several other hits, including "Little Things."

He is currently on a tour of the Middle West and East doing concerts and clubs in conjunction with his latest release, "It's Too Late," and his new album, "Broomstick Cowboy."

Let's hope he gets all his performances done before the World Series starts this Spring.

'Noted In The United Kingdom' By Gil

FRED LENNON (JOHN'S father) will have his record "That's My Life" released in the United States after all . . . THE WALKER BROTHERS deny any split but GARY has recorded a single entitled "You Don't Love Me" . . . ROLLING STONE KEITH RICHARD has produced an album entitled "Today's Pop Symphony" which features English hits of 1965. Keith directs the orchestra and hits by the BEATLES, the STONES and SONNY and CHER are given the classical treatment . . .

* * *

The ROLLING STONES still refuse to reveal any part of the plot of their first movie. The movie, which is tentatively titled "Back, Behind, and In Front," is probably based on "Goon" humor. "Goon" humor originates from an old British radio show, which starred PETER SELLARS. PETER also made a "Goon" flick, entitled "The Running, Jumping, Walking, Standing Still Film," which was directed by RICHARD LESTER. . . . THE ANIMALS "big band" sound could be very big for them in '66. Figuratively speaking, the band is pretty big right now—even COUNT BASIE might blink . . . The SPENCER DAVIS combination has for some time been acknowledged as far superior to many of the groups who consistently make the charts with new releases, so it is really fab to see SPENCE himself with a big hit in England. The record, "Keep On Running" has been released in the United States and if given a fair amount of air play should be a big hit . . .

* * *

JOHN LENNON'S new book may shock some citizens (senior and otherwise) out of a few years growth . . . PETER & GORDON deny numerous rumors pertaining to a split. You don't have to look very hard for the origin of these rumors. PETER & GORDON remain very uncomplimentary to each other in public . . . It appears that the BEATLES have finally found that elusive Western movie script. As four individual badmen, they will meet up in midscript. PAUL will definitely have a girl, but it is still uncertain about the others. This will be the first movie that BEATLEMANIACS have had an opportunity to judge each performer separately. Speaking for myself I just can't wait for it, imagine the BEATLES in a Western!! I can see GEORGE riding out with Custer to meet the Indians—with a guitar strapped to each leg. I can see RINGO being run out of town. And I can see JOHN leading the Indians . . .

* * *

The BYRDS have made some very good records, and next to the VEJTABLES are my favorite American group, but why do they persist with such unoriginal openings to their records . . . The WALKER BROTHERS claim to want both American and British citizenship. If this is so they are in for a surprise. Under American law, dual-citizenship is normally not permitted—as ELIZABETH TAYLOR found out to her regret. Winston Churchill is the only man who has ever possessed both American and British citizenship at the same time—and that took an act of Congress . . .

* * *

A U.K. radio station polled it's listeners to find out the top five favorite BEATLE songs. The following was the result: 1. "If I Fell" 2. "Yesterday." 3. "Eight Days A Week." 4. "You've Got To Hide Your Love Away." 5. "From Me To You." Other hot favorites were: 1. "I'm A Loser." 2. "We Can Work It Out." 3. "Norwegian Wood." . . . "Drive My Car" which was on the English "Rubber Soul" is not an invitation to take LENNON'S Rolls Royce . . . English Popular music fans may soon be able to pick up a telephone and dial any hit record they want to listen to. The cost will be around five cents . . .

* * *

ERIC BURDON feels as strongly as RINGO STARR about racial prejudice . . . The popularity of CLIFF RICHARD has notably declined in the U.K. since the advent of the "long hairs." Somehow clean-cut CLIFF just doesn't fit in. Actually his material has been very weak of late. RICHARD came in as the English answer to America's ELVIS PRESLEY, but in the last few years has quieted down very much. He now prefers beat ballads. Maybe LENNON and McCARTNEY can come up with something for him. Their names as composers are usually all that is required to send a record to the top . . .

* * *

Whatever happens, the BEATLES are sure of another fantastic welcome in the USA. Their popularity, far from diminishing, is increasing all the time.

It's no skin off my nose, but the BEACH BOYS must be crazy to release a record as inept as "Barbara Ann" . . . When the BEATLES tour the United States in 1966 let us hope that promoters will shell out enough money to provide an adequate microphone system for the boys . . . Will the BEATLES ever do a song by DYLAN? When asked this question JOHN said: "No! He's got too much money as it is, besides PAUL and I are capable of writing our own songs thank you." . . . LENNON'S witticisms are usually 'a bit of a giggle.' But on occassion, even JOHN'S mind is a bit dry. While in Liverpool JOHN said that the BEATLES needed a new drummer because . . . "RINGO'S got the ZAK." . . . After that one I think that I had better split until next week.

SIMON AND GARFUNKLE made some very important sound-dents on the music charts in the nation with their first Columbia release, "Sounds of Silence." Now, they have released their second record and seem to be headed in pretty much the same successful direction. "Homeward Bound" is another tune penned for the duo by Paul Simon, who writes much of their material, and this brand new disc by the talented artists seems definitely bound in the direction of lasting success. At present, many of their tunes are also being recorded by other artists who favor their unique and beautiful musical compositions.

KRLA ARCHIVES

BEAT Prediction

'Way Out' Will Be Way 'In'

Since "Shindig" first hit our television screens we have had countless pop shows crammed down our throats by ambitious individuals trying to cash in on a good thing. And the teen market is about as good as you can get.

Some were excellent, some mediocre and some downright horrible. The bad ones didn't even attempt to disguise their motives, their formats were almost identical and most didn't last long. Even "Shindig" didn't make it.

Now Four Star is coming out with a brand new type of pop show, an original and fresh idea which is titled very appropriately, "Way Out."

The half hour color show has Joey Paige as host with several different guest stars each week and a resident group in The Bees. What's so different, original or fresh about that you ask? Well, not much—it's the "way out" shots and gimmicks employed in the show which make it so completely alien to any pop show which thus far has found it's way on television.

It's difficult to explain. It doesn't sound nearly as funny in words as it is when you actually see it. Of course, we don't want to give the whole thing away because then someone else would immediately jump on the bandwagon and air an identical show before "Way Out" is officially on its way. But we *will* give you a rather brief idea of what you can expect to see on the show.

They'll have all kinds of crazy shots of dancers blinking across the screen so fast that you really can't see them at all. Sound weird? Well, it is, believe us, it is!

There is the spot in which Joey introduces one of his guest stars and proceeds to bite hungrily into the microphone. There are dancers painted entirely in the color they're wearing. And you'll have to admit that you rarely see an all green girl!! But if you tune into "Way Out" you'll see even wilder things than that.

Mel Carter drew the only "straight" number in the pilot. Chad Stuart and Ian Whitcomb weren't so fortunate—they were directly involved in paintings, dancing and dunkings.

That gives you a small idea of how really "way out" the show is and it continues right along that way until the credits come up at the end of one of the funniest half hours you've ever seen.

The whole thing looks like *Mad Magazine* set to life. So, if you dig that kind of humor (and who doesn't?) don't miss "Way Out." It's due to air in April and with any luck at all stands to be one of the biggest shows to come along since "Batman."

If it does nothing else it has *got* to make a tremendous success out of Joey Paige. It's been a long time coming but with "Way Out" Joey just can't miss. Besides being the show's host, Joey will sing at least two numbers each week as well as take an active part in most of the gimmicky shots.

And who knows, Joey just may emerge as a dual personality—singer *and* comedian! Anyway, give it a watch. We don't think you'll be disappointed—we know we weren't.

It feels good to see a pop show with a little originality for a change and originality is one thing which "Way Out" has lots of. Green girls, eatible microphones—*that's* originality whether you view it in black and white or color!

...AND HERE WE ARE, THE BEES.

...JOEY PAIGE, "WAY OUT" HOST.

...IAN WHITCOMB AND A ONE-LEGGED GIRL?

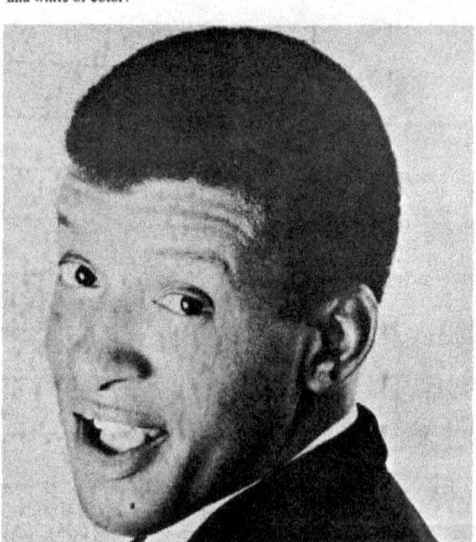

...MEL CARTER—ONLY "STRAIGHT" NUMBER.

..."WHERE DID THIS COME FROM?" ASKS CHAD.

KRLA ARCHIVES

The Adventures of Robin Boyd

By Shirley Poston

Chapter Seventeen

Robin Boyd was a nice enough kid, but she was certainly no angel. And, had she not seen "Help" some 4,000½ times (the ½ explained by the time her mother literally yanked her out of a theater at approximately 2:13 a.m.), she would surely have taken up swearing that Saturday.

However, she had. Seen "Help" 4,000½ times, that is, and had learned that even Oriental thugs stuck to expressions such as "gosh" and "my goodness" (when anyone was listening).

And, anything any Oriental thug could do, Robin could do better.

"*Golly-gee-whiz-bang not to mention ratzafratz!*" Robin screeched, searching wildly about in her closet. But, it was no use. Mick's ring simply was not there. It was, in fact, *nowhere!* And so was she. With the possible exception of up seventeen creeks without a paddle.

A second later, her mother came racing into the room. "Robin Boyd," she said sternly and not without good reason as this happened to be her daughter's name. "Stop screeching in that closet!"

Total Chaos

Wanting to ask what closet she *should* screech in, Robin decided against it (she bruised easily) and banged the closet door shut before her mother started screeching about the total chaos therein.

"What are you looking for anyway?" her mother asked, gentling her tone at the sight of her daughter's stricken face.

"My marbles," Robin muttered. Her mother nodded. "I believe it," she muttered back.

Then Robin brightened a bit. Maybe she'd dropped the ring somewhere around the house! Maybe her mother had picked it up (and with Robin's luck, pawned it!)

"Mum," she bagan cautiously, knowing it would be better to say no more than too much. "I seem to have misplaced a ring of great value . . . er . . . great *sentimental* value. Did you by any remote chance find it, I hope, hope, hope?"

Her mother shook her head (her own, not Robin's.) "I did not, not, not," she answered, at which time it was her turn to look stricken.

"What am I *saying?* I mean, no I did not find it!"

Robin moaned out of desperation. Also out of agonizing pain because she could no longer resist the urge to bang her head against the closet door.

Pay-Off

Darting terrified from the room, her mother soon darted terrified back into the room, clutching a handful of money.

"*Stop that!*" she bellowed at her daughter who was still banging away. With this, she thrust the several dollars at Robin.

"What's that for?" Robin blithered, pausing in her snit to greedily eye the greenbacks.

"Go to a movie," her mother begged. "Go *anywhere!* Just stop that screeching and banging. It's giving me a headache!"

This being the best offer she'd had all day, Robin grabbed the loot and was half way down the block before she paused to say in tones of amazement, "it's giving *you* a headache?"

Mrs. Boyd watched sadly until her daughter was out of sight. Then she poured a cup of coffee, opened the yellow pages to the well-thumbed psychiatry listings, and bravely prepared to make the final choice.

Several hours later, Robin crept nervously out of the neighborhood theater where she had just witnessed a double feature entitled "Cannibals A-Go-Go" and "Eat Your Heart Out."

"Crikeys," she breathed in horror. "It's *dark* outside."

And, it was. As pitch. Almost as dark as it had been *inside*. And although Robin generally found nothing frightening about horror films (with the possible exception of the acting), she was, at present, about as calm as a Fizzes factory during a flash flood.

Straight Ahead

Tippy-toeing down the deserted street, Robin swore a solemn oath (not the kind *you're* thinking, either) to look straight ahead all the way home. There was no sense in encouraging the cannibals who were following close behind her.

Then she retracted the promise. What difference did it make anyroad? She'd lost the ring, which meant she couldn't return it to Mick, which meant she had also lost her magic powers forever, not to mention her luvley Liverpudlian genie named George. What was the point in living when one could no longer turn oneself into a *real* Robin and fly off to terrorize - er - visit the Beatles and other faves?

There was only one sensible thing to do when all was lost with no help in sight! Save oneself the trouble of finding a cliff and get it over with.

Turning around, Robin looked encouragingly in the direction of the cannibals, who had conveniently leaped behind palm trees. (Ordinary cannibals are bad enough, but when they're skinny enough to hide behind *palm* trees, say your prayers.) (Grace would be appropriate.)

But Robin merely laughed in the face of danger. They could *broil* her for all *she* cared. And she continued to look back encouragingly every few steps. Which is probably why she ran smack into someone.

"Yeeeeeek!" she screamed, but her panic was short-lived. "Oh, excuse *me*," she said aplogetically to the aforementioned someone.

"Whew," she breathed, walking on. For a second there, she thought she'd run right smack into a *cannibal* or something.

Fortunately, it had only been a tall man wearing a strange mask . . . and . . . a . . . swirling . . . CAPE?"

It was then that Robin knew what she must do. She only hoped that she would do it gracefully. (She didn't, but don't go blabbing it around.)

When Robin regained consciousness, she was riding in a strange car, sandwiched between a tall man wearing a strange mask (and a swirling cape) and a boy wearing an average mask (and a swirling cape.)

And Panic Again

There are some people in this world who would panic shortly after finding themselves in this particular sandwich (or, for that matter, *any* sandwich). And Robin Boyd was one of them.

"LEMMEOUTAHERE!" she shrieked, causing the driver of the strange car (a tall man wearing a strange . . . oh, you know) to graze a palm tree.

Suddenly, Robin smiled.

Not only because the holy heck had just been scared out of a skinny cannibal. Also because she had just recognized the masked man and his faithful un-Indian companion.

Help had arrived (and not the one she'd seen 4,000½ times, either!!!) All her problems were about to be solved!

How, you ask?? With the greatest of ease!

The case of the missing ring would be no job at *all* for Batman and Robins!!!

...THE SPENCER DAVIS GROUP

New Group For The U.S.

By Kimmi Kobashigawa

Have you heard about the latest, greatest, fabmost group from England yet? Their name is The Spencer Davis Group, and they have recently been the occupants of the topmost spot on all of the English charts with their smash hit—"Keep On Running."

The Spencer Davis Group all hail from Birmingham, England which is now referred to—affectionately, of course!—as Spencerland, due to the overwhelming popularity the boys built for themselves in their native city.

Rumor from across the big surf has it that there is one member of the Spencer Davis Group who is a dead ringer for a certain Paul McCartney—of the MBE set—however, we will all have a chance to determine this for ourselves when the boys make their first trip to Uncle Samland sometime this month.

They played a date at Yale University on February 25, and as far as we're concerned—the long hairs never had it so good!!!

KRLA ARCHIVES

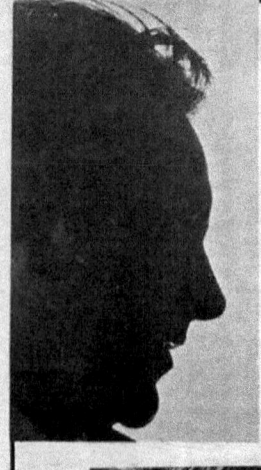

BEAT Goes To The Movies
'THE SPY WHO CAME IN FROM THE COLD'

THE DRAMATIC CONCLUSION of this Paramount thriller as British spy Alec Leamas helps his girl over the infamous Berlin Wall. But can the West really allow her to get back safely, with all she knows? The answer forms one of the most gripping parts of this photoplay.

By Jim Hamblin
The BEAT Movie Editor

ACKNOWLEDGED TO HAVE one of the finest speaking voices in the world of entertainment, Richard Burton portrays a man whose life is used as a pawn in an international intrigue, between East and West. Burton brings to this low-key story a certain sublime drama that proves again his ability to "live" each role.

HOLLYWOOD—First of all, every theatre marquee boy in the country hates this movie, because the title won't fit!

But for some amazing reason film critics the world over have gathered around this movie like it had finally answered all their dreams of how a picture should be made. This attitude is especially strange since so many people have been panning Burton's other recent flick, THE SANDPIPER. As he always does, he turns in a beautiful acting job on both, and for the life of us we cannot see why there are so many raves about this newest spy picture, and so much bad-mouthing of the Sandpiper. Except that Elizabeth Taylor also stars in the former, while she is not seen in SPY WHO.

We shall take this opportunity to highly recommend THE SANDPIPER to you, if you have not yet seen it, particularly if you're a *BEAT* reader in the Bay Area. The film captures the magnificent Big Sur coastline and instantly produces a case of wanderlust, among other things.

But on with the spy epic we started out to talk about. It is, by way of introduction, the filmization of the best selling novel of the same name, written by a former British Foreign Service officer who is now jetting around the world appearing on the telly, standing with glass in hand at parties, but more generally enjoying all that money! His name is really Cornwall, but as an author he is known as John Le Carre.

We had lunch with Le Carre recently at the Beverly Hills hotel, out by the pool, and talked about the book.

"It's not really very good, you know," he volunteered, "but it seems to be what people wanted to read. And I think it captures something of the real spy business."

The book has indeed been a runaway best seller, and for the millions who will see the movie after reading the book, they will not be disappointed.

But the severest critic of that would be the author, and we asked him if he liked what Martin Ritt and Paramount Pictures had done to his story. He looked up from his glass, studied a lovely blonde bobbing across the pool deck for a moment, and wistfully replied, "Yes. Yes, I did like it. The whole thing seemed to come alive on the screen."

SPY is a cold and bleak movie, and the worst mistake anyone could make is going to see it expecting a James Bond thriller with sex and gore, flashy cars and little devices for doing people in.

That's not the real world of international espionage, and that's not what we see. We see a more chilling and realistic portrayal of the cold-blooded reality of men whose lives are used up like Kleenex to make a few points in the Cold War.

The picture has a surprise ending with a surprise ending of its own.

You will leave the theater with a new respect for the dedication some men have, and you will leave perhaps a little depressed by this glimpse of a twilight life we so rarely hear about.

The Kingsmen Win Law Suit

The Kingsmen have won their law suit with former group member, Jack Ely. The decision was handed down by the Circuit Court in Portland, Oregon.

As you may remember, Ely was with the Kingsmen when they first began hitting the charts. However, he split with the group to go back to school. Then he appeared on the scene again with his own group which he deceptively billed as "The Kingsmen."

The original Kingsmen were naturally upset about this development because audiences who had never seen the real Kingsmen were confusing the second "Kingsmen" with them.

They brought the suit to stop Ely from using the name "Kingsmen" at all, except to say that he was formerly with the group. The Oregon court agreed whole-heartedly with the Kingsmen and, therefore, restrained Ely from performing as "The Kingsmen, or under any name using the word 'Kingsmen' or any deceptively similar word."

The Kingsmen told *The BEAT* that they'd be happy to take any damages awarded them by the court but that they really only wanted Ely to stop using their name.

HOTLINE LONDON
(Continued from Page 1)

is there, good and strong, but it also tends to get a bit obscured. One of our reviewers doesn't dig this at all — but a million fans will." *Disc Weekly* complained about "straining to hear Mick's voice surface from the backing" whilst *New Musical Express* summed up the disc as "better than 'Cloud' – at least a No. 1, might even make No. 1-1/2!"

NEWS BRIEFS . . . Brian Epstein's latest signing is Tony Rivers And the Castaways, a six-man combo with Britain's nearest replica of your California surfin' sound. They've recorded the Brian Wilson composition "Girl Don't Tell Me," produced by Andrew Loog Oldham for his Immediate label . . . Strongest TV rumour of the week in London is that America's ABC network may screen our weekly "London Palladium Show" this summer when "Hollywood Palace" comes off. Meantime, Pat Boone heads the "London Palladium Show" bill this Sunday and Cilla Black is the star the following week . . . Forget those rumours that Mrs. John Lennon, Mrs. George Harrison and Mrs. Ringo Starr plan to make a girlie-group vocal record. They started with George making a joke answer to a reporter's question. But he added: "Don't put that down – I'm only joking" . . . Sudden onslaught of American soul singers for British dates. Included are Lee Dorsey, The Vibrations, Otis Redding, Wilson Pickett, Joe Tex and Stevie Wonder. The pop pirate stations, Radio Caroline and Radio London, have been hard-selling all these artists in recent months . . . To coincide with the release of their new single "Inside – Looking Out," The Animals will be seen on all British top TV pop shows as soon as they return from New York . . . P.J. Proby plans to record and make a thirty-minute film on your side of the Atlantic when he tours in April . . . Much controversy over promoter Tito Burns' decision to give priority allocation of Bob Dylan concert tickets to people who come and see a 'specialist' folk tour which Burns is staging in nine cities this month. Many Dylan fans who are disinterested in the folk show may buy tickets solely for the purpose of getting to see Dylan later in the year! . . . Rising singles in our Top Twenty include "Get Out Of My Life Woman" by Lee Dorsey, rival versions of the Lennon/McCartney ballad "Girl" by The Truth and the St. Louis Union plus "Up Tight" which makes Stevie Wonder the only current Tamla Motown representative amongst our best-sellers.

KRLA ARCHIVES

Dave Hull's HULLABALOO
The Rock & Roll Showplace of the World
6230 SUNSET (AT VINE) HOLLYWOOD, CALIF.

FEBRUARY 18 AND 19

DICK & DEE DEE
THE SHINDOGS
THE PALACE GUARD

FEBRUARY 25 AND 26

THE NEWBEATS
Doing Their Hit — "Run Baby Run"

THE PALACE GUARD

BEGINNING THIS SUNDAY MATINEE —
"MOVIES"
IN ADDITION TO OUR EXCITING LIVE STAGE SHOW
THIS WEEK, THE 20TH
"DRACULA" & "FLASH GORDON"
CARTOONS
—"DOOR PRIZES"—   —"DRAWINGS"—
— FREE RECORDS —

THIS CHIP WORTH 50¢ OFF ON A HULLABALOO PIZZA

"COMING ATTRACTIONS"

March 4, 5, 6	— APRIL —
THE ASTRONAUTS	**THE HOLLIES**

MAKE RESERVATIONS — HO. 6-8281

KRLA ARCHIVES

America's Largest Teen NEWSpaper 15¢

KRLA Edition BEAT

MARCH 12, 1966

BEAT Camera Art: Charles (Tiny) Caubet

Three Faces Of Paul McCartney

KRLA BEAT

Volume 1, Number 52 — March 12, 1966

HOTLINE LONDON

Strangers Sleeping On Ringo's Lawn

By Tony Barrow

Richard and Maureen Starkey — Ringo and Mo to you — seem to be settling in very comfortably at their new and very secluded hideaway home close to the Lennon property at Weybridge in Surrey. They have a nanny to look after baby Zak but she takes two evenings off each week and then Ringo and Mo stay in, firmly avoiding the idea of bringing in baby sitters although a million fans might gladly accept the task!

Ringo spends most of his afternoons at John's place. Maureen enjoys a weekly shopping trip to London's West End.

Beatle People who have been ambitious enough to seek out the Starkey house come away with stories of a strange caravan (that's a trailer to you!) parked in the garden. Each night five or six men sleep in that caravan and what the fans don't know is that these are labourers who are still working on internal re-construction and improvements to the house.

The Starkeys thought all the work would be complete but they fixed their Christmas move-in schedule long before the men were ready to leave. The team of workers live about fifty miles from Weybridge — right over in the county of Kent — so Ringo arranged for them to set up the king-sized caravan in his garden so that they could sleep right there beside the house until the job is complete.

AND THAT'S ONE REASON WHY RINGO CAN BE FOUND AT JOHN'S HOUSE ALMOST EVERY AFTERNOON OF THE WEEK — HE CAN'T STAND THE NON-STOP NOISE OF HAMMERING AND DRILLING AT HIS OWN PLACE!

Incidentally, it doesn't seem like a whole year since Ringo married Maureen does it? In fact the couple celebrated their First Wedding Anniversary on Friday, 11 February!

More Beatle Music

An hour-long television spectacular, "The Music Of Lennon And McCartney," screened in Britain last December and now being made available for showing throughout the world, will represent the U.K. in this year's Golden Rose Of Montreux contest. The annual television festival at Montreux features special programmes entered by numerous TV companies from various countries.

A long list of international stars are featured in "The Music Of Lennon And McCartney." They include Henry Mancini, Esther Phillips, Peter And Gordon, Marianne Faithfull, Peter Sellers, Billy J. Kramer With The Dakotas, Cilla Black, Dick Rivers, The George Martin Orchestra and Antonio Vargas with his Spanish Dancers. John and Paul act as comperes and the show includes fifteen Lennon/McCartney compositions presented in as many different styles. One hundred singers, dancers and musicians are involved in the fast-moving production. The Beatles make two appearances to perform their latest numbers, "We Can Work It Out" and "Day Tripper."

The 1966 Golden Rose festival takes place in Montreux in Switzerland throughout the final week of April.

Keith Produces

Keith Richard has recorded an album of instrumental tracks in which he conducts "The Aranbee Pop Symphony Orchestra!" The ten tracks include "We Can Work It Out," "There's A Place," "I Got You Babe," "In The Midnight Hour" and "Rag Doll."

In the meantime, The Stones have not been short of press publicity to tie in with the U.K. release of "19th Nervous Breakdown" which smashed into our charts at Number Two less than a week after release. Suddenly, after a quiet spell, the fivesome (plus Andrew Loog Oldham) became available for interview and every pop paper in London took advantage of the situation, splashing pix and stories across their pages.

Almost immediately after his solo stint as a panel guest on "The Eamonn Andrews Show" (like your Carson programme), Mick Jagger flew to New York ahead of the group. Before he left he had this to say about "19th Nervous Breakdown:" "It's not supposed to mean anything. No, it's not intended to be a social comment at all. I thought of the title and then started to write around it. It's about this bird who is neurotic."

Andrew has cultivated a very fine and very ginger-coloured moustache which spreads out like a pair of immobile wings beneath his nose. With this he uses thick-rimmed glasses and an enormous tie. Bill Wyman has also taken to wearing a moustache but on their behalf, Mick assures everyone that neither Andy nor Bill were influenced in their decision to grow whiskers by the briefly displayed and hastily shaven beard of Ringo Starr!

(Turn to Page 4)

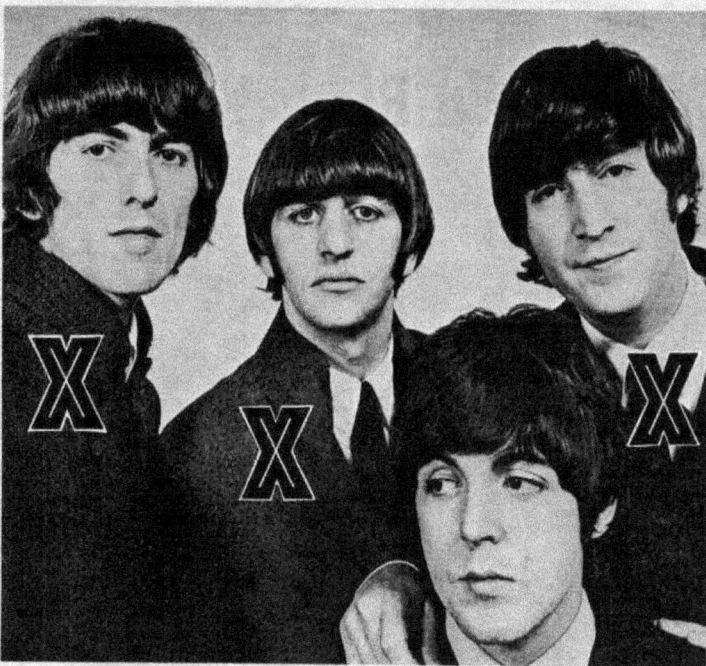

...GEORGE, RINGO AND JOHN OFFER PAUL THEIR CONDOLENCES ON HIS BACHELORHOOD.

Now Only Beatle Left

What Will Happen To Paul?

By Louise Criscione

And now there is only one — unmarried Beatle, that is. What will become of Paul McCartney now that he is the sole eligible (?) bachelor? To say the least, Paul is not over-joyed with the situation.

Up until the Beatle world got wind of George and Patti's marriage, Paul was forced to carry the burden of being the "charming" Beatle, the one who soothed over any irritation caused by the other Beatles' (but particularly John's) sharp-tongued remarks.

He was the one who could be counted upon to wink at the girls in the audience with an amazing amount of regularity. He was indeed the charmer.

That alone was enough to keep Paul busy but he had one extra little quality which caused him to work harder than his three companions. When the Beatles first visited Stateside Paul was awarded the title "Most Handsome Beatle." An honor? Well, yes and no. No, because it meant that Paul always had to look sharp.

Never Paul

Ringo could grow a beard, John could forget to shave, George could let his hair grow untidy, but Paul had to look great no matter what. Think back. Have you ever seen Paul's hair too long, his clothes too messy or his beard too noticeable?

So, there was Paul the charming and polite young man and Paul the handsome Beatle. Paul who was funny even when he was being sarcastic and cutting. He probably got tired of smiling. He was the only Beatle who continually wore a smile across his handsome face.

The others got neatly out of the smiling bit. Ringo became known for his usually deadpan expression, George took to not talking much and smiling even less and John — well, John did just as he pleased. Sometimes he laughed the loudest, cracked the funniest jokes and produced the widest grin. Other times he neither laughed, nor smiled. But what ever he did was accepted as easily as a Beatle's autograph. After all, he was John Lennon — the unclassifiable Beatle.

That left only Paul to keep the smile on. Tired, hungry, sick — it didn't matter, he *had* to smile and be friendly. He wasn't allowed to let the Beatle image be covered by even a hint of a shadow.

That Day

It was Paul too who carried the brunt of the Beatle marriage rumors. I don't suppose Beatle fans will ever forget the day they opened their morning papers in February of '64 to be faced with the "news" that Paul and Jane Asher had gotten married.

Beatle fans read the short story with a sinking, sort of everything-is-lost feeling. Was it true? It was by-lined by Walter Winchell and whether it was true or not it had the strength of having been written by a world famous and powerful newspaperman.

It goes without saying that plenty of tears were cried and thousands of Paul McCartney pictures were torn to shreds before Paul ever got around to denying it. And even when he did there were those who doubted his word.

They couldn't help it — they had just become aware of the Beatles and they didn't know much about them, except that they were the most exciting act to hit the pop scene since Elvis Presley had first wiggled his hips and shocked the life out of parents whose teenage daughters seemed to actually *like* this side-burned, guitar-toting character with the unlikely name of Elvis.

Always Present

On the boot heels of that very first Paul-Jane marriage rumor came a score of others. They didn't have nearly the impact of that first one but they were there just the same.

Along about this time the romance of Ringo and Maureen became known so the rumor-mongers took to making up stories about them. And then along came George and Patti and some more rumors. You couldn't say that Paul *wished* the rumors on Ringo and George but then you also couldn't say that he wasn't relieved to have someone else sharing the marriage rumor business with him.

It gave Paul a welcome rest. But one year ago Ringo and Mau-

(Turn to Page 11)

Inside the BEAT

Johnny Rivers — Live! 3
Al Martino Greets Success 4
Pop Comic Strip 5
Jackie Lee Ducking 6
Boy Wonder Sings 7
Byrds Interviewed 10-11
Cher 'Shot Down' 12
Girls in Beatles' Lives 13
BEAT Goes To The Movies 15

The BEAT is published weekly by BEAT Publications, Inc., editorial and advertising offices at 6290 Sunset Blvd., Suite 504, Hollywood, California 90028. U. S. bureaus in Hollywood, San Francisco, New York, Chicago and Nashville, overseas correspondents in London, Liverpool and Manchester, England. Sale price, 15 cents. Subscription price: U.S. and possessions, $5 per year; Canada and foreign rates, $9 per year. Application to mail at second class postage rates is pending at Los Angeles, California.

KRLA ARCHIVES

Yeah, Well Boss...
You Kinda Blew Your Cool

By Tammy Hitchcock

Yeah, well the boss lost her car. Actually, she didn't *lose* it—she more like had it *stolen*. At first I didn't believe her when she told me because of that incident at the Stones' press conference.

You see, the boss and I had gone over in her Stingray and wonder of wonders (and I kid you not!) we hadn't gotten lost. But the boss decided it would be stupid to park in the hotel parking lot when we could park a block away (*she said*) for free. It's not that the boss is cheap or anything, it's just that if it's at all possible she'd rather spend a dime than a dollar which is really very wise when you stop to think about it.

Anyway, she parked the car and we started walking the block to the hotel, except that it turned out to be around the corner and down *six* blocks! But we overcame that obstacle and arrived at our destination with sore feet and messed up hair but otherwise all present and accounted for.

The press conference turned out to be quite long and after the questioning was finished the press was supplied with food and drink. So, it was already dark when the boss and I finally left. We walked out of the doors together and then the boss turned *left* while I turned *right*.

Wrong Way

"Where are you going now," she wanted to know. "To the car," I answered simply (you see, every once in a while I do come out with a logical answer to a question. Not every often but occasionally.)

"Well, if you're going to *my* car," said the boss, "you're headed in the wrong direction."

Being as I have a mental block about directions I assumed the boss was right so I followed along behind her. Well, we walked the six blocks and then rounded the corner. No car!! The boss let out a shriek similar to those heard at a Stone concert. She scared me half to death—I thought maybe she had seen Mick Jagger or Keith Richard or somebody.

On second thought I decided it couldn't possibly have been either Keith or Mick. The boss wouldn't scream nearly that loud for them—it must be Frank Sinatra. For Sinatra the boss would scream, yell, faint, and maybe even considering chasing him down the street! That's how far gone she is on The Chairman of the Board!!!

Personally, I had hoped it was Mick or Keith. Fact is, I would have settled nicely for Sandy Koufax. "Who do you see," I whispered (not wishing to sound like an idiot if whoever she had seen happened to be within hearing distance).

See Who?

"What do you mean, who do I see?" the boss screamed — only at me this time.

"Is Frank Sinatra around here?" I asked, completely stumped by the boss' behavior.

"Frank Sinatra!!!!!!" the boss screeched louder than ever. "Where?"

Then she started fixing her hair and asking me out of the corner of her mouth where he was and was

...THE BOSS

he coming toward us and how was her hair and was her lipstick on straight. I assured her that she looked great and then I started searching around frantically for the Leader.

Yeah, well there was the boss trying to look nonchalant and there I was looking in every conceivable direction for Frank Sinatra when I came eye to eye with a policeman.

"Did you lose something?" he asked.

"Yeah, Frank Sinatra, did you see which way he went?" I said before thinking that he must have surely thought we were out of our minds.

The boss gave me a good poke in the side and informed the officer that we really hadn't lost anything at all. He gave the both of us a funny look and then walked away.

Blew Her Cool

I guess it was then that it hit the boss again because she let out another scream and went running after the policeman waving her arms in the air. I really felt sorry for her—I thought she'd lost her mind! The sight of five "live" Rolling Stones had done it, I was positive.

But being a loyal employee I ran after her, making up a huge whopper in my mind to tell the policeman about the boss not usually acting like that. Well, by the time I had caught up with the boss, she had already caught up with the officer.

Too late, I *thought*, he'd put her in the nut house for sure. However, when I got there I heard the boss saying something about parking her car right there not an hour ago—well, maybe *two* hours ago. It was more like three but what difference does an hour make anyway? Her car had vanished!

Yeah, well the policeman was very nice and he took the boss and I back to the hotel in the police car which I thought was pretty exciting except that I was sitting in the back seat and therefore looked like a criminal.

Wearing Black

When we finally reached the hotel it occurred to me that I had headed *right* and the boss *left* when we had first come out. So, I did all sorts of things to get the boss' attention but she was too busy mourning the loss of her Stingray.

I decided that I just couldn't wait any longer so I blurted out, "Boss, I think you parked the car down the other way."

"Nonsense, I should know where I parked my own car—*I think*."

If you've ever been so embarrassed that you fervently prayed the ground would just open up and swallow you whole you will know approximately how the boss and I felt when the policeman drove us down six blocks the other way, around the corner and sitting right there where we had left it was the car!

The boss and I didn't do much talking on the way home (we were too embarrassed) not even when we passed a car bearing a man who must have been Frank Sinatra's twin brother if it wasn't the Chairman himself.

Really Stolen

Yeah, well that's why I didn't believe the boss at first when she said that the car had been stolen. But I changed my mind in one big hurry when I had to start driving the boss around in *my* car, which you know if you read this column is no great pleasure—my car, not driving the boss.

Anyway, you can relax, I won't be menacing the highways anymore. The boss and I payed a little visit to the local police station and returned with her car—intact.

Yeah, well the moral of this story is to remember where you parked your car and if you can't remember, for heaven's sakes don't go looking around for Frank Sinatra. How would he know what you did with your car anyway?

On the BEAT

By Louise Criscione

George Harrison declared that he and Patti's trip to the British West Indies was a "non-honeymoon vacation." Asked how married life agreed with him, George replied: "It's great, lovely. We haven't had any tiffs."

Bob Dylan has written a song for the Paul Butterfield Blues Band. Paul and Dylan have discussed the number at length and the group has definitely decided to go ahead and cut it. If R&B is the next big musical trend, as many record people are predicting, we might be hearing a lot from Paul Butterfield.

The Supremes, who are always busy enough for sixty people, have volunteered to sandwich in an appearance for our troops at Guantanamo sometime in April. It goes to show that some entertainers will give of their valuable time for a good cause, others only count the dollar signs before agreeing to appear *anywhere*.

STONE NOTES: Stones have won a Gold Record for their "December's Children" LP. They've also won the coveted Gold ones for "Out Of Our Heads" and the classical "Satisfaction" ... Brian admits that he "made a mess" out of his earlier life ... Mick believes the worst career move the Stones *ever* made was appearing on "Hollywood Palace" during that first Stateside tour, terms the experience "embarrassing" ... Keith says during that first tour "we were just ignorant" ... Brian's trading in his Rolls for a Mini ... Saw a great pix of Keith in one of the English

...MARY 'SUPREME'

trades reading a copy of *The BEAT!* I'm surprised they printed it but glad they did ... Brian is pleased that the Stones didn't receive hundreds of angry letters over his publicity in the English papers concerning court orders to pay support for his children.

Design Your Own

Dave Clark has designed his own home which, believe me, is pretty wild for the conservative Mr. Clark. Ceilings are black, carpets and drapes are scarlet red. The walls are adorned with Dave's antique pistols, swords and coaching horns.

Dave has also strategically placed three hi-fi sets throughout his house. He admits, "I wouldn't mind settling down on the West Coast with all its sun, sea and surf" but then adds that it would probably always be England for him.

Byrds are really doing well—so far they've gone over big in Spillville, Iowa, Sandusky, Ohio and now they're headed for White Fish Bay, Wisconsin. And that's the truth!

Looks as if the Hollies have finally set a definite date to tour the U.S. If all goes as planned (which it very conceivably won't) they fly out on March 27 for a six week tour which would include radio and TV dates as well as stops along the college circuit.

School For Singers

Len Barry is so disgusted with the stage performances put on by a lot of Top 40 entertainers that he is considering opening a school someday to teach them a little bit of stage presence. It's a good idea—I've seen quite a few performers who could use a little brushing up. Bet you've seen plenty too.

An English pop paper got a little confused and printed that the Liverpool Five are an *American* group. Not true. They do possess permanent visas and make their home in Southern California but they all hail from England—which makes them English, *I think!*

The hard core of "admiring" fans are getting worse and worse, if that's possible. At one of the Byrds' dates at a Hollywood club one such fan attached an endearment to a real live brick and hurled it at the stage. It missed it's intended target and instead hit a waitress in the head.

Terrific—keep it up fans and see how long groups coninue playing those dangerous dates.

Danny Hutton ("Roses And Rainbows") has come up with a novel idea—he wants to use taped instrumental tracks to back his voice on personal appearances. Don't know how well this idea will

...DANNY HUTTON

go over with audiences. They pay to see a *live* show not a lip-synced version. Of course, it *would* rid entertainers of the very real problem of bad sound systems.

KRLA ARCHIVES

Johnny Rivers — Completely Live

By Jamie McCluskey III

And now, ladies and gentlemen — coming to you LIVE from *The BEAT* — on the famed Sunset Strip *BEAT* — Johnny Rivers!!!

Well, . . . would you believe Johnny Rivers on a *delayed tape* from *The BEAT*? So, settle for an *almost*-live interview in this column already, and let's get on with it, okay??

Born November 7, 1942 in Baton Rouge, Louisiana — Johnny Rivers is a *very live*, blue-eyed, all-American male. And he sings, too! In fact, when we asked him to pin a label on his own unique sound, he promptly dubbed it "Many-years-of-hard-work-type-sound!"

This live young man is very much on the move — so much so that he has recorded his latest album all over the country. Seriously! "The album is called, 'I Know You Want To Dance,' and it was recorded in New York, San Francisco, Las Vegas — little pieces of live recordings from different places. It's all done live."

With all of this traveling, Johnny has an opportunity to observe the nation's pop music in many different areas of the country. I asked Johnny what sort of new trends in pop music he saw heading our way: "New trends? No, I don't know. I think rhythm and blues is just as strong as it ever was, and the protest songs — I'm pretty sure — are on their way out.

"Folk tunes will always hit if they're a good one — ballads will always hit if they're good, and country songs will hit if they're good. So, it's just back to where it was — you have to have a good sound and a good song."

Johnny came very much alive when he began to discuss the Beatles and their influence on pop music, and his baby blue eyes were very sparkly and enthusiastic as he explained: "The Beatles have *definitely* had a big influence. They have probably given pop music the biggest shot in the arm it's had since Elvis Presley. They've really gotten records to sell again — they've been great for the record business."

From the four Leading Liverpudlians, Johnny's speeding train of thought raced back across the Atlantic to *The* Leader, himself — Bob Dylan. "Bob Dylan has been good; he's gotten people to listen to the lyrics. One thing that does disappoint me about Bob Dylan is that I liked him better when he was just really Bob Dylan playing rhythm guitar and a harmonica, rather than trying to be a regular rock 'n' roller, or something.

I just think of Bob Dylan as a guy that goes in and does a concert by himself on a stage with just a guitar and a harmonica, and people just come to listen to his songs and his words; sort of like a poet."

About a year ago, Johnny joined the National Guard, which means that he must spend a certain amount of time every year for the next six years with Uncle Sam and friends. But Johnny is working for the government in other ways, as well. On March 8 he began an eighteen-day tour of Viet Nam with Ann-Margaret.

Johnny settled back in his chair for a moment and gave some further consideration to the world of music in which he is involved, then said: "Songs are getting better, I think, lyric-wise and melody-wise which is good. The Beatles are doing things like 'Michelle,' and pretty songs — and they have a big influence on the whole market.

"I dig that, 'cause I'd love to see that happen. It eliminates a lot of people that are making it who more-or-less just got lucky on a few songs. And lately, within the last six months — rock music has really become accepted in the top night clubs around the country where two years ago it was unheard of."

Johnny's latest single was written by Oscar Brown Jr., and is entitled "The Snake," and once again Johnny has gone back to his original "live" sound. It's a *very* live, very exciting sound and it looks like another hit for the handsome young man with the Southern accent. But then — he's a very live and exciting young man — with or with*out* his accent!

The Beauchemins 'A Beautiful Way'

They call themselves the "Beauchemins" (which means "A beautiful way")

Lee Kriske, age 18, sings tenor and plays guitar and is the tallest member of the group.

Pam Funkhouser, age 19 sings soprano and plays the biggest tambourine you've even seen and has bruises on her leg to prove it. An expert dancer and choreographer, she eats all the time but doesn't show it.

Nancy Burba, 17 years old sings alto. She has long blonde hair and has modeled for some of Hollywood's top photographers.

Vern Willis, 17 years old, plays the banjo and sings bass or baritone. He is called the smart one as he plans to teach math.

Last we have the youngest member, Paul Marshall. Though only 16, Paul is the one responsible for writing the songs and arranging them. He also plays guitar and harmonica and is the lead singer.

The Beauchemins are all from the same High School. They formed the group about a year ago and feel after a year of practice and hard work they have acquired the sound they were searching for and have just recorded "My Lovin' Baby" penned by Paul.

...THE BEAUCHEMINS

KRLA ARCHIVES

Al Martino Ready For Success Now

Back in the mid-50's, a young Philadelphian by the name of Al Martino thought he had it made. He was at the top of the ladder with a million-seller, "Here In My Heart," and as far as Al was concerned he was there to stay.

"But," he confessed later, "it all happened too fast and I was too young to cope with it. In the years that followed it was one frustration after another." Al's frustrations were plentiful. After "Here In My Heart" he produced several more hits for Capitol – "Take My Heart," "Wanted" and "Rachel," then the decline started.

First, his record sales came to a complete stop and, as Al puts it, "I had to leave Capitol Records by popular demand." Next his marriage ended in divorce. By 1957, Al Martino was a forgotten name. Everything he attempted seemed to end in failure.

For the next few years, Al tried a number of different roads to the top. He entered the construction business (he had been in it with his father when he was a youngster in Philadelphia) in California but he lost money.

To England

Then he went to England and for the first time in several years he was able to make a living at his first love – singing. When Al remarried in 1959, he still had the hope that someday he would make a comeback.

That day came in 1962 when Al borrowed $14,000 to make a comeback album. He took the LP to Capitol A&R man (now Vice President) Voyle Gilmore who had produced Al's previous recordings for Capitol in the early 1950's.

Gilmore was so impressed by the performance he heard that he bought the album and signed Al to a long-term contract. On October 1, 1962 "The Exciting Voice of Al Martino" was released. "It had just enough success to give Voyle the confidence to let me record four singles."

One of those singles was "I Love You Because." "If that hadn't scored," Al said, "I would really have been in the soup." But the Martino luck had changed and "I Love You Because" did score, almost as big as "Here In My Heart" had 12 years earlier.

A String Of Hits

Al followed this with a string of hit singles and LPs – "I Love You Because," "Painted, Tainted Rose," "Living a Lie," "I Love You More and More Every Day," "We Could," "My Cherie" and suddenly he found himself back at the top with records and in nightclubs (he was booked into the Copacabana where he received tremendous notices and then the Cocoanut Grove).

In less than twelve years he had traveled a full 360 degrees – from the top to the bottom and finally back to the top, where he intends to stay.

Al Martino was born Alfred Cini on October 7, 1927 in South Philadelphia. His family originated in Abruzzi, Italy, and the Italian love song was a strong influence in the family. "We used to sing all day and go to the opera at night," recalled Al.

In The Army

At 15 he joined the Navy and served throughout the Pacific in World War II. Afterwards he joined his father, Jasper Cini, and brothers in the family construction business. During the day he was a bricklayer but his nights were occupied with singing at local clubs.

In 1950, an old boyfriend and singer, the late Mario Lanza, gave Al all the encouragement he needed. He headed for New York and won one of the first of Arthur Godfrey's "Talent Scout" shows. His big break, however, was the discovery and recording of the song "Here In My Heart."

Al recalls that he heard Lanza was going to record the song first. He asked Lanza if this was true and the famous singer said it was, but he agreed not to make the record so that Al could have a clear shot at what surely was his big chance.

Al still lives in Philadelphia with his wife, Gwendolyn, and their daughter and son.

As for the future, Al says, "I plan to take advantage of every opportunity that's offered to me. And I'm going to be very careful in selecting material for future recordings. A lot of performers feel they can sell anything they put on wax, after they have a hit. This may be true for some, but it's a long shot at best."

...AL MARTINO

L.P. Corner

By Tracey Albert

L.P. buyers are in for some good listening as there are some fab new albums out now. One of the best of the bunch is the Knickerbockers' first long-play attempt, "The Fabulous Knickerbockers – LIES."

The ten cuts are really a showcase for the many talents of the Knickerbockers. Track one is, of course, their smash single, "Lies," but the rest of the album is a mixture of the old and new, the slow and the fast.

In my opinion, the greatest cut is an almost 4 minute version of "Harlem Nocturne" which is absolutely guaranteed to blow your minds. It's that good.

Also included on their first L.P. is "I Can Do It Better," "Please Don't Fight It," "I Believe In Her," "You'll Never Walk Alone," "Your Kind Of Lovin'," "Just One Girl," "Can't You See I'm Tryin'," and "Wishful Thinking." They all add up to an album well worth your money – don't miss it.

Walkers Arrive

Smash Records has finally released the long awaited Walker Brothers' album, titled strangely enough, "Introducing The Walker Brothers." The L.P. features all of the Walker's single efforts, "Pretty Girls Everywhere," "Love Her," "Make It Easy On Yourself" and "My Ship Is Comin' In."

John, Scott and Gary skip effortlessly from a rocking "Dancing In The Street" to a slow and extremely pretty "I Don't Want To Hear It Anymore." They've also added hits by other artists but with a definite Walker Brother sound. You'll hear "Love Minus Zero," "Land Of A 1,000 Dances" and "There Goes My Baby."

More Lettermen

The Lettermen have always done well with their albums, much better than their singles really. People in the business seem to chalk this up to the Lettermen's appeal to the college crowd rather than the teen market.

Anyway, Capitol has again released a Lettermen gold mine in the form of "More Hit Sounds Of The Lettermen." However, the title is a bit deceptive. The tracks included on the L.P. were all big hits – but hits for other artists.

Nevertheless, the Lettermen do them so well that it makes you wonder why they can't come up with a smash single of their own. All three of the Lettermen take turns soloing with Tony taking the lead in "Yesterday," Jim in a beautiful "And I Love Her" and Bob in a fantastic version of Bobby Vinton's oldie, "Blue Velvet."

Tony, Jim and Bob join up again for such recent hits as "Mr. Tambourine Man," "Cryin' In The Chapel" and "Turn, Turn, Turn." Other tracks are "Secretly," "The Things We Did Last Summer," "Sweet September," "You Were On My Mind" and "Save Your Heart For Me."

McCallum Too

Everybody's favorite UNCLE, David McCallum, has a beautiful picture of himself stretching across a Capitol release, entitled, "Music – A Part Of Me – David McCallum."

On the liner notes David himself explains the album and his reasons for selling the idea to Capitol. It seems that when David was very young his family encouraged him to play a musical instrument, which he eventually did by taking up the oboe and the English horn.

However, David was forced to make a choice between music and acting and he chose the latter, selling his oboe and horn because he needed the money. But he never forgot music.

Now David has money so he has returned to music as the conductor of "Music – A Part Of Me." The album features 12 cuts all of which are instrumental. David conducts the orchestra in such hits as "1-2-3," "The 'In' Crowd," "A Taste Of Honey," "Satisfaction" and "We Gotta Get Out Of This Place."

We think you'll enjoy the unique interpretations of these hits and if you don't you can always just sit and look at the huge color photo of David which Capitol has conveniently placed inside the album. That *alone* is worth the price of the album!

HOTLINE LONDON

(Continued from Page 1)

NEWS BRIEFS ... "These Boots Are Made For Walkin'" has taken Nancy Sinatra to Number One in the U.K., the first time in years an American songstress has topped our charts! ... On April 12 at London's Prince Of Wales Theatre, Princess Margaret will watch a charity preview performance of "Funny Girl" starring Barbra Streisand ... British girl Kathy Kirby has recorded a vocal version of the international Herb Alpert hit "Spanish Flea" ... Tommy Quickly, first solo singing star to be signed by Brian Epstein way back in June 1963, is no longer handled by the Epstein organisation. 20-year-old Tommy visited Los Angeles for promotional radio and TV appearances just over a year ago. He has a thriving Californian fan club run by Jeannie Anderson. Now managed by London's George Cooper Organisation, Tommy is expected to make a new recording shortly ... Burt Bacharach is expected in London to attend forthcoming Cilla Black recording session. Burt has penned a new ballad especially for Cilla whose current U.K. hit, "Love's Just A Broken Heart" reached No. 2 on our charts ... Ringo is not in favour of the large number of Lennon/McCartney cover versions being produced. Says the only Beatle who has NOT written any origianl songs of his own to date: "There are hundreds of 'Michelles' and 'Girls' coming out. Now it looks as though everyone is going to have a go at 'Norwegian Wood.' There's nothing wrong with cover versions in moderation but this is ridiculous!" ... The number of pirate radio stations broadcasting from ships around the British coast increases all the time. Apart from the originals – Caroline South, Caroline North and Radio London – we've got Radio City, Radio Scotland, Radio 390 and Radio Channel. And there are others in the offing.

KRLA ARCHIVES

Why Not Popsters As Comic Heroes?

By Tammy Hitchcock

Now that we've been blessed with "Batman" The BEAT sees no reason to discriminate againt the rest of our great comic book heroes. After all, that would be un-American in the extreme. Television officials are busily buying up the rights to all our comic strip favorites so be prepared for an onslaught on all stations next season.

Since it is a foregone conclusion that such heroes as Charlie Brown, Snuffy Smith, Wonder Woman and the Human Torch will shortly be coming to life we thought that the very least we could do would be to help the television people cast their up-coming rating-grabbers with our Top 40 performers. A wild idea, right?

So, here is a list of pop artists who we are convinced would make fab comic book heroes. Let us know if you agree, disagree or can come up with some even crazier suggestions.

The BEAT Suggests

Mick Jagger as The Human Torch
Tom Jones as Captain Marvel
Nancy Sinatra as Wonder Woman
Keith Richard as Flash Gordon
Jim McGuinn as The Submariner
Bill Wyman as Spectre
Lou Christy as The Green Lantern
Donovan as Hawkman
Barry McGuire as Captain America
Bob Dylan as The Plastic Man
Roger Miller as Little Abner
P.J. Proby as Superman
Keith Relf as The Spirit
Cilla Black as Little Lulu
Brian Jones as Dennis The Menace
Dino, Desi or Billy as Archie
Leslie Gore as Orphan Annie
David McCallum as Dick Tracy
Jeff Beck as Beetle Bailey
Joan Baez as Brenda Starr
Eric Burdon as Prince Valiant
Paul Revere & The Raiders as Terry & The Pirates
Jackie DeShannon as Blondie
Ringo as Dagwood
Herman as Charlie Brown
Elvis Presley as the Phantom
Paul McCartney as Daddy Warbucks
John Lennon as Snuffy Smith
Sonny as Popeye
Cher as Olive Oil
Simon & Garfunkel as the Katsunjammer Twins
Brian Wilson as Joe Palooka

KRLA ARCHIVES

Jackie Lee 'Ducks' Into a Double Life

By Marsha Provost

... JACKIE LEE

Take half of a successful singing duo, give him another name and have him write a song that starts a dance craze and what do you have?

Jackie Lee.

As Earl Cosby he is half of the team of Bob and Earl whose hits have included "Don't Ever Leave Me," "Deep Down Inside" and "Harlem Shuffle."

He was born and raised in California as Earl until last year when he wrote "The Duck" and became Jackie Lee.

Jackie wants it made very clear that Bob and Earl have *not* split up, in fact they are doing their own version of "The Duck" for release soon.

Over lunch during a break in recording sessions recently he explained how Jackie Lee and "The Duck" came about.

"I didn't create the dance. I saw kids doing it and I wrote the song. Some people at Mirwood Records liked it and said great, we'll put the name Jackie Lee on it."

So they cut it, released it and it became a smash. Earl became Jackie and started on a string of one nighters.

After being with a duo many performers might worry about going solo but not Jackie. "I love it," he says. "I don't have to worry about what anyone else is doing on stage and if we're together."

But once again he wants to make sure everyone knows he and Bob are still together.

Jackie's a prolific writer, mostly ballads, and he hopes to record some of his own writings on his next album. His one great desire now is just "to sit alone on stage and sing my ballads" whether as Earl Cosby or Jackie Lee.

But right now he's doing more recording as Earl of Bob and Earl and he has his second record out as Jackie Lee. It's called "Your Personality" with "Try My Method" on the flip side.

Jackie's an athletic young man who was all city champion in the 100 yard dash and broad jump when he was in high school in California but he has one fear, and that's airplanes.

He can't stand to fly unless he *absolutely* has to. Right now he's somewhere between California and New York in a car with a couple of other guys. He's been booked for a show in New York and is *driving* all the way so he won't have to fly. And after he finishes *that* show he'll drive to St. Louis for his next appearance.

He doesn't seem to mind long drives just as long as he doesn't have to fly. He says nothing helps him relax when he *is* forced to fly due to lack of time to drive cross country. The movies don't help, he can't sleep and even tranquilizers don't help. One good thing about it though, he's probably seen more of the country in his travels than most performers do on tours.

Jackie is a quiet young man who's easy to like and who likes easily. He's a fan of James Brown, Aretha Franklin, Sammy Davis and Andy Williams. As much as he hates planes he loves ships and he has a passion for casual clothes, particularly velour shirts and soft leather jackets.

And he's a mover. He knows you can't get ahead by standing still so he works hard all the time.

"If you're not running and moving all the time you're just not with today's teenagers," he says.

So watch for Jackie Lee and/or Earl Cosby – he'll be in there running and moving with the best of them.

For Girls Only
By Shirley Poston

Hmmmmm . . . I'm confused. Which isn't exactly *news* if you're a regular reader of this column. (And, if you aren't, you don't know how fortunate you are.)

Actually, what I'm trying to say is that I'm even more confused than usual. While a certain person (ahem) was on his honeymoon, I was somewhat off my rocker and I've completely lost track of a number of things (including several marbles.)

Tell me, did I or did I not ever have that Herman contest? The record album one, I mean. Or did I just rave about it? If someone doesn't hurry up and clue me in, I'll have to read through all my recent columns, and would you do a thing like that to a nice kid like me? You would? It figures.

Speaking Of . . .

Speaking of figures (thought I was going to say something else, didn't you?), that same certain person also caused me to lose six pounds! Here's hoping he gets married more often. (To me, for istance.)

Ratzafratz (sorry about that, Robin), I've completely forgotten what I was going to say next. Oh, it just came back to me. (I realize that most people don't put that sort of thing on paper. They just sit there and think until they can remember what was on their mind, and don't bore everyone else with their problems. But, oh well, sanity isn't everything.)

Anyway, here's what I was going to bore you with before I bored you with that.

I had dinner with a rather ghastly boy last night, in a rather nice restaurant. You know the type. So aggravatingly proper and polite you just want to lean over and rumple his crew-cut. Well, when I spilled a glass of water (coordination is not among my many virtues), he about had a relapse.

While he was writhing about, I happened to notice the couple at the next table. They were also mis-matched, only in that case, the girl was a creep (modesty is also not among my many virtues.) And she started writhing about because her date was laughing at the way I was trying not to laugh (about the water in case you've forgotten) (my writing has a tendency to make you forget what you've just read) (or wish to high Heaven that you could.)

Anyroad, a few moments later I heard her getting after him again. "Do you always put your elbows on the table?" she hissed.

The boy looked right at me and I looked right back and he said, so loud you could hear it practically all over the room, "No, I seldom put my elbows on the table. It doesn't leave enough room for my feet."

Die Laughing

Well, I thought I was going to die laughing, and so did everyone else in a ten-mile radius, except for those two aforementioned people who were surely meant for each other.

If that boy (the un-creep) is reading this column, I have news for him. I know of two *other* people who may just be meant for each other.

Speaking of gentle (as in brick) hints, I just had one. When I was writing that *fascinating* little anecdote (antidote?) (I always forget which is which) (which figures), I had the strangest feeling it had happened before. That feet-on-the-table bit, I mean.

If it did, and I've written about it before, do you suppose that boy read it and was trying to give me some kind of a signal because he's *following* me?

I dearly hope so.

Another Boy

I've raved on too long to tell you about another boy who may have also been meant for me, but I will next week. Let it suffice to say that his unusual "accidents" makes the time I shut my ear in the car door sound *sensible!*

Truthfully, there's plenty of room to talk about him now, but if I do that, I won't have enough space to say what I've been thinking about ever since I started writing this week's blitherings, which is, as everyone knows . . .

SPEAKING OF GEORGE!! That dark hair . . . that grin . . . and those *eyes!* Why, I'll bet you could get lost in those eyes for about seven years and . . .

What am I *saying?* I didn't mean to get quite *that* carried away! It's just that I haven't said Speaking Of George all column and I guess it was too much for me.

So what if he is married? John Lennon's married and I still like him. (Welcome to the understatement of the year.)

Down, Shirl. I don't know what *happens* to me when I so much as mention the name of George P. (as in Pant) Harrison. Come to think of it, I *do* know, and will now change the subject in one large hurry.

Well, this isn't exactly changing the subject, because it's about the Beatles, but you can't have everything (blast it all.)

I've just heard about the greatest Beatle fad I've ever heard of! (Welcome to the world's most ungrammatical sentence.) If you're the sort of person who goes around wishing you were married to a Beatle (Shirley, I'm *warning* you), why keep it a secret?

If you want everyone to know that you're sort of taken with one of the fab four (and that someone is coming to take you away soon) (in a net), all you have to do is stalk to the nearest dime store and buy a wedding band.

After you've scratched or written or pasted or something the name of your Beatle on the inside of the band, wear the ring on the little finger of your right hand. (It would be nice if you paid for it first, though.) (The ring, not the finger.)

Isn't that the fabbest and/or gearest idea yet? It sounded kind of strange at first, but about two seconds later, I ran about six miles trying to find a dime store. And I'm never going to take it off, *ever!* (The ring, not the dime store.) At least not until August, if you see what I mean.

Whoops! Outa room! See you next *BEAT!*

British Top 10

1. 19TH NERVOUS BREAKDOWN ...... The Rolling Stones
2. THESE BOOTS ARE MADE FOR WALKIN' .... Nancy Sinatra
3. YOU WERE ON MY MIND .... Crispian St. Peters
4. GROOVY KIND OF LOVE The Mindbenders
5. MY LOVE .... Petula Clark
6. LOVE IS JUST A BROKEN HEART .... Cilla Black
7. MICHELLE .... The Overlanders
8. MIRROR, MIRROR ... Pinkertons Assorted Colours
9. SPANISH FLEA .... Herb Alpert
10. OUTSIDE LOOKING IN ... The Animals

KRLA ARCHIVES

Burt (Robin) Ward To Sing

By Carol Deck

...BURT THE ROBIN

...BURT THE SINGER

Holy hit records!!! Guess who's taking up singing?

Half of the dynamic duo, battler of bad guys, Boy Wonder—Robin—also known as Burt Ward, has been signed to an exclusive recording contract by ABC-Paramount Records.

Now while tearing through the night with the Caped Crusader in the Batmobile, he can set his pitiful puns and rip-roaring riddles to music to further confuse and confound the villains.

He's cutting a record this week that will probably be rushed into release as soon as possible. It's his very first professional singing job but then "Batman" was his first professional acting job and look what he's done with that.

Burt had had no acting experience at all when he got the "Batman" job but he did have one thing the producers were looking for, for the part—he was very athletic.

He was an accomplished ice skater at the age of two. "That came naturally," he says. "My dad was owner and operator of one of the greatest ice shows," "Rhapsody On Ice."

He pitched several perfect games in the little league and set a school record of six seconds flat for the 50 yard dash in the eighth grade. In high school he lettered in track, wrestling and tennis and then took up karate.

The karate was what really got the part for him—he cracked a brick with his bare hands as part of the screen test.

"I knew from the comic book that Robin does all kinds of things like climbing walls, jumping off buildings, fighting bad guys twice his size and I wanted to show the producer that I can do all that stuff myself," he explains.

And he very well can do "all that stuff" by himself, but Adam West, who plays Batman, seems to have a little rougher time of it.

West just spent five days in the hospital for over-work, exhaustion and the flu.

He's back at work now, still a little on the tired side, but he'd better watch it—while he was resting up in the hospital, they signed his side kick to a singing contract.

Heaven only knows what might happen if Adam decided to take a nice long vacation. Burt might show up in a Broadway play or something. You have to watch these Batman people—they're sneaky.

The Adventures of Robin Boyd...

By Shirley Poston

Chapter Eighteen

Robin Boyd smiled sneakily in the darkness of the speeding Batmobile. For two reasons.

One—not everyone in this world had the good fortune to be chauffeured home by none other than Batman himself.

Two—Robin Boyd, not being the sort of person who would let such an opportunity go to waste, had something up her sleeve besides a reasonably well-shaped (if she did say so herself) (and she has been known to) arm.

"Batman," she purred, in her most effective (or was it affected?) (details, details) tone. "I'd like to ask a favor."

The masked man to her left swallowed with some difficulty as the masked boy to her right began to pluck nervously at the hem of his cape.

Robin (As In Boyd) paled, thinking she had gone too far, but her fears vanished when the masked man to her left spoke.

"Would you mind plucking nervously at the hem of your own cape?" he asked, directing the question at the masked boy to her right. "You're choking me."

The M.B.T.H.R. (Masked Boy To Her Right) blushed apologetically. "Holy... ah... holy..."

"Ratzafratz?" Robin (A.I.B.S.) (As In Boyd, Stupid) interjected generously, causing the M.B.T.H.R. to glare at her in utter distain as he began to pluck nervously at the hem of his own cape.

"What kind of favor?" queried the M.M.T.H.L.

"I've lost a ring," Robin (A.I.B.) re-purred, batting her eyelashes hopefully. (To be perfectly honest, she was mostly hoping they wouldn't fall off.) (No one is perfect.)

"And you want us to help you find it," finished the M.M.T.H.L., plucking nervously at everyone's capes.

Robin (A.I.B.) smiled sneakily-er. "You said it," she breathed. "Purty please with gleeps of sugar on it," she added.

The Batmobile swerved. I don't think you quite understand," said the M.M.T.H.L., grazing a pink Cadillac (sorry about that, Elvis). "It's only a television show, you know. We were just on our way home from the studio when..."

"It is NOT only a television show!" Robin (A.I.B.) interrupted fearfully (fearful, that is, of her sanity on account of because she firmly believed every word she was about to say.) "It is the triumph of good over evil," she raved. "It is faith and hope and charity and..."

"Holy baloney!" exclaimed the M.B.T.H.R. "She's one of us!"

"And therefore," contemplated the M.M.T.H.L., "it is our responsibility to..."

"Exactly," Robin (A.I.B.) said smugly. "And it shouldn't be too difficult. I lost the ring somewhere in the house."

"Did you look under the bed?" asked the M.M.T.H.L.

Robin gave him a look. "Of course," she replied. "What do you think I am, batty or something?"

The M.M.T.H.L. and the M.B.-T.H.R. turned a rather attractive shade of purple. So did Robin (A.I.B.).

"I'm sorry," she blurted. "I didn't mean..."

Suddenly the Batmobile turned a familiar corner and drove into a familiar driveway and Robin (A.I.B.) panicked mid-way in her heartfelt apology.

"I also looked under all the furniture and in the vacuum cleaner and in the garbage disposal," she rattled. "I also looked in..."

"Stop!" cried the M.M.T.H.L.

The M.B.T.H.R. looked startled. "Am I plucking nervously at the hem of your cape again?"

The M.M.T.H.L. shook his head, which was clad in a midnight blue cowl (not to be confused with animals that say "mool.") "No, no, it's not that! It's the ring!"

"Where, where?" cried Robin (A.I.B.).

"There, there!" replied the M.-M.T.H.L. pointing at the familiar house. "Safe and sound in... are you ready for this?... in an English tea pot!"

Robin (A.I.B.) leaped to her feet (which ain't easy in a Batmobile) (welcome to the understatement of the year.)

"A tea pot?" she shrieked, mangling both the M.M.T.H.L. and the M.B.T.H.R. as she catapulted gracefully (she hoped) through the window of the car.

"Yes, a tea pot," muttered the M.M. to the left of the M.B. at the right, "But how did I know that?"

As Robin (A.I.B.) dashed wildly into the house, waving a hurried but fond farewell to her heroes, the M.B. at the right turned to the M.M. at his left.

"Holy ratzafratz," he said reverently. "You knew it because you know everything."

"Oh," said the M.M. to the left of (oh, forget it)... said the M.M. to the M.B. And, grateful for this explanation (because it explained things), he touched a gloved hand to the gears and the Batmobile took off like a bat out of Dingle Vale.

Immediately after bursting through the front door, Robin mowed down her twelve-year-old sister.

"Ringo!" she thundered. Watch where you're going!" (Anyone wishing to comment upon the fact that hardly anyone has a sister named Ringo is invited to take the matter up with Ringo Boyd, who is large for her age.) (Who is also, come to think of it, large for any age.)

But, instead of spearing her older sister with the Ludwig "droomstick" she wore about her neck (on a chain, on a chain) Ringo picked herself up and gave Robin a stricken look.

"Please tell me I didn't just see you leap out of a Batmobile," she begged, fearing for her sanity.

"You didn't just see me leap out of a Batmobile," Robin said agreeably, rushing to the empty mantel. "But you did see my tea pot, didn't you?"

Ringo shrugged. "Don't fret your fretner," she said calmly. "Mom has it in the kitchen."

Robin jumped sixteen feet into the air (which is difficult in the average living room) (which, come to think of it, is difficult, period.) "Why does she have it in the kitchen?" she bellowed.

Ringo re-shrugged. "I guess she's makin' herself a cuppa to settle her nerves."

Gasping for dear life, Robin reached the kitchen in a single bound (not to mention faster than a speeding bullet.)

But she was too late. Her mother had just filled the tea pot with boiling water and was replacing the lid.

"Mother!" shouted Robin, grabbing the pot and dumping the contents into the sink.

"Oh, NO!" she added shortly thereafter. For, just as she had feared, the contents were not of tea-type-hue. The liquid was instead darkish.

The same color as her beloved Liverpudlian genie's beautiful black hair and leather jacket!

Bursting into noisy blithering, Robin was barely conscious of the fact that her mother was plucking nervously at the hem of her cape ...whoops...sweater.

"Robin!" her mother insisted. "What is the matter with you? Now," she added wearily.

"GEORGE!" wept Robin bitterly, watching the last drop of him go down the drain. "You almost drank George!"

(To Be Continued Next Week)

KRLA ARCHIVES

Paul Newman is 'Harper'

This is a different kind of cat named Lew Harper... and excitement clings to him like a dame!

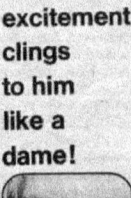
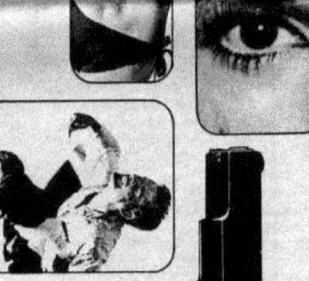
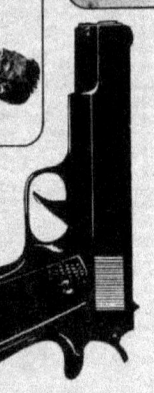

A GERSHWIN-KASTNER Production
CO-STARRING (IN ALPHABETICAL ORDER)

**LAUREN BACALL · JULIE HARRIS · ARTHUR HILL
JANET LEIGH · PAMELA TIFFIN · ROBERT WAGNER
SHELLEY WINTERS**

Screenplay by WILLIAM GOLDMAN · Produced by JERRY GERSHWIN and ELLIOTT KASTNER · Directed by JACK SMIGHT
TECHNICOLOR® PANAVISION® FROM WARNER BROS.

EXCLUSIVE ENGAGEMENT
NOW PLAYING!
PACIFIC'S **PANTAGES** THEATRE · HOLLYWOOD
HOLLYWOOD BLVD. near VINE · HO 9-2211

Inside KRLA

Just as it was last year, the Valentine contest at KRLA was a huge, smashing success. In fact — in some cases, it was even *too* huge. Dick Moreland confided to *The BEAT* that there were over 40,000 entries in the contest this year and they were even *larger* than last year!

For example, the first prize entry was a heart which looked very similar to a Rose Parade float! It was a heart which opened up with lights all over it. It was so large that it couldn't be taken inside the building, and had to be kept in the garage underneath KRLA.

The second prize entry was also a gigantic heart-shaped affair which opened up to reveal real, live *doves* flying around!

One of the many third prize entries was an upside-down, hanging bat! Now that's what we call loyalty!!!

In case you missed the announcements on the air, we have listed here all of the first, second, and third place winners and their prizes. By the way — the third place prizes were created due to the fantastically large numbers of great valentines which poured into KRLA.

First Prize ($1,000) was awarded to Pat Jamieson of Newhall.

Second Prize ($500) was awarded to Cindy Littlefield, of Glendora.

Third Prizes ($50) were awarded to: Jim Rumph, of Pacific Palisades; Frank Salvucci of Los Angeles; Jerry Lazar, of West Los Angeles; Gene Shusko of La Verne; Dennis Roof, of Pacific Palisades; Debbie McCluskey, of Anaheim; Lee Fitzgerrell, of Occidental College; Joe Stuben, of Los Angeles; James Edson, of El Monte; and a very good friend of *The BEAT* staff: composer, poet, songwriter, and great human being — Mason Williams.

Mason's very unusual entry — a very beautiful and indescribable window of love — is now hanging in a place of honor in our offices, so I guess that now we can truthfully say that *everyday* is Valentine's Day at *The BEAT!!*

For a period of four days during the flu epidemic which affected just about *everyone*, KRLA awarded $11.10 in KRLAid to the first person who could call the station and tell them just exactly how they felt — in *one* word!

The entire project was affectionately referred to by the KRLA DJ's (three of whom were caught by the bug, themselves) as "Something Special for KRLAsian Fluser-Losers." Personally, I think they should have awarded a very special prize to anyone who could even *say* all that!

Here's an important announcement. Bob Eubanks has decided to advertise in *The BEAT* due to the fact that he didn't have much success advertising on his own nightly 6:00 to 9:00 show on KRLA. I guess I'd better explain. You see, Bob proposed to Nancy Sinatra on the air one evening recently because he was unable to obtain Miss Sinatra's home phone number.

But since he hasn't received an answer to his proposal as yet, we will just have to assume that she simply couldn't get a hold of *his* home phone number! Well, *The BEAT* is very pleased to inform both of the young lovers that we will be more than happy to act as a middle-man in this blossoming new romance! So if Nancy would like to reply to Bob — our pages are at her service. Good luck, Bobby-baby!!!

And what of Our Groovy Leader — The BatManager himself — John Barrett? We still haven't been able to discover the fiendish culprit who planted that insidious BatManager sign on John-John's door. However . . . we have noticed that Our Cool and Groovy Leader of us all has been in the constant companionship of a new-found friend of late. Don't know who he is, but I *can* tell you that he is young and his last name is "Wonder." I'd probably be able to tell you more, but John only refers to him as "Boy."

KRLA BEAT Subscription
SAVE 33% Of Regular Price

☐ 1 YEAR — 52 Issues — $5.00   ☐ 2 YEARS — $8.00
☐ 6 MONTHS — $3.00

Enclosed is _____   ☐ CASH   ☐ CHECK
PLEASE PRINT — Include Your Zip Code

Send to: .... Age: ....
Address: .... City: ....
State: .... Zip: ....

MAIL YOUR ORDER TO: KRLA BEAT
6290 Sunset, Suite 504
Hollywood, Calif. 90028

Foreign Rate: $9.00 — 52 Issues

KRLA ARCHIVES

Hearts Full Of "Gold" At KRLA

The KRLA Fifth annual Valentine contest is over now, and all the prizes have been awarded to the winners. The contest, as a whole, was a huge success, and some of the most beautiful, most unusual — as well as some of the *largest* — valentines in history were received by the station during the contest.

The First Prize winner was a cute Southern California teenage miss named Pat Jamieson who lives with her family in Newhall. Pat was the lucky recipient of $1,000 awarded to her for her outstanding work on a huge, intricately-decorated valentine.

Pat's entry was a huge heart-shaped affair which opened up, and featured lights, and decorated drawings all of which she had done herself.

KRLA DJ, Charlie O'Donnell presented a check for $1,000 dollars to a very proud and happy Pat — in the *garage* beneath the station! The reason for this was that Pat's Valentine entry had been just too large to get inside of the studios.

It was a happy Valentine's Day for many people, and KRLA would like to extend their thanks to all of the people in KRLA-Land who entered and made this contest the most successful Valentine Contest ever conducted by a Top 40 Radio station.

...CHARLIE O'DONNELL PRESENTING $1,000 TO PAT JAMIESON

KRLA Tunedex

This Week	Last Week	Title	Artist
1	1	THESE BOOTS ARE MADE FOR WALKIN'	Nancy Sinatra
2	3	CALIFORNIA DREAMIN'	Mamas & The Papas
3	8	LISTEN PEOPLE	Herman's Hermits
4	2	YOU BABY	The Turtles
5	7	I AIN'T GONNA EAT OUT MY HEART ANYMORE	The Young Rascals
6	15	HOMEWARD BOUND	Simon & Garfunkel
7	5	A WELL-RESPECTED MAN	The Kinks
8	17	THE BALLAD OF THE GREEN BERET	Sgt. Barry Sadler
9	13	TIME	Pozo-Seco Singers
10	6	FIVE O'CLOCK WORLD	The Vogues
11	4	ZORBA THE GREEK	Herb Alpert And The Tijuana Brass
12	20	I'M SO LONESOME I COULD CRY	B.J. Thomas
13	3	JUST LIKE ME	Paul Revere & The Raiders
14	21	SET YOU FREE THIS TIME	Byrds
15	11	ELUSIVE BUTTERFLY	Bob Lind
16	10	LOVE MAKES ME DO FOOLISH THINGS	Martha & The Vandellas
17	22	WORKING MY WAY BACK TO YOU	The Four Seasons
18	18	BATMAN	Neil Hefti
19	29	WOMAN	Peter & Gordon
20	38	19TH NERVOUS BREAKDOWN	The Rolling Stones
21	14	MY BABY LOVES ME	Martha & The Vandellas
22	23	KEEP ON RUNNING	The Spencer Davis Group
23	31	SHAKE ME, WAKE ME	The Four Tops
24	39	DAYDREAM	The Lovin' Spoonful
25	27	DARLING BABY	Elegants
26	30	LOVE IS ALL WE NEED	Mel Carter
27	24	ANDREA	The Sunrays
28	25	LOOK THROUGH ANY WINDOW	The Hollies
29	28	THE CHEATER	Bob Kuban
30	26	AT THE SCENE	The Dave Clark Five
31	32	HUSBANDS AND WIVES	Roger Miller
32	40	CALL ME	Chris Montez
33	—	WALKIN' MY CAT NAMED DOG	Norma Tanega
34	34	BABY SCRATCH MY BACK	Slim Harpo
35	35	IT'S TOO LATE	Bobby Goldsboro
36	—	LOVE MAKES THE WORLD GO ROUND	Dion Jackson
37	37	THE ONE ON THE RIGHT IS ON THE LEFT	Johnny Cash
38	—	FOLLOW ME	Lyme & Cybelle
39	36	PROMISE HER ANYTHING	Bob Jones
40	—	BANG, BANG	Cher

DAVE HULL

BOB EUBANKS

DICK BIONDI

JOHNNY HAYES

EMPEROR HUDSON

CASEY KASEM

CHARLIE O'DONNELL

BILL SLATER

'Battle Of Beat'

Cash prizes and musical equipment totaling $700 will be awarded to the top three bands in the fifth annual "Battle of the Beat," one of the highlights of the Teen-Age Fair, which will be held April 1-10 at the Hollywood Palladium.

Southland instrumental groups desiring to enter the competition may do so by calling Mrs. Bush at HO. 2-6464 or by writing Teen-Age Fair, 6290 Sunset Blvd., Hollywood, Calif.

Bands will be judged each day during the Fair and finalists will compete for the bounty of prizes on Sunday, April 10. The winning group will receive a cash prize of $150 plus musical equipment from the Fender Guitar Co. valued at $400. Cash prizes of $100 and $50 respectively will be awarded to the second and third place winners. Handsome trophies and participation plaques also will go to the winning groups.

A panel consisting of professional musical authorities and executives of leading recording companies will judge the competition, which is being sponsored by Fender Guitar Co.

Eve's APPAREL
See if you can BEAT our prices on our new Jr. and missy lines. Samples at wholesale or less.
1800 N. Vermont NO 3-4456
Hollywood, Calif.

MEET YOUR NEW LEADER, DAISY CLOVER

Natalie WOOD
CHRISTOPHER PLUMMER

IN A PAKULA-MULLIGAN PRODUCTION

inside DAISY CLOVER
the story of what they did to a kid...

ROBERT REDFORD · RODDY McDOWALL · RUTH GORDON
Music: André Previn
Screenplay by GAVIN LAMBERT Produced by ALAN J. PAKULA Directed by ROBERT MULLIGAN
TECHNICOLOR® PANAVISION® FROM WARNER BROS.

Starts WEDNESDAY, MARCH 9th!
IN A THEATRE OR DRIVE-IN NEAR YOU!

KRLA ARCHIVES

Three Fans Interview Two Byrds

Every now and then The BEAT staff gets a little lazy and lets fans do our writing for us.

The following interview with Gene Clark and Jim McQuinn of the Byrds was sent to us by three of their fans. We'd like to thank Debbie Weller, Margie Hoeft and Hillary Bedell for this look at a top group by some average teenagers.

As you know, "Rock-and-Roll," has been long gone from the musical scene. The current rage is "Folk-and-Roll." But, now, there is a brand new, explosive type of music by that fantastic new group, The BYRDS. With a sound of their own, they have flown themselves to stardom.

It was eighteen months ago in a small coffee house, "The Troubador," where the members of the group first met each other. After trying a handful of different names for the group, they selected the most fitting name, The BYRDS. Although Gene Clark and Jim McGuinn (lead of the group) sing a sort-of-folkish music, their favorite types of tunes are jazz. Jim also enjoys Indian type music; especially, when it is written by Ernest Minj, his favorite Anglo-Indian writer.

Many people think of Jim McGuinn when they see the new rage in glasses, the "Ben Franklin" specs'. He is thought of as the originator of the glasses. But, according to him, one day he went to a store and discovered them there. Jim now has three different pairs of these specs'. They are in a rose color, cobalt blue, and neutral colored Air Force corrective grey.

According to Gene, the Beatles had little to do with the group's long hair. All of the group had let their locks grow long, before they had joined together. Gene, himself, had long hair far before the Beatles were ever popular.

Eighth Wonder

To many BYRD fans, the eighth wonder of the world is why Chris Hillman, bass guitarist, never smiles. It isn't that he is unfriendly, he is just a very serious musician. And likes to concentrate on his work so he can give the BYRD fans the great entertainment they come to hear.

Have you ever been in an embarrassing predicament? Gene Clark says his is yet to come. But Jim McGuinn confesses his is when he appears on stage and his guitar is out of tune.

Many stars are changed for the worst when they become successful and popular. The BYRDS admit that their personalities have changed a lot since their popularity, but for the better. Now, the group has much more confidence. Also, material items mean much less than they did before.

Is T.V. for the birds? . . . Well, these BYRDS like it! One of Jim's favorite television shows is "The Man From U.N.C.L.E." Gene enjoys watching "The Lloyd Thaxton Show," and "The Bullwinkle Show." Jim enjoys watching his favorite T.V. program and many others on two television sets at the same time; one being black-and-white, and the other in color. It's sort of a "stereo television."

You fans don't have to worry about screaming at BYRD concerts. The BYRDS see it as a showing of appreciation. But, don't scream too loud, or you won't be able to hear the concert! We know all of the BYRD fans never mean to do any harm to the group, but occasionally they receive minor injuries from excited admirers mobbing them.

Recently, at a concert in La Jolla, the BYRDS were mobbed and left with a missing left windshield wiper and a torn off license plate from their car. Jim's glasses are the main item that fans try to get at, but every time a fan grabs them, he manages to get them back.

The group spends most of their money on such items as radios, tape recorders, color T.V.'s, and automobiles. They mainly like compact, and foreign model type cars. Most of the group likes Porsches, Ferrari's, and XKE's. Jim drives a new red Porsche with black interior.

Burn Incense

When the BYRDS have any time to spare, which is very seldom, they usually just stay at home and relax. When they are completely alone, they light candles or burn incense. Or they just lounge at home and watch the television.

Sometimes Jim fools around with his favorite hobby, electronics equipment. One of his future ambitions is to have his own electronics lab. Gene likes to walk and to drive as his hobbies.

Most of the time, the BYRDS eat at home, because it is hard to go to restaurants. Occasionally, they would take a trip to "Ben Frank's," famous coffee shop of the "Sunset Strip goer's." They rarely go now, because it is inconvenient. You may see Gene and Mike at the beach sometimes. They enjoy surfing when they have a spare moment.

The BYRDS not only sing and surf, but they will also be acting soon. The group is going to be shooting a movie in about six months, and it should be released shortly after.

Every time the BYRDS get a number one hit it is an exciting moment. But they say the most thrilling moment was when "Mr. Tambourine Man," a song of personal freedom, became a number one hit in both the United States and England.

Gene entered show business after he finished high school at Bonner High School of Kansas City, Missouri. The last Jim ever saw of school was the Latin School of Chicago. Jim was educated musically at the Old Towne School of Folk Music. Gene had no musical education.

"Bongo" Clarke

Mike Clarke, handsome drummer of the BYRDS, has a nickname very fitting to him. Many of his friends call him "Bongo." They sometimes call Chris Hillman, "Herman." When we asked Gene Clark if he had a nickname, he said "yes" and began laughing. He said it was too embarrassing to say.

If you were to look through Gene Clark's closet you would probably find many items of suede and denim material. These are what his favorite clothes are made of. Jim enjoys wearing any type of clothes, as long as they are in good taste.

Jim likes everything, except negatives. He hates fear, worry, hate, distrust, anxiety, and other pessimistic forms. Gene likes everything except bugs.

Some of Jim's likes are love, creating, trusting, growing, and moving forward. Gene likes everything, as I said before, except for those creepy crawlers (bugs)!!!!!!!!

From complete unknowns in small coffee houses, to performers of many hits, such as "Turn, Turn, Turn," and "Mr. Tambourine Man." The BYRDS have acquired a style of their own, which has caught the ears of teenagers all over the world.

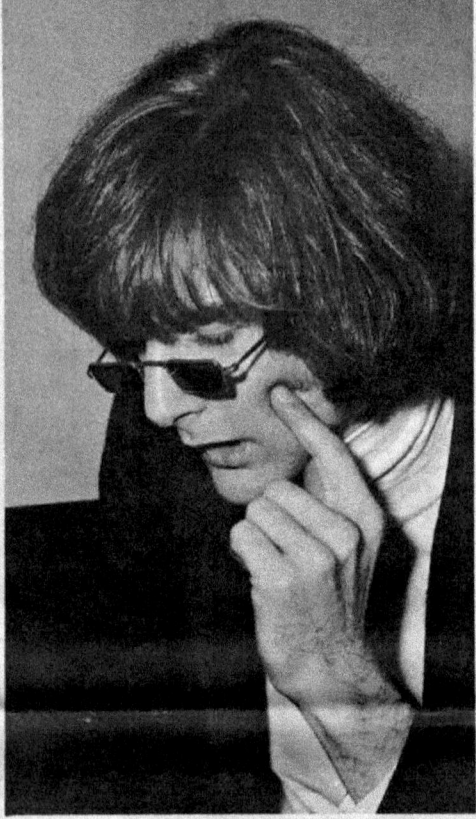

... JIM McQUINN

... GENE CLARK

THE LUCKY fans who talked to Jim McQuinn and Gene Clark of the Byrds also talked them into posing for a picture with them. That's Debbie and Hillary with Jim, Margie in the center, and a friend, Sherry, with Gene. We're still wondering who took the picture for the girls.

KRLA ARCHIVES

BEAT Reporter Catches Another

By Kimmi Kobashigawa

Now, I know it may not make any sense to *you* — but really, I just can't help myself. Everytime I hear the Byrds I think of *bells*. I mean it . . . *bells!!* I'm not in love with them or anything, and I'm not even insane — although there *are* those who might disagree! It's just that the five Byrds make me think of bells. So you can imagine what it was like the other night when I interviewed David Crosby — total ring-a-ding-ding!!!

The Byrds were preparing to do one of their rare concert appearances and David and I trudged to the very back of the huge night club in order to find a spot quiet enough to conduct an interview.

He was, as usual, wearing the cape for which he has become famous — and that, too, reminds me of bells. It makes me think of the Hunchback of Notre Dame as he climbed up in the bell tower. Of course, David doesn't bear any resemblance to the Hunchback — he looks somewhat more like a very affectionate puppy.

An Accent?

He smiles often, and very sincerely — and when he speaks to you, his voice is tinged with the slightest hints of accent . . . one quite hard to define. But it is a voice of authority and certainty with which he relates his own opinions to you. He spoke to me of Dylan: "Yes — he's improved the lyrics in pop music tremendously.

"I think we were the first ones to do his stuff — successfully — in the pop world. That's why we did Dylan songs — because there wasn't anybody else writing songs that were as good."

Onstage, the Byrds sing songs such as "The Chimes of Freedom," and "The Bellys of Rhymney" (David's favorite Byrd recording), and these also lend a chime or two to the sounds of bells I hear when near a Byrd. But these songs do much more; they carry with them a message, and often the Byrds are asked to define for their public just what the message which they wish to convey is. What is it they're trying to say?

I asked David if these songs which the Byrds sing have political overtones, and if the Byrds were using them as a means of political communication. He thought about that for a while, and then replied quite honestly: "We — as a general rule — feel that we're musicians and that we have sort of a universal distaste for politics of *any* kind. Between all of us — I don't think *any* of us are political at all. We're certainly anti-Establishment; but we're not political at all.

"I haven't heard of a political party that wasn't just as silly as all the others yet. I haven't heard of one that had anything to say that involved truth, or reality, or love, or anything I was interested in."

Their Themes

What then, are the themes which the Byrds are carrying in their music? *Is* there, in fact, *any* themes which run throughout their songs? "Yes — there are several. First — and the biggest one — is freedom; personal freedom, freedom of the thinking, freedom of the being. Then there's *love* — and that's where it's at. And there's motion, too — there's a lot of motion. Sometimes it's trains, sometimes it's horseback, mostly it's jets . . . 'cause that's mostly what we ride, that's where our heads are at!

"Those things run through it. You won't find an intellectual conscious stream running through it — but you will find those characteristics. We don't have a specific intellectual thing that we want to get said — we'll just do whatever songs we feel like."

On the floor all around us, there was a multitude of confetti which someone had strewn all over with gay abandon, and for a moment — David gayly abandoned our interview in order to collect several handfuls of the colored stuff which he later threw all over me and several other innocent bystanders.

Stooping And Swirling

As he stooped down to gather up the little bits of paper, the motion of his cape reminded me of the swirling movements it makes on stage as David plays his guitar. It made me think of their unique sort of 12-string-sound, and suddenly I could hear them singing the "Chimes of Freedom." David returned to me then, and we spoke a little of that freedom.

"If there's enough of it, it'll take us out of a place where we want to make wars and — probably — off the planet, and out. That would be a nice way for us to go. I don't know what's going to happen; I'm not a prophet or a seer — I just live here.

"Freedom is something I see to be a good thing — not a *comfortable* thing, not a *satisfying* thing — it's a *hard* thing that you've got to pay dues for all the time. But it's *freedom* — and I like it! I guess *every*body that gets a taste of it in their thinking is going to think differently than things have been lately.

Real Love

"I think things are going to change a lot. You know — I really *love* this country for giving us the room to be what we are. I really love it — I would never put down this country. I disagree with some of the things — obviously. *Every*body disagrees with *something*, you can't please everybody. But it's nice that we can get as far out and explore as much as we have. I hope that we can go a lot further — soon."

He smiled at me again, then — he asked if there were any other questions which I really wanted to ask. But it was time for him to go onstage, and so I thanked him for his time and prepared to leave. David said thank you and smiled his puppy dog smile just once more — than vanished out the huge concrete opening with a flashing of his cape.

I gathered up my belongings and followed his trail of confetti until I came directly to the site of his first victim — Cass, of the Mama's and Papas — who visited the Byrds backstage. Within seconds and just a flash of his hand — I became confetti victim Number Two!

But then I began to hear bells again — this time they came from the stage, and from five very musical Byrds.

. . . DAVID CROSBY BEAT Photo: Chuck Boyd

The Only Single Beatle

(Continued from Page 1)

reen made the rumors fact leaving George and Paul wide-open to face the rumors alone. And then George went off and got married and once again only Paul was left for the rumor people to carve up.

If you think this rumor business isn't a very real problem you're off your rocker because it most definitely is. Even though Paul was very happy for George and Patti, he commented to the reporters gathered outside the registry that he supposed *he* was now in for an onslaught of newly made-up marriage stories.

Hounded

Even George felt badly about leaving Paul the only bachelor Beatle: "Actually, I feel sorry for him. He'll be hounded to death now us other three are married."

But surprisingly enough a whole month has passed and not one single rumor has hit the papers. Maybe none will, but don't bank on it. There is always someone around to stir up trouble, always someone who thinks he can sell a few more papers or boost his magazine's circulation by printing a huge spread on Paul and Jane's "marriage."

And, of course, there is Jane herself who continues to insist that she and Paul are getting married while Paul is equally firm in insisting that he has no marriage plans.

Where it will go from here is anybody's guess. Probably even Paul isn't sure. About the only thing in the whole mess is that the Beatles will be around the pop scene for a long, long time to come — whether Paul stays the charming, handsome, bachelor Beatle or not.

Say you saw it in The BEAT

. . . THE BYRDS ON STAGE

KRLA ARCHIVES

IN SEARCH OF FOLK

Buffy Still A 'Loner'

By Shannon Leigh

Philosophers have, for centuries, questioned the human existence and the proof of that existence—how do we know that we really exist? Many have concluded that it is only through those sensory experiences peculiar to human beings that we can approach any certainty of our own personal existence.

It is, then, quite understandable that we relate many of our everyday experiences to the sensory perceptions and experiences immediately involved. We remember the way something looked, the way it felt, the sounds we heard at a particular moment, the taste of something, and the way something smelled.

The word *smell* is not generally associated with anything delicate—for that connotation we usually resort to something like "scent," or "fragrance." But things *do* smell—both good and bad, and we remember certain experiences through the smells associated with them.

This week, our search leads us to a talented, "magical," unusual young woman who is quite frequently referred to as a "folk singer." She is a lot more than just that ... mostly, she is Buffy Sainte-Marie.

Canadian Cree

Many members of her audiences are aware that Buffy was born in Canada of Cree Indian parents, and it is this knowledge which deeply affects their interpretations of her performances. I found myself influenced by her background, and my impressions seemed to center around that basis.

The overall setting on this evening was a darkened folk-club, crowded with people anxiously awaiting Buffy's performance. It was dark, and pervaded by a muffled din of pre-show chatter.

The warm-and-honey-eyed smells of coffees—some exotic—passed us by, and then were joined by sweeter wisps of cider floating on the smoke-filled air.

A brief announcement by an unseen voice—and a small, raven-haired girl stepped on stage. Delicate, and yet strong as all the ages, and certain of herself as she began

BUFFY SAINTE-MARIE

to sing. There wasn't a breath wasted in the audience; they were enveloped by her spell.

And I remembered what she had said: "I'm not in any kind of movement—I'm trying to awaken the interest in everyone." I thought of this as she sang songs of people—and I thought of this as she sang songs of *her* people . . . the Indians. Songs of a people too often ignored, songs of the injustices which they have suffered.

The fresh, stinging air of the prairie in the morning—I could smell the tingling of the pine needles in the forests. Places far away and near.

She sang of "piney woods," and we were there. But not with Buffy—for Buffy goes alone. There are some who call her "loner," but that is only because they cannot follow behind. She tells us, "I spend a lot of time *alone*, but I never get lonely. I enjoy solitude, I like being alone. What can I do when there are a thousand people around? I can't do very much! So, what I do is take off for long spouts of time at once, and I'll go wherever I'm going.

"Like, I went to Spain for three months this summer—and I just went. I didn't tell anybody and nobody knew where I'd gone. I *told* them I'd be back in three months—and in three months . . . I came back!"

Dazzling Heat

I could somehow feel the dazzling-white heat on the sun-drenched roads in Spain, and when she sang her own composition, "Los Pescadores," (The fishermen) I could smell the wharf and salt sea air rushing past me in that darkened night club.

Jasmine incense crowding in with smells of something foreign, something of another place . . . something in the mystic East that clasps you by the mind-strings which you have left to dangle and then takes you on a dream-like journey of some other-where.

All of this while Buffy sang songs of different nationalities, songs which spoke—for her—of life. Later, when she spoke to me, she would tell me of her writing—and still it seemed as though she came to us from some far-distant land.

"I've been composing all my life and I've been making up poetry and stories and writing classical-type things and songs. I started when I was about three. When I put out a book of my poetry or songs, I'd like to illustrate it; I like to do illuminated manuscripts like they used to illuminate Bibles. If I put out a book of poetry, I'd like to make it beautiful, and put it out as a complete work of art."

Sweet Candy

Chocolate—sweet and candied—seemed to dominate the tiny little dressing room. Only in a box on the table, it reached out and offered its sugared-treats to everyone who came near.

Buffy called the heart-shaped box of Valentine candy on the dressing room table "movie star candy"—Gilbert Roland had sent it over to her. She insisted that everyone present share it with her, share the sweetness of just a little taste of chocolate—and she was like a little girl.

But Buffy believes her five-feet-and-two-inches with her talent so like an ivory tower—so beautiful, so out-of-reach, so very much alone.

She speaks Cree—several different dialects—English, French, Spanish, a little Russian, Hindie, and she is learning Italian. She can play the banjo, the guitar, the mandolin, the fiddle, piano, and the mouth bow, and during the summer just past she began an opera and finished a concerto for guitar and orchestra. Her songs have been recorded by many of the top artists—folk and otherwise—in the industry.

Stage Language

And over the friendly warmth of coffee she explains in final summary: "I don't really have anything to say in interviews. I say what I'm saying *onstage*. What you see onstage is a very well-edited version of who I am, and what I want to tell people."

Sweet things like roses blooming, and foreign smells of Jasmine tempting us to roam incessantly as she does; piney smells of far-off woods, and rougher smells of cowhide from a distant reservation.

Who is she? What does she say to people from that stage? What words does she use to capture all who see her and cause them to be firmly entranced, as though she were some mystic? It is only her music, and the way in which she shares it with others—it is only that she seems to say to all who come to see her: "My name is Buffy Sainte-Marie, and I'll spend this time with you. Who are *you*?"

Cher 'Shot Down' As Flu Bug Strikes

By Eden

It was a time of illness for everyone—the flu bug had struck the Southern California area very hard for the second time in a decade. It was labelled Type A Asian flu by the physicians—and labelled just plain *bad* by all of its victims.

Many of those stricken were among the people in the field of entertainment including a girl named Cher. Unfortunately however, Cher was caught by the more serious complications of the disease.

We learned of Cher's illness about noon on a Friday afternoon at *The BEAT*, and naturally very concerned—we immediately called Sonny to check on her condition. We knew that she was suffering from acute Asiatic flu as well as Bronchitis, but Sonny assured us immeidately: "She's sick today—but she feels pretty good under the circumstances. She will probably only have to be in the hospital for two or three days—I hope!"

At the time, Sonny and Cher had been scheduled to make some personal appearances in St. Louis and Chicago—both dates, of course, had to be cancelled. Sonny told me that he hoped that he and Cher would be able to make both engagements at a later date, but explained with a note of worry in his voice: "The doctor says that if she'd gone on the road now she would have gotten pneumonia! Right now, her cold is bronchial."

I asked Sonny if Cher had a history of poor health, and he explained: "She's not as strong as me. It's do demanding now—we're going, going all the time—and if you're not a strong person, it's very taxing. I can go for a long time and not get sick—knock on wood!—but when Cher gets tired, she gets sick."

Sonny tried to give me a little idea of just how hectic their schedule was at the time by telling me of all the things which they had been doing. At the same time, they were involved in cutting two new albums—one for Cher, and one for both of them—as well as doing all the preparation work for their first movie which will begin shooting on the 14th of March.

Sonny confirmed that he definitely was doing all of the songs and scoring for the movie, and that he had collaborated with a writer on the basic script, which would receive only polishing up from a second writer.

The movie is going to be rushed through production so that it will be ready for release some time in May. It will be about Sonny and Cher making a movie, and Sonny will be doing such unbelievable things as riding a horse and wrestling a lion! "Of course, we have a lot of preparation work to do before we start filming the movie. I have to meet the lion and get kind of friendly with him, 'cause I'm not going to use a stunt man!" Here's to a warm friendship, Sonny!

As soon as the movie is completed, Sonny and Cher are off to Europe on a whirlwind personal appearance tour, during which time they will appear on several European TV shows.

Then, believe it or not—they will finally get an opportunity to take a much needed and well-deserved rest.

Until then—the entire staff here at *The BEAT* sends its very best wishes to Cher (she is now out of the hospital) for a healthy and speedy recuperation.

DRUMMERS

YOU HIP TO METAL DRUMSTICKS?

Experts agree . . . Practicing with these weapons will do these important things for YOUR BEAT!

- Give you more **power**—to make yourself heard above amplified instruments.
- Give you new **stick control**—to play today's beat with more precision and fire.
- Give you more **endurance**—to keep excitement at its peak all nite long.

Try 'em and see for yourself what fantastic results will follow. **ORDER YOUR PAIR NOW!**

$5.95

Harriman's
1884 Pandora Avenue
Los Angeles, Calif. 90025
(Sorry, no C.O.D.'s)

THE BEATLES: The Girls In Their Lives

By Sue Barry

There is probably no group of people more talked and written about than those four young men collectively known as the Beatles. In fact, if there was one, I am sure these boys would walk away with the award for the largest number of words written on one subject in a short span of three years. Yet, for the millions of words printed about these four there remains a cloud of mystery over one aspect of their lives. This concerns their relations with the opposite sex and, in particular, Cynthia Lennon, Maureen Starkey, Pattie Harrison and Jane Asher.

It is no accident that these girls have been carefully guarded from the spotlight. For there is an unwritten agreement among John, Paul, George and Ringo that their private lives are indeed private and should be kept from the spying eye of the press. One has to admire the boys for this policy. They have protected their girls from the needless and unnecessary hurt that so often arises out of "scoop" stories written by so-called fan magazines.

Yet, one cannot help but wonder about these girls. After all, fans are fans and although they don't wish to pry they do like to know about these all-important femmes in the Beatles' lives. So we of *The BEAT* have decided to give you a little of each girl. We do not mean to pry, nor do we want to spread any falsehoods, but wish to share with you the girls in the lives of the Beatles.

BEAT Photo: Robert W. Young

"My girl was at home in Liverpool. I'd met her one day and we'd suddenly fallen in love. A little while later we were married. I love her." The man speaking was John Lennon once pegged as the "married Beatle." The girl he spoke of is, of course, his wife Cynthia.

Theirs is a story of love and one any girl would delight in telling. In a way it's like a fairytale come true. But perhaps it would be better for you to find out for yourself. Let us go for a moment into the world of John and Cynthia Lennon.

They first met in art school. John was a young man struggling between his love for a guitar and art. Cynthia Powell was a quiet, intelligent girl. They met and as John says, ". . . suddenly fell in love." It must have been evident for a Mr. Ballard who tutored John at art school has this to say: "She was his guiding light, and even though she was the top girl in her class, she always managed to spare time for John. Even in those days they were really made for each other." Yes, they were made for each other and when John finally quit school to devote all his time to his music Cynthia encouraged him. Often she would travel up to thirty miles from her home on Trinity Rd. in Hoylake to hear John and the other boys play. A friend recalls how during breaks John would sit on the edge of the stage quietly talking with her.

But times changed and when they married on August 23, 1962 it was decided that the best thing was not to let out word of their marriage. The Beatles were on the road up and a marriage in the group might have caused them to lose a great amount of popularity. Perhaps this was the hardest time of their marriage—that first year or so when it seemed so important that John's marriage be kept hidden. They lived at John's aunt Mimi's. During their stay, a baby, John Julian, was born on April 8, 1963.

It wasn't too long after this that pictures of Cyn appeared in the papers. The truth was out! And what did John have to say? "I never denied it at all. It's just that nobody asked me." A typical straight forward Beatle answer!

Cynthia remarks: "At first it was horrible. John used to get terrible letters and if I'd been unstable, I would have been terribly upset by them. But afterwards the friendly ones far out-numbered the unpleasant ones."

And so there was one married Beatle. John was careful not to let the press get to his wife, "I haven't deliberately hidden her from the public . . . but I have tried to keep her away from the press. I don't see why they should treat her like a freak just because she married a Beatle."

But what is this woman like? Cynthia had remained the same girl from Liverpool although her tastes run expensive now that she has the money. She is a shy, quiet girl who likes to spend her time at home with her young son. In fact, she recently let her cook go, deciding she would be happier cooking her own meals, taking care of her home. Her love of art still remains and she often finds time to put her brushes to use. Cynthia's flair for fashion is evident to anyone who has seen this lovely blonde, blue-eyed woman. She once said of John, "I understand everything he does. He may surprise many, but he never surprises me."

But perhaps the highest compliment ever paid her was when a friend said of John and Cyn, "I don't think he would have been half so good if they had not met."

(Series To Be Continued)

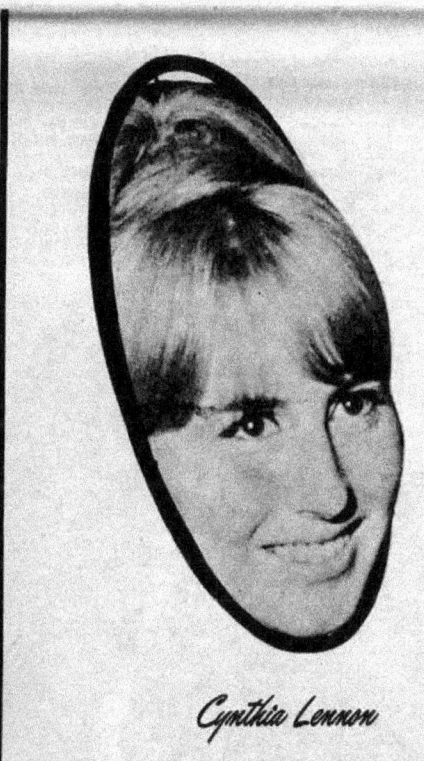
Cynthia Lennon

KRLA ARCHIVES

...FREDDY CANNON

Freddy's Dedicating Songs To Everyone

By Carol Deck

Freddy Cannon took us "Where The Action Is" and now he's back dedicating songs to everyone in town.

He's adding "The Dedication Song" to his remarkable string of hits that started way back with "Tallahassee Lassie" and has included "Way Down Yonder in New Orleans," "Chatanooga Shoe Shine Boy" and "Abigail Beecher."

Freddy's a slender young man from Massachusetts with wavy brown hair, sparkling brown eyes and a very contagious grin. He's got a voice that's instantly recognizable, particularly when he throws in his "wows" in the middle of numbers.

He's been in this business for a while, but then he got his start real early. At the age of seven, when he was living in Revere, Mass. with his parents and sister, he decided he wanted to have a combo like his truck driver father, who still plays lead trumpet in a group called Freddy Carmen and his Orchestra.

Wanted Snap

But his father was more interested in the Guy Lombardo-Lawrence Welk sort of music with a slower beat. Freddy, who was still using his real name of Freddy Picariello, was looking for something with a little more snap to it.

He spent hours listening to people like Hank Williams and Chuck Berry and when he was 15, he and a couple of school chums formed a little band.

After the group, with Freddy on guitar and as lead singer, had reached the top of the "most wanted" list for local teen parties, friends began urging them to try for record hops.

When he was 16, Freddy played his first record hop, and he hasn't stopped since. But it wasn't all fun and games.

Audiences were enthusiastic and seemed to enjoy hearing the group but the group couldn't seem to get anything better than record hops.

At The Bottom

They stayed at the bottom of the rung for almost three years before a couple of record producers finally saw Freddy perform and offered to collaborate with him on a demonstration record.

The result was "Tallahassee Lassie" and within a month it was on the charts around the world and it raced into the top five in the country.

He followed that with hit after hit including his latest—"The Dedication Song."

Somehow, at the end of the record when he says "Ah, ah, ah, ah ... don't touch that dial. I'll be back in a little while," you know he means it.

He'll be back, again and again, with hit after hit. It's become a habit with this young man.

What It Takes To Have A Hit Record

In this second article in our series on record producers, we are going to speak with three of the top young producers in the field of pop music currently. The first two are a team of young men, already familiar to the general public as having been the managers for one of the most popular sining duos in pop music—Sonny and Cher. Their names are Charlie Green and Brian Stone, and they are also the guiding force of their own successful music company, for which Sonny and Cher still record.

In seeking for some workable definition of a good record producer, Brian offered a few of his own, many thoughts on the subject. "A *really* great record producer has an excellent knowledge of music to start with. For example, Spector, Nitzche, Bacharach. That's the upper echelon of record producers. That's one of the necessary ingredients.

"There *are* record producers who don't necessarily have an actual formal knowledge of music—people in this category are able to go into a studio and just be able to recognize it when they hit the right thing."

Special Techniques

I questioned Charlie and Brian as to their own, special techniques of record producing, and Brian explained: "I don't think we use techniques necessarily peculiar to *only* us; I think *our* techniques are similar to other producers. I'd say that our style is a style which is combined of a *number* of other producers'. Almost *everybody* picks up things from other people. And you take the greatest of them—*they've* learned from *somebody*; they've been around sessions, and they pick up little things, and so forth.

"When we go into a studio—when we're actually producing a date—*our* style and technique is similar to, or a combination of, that of other producers."

Although Brian and Charlie refuse to classify themselves in that upper echelon of record producers, they do have their own ideas and theories of how a hit is made: Just briefly, they explained to *The BEAT*—step by step—just how *they* might approach the production of a record.

For A Start

"Usually, when we start, we're either given a song or given an artist. Let's say we hear a song and feel it's great—it's a hit song—then we decide which artist to use on this song. If we haven't got one who's right for it—then we will eventually find an artist who is right for it.

"Then, we'll sit down with an arranger and go over *our* ideas for the arrangements. But basically, we will not come up with formal arrangements most of the time. We'll go into a studio and kind of *ad lib* a little bit! This is a style that Sonny uses.

"Also, when we go into a studio—we go in to cut *only* one song. If we believe in a song, then that's what we go in to cut—*one* song. This is something which Phil Spector does—this is what I mean when I say we employ elements of other people's style. So, we'll go in with a song and chord sheets—then, in the studio ad lib arrangements, and come up with ideas we have, blended with some basic ideas. We'll know in front what kind of instrumentation we want.

What's Needed

Brian and Charlie both seemed to agree that a producer must have a number of abilities in order to produce a really good record today, and Brian attempted to sum up their feelings for us: "A really fine record producer has got to have a knowledge of a great many things. I mentioned before a knowledge of music; he also has to have a tremendous knowledge of what's really *happening* in music today, and got to have a knowledge of various studios and kinds of sounds which you can get out of them.

"He has to have a knowledge of how recordings are made, and he needs a rapport with everyone in the studio. Actually, you've got to have a team of *everybody* together—and that includes your engineer, and your leader, and the arranger, and musicians—the song and the artist, and it's a combination of everything together.

"What I'm talking about is a *really* fine producer—he's got to know how to create that sound that he wants to get. This is that A-1, above average class producer—the guy who has a knowledge of *all* of these elements and knows how to utilize them all and put them all together into one thing. *I* believe that the finest producers are those who have a *complete* knowledge of *everything*."

Finished Product

And what about the finished product? What really *is* a good, hit record? Well, according to mssrs. Greene and Stone: "What we feel constitutes a good, hit record—the elements are, Number One above everything is the song itself. Number Two is the arrangements and production. Number Three is the artist, and Number Four is the promotion of that record. There are actually so *many* elements to a hit record that it's very difficult to list them."

After contemplating the subject for a few moments more, Charlie and Brian finally concluded: "Very few people realize how complex record production is. It's an enormous topic."

Truer words have seldom been spoken! But, nonetheless—we will have a few *more* words being spoken next week when Brian Wilson and Steve Barri give us a further look behind the scenes of record production.

...SONNY, BRIAN STONE, CHARLIE GREEN AND CHER

KRLA ARCHIVES

...PAMELA TIFFIN COMFORTS ROBERT WAGNER.

...PAUL NEWMAN — HARPER.

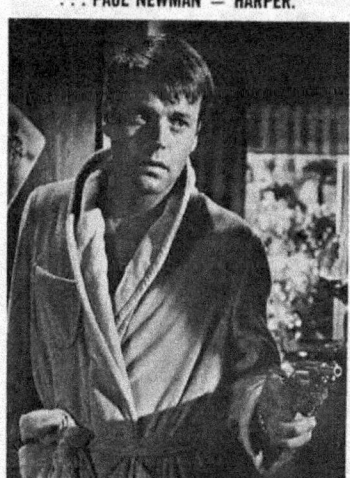

...WAGNER TAKES DEADLY AIM.

THE BEAT GOES TO THE MOVIES
'HARPER'

By Louise Criscione

If you're the type of person who sits up nights reading mystery books just to find out who-done-it, then don't dare miss Warner Brothers' "Harper." The movie is sort of a thinking man's James Bond but the plot is so complicated that perhaps even the great James Bond himself couldn't figure it out!

Handsome, Paul Newman is the hip private-eye, Lew Harper, who through the recommendation of his friend and attorney, Albert Graves (Arthur Hill), agrees to investigate the disappearance of Elaine Sampson's (Lauren Bacall) husband.

And this is where the murders, kidnappings and beatings begin. In fact, so many people meet their deaths that at the end of the movie about the only character left alive is Harper himself and the "bad guys" try their best to rectify that situation.

"Harper" sports an extremely long cast with at least 13 other major characters besides Harper involved in the story. Beautiful Pamela Tiffin, who I'm sure you remember for some of her roles in Beach Party type films, plays Sampson's wayward daughter, Miranda.

Robert Wagner, probably (though unfortunately) best known as Natalie Wood's ex-husband, is Alan Taggert — Sampson's pilot.

Probing deeply into Sampson's life, Harper discovers a photograph of a former movie star, Fay Estabrook (Shelley Winters) in Sampson's Bel Air Hotel suite. Following the lead, Harper pays a visit to Fay and while there receives a mysterious phone call informing him that "the truck is coming through."

Being a proper detective, Harper dutifully traces the call and finds that it came from The Piano Bar. When Harper arrives at The Bar, he finds singer Betty Fraley (Julie Harris) just completing her number. A talk with Betty sheds little light on what Harper now considers Sampson's kidnapping but does cause Harper to be beaten up by the club's bouncer.

Searching still further, Harper learns that in a drunken moment Sampson has given a mountain top to a religious sect. When Harper checks out the Temple In The Clouds he notices the indicative tire marks of a truck firmly emplanted on the driveway.

It would really be unfair of us to reveal any more of the plot to you, but The BEAT strongly suggests that you go and view "Harper" for yourself. Even if you don't care to find out who-done-it, at least you can sit through "Harper" and drool over Paul Newman. That in itself is well worth the price of admission we assure you!

"Harper" opens nation-wide during Easter Week and once again we advise you not to miss it.

...HARPER RESCUES JULIE HARRIS.

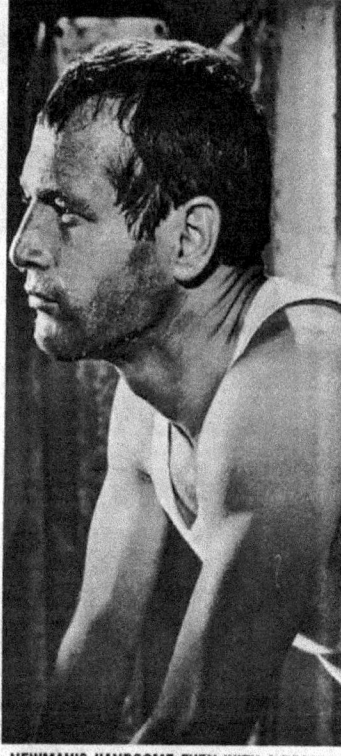

NEWMAN'S HANDSOME EVEN WITH A BEARD.

KRLA ARCHIVES

COMING IN APRIL — THE HOLLIES

Dave Hull's HULLABALOO
The Rock & Roll Showplace of the World
6230 SUNSET (AT VINE) HOLLYWOOD, CALIF.

PRESENTS IN CONCERT

FOR THE FIRST TIME ANYWHERE THE TWO MOST EXCITING GROUPS IN AMERICA

PAUL REVERE & THE RAIDERS

plus

THE PALACE GUARD

THIS CHIP WORTH 50¢ OFF ON A HULLABALOO PIZZA

ONE DAY ONLY 4 P.M.–8 P.M. — SUNDAY, MARCH 13

MARCH 4-6	MARCH 19-20
THE ASTRONAUTS	CHAD & JEREMY

plus

→ **THE PALACE GUARD** ←

MOVIES EVERY SUNDAY *plus* **STAGE SHOW**

MAKE RESERVATIONS — HO. 6-8281

KRLA ARCHIVES

America's Largest Teen NEWSpaper

KRLA Edition BEAT

MARCH 19, 1966

From Taxis To Fleas—What Now Herbie?

KRLA BEAT

Volume 2, Number 1 — March 19, 1966

BEAT Exclusive

Enter the Young

BEAT Photo: Robert Custer

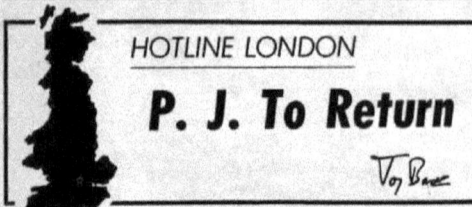

HOTLINE LONDON
P. J. To Return

By Tony Barrow

When his current work permit expires at the beginning of April, P.J. Proby will head for America. Before his departure he plans to play a series of special farewell concert engagements in key cities like Liverpool, Birmingham, Newcastle and Bristol. These shows will be staged at independent venues. The ban placed on Proby by Britain's major theatre chains more than a year ago is still in force.

At the moment, Proby is doing cabaret dates and his act has been toned down to include a string of stylish standards like "Let There Be Love," "I've Got Rhythm" and "Maria."

Dave Berry, David And Jonathan plus Pinkerton's Assorted Colours will be the supporting acts when Herman's Hermits undertake their lengthy U.K. concert tour in April. During his recent Down-Under visit Herman collected a deep sun-tan on the silvery sands of Australia's beaches. With him was Tom Jones and the entire party spent most of their off-duty hours swimming and sunbathing. I guess that's exactly the sort of pastime which has been pleasing The Stones in the last couple of weeks. Before they left London, Mick claimed he'd fit in a bit of surfing and a bit of water-skiing while in Australia. You'll see him in L.A. before we do so I expect he'll tell you all about it.

When The Stones come home to London they'll have a brief break before starting a European tour.

Hey, do you know where The Action is? Right here in London! The Action is a wild new group which is causing the biggest stir of the year on our pop scene. Lead singing man is Reggie King (20); the rest of the outfit consists of four 19-year-olds who produce one of the wildest instrumental sounds around.

The Action have collected high praise from a host of top pop folk – including The Beatles.

Their recording of "I'll Keep Holding On" is to be released in America at the beginning of April when The Action will be on your side of the Atlantic for several impressive television dates.

NEWS BRIEFS... Donovan made a transatlantic call from New York to say how excited he was about the success of his Carnegie Hall concert. At the end of his current coast-to-coast U.S. tour he's playing your Trip Club for ten days and doing two concerts in San Francisco. Donovan's latest U.K. single is "Josie" which he recorded a year ago when "Catch The Wind" was a chart smasher... After Cilla Black's bill-topping appearance on television's "London Palladium Show," she was guest of honour at a celebrity party thrown by Brian Epstein.

'Dance-In' At Cavern

LIVERPOOL – An era came to an end as police closed the famous Cavern Club – birthplace of the Beatles and the British beat – but only after a spirited protest by determined teenagers.

About 100 of them barricaded themselves inside the club to prevent police from closing the club for debts owed by the owner.

Many of the teenagers had been in the Cavern all night. They danced up to the last minute to beat groups pounding out the Liverpool sound from the little stage that gave the Beatles and many others their start on the road to fame.

They barricaded themselves inside when the official bankruptcy receiver went to the Cavern with his assistants to take over the place because a building company had applied to the courts to recover $42,000 owed to it by owner Ray McFall.

Finally police got in through a back door after failing to clear the furniture blocking the narrow stone stairs at the front entrance. Then an era came to an end as the teenagers streamed out in response to an appeal to leave quietly.

Inside the BEAT

Million Dollar Trumpet	2-3
The Love of Sonny and Cher	5
The Music of Miller	6
For Girls Only	7
Adventures of Robin Boyd	10
Spencer Davis On The Run	11
Stoned!!!	12
Yeah, Well Stones	13
Beat's Academy Ballot	14

The BEAT has, in the past, printed the lyrics to what we have felt to be significant songs appearing in the field of contemporary music.

This week we have published the lyrics to a song entitled "Enter The Young." This tune, written by Terry Kirkman of The Association, has not yet been recorded – however we feel that the message contained within its lines are significant enough to be noteworthy.

The song speaks *of* the younger generation, and it speaks *for* the younger generation, and it is spoken *by* a member of that same younger generation. It isn't another of the endless tirades upon the youth of today launched by a stuffy, straight-laced, nameless person with little rhyme or reason.

Instead, it is a simple, straight-forward definition of what seems to be "happening" among our younger citizens. Yes, they *are* thinking – they are doing a great deal of very important thinking these days, and they are *caring* about many of the things which they are thinking about.

Then, after they have done some thinking – they are *doing* something about those thoughts. And that is very important. Idle thoughts alone won't build a world, though they might make some useful contribution in combination with a little positive action.

We, here at *The BEAT*, feel that these words are important enough to warrant a little bit of thought on *our* part – and possibly on *yours* as well. So, we are presenting them here for your consideration... and thought.

Words and music by Terry Kirkman

HERE THEY COME
HERE THEY COME
HERE THEY COME
SOME ARE WALKIN' SOME ARE RIDIN'
HERE THEY COME
SOME ARE FLYIN' SOME JUST GLIDIN'
RELEASED AFTER YEARS OF BEIN' KEPT IN HIDIN'
THEY'RE CLIMBIN' UP THE LADDER RUNG BY RUNG

*ENTER THE YOUNG...YEAH THEY'VE LEARNED TO THINK
ENTER THE YOUNG...MORE THAN YOU THINK THEY THINK
NOT ONLY LEARNED TO THINK BUT TO CARE
NOT ONLY LEARNED TO THINK BUT TO DARE

HERE THEY COME
SOME WITH QUESTIONS SOME DECISIONS
HERE THEY COME
SOME WITH FACTS AND SOME WITH VISIONS
OF A PLACE TO MULTIPLY WITHOUT THE USE OF DIVISIONS
TO WIN A PRIZE THAT NO ONE'S EVER WON
ENTER THE YOUNG.........REPEAT CHORUS

HERE THEY COME
SOME ARE LAUGHIN' SOME ARE CRYIN'
HERE THEY COME
SOME ARE DOIN' SOME ARE TRYIN'
SOME ARE SELLIN' SOME ARE BUYIN'
SOME ARE LIVIN' SOME ARE DYIN'
BUT DEMANDING RECOGNITION ONE BY ONE
ENTER THE YOUNG.........REPEAT CHORUS

*CHORUS

KRLA ARCHIVES

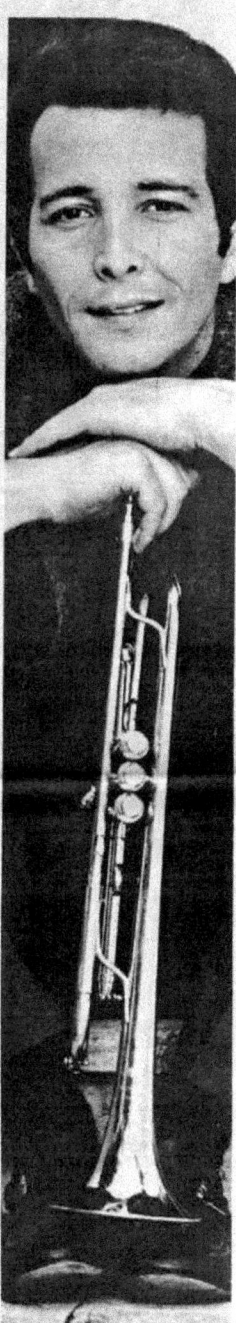

"You have to know where you're going"

■ HERBIE and his horn.

... HERB proudly displays his two BEAT awards.

the million dollar TRUMPET

■ HERB and the TJ Brass receive the cheers of the crowd.

By Louise Criscione

■ They say that in order to make a lasting name for yourself in the music business you've got to come up with something which is original and fresh. Of course, that new "something" has also got to catch the public's listening ear and force them to delve into their wallets and part with a few of those greenbacks.

Herb Alpert is one man who has accomplished all of those things with his Mexican-flavored musical arrangements. Herb calls it "Quasi-Mexican; a combination of American and Mariachi." But the whole idea was an impulse with Herb, sort of a spur of the moment idea which actually came about by accident.

"One night a friend of mine, Sol Lake, was playing a tune on the piano—something called 'Twinkle Star,' one of those persistent melodies that pops into your head when you wake up and refuses to go away," recalled Herb.

"It seemed to me to lend itself perfectly to a Spanish tempo. We worked with it for awhile adding trumpet, piano, bass drums and mandolin, using my voice and that of the mandolin player, plus a girl singer.

Excitement

"Then we incorporated the sounds of the Tijuana arena—the trumpet call as the bull comes out, the roar of the crowd, all the noise and excitement of the bull ring," finished Herb.

And what he eventually came up with was his first smash single, the one that brought his name, his trumpet and his Tijuana Brass to the attention of the public. The record, of course, was "The Lonely Bull."

That first inspiration came about by accident but Herb's musical ability and his way with a trumpet were anything but accidental—they were plain hard work.

"You have to know where you're going," Herb believes. And he certainly knows where he's headed and he knows where he came from too—a musical family. His mother played violin, his father the mandolin, his sister the piano and his brother the drums.

"We could have had our own orchestra and doubled as a basketball team," laughs Herb.

KRLA ARCHIVES

Unusually enough, Herb's prowess on the trumpet was aided along by his two year stint in the Army which he spent as the solo trumpeter with the Sixth Army Band at the Presidio in San Francisco. You may consider that an easy job until you learn that Herb's assignment often meant playing taps for as many as eighteen funerals in one day!

Since "Lonely Bull" Herb and his Tijuana Brass have been nothing but busy. They're released several follow-up singles, the latest being a fantastic version of "What Now My Love," and all of which have repeated Alpert's first taste of record success.

Albums have not been overlooked by Herb either. So far, he has released five long-players, four of which are currently in the nation's top 15 best selling albums.

BEAT readers started Alpert's award winning ball off by voting Herb and the Brass the most popular instrumental group and choosing "Lonely Bull" as the best instrumental single record of 1965 in the BEAT's First Annual International Pop Music Awards.

More Awards

Herb's latest award was made recently by Ricardo Montalban. It was a citation from Los Angeles' mayor, Sam Yorty, praising Alpert on his award from the Mexican Government "for promoting Mexico and Mexican folk music throughout the world in concert, on television and through recordings."

Although Alpert's dark and handsome features make Herb appear to have actually come from South of the Border – he did not. In fact, he is a graduate of L.A.'s Fairfax High.

Still, Herb *has* promoted Mexican music throughout the entire world. His latest conquest was Holland where his discs have just been released and are ascending the native charts so rapidly that it's almost unbelievable.

There is practically nothing which Herb hasn't already done or is not about to do. He has just completed a one night tour which would stagger a smaller entertainer and is currently out on the road with another set of one night stands which would make most performers drool.

On March 10 Alpert and the T.J. Brass were in England for three days for a gigantic concert sponsored by Brian Epstein as well as some spots on the BBC.

White House

Stateside again, Herb has been asked by President Johnson to be the sole entertainment at the White House Press Ball on March 25 – an achievement for *any* American.

March will also bring Herb to both the Dean Martin and Danny Kaye television shows and will see Herb release his sixth album. I say *Herb* will release the album because, you see, he and Jerry Moss own the record company, A&M Records, for which Alpert cuts.

And that's not all – on April 12 Herb will headline a show at Carnegie Hall and throughout the rest of April Herb will be busy on a one-night stand tour of the Eastern U.S.

A busy, talented, genuinely nice human being. Put them all together and they spell Mr. Herb Alpert – a gas of an entertainer.

OLE! OLE!

KRLA ARCHIVES

"THE MAN FROM CAPITOL" — David McCallum — ventured forth with some copies of his first LP, "Music — A Part of Me," recently in order to meet his fans, and to autograph their copies of his LP and his latest single. The autograph party was a huge success, attracting hundreds of fans, and was soon repeated in subsequent appearances. Ah, well — it's a spy's life!

Art Of Autograph Hunting

What's your favorite sport? If it's fishing, baseball or ping pong, this feature may not be exactly your dish of tea. But, if it's autograph hunting, you've come to the right place! Here are ten simple (we said it, you didn't) rules to help you bait the trap, and they're *guaranteed* to help you bag bigger and better catches!

1. First and foremost, don't feel silly about asking a star for his autograph. Many hunters miss the chance and the signature of a lifetime because they're afraid of acting like a "fan." There is nothing nitty about being a fan. If you ever need to be reassured of this fact, stop and think where our faves would be *without* us. When you request an autograph, you're paying the star a compliment. If you're concerned that you might see him again, and would rather he didn't remember you as an "autograph hound," stop worrying. And start hoping he'll remember you, period!

2. Never tell a star the autograph is really for someone else, even if it is. People who say "this is for my Aunt Mable's Uncle Agnes," or some such, are a standing joke in the entertainment field.

3. If you want the star to sign the autograph to a particular person (yourself, for instance, or whomever) say so immediately, before he starts writing. Don't tell him what message to write. Just say "please sign this to so-and-so" and spell the name if it's an unusual one.

4. When you go autograph hunting, go armed! And prepared! (Would a fisherman leave rod and reel at home?) Take a pencil or a pen (incidentally, a star will be more responsive to signing with pencil than with pen), and a small tablet (with a hard back) or an autograph book. Top-notch hunters keep this equipment on hand at all times, just in case. It's best not to ask unless you can provide the necessary materials. Many stars have to refuse not out of choice, but simply because there's nothing to write on or with.

5. If you are caught unprepared, there is one way out. Round up a ball-point pen and ask him to sign the back of your hand. The signature can be transferred by pressing it very hard against paper.

6. Don't ask for an autograph when a star is going every whichway, or when he is in the middle of a meal or a conversation. Timing is just as important in autograph hunting as it is in any other sport.

7. Speaking of sports, if a star says no to your request, be a good one. Don't go away mad, just go away. This sort of thing doesn't happen without a reason, and since you have no way of knowing what that reason may be (unless it's painfully obvious and someone has just torn out a large handful of his hair), respect his wishes and he'll respect you for it.

8. Any star with his wits about him will refuse to sign a large sheet of paper that is otherwise blank, for various and assorted legal reasons. If this is the only size paper you have with you, tear it in fourths before making your request.

9. Autograph hunting by mail is often more successful than the in-person plan. State your request briefly, and enclose a stamped, self-addressed envelope, along with a small sheet of paper for the signature. The simpler you make this task for the star, the better your chances.

10. Make things even simpler by writing the following on the outside of the envelope (front left hand corner is a good spot, at the bottom of the envelope): *Request — Autograph Only. Return Envelope Enclosed.* Remember, a star has very little time to read his mail, and even less to answer it. If he's in the mood, or has a few moments to reply, he will naturally choose those letters which will require the least time and effort.

P.S. — Happy hunting! No, make that *happier*!

On the BEAT

By Louise Criscione

Is Chrissie Shrimpton or is she not accompanying Mick Jagger on the Stones' Australian tour? Pictures taken at London Airport seem to indicate that she definitely is.

John Steel is leaving the Animals just as their latest hit, "Inside Looking Out," is bounding up the charts. His reason for splitting is simple and has nothing to do with inner-group feuds or anything like that. It's just that with the hectic life lead by the Animals, John found very little time to spend with his wife and daughter. So, he decided to chuck his career for a decent family life and will return to Newcastle (Animal's hometown) as the manager of a boutique.

Herman reveals that he had a fantastic time during his first visit to Australia and the Far East. Says that in Japan all of the Hermits purchased those ceremonial masks to "improve our looks!"

Although full-scale tours of Britain have slackened off considerably, Herman will undertake one this Spring along with the Mindbenders and Pinkerton's (Assort.) Colours. The tour kicks off on April 7 at Dover and winds up on the 20th in Edinburgh.

...JOHN STEEL

Cilla's Comin'

Watch for Cilla Black to return Stateside next month for appearances on "Ed Sullivan" and "Johnny Carson." Cilla has previously guested on both shows and quite obviously they'd like her back — and so would we. She's great!

Have to admit that I (along with Susie, our receptionist) goofed a good one when we received a copy of Slim Harpo's "Baby Scratch My Back." Neither of us had ever heard the record before but just by looking at the label we cracked up!

But after hearing the disc we are now both properly ashamed. It's one of the best records out today — and to think we actually *laughed*!

Dionne Warwick went down fabulously in Paris but I'm afraid her remarks in England won't win her any "Best Liked Female" award. She knocked several fellow entertainers as well as stating that no one except a Negro could possibly achieve what is referred to in the business as the "colored sound."

It drew quite a bit of response from irate readers — one of whom went so far as to say that Dionne herself sounds white!

"Soul" For Len

Speaking of the "colored sound," Len Barry thinks he has it. "I do a very different act from most white people," said Len, "I don't sing well enough to stand still and sing for forty minutes!" Perhaps that's the reason for people suddenly tagging Len, "Mr. Excitement."

The British television spectacular, "The Music Of Lennon and McCartney," has been entered for the Golden Rose Of Montreux International TV Festival which will take place from April 22 to April 30. *The BEAT* wishes you the best of luck, boys.

Wayne Fontana, very much minus the Mindbenders, is negotiating a tour of the U.S. for 15 days beginning in late March. However, since Wayne has had only one previous Stateside hit, "Game Of Love," it is quite likely that the Union will not issue him a work permit. It's happened before, you know.

Eric Burdon certainly has an outspoken nature. He recently criticized all American acts, "with maybe just a couple of exceptions," for their pre-arranged stage acts.

In The Mirror

Eric is entitled to his opinion, of course, but before he makes remarks like that he should look at himself on stage. On records the Animals sound great but their stage act (which quite obviously has *not* been rehearsed) leaves much to be desired.

I saw them "live" and to say that they could have done with some polishing up would be the understatement of the century!

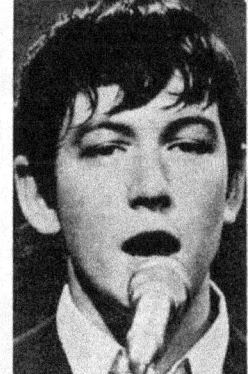

...ERIC BURDON

I don't mean that they should all learn little dance steps or anything like that, but the long minutes of Animal discussion before each number could be eliminated by simply knowing what songs they are going to do before they ever set foot on stage. It's called professionalism, Eric, and it's worth a lot.

KRLA ARCHIVES

ℒove, ℒove

"I'm more comfortable with kids than with anyone else. Kids are so open, and they're more eager to *give* love and to *receive* love, and they like to *see* love. I think it's very important for the kids to be able to see two people who are married and who are very much in love."

These are the words of Sonny Bono—one half of a very *loving* couple. Both Sonny and his beautiful wife Cher believe in the great powers of love, and try constantly to communicate their love for one another—as well as their very genuine love for their fans—to all of their many fans.

It is a very honest sort of love which Sonny and Cher have for their fans, and Sonny is very sincere when he tells you: "It's really nice when you don't have to put it on. The kids know when you're putting them on and when you're not. I think that we have a lot of respect from them, and I appreciate it. I *know* we have a lot of respect for *them*. I love 'em!!"

It is this honest sort of a relationship which Sonny and Cher have with their fans which has endeared them to so many and formed a bond of loyalty between them. Sonny takes great pride

(Turn to Page 6)

BEAT Photo: Robert Custer

KRLA ARCHIVES

his kind of MAGIC

By Shirley Poston

The first time a lot of people saw Roger Miller, he was toting luggage, and lots of it. Because he was a bell-hop at the Andrew Jackson Hotel in Nashville, Tenn.

The first time I saw Roger Miller, it was eight years later and he was carrying six chairs. Because he was a nice guy.

The latter happened in 1965, at the filming of the "Million Dollar Music" TV spectacular.

"Hi, Pat!" I said, smiling as he passed by me.

"Hi," he answered, nearly dropping at least four of the chairs.

Just then, a nearby friend gave me a crashing stomp on the toe. "What do you mean 'hi, Pat?'" she hissed.

I returned the stomp. "Wasn't that Pat Boone?" I hissed.

"No, you nut!"

"Well??? Who was it then?"

"I don't know," she replied. "But I do know it wasn't Pat Boone."

About an hour later, after having walked several thousand miles up and down the corridors of the television studio, falling over some cables and leaping over others, I saw "Pat" again.

He was carrying more chairs. Eyeing them greedily, I smiled again. "Do you think I could have one of those?"

"They're for inside," he answered pleasantly, gesturing toward the filming area. "But I'll help you find one in a minute." And, in a minute, he did.

The next time I saw him that evening, he was before the TV cameras, singing "Dang Me." And dang me if I didn't almost fall over the aforementioned chair.

That wasn't Pat Boone! Nor was it a helpful studio employee! That was the famous Roger Miller!

I couldn't help but wonder why the famous Roger Miller had been doing double duty as usher and official chair-finder, but I found out about two seconds later.

He was well into his song when the cameras suddenly ground to a halt. And, due to some too-technical-for-me problem, the filming did not resume until some forty-five minutes later.

During that wait, Roger didn't rush off to the nearest coke machine. He stayed on stage, doing songs and comedy routines for the audience, and when we were ready to roll again, every teenager in the place leaped up and gave him a standing ovation. Which I, needless to say, joined.

...ROGER MILLER
BEAT Photo: Robert Custer

Roger has had much the same effect on everyone who has come into contact with the Miller brand of magic. With the exception of the Grand Ole Opry where he tried and failed to get his start.

This hometown boy just didn't make good in the Grand Ole. He was, as one friend put it, "too in and too far out to buck the Opry's conservatism."

Even his on-the-house performances at "Tootsies," a lounge in Nashville which has long been a home away from home for the country music clan, didn't spark an interest in his antics.

But, when the record-buying public got a look and a listen, things changed. Roger Miller stepped out of the sidelines to become the biggest thing to hit pop music since the Beatles.

Last year, which was his first as a star, he literally stole the show at the Grammy Awards, walking off with five, count 'em five of the six C&W awards.

And it looks like he's about to do it again. This year, he's been nominated in *nine* categories!

His "King Of The Road" netted him five of these nominations. Record of the year, song of the year, best male vocal performance, best contemporary record, and best contemporary male vocal performance.

He was also nominated in four C&W categories. Best C&W single, best C&W male vocal performance, best C&W song (all three for "King Of The Road") and best C&W album ("The Return of Roger Miller.")

Although he is most assuredly at the top, Miller remains very down to earth. Everything around him has changed, but he hasn't. Progressed, of course, but not changed.

Just as an example, to this day he still employs the same musicians who backed him on his first hit. He won't record unless they're right there with him.

It's my guess that Roger Miller will be carrying on for years to come. And that he'll never be too much of a "King" to carry a few chairs while he's at it.

The Lasting Love Of Sonny And Cher

(Continued from Page 5)

in telling you, "The most gratifying thing of all is that people have accepted us and like us for what we *are* – not for our next record."

Nearly everyone in the music industry predicted the largest hit ever for Sonny and Cher with "What Now My Love?" and it is still a mystery to many as to just why it never made it to the Number One position on the charts. When we suggested to Sonny that possibly the theme – that of breaking up – was so contrary to their own image that it upset people, he thought about it for a moment and then disagreed.

"I don't think so. Just look at Cher's latest record, "Bang, Bang" – that has the same theme, but that's a hit. But then, there's a contradiction for everything you say in the record business!"

Sonny finds it difficult to understand why some people insist upon taunting and harassing people, such as himself, who wear their hair in a long style. Then he notes that they usually wait until they have you on "unequal terms – usually when you're sitting all by yourself in a corner minding your own business."

Instead of making fun of everyone else around you, Sonny seems to find it much more agreeable to simply *accept* the other people and understand that we are all just a little bit different in our own individual ways.

Sonny might remind you of a very lovable little puppy dog – with his huge brown eyes and long brown hair, and I couldn't help feeling a little sad when he explained to me how lonely he had been when Cher had to go into the hospital for a few days recently when she was suffering from acute influenza and bronchitis. He looked up with a very sad expression and explained, "I don't like to be alone, and I missed her very much."

When both Sonny and Cher are at home, they frequently play host and hostess to many of their fans who have, in one way or another, managed to locate their new house. There are many other top name entertainers who would be quite perturbed at having their privacy continually violated, but Sonny actually enjoys having an opportunity to get to know their fans.

Very often, if they are not extremely busy, Sonny and Cher will invite their visitors inside and will show them around their lovely new home – of which they are quite rightfully very proud – and will spend some time speaking with them.

But Sonny explains gratefully that all of the kids who come to visit them have been very well-mannered and respectful of their privacy. "They never insist on coming in if I explain to them that we are hung up at the moment and ask them if they could come back later."

In fact, just recently Sonny bought himself a brand new motorbike – and immediately shared it with all of his fans! "I bought a new motorcycle and that was the big event of the day around here! So I took a whole bunch of the kids who came over out riding with me. It was great – we really had a ball!"

Many have commented on Sonny and Cher's unique style of dress, and especially upon the *absence* of Cher's *dresses!* But when I asked Sonny whether or not it was an absolute impossibility that Cher would ever wear a real, honest-to-goodness dress, he laughed and said, "She *would* wear a dress if there was really a good reason for it. If the occasion called for it, I might even put on a tux!"

Now *that* definitely *would* be wild! Can you see Sonny and Cher in a dress and a tuxedo??!!! At any rate, they are designing their own line of clothes now which are being put on the market by one particular manufacturer. Sonny explains, "Cher designs all of her own clothes and most of these clothes. But we won't let anything go out if it's trash. If we wouldn't wear them or if we couldn't want them, then we won't let them go out."

Currently, Sonny and Cher are living a hectic life in which their daily schedule is utterly chaotic. At the same time, they are trying to make their very first movie – for which Sonny has collaborated on the script, and is writing all of the music and doing the scoring, producing two new albums – one for Cher and one for both of them, preparing for a European tour, scheduled to begin as soon as the movie is completed, and appearing on various television shows.

It is a hectic, whirlwind life sped up to a truly jet-age pace, but one which they enjoy. It is a life of creativity, and of love; a love which they share in their marriage, and a love which they reserve exclusively for their public. Sonny says quite earnestly of all of their fans: "They're the ones who put us there, and we can never forget that!" And it is for certain that they won't – this is one marriage, private *and* public – which will last forever.

More Movies Set For Elvis

Elvis Presley has just been signed by MGM for four more movies. With the two he's already set for, this brings to six the number of Presley pictures we can await.

The King starts filming his latest, tentatively titled either "Jim Dandy" or "Never Say Yes," this month. The second film set for this year is called "It's Killing Me" and will be filmed this summer.

The latest contract signed by the King with MGM calls for two pictures a year over three years and means that by 1969 he will have starred in 12 movies for MGM.

KRLA ARCHIVES

Grammy Nominees Poised And Ready

Each year as the motion picture industry is preparing itself for the big night of the year, Oscar night, the music industry hands out its awards for the best musical contributions of the year.

To the recording artist, the Grammy is as prized as the Oscar is to the movie star. Perhaps even more so because there are more records put out in one year than there are movies put out in *six* years! So, to capture a Grammy one must really shine.

This year a country singer, a Mexican-styled instrumental group and an English, instrumental-singing quartet top the list of candidates awarded by members of the National Academy of Recording Arts and Sciences (nicknamed the NARAS).

The singer is, of course, Nashville's Roger Miller whose "King Of The Road" recording has popped up in *nine* different categories. It was Roger who last year walked off with the most Grammy awards, winning in practically every single category in which he was nominated.

Alpert Too

The instrumental outfit is Herb Alpert's Tijuana Brass which has drawn enough votes in the next-to-final round to place in six different divisions.

And the English group, as I'm sure you've already guessed, is the Beatles. Their single, "Yesterday," captured six spots and their album "Help," won four more nominations giving the Beatles a chance to win in *ten* categories.

All three—Miller, Alpert and the Beatles—have been nominated for "Record Of The Year" honors along with the Ramsey Lewis' recording of "The 'In' Crowd," and Tony Bennett's version of "The Shadow Of Your Smile." The Bennett single also shows up in five additional categories including "Best Song Of The Year."

Miller, the Tijuana Brass and the Beatles have also qualified for this year's "Album Of The Year" Grammy. Here they are joined by the sound track album for "The Sound Of Music," Eddy Arnold's "My World" and Frank Sinatra's "September Of My Years."

Sinatra In Six

Besides "Best Album Of The Year" Frank Sinatra appears in four other categories with his "September of My Years" while his smash single, "It Was A Very Good Year" racks up two more award nominations.

The Grammy Awards, which incidently are based on quality of performance rather than the quantity of sales, encompass 47 different categories ranging from strict pop and contemporary to jazz, folk, country and western, rhythm and blues, Broadway shows, spoken word, religious, children's and classical music with eleven categories devoted entirely to the serious music field.

The end of February is the deadline for Academy members to return their ballots to the independent accounting firm of Haskins and Sells for tabulations. Winners of the Grammys will then be announced on Tuesday evening, March 15, at star-studded award ceremonies in New York, Los Angeles, Chicago and Nashville.

In addition to the top categories of "Best Record," "Best Song," "Best Album" and "Best Vocal performance—Male and Female" interest is running exceptionally high this year in the category of "Best New Artist" with such people as the Byrds, Herman's Hermits, Tom Jones, Sonny & Cher and Glenn Yarbrough all giving it a run for their money.

March 15 will tell the tale and you can bet that all of the nominees are sitting on pins and needles waiting to see if their name will be called as winner of one of the precious Grammys.

For Girls Only
By Shirley Poston

Would anyone care to join me in a teacher roast?

Boy, am I mad!! And I don't mean as a March hare, although there's a nasty rumor going 'round that I'm that, too. (Not a March hare, as mad as one.) (I hope.)

I won't bore you with the endless details of what a certain very young and very handsome English (yeah, yeah, yeah) teacher was doing at our house the other night, but I'm about to bore you with what happened!

I wasn't there when he arrived, and during a lull in the conversation with my little brother (which accounts for the lull in the conversation in the first place) (huh?), he just happened to pick up one of the several million Beats which just happen to litter the old homestead beyond belief.

Then, a few moments later, I walked in. And what were his first words to me? (I ask you?) After all, we'd met before. He could have at least started with "hullo." But, no. Instead he looked up and said: "This is the silliest thing I've ever read in my life."

"The BEAT?" I bristled.

Scatter Brain

"No," he replied. "A column called 'For Girls Only' written by a scatter-brain called Shirley Poston."

Well! (Not to mention thanks a lot and I'll try to do the same for you sometime, fella.)

Of course, he had no *idea* that *I* was the scatter-brain called Shirley Poston. (As I've told you previously, for various and assorted reasons, S.P. is my "pen name." (Among those reasons is the fact that I'm a coward.)

But that's beside the point. He was also absolutely *right*, but that's beside the point too! My brother knows, and you should have *heard* him egging "Teach" on!

Want to hear his final analysis of me? I am, and I quote, "a very sick eleven-year-old."

Well, I'll have him know that I am most certainly *not* eleven. (I was once, but that is certainly none of *his* business.)

I just read all this over before continuing to rave and I have come to the following conclusion. The point all this is beside is right square on top of my head. Crikeys, I was only going to write a couple of paragraphs about this incident, and really fix those two louts, and I've written a *novel* instead (I can hardly *wait* until they make it into a movie) (however, something tells me I'm going to have to, for a *very* long time.)

Unfolds His Hair

Now, about that fixing. The English teacher in question is not as dull as he may sound. Every morning before school, he gets up an hour early to comb his hair. Why??? Because it is *disgracefully* (otherwise known as *marvelously*) long and the short-locks rule at his school applies to teachers as well as students. Then, after work, he spends another hour *unfolding* his hair! So *there!!*

As for my brother, some of his deep, dark secrets are: (1) He smokes pretzels. (I am *not* kidding! He calls it "practicing up.") (2) He has a desperate crush on Cynthia Lennon, and spends hours dreaming up ways to take her away from John (hopefully, he will someday succeed). (3) He has an English china tea pot on his dresser with a picture of himself in it! (He got the idea from several of you who've written to me, saying you're giving tea-pots-with-pix-of-special-faves-inside as birthday gifts.) (Which makes absolutely no sense whatsoever if you don't happen to be acquainted with a rare bird by the name of Robin Boyd.) (And if you aren't, you haven't lived.) (Modesty does not number among my many virtues.)

Jeez. Who was I talking about before all *that?* Oh, yes. That wretch who shares my roof. The only good thing about him is a *disgracefully* long lot of blond hair. By the way, he's sixteen, and if anyone would like to write him a note (enclosing a bomb), send same to Jimmy J. Poston (the J. stands for JERK) in care of me in care of *The BEAT*, whatever *that* means.

Now, enough of this sensible, rational palaver. And on to ... you guessed it ... speaking of George!!

Just think, somewhere he's *breathing* ...

Sorry about that. I have a tendency to get carried away. By men bearing large nets, that is.

But, I do have a new Beatle idea for you. Remember a few million columns ago when I raved on indefinitely about Bear Scares? In case you haven't the foggiest of what I'm blithering about (join the crowd), a Bear Scare is an Indian charm which is supposed to ward off evil and make wishes come true as well.

But, someone has thought up something even better called a Beatle Scare! Here's what you do. Take a piece of rawhide and tie four knots in same. Then tie it around your right wrist. The fifth knot is for yourself, signifying that you wish for the safety of the foursome.

Stop Caring

And the most beautiful part about the whole thing is the remark this someone made when I asked her when you were supposed to remove the Beatle Scare.

She just looked at me and said: *"When you stop caring."*

This is really maudlin and grotty and all that, but I put my Beatle Scare on the night some real pal came running up to me with the good news that one of the Beatles had been critically injured and was nearing death's door. It turned out to be the non-critical McCartney Vs. Motorbike incident, but all the same, I about had a relapse.

I can't exactly say I believe in magic (Sorry about that, Lovin' Spoonful). But I do believe this. The more people who wish you well, the well-er you are. Oh comma brother, I'm a *writer??* But you know what I mean. I don't know why I always try to explain stuff to you ... sometimes I think you know me better than I know myself ... and that in a funny way, we're all the same person.

Good as in gravy, what am I raving about *now?* Anyway, don't hesitate to wear a Beatle Scare (or an any-other-star-Scare) because it can't be removed. I had (and I *do* mean *had*) to attend a very formal (not to mention fiendish) thingy a few nights back and several simps simpered: "Ohhh, what a perfectly divine leather bracelet!"

Just watch it when it's your turn to do the dishes. Rawhide stretches! Speaking of rawhide (thought I was going to say George, diddanya?), if you can't find so much as an inch (I realize it's somewhat difficult to walk into a department store and say "I'd like enough rawhide to go around me right wrist."), just send me a stamped, self-addressed envelope and I'll provide same.

Put the letters R.H. in the lower left hand corner of the envelope (the one you send the self-addressed one in) (I repeat, I'm a *writer??*) and I'll send you enough rawhide to fashion your own Star Scare (I'll send it faster if it's for a Beatle scare). (It isn't necessary for you to send a letter in return saying "thongs a lot," but it would be nice.) And don't forget to make a special personal wish, in addition to hoping for the safety of your faves, when you tie the knots.

Also, don't forget to read my column next *BEAT*. In it, I hope to mention all the sensible, rational items which I can't seem to remember for the life of me.

BRITISH TOP TEN

1. **19TH NERVOUS BREAKDOWN**
   The Rolling Stones
2. **THESE BOOTS ARE MADE FOR WALKIN'**
   Nancy Sinatra
3. **GROOVY KIND OF LOVE**
   The Mindbenders
4. **MY LOVE**
   Petula Clark
5. **YOU WERE ON MY MIND**
   Crispian St. Peters
6. **SHA LA LA LA LEE**
   The Small Faces
7. **INSIDE LOOKING OUT**
   The Animals
8. **BARBRA ANN**
   The Beach Boys
8. **LOVE IS JUST A BROKEN HEART**
   Cilla Black
10. **MIRROR, MIRROR**
    Pinkertons Asst'd Colours

DRUMMERS

YOU HIP TO METAL DRUMSTICKS?

Experts agree... Practicing with these weapons will do these important things for YOUR BEAT!

- Give you more **power**—to make yourself heard above amplified instruments.
- Give you new **stick control**—to play today's beat with more precision and fire.
- Give you more **endurance**—to keep excitement at its peak all nite long.

Try 'em and see for yourself what fantastic results will follow.
ORDER YOUR PAIR NOW!

$5.95

Harriman's
1884 Pandora Avenue
Los Angeles, Calif. 90025

(Sorry, no C.O.D.'s)

KRLA ARCHIVES

KRLA Tunedex

This Week	Last Week	Title	Artist
1	2	CALIFORNIA DREAMIN'	The Mamas & Papas
2	1	THESE BOOTS ARE MADE FOR WALKIN'	Nancy Sinatra
3	3	LISTEN PEOPLE	Herman's Hermits
4	24	DAYDREAM	The Lovin' Spoonful
5	8	THE BALLAD OF THE GREEN BERET	Sgt. Barry Sadler
6	41	NOWHERE MAN	The Beatles
7	20	19TH NERVOUS BREAKDOWN	Rolling Stones
8	5	I AIN'T GONNA EAT OUT MY HEART ANYMORE	Young Rascals
9	6	HOMEWARD BOUND	Simon & Garfunkel
10	4	YOU BABY	The Turtles
11	12	I'M SO LONESOME I COULD CRY	B.J. Thomas & Triumphs
12	40	BANG BANG	Cher
13	19	WOMAN	Peter & Gordon
14	11	ZORBA THE GREEK/TIJUANA TAXI	Herb Alpert & T.J. Brass
15	16	LOVE (MAKES ME DO FOOLISH THINGS)	Martha & The Vandellas
16	9	TIME	The Pozo-Seco Singers
17	14	DON'T MESS WITH BILL	The Marvelettes
18	33	WALKIN' MY CAT NAMED DOG	Norma Tanega
19	25	DARLING BABY	The Elgins
20	29	THE CHEATER	Bob Kuban
21	18	BATMAN THEME	Neal Hefti
22	23	WAKE ME, SHAKE ME	Four Tops
23	17	WORKIN' MY WAY BACK TO YOU	The Four Seasons
24	32	CALL ME	Chris Montez
25	22	KEEP ON RUNNING	Spencer Davis Group
26	34	BABY SCRATCH MY BACK	Slim Harpo
27	31	HUSBANDS & WIVES	Roger Miller
28	36	LOVE MAKES THE WORLD GO ROUND	Deon Jackson
29	—	SOUL AND INSPIRATION	The Righteous Bros.
30	—	THIS OLD HEART OF MINE	The Isley Bros.
31	—	INSIDE-LOOKING OUT	The Animals
32	38	FOLLOW ME	Lyme & Cybelle
33	—	SURE GONNA MISS HER	Gary Lewis & The Playboys
34	35	IT'S TOO LATE	Bobby Goldsboro
35	—	KICKS	Paul Revere & The Raiders
36	—	ONE TRACK MIND	The Knickerbockers
37	—	SPANISH FLEA/WHAT NOW MY LOVE	Herb Alpert
38	10	FIVE O'CLOCK WORLD	The Vogues
39	13	JUST LIKE ME	Paul Revere & The Raiders
40	7	A WELL RESPECTED MAN	The Kinks

DAVE HULL

BOB EUBANKS

DICK BIONDI

JOHNNY HAYES

EMPEROR HUDSON

CASEY KASEM

CHARLIE O'DONNELL

BILL SLATER

Holy Rock And Roll!

Holy rock 'n' roll, kiddies! — the Marketts have done it again!!! These six talented Hollywood musicians have once again crashed (zock, poww, bamm!) to national prominance with their single recording of the Batman theme.

Their first smash hit was a tune called "Out Of Limits," which has now sold well over one million copies in the United States and around the world. Now the boys are on their way to another disc success with their instrumental recording of the theme song that rocked the world . . . of rock 'n' roll!

Under the direction of Dick Glasser, the Marketts raced into a recording studio just one night after the "Batman" series made its TV debut, and in just 24 hours — recorded, mastered, and shipped the finished product to disc jockeys all across the nation.

KRL "Art"

Pictured here at right are just a few of the more than 70,000 entries which were received in the Fifth Annual Valentine Art Festival.

The contest was a smashing success, and so was the showing of many of the entries held later at Bob Eubank's Long Beach Cinnamon Cinder.

One of the most unusual entries received during the duration of the contest was a 15-foot, upside down hanging red and white bat! The friendly creature is now hanging decoratively in the lobby of KRLA's popular studios.

Pictured on the opposite page is one of the entries submitted to the contest, created by Mason Williams, a talented composer-author-singer from Hollywood. One of the most unusual entries — and also one of the most beautiful, with three verses of poetry hand-printed on three of the window's panes.

The entry which finally walked off with the first place prize of $1,000 was submitted by Pat Jamieson of Newhall, and featured a dazzling array of lights on a huge heart which actually opened up.

All in all, the contest was a huge success, and as soon as all of the KRLA DJ's can finish clearing out the upstairs Bat Cave of all the 70,000 entries — we can begin anticipating *next* year's contest!!!

PARIS SISTERS stop by KRLA and capture disc jockey, Casey Kasem.

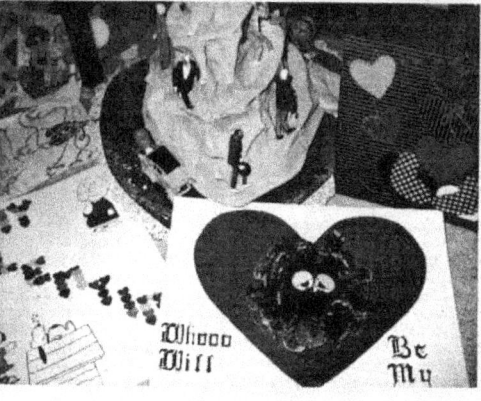

KRLA ARCHIVES

Inside KRLA

Believe it or not... KRLA *still* hasn't recuperated from Valentine's Day! Still very much present in the lovely foyer area of the illustrious studios is the red and white, upside-down hanging bat, which "hangs" about 15 feet tall! Actually it really *is* quite impressive to walk in the door and immediately be greeted by a red and white upside-down creature dangling high above your head!

This has been a week of many questions, both in and of the BatcAve-RLA. For example, do *you* know just exactly what is in the mysterious, camel-guarded closet in the upstairs Bat Cave? It is rumored that several top Hollywood personalities have been seen quietly leaving the Cave of late... but *no one* is talking about it!

Another prominent question on the minds of many this week is a true-and-falsie: Is it really *true* what they say about the boiling feud between Bob Eubanks and Dick Biondi? Also, what is the real story—black though it may be—behind John Barrett's matchsticks?

A Eumephowl??

And, most important of all: What—that is, just *what*—is a Groovy Eumephowl?? (Only our Groovy Leader knows, and he won't even tell his hairdresser!!!)

Memo from the Bat Cave: The Bat Kits are now in their third printing; word about town is that copies of the first edition are now collector's items! (If anyone should come across one such item, please forward it to Dick Moreland, along with any spare sticky Bat Dealies you might have laying around as the poor soul has been unable to obtain any of his very own!)

Then there's poor Bob Eubanks, who seems to have to suffer far more than his own fair share of trouble and woe! You may remember last week when we explained the sad story of Bob's rejection by Nancy Sinatra. You would most certainly think that it would be enough to have your most heartfelt, and sincere proposal of marriage completely *ignored*—but, no! Fate is not yet done with our boy Robert.

You may, or may not, be aware that Bob has been driving a new white Cadillac for some time now. Well, through no fault of his own, Bob and his beloved auto have come to a parting of their ways. It wasn't that he didn't love his car—but they simply weren't destined to stay together, so Bob was forced to purchase a brand new, 1966 maroon-colored Cadillac. *Really*—there was no other way out for him, the original car had just become impossible to drive. You see, the ash trays had—after a whole year—finally gotten full!

Plans For Fair

Everybody here at KRLA is occupied making plans for the Teen Age Fair at the Palladium in Hollywood on April 1. Projected plans for the festival this year include having Dick Biondi in a cage attempting to type K-R-L-A. Hmmmm—wonder if he'll make it??!

Paul and Barry Ryan—a successful pair of English twins who have formed a great singing duo—visited the Hallowed Halls of KRLA last week, and were an instantaneous hit with everyone. These two boys seem definitely headed for the top on this side of the Surf.

Once again, folks, it is time to resume our trail of clues in the mystery of the BatManager sign on the door of our Groovy Leader's office. When we left John-John last week, you may remember that he was in the company of a certain young lad whom he referred to as "Boy." Well, he has taken to calling the youngster "Tad," this week, and just yesterday I witnessed the two of them creeping silently out of the upstairs Bat Cave, loaded with an armful of long-stemmed red roses which oddly enough—smelled very strangely like Limburger cheese!!

I don't know what our Groovy Leader is up to—but whatever it is, we need to know... and we *need* to know *now!!!* Stay tuned for next week's exciting developments.

Roy Orbison To Tour With Walker Brothers

Writer and singer Roy Orbison has been signed for a return trip to Great Britain beginning March 25.

Roy, currently on the charts in England with "Breakin' Up Is Breaking My Heart," has had a string of big hits over here including "Only The Lonely," "Running Scared," "Candy Man," "Mean Woman Blues" and "Pretty Woman."

He will make this tour with the Walker Brothers, one of the hottest American groups in England today.

THE YOUNG MAN AVIDLY READING THE BEAT with KRLA's own Charlie O'Donnell is Charles Christy, a talented young singer from Ft. Worth, Texas. If you remember a recording duo named Skip and Flip from a few years back, you may remember a song which they recorded entitled "Cherry Pie." Charles has re-recorded the tune in his own style now, and is enjoying a growing success across the nation with his first disc attempt. He records with a group called The Crystals, who are also from Fort Worth, Texas.

THIS VALENTINE WINDOW was submitted to the Fifth Annual Art Festival at KRLA by a young man named Mason Williams. The three verses of poetry on the panes of the window are excerpts from his book, "By The Window."

The KRLA contest judges were so impressed with the originality and beauty of Mason's unusual entry that they decided to award him a special Third Place honorable mention prize.

KRLA BEAT Subscription
SAVE 33% Of Regular Price

☐ 1 YEAR — 52 Issues — $5.00   ☐ 2 YEARS — $8.00
☐ 6 MONTHS — $3.00

Enclosed is _____ ☐ CASH ☐ CHECK
PLEASE PRINT — Include Your Zip Code

Send to: _____ Age: _____
Address: _____ City: _____
State: _____ Zip: _____

MAIL YOUR ORDER TO: **KRLA BEAT**
6290 Sunset, Suite 504
Hollywood, Calif. 90028

Foreign Rate: $9.00 — 52 Issues

Eve's APPAREL
See if you can BEAT our prices on our new Jr. and missy lines. Samples at wholesale or less.
1800 N. Vermont
NO 3-4456   Hollywood, Calif.

New Teen Spot
Di Gati's Di Go-Go
230 West Whittier Blvd.
La Habra, Calif.

Top Entertainment Nightly

MINIMUM AGE - 15
$1.00 Admission

UNLIKE ANYTHING YOU'VE EVER SEEN!

WARNER BROS. SUPER CINERAMA PRODUCTION
BATTLE OF THE BULGE

PACIFIC'S Magnificent CINERAMA DOME Theatre   **NOW PLAYING!**

MAR 8-13 — ONE WEEK ONLY

EDDIE BROWN
OF
JOE & EDDIE

MAR 18-27 BROTHER DAVE GARDNER

AT DOUG WESTON'S
Troubadour

RESERVATIONS
CR 6-6168
9083 SANTA MONICA BLVD.
L.A. NEAR DOHENY

TV'S FUNNIEST BROTHERS — THREE DAYS ONLY
MAR 15, 16, 17 — PHONE NOW CR 6-6168

KRLA ARCHIVES

... TAMMI TERELL

Tammi Terell – From Medicine To Music

Some people fade into a crowd and some just naturally stand out. Tammi Terell is one of those who stand out.

This 22-year-old Detroit singer burst on the scene with her first release, "I Can't Believe You Love Me," and she still can't believe it.

There are a lot of things that make Tammi stand out in a crowd but the most obvious is the variety of hair styles and shades that she sports. Her hair styles change with her moods and she never quite looks the same.

And then there's the variety of clothes she's been seen in. This girl is equally at home in white boots and jeans or flowing evening dresses.

The Philadelphia-born singer is the daughter of a former actress and feels that show business is definitely her way of life.

Lived and Loved

"I just wouldn't be happy doing anything else," she declares. "I've lived and loved this business for too long not to be a part of it."

However, if she hadn't gone into entertaining she might well be on her way to practicing medicine.

She spent two years at the University of Pennsylvania in a pre-med program with a major is psychology. Tammi was very active in everything from dramatics club and choir to meetings of chemistry, physics or biology groups. She seemed to enjoy the challenging courses, like math and science best.

But at the same time she was gaining some very valuable experience in show business too.

She started by entertaining at children's parties, singing in the choir and giving piano recitals. She also took dancing lessons for about 13 years.

First Break

She got her first big professional appearance after winning a talent contest, and shelved her career as a psychologist, although she still feels that psychology is an important thing for people to study. She says, "No matter how many people you meet, you never find anyone with the same personalities or thoughts."

In her spare time she enjoys reading and writing songs and short stories. Her tastes in music run from the Supremes and Marvin Gaye to Dave Brubeck and Barbra Streisand.

She's gone a long way since she changed her name from Thomasina Montgomery and took up singing. She's played the Apollo Theater in New York, the Civic Center in Baltimore and the Riviera in Las Vegas.

It looks like those Tamla-Motown people have come up with another winner in Tammi Terell.

Adventures of Robin Boyd

By Shirley Poston

Chapter Nineteen

After the last of George had gone down the drain, Robin stopped standing by the sink, screaming hysterically. Instead, she sat at the kitchen table, screaming hysterically.

By this time, her mother was beside herself (and they made a lovely couple.)

"Robin," she begged, hovering over her sobbing daughter. "Tell me what's wrong!"

Robin wailed. "George was in that tea pot," she babbled.

Mrs. Boyd looked helplessly to her younger daughter for help (which somehow figures.)

"Ringo," she begged, addressing the sturdy (and I use the term kindly) twelve-year-old who was staring plumply from the doorway. "Who is George?"

Ringo shrugged. "George Harrison?" she offered, twiddling the Ludwig droomstick she always wore about her neck (on a chain, on a chain).

Mrs. Boyd looked blank. "Who is George Harrison?"

While Robin proceeded to scream hysterically-er, Ringo burst into noisy laughter.

Two Nuts

Mrs. Boyd stared from daughter to daughter. And her eyes widened in stark terror as she, for the first time, realized that there was not one nut in the family. There were two.

"Stop it, dear," she urged gently, patting the stricken Robin. "There was no one, I mean nothing, in that tea pot, I swear!" (And, at times like these, she added to herself, I wish I could!)

Robin raised her head and sniffed in an unladylike manner. "You couldn't have seen him," she blabbered, immediately wanting to take her big fat mouth out into the back yard and bury it. "I mean, why was the tea all black and foony - er - funny looking?"

Mrs. Boyd gave a sigh of relief. Why, she wasn't quite sure, but she gave one anyway. "That wasn't tea! That was a disinfectant I was using to sterilize the pot. You did swipe - er - rescue it from a garbage can, didn't you?"

Nodding, Robin re-sniffed. George hadn't been brewed after all. He'd been disinfected! And, at the very thought of same, she looked out the kitchen window in the direction of the rising moon and howled openly.

"Wait!" cried Mrs. Boyd. "I'd completely forgotten. I took George out of the pot!"

Robin leaped several feet into the air, chair and all. "You did what?" she bellowed.

Mrs. Boyd dashed to the cabinet and returned with something clutched in her fist. "This, I assume, is George, isn't it?" she said, opening her hand.

Mick

But, she was wrong. It wasn't George. It was Mick. At least that was what Robin called it as she scooped up the object in a frantic paw and fled from the kitchen, shouting "Batman was right!"

Helping Ringo to her feet (when Robin fled from a kitchen, Robin fled from a kitchen), Mrs. Boyd walked resolutely to the telephone.

Lifting the receiver, she stood there for a moment. "George?" she muttered. "Mick?" she muttered. "Batman?" she muttered.

When Robin was safely in her own room with the door double-bolted, she shined the ring until it shone (or, if you prefer, shone the ring until it shined) and plopped it into the special box she'd made for its return flight to England. Of course, the service on this trip would be a little less personalized, as the ring would have to settle for plain old air mail, but one couldn't have everything.

After she'd tied and addressed the small (but mighty) parcel, Robin pasted on a few million of the stamps she'd snitched - er - borrowed from her father's desk. Then, putting Mick Jagger's jacket on for warmth (not to mention effect), she set out to find the nearest post box.

Fortunately, she remembered having seen one just down the street. However, with her luck, it had probably been an unslender neighbor, waiting for a bus, clad in a blue and red suit (the neighbor, not the bus).

But, she'd find one if it took all night! She had to get the ring on it's way to Mick before something else happened to it.

On her way out, she passed through the living room where her mother was sitting on the couch, trembling a lot.

"Where are you going?" Mrs. Boyd squeaked.

Robin smiled at her unnerved parent. "I'm going to mail this ring back to its rightful owner before I lose it again," she explained casually.

Her unnerved parent re-trembled and Robin suddenly wished she could tell all so her mum would stop thinking she'd dropped one (and know she'd dropped one.) But, since that was impossible, Robin summed up another smile.

"I'll be right back," she promised. "And I am not what I seem," she added gently.

Although it had been less than an hour since she had crept terrified down these same dark streets (having witnessed a delightful double feature about cannibals that afternoon), Robin now stalked fearlessly.

Neither rain nor snow nor hail nor sleet were going to keep her from her appointed rounds. For that matter, an Oriental thug could rush up and paint her red for all she cared. She would still find a post box.

George's Back

Finally, she did. Double-checking to make sure it wasn't an unslender neighbor clad in a red and blue suit, she poked the package through the slot and took a deep whoosh of night air.

Then she looked plaintively toward the Heavens. "Now can I have my magic powers back?" she whispered. "Not to mention my George?"

"Would you settle for a skinny cannibal?" came the answering whisper from behind a nearby palm tree.

Robin clutched the post box in stark terror, wishing now that it were an unslender neighbor clad in (oh, you know), but suddenly she giggled.

What she knew about cannibals could be engraved on the head of a pin, but there was one thing she was certain of. Cannibals, skinny or otherwise, did not speak with a Liverpool accent!

Racing to the nearby palm tree, Robin threw her arms about it. Also about a tall, dark-haired genie who was lurking in its shadows.

"George," she breathed soulfully, staring up into his lean, luvley face.

"Marcia," he chortled.

Ignoring his sally (by the way, did anyone ever find out what actually did become of Sally?), Robin hugged him bone-crushingly.

"You're back!" she blithered joyously. "I thought I'd never see you again! I thought my mother disinfected you and . . ."

"Shurrup," George interrupted, grinning.

"And give us a kiss!" they chorused together. Shortly before they both shurrup.

(To Be Continued Next Week)

OUR HERRINGBONE IS WAY IN

SUEDES AND CORDS TOO

LENNY'S BOOT PARLOR
1448 GOWER STREET
JUST SOUTH OF SUNSET
HOLLYWOOD ★ 466-7092
Mail Inquiries Invited For
'OUT OF TOWNERS'

KRLA ARCHIVES

Running and Running

By Phyllis Pace

The Spencer Davis Group has been running and running for some time toward a hit record and have finally reached their goal—but they aren't prepared to stop just yet. They're going to "Keep On Running."

After replacing the Beatles in the Number One spot on the British charts in February they are steadily climbing the National Charts with their first American release. "Keep On Running" is the group's own arrangement of "The Hammer Song."

While still on the charts with their first hit they've already released another single in England titled "Somebody Help Me," which has a lighter, more swingin' sound than "Keep On Running" and promises to be an even bigger hit.

Spencer, Steve, Peter & Muff have been popular among many British Groups who recognized their talent long before the record buying public became aware of them. The Rolling Stones and The Who are good friends of the SDG — in fact, The Rolling Stones *loaned* their limousine to the group recently.

Looks like the Spencer Davis Group is following closely in the footsteps of the Yardbirds. Last year, the Yardbirds were unknown (to everybody but *The BEAT*, that is) and when "For Your Love" was released they had just completed a season with the Beatles. The record zoomed up the charts and The Yardbirds quickly followed it up with two more Top Ten Hits.

Likewise, "Keep On Running" was released right after The Spencer Davis Group finished a tour with the Rolling Stones and they're on their way to a smash follow-up with "Somebody Help Me." Put this one in the Top Ten boys and you only have one more to go to reach the fame of the Yardbirds.

A lot of people are comparing The SDG's success with that of Georgie Fame's success last year. To do this you would have to compare "Somebody Help Me" with Fame's follow-up — "In The Meantime" — and how can you?

"The SDG has a spokesman (Spencer), an image (Steve), a publicist (Pete) and a business man-me," explained Muff who is sometimes jokingly referred to as "Scrooge" by the rest of the group. Wonder why?

Bookings are already coming in for the very popular and talented group. They're set to join The Who on a week's theatre tour in April and a 35 night tour in the Fall. Overseas offers are currently flooding in including two German TV dates, and Scandinavian and Australian tours.

...SPENCER DAVIS GROUP

Peter & Gordon Aided By Unknown

By Susan Frisch

Well, it looks as though Peter and Gordon have scored another hit with "Woman." But *The BEAT* has learned that the British duo were aided by a certain John Doe.

How's that? Apparently, a dub of "Woman" was delivered to their office by some unknown but certainly talented song-writer. Peter and Gordon listened to the dub, dug the song and immediately set out to find its writer—but without much luck.

So, they went ahead and cut "Woman" and have succeeded in sending it bounding up the nation's charts. In fact, the duo are keeping their fingers crossed for a Gold Record—and if sales continue along as they have been doing since the record was released it's quite likely that they'll get that Gold One yet!

London-born Peter Asher and Scotland-born Gordon Waller seem to have something of a Midas Touch when it comes to turning out hit records, though during the last few months they sort of lost it!

A "Cocktail"

Both Peter and Gordon describe their music as a "strange cocktail of sound." They are rather reluctant to label it but they agree that they are definite rhythm and blues addicts but also "middle of the road pop buffs and rock fans."

They enjoy wild, exciting concerts but there are times when they wish they just hadn't gone on at all. Those are the times when the show had to be stopped prematurely because the audience got out of control.

The screaming and yelling bit witnessed at practically every "live" performance is harder to take for Peter and Gordon than for most pop entertainers because the duo would really rather have their audience *listen* to what they're singing and then scream when they're finished.

Peter and Gordon have spent most of their time in the U.S. lately, especially in Hollywood where it is not at all unusual to spot either Peter or Gordon browsing in a record shop or having lunch in a local restaurant.

Never Made It

There are several reasons for their long Stateside stays. First off, they never really made it in England. They had their share of hits but they never were able to muster up enough of a fan following to sell-out concerts or club dates.

Secondly, they don't believe touring in England is worth the trouble not only because of the money (which is much lower than wages paid on an American tour) but also because of the poor management of the tours themselves.

They'd much rather stay here and tour with the Dick Clark Caravan where, incidently, they've done very well for themselves.

Even though Peter and Gordon are not positive about what the future may bring them (but then who is?), they will definitely stay in the entertainment business—even if it means singing in tiny coffee houses or poor-business night clubs.

Conceivably, they could play anywhere since they know hundreds of different songs for any type of show possible. Anyway, whatever they do *The BEAT* hopes they will continue producing hits like "Woman." And with the help of the John Does everywhere I'm sure they will!

...GORDON AND PETER

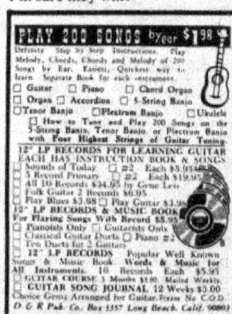

KRLA ARCHIVES

STONED!

(Ed. Note—These two articles were written by teenage fans of the Stones and readers of The BEAT. You know what we think of the Stones so we thought you might like to see how our readers feel about the fab 5.)

By Cari Beauchamp

Since the Rolling Stones are, in my opinion, just about the most popular group around today I thought I'd write an article on my favorite Stone, Keith Richard, whom I was fortunate enough to meet personally.

The meeting happened sometime ago but I never thought about writing it until just recently, although I admit I spread it around plenty by word of mouth.

The Stones played San Jose on December 4, 1965. My girlfriend and I were staying with a mutual friend in San Francisco. We had arrived Friday afternoon and were planning on spending the next day in the city.

Needless to say we were up early Saturday morning and set out to visit some of the exclusive clothes stores. Our first stop was at the Town Squire, a really way out place. We were trying on all sorts of weird clothes—I remember that I had on a paisley shirt and a wide wale corduroy pair of bell bottoms when who walked in the door but Brian Jones and Keith Richard.

Never Find 'Em

We couldn't believe it! We knew that the Stones had come into San Francisco from Sacramento the night before but we had decided that it would be more than senseless to try and find them in a city as big as San Francisco.

So, there I was standing there in my tried-on outfit when Keith came up to me and absolutely flipped over it! He quickly grabbed up some wild checked pants and a suede vest which he tried on and looked terrific in. He finally ended up buying four shirts and three pairs of pants.

Naturally, since Keith had bought some clothes and since he had liked my outfit I purchased it—even though I really couldn't afford it. Altogether we spent over an hour in the shop and when we were leaving Keith asked us if we'd like to come back to their hotel with them for some cokes.

Of course, we said yes!!!! So, we followed them back and by the time we got there it was after 3 o'clock. Ordinarily time would make no difference to us but we had tickets for the Stones' concert that night at nine.

Mick Too

Luckily, there were no fans gathered around the four rooms in the hotel and when Keith opened the door for us there sat Mick reading a newspaper. He looked up, smiled, grunted a greeting and went back to reading his paper.

We sat down, Keith ordered some cokes and then picked up one of the three guitars which were laying around and began strumming. He explained that there would be no rehearsal for the evening's show but that he just liked to play anyway.

Keith told us that he owns over 50 guitars and totes along six of them when they go on tour. At first Keith seemed awfully shy but then after awhile he began joking around and laughing it up.

What impressed me the most about Keith was his real interest in us, our schools and our families. He made me feel like he cared about us as individuals. He wasn't swell-headed, nor did he sit and talk about himself as so many artists are inclined to do.

All of a sudden Keith realized that he hadn't seen either Charlie or Bill all day long. He checked the other rooms but they were nowhere to be found so we launched a search for them—finally discovering both of them in the hotel restaurant.

Keith said he didn't know how they could possibly eat before a show because he is always terribly nervous before the Stones go on.

Shockin' Keith

It finally came time for us to leave, for both the Stones and the two of us had to travel to San Jose for the show. Keith wasn't too happy about the idea of going on stage that night for the previous evening he had received quite a shock from a loose wire in his microphone.

We arrived at the auditorium around 8:30 and quickly found our seats. We didn't bother telling anyone else about our fabulous afternoon for we still couldn't believe it ourselves!

The show was fantastic. Mick put on his usual wild performance but I couldn't take my eyes off Keith. As always happens with a great show—it ended all too soon for us. But we knew the Stones were going directly to the airport so we followed them to the San Jose Executive Terminal.

Brian and Mick hopped aboard a small private plane but Keith, Charlie and Bill got on a much larger plane along with the rest of the tour. Keith looked out the window, spotted us and blew me a kiss good-bye as the plane began taxiing off.

What a day!!! We hadn't even found them—*they* had found *us*! The Stones had always been one of my favorite groups but ever since that day the Stones—and especially Keith—will have a very special place in my heart. They're great!

By Jill Richard

Without a doubt, The Rolling Stones are the most controversial group on the pop scene today. Why is this? Obviously it is not the quality of their music, as the Stones' record sales run second only to The Beatles. It must then be the Stones themselves. Let's take a trip to a Rolling Stones Concert and examine the reasons for all this controversy.

The scene outside the auditorium is quiet enough. Groups milling about; vendors with programs and buttons. Surprisingly, there is very little talk about what is soon to happen inside.

There is a bit of pushing as the doors open, and, as seats are located moans and exclamations of happiness are heard, depending on how early the seats were purchased.

The show is a few minutes late in starting so clapping and chants of "We want the Stones" continue until the local disc jockey comes on to warm up the audience and introduce the first act.

The three backing acts are excellent and receive generous applause. As the Stones gear is being set up there is a restless, tension-filled intermission.

Here They Are

By now the fans are quite 'warmed up' and are only anxious for The Stones to appear. Five minutes later, as the announcer comes back on stage, he is aware of the feeling, so with as few words as possible, namely "And now, The Rolling Stones," the curtains part on the five most talked-about musicians in show business.

The loud speaker system had been so loud throughout the show it was deafening if you happened to be right under one. But the reason for that became apparent as the Stones were nearly drowned out by screams.

Opening with "Everybody Needs Somebody" a favorite stage number, lead singer Mick Jagger attracts your attention first. Taking a quick look over the other four, our eyes are riveted to blond, pale faced Brian Jones. This quiet-looking lad causes a mild sensation in what appear to be corduroy pants in the wildest shade imaginable, somewhere between red and orange. Worn with his 'trademark' shirt, a brown turtleneck, he is an arresting sight.

Drummer Charlie Watts, the best dresser of the group, is conservatively clad in a grey suit and dark blue shirt (to accent his blue eyes, no doubt.) Nothing in this staid Britishman to cause any raised eyebrows.

Keith Richard, lead guitarist, is another story. On top of his long, thin figure is a sudden splash of color in what he calls his "Draught-board" jacket. Made of squares of soft, bright colors, it is, to our delight, very attractive.

On bass guitar, another conservative, Bill Wyman, in brown suit and yellow shirt.

So far there has been nothing extremely unusual about these musicians. Perhaps some of the clothes are unique, but seeing someone in the same outfit walking down the street, would not cause one to stop and stare, or think 'there goes a freak.'

As for the hair. Well, that's rather cliche, don't you think?

While he is wailing "Mercy Mercy Mercy" and "Play With Fire" let's take a closer look at Mick Jagger.

His jacket is brown and his pants, hipsters of gingham-type brown check. But his clothes are not what stand out about this Stone. It is his movements, his complete control of the audience—and his earthy, blues based voice. He sings with his entire body, not just his voice. His feet twitch, his rubbery legs wobble, his skinny hips move and shake and his hands are clapping or holding the mike or tambourine or maraccas, or beseeching his audience. For undeniably this is HIS audience. And this must be what all the uproar is about. This dancing, singing, clapping, swinging, shaking, wild, happy kid.

The Voice

He turns his back to the crowd and shakes his hips like his own maraccas. He almost manages the splits. He sits on the edge of the stage. He gets down on his knees. He lifts the mike over his head. He jumps in the air. He does his "will he throw it or won't he" bit with his jacket. He walks to each side of the stage, shades his eyes with the tambourine, and looks at the people who pay to look at him. He sings and shakes. And he makes thousands of girls and boys a little bit happier.

So what's wrong with this dancing and singing-shaking? Admittedly, a few girls are turned into a raging, dangerous mob, but note that this is only a small percentage of the audience. Most fans stay in their seats, if not calm, at least not rushing the stage.

Perhaps more people who find the Rolling Stones offensive should go to one of their concerts. Talk with the fans. Listen, really listen, to the music. Of course, you will find the looks of the Stones important to the girls. Handsome faces are always pleasing to look upon. But the basic reason for the devotion given these five is their music.

Can you deny the pleasure this music, these boys, bring to their fans? In a world taut with fear, torn by war, be glad young people have this to turn to.

Fairness to the Rolling Stones, judging them as musicians, by their music, will lead to only one conclusion. As a lady in her seventies so nicely put it—"I see nothing wrong with them. There's good and bad in all of us. You don't have to have your hair short for that!"

KRLA ARCHIVES

YEAH WELL

By Tammy Hitchcock

Due to popular demand (my own) we are going to see if the Rolling Stones will squirm on our "Yeah, Well Hot Seat." Actually, the Stones are my favorite group and so naturally I'm always on the look-out for excuses to write about them.

This time I've come up with a beaut (if I do say so myself—and I just have.) You see, the Stones sent me a new bio and from the sound of it I'm sure they wrote it themselves—which is a marvelous excuse to write about them, right? Too bad—they're going on the "Hot Seat" anyway.

Seriously, though, this bio is really too much. It's all done in the standard biography form but the answers are hilarious (if not true.) For instance, Mick Jagger states that his professional name is Vince Whirlwind!

Yeah, well I don't know about Vince Whirlwind but would you believe Mick "Lock-kneed" Jagger?

Mick says that his present home is in a place called Golders Green and since I've never been to England I'll have to go along with that through ignorance but when he names his compositions as "Blue Turns To Grey," "It Should Be You" and "for George Bean and others ask for list" then I draw the line!

Yeah, well who other do I ask for a list of your compositions, Mick—your dog, Theodora????

You're Kidding

If you think Mick's professional name is wild you should hear Keith's professional moniker (or so *he* says.) Are you ready for this one? His stage name is Valerie Masters!!!

Yeah, well even *I* don't have a suitable answer for that one.

Keith is really a doll and I must admit that I dig him the best of all the Stones *but* I'd just like to know why he wrote neatly next to Present Home—"None of your business."

Yeah, well that really hurt, Keith. I mean, you know me and my sense of direction. If I ever *did* get to England (which is about the remotest possibility possible) I'd *never* be able to find your present home anyway. Heck, I can't even find you when you're right here in *my* hometown!! I wonder why that is, Keith. You're trying to tell me something, maybe?

Even though Keith says it and I always believe what Keith says, I sort of doubt that his former occupation was "tram driver in Instanbul."

Yeah, well I honestly hate to doubt you Keith, but a *tram driver in Instanbul?* Now, if you would have said a *camel rider* in Instanbul—that I would have believed.

And there is one other little thing which upsets me, (not that you care, I'm sure), and that is that Keith has listed meeting Charlie Watts as his Biggest Disappointment. Come on now, Keith, Charlie's a nice guy. One time he even let me try on his cowboy hat which was extremely generous of him considering the fact that I had just sat on it and flattened it out to the approximate size of an overly-ripe pancake.

All's Well

Yeah, well you're forgiven, Keith. I just read a little further down in your bio to the part about your Best Friend and although I'm hurt that I don't find Tammy Hitchcock listed there at least I'm proud to see Charles Watts residing in that category. He really is nice, you know. It's not everyone who would let me try on a squashed cowboy hat.

For those of you who didn't know it, Keith has a dog named Ratbag. Yeah, well that's fair I s'pose because I have a dog named Keith.

All right enough said about Keith has listed meeting Charlie cidently, outdid himself in this bio business. He says that he entered show business at the ripe old age of four months at a baby show at West Gloucestershire Women's Institute Annual Show.

Yeah, well what did you do on the show, Brian, play a chorus or two of "Little Red Rooster"—or was it "Little Red Riding Hood" or would you believe "Papa's Got A Brand New Bag—Part 1?"

Brian says that he has a Rolls but would very much like to own an American Toronado. Yeah, well how about a '56 Chevy—real cheap?

Brian lists his biggest disappointment as "never having been to Korea." Yeah, well you've been to Japan and if you've been to Japan you've seen Korea. So, how about seeing me?

For Once

Brian's miscellaneous dislikes are "people who ask what I think about the Beatles getting their M.B.E.'s" Yeah, well for once I don't fit into the category mentioned. I never once said a word to Brian about the Beatles getting theirs, I only asked when *he* was getting *his*—that's all.

What is this giant conspiracy against Charlie? Bill followed right along in Keith's footsteps and said that his biggest disappointment was in meeting Charlie Watts. How could you possibly say that, Bill? Just because Charlie didn't let you try on his smashed cowboy hat—you shouldn't hold a grudge.

I will say one thing for Bill—he takes you literally. I mean, you ask him his miscellaneous likes and he makes them miscellaneous. He officially digs "young ladies, cashew nuts, R&B, tape recorders and chewing gum."

Yeah, well I don't know about the rest of them but the chewing gum bit I believe, I believe.

Bill reveals that his favorite food is "cheese on toast." Yeah, well they serve that here in the U.S. too, Bill, only they put a fancy name on it—Welsh Rarebit.

And I know too. About a week ago I went into this restaurant and ordered Welsh Rarebit thinking that I was going to get some meat sandwiched in between the cheese and the toast somewhere. Yeah, well.

Forgetful

And that leaves only Charlie. I've saved him for last because I'm not exactly sure what to write about him 'cause he has "don't know" written on his bio five times, "haven't one" listed six times and "can't remember" written twice.

However, Charlie states with an enormous amount of certainty that his real name is Charles Robert Watts, he was born on June 2, 1942 in Islington, stands 5 ft. 9 in., weighs 10 stones 3 lbs. (whatever that may mean), has blue eyes and brown hair, and a wife named Shirley and a mother and father named Charles and Lily (only I think he means his mother's name is Lily and his father is Charles), has a sister named Linda, went to Tylers Croft School, plays drums with a group called the Rolling Stones, likes jazz, has a pony, a cat and a collie dog and was once a commercial artist.

Yeah, well when they're all listed down that way Charlie knows quite a lot, doesn't he?

P. S. to Betsy: Afraid they didn't squirm much, did they?

And for those of you who don't know who Betsy is, just label that last sentence an "in" joke. Well, we've got to get our kicks someway you know!

KRLA ARCHIVES

WHILE IN AMERICA to sign a new movie contract, The Dave Clark Five introduced their latest release "At The Scene" on the Ed Sullivan Show. This made their tenth appearance on the Sullivan Show, making them the most often featured of the British groups. "At The Scene" is expected to equal the success of their last single, "Over And Over," which was number one on the national charts.

Vote For Your Favorite Movie And TV Stars

It's almost that time of year again. Academy Awards time, that is. And all of Hollywood is starting to hold its breath, wondering who will take home the prized statues come Oscar's big night.

The only problem is, a large majority of America's moviegoers *aren't* holding *their* breath. Because that majority is made up of teenagers, and our favorite films and performances often don't even get a mention on the nomination roster.

As you know, the winners of the Academy Awards are chosen not by the people who attend movies, but by those who make them. Actors, actresses, screenwriters, directors, producers, etc.

Wouldn't it be great to do an about face and have the champs of the year selected by the ticket-buyers who plunked down their allowances to view 1965's film fare?

We think so, and we bet you'll agree.

Since we don't think it would do much good to show up at the Academy, en masse, on voting day, here's what we're going to do instead—sponsor our own ballot! The Beat's Pop Music Awards were a smashing success, and we know this new venture will be just as much of a ball for all.

Now, why don't we stop talking about it and start moving? Good idea!

Right here on this page you'll find your official Beat Ballot. We've started the ball rolling by nominating ten movies that went over big with teenagers during 1965, and in case we didn't mention your favorite, we've left room for you to write in your own choice.

Same goes in the Best Actor and Best Actress categories. We've nominated five in each, and left room for you to fill in your special candidates.

While we were at it, we had another brainstorm. Why not include the TV industry, we asked ourselves. *Why not,* we answered. So, you'll also find a special television section on your ballot, with nominations made and space for write-ins.

After you've marked your ballot, drop it in the mail to *BEAT* Ballot c/o *The BEAT*.

And, just in case you think you've heard everything, wait until you hear what the Beat Award is going to look like! We'll be telling you all about that soon, so stay tuned.

OFFICIAL BEAT BALLOT

BEST MOVIE OF 1965: Vote for one nominated film or write in your fave.
- ☐ "Help"
- ☐ "Billie"
- ☐ "Goldfinger"
- ☐ "Ski Party"
- ☐ "That Darn Cat"
- ☐ "Where The Boys Meet The Girls"
- ☐ "Ferry Across The Mersey"
- ☐ "Catch Us If You Can"
- ☐ "Beach Blanket Bingo"
- ☐ "Harum-Scarum"
- ☐ _____

BEST ACTOR AND ACTRESS OF 1965: Vote for one film star in each of these two categories. Choose from those nominated or write in your candidate.
- ☐ Paul McCartney
- ☐ Elvis Presley
- ☐ Peter (Herman) Noone
- ☐ Ringo Starr
- ☐ Sean Connery
- ☐ _____
- ☐ Patty Duke
- ☐ Annette Funicello
- ☐ Connie Francis
- ☐ Deborah Walley
- ☐ Hayley Mills
- ☐ _____

BEST TV SHOW OF 1965: Vote for one nominated show or write in your fave.
- ☐ "The Man From U.N.C.L.E."
- ☐ "Shindig"
- ☐ "Hullabaloo"
- ☐ "Where The Action Is"
- ☐ "Gidget"
- ☐ _____
- ☐ "I Spy"
- ☐ "Bonanza"
- ☐ "Peyton Place"
- ☐ "Tammy"
- ☐ "Get Smart"
- ☐ _____

BEST TV ACTOR AND ACTRESS OF 1965: Vote for one TV star in each of these two categories. Choose from those nominated or write in your candidate.
- ☐ David McCallum
- ☐ Robert Vaughn
- ☐ Michael Landon
- ☐ Bill Cosby
- ☐ Don Adams
- ☐ _____
- ☐ Patty Duke
- ☐ Mia Farrow
- ☐ Sally Field
- ☐ Debbie Watson
- ☐ Pat Morrow
- ☐ _____

Pop Talk

JANE ASHER set for an important role in the upcoming flick, "Cleo," to be filmed in this country. I wonder if that means our sunny shores will be graced by another long-haired visitor (man-style) at the same time?

MARIANNE FAITHFULL is sporting a brand new hairdo these days but you probably haven't had an opportunity to see a picture of it. She certainly did a great deal to popularize the sweet, ethereal look when her hair was left to flow gracefully to her shoulders. Now she has cut all of her locks off and is wearing a style very similar to the one which Cilla Black had designed for her some time ago. It is combed to the side and has a little wave coming over the cheek extending almost to the lip-line. Very pretty. But, almost anything would be on Marianne.

THE SUPREMES have reportedly 'shut-down' a recent offer to lend their super name to a Detroit discotheque. Rumor has it that the "No" they gave was the negative answer (given them) to a six-figure positive planned for the projected nitespot.

PAT BOONE was the only one of the British or American entries who scored much of a victory for the pop field at the San Remo Festival. Oddly, British duo Chad and Jeremy, were officially listed as U.S. entrants while American-born P.J. Proby represented Great Britain.

THE DAVE CLARK FIVE recently appeared on The Ed Sullivan Show for the tenth time, setting a record on the show for appearances by any pop group. Sullivan's Show owes a great deal to the Beatles: After presenting them, he suddenly gained an entire nation of younger viewers who began tuning in weekly. Now he has one of the most successful, teen-age pop shows on television!

S/SGT. BARRY SADLER has become the only recording artist to equal a remarkable feat of The Beatles. His "Ballad of the Green Berets," which concerns the conflicts in Viet Nam (of which he is a veteran) has been awarded a gold record for both the single and album by that name. The only other time this has happened was when The Beatles recorded "Help!" as a single and the soundtrack LP of the same name was released.
And Barry's LP is selling 50 percent faster than "Sound of Music!"

JOHNNY CASH is reportedly suing the Klu Klux Klan for $25 million because they allegedly distributed leaflets which he claims contain "attempts to make my children ashamed they were born." He also said if he wins the money, he'll donate it to the defense budget.

POOR P.J. PROBY! Regardless of *which* country he decides to owe allegiance to now, he is going to owe some international-style money to Italy. Seems that Mr. Proby lost 500 pounds (about $1400) in a San Remo casino in just *one hour*.

MARY TRAVERS of Peter, Paul and same might have the answer to what has happened to the "pure folk" craze which swept our pop nation a couple of years ago. About the change, Mary has this to say: "The great boom in folk music is over because mass media allows and encourages a total exposure of cultural roots. It isn't an oddity or a fad anymore; now it's an established form of musical expression like jazz or contemporary classical music."

THE SUPREMES will become the latest on the list of artists to record a Lennon-McCartney tune when their new album, including "Yesterday," is released. Then of course there is David McCallum who is cutting an entire LP of John's poetry. That should be wild!

SIMON AND GARFUNKEL are rapidly becoming one of the most popular singing duos in this country as well as in Great Britain. Paul Simon is also becoming one of the most popular songwriters around and is already hosting long lines of artists who want to record his material. Artists already lined up to wax some of his effortations include the Bachelors, Moody Blues and the Hollies.

KRLA ARCHIVES

The BEAT Goes To The Movies
"BATTLE OF THE BULGE"

By Jim Hamblin
(BEAT Movie Editor)

Hollywood has created just about everything from Adam and Eve and Noah's Ark, to a space trip to outer galaxies—Now one of America's biggest studios drops some of the bloodiest parts of World War II in your lap!

THE BATTLE OF THE BULGE is not about someone using Metrecal and trying to lose weight. The location is Europe, and the time is 1944. The American Army figures it's got it hacked, that the Germans are washed up. So much so, they are talking about going home for Christmas. Well, that was all before December 16th. Henry Fonda tried to tell 'em, he warned and pleaded and cajoled, but nobody would listen. "The Germans are massing heavy armor for a surprise attack on our whole 85 mile front," says Fonda, who should know because he has been in so many of these war movies. But they didn't listen. And the attack came.

The trick in making a movie like this is solving the problem of keeping up the suspense. After all, just who lost the war is not exactly a secret. But what was the enemy doing with those funny rubber hoses? Was their attack ever going to slow down?

The producers of this picture were a little worried that the Viet Nam war would dampen audience enthusiasm at the box office, but so far that has not been the case. And we hope it never is. War is not a pretty thing, and this is a realistic film. But if we might be permitted an editorial comment, we think everyone needs to be reminded once in a while about that war, and all the other wars—and when you hear somebody say, "Aw, it can't happen here," it's a good time to recall the fact those were the exact words we heard up until December 7th, 1941.

TWO OF THE PICTURE'S STARS—Henry Fonda and Robert Ryan—taking a break from action in the middle of a very hectic World War II!

...DANA ANDREWS   ...ROBERT RYAN

HAND TO HAND COMBAT WITH A GERMAN TANK, ANYONE? That might not provide very good odds for this soldier—George Montgomery—but then, that was about the only style of fighting left after the American Army was over-run by the German attack along the entire front. This one-man attack is just one of many exciting scenes from the Cinerama Technicolor production for Warner Bros., "Battle of the Bulge."

THE BIG NEW GERMAN TIGER TANK was almost unstoppable; here the huge German tank crashes through the Allied lines in the Belgian town of St. Vith as a part of a massive last-ditch attack.

KRLA ARCHIVES

KRLA BEAT Edition
America's Largest Teen NEWSpaper
MARCH 26, 1966 — 15¢

if you can BELIEVE your EYES and your EARS (pg. 14)

KRLA ARCHIVES

KRLA BEAT

Volume 2, Number 2 — March 26, 1966

A Very Important 'PUSSYCAT'

HOTLINE LONDON
Dylan On Tour

By Tony Barrow

Some of London's music business moguls look upon Capitol's signing of balladeer MATT MONRO as an indication that the label expects him to follow in the worthy steps of former Cap giants of Sinatra and Cole calibre. Despite the new 5-year contract, Matt will continue to record under the supervision of George Martin who makes records with THE BEATLES, CILLA BLACK, GERRY AND THE PACEMAKERS, PETER SELLERS and many other big names. Matt is expected to make his first Capitol album in Hollywood at the beginning of May. In the meantime his first single since the label switch is "Born Free," title number from the movie chosen for London's 1966 Royal Performance.

BURT BACHARACH arranged and conducted the orchestral accompaniment at EMI's London studios when CILLA BLACK recorded his ballad "Alfie," a composition inspired by the movie of the same name. The adults-only picture—starring Michael Caine, Millicent Martin, Shelley Winters and Jane Asher—has a March 24 London premiere. Immediately afterwards Cilla flies to New York where she'll preview her "Alfie" single for you via "The Ed Sullivan Show."

Bob Dylan Dates

Impressario Tito Burns has just announced the rest of his BOB DYLAN dates and venues. The complete tour schedule runs like this:—Dublin (May 5), Belfast (6), Bristol (10), Cardiff (11), Birmingham (12), Liverpool (14), Leicester (15), Sheffield (16), Manchester (17), Glasgow (19), Edinburgh (20), Newcastle (21), London's Royal Albert Hall (26).

THE BACHELORS have made a Decca disc of the Simon/Garfunkel song "Sound Of Silence" and Irish balladeer VAL DOONICAN has covered "Elusive Butterfly" for the same label. "Blue Turns To Grey," penned by MICK JAGGER and KEITH RICHARD, is the March 18 single release in the U.K. by CLIFF RICHARD AND THE SHADOWS. Cliff is currently packing London's "Talk Of The Town" niterie where his season has been extended. In April Cliff and The Shads will star in an hour-long BBC television spectacular. Incidentally VIKKI CARR is next in line for "Talk Of The Town" cabaret and JOHNNY MATHIS goes in there for the month of August.

NEWS BRIEFS . . . In U.K., about 8 cents added to the retail price of singles bringing the new total to just under one dollar . . . PET CLARK and husband Claude hope to purchase L.A. home — Pet's sister Barbara already lives in your part of the world . . . In press interview here LEN BARRY described THE STONES' "Get Off Of My Cloud" as trash! . . . May U.K. visit probable for MITCH RYDER . . . Get-

(Turn to Page 14)

Where Will Pop Go From Here?

By Louise Criscione

The question of the month seems to be — what trend will the pop scene take now? The question has been asked repeatedly but so far no one has been able to come up with any sort of concrete answer. There is little wonder the future of pop is so hard to predict for no one can read the millions of minds of the record buyers.

But if several records appear on the nation's charts, all with a marked similarity it is usually safe to say that a trend will develop because there are always plenty of entertainers willing and most eager to jump on the bandwagon. However, the record scene of today is even defying *that* avenue of prediction by the emergence of strong regional trends which fail to catch on in the rest of the nation.

A perfect example is the Beach Boys' latest, "Barbara Ann." The disc sold enough records around the nation to send it all the way up to number three in the U.S. charts.

But in Southern California, the place which started it all for the Beach Boys and their surfing sound, the record failed to even dent the local charts. There were two reasons for this: first off, there was not enough of a demand from listeners to warrant the radio stations giving the disc much air play, and secondly the actual sales of "Barbara Ann" were very slow and rather inconsequential.

Actually, the sale of singles itself is currently in a serious slump.

(Turn to Page 11)

Tom Jones is telling us all to "Promise Her Anything," and with a voice like his . . . she'd probably *believe* it, too!

In the last year or so, Tom has become one of the most popular singers on the pop scene for his rugged good looks and powerful "tiger's" voice. But Tom was not always a singer, and there was a time when he wasn't really just the "Jones boy next door."

He was born Thomas Jones Woodward in Pontypridd, South Wales, on June 7, 1940. He was born in a mining town, and claims that his interest in show business began immediately after he first realized "how heavy a Hod was." A "hod" is a board which is used by builders to carry cement.

As a youngster, Tom's only real contact with the worlds of music and "show business" came when he sang in the chapel choir at Treforrest Secondary Modern School.

For a time after he finished school, Tom held a number of jobs in a very short period of time, which included working as a miner, a dump truck operator, a door-to-door vacuum cleaner salesman, and a construction worker. Then finally he began his career as a performer when he began playing drums in various clubs in and around South Wales.

The only problem was that all this time Tom was only playing drums, and was never given an opportunity to sing. It wasn't until he formed a group of his own — which he called The Playboys — that he was given an opportunity to turn his Golden Tonsils loose.

And turn them loose he did — all over London! Shortly after after arriving in London — where he substituted for a star act at a fashionable West-End night club on only 30 minutes notice! — he received his first professional date... which turned out to be in Swansea, Wales!! And as he turned around and headed back toward his home he simply murmured philosophically to himself, "Ah well, that's show business!"

Yes, that *is* show business and it is now a world in which Tom Jones is a VIP—Very Importan "Pussycat." So, what's new?

What's New?

I'll tell you what's new — Tom's house in Shepperton! The Jones family (Tom, his wife Linda and their eight year old son, Mark) moved into the dream house ($24,000 worth!) recently and are thrilled about having their own home after living in apartments all of their married life.

The house is really something else, with a huge picture window running the entire length of the ground floor, built-in fireplaces, a king-sized master bedroom, under-floor heating and double-glazed windows.

When Tom and his wife made the trek to London they were

(Turn to Page 10)

Inside the BEAT

Newsmakers	2
Dirty Unkempt Stones	3
Two Down—Now What?	4
George Speaks	5
Men and Green Berets	7
Walkers 'Hairy' Shows	10
Nancy Sinatra	11
Teen Club Directory	12
Another British Invasion	13
Adventures of Robin Boyd	14
The Temptin' Temptations	15

The BEAT is published weekly by BEAT Publications, Inc., editorial and advertising offices at 6290 Sunset Blvd., Suite 504, Hollywood, California 90028. U.S. bureaus in Hollywood, San Francisco, New York, Chicago and Nashville; overseas correspondents in London, Liverpool and Manchester, England. Sale price, 15 cents. Subscription price: U.S. and possessions, $5 per year; Canada and foreign rates, $9 per year. Second class postage prepaid at Los Angeles, California.

KRLA ARCHIVES

Letters TO THE EDITOR

Paul And Jane
Dear *BEAT*:
I've read over and over again about Jane Asher and Paul McCartney getting married. I don't suppose many Beatle fans are too happy about the prospect but what are you going to do?

My own personal feelings are like this. I don't like Jane, mostly because I heard some of her honey-sweet remarks about Beatle fans and her "marriage" to Paul.

I heard her speak the following words on a television show. "I think they're (meaning us) a little soft in the head to chase in the streets after those men. People ought to be able to control themselves. Those girls are simply jealous because I've got something and they might as well just face it — they never will have.

"As for my marriage to Paul — no, we are not married but I couldn't hold my breath."

Jane was overly sweet and kept throwing her hair around. About the M.B.E. awards she managed to sigh (as if it were nothing), "It's marvelous. They deserve it all the way."

She had to be honest and say she didn't like the songs in the Beatles' movie, "especially well."

I couldn't believe it. Paul must be blind to her. She can't be like that off screen, can she? I hope not. Maybe she can make Paul happy — maybe not. But I hope so, I really do.
R.A.

— HERMAN, LUV
By Mary Gray

Who has the bluest eyes?
   The cutest nose?
The fairest hair?
   The nicest clothes?
The sweetest voice?
   The biggest smile?
The dearest ways?
   The neatest style?
I know, don't you?
   It's Herman, that's who!

Stones' Gettysburg Address
Dear *BEAT*:
I have made an address to the Rolling Stones which is really the Gettysburg Address.

Two years and seven days ago our sisters brought forth upon this nation a new group called the Rolling Stones. Conceived in fainting and dedicated to the proposition that all girls will scream.

Now we are engaged in the great performance on that stage testing whether that group is good enough. We are met on that stage as a final resting place for those girls who fainted so that that group can stay popular all along.

But in larger sense they can sing! They can dance and they can even think. The brave girls, living and screaming, who have struggled here have consecrated it far above our power to stop them.

The world will very little note nor long remember what they said here but they will never forget when they sang "Satisfaction."
Edward Brita

Black Plague
Dear *BEAT*:
I think that Canada's top male singer, Terry Black is the greatest thing since R&R! Every record which Terry has released has hit the top ten in Canada and "Unless You Care" did nicely here.

Terry caused the greatest epidemic in Canada's history — *The Black Plague*, which is the name of his first album. It will not be long before the disease strikes here.

Why not stay one step ahead and prepare the world for this fine and talented singer? An article would be appreciated or even just a picture. Don't let the world suffer one more minute — time is running out!
Chrissie McDonnell

A Modern Fable
By Leona

One day near a rocky hill, a Hermit that had a bad case of the Uglies that day threw a Fortune Cookie away. Some Beatles happened along and saw it.

"Who dropped this Cookie?" they said. No one spoke up so the We Five started to eat it.

A hungry Byrd, Who was a Yardbird but escaped, saw the Beatles and ate Them for he was a Cannibal.

Now this Byrd made a terrible Sound while eating and he distrubed an Animal, Who had the Measles. The Animal got sore and stomped on the Byrd. All this stomping caused a landslide and the Animal was hit by a Rolling Stone which knocked him Kink-y and he Bee-came Zombie-like.

This Pretty Thing was a Walker so he Zombie-strolled across a road and was hit, Fourmost, by an M.G. driven by a Girl Playboy on a Surfari.

She stopped the car near some Grass Roots and was immediately robbed and clobbered by some Small Face-d Raiders, Who wore Mojos.

The Raiders rode away on their Kubas, a type of beast that says "Gonk," and came upon a Turtle eating the rest of the Cookie. They dismounted and stomped on the Turtle. This stomping also caused a landslide and the whole mess was buried by Rolling Stones.

A Hollie wreath with black Leaves was placed over the slide by some Undertakers.

MORAL: Today's musical groups are getting away with murder!

Parents Not So Bad
Dear *BEAT*:
I would just like to say that parents deserve a lot more than our teen generation gives them.

Many teens do not realize what we owe our parents. Many times when we have fights with our "old men" or our "old women" we tell them they don't know where it's at. But we (and I include myself) forget that at one time our parents were teenagers too.

They might not have had grannies and mop-like haircuts and they didn't have the jerk, the watusi or the swim but the fact remains that they were teens.

More important than any of these things is the fact that one day we shall become parents (99% of us anyway) and we shall bawl out our teens in the same manner that we are being bawled out now.

And so to end, I say that you don't have to be a jerk, or a square, or a creep — you just have to have a little understanding for your parents.
"Porky" John

Thanks Pop People
Dear *BEAT*:
I hope very much that you will print this letter because I want anyone in the pop music business reading *The BEAT* to see it — no matter how famous or how unknown they are.

I want very much to thank these people for making my life so much brighter. They help me everyday to forget my troubles. When I come home after some seven hours of school I always know that I can run upstairs and turn on my radio. Then I get completely caught up in the magic spell of this music I love so much.

While I'm at it I also want to thank *The BEAT* for it is you people who keep me informed on the happenings in the music world.

Since I've taken up so much of your valuable time, I'll flake off now. Thanks for everything.
"Me"

Fussy Adults
Dear *BEAT*:
I get very amused when I think about all the fuss adults are making over a simple, unimportant subject such as long hair. Here we are, practically in the middle of a war and some adult who thinks that just because he's 45 years old he has the right to yell, "cut that idiotic hair!"

I feel that there are many reasons why a boy should be allowed to wear his hair long without being forced to cut it and being kicked out of school.

First, it is his right to wear his hair the way he pleases. If the Constitution declares that everyone in the U.S. has the same equal rights regardless of race, color, creed or religion then aren't adults taking this boy's rights away? The right to be himself.

Secondly, if teenagers didn't have the urge to be different from their elders, what would we all look like? Mass produced human beings is the answer. It would get to the point where we really couldn't tell mother from daughter. Uniqueness is what we're told to strive for — for to be unique is to be different.

Last of all, long hair is a sign of rebellion. Rebellion against this whole crazy mixed up world that no one seems to understand. Short hair is a symbol of the adult's world and we don't want any part of it. Adults may ask, what's wrong with this world? Nothing much, except poverty, hate, war, suicides... Somewhere something's wrong if thousands of people hate themselves and the world. Somewhere someone failed.
"Milicent Emerson"

NEWSMAKERS

PAUL REVERE AND THE RAIDERS were recently snowbound in Chicago and indirectly gave a new group, the **Little Boy Blues**, a boost in their career. A local disc jockey who emceed the show the Raiders missed aired the stand-in group's record, "I'm Ready" and it was voted the best record of the week.

LEN BARRY is currently on a cross-country tour with **Gene Pitney**.

BARRY McGUIRE is in the news again. This time in Oslo, Norway. His Recording of "You Were On My Mind" (taken from his LP) has taken over the No. 1 spot from the Beatles who reigned for 12 weeks at the top of Oslo's chart.

JEFFERSON AIRPLANE just completed a highly successful stay at San Francisco's Matrix club. Their first single, "It's No Secret" b/w "Runnin' Round the World," is now on the record stands.

THE VENTURES are firming up their National Ventures Fan Club by opening offices at the Tokyo Hilton Hotel — in Tokyo.

THE SUPREMES will be working almost every day until mid-October. Thei appearances include a tour of the Caribbean Islands in April, taping an Ed Sullivan Show in May, an appearance at San Francisco's Fairmont Hotel (May 19-June 8) and the Flamingo, Las Vegas (Sept. 29 - Oct. 19).

SIMON AND GARFUNKEL have been awarded a gold record for their single, "The Sounds of Silence." The song was an original by **Paul Simon** and launched their career. Their belief in the song has led them to include it in both their albums — "Wednesday Morning 3 A.M." and "The Sounds of Silence."

DONOVAN has made all necessary financial settlements with his former manager and now is being managed by his father, **Donald Leitch**, in association with the **Vic Lewis** organization (which is, in turn, connected with **Brian Epstein**.)

GARY LEWIS AND THE PLAYBOYS and **THE KNICKERBOCKERS** join Dick Clark's "Where The Action Is" troupe on their national five-week concert tour leaving April 9. Also on the tour will be Paul Revere And The Raiders, Billy Joe Royal and the Viceroys in addition to the regular cast.

PETULA CLARK also set for a U.S. return. She opens at the Cocoanut Grove in April.

VIC DANA known here as both a dancer and a singer is known in Italy for only two recordings. He is now, however, in Milan to record all his hits in Italian.

FRANK SINATRA is having a world-wide birthday party. Nippon Victor (Record Company) in Japan is sponsoring a "Sinatra Fair" until April 20.

JACKIE DESHANNON filming "C'mon Let's Live a Little" for Paramount.

BOBBY VEE co-starring in the film with **Jackie**. Also in the movie is Eddie Hodges.

BOBBY RYDELL has just returned from a 17 day tour for GI's in Vietnam. His troupe travelled to performances by any means of transportation (including a tank) and performed for as few as 25 and as many as 7,000 GI's.

KRLA ARCHIVES

"The dirty, unkempt Rolling Stones..."

BEAT Photo Supplied by Tony Macarthur

By Gil McDougall

They're at it again! Don't they make you sick? I am talking about the international union of sour people! The people who belong to the union are those who criticize people and things purely for the joy of doing so.

When the Beatles first emerged with their long hair, they were the number one target for the union. But much to the surprise of the sour people the Beatles turned out to be very talented young blokes. So talented, that it was just not possible to criticize them unfairly.

With their number one target taken away from them, the international union of sour people decided that if they wanted to remain 'hip' (a hip sour person is one who spends all of his spare time worrying about whether his tastes are 'in.' Consequently he is usually 'out') they would have to find someone else to pick on. And then they found the Rolling Stones.

The union has decided that the Rolling Stones are dirty, unkempt, illiterate and definitely rebellious. Why have they decided this? Why because the Stones don't conform, of course!

In reality, the Rolling Stones don't come under any of the above classifications. Actually, the Stones are literate and very, very clean. As far as it goes, they also have more than their fair share of intelligence.

Mick Jagger spent two years at the London School of Economics. All of the Stones have had considerable schooling, and their artistic and literate achievements are very impressive.

Thankfully, the Rolling Stones (like the Beatles) refuse to conform to the traditional image of the Hollywood Star. They are not of the clean-cut school but remain individual regular type human beings (like you and me.) The Stones refuse to be typed, classified, or categorized and so, therefore, they are a prime target for the international union of sour people. Speaking for myself I am right behind the Stones, and if you have read this far you must be as well. (There will now be a short pause so that we can all jump up and down as we shout together—Rolling Stones forever.)

Musically, the Rolling Stones are very talented. The Keith Richard-Mick Jagger composition "As Tears Go By" was an excellent melody. They are at their best, however, when performing a fast mover such as "Get Off Of My Cloud." All of their records contain original sounds, plus an excitement that few other artists can put onto wax.

Charlie Watts is perhaps one of the most talented drummers on the entire popular music scene. He had already achieved a fair amount of fame, as a jazzman, before the Rolling Stones, as a group, were even professional musicians. In fact, the rest of the group were a little apprehensive about asking him to join the Rolling Stones—they thought that he would cost too much!

In those days Bill Wyman and Charlie Watts were the only two members of the group who were actually employed. Keith, Mick, and Brian wanted to spend all of their energy on making the Rolling Stones successful, but Bill and Charlie preferred to hold onto something a little more concrete until they broke into the big time. It is just as well that they did. Otherwise, Mick, Keith and Brian might have starved to death.

Perhaps the most enduring trait of the Rolling Stones is their completely honest attitude to life. If they think that you are a fink, you had better expect them to tell you so. They are outspoken about everything. From the people who make music to the people who buy what is made.

Keith Richard recently said of contemporary jazz: "They're all round the bend. Not every creative artist, of course, but a lot of people are getting away with rubbish. I was in a record shop a couple of days ago and watched a couple of way-out jazz fans saying how great a record was. It was an LP, and they were playing it at 45 speed!"

I don't know whether the two people that Keith talks about really knew what they were doing, but there are many people around today who make a big deal out of jazz and look down on Rock 'n' Roll purely because they think that it is the sophisticated thing to do.

You can find a lot of people who think this way at Bob Dylan concerts. At least you could before he picked up that beat. Now they think that it is sophisticated to knock Dylan's music. This kind of person is usually a charter member of the international union of sour people.

The Rolling Stones are soon to make a motion picture—about which they will not reveal a cotton-picking thing—and I feel fairly safe in saying that it is a pure success already. When you put a bunch of individualistic nuts such as this in one movie, something great is sure to happen!

Maybe their cinematic efforts will convince the international union of sour people that the Rolling Stones are not dirty, illiterate, or unkempt. As to their being rebellious and outspoken—I can think of a lot of things that I don't like too!

Two down - Now what?

...PAUL havin' "A Hard Day's Night."

WALTER SHENSON and the Beatles take time off in the Bahamas during the filming of their second motion picture together, "Help."

On a spring day in 1964, a young film producer named Walter Shenson raised a weary head from a cluttered desk and cast a wary eye at his visitor.

"You want me to produce a movie starring *what?*"

The visitor, a representative from United Artists, smiled patiently. "The Beatles" he repeated.

Shenson shrugged. "Who are *they?*"

The visitor went on to explain they were a rock and roll group that had taken England by storm, and that they appeared to be working the same magic all over the map. They had wild hair, a wild beat, and were, well...just wild.

"Sorry" said Shenson. "Not interested."

And he went on to explain that what he wasn't interested *in* was making an ordinary little pop musical.

While this particular scene was taking place in London, a similar discussion was being held in London.

"You want *who* to produce a movie starring us?" four Beatles chimed in unison.

"Walter Shenson," came the reply.

"Who's *he?*" chorused John, Paul, George and Ringo.

However, several weeks later, five strangers by the names of Lennon, McCartney, Harrison, Starkey and Shenson joined forces to film the most *extra*ordinary little pop musical in motion picture history.

It was titled "A Hard Day's Night," but it wasn't one. It was ninety low-budget minutes of pure delight.

How did this manage to happen considering that not so long ago, the foursome didn't know the fifth from Adam and the feeling was mutual?

First off, there was a good reason why Walter Shenson had never head of the Beatles. It all started seven years ago.

Seven years ago, Shenson was not the creator of avant garde films. He was the bright, young European Publicity Director for Columbia Pictures. The brightest and youngest thing about him at that time being the fact that he did not intend to *remain* the European Publicity Director for Columbia Pictures for the remainder of his days.

Someday he would *produce* pictures for Columbia. Not publicize

...PAUL prepares for a western?

them. But, through a twist of fate, he found himself out of the publicity racket long before entering the producing game.

You see, there was this book. You know, one of *those.* Not the kind you read and think "hmmmm, would that ever make a great movie." The kind you read, and if you are Walter Shenson, think, "I will make this into a great movie, or else."

At the outset, Shenson contacted the author and purchased the movie rights. (With his own money.) Then, with a star already in mind for the lead role, he hired a screenwriter and had the book scripted. (Using what was *left* of his own money.)

Then he took the project to the head of Columbia Pictures.

"This is it," said Shenson, handing over the manuscript.

"No it isn't," said his employer, returning the manuscript.

A bit of fencing followed. Shenson stood his ground firmly. It *was* a good idea. It *would* make money.

His employer paried, with a no

By Tony Barrow

There is only one man in the world qualified at this time to give an up-to-date progress report about the search for a suitable script for the third movie to be made by the Beatles. He is producer WALTER SHENSON, the man who is doing all the searching.

Shenson has read scores of scripts and story ideas submitted by American and British writers. He has held extended meetings with the Beatles. As I write, he is still waiting to find the right material for the foursome's vitally important third motion picture.

Today I talked with Walter and here, to set the record straight, are the facts as they stand.

WHEN WILL THE NEW MOVIE GO INTO PRODUCTION? It will not, says Walter, until the right story is found. He goes on: "It must be a subject which we feel is dead right for the Beatles. It must be something we all have a lot of enthusiasm for. We're not going to rush into something just for the sake of getting a shooting schedule under way."

WILL THE STORY BE A WESTERN?: "Probably not. The Beatles themselves can see plenty of good comedy situations in a Western setting. So can I. Someday I'm sure they'd like to try a Western. I doubt if they'll do so just yet. Right now the subject could be anything. Writers are working on ideas but at no time have I suggested that I am especially anxious to see Western ideas. All this dates back to the period when 'A Talent For Loving' was under consideration."

WILL DICK LESTER DIRECT THE THIRD MOVIE?: "That will depend on two things – whether Dick likes the script we finally choose and whether he's available at that time to direct the picture."

WHY HAVE SO MANY STORY IDEAS BEEN TURNED DOWN?: "For a variety of reasons. For one thing, so many writers have been basing their ideas on 'A Hard Day's Night' or 'Help!' or a combination of both scripts. As first and second pictures, these were fine. Now we want to find something completely original for the third one. To repeat the same ideas would be to look backwards instead of forwards. The boys want to have four completely different parts to play in their next film. They can still be John, Paul, George and Ringo but they needn't even be the Beatles. They need not be together when the story opens. They can come together as the story progresses. What we're after is a story which will put the boys in the centre of the action but a story which is strong enough to stand up as an entertaining picture in its own right."

THIS IS HOW WALTER SHENSON SUMMED UP: "We don't have a subject. As soon as we do, we'll move forward into production as quickly as possible. I know just how many rumours and bits of false information there are in circulation but all I can do for the moment is answer with negatives. As soon as there is something positive the full details will be announced – both from me and from the Beatles' office. There's no question of holding back information."

In the meantime, the Beatles' vacation is coming to an end. Within the next few weeks they will be getting down to work on something like fifteen new compositions – material for their first new album of 1966 plus two numbers for another single.

Until now, the boys have done most of their composing at home. In the future they are anxious to put greater pressure on themselves by fixing definite working hours.

Says John: "We don't really think up new songs on the spur of the moment. We need to go into a room, sit down and decide to spend a day writing. That's the way we'll work on the new album. We'll fix dates and times and stick to them. It's like any other job of work – you've got to discipline yourself."

on both counts. Then came his final thrust. In Shenson's opinion, was the idea worthy enough for him to consider resigning his present position in order to produce it?

It was, jabbed Shenson.

"Good luck, then," said his former employer. And that was that.

But what does all that have to do with Shenson's lack of Beatle knowledge?

(Turn to Page 12)

KRLA ARCHIVES

GEORGE SPEAKS!

By Gil McDougall

The quiet Beatle. The boy next door. These are some of the descriptions that reporters often apply to George Harrison. Well, I've got news for them! Mr. Harrison is sick and tired of being known as the do-nothing, know-nothing type of person.

George never was satisfied as being known as the boy next door. The idea is pretty crazy anyway. After all, how many people have such a rich and famous neighbor?

Possibly his marriage to Patti had something to do with it, but even if this is not so, George is now more determined than ever to speak his mind when he feels like it. Of course, like the other Beatles, George has always been known to speak out when the occasion called for it. Today, however, he is much more forward with his thoughts and ideas.

These new vibrations emitting from the Harrison Household tend to shatter previous conceptions of George's personality. People are now saying "maybe he isn't so quiet after all."

One particular myth that went quickly to the dogs was the much publicized "Harrison Guitar." According to his press agent, George had been steadily working on a new type of guitar that was soon to be put on the market. George killed this with: "There is no guitar. It was just a publicity thing."

Like John Lennon, George isn't particularly worried about his image. This kind of honest attitude is perhaps very seldom found among recording stars. Now, of course, George is married (sorry if I keep bringing it up) but before he and Patti took the vows he was asked if traveling with his girl hurt his image. George's answer was typical Beatle: "I don't know what you mean. We don't have an image. We don't believe in images."

Ignorant Reporters

Some people attending Beatle press conferences are not that familiar with the facts of life pertaining to the group. This irritates George very much, and he has often complained about reporters who try to interview him but are actually ignorant of facts about the Beatles. Some are so completely ignorant that they can not even tell one Beatle from another. This often results in quotes being ascribed to the wrong person.

Before getting married, George enjoyed living it up in London's great clubs. Even while on tour he enjoyed a little life now and again. He has visited the "in" places in many major cities. New York's discotheque, Arthur, did not impress him very much however. On Arthur, George said: "The discotheque in New Nork called Arthur is just a bad copy of an original. I'm talking about the Ad Lib. I was not very impressed with Arthur. They should chase out all the people who go there, turn the lights down and change the sound."

Being a married man now it will be some time before George is able to hit his favorite club again. He is more than occupied with his duties as a husband. He and Patti have done considerable redecorating in their Surrey bungalow. George has lived there for some time, of course, but as he recently said: "It was like a flat before I got married, but now it seems like a home. I'm not very hard to please when it comes to food, but Patti is a good cook anyway. She's not spectacular, but she is finding out a lot from this big cook book that she has."

Patti usually just lets her husband talk to the press, but she had plenty to say on her new way of life: "There is a lot to do in the house, and it is really a lot of fun. Sometimes it is a little bit difficult to believe that we are man and wife. We were going steady for two years."

Marriage

On the subject of going steady George revealed that he was very pleased that he and Patti had waited as long as they did. George explained: "Marriage is a very final thing and you should know about each other's peculiarities. I think that all people getting married should make a point of really knowing about their future husband or wife. Sometimes I forget that Patti and I are married. Every now and then I have to remind myself that Patti is my wife and not my girl friend."

With only one single Beatle left many people expected a lot of nasty letters to be sent to Patti and George. But as it turned out, the fans were very understanding. Patti especially hoped that there were no sore losers. She said: "I hope that we didn't break any hearts. I never think of George as a Beatle. When we are at home I just think of him as George—my husband."

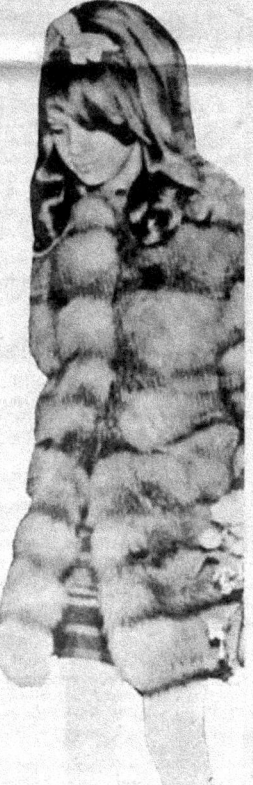

By Sue Barry

"My own tastes run to small blondes who can share a laugh with me. That sense of humor is all important to me... Anyway, I so date as often as we get a night free or an hour off."

So it was that George Harrison once spoke of his dream girl. He hadn't found her, but dated as often as possible in hopes that one day the right one would come along. It wasn't Estelle Bennet, Sally Anne Shaw or any of the other lucky girls who found themselves on a date with the "quiet Beatle."

George was the youngest of the quartet, in no hurry to marry. He once said when asked about another marriage in the group, "I don't think one marriage has hurt us. I don't think John was wrong to marry, one marriage out of four's all right, but two marriages or three, I'm not sure. I'm inclined to think it would hurt us."

And then one day he met Patti Boyd. She was one of a group of girls chosen to be in the Beatle's first film, "A Hard Day's Night." Patricia Ann Boyd was not what you'd call a beautiful girl, but she was a typical "dolly," a person of the moment. With her 5 ft. 6 in., 34-23-35, 110 lb. frame she seemed to fit in perfectly as a "Beatle girl." She and George were attracted to each other.

Tina Williams who worked with Patti in "A Hard Day's Night" put it this way, "I found that he (George) likes to sit and have long conversations and he prefers to talk about you rather than himself.

"I think this may be what attracted Patti particularly, as she is so reserved. But I noticed they always seemed to have plenty to say to each other."

But it wasn't love at first sight. They dated often, but only because they enjoyed each other's company. Said Patti: "George is tremendous fun to be with. We want it to stay just fun without having to talk about engagements and marriage."

It was not long after that, that Patti accompanied George, John and his wife Cyn to Ireland for five days. The public began to take notice of George and his steady. Once, when they dined at the Pickwick Club, George held Patti's hand and announced, "I'm old enough to go out with girls!"

Then in May of 1964 George and Patti vacationed once again with John and Cyn, this time in Taiti where they spent twenty peaceful days on a cruise of the Polynesian Islands. On a stopover in Los Angeles George smilingly introduced Patti as his "chaperone."

It became apparent that perhaps George had found the girl he was looking for in Patti. The same girl, was once spoke of as, "... a thoroughly nice person." They shared many interests—among them cars, watching movies and that all important sense of humor—Patti is easy to amuse.

Eventually the question of marriage popped up. George said, "Well, I can tell you I'm not going to end up like Elvis and think I'll wreck my image if I get married before I'm forty. Who will I marry? Well, that's obvious isn't it? You don't go around with a girl for months and months if you don't feel serious about her."

He went on to say, "Patti and I are not engaged. What is the use of engagements? It's just a way of telling people so they can save up for presents. And I don't want a white wedding—all that business with vicars and snivelling people."

And so it was that on January 22 of this year George married Patti in a quick simple ceremony in Epsom, Surrey.

Patti is a typical mod. She wears her blonde hair long, has blue eyes and enjoys a wonderful sense of fashion. Simple, loose-fitting dresses are her favorite.

She is, as has been said, a very quiet person which comes as a surprise for someone who lives in a world of constant excitement—she is one of the best fashion models in the London area.

Mick Curtis who has worked with her has this to say: "Patti is very quick, professional and punctual. She's very quiet, never says what her aims or ambitions are. I tried to talk to her about this once but didn't get very far. She doesn't talk about George either."

This young woman has come a long way from the farm in Kenya where she spent much of her childhood. Not only has she become a leading fashion model, but also has become one of the most envied girls in the world—wife of George Harrison, a boy from Liverpool made good.

For Girls only

by shirley poston

It's sure a good thing you're used to me by now.

I mean the way I always sound like I'm running a temperature. On account of today I am kind of delirious for real, thanks to a large bite from the flu bug.

At least I accomplished one thing during my agonizing sufferings (oh comma brother.) I have again managed to dream about the Beatles! *Really*, that is, and not just a made up one.

Anyroad, I did dream about them and it was fabulous. I actually was on the Beatle tour!! The dream took place in the plane, and it started when I was cowering under a seat during a take-off. (I'm deathly scared of flying.) (In planes, that is.)

And what did my dear Beatles do but rescue me. They all gathered around and made comforting remarks like "We aren't going to crash for at least an hour," etc.

I can't remember much of what they said, but their faces were so plain I still flip every time I think of the dream.

Then, all of a sudden, the pilot came running out of the cabin telling us to put on our parachutes and bail out. Only problem was, I didn't have one. I guess I wasn't really supposed to be there or something, which figures.

Anyway, John Lennon told me to hang onto him and out we jumped. At first, the parachute wouldn't open, but it finally did, and it seemed like *hours* before we hit the ground (you can about imagine how I hated *that*.)

I woke up the second we touched earth, but not before I heard John say the funniest thing. He said, and I quote, "how can you laugh when you know I'm down?"

Isn't that weird? I wish I could interpret dreams and that sort of thing. If anyone reading this can see any hidden meanings, please let me know.

In the meanwhile, I'll keep busy re-dreaming (day-fashion) that it was really George whose parachute I shared, and that we landed right in the middle of a deserted desert island, etc.

While I was nearing death's door (lay it on thick, kid), I also watched about ten thousand old movies on the telly. And I swear every single one of them was about some rare illness. I don't need to tell you that I had every single symptom of same. Do you do that? Immediately come down with everything you see on the screen?

I've done the same thing in school, too. About five seconds after we start reading about the Black Plague or something, I'm ready to be rushed to the hospital.

About the only good thing I saw (besides those fab, fab, fab Beatle cartoons on Saturday mornings) was this commercial. It makes up for all the creepy ones.

The one I'm raving about is for Gold Medal Flour. I'm sure you've seen it. This woman comes on and tells how she used to lack faith in her cooking until Gold Medal gave her connnnfidence! That has to be the all-time classic.

I shouldn't tell you this, 'cause it's sort of gory, but in one movie I saw, there was this horrible fire with everyone turning into crisps. Then, right after that scene, there was a commercial about shish-ke-bob on a flaming sword. I had to laugh, I couldn't help it. I'll bet everyone at the TV station about had a relapse over that one.

Oh, before I forget, I'd like to thank a girl named Ann (who lives in New Hampshire and writes to me every week) for knitting me a Beatle thingy.

Beatle Thingy

In case youre wondering (and I hardly blame you), a Beatle thingy is a knitted thingy about the size of a half-dollar. You name it after your favorite Beatle (guess what I named *mine*) and then you keep it with you at all times. It's supposed to bring good luck to both you and your fave.

Another fascinating item (oh, *sure*). My brother has finally managed to say something slightly humorous. One of his friends said something really uncool, and with a snarl, my brother replied: "Oh, go heat a building."

Say, I've been meaning to tell you this for years (a slight exaggeration.) I got the greatest letter awhile back from two girls named Sam and Aron.

No, I haven't completely cracked up. That's how they signed it ... two girls named Sam and Aron. (No one is perfect.)

Anyway, the letter was written by both of them, with two different colored pens. The ink was a different color, I mean. CRUMBS! We're getting nowhere fast!

What I am *trying* (very) to say is that one girl wrote in red ink and the other girl wrote in black. They sort of alternated paragraphs and traded remarks, and if you have the slightest idea what I'm blithering about (I certainly don't), give this idea a try.

The letter was lots of fun to read, and probably was even more fun to write.

Well, at least I didn't blabber about orange popsickles and feet. I'm saving those for next week. See you then?

Pop Music Hall Of Fame

Baseball has its Hall Of Fame, Hollywood has its Graumen's Chinese Theater—so why not a pop music Hall Of Fame? There *is* no reason why not and so Hollywood's newest teen night club, The Hullabaloo, is starting its own Hall Of Fame.

The Hall will be located in the lobby of the club and will feature moementoes, the star's handprints and autographs in concrete as well as all those other little goodies which are traditionally found in a Hall Of Fame.

The club does have one slight problem, however. One which it will be up to you to solve—and that is, who will be enshrined in the Hullabaloo's Hall Of Fame?

All readers of *The BEAT*, regardless of where they may live, will have the opportunity to vote for three artists who you feel deserve to find their way into the Hall Of Fame.

Since it is a teen club and since pop music really *does* belong to teenagers, you are the only ones who will be able to dictate what artists should be awarded a place in the Pop Music Hall Of Fame.

There will be three categories and all you have to do is list what American group *and* single artist and what International group *or* artist you would like to see in the Hall for 1966.

Your votes should be mailed to the Hullabaloo Club, 6230 Sunset Blvd., Hollywood, California. The deadline for votes will be April 7, after which all of the votes will be tabulated and the winners will be properly placed in the Hall with all the flourish and glitter of a Hollywood ceremony.

Please do vote, though, because it is *your* Hall Of Fame and it will be you and no one else who determines who goes in and who remains out—until 1967 at least!

SEND BALLOTS TO:
HULLABALOO CLUB
6230 SUNSET BLVD.
HOLLYWOOD, CALIF.
PLEASE CAST MY HALL OF FAME VOTES FOR:

AMERICAN ARTIST: _____

AMERICAN GROUP: _____

INTERNATIONAL
GROUP OR ARTIST: _____

RON STENDER (now Pvt. Ron Stender, U.S. Army). This picture was taken just prior to his departure for service in the Army.

A Pop Musician Experiences Draft

Staff of The BEAT: as I was reading the new BEAT last night, I noticed a small article on the draft. As a former member of the Barons and the Pyramids, and just finishing my Basic Combat Training, I have written the following letter in hope of giving BEAT readers my side of the draft as it happened to me.
Sincerely .. Pvt. Ron Stender
US ARMY

Hello *BEAT* readers. This letter may come as a surprise, but I feel it may ease some of your tensions over the draft.

Before my departure last December, I found myself a busy leader, singer and sax player in The Barons, and a replacement in The Pyramids. Both groups played such places as Disneyland, Rendevous, Retail Clerks stores and thousands of schools and dances throughout California and the Western United States.

As a member of the Barons, I engaged in many back-up jobs with such stars as Bobby Day, The Rivingtons, Dick & Dedee, Mary Wells, The Olympics, Otis Redding, and many more. On December 21, 1965, I found all of this lifted out from under me completely, and found myself on the way to Fort Bliss, Texas for my Basic Combat Training as a member of the US ARMY. I soon found that I wasn't in a boat by myself, as non other than Johnny Crawford was right across the aisle. This helped my attitude greatly, though I knew it would still be a rough, long road.

To put it short, Basic was the roughest 9 weeks of my life, but actually was fun as well as interesting. When I first left, I thought I had left everything by leaving the band, and my girlfriend behind, but now I think I see the light. We must remember that if our country wasn't free, that we wouldn't have rock & roll music, free radio and television, records, and no tours and appearances by American and English artists. We wouldn't have much of anything to enjoy as we do today.

Well my outlook is, that we that live on music must help to protect it, right?? So, if this is the cost, it can't be so bad to take a 2 year vacation. Right again??

Besides, I found out that the ARMY has some really great areas for learning, so you get something more in here than what you think. Just because you get drafted doesn't mean that you're getting a free ticket to Viet Nam. What it means is that no matter what you do, or who you are on the outside, that you are needed by your country in any one of thousands of different occupations, be it a Gorilla Figher or a Mess Cook.

In summarization, I'm glad that I'm getting it over with. Besides, I think I'll be twice as aggressive with music when I get back, than I ever was before.

So when your letter comes, take it with a grain of salt; some of us have more to leave than you, and we've even found it tasty.
Sincerely,
Pvt. Ron Stender

BALLADS:
OF MEN AND GREEN BERETS

The "Green Berets" are a special group within the Army who carry out special missions beyond the scope of regular troops. The range of their skills and the fantastic, knife-edge sharpness to which they are honed would make some of the most famed fighting men of old look like amateurs. Chosen from men in the topmost range of physical, mental and personality qualities, only *three* "Green Beret" candidates out of a *hundred* applicants survive the long, arduous training course.

The men who emerge from it are, competent fighting men, thoroughly trained in all scientific methods of combat, including karate and judo. In addition, each man of a 12-man squad is expected to be completely skilled in at least two areas of specialization, selected from the following group: communications, medics, demolitions, operations and intelligence, and weapons.

In the field of pop music, we are used to hearing songs about love and dating and other generally light, non-serious subjects. Obviously, the war in Vietnam is not generally considered to be subject matter for Top 40 material.

But, out of that cold and dirty war "so far away," has come a group of the first war songs in two decades, and they have come from a young man named Barry Sadler. A young man who proudly wears The Green Beret.

Until the late Spring of 1965, Barry had been stationed in Viet Nam. It was at that time that he was wounded while leading a small combat patrol; he operated on himself—cleaning the wound between fainting spells—until some members of his patrol found him and carried him to safety.

Somehow, during the long months that Barry was stationed in Viet Nam, he found time to compose several tunes about the war which he was fighting with so many others. They were songs about the perils and dangers faced by our fighting men in defense of our precious liberty, songs about the very human aspects of war.

After his injury, Barry was eventually sent back home to the States for a complete recuperation, and it was after his arrival that some of his songs were brought to the attention of RCA Victor.

Barry was immediately put under contract to the company and within a short time recorded his first record — one of his own compositions, written on duty in Viet

Nam — "The Ballad of the Green Beret." The song went almost immediately to the Number One spot on the nation's pop charts—put there by a predominantly young record-buying public who had been accused of "not caring;"

and following that reception, Barry released an album—"The Ballads of the Green Beret"—containing a total of 12 of his compositions.

Twenty-five years old, the father of a year-old son, Thor, a Black Belt in judo, an experienced paratrooper, a trained Army medic who aspires to be a full-fledged musician . . ., a highly-skilled, superbly trained young man who wears the Green Beret. This is the voice behind the Ballad . . . this is Barry Sadler.

Our Fighting Men in Action...

Qualifications

What does it take to be a man in the special forces of the U.S. Army?

- *He must be in good shape.* There's no tougher fighting man in any Army, anywhere in the world than a Special Forces soldier.
- *He must be intelligent.* A Special Forces soldier must be smart enough to learn a great deal, to think for himself, to invent and improvise when needed.
- *He must be a trainer.* In Special Forces, his mission will require that he teach what he knows to others—so that they can defend themselves against aggression or fight against those who would deny their freedom.
- *He must be a double volunteer.* He must volunteer for Airborne training, and for Special Forces duty. When he does this, he agrees to go anywhere in the world, on a moment's notice—no questions asked.

KRLA ARCHIVES

STAMP OUT STIFF HAIR.

Caryl Richards

★ Caryl Richards ★

Student Discount Exchange Coupon
Exchange this coupon and $1.25 (tax incl.) at Box Office. Save 50c on $1.75 admission (one admission with each coupon)

WORTH 50¢

EASTER VACATION FUN

★ **TEEN-AGE FAIR** ★
THE WORLD'S FAIR FOR TEEN-AGERS
HOLLYWOOD PALLADIUM
APRIL 1 thru 10, 1966
Doors Open Daily: Noon to Midnight

SEE...IN PERSON... • SONNY & CHER
• The REGENTS • The CHALLENGERS • JOEY PAIGE
• SAM RIDDLE'S TV SPECIALS • TOP TV, RECORD & MOVIE STARS

OVER $3,000,000 WORTH OF FABULOUS EXHIBITS & ATTRACTIONS
Fender Battle of the Beat — Model Car Drag Strip Racing — Custom Car Caravan — Surfing Movies — Miss Teen International Pageant — Harmony Folk Festival — Guest stars in Person from Movies, T.V., Records and Radio (Top D.J.'s) — Beauty Clinics — Judo — Karate Thrill Shows — Photography and Home Movie Exposition — Fabulous Fashion Shows — Dream Cars of the Future — Bands and Drill Teams — Free Prizes and Gifts — Nonstop Record Hop
All above events and attractions included in admission price

★ VISIT CARYL RICHARDS' BOOTH AT THE FAIR ★
WIN HUNDREDS OF DOLLARS WORTH OF PRIZES

KRLA Tunedex

DAVE HULL

BOB EUBANKS

DICK BIONDI

JOHNNY HAYES

EMPEROR HUDSON

CASEY KASEM

CHARLIE O'DONNELL

BILL SLATER

This Week	Last Week	Title	Artist
1	1	CALIFORNIA DREAMIN'	The Mamas & Papas
2	6	NOWHERE MAN	The Beatles
3	2	THESE BOOTS ARE MADE FOR WALKIN'	Nancy Sinatra
4	4	DAYDREAM	The Lovin' Spoonful
5	12	BANG BANG	Cher
6	7	19TH NERVOUS BREAKDOWN	Rolling Stones
7	3	LISTEN PEOPLE	Herman's Hermits
8	5	THE BALLAD OF THE GREEN BERET	Sgt. Barry Sadler
9	11	I'M SO LONESOME I COULD CRY B.J.	Thomas & Triumphs
10	9	HOMEWARD BOUND	Simon & Garfunkel
11	8	I AIN'T GONNA EAT OUT MY HEART ANYMORE	Young Rascals
12	13	WOMAN	Peter & Gordon
13	18	WALKIN' MY CAT NAMED DOG	Norma Tanega
14	29	SOUL AND INSPIRATION	The Righteous Bros.
15	10	YOU BABY	The Turtles
16	19	DARLING BABY	The Elgins
17	23	WORKIN' MY WAY BACK TO YOU	The Four Seasons
18	20	THE CHEATER	Bob Kuban
19	24	CALL ME	Chris Montez
20	26	BABY SCRATCH MY BACK	Slim Harpo
21	28	LOVE MAKES THE WORLD GO ROUND	Deon Jackson
22	32	FOLLOW ME	Lyme & Cybelle
23	30	THIS OLD HEART OF MINE	The Isley Bros.
24	22	WAKE ME, SHAKE ME	Four Tops
25	31	INSIDE-LOOKING OUT	The Animals
26	27	HUSBANDS & WIVES	Roger Miller
27	—	WHAT GOES ON	The Beatles
28	34	IT'S TOO LATE	Bobby Goldsboro
29	33	SURE GONNA MISS HER	Gary Lewis & The Playboys
30	35	KICKS	Paul Revere & The Raiders
31	36	ONE TRACK MIND	The Knickerbockers
32	37	SPANISH FLEA	Herb Alpert
33	—	SHAPE OF THINGS	The Yardbirds
34	37	WHAT NOW MY LOVE	Herb Alpert
35	—	YOUNG LOVE	Lesley Gore
36	—	SECRET AGENT	Johnny Rivers
37	—	LULLABY OF LOVE	The Poppies
38	—	YOUR PERSONALITY	Jackie Lee
39	—	MAGIC TOWN	The Vogues
40	—	WOULD YOU BELIEVE	Jerry Naylor

WANT TO PLAY GUITAR?

We help you organize and promote your own group.
Call 793-6862 RIGHT AWAY! We have a few guitars to lend to beginning students to play at home.
Our pro teachers will show you how easy it is to play the top tunes now on KRLA.
COMPLETE RECORDING FACILITIES
We sell all types of guitars and amplifiers. You can take three years to pay!

The FLAHERTY SCHOOL OF MUSIC
129 N. Hill Avenue — Pasadena

Spy-Spoof Car At The Teen-Age Fair

If you want to see the spy-spoof car of the year then don't miss the Teen-Age Fair, which will be held April 1-10 at the Hollywood Palladium.

The fantastic spy-rod is George Barris' ZZR and it will be shown for the first time at the Fair. The way-out machine was built for the movie "Out Of Sight," which will be released during the summer.

The ZZR will be the highlight of a one-million dollar display of custom cars and bikes built by Barris. Also on display will be the Flaky T, the Beau T, The 003 Mustang, the Apartment Station Wagon, the Silencer Car, the A Go Go Rod, two customized Yamahas and the Ferrina, a miniature Italian grand prix car.

Utilizing the latest in rod design, the ZZR has two 340 cubic inch 1966 Buick engines with a total of 800 horsepower. Mounted on the rear is an arsenal trunk locker complete with machine guns, pistols, silencers, rockets, flares, grenades, knives, brass knuckles and a skid juice spreader (toys, of course.)

In Barris' cars, the Teen-Age Fair has obtained the finest custom cars in the world. His reputation has spread throughout the world on the strength of cars he has customized for movie personalities and for TV shows.

The custom car display will be just one of many highlights of the Teen-Age Fair. Among the hundreds of things to see and do will be: acres of amusement rides imported from Europe; a hall of the unexplained; an operative laser beam; continuous surfing movies; live television shows; the "Miss Teen International Pageant," appearances by motion picture, TV and recording stars; autograph parties; the "Battle of the Beat," and the American debut of French parapsychologist Paul Goldin, entertaining four times daily with the fantastic powers of the sixth sense.

Paul Newman is 'Harper' ...a different kind of cat!
BACALL • HARRIS • HILL • LEIGH • TIFFIN • WAGNER • WINTERS
PACIFIC'S **PANTAGES** THEATRE HOLLYWOOD
HOLLYWOOD BLVD. near VINE — HO. 9-2211
EXCLUSIVE ENGAGEMENT NOW! CALL THEATRE FOR SHOW TIMES

KRLA ARCHIVES

Inside KRLA
By Eden

Well, Super Sissy has struck again. Now a permanent member of the KRLApes basketball team, Super Sissy can be found at every game running rampant on the basketball court.

The only problem is that he seldom contributes much to the game as he is usually too busy running about tapping people on the soulder and calling them "silly savages."

B.J. Thomas—the young man who sings "I'm So Lonesome I Could Cry"—visited the studios of KRLA this week, along with everybody's favorite people, nice-guys Joey Paige and Jerry Naylor.

Incidentally, Jerry has a brand new record out, entitled "Would You Believe?" Well, yes Jerry—we *would!* We would even go so far as to believe a very large, super-sized type of hit for you with your latest disc.

It has just a little of the country and western flavor which has become so popular, and a lot of great singing—which is *always* nice. And, it is more than high time that Jerry Naylor had a hit. He's not only one of the nicest young men in the industry—but he is also one of the most talented.

Old Uncle D.M. has been walking around looking somewhat forlorn lately. It's very sad, actually; you see, his membership drive for the Mouse Fan Club of America and New Zealand—of which he is the President, Secretary, Treasurer, and sole member—has been a total failure.

He had hoped that possibly he might be able to recruit at least one more member—you know, someone to be Clean-Up Chairman—but even that just didn't work out, and Dick will just have to continue being stuck with all the dirty work involved in running a big time fan club. Oh well, Richard—in this life, we must learn to accept the sweet with the bitter... no matter *how* sour the lemon turns out to be!

In a survey conducted by Billboard magazine recently, KRLA was listed as the most important station in Los Angeles in breaking records. Also, KRLA DJ's Dave Hull, Bob Hudson, and Dick Biondi were cited as the most influential DJ's in the City of the Angels in playing new records and introducing them to the public.

Just recently, a large high school convention—which included several lectures for its participants—was held at the hotel adjacent to KRLA. Funny thing was that not many people seemed to be attending those lectures—for some reason, the entire membership of the convention re-located itself in the lobby of the KRLA studios where they proceeded to watch all of the on-the-air proceeding while in progress.

And once again we come to our favorite time of the column; yes, folks—it's time to revisit your favorite BatManager—and *his*—John-John Barrett.

However, before we give this week's clues to our BatManager mysterious mystery, we'd like to answer some questions. Our *BEAT* offices have been beaten under with mail of late asking us just *who* John Barrett is, and how he happened to become the now world-infamous BatManager.

Well, John in the General Manager of Radio Station KRLA—which incidentally, had nothing whatsoever to do with his obtaining the position of BatManager. That is definitely a position held in high esteem, but as to just how John-John was able to secure it... well, that is all part of our huge and insidious mystery.

Rumor this week around the ol' Bat Cave has it that some pieces of green felt have been found lying around outside of the Upstairs Bat Cave at KRLA; but that's not all. Oh no—it has also been mentioned in some circles (strictly on the *square* of course!) that John has been spotted stealing stealthily from his Gold Leaf-and-Velvet office wearing... Holy BatManagers, yes!... wearing a *green felt cape!!!*

Now I have never been one to jump to conclusions, but I should definitely think that there is something to all of this. Not only that, but I know for a fact that John has had lunch—on *three* different occasions!—with someone who very distinctly resembles Super Sissy.

Will we ever find out about the BatManager sign on John's door? Will we ever know who put it there? And was that person responsible for the Green Felt episode outside the Bat Cave? Tune in next week, children, same Bat Time, same Bat Channel, same Bat Kave-RLA!!!!!!!!!!

SONNY BONO got so lonely while wife Cher was in the hospital with the flu recently that he felt he just had to get out among his fans. He and a friend, Terry Dene, examine a menu at Dave Hull's Hullabaloo in Hollywood while the delighted fans look on during Sonny's surprise visit to the pupular teenage club.

THE ONE ON THE LEFT'S singer Johnny Cash and the one on the right's a deejay who is undoubtedly in love with Nancy Sinatra.

New Teen Spot
Di Gati's Di Go-Go
230 West Whittier Blvd.
La Habra, Calif.
Top Entertainment Nightly
MINIMUM AGE—15
$1.00 Admission

March 8-27
THE ASSOCIATION
also
Texas Twosome
ends March 13
also
Danny Cox
March 15-27

The ICE HOUSE GLENDALE
folk music in concert
phone 245-5043 for reservations

KRLA BEAT Subscription
SAVE 33% Of Regular Price

☐ 1 YEAR—52 Issues—$5.00   ☐ 2 YEARS—$8.00
☐ 6 MONTHS—$3.00

Enclosed is: ☐ CASH   ☐ CHECK
PLEASE PRINT—Include Your Zip Code

Send to: .... Age: ....
Address: ....
City: ....
State: .... Zip: ....

MAIL YOUR ORDER TO: KRLA BEAT
6290 Sunset, Suite 504
Hollywood, Calif. 90028

Foreign Rate: $9.00—52 Issues

Surf with Mike Doyle (2 Sessions)
JOIN THE SURFARI
SOUTH OF ROSARITO BEACH, MEXICO THIS EASTER VACATION... Co-ed fun in the Baja sun.
Call or write for information—CR 1-4843, SURFARI, 9000 Sunset Blvd. Los Angeles, Calif. 90069

UNLIKE *ANYTHING* YOU'VE EVER SEEN!
WARNER BROS. SUPER CINERAMA PRODUCTION
BATTLE OF THE BULGE
PACIFIC'S CINERAMA DOME Theatre
NOW PLAYING!

KRLA ARCHIVES

Walkers' 'Hairy' Shows

By Gil McDougall

Perhaps I had better qualify the title of this article. The Walkers probably have the most hysterical fans around (that's if you don't count Beatlemaniacs). When they appear on stage, there is a sort of frenzied charge from the audience to the performers. The situation, however, sometimes prevents the Walker Brothers from giving as good a performance as they would like. Most of the time they never stay on stage more than twenty minutes.

Gary Walker, being the drummer, is usually safer than the other two but he still remembers the time that a man ran up past Scott and John and then proceeded to punch him! Some of the concerts by the Walkers are almost unbelievable. Gary explained: "It's getting really hairy on stage. They tear our shirts right off our bodies. When they get to me it is the end. Usually Scott and John get it all. They are in the front and I'm back there on the drums. They just run up there and grab us."

The Walkers also have that seemingly age old problem that the Beatles, Stones, and others always complain about: The fans enjoy throwing things at them. Not from anger, of course, from appreciation! Personally I wouldn't want people chucking objects at me—regardless of the reason. The objects are never hard or heavy, but even so can cause serious damage to the performers. That is something that fans seem to forget about in the excitement.

Teabags Thrown

On several occasions the fans have dragged one or more of the Walkers right off the stage! Usually they are content to throw teabags (the Walker Brothers once stated a preference for them) or just mill around the stage and scream.

Two years ago the Walkers were completely unknown in the U.K. Two months ago they were voted second place in a poll for the most promising new group of 1965.

There was a time when Gary Walker thought that he wasn't getting enough attention. He clarified: "I was going to become a dancer so that people would see me. Scott and John are always on the scene but I hardly ever get noticed being at the back all the time. The dancers get noticed so I was going to join them."

The success of the Walker Brothers in pop-conscious Britain is surprising when you consider the fact that they are all Americans. Scott Walker (real name Scott Engel) who is six foot one inch was born on January 9th, 1944. His birthplace was Hamilton, Ohio. His first public appearance, at the age of eighteen, was at the "Hollywood A-Go-Go."

Drummer For Elvis

John Walker (real name John Maus) was born in New York City, and his first public appearance was also at the "Hollywood A-Go-Go." Gary Walker (real name Gary Leeds) was born in California and has been playing Rock 'n' Roll for some seven years. He once played as a substitute drummer for Elvis Presley.

The Walker Brothers may be American but they have settled down to the English way of life with great enthusiasm. According to Gary: "We love the whole scene. The people are friendly—you can get to know them. The country and everything is great."

After returning from his recent vacation in the U.S. John arrived in the U.K. and expressed surprise over the scene in America: "The groups and teenagers over there have British style long hair. Out of the top hundred in the States only about five were worthy of their positions. The groups there try to copy the Kinks, Beatles and others."

The Walker Brothers have an apartment located in Chelsea, which is an "in" place to live in London. They finally had to get an unlisted phone number last month. So many fans were calling them that it really got to be pretty much of a drag. Some excited young female fans would call the boys up, and then when one of the Walkers answered they would be too flustered to talk at all!

On some occasions the Walker Brothers have to be protected from people who aren't fans of theirs. The man who usually comes to the rescue is their organist, Johnny B. Great. He just happens to weigh a hefty two hundred and fifty pounds! At one Walker concert Johnny had to protect the boys from the promoters of the show. One of these promoters tried to get nasty with Scott and according to Scott "I told them that I would get someone to kill them. Along came Johnny, and that was that."

The Walkers are looking forward to doing "some films" but they have no concrete plans at the present time. They will continue to do television and live performances throughout the U.K. Providing that they don't get killed in the process that is. Their next tour will be with Roy Orbison and that should be "a real gas." Undoubtedly, the press reports of the tour will tell of riots, cavalry charges and general mass hysterics. The Walkers will be dragged from the stage and have their shirts torn from their backs. Gary might even get involved in a punch-up again. What a way to make a living!

Tom Jones—V.I.P.

(Continued From Page 1)

forced to leave Mark with his grandparents in Wales due to the fact that they were living in other people's flats. Now that they have their new home they have brought their son to live with them which is something that they have wanted to do for so long.

Tom is rather old-fashioned in so far as he believes children should be raised by their parents so he is naturally very happy to not only have an ultra-fab new house but also to have his son sharing it with him and Linda.

On the BEAT

By Louise Criscione

Sad news for Byrd lovers—Gene Clark is suffering from "nervous strain" and has been advised by doctors not to undertake any further personal appearances with the group for the next several weeks.

Byrd's manager, Eddie Tickner, revealed that: "He's clearly not well enough to cope with the pressures and strains of one-night stands and cross-country travel. Gene, of course, remains a member of the group and will continue to write songs and work with them on their recordings."

Gene's "illness" will force him to miss the remainder of the Byrd's cross-country tour which began on March 3 and winds up in early April.

Herman's Gold Taken

Herman is having his share of problems too. When he arrived back in London, after a brief stopover in L.A., British custom officials confiscated his Gold Record at the airport! Their reason? The disc, an award from the American record industry for sale of a million dollars of the group's records here in the U.S., will have to be valued and the proper amount of duty paid on it by the group.

... GENE CLARK

Naturally, Herman, the Hermits and their management are furious at the confiscation protesting that an award for export earnings should not be dutiable.

I admit to almost total ignorance on the subject but it seems to me that this whole thing is something of a fiasco and a particularly lousy deal for Herman.

Congrats to the Righteous Brothers for a lot of things but especially for their fantastic new record, "Soul And Inspiration." I'm glad to hear both Bobby and Bill's voices on the disc—sounds great for a change.

However, someone certainly steered the Brothers' publicity people the wrong way. A release states that Bobby and Bill are the only recording artists in history to ever have three LP's in the Top 15 best selling albums at the same time.

Four For Herbie

No so. Herbie Alpert has done it before and, in fact, the talented Mr. Alpert and his T.J. Brass currently have *four* albums residing in the Top 15 in the nation!

The Young Rascals have a brand new one, "Good Lovin'," which is already a smash in New York and promises to be just as big all across the nation. I heard a sneak preview of the new song about a month ago when Eddie sang it to me right here in *The BEAT* offices.

It sounded like a winner then and I certainly hope it is because these five Rascals are one of the funniest groups on the scene—also one of the most talented. So much so that I have finally completely forgiven them for keeping me waiting four hours for an interview that time!

Britain's Musician's Union is considering a proposal to ban miming on television shows which would drastically effect the current crop of English pop shows.

In the first place, only the groups who are able to reproduce their record sound "live" will come out sounding half-way decent on the shows. And secondly, the television shows themselves will be forced to go to considerable expense to hire an orchestra to back up their guests which is, of course, exactly what the Musician's Union has in mind.

"Heartache" for Marvin

Marvin Gaye has another smash in "One More Heartache," which is not at all unusual for a Motown artist especially for one of Marvin's calibre. As also befits a member of the Motown family, Marvin has lined up a busy schedule for himself.

He'll play Vancouver's Cave Supper Club, Bimbo's in San Francisco, the Whiskey A Go-Go on Hollywood's Sunset Strip and New York's Copacabana.

Marvin will also be on "Ed Sullivan" in June and is currently in New York cutting his next album which will be predominantly blues with such tracks as "Night Life," "This Will Make You Laugh" and "Funny" included on the LP.

... MARVIN GAYE

KRLA ARCHIVES

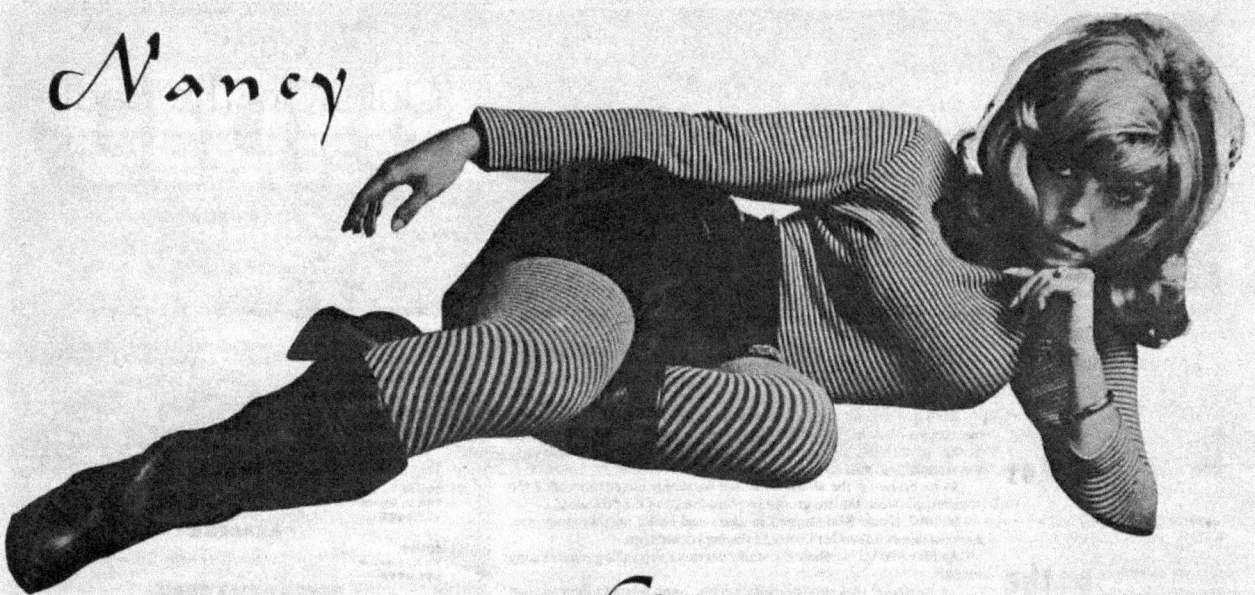

Nancy Sinatra

HOLLYWOOD, (U.P.I.) – Dark-haired Nancy Sinatra is riding the record crest with her "These Boots Are Made For Walkin'," which just won a gold record for her, and no one is happier than her famous singing father, Frank.

The 25-year-old daughter told U-P-I's Vernon Scott in Hollywood ... "When they bring in the sales charts of daddy's records he merely says 'The heck with mine ... let me see how Nancy is doing'."

Nancy, who wears eye glasses to correct a far-sighted condition, works for Reprise Records, which is owned by her father. The "Walkin' Boots" song sold more than 500-thousand records the first seven weeks it hit the stands. Nancy also has a "Boots" album being released this week and combined with the single she could make about 100-thousand dollars in the next few months.

Nancy says father Frank has never tried to help with her voice or singing career. Composer-arranger Lee Hazelwood is her professional teacher.

Says dark-eyed Nancy ... "I'd describe my voice as a new sound, a calculated sound. It's not the nice little girl, or all-American girl sound."

Nancy was divorced in 1965 from singer Tommy Sands after five years of marriage. She lived with her mother and 17-year-old sister Tina for a time but shortly before Christmas bought a new three-bedroom home in Coldwater Canyon. She dates occasionally but has no steady boy friend.

The rising singing star insists her parents' divorce didn't hurt her, Tina or Frank Sinatra, Junior. Nancy explains ... "They had already given us a set of unshakable values that will serve us well the rest of our lives."

Nancy goes on ... "I'm proud of the show business tradition in the family. Frank, Junior, is doing well singing and Tina is directing high school shows. I think Tina will be the biggest talent in the family. She doesn't want to sing and won't have to. She'll go into the biggest movie of 1968 or something."

Nancy Sinatra was asked what she would do with all the new found wealth. She replied ... "I dream about furs and diamonds. But my business manager dreams of stocks and bonds and orange grove investments."

She adds ... "Actually my way of living won't change very much. Some day I'd like to marry and have children. Until then I'll continue to work ... and put a little money aside for my father's old age."

Pop Music is Heading Where?

(Continued From Page 1)

Up until today singles were the big sellers and albums the poor sellers but now the trend has reversed itself with albums recording the biggest sales and singles coming in a poor second.

People in the industry accord this phenomena to the fact that the Beatles made the teen market very much aware of albums. Before the Beatles appeared, teens spent the greater amount of their money on singles where now they wait to purchase the hit singles on albums.

This, of course, is due in part to the recording companys' trend of following up a hit single with an album of the same name including the single as well as 11 other tracks. If the teens wait for these albums to be released they get more for their money.

In today's market only the top ten singles receive good sales returns while the sales for the rest of the singles' market has stooped so low that sales of thirty or forty thousand are enough to warrant a "hot" mark on the nation's top hundred charts.

Getting back to trends in records themselves, it is safe to say that the year of folk has officially ended. Folk has always, and will continue to have a certain share of the market but the day of protest records has ended.

Barry's Bag

Barry McGuire can certainly attest to this. His "Eve Of Destruction" was one of the biggest sellers of '65 but since then Barry has been unable to come up with any sort of hit follow-up since most record buyers have placed him exclusively in the protest bag.

Barry himself was afraid this sort of thing would happen and so was not overly surprised when it did. It's the price an artist pays when he allows himself to be categorized and stereotyped.

The king of folk, Bob Dylan, has always had his hard core of followers. And although I'm sure he will continue to produce hit albums it is doubtful that his singles will have the impact and immediate sales which his "Like A Rolling Stone" demanded a few short months ago.

Again like folk, country and western music has its own followers and its own market. It even has its own charts and artists frequenting the C&W charts seldom find their way onto the pop charts. Of course, there is one notable exception in the person of Roger Miller.

Miller, time after time, comes up with singles which are acceptable to both the pop and country markets, thus assuring him of double sales. His current "Husbands And Wives," is climbing up both charts with amazing speed and will most probably make the top ten in both fields.

That leaves us rhythm 'n' blues. The sound of the future? Possibly. It's strange that the pop market had to be conditioned for R & B by the English groups but that is exactly what has taken place.

Especially the Rolling Stones have enabled the teen market to tune its ears to the American blues. Before the Stones, most teens had never even *heard* of the great R&B entertainers but by the constant praise of the Stones people such as Muddy Waters, John Lee Hooker, Jimmy Reed and Otis Redding became familiar names.

And now that they are familiar names they just might become prominent record sellers. Otis Redding has waxed his version of the Stones' "Satisfaction" which he calls a tribute to the Stones' efforts to popularize rhythm 'n' blues.

In fact, R&B has already become so widely accepted that songs which normally would never have ventured out of the R&B market have shown up on our pop charts. Examples on today's charts show such singles as "Baby Scratch My Back," "Up Tight," and "Cryin' Time" ascending both the R&B and the pop charts.

Ignored

Perhaps then as 1965 was the year of folk, 1966 will be the year of rhythm 'n' blues. Let's hope so anyway for R&B is an American institution, one which has been with us probably longer than any other form of music but which has just as long been ignored by the mass of record buyers.

It is time that R&B was accepted by the general record-buying public. For when you come right down to it there is nothing with the feel of R&B, the place where "soul" really is.

Say you saw it in The BEAT

BRITISH TOP TEN

1. 19TH NERVOUS BREAKDOWN..........The Rolling Stones
2. THESE BOOTS ARE MADE FOR WALKIN'..................Nancy Sinatra
3. GROOVY KIND OF LOVE...The Mindbenders
4. SHA LA LA LA LEE............Small Faces
5. BARBARA ANNE..............Beach Boys
6. BACKSTAGE..................Gene Pitney
7. MY LOVE....................Petula Clark
8. INSIDE LOOKING OUT.........The Animals
9. LIGHTENING STRIKES........Lou Christie
10. I CAN'T LET GO.............The Hollies

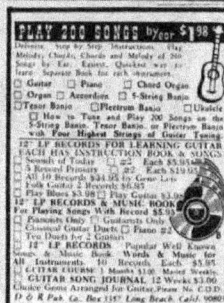

KRLA ARCHIVES

joe long Joins the 4 SEASONS

By Carol Deck

For the first time in their ten year highly successful history there has been a personnel change in The Four Seasons.

Early last month bass player Nick Massi decided to make like a homebody and returned to his home state of New Jersey rather than continue with the world wide traveling of the Seasons.

The other three Seasons also returned to New Jersey, but only long enough to collect Nick's replacement, Joe Long.

Joe's only been with the group for a very short time but he's already worked on their current smash, "Working My Way Back To You."

Joe was born, raised and still lives in New Jersey, keeping the Four Seasons the favorite sons of that state.

Only Bob Gaudio, who was born in the Bronx, New York, is an out-of-stater by birth, but he migrated to Jersey some years ago. Both Frankie Valli and Tommy de Vito are natives of New Jersey.

Joe's had a good deal of professional experience both in the state and nationwide. He started his own five piece group, the Rockets, which broke up in 1961 when Uncle Sam called several members into the service.

So he broke up the all-male act and formed a mixed act called the Accents. Between the two groups he played in 25 of the 50 states.

In 1962 Uncle Sam stepped in again and broke up this group too. Joe then joined Al and Jet Loring, a singing comedy act.

And now he's a member of one of America's top selling male singing teams.

Joe originally took up the accordion but when a hand injury in high school impeded his accordion playing he turned to bass.

He also took up singing in high school as a baritone in his high school glee club.

This 24 year old, six foot, black hair, brown eyed addition to the Seasons is also an avid amateur photographer and promises a flood of pictures of the group for their fans.

When not playing around in his own dark room he can often be found building and improving his own stereo sound system or watching baseball games on television.

So let's welcome a new Season to the scene.

VETERAN MEMBERS OF THE 4 SEASONS—Frankie Valli, Bob Gaudio and Tommy de Vito

Teen Directory
Clubs On The Beat

The BEAT receives numerous questions about where teens can go see their favorite acts and dance to top groups. For your convenience we are now starting this directory of current top pop spots.

We recommend that you call a club beforehand regarding reservations and possible changes in prices.

HOLLYWOOD

ASH GROVE
8162 Melrose
653-2070
(no age limit, adm. $2.00, open 8:30 p.m. Fri., Sat., Sun.)

DAVE HULL'S HULLABALOO
6230 W. Sunset
466-8281
(min. age 15, adm. $1.50, $2.50, $3.50, open 7:30 p.m. Fri. and Sat., 1:30 p.m. Sun.)

THE TRIP
8572 Sunset
652-4600
(min. age 18, adm. $2.00 week nights, $2.50 Fri. and Sat., open 8 p.m. nightly)

THE TROUBADOR
9081 Santa Monica Blvd.
CR 6-6168
(min. age 18, adm. $2.50, open 8:30 Fri. and Sat., 9 p.m. week nights, hootenannies Mon. nite, adm. $1.00)

WHISKEY A GO-GO
8901 Sunset
652-4202
(min. age 18, adm. $2.00 week nights, $2.50 Fri. and Sat., open 8 p.m. nightly)

GLENDALE

ICE HOUSE
234 S. Brand
245-5043
(no age limit, adm. $1.25 week nights, $1.75 Fri. and Sat., open 8:30 p.m. nightly)

PASADENA

ICE HOUSE
24 N. Mentor
681-9942
(same as Ice House, Glendale)

NORTH HOLLYWOOD

CINNAMON CINDER
11345 Ventura Blvd.
877-9971
(min. age 18, adm. $2.00, open 8:30 p.m. Weds. through Sun.)

LONG BEACH

CINNAMON CINDER
4401 E. Pacific Coast Highway
877-9971
(min. age 18, adm. $1.50, open 8:30 p.m. Weds. through Sun.)

LA HABRA

DI GATI'S DI GO-GO
220 W. Whittier Blvd.
687-6219
(min. age 15, adm. $1.00, open nightly)

SAN FRANCISCO

BIMBO'S THREE-SIXTY FIVE CLUB
1025 Columbus Ave.
(no chaperone necessary, dinners, floor show and dancing)

BORA BORA CLUB
1040 Columbus
(must be accompanied by an adult, dinners and floor show)

THE VENETIAN ROOM
Fairmont Hotel,
California & Mason
(no chaperone necessary, dinners, name attractions and dancing)

GOMAN'S GAY NINETY
345 Broadway
(no chaperone necessary, dinner and dancing)

THE COMMITTEE
622 Broadway
(no chaperone necessary, dinner and name attractions)

THE HUNGRY I
599 Jackson St.
(no chaperone necessary, dinner and name attractions)

BASIN STREET WEST
401 Broadway
(no chaperone necessary, dinner and name attractions)

PUSSYCAT A-GO-GO
2215 Powell
(16 year olds admitted until 10:00 p.m., 18 and up until 2:00 a.m.)

WHISKEY A-GO-GO
568 Sacramento
(okay on Sundays from 5:00 to 1:00 a.m.)

CASA MADRID
406 Broadway
(okay anytime)

Clubs wishing to be listed may contact The BEAT at either 6290 Sunset, Suite 504, Hollywood or No. 1 Nob Hill Circle, San Francisco.

The Beatles And Shenson
(Continued From Page 4)

A great deal. The script in question finally was produced by Shenson, and it just happened to be "The Mouse That Roared," the Peter Sellers starrer that skyrocketed that multi-talented Englishman to universal fame.

After that, Shenson was up to his eyebrows in the film world. Rushing between New York and England, not to mention points East, West, North and/or South. Too busy to even take note of the four shadows which were looming large on the international music horizon.

The Beatles' lack of Shenson awareness is as easily explained. Where they were able to rattle off the exact fingering for approximately 3,421 guitar chords, they were less up on the contents of the Producer's Association Handbook.

But, when Shenson heard more about the Beatles, and they heard more about him, including the just-mentioned film which they had seen and dug (being avid Peter Sellers fans), a meeting was arranged and it was luv at first sight.

"We don't want to do an ordinary little pop musical," warned the Beatles.

"They'll be sensational," smiled Shenson.

After "A Hard Day's Night" brought back twenty times its original cost, the Shenson-Beatle combination added another brainchild to their film family.

The movie of many titles which ultimately came to the screen as "Help," and certainly didn't need any of same to become another giant hit.

Will Shenson, who has gained additional fame with his Rita Tushingham classic titled "The Knack," have a hand in the third Beatle flick which is scheduled to start rolling in June?

That remains to be seen. But, we number among the millions who surely hope so.

KRLA ARCHIVES

Another British Invasion This Time, It's By Twins

Attention all red-blooded American females (especially those between the ages of one and 17!): you are about to be faced with another British invasion, this time with a double front. Yes, it's true: our own dear red, white and blue-type hearts are about to be threatened with capture, and our potential captors are none other than Paul and Barry Ryan.

Who and *whoey* Ryan, you ask? They are Paul and Barry—they are very British—they are twins (not identical) — and they are 17 years of age. And that should be just about enough to get you interested in making a few war-like preparations. If not, just take a quick glance at their picture on this self-same little page . . . and I guarantee that you will be in full battle array within five and one half seconds!!!

Just recently, I attempted (and I use that term quite loosely!) to obtain an interview from these two charming—and very *mischievious*—young men. But it was all in vain; about all that really happened was that they interviewed *me*—as well as themselves, their road manager, a few of their fans, and a small, new-found friend known to one and all as a *slurp*. But please —hang on, Slurpy!—we'll have more about that later!!

Telly Nuts

Our interview began in the plush surroundings of their hotel suite, as we all sat 'round a small, marble television—I, with tape recorder in hand, and they, with eyeballs glued on the "telly." These Ryan boys are some kind of TV-Nutniks! The absolute lunacy of the situation, was characterized by the way they told me when and where they were born.

Barry: "We were born in Leeds . . ." Paul: "*Were* we?" Barry: ". . . that's right, on the 24th of October, 1948 . . . and Paul is 10 minutes older than me."

Okay, see what I mean? Total unbelievability!

Paul and Barry went to private boarding schools and after completing their elementary education, went on to one of the art colleges in London for about six months. At that point they decided once and for all that they had been destined to become singers, and began to devote their full attention to that end.

They have since become one of the hottest new singing duos in all of Britain and their first record enjoyed a large chart success. As Paul looks over the pop scene in this country and his own, he says: "I was quite surprised when we came over here. The competition is much stronger now than it used to be. There are a lot of very good records out at the moment."

Group Scene Dying

But England is something else again: "It's changed quite a bit now, y'know. The established groups are staying in but it's a lot more difficult to get a record out nowadays. We have a lot more trouble with getting television shows and everything because the group scene is dying out now a lot; because it's got so flooded now, that only the best ones are surviving. And especially now, because miming in the next few months is going to be banned in Britain, so only the good groups can stay."

For a few moments then, the boys became very much absorbed in the TV set in the corner, and began joining in with the actors on screen—which included laughing, shouting, singing, and pummeling one another about the head and face!

Then just as though there had never been any sort of interruption, Paul turned right 'round to me and began to discuss a new trend in music: "There's a new style now called 'Op Art;' things like The Who. More sound effects—it's not singing, it's just *sound effects* with guitars and things.

"Jeff Beck (Yardbirds) is very influential in Britain. He's one of the best guitarists in Britain. George Harrison copies all of his music . . . the *way* he plays, because he's by far probably the best guitarist in Britain."

Gimmick Or Not

Then I asked about their very obvious "twinship;" mistake Number One!! Paul started out saying, "It's a bit of a gimmick, isn't it? Well . . . not *really*." At which point Barry insisted, "Yes, t'is!" Paul—"It's *not!*" Barry: "*It's a bit of a gimmick!!*" Then Paul began to sob violently: "*Tisn't, Tisn't,* Ahhhh!"

And before I could try to comfort the dear boy, both Paul and Barry had become quite serious—almost *mysterious*—once again, and were telling me in hushed voices: "We're quite telepathic sometimes, y'know. Especially when we're singing. Like, this morning when we were in the bathroom—I walked past and Barry just started singing a song and I started singing exactly the same song—*exactly* the same words, *exactly* the same moment. It was a song I hadn't sung for years before and I just started singing."

Both Paul and Barry are very creative, and if and when they are able to find two or three free minutes they enjoy drawing and painting. They also design all of their own clothes, and after Barry had told me this . . . he couldn't wait to dash straight off to the closet to bring out every article of clothing he had ever designed for my approval. In all honesty, I must say that I *do* approve! They have

PAUL AND BARRY pose in their self-designed jackets.

come up with some really great designs, and I'm currently trying to figure out how to earn enough money to hire them as my own full-time personal designers.

Suddenly, there was a phone call from the lobby, then moments later—a group of female fans rushed in carrying with them a gift for the boys. It was a "Slurp." Nope—*your* guess is as good as mine! It was blue, very furry, had bloodshot eyes and yellow paws, and for the next 30 minutes Paul and Barry sat around brushing it into all sorts of weird positions.

When the Slurp was just about all brushed out, Paul and Barry's mysterious road manager made a sudden appearance to tell the boys that they were about to be late for a television show, so I decided to make a hasty disappearance.

We said good-bye at the door, and Paul said to be sure to look them up the next time they came into town. But I have a feeling that the next time these boys come back it will be just a little more difficult to get near them, 'cause they are gonna be very big stars.

Well, I just thought that I'd tell you so you could clear a large space on your wall well ahead of time where you will be hanging their picture very soon.

You Can Interview Your Fave

By Shirley Poston

Here's the feature we promised a few *BEATS* back. Ten tips on the fine art of interviewing a star! Even if you live in an area where there isn't a star in sight, we suggest you digest this article.

You just never know when you might find yourself face to face with a fave, and there's nothing like being prepared for the best!

1. First and foremost, start the interview off on the right foot. Don't begin firing questions immediately. At least introduce yourself, or talk about the weather or something. But don't let the warm up take more than a couple of minutes. Most stars are in a hurry 24 hours a day, and can't afford to waste what time they do have. It might be a good idea to ask him how much time he *can* spare you. That way, if you won't have a chance to ask all your questions, you can choose those which are most important.

2. Don't make the mistake of not making up a list of questions before the interview. Although you might think the subjects will come naturally once the two of you get to talking, don't count on it. Unless the star is a brand new personality, stay away from the typical where-were-you-born and how-did-you-get-started inquiries. Everyone already knows this information. Try to think of questions and topics that haven't been printed before.

3. Tell the star, at the beginning of the interview, where his answers and comments will appear. If you're interviewing on a "free-lance" basis and don't have a specific publication in mind, at least have some idea of where you'll be trying to sell the finished product. Pass this information along. It will help him decide how to answer your queries.

4. Just plain conversation, without notebooks or tape recorders, is the most relaxed sort of interview. But, unless you have a memory that just can't fail, don't rely on same. You might forget a great remark, and you might also unintentionally misquote the star. A tape recorder would be the first choice. Second is a notebook with one or two questions (written in advance) on each page. This gives you room to expound on a subject if he does. There's no need to take down every single word. That makes both of you nervous. Just take notes and translate them later.

5. Assure the star that you won't print every syllable he utters unless he gives his okay. Tell him to let you know when and if he says something that's intended for your ears only. This will keep him from feeling like he's on the "hot seat." Also, offer to show him the final draft of the interview. He probably won't take you up on it, but will be more relaxed because you did make the offer.

6. If the interview, at any point, turns into more of an exchange of ideas than a question and answer session, don't ramble on unless the star encourages you to do so. Express your own opinions if he's interested in hearing them, but be brief.

7. Chances are, you won't see the star alone. An agent or some such representative is usually present at most pre-arranged interviews. But it's best that you *are* alone when you see the star. If you're interviewing a group, check beforehand to see if you can bring a friend to help you take notes. But never bring more than one other person, and then only with permission.

8. Don't ask too-personal questions. Anyone resents this sort of thing, and a star is no exception. For example, say the star is constantly being asked if he's married or engaged to so-and-so, a question he always answers with a no. If you bring up the subject at all (and it's best not to), you might ask how he feels about the rumors concerning his supposed marriage or engagement. But don't come right out and inquire as to whether the rumors are fact.

9. Don't ask *silly* questions. But you might ask the star if he'd mind answering a few funny ones. Kooky questions always liven up an interview, both when it's taking place and when it appears in print. However, be sure to warn the star when you're about to begin a lighter approach. Remember, he is used to being asked utterly moronic questions in all seriousness, so don't leave it up to him to decide whether or not you're kidding.

10. Always give the star your name, address and telephone number at the close of an interview. That may sound awfully forward, but it won't when you hear the reason why. How many times have you thought about a previous conversation and realized you've said something you didn't mean, or that you could have said it so much better? This happens to stars too, and since what they've said is going to appear in print, they might like to change or rearrange a comment. Tell the star you are giving him this info in case he wants to make some revisions. If he's just passing through town, provide a stamped, self-addressed envelope.

KRLA ARCHIVES

the MAMAS and PAPAS

By Kimi Kobashigawa

For those of you who find yourselves ready and willing to believe your eyes and ears—may we present . . . The Mamas and The Papas.

Let's see . . . would you believe . . . *four* of them? Four unusual—and unusually *talented*—people who make their way of life in a world inhabited by cuckoo clocks, antique lamp shades, Indian boots and John Lennon, semi-existentialism and various shapes and forms indescribable!

There is one Papa who goes by name of John Phillips—definitely the tall, quiet member of the group. But no one really minds his silent ways, 'cause he is also the one responsible for writing much of the music being sung by the group. And the results of his musical masterpieces speak loudly enough for *both* of them.

Besides that . . . John also happens to be married to one of the Mamas, Michelle. And she is just pretty enough to make all of the Papa-type fans out in record-land wish that John would be very quiet.

There is another Mama; they call her Cass. Cass of the heart of gold—a golden heart which finds "lovely" room for such faves as Whispering Paul MacDowell and somebody named J. Lennon, MBE. Cass has been supplied to the listening public in the large economy package (a container currently undergoing refurbishing, de-carbohydrate-style) but that is only in order to provide people with more and more of her great voice.

And then someone said, "Let there be a Denny" . . . and somehow, there *was*. He's the second Papa in the group, with a fine enough voice to insure that he will never be a fifth wheel with *any*one. Denny is semi-nonconformist and handles all of the group's feelings of rebellion for them.

He accomplishes this by looking very much like an "insolently handsome young Canadian," which, by the way—he is. Handsome, young, Canadian . . . and on occasion, insolent.

The Mamas and Papas have already enjoyed one Number One smash hit with their first release on Dunhill: "California Dreamin'," a tune penned by John and Michelle. Now they are practicing being excited about the fantastic reaction to their very first album—"(If You Can Believe Your Eyes and Ears) The Mamas and the Papas;" actually, it's only a warm-up for the foursome, 'cause from now on they're gonna have a *lot* of practice being excited about their success.

In England, The Mamas and Papas have become the latest "in" thing among the various English groups on the pop scene—and they are definitely becoming *very* "in" on all of the charts—English *and* American. Although there has been talk of a European tour sometime in April, as of this writing—nothing has been confirmed.

The four arrived in Los Angeles many months ago with no car and no clothes—theirs had been stolen from a Rent-A-Car they were driving. Now, they each have a house and the two Papas have even indulged in the luxury of brand new motorcycles.

Wild, wonderful, talented, witty, unusual, pretty, weird, uptight (as in, *out of sight!*), and "cool camp—to the eighth power" . . . The Mamas and Papas are yours for the taking. That is, *if* "you can believe your eyes and ears!!!"

Adventures of Robin Boyd
By Shirley Poston

Chapter Twenty

Robin Boyd's spoon clattered to the table.

"Did I just hear you correctly?" she whispered in shocked disbelief.

Mrs. Boyd nodded. "If you have any plans for the day," she repeated, "they'll have to be cancelled."

Robin glared. (If she had any *plans* for the day . . . like going to England to see the Beatles, for instance.) "May I ask *why?*" she tried to say in a civil tone and failed.

"Because you have a doctor's appointment."

Robin re-glared. "May I ask *why?*" she repeated, having a tendency to become repetitious shortly before becoming violent.

"Because you're sick . . . I mean . . . because you don't look well," her mother struggled. "You don't eat right," she finished, gesturing at Robin's untouched breakfast.

Grabbing her bowl of Soggies, Robin consumed them in three gulps. (She could have done it in two had she also thought to grab the spoon.)

"I feel *marvelous*," she insisted, downing Ringo's glass of milk as en encore.

As Ringo succeeded in spearing her older sister with a Ludwig droomstick, Mrs. Boyd tried again.

"You just don't seem to have any energy lately," she offered.

Leaping to her feet, Robin chinned herself ten times on the door jam and somersaulted back to the table (landing right on Ringo's left toe.)

Marvelous

"I *told* you I felt marvelous," Robin puffed, fearing she was about to leave the repetitious stage and go on to bigger and better (not to mention noisier) things.

"You *still* have a doctor's appointment," her mother said sternly.

And, that did it.

"NUTS!" shouted Robin. And while her mother fought to keep from saying "you took the words right out of my mouth," Robin slammed violently out of the kitchen. She then proceeded to slam violently through the living room and slam violently into her own room.

Once there, she slammed violently the door (huh?) and slammed herself face down onto the bed (violently.)

"Ratzafratz," she sobbed, among other things. Why did everything always have to happen to *her*, anypath? It was always *something*.

First it had been *George*.

You would have thought that after they'd been apart two whole weeks, he would have agreed to *anything*, just to make her happy. Especially after that fond greeting (welcome to another understatement of the year) she'd given him, proving beyond a doubt that her affection for that luvley Liverpuldian genie had progressed well beyond the point of palship.

But *no!* The very *minute* she had even *mentioned* that since her magic powers had been returned, she was going to start all over and re-visit the Beatles, taking care this time not to drive them to distraction (not to mention drink), George had turned positively *green*. (A rather attractive shade of avocado, actually.)

"Why the *Beatles?*" he had snapped jealously. "What's so great about them, anyway?"

Robin had sighed. (Why is it that every Englishman in one's life wants to be the *only* Englishman in one's life?) (Ah well, that's the way the crumpet crumps.)

Well, to make a long story longer, it had taken one solid *week* to convince George that her feeling for the foursome was in no way, shape or form like her feeling for *him* (what George didn't know couldn't hurt him.)

Having finally succeeded, they had planned to leave this morning. And George had promised to spend the day with friends in Liverpool while she flew about terrorizing - er - visiting her faves.

Then *this* had to happen. And Robin was seriously considering hurling herself out of her bedroom window (a death-defying three-foot drop) when her blitherings were interrupted by a brisk knock on the door. (Well, it was actually more of a hysterical banging, but there's no point in shattering Mrs. Boyd's calm, cool image.)

"Stop that blithering," Mrs. Boyd ordered (Robin had to admit, her mother certainly had her down to a science.) "We're leaving for the doctor's office in five minutes."

Sad News

Five minutes later, during which time the lid of a certain tea pot was lifted and the sad news related, they left. Robin, who bruised easily, knew better than to try her mother's patience any further (she hadn't learned her violent slamming techniques from any stranger), so she soggily (using the term literally) submitted to being herded into the family station wagon.

After driving in stony silence (also California) for about ten minutes, Mrs. Boyd careened to a stop before an impressive-looking building.

"Go to suite 618," she commanded, handing Robin a clink of change. "Take the bus home, *straight* home, after the . . . examination," she further commanded.

"That's Paul McCartney's birthday," Robin mused, greedily pocketing the money as she got out of the car.

Her mother gave her a don't-look-now, but-you've-just-dropped another-one look. "Of *course* it's Paul McCartney's birthday," Mrs. Boyd said soothingly. Then she sped away from the curb like a bat out of Weybridge.

Robin stared at the diminishing wagon. She started to call out that she'd only meant that 618 was *like* Paul McCartney's birthday because he was born on 6-18-42, but she decided to forget it. If her mother didn't know where it was at, that was her mother's problem. She had quite enough of her own, thank you. (You're welcome.)

Suite 618

After a couple of side trips (one to buy a bar of chocolate) (another to wash up after same had succeeded in melting in her mouth *and* in her hand), Robin stood poised before the door of suite 618.

Groping in the ole kit bag for a mirror, she arranged her bangs so that she could see out without anyone being able to see in.

Then she stood there for several moments, deliberately rasping at her hair with a comb, in hopes that Wanda The Witch would show up and spray her to death. But, when nothing happened, she finally trudged into the empty waiting room and sank into a mighty leather-chair.

Nothing continued to happen. There wasn't even a nurse who came round for that self-conscious but inevitable little chat about who (or is it whom) (just as long as it's *someone*) would be paying the bill.

So, after ruffling through a pile of magazines published by people who had obviously never been teenagers, she began flicking through a small pile of cards on a nearby table.

Shortly thereafter she stopped breathing. For the cards read, A. G. Andersrug, Psychiatrist!

Psychiatrist!

"*Psychiatrist?*" Robin shouted, and it was then that she knew what she must do.

Unfortunately, she was just a little too late. Just as she reached the only available exit in a single bound (not to mention faster than the speed of light and hearty as a Hi Ho Silver), Robin heard a sneaky click.

And although she wrenched furiously at the locked door, hoping to pull off an escape that would make the "Man From U.N.C.L.E." look like kid stuff, all she succeeded in pulling off was the knob.

(*To Be Continued Next Week*)

Hotline London
(Continued From Page 1)

Well-Soon telegram went to songstress ALMA COGAN in London hospital from MAUREEN AND RINGO . . . MARIANNE FAITHFULL tested for screen role in "The Taming Of The Shrew" to be shot this April in Rome with cast headed by LIZ TAYLOR and RICHARD BURTON . . . Your sensationally talented writer/singer BOB LIND here for TV during second half of March. I see his "Elusive Butterfly" as the U.S. answer to the equally vivid lyric-writing of our Jonathan King . . . THE STONES thoroughly unimpressed with Australian food . . . "Homeward Bound" by SIMON AND GARFUNKEL just issued here with cover version by THE QUIET FIVE . . . THE LOVIN' KIND, heard behind FRED LENNON on "That's My Life," just out here with "Accidental Love" and getting plenty of deejay exposure from the pirate ships . . . "Backstage" is GENE PITNEY'S fastest-selling U.K. single to date and could make Number One . . . Wild new combo THE ACTION currently touring Britain with the P.J. PROBY/SEARCHERS package . . . U.K. concert tour later this year for LOU CHRISTIE visiting us this month to plug "Lightnin' Strikes" single . . . HERB ALPERT'S "Spanish Flea" has sold 300,000 copies in U.K. to date .

The Temptin' Temptations

By Lincoln Culver

HOLLYWOOD — "Soul" — a word without a definition. **Temptations** — a group with a whole lot of soul. This soulful group — defies all description.

No one seems to be able to tell you just what "soul" is, but there are a number of people around who have it . . . and some, in very large quanitites. The Temptations seem to have a small monopoly going on it!

Sometimes, when trying to understand something, it is helpful to break it down and work on one thing at a time. Individually, the "souls" in the group are, Otis Williams — baritone singer, also capable of playing the tuba; Paul Williams, graduate of many school choirs; Eddie Kendricks, also a "natural" singer; Dave Ruffin, a tenor singer and a great drummer; and Mel Franklin, who "plays at the piano."

Although there are several instruments played within the group, Melvin explains that the group now plays infrequently: "We have had occasion to do so. Often times we go somewhere where we have a band that aren't true musicians, who can't read, and we'll play. But now we don't do it as much as in the past because we have a fantastic trio."

'Rehearsal'

I asked Melvin what the most important element of the Temptations' music was, and he rapidly replied: "Rehearsal!!" He then went on to say that "everybody" — each member of the group — constitutes the most essential elements of their sound.

The Temptations are a group of truly good singers as well as fine musicians, and they continually improve upon their own act and talents by watching and analyzing the performances of other members of their profession. As far as any new trends in the field of pop music are concerned, Melvin sums up the feelings of the group by saying:

"I believe that not only with rhythm and blues, but *music itself* — the world is becoming more educated now and people are just accepting good music, be it pop, country and western, rhythm and blues, classicals, or what have you. People are just starting to enjoy good music."

And the Beatles? Melvin smiles quite broadly and says, "I love them! We *all* do; anything that's unique, we love."

Aid From Smokey

After watching the Temptations put on an exciting — and *exhausting* — performance at The Trip, a top Hollywood night club on the Sunset Strip, I remarked to Melvin that one of their numbers in particular had reminded me of Smokey Robinson and the Miracles.

Melvin smiled and explained: "Smokey has been very, very instrumental in our success. He writes all of our current hits, ever since "The Way You Do The Things You Do," which incidentally, was our first big record, although we had been recording for years before that. This may be the reason we have a similar sound to the Miracles on *certain* records; groupwise, I don't think we sound alike at all."

In the Fall, the Temptations will do an extensive tour in Europe — their second in two years — with Sam the Sham and the Pharoahs, and will be playing individual engagements for most of the time until then right here at home.

We spoke about it, we had listened to it, we heard the word used all around; but finally I asked Melvin what exactly it meant. Just what is "soul?" "Soul is like the word *love;* it's a four-letter word that really can't be defined. It's just a *feeling* — a feeling beyond reproach. Like *liberty* or *freedom* — these are things that we all understand, but you can't really definitely say what it is. *Soul* is just something that you're *born* with!"

Melvin is definitely the man with the quick wit and easy smile, and when I asked if anyone in the group was writing — other than music — he immediately said, "Yes — lots of *love letters!*" Just back from New York and an extensive press conference at the time we spoke, Melvin told me, "I believe they asked us *everything* in the world! Including the design of our fingerprint!!" (Which he later confessed was *paisley!!!*)

There was just one final thing that Melvin wanted to say, for himself and for the entire group: "I don't think there's anything else we missed — other than our gratitude to the public for sticking with us and for helping to put us where we are; and if they keep up the same enthusiasm toward us, we can't help but keep up the same enthusiasm toward them. God bless everybody and we love them!"

Five very talented young men called The Temptations: an *indescribably* great group with a whole lotta *soul!!!*

... "SOUL" AT THE TRIP — TEMPTATION STYLE.

... COWBOY TIME WITH "WAGON WHEELS."

... SHE'S "MY GIRL."

KRLA ARCHIVES

COMING IN APRIL – THE HOLLIES

Dave Hull's HULLABALOO
The Rock & Roll Showplace of the World
6230 SUNSET (AT VINE) HOLLYWOOD, CALIF.

IN CONCERT — MARCH 13 — 4 P.M. AND 8 P.M.
TOGETHER — FOR THE FIRST TIME ANYWHERE
The Two Most Exciting Groups In America

PAUL REVERE
& The Raiders ▶▶▶▶

plus

THE PALACE GUARD

▶ FRI. & SAT. MARCH 18 and 19 ◀

CHAD & JEREMY
▶▶▶▶▶▶▶▶▶▶▶▶▶▶▶▶▶▶▶▶

FABULOUS EASTER WEEK EXTRAVAGANZA

CONTINUOUS SHOWS 12 NOON TO 2 A.M. APRIL 1-10
PRESENTING THE WORLD'S TOP ROCK & ROLL ARTISTS

THE TURTLES – THE HOLLIES
DICK DALE – JOEY PAIGE – THE PALACE GUARD
AND STILL MANY MORE OUTSTANDING ACTS TO BE ANNOUNCED

MAKE RESERVATIONS – HO. 6-8281

KRLA ARCHIVES

America's Largest Teen NEWSpaper

KRLA Edition BEAT

APRIL 2, 1966

Pop Lennon Vs. Lennon Pop

BEAT Art: Jan Walker

KRLA ARCHIVES

KRLA BEAT

Volume 2, Number 3   April 2, 1966

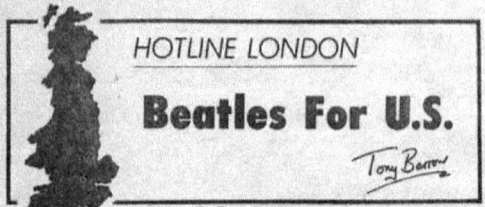

HOTLINE LONDON
Beatles For U.S.
Tony Barrow

By Tony Barrow

Although definite dates remain unannounced pending progress on the search for a suitable movie script, BRIAN EPSTEIN has released initial information about his 1966 plans for THE BEATLES. They'll be back in America for sure this summer. Brian has been asked to consider the idea of the group undertaking two concerts at New York's mighty Shea Stadium but he has rejected the double date and is thinking in terms of just one performance at the venue.

Before coming to America, The Beatles will undertake short tours in Germany and Japan. It is unlikely that the third movie will move into production before late summer or early autumn but at the end of the year The Beatles will certainly go out on another tour of Britain.

Their most recent U.K. concert tour took place just before Christmas when John, Paul, George and Ringo played 18 concerts in eighty key centres up and down the country.

Keith Relf Married

Keith Relf, lead singer with THE YARDBIRDS, was secretly married on the morning of Thursday, February 24 at Paddington Registry Office in central London. His bride is former riding instructress April Liversidge, 19, who came to England from Kenya in 1964. Keith and April met for the first time the following Christmas when ardent Beatle fan April went to see "The Beatles' Christmas Show" at London's Finsbury Park Astoria. The Yardbirds were amongst the show's supporting acts.

Poor old HERMAN had a hunk of hard luck when he flew into Manchester at the end of his trans-global concert tour. The customs people seized the Gold Disc he'd collected for million-dollar album sales in the U.S. They'll return the award to him when they figure out how much customs duty Herman has to pay. Meantime Herman had to write out

(Turn to Page 4)

... PAUL REVERE & THE RAIDERS (l. to r. Drake Levin, Phil Volk, Mark Lindsay and Mike Smith. In the chair, Paul Revere) getting their kicks, or getting ready to give Paul his!!

Did you ever wonder how a pop group gets their kicks? Well, Paul Revere and the Raiders recently got their "Kicks" by visiting Santo Domingo.

It's always surprising to me that at least one member of a top group can be easily reached by a simple phone call. And that's all it took to get Mike Smith of the Raiders on the line. Once on the phone Mike eagerly began telling me all about the group's trip to entertain U.S. troops.

"Santo Domingo was a mystery to us," began Mike. "We started out in Los Angeles, then on to Albuquerque, Dallas, San Antonio and to New York to do 'Hullabaloo.'

"Then we went to Florida to an Air Force base where they loaded us onto a C-130, which is really a flying box car. We sat on the paratrooper seats and it was sure a change of pace for us.

"Anyway, we landed at night and all the lights on the runway were off," continued Mike, "because there had been a flare-up in Santo Domingo where the U.S. Army had shot some rebels. So, we had guards all around with guns and they snuck us from the base to the Americana Hotel. You know, that's where all the tourists were pinned down with rebels shooting at them during the revolt.

"The first thing we got was a briefing by Sgt. Pratt about what to do and what not to do. We were one mile from the rebel zone and we weren't supposed to drink any of the water. We could take showers and go swimming but they brought us up purified water to drink.

Tanks And Guns

'We were on the ninth floor of the hotel and we could look out and see the U.S. Army base and across the street was the Commander of the Dominican army with tanks in the back and pointed guns.

"They really seem to hate Americans down there and there are signs all around saying, 'Yankee Go Home.'

"But Drake and I went into the rebel zone carrying cameras. The only way to save yourself is to have a camera because they love to have their pictures taken! We went to a cock fight which was interesting but we could only stay

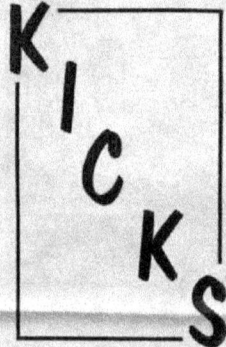

for one because the crowd got worked up. So, we had to leave but we did get some pictures of all that.

"We did USO shows for the troops down there—two shows a day for four days. One day we had off though, because Paul drank the water anyway and got dissentry but I guess we shouldn't go into that!

"We didn't have any girls with us, as Bob Hope always does, so we had to work extra hard during the shows. Most of the service men were young and they really have a poor time down there. You see, the U.S. has seized the land—everything. Therefore, every Santo Domingan hates all Americans. So, the soldiers are very restricted. They don't have any entertainment, only a few USO clubs.

"We had been doing volunteer work for the Job Corps and we had some friends in the White House so when they were putting this tour to Santo Domingo together they asked us to go.

(Turn to Page 6)

Riot At Byrd's Concert

CHICAGO—The Byrds refused to take flight as 300 screaming female fans stormed the stage of the Civic Opera House in one of the wildest rock shows which this city has yet to witness.

The Byrds continued performing and absolutely refused to vacate the stage even when House employees rushed from the wings and attempted to unplug the group's electric guitars.

In the end it took a total of 30 policemen to quell the screaming audience as the Byrds calmly sang "Mr. Tambourine Man." Ushers were pushed aside like cardboard boxes as about 20 of the girls managed to make it on stage to their heroes.

One girl in the audience received a bruised back and two other members of the Byrd audience were arrested—the first for disorderly conduct and the second for simple assault.

The police lieutenant stated that he made the second arrest after being kicked twice in the leg.

The audience was primarily female and many wore buttons proclaiming, "I'm bold," which had to be the understatement of the century!

Questioned after the concert most declared that they had been pleased with the show but apparently the police had other ideas and so stopped it when it was about half over.

In the meantime, Gene Clark is in Los Angeles getting over his nervous strain. Byrd's manager states that Gene will return to the group within the next five or six weeks but a nasty rumor buzzing around the business is that Clark is out for good.

The BEAT is currently checking this rumor and we will, of course, let you know as soon as we find out for sure but as of right now it is *only* a rumor.

Inside the BEAT

On The Beat	2
Beach Boys Visit Animals	3
Adventues of Robin Boyd	4
The Genius of Ray Charles	5
Noted In the United Kingdom	6
Fashionable Turtles	10-11
Yardbirds Speak Out	13
The London Scene	14
Cash On the Right	15

The BEAT is published weekly by BEAT Publications, Inc., editorial and advertising offices at 6290 Sunset Blvd., Suite 504, Hollywood, California 90028. U.S. bureaus in Hollywood, San Francisco, New York, Chicago and Nashville, overseas correspondents in London, Liverpool and Manchester, England. Sole price is 15 cents. Subscription price: U.S. and possessions, $5 per year; Canada and foreign rates, $9 per year. Second class postage prepaid at Los Angeles, California.

John's Father Wants To Knock Off Beatles

By Gil McDougall

When John Lennon was five years old, he and his mother were deserted by his father Freddie Lennon. John has been pretty bitter about this for most of his life. His notable cynicism may be partly rooted in this early shock. Perhaps Lennon's biggest shock since, regarding his father, was to discover that Lennon had embarked on a singing career.

From when he was five 'till he was famous, John didn't hear from his dad, so when Freddie did try to get in touch with his famous son, John was skeptical of his father's reasons. Eventually however, Brian Epstein took the initiative and arranged a meeting between father and son. According to Freddie the conversation was a bit strained. He later stated: "Neither of us knew what to say, but we had a bit of a natter." John's father was also mystified as to John's accent. He said: "I couldn't understand where John had got his Liverpool accent. The last time that I saw him he had a very proper English accent."

This session in Epstein's office was some time ago, and since this occasion the two have not met. John remains very touchy on the subject. During the 1965 Beatle tour he answered a reporter's "how's your father?" with: "Pregnant for all I know, how's yours? My private life is my own concern."

Now that Freddie Lennon has started on his own recording career the fan following of the Beatles is very critical because they think that Freddie is trying to cash in on his son's success. Lennon's pop answers these comments with: "They think that it's just a stunt. I expect to get knocked. I've always enjoyed folk and country and western music. I would like to be judged on my own records."

Despite the fury of Lennon's followers, and the jibes of the press, Lennon senior is very enthusiastic about his new disc career. This is understandable as his last job was washing dishes. He states that he is just waiting for a chance to "knock the Beatles off the top of the hit parade."

Somehow I can't help feeling that he has got quite a long wait.

KRLA ARCHIVES

On the BEAT
By Louise Criscione

Paul McCartney is indirectly responsible for the covering of the Beatles' "Girl" by The Truth. What actually happened was that the Truth's manager, Jeff Cooper, was in a music publisher's office when Paul walked in, tapped Jeff on the shoulder and asked for a light.

Jeff felt that it was a good omen and so The Truth went ahead and cut "Girl," sent it bounding up the British Charts and thereby the group acquired their first smash.

Pop marriages are sprouting up all over the place again. Congratulations go to Keith Relf and his new bride, April Liversidge, and to Glen Dale of the Fortunes and his wife, Janice Hoole.

Joan Baez, queen of folk, would like very much to switch bags and cut an album with a rock group! Says today's rock is too "tame" and she would like to liven things up a bit. Should be interesting.

Tom Is Comin'

Tom Jones is flying into Hollywood to attend the Academy Awards as a guest of Burt Bacharach whose "What's New Pussycat" is up for an award. Three days after the Awards, on April 21, Tom is scheduled to sing before the Duke of Edinburgh in London. A busy "pussycat" – Tom.

Thanks to her electrician brother, 23 year old Bobbie Miller has recorded her first record, "Everywhere I Go," with Bill Wyman acting as producer.

It seems that her brother fixed Bill's faulty amp during a Stone concert and afterwards told Bill about his musical sister. Bill liked what he heard and so went off and A&R'd Bobbie's debut sound! Just goes to show...

...JOAN BAEZ

Speaking of the Stones, their Australian tour went down a smashing success—so smashing, in fact, that Keith had to go to the hospital to have his cut eye taken care of. Some female type fans got a little carried away when they actually saw Keith in person, rushed the stage etc. and Keith came off with a cut eye.

"Puncy" Charlie

Quiet New Zealand was the scene of some action for the Stones—at least, for Charlie it was. Mick says that some man kept knocking on Charlie's hotel room door and each time Charlie opened it he was met with all sorts of verbal insults. Finally, the usually quiet and rather reserved Stone had had enough so he calmly opened the door and punched the intruder in the nose! The incident surprised Mick because "the fellow was a foot taller than Charlie!"

England thinks that they have come up with an answer to Herbie Alpert and his T.J. Brass—a group appropriately (if not suspiciously) entitled, Richito's Golden Brass.

The Knickerbockers have done almost the impossible with their latest disc, "One Track Mind." This time around they not only sound like the Beatles but their instrumental is definitely Yardbird inspired. With all the talent in that group I can't understand why they can't come up with an original sound all their own.

Keith's Kick

Keith Moon of the Who has a new kick—he's crazy over Jan and Dean! He wants a skateboard, as well as some Jan and Dean tee shirts shipped over to him in England. However, the Who will be Stateside shortly so Keith can pick up some J&D gear in person.

Jeff Beck, Yardbirds' lead guitarist, was recently pondering today's scene and exactly how much of the audience actually knows what's going on.

"I feel that probably fifty per cent or more of an audience don't understand what it's all about. They come to see Keith Relf, the singer, still they pay their money I suppose," says Jeff.

And he ought to know, I guess, since he occasionally tests his audience's knowledge by bashing open chords and more times than not the audience doesn't even realize what he's up to. Still, Jeff is one of the best guitarists around and I know of plenty of people who pay to see *him*.

IT'S AMAZING WHAT YOU CAN FIND IN SOME ZOOS.

LET'S SEE NOW, ONE FOR YOU AND ONE FOR ME AND...

...JEFF BECK

KRLA ARCHIVES

The Beach Boys Visit The Animals

By Eden

Actually, I don't *usually* go flying around in airplanes with five Beach Boys—I mean, not *usually*; but this was sort of an exception. It was also extreme exhaustion, total hysteria, and complete pandemonium by the time it was all over. But then—I am getting a little ahead of myself. So, let's go back to the fateful day just recently when your favorite *BEAT* reporter and mine—namely *me!*—agreed to accompany all of the Beach Boys on a trip to the San Diego Zoo.

It all started when Brian Wilson informed me that he thought it would be a good idea if I tagged along as all five of the boys trooped down to the world-famous zoo where they were going to shoot pictures for the cover of their up-coming album. It sounded like fun—to an innocent bystander, such as myself!—so I agreed to go.

I joined Brian and his cousin Steve, brother Dennis Wilson, and a friend of Brian's named Marilyn, at Brian's palatial estate in the Bel Air hills of Southern California bright and early on Thursday morning. Brian wasn't yet ready, and as Steve was the man in charge of getting everyone to the airport and safely aboard the plane on time—he was rapidly on his way toward obtaining his first coronary seizure.

After nearly an hour of waiting—during which time Steve developed four and a half new ulcers and Dennis composed three new jazz sonatas on Brian's piano—we finally made it out to the driveway, where all five of us piled into Brian's bright, yellow Mark IV Jaguar . . . and that ain't easy!

Steve and Dennis both took it upon themselves to instruct Brian as to the shortest and quickest route to the airport—at the tops of their lungs!—while Brian calmly *ignored* them both, and at a leisurely 98 miles an hour, blazed his own trail-way through the heavens to the airport.

When finally we arrived at L.A. International—we discovered that we were just in time to wave good-bye to our plane, which had just taken off! At this point, Steve simply collapsed in a puddle of tears, while the rest of us walked merrily off to join the other Beachboys, the photographers, some press agents, and a few other girl friends who had come along.

AND BRIAN SAID "LET THERE BE GOATS."

Eventually, we managed to get the entire party of 15 downstairs and safely aboard the huge jet which would carry us to San Diego. We settled back comfortably in our seats, and waved good-bye to sunny Southern California.

Twenty-two short minutes later, we landed in a grey, and over-cast San Diego, with the threat of rain hanging ominously over us.

It took about half a million cabs to get us all to the zoo (would you believe about *seven* cabs??), where we discovered that nearly everyone there knew of our arrival, and had their pens and albums ready to be autographed by any one of the five Beach Boys. Once inside the zoo, we headed for the children's zoo where we were led into a huge pen which contained various odd species of lambs, goats, llamas, and a few other animals which defied *any* sort of description!

We spent quite a bit of time inside the cage feeding the animals while the photographers click-clicked away, capturing some of the most unusual pictures of the Beach Boys and friends ever to be seen. Then, we left that area and began to explore the other areas of the vast zoo. We stopped at nearly every cage to examine its occupants, and the Beach Boys stopped at nearly every hot dog stand to *buy* some of *its occupants!* You probably wouldn't believe the quantity of food which was eaten by the Aquatic Five that day!

Several million pictures and some very tired feet later, we found ourselves in the general vicinity of a baby elephant, who just happened to be wandering around near the kitchen in the Children's Zoo. So deeply engrossed in petting the little darling were we, that we didn't immediately notice the torrential wind which sprang up from the North (or wherever it is from which those things spring up!).

COME ON, PLEASE, COUGH UP THE CAR KEYS.

Within seconds from the moment when we first noticed that all of the trees were bent in half and our hands were blue with frost bite, it began to pour huge drops of rain all over us. Granted, the boys *do* call themselves the "Beach Boys," but this much at home they didn't have to make us feel! One might think that under such wet conditions, the obvious thing to do would be to run for cover, wouldn't one?

Forget it! The head photographer-type took one look at the overflowing skies, then in his loudest tones yelled out for us to follow him to the uppermost level of the zoo for some more pix! Holy woodies, surfer-buddies—there's just nothing quite like a photographic session in the rain!

Somehow or another, 5:30 that evening found all fifteen of us at the airport in San Diego awaiting the plane which would return us to our happy homes. It was an especially crowded flight and we had a long delay before take-off. Finally air-borne, we soon began to wish we weren't!!! It turned out to be a very rough and rugged flight home, and there was more than one queasy tum-tum as we set down for a landing on the darkened field, lit by several thousand sparkling colored lights.

It had been a wild and wonderful day. A day which found Dennis sharing a hot dog and fritos with a llama; a day which saw Brian in his first face-to-face encounter with a curious giraffe; a day which watched Mike eat every hot dog in the entire zoo; a day of Beach Boys, and a day which won't be soon forgotten.

HEY, WHO TOLD YOU YOU COULD HAVE A BITE OF MY HOTDOG?

WHAT'S THIS? Some kind of a dream — a nightmare maybe? Nope, it's a "Daydream" and it's vaulted Joe Butler, Steve Boone, John Sebastian and Zal Yanovsky — The Lovin' Spoonful — right into the top ten again.

HOTLINE LONDON
The Lasting Success Of Three Bachelors
(Continued From Page 1)

a check for nearly a thousand dollars before he could pass through the airport customs area. This was the duty due on his huge pile of gifts — including cameras and souvenir guitars — bought during the tour.

In the summer of 1962 I was working for Decca Records in London. I met two different groups who were about to make their disc debut. One was a singing threesome who had come across the Irish Sea. The other was a four-man vocal and instrumental unit who hailed from Liverpool.

The trio was called THE BACHELORS and it earned itself a recording contract with Decca. The quartet was called THE BEATLES and it was turned down by Decca. I hasten to add that I was not in any way conceerned with Decca's decision not to sign The Beatles — the label was to regret its action less than six months later when The Beatles were with E.M.I. and had taken their recording of "Please, Please Me" to the top of our charts. That, incidentally, was when I left Decca to become Brian Epstein's Press Officer.

Back to The Bachelors. All through Britain's big beat boom, its folk-rock craze, its protest period and just about every other passing pop phase we've known in the last couple of years, The Bachelors have maintained their steady popularity. Most of their singles make our Top Ten. The three boys — brothers Con and Dec Cluskey plus John Stokes — are as big with the mums 'n' dads generation as they are with the screamagers.

As I write, their latest release — it revives the oldie ballad "Love Me With All Of Your Heart" and covers the U.S. chart-topper "The Sound of Silence" — is climbing rapidly.

Two bits of bad luck have bugged The Bachelors this month. John has been in the hospital for an operation and Dec smashed up his car and had to have twelve stitches sewn into his head. But there's also a bit of good news on the Bachelor front. The trio are all set for a trip to America in May.

I talked with their manager, Dorothy Solomons, this week.

Says Dorothy: "When The Bachelors did the Sullivan Show last year I was flooded with requests from other U.S. television producers. They didn't believe me when I told them that the boys had a solidly filled diary for the following twelve months. Now, at last, I've been able to fit in some new American dates. I'm about to sign the contract for them to star in the Ed Sullivan Show on May 15. Immediately after that they'll do a short series of concerts, possibly at colleges where they are in great demand."

When The Bachelors get back to Britain they have a 16-week summer season at Blackpool where they co-star in "Holiday Startime 1966" with Cilla Black.

The Adventures of Robin Boyd
By Shirley Poston

CHAPTER TWENTY-ONE

There are some people in this world who would become panicky upon finding themselves behind locked doors, at the mercy of someone (or some*thing*) named Dr. A. G. Andersrag, Psychiatrist. And Robin Boyd was one of them.

But, shortly after pulling the knob right square off the door, Robin suddenly pulled herself together.

Later with all this clawing and wrenching! All she had to do to get out of this jam (or, if you prefer, jelly) was say the right thing. And that right thing was, of course, "Liverpool." So, which somehow figures, she said it.

Meanwhile, behind the closed doors of his private office, Dr. A. G. Andersrag, Psychiatrist, sulked stylishly behind his $2,000 desk.

So what if he had another one bagged in the waiting room? The thrill of knowing that some poor confused dolt was clawing and wrenching about no longer sent him.

Listlessly humming "kicks keep on gettin' harder to find," the doctor opened his appointment book.

Robin Boyd, he mused. Age sixteen. Worried parent fears the child is off her nut.

The doctor chortled. Of *course* the child was off her nut! *Every*one was off their nut! If only they'd stop *fighting* it and learn to *enjoy* being a lunatic!

Then he stopped chortling in one large hurry. No, that would never do. If they did *that*, they'd stop coming to *him!* And before he knew it, a large man would be coming round to repossess his $2,000 desk (not to mention his mink coat) (no one is perfect.)

Yawning, the doctor got to his feet and opened the door to the outer office. Which, of course, appeared to be empty.

"Come out from under the furniture," he simpered according to Plan One. "I'm here to *help* you," he further simpered.

When nothing, however, crept out from under the aforementioned furniture, the doctor sighed. A *stubborn* psycopath, yet. Exactly what he needed today like a(nother) hole in the head.

Smiling fiendishly, he went on to Plan Two, and pressed the button that raised the couch, table and chairs several feet off the floor.

Then he stopped smiling fiendishly. He also ran sobbing into his private office, flang himself to the floor and kicked his heels soundlessly on the deep cashmere carpet. (An act which will henceforth be referred to as Plan Three.)

And his consternation (actually, it was a tantrum, but we wouldn't want to blow the good doctor's cool calm image) was understandable!

The waiting room didn't just *appear* to be empty. It *was* empty! Which was impossible because the lock (unlike some jewelers we could mention) never failed! No victim . . . er . . . patient had ever escaped before!

And to make matters worse, the potted plant in the corner of the outer office had *giggled* at him!

After a few more kicks of the olde heel, the doctor straightened his $2,000 tie (which was subtly decorated with the hand-painted figure of a $2,000 hula dancer,) he raced to the telephone. Whereupon he dialed *his* psychiatrist and begged for an appointment that afternoon.

At this point, the potted plant in the corner stopped giggling and cracked up. In fact, Robin laughed so hard she lost her balance (not to mention her Byrd glasses) and fell off the leaf she'd been clinging to.

This certainly was a switch! Just moments ago she'd been terrified of the very same doctor who was now fearing for *his* sanity! Why, this was almost as much fun as terrorizing - er - visiting the Beatles!

Suddenly, Robin ceased cackling. There was only one problem. The doctor was certain to call her mother and blab everything. And since the rather rattled Mrs. Boyd was already nearing the breaking point (the point of breaking some large object over Robin's head), it was pointless to further convince her that her poor confused dolt of a daughter was fruitier than a nut cake.

It was then that Robin knew what she must do. She must convince the doctor (and in turn, her mother) otherwise!

Crossing her fingers (which ain't easy for a *real* Robin) she chirped the magic word. This time she had no trouble saying it. The good old days of flapping hysterically about on the floor of the Beatles' garage, trying to pronounce "Worcestershire" were gone forever. She had managed to wheedle George into changing the magic word to "Ketchup."

When her genie-given powers immediately turned her back into her sixteen-year-old self (yes, yes, they also turned her *front* into her sixteen-year-old self), she knocked gently at the doctor's door.

"Go away," said the doctor in a strangled tone. And Robin, having been the champion class-cutter at obedience school, stalked bravely into his private office.

As she slipped into a chair, the doctor raised his formerly brunette now gray head from the desk and looked at her wearily. (For those interested, the wearily is located just slightly to the left of the clavicle.)

"Challo!" she said cheerfully, "Sorry I'm late."

"Late?" the doctor echoed disinterestedly.

Robin gave him a bat of the olde eyelash. "You know, for our appointment."

"Appointment?" the doctor echoed disinterestedly.

Robin, who was long on eyelashes and short on patience when batting same about failed to work, stamped her foot.

Retrieving her leg, which had sunk into the carpet up to the knee, she stared waspishly at the doctor. *Ratzafratz*, she thought. Why was he delaying her with all this nonsense when she was supposed to be on her way to England at this very moment? In the company of her jealous but otherwise luvley Liverpudlian genie (gasp and pant, not to mention rasp.)

"Yes, *appointment*," she snapped. "And if you think I'm going to sit through much more of *this*, you'd better have *your* head examined too!"

Suddenly, the doctor smiled.

(Turn To Page 6)

KRLA ARCHIVES

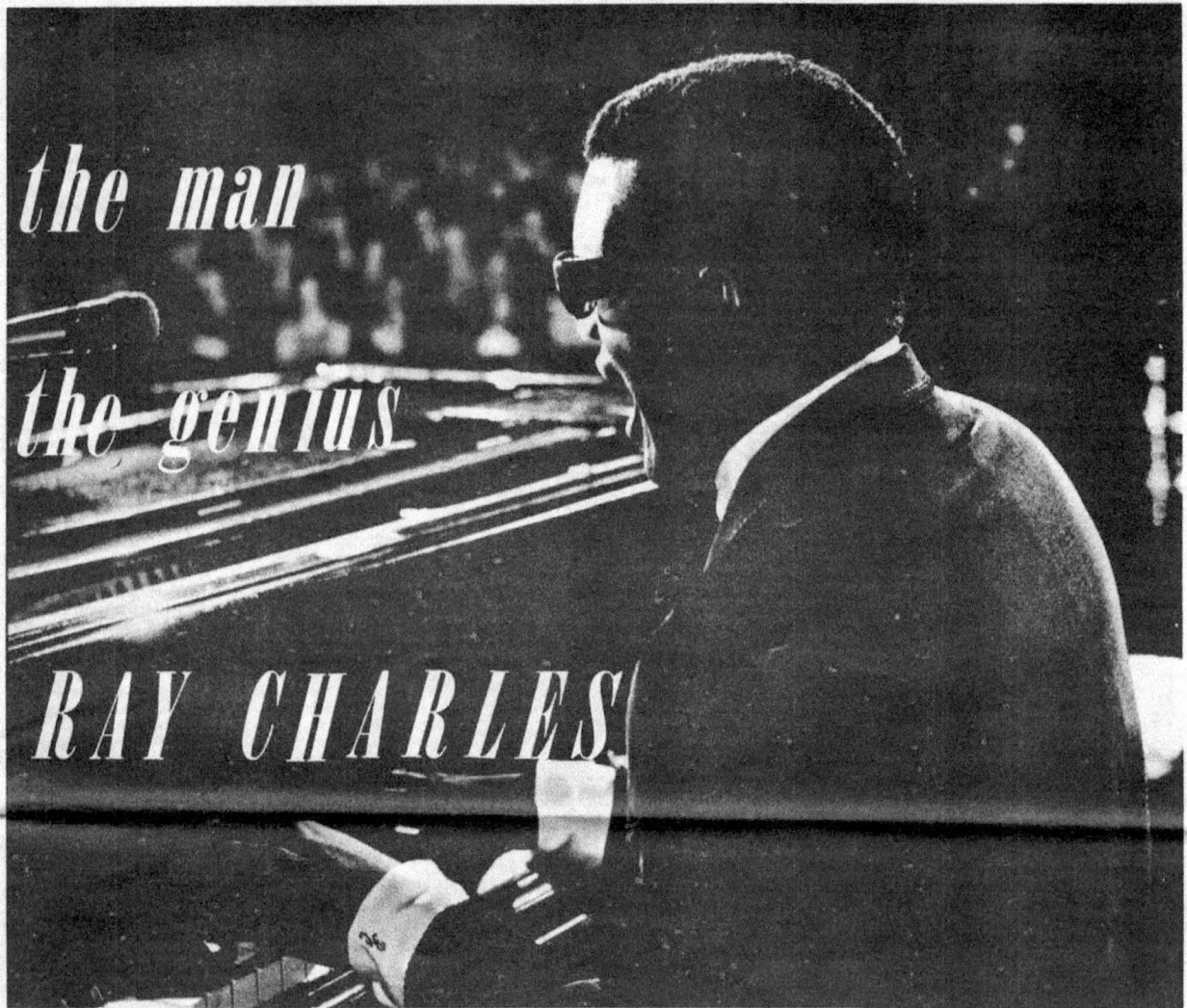

the man the genius RAY CHARLES

The story begins in Albany, Georgia in the year, 1932; Ray Charles was born. Six years later, the story—and the Charles family—had moved to Greenville, Florida where tragedy struck its first piercing blow. The small boy they called Ray was blinded—totally—with positively no hope for recovery.

Perhaps it isn't quite fair to call this a story; in all truth, it is a legend, for the man they call The Genius of Ray Charles is truly a legend in his own lifetime. But even legends have a tale to tell, and for Ray—it is a heart-warming story of almost epic proportions.

After learning of his permanent handicap, Ray's family sent the six-year old child to a special school for blind children in St. Augustine, Fla. Here he stayed until the age of fifteen when once again the claws of fate stabbed into Ray's darkened world to pierce his heart with the deaths of both his parents. Blind, and orphaned—a young boy left completely alone in a world of constant night—Ray stood up and "looked" around him, and then began a steady walk toward a far-distant shining light of life . . . *his* life; it is a walk he has never ceased.

While he had been at the school, Ray had acquired a certain amount of musical knowledge, and when he made the decision to leave—he immediately found himself playing with a great number of bands in the Florida area.

At 17, he organized his first trio—a bass and a guitar to blend with his own sax and piano, and within a short time became one of the most popular acts in Florida.

So much so that the trio soon found itself settled in Seattle, Washington where they appeared on a regular radio show, and went on to become the first Negro act to have a sponsored television show in the Northwest. Ray has since described the experience as having been his greatest thrill while in this business.

Ray is a perfectionist with his music—and with nearly everything he does. When he speaks about his world of music, he explains: "I want people to feel my soul. I try to bring out my soul so that people can understand what I am." And, just what *is* Ray's "soul?" What *is* Ray Charles?

He is a man of boundless energy and determination, a man of amazing ability who remains nearly unhindered by a physical handicap which would cripple many others. He is a man of dedication—to the music he creates, to any of many hobbies in which he occasionally indulges.

Although he is totally without the benefit of sight, Ray is capable of building (from the ground up) and repairing complete television sets, tape recorders, high fidelity sets, and can repair almost all parts of an airplane, including many pieces of complex and intricate portions of its immense engine.

Ray has one of the most sensitive ears in all of show business; he can hear a note which goes even *slightly* off-key—even though it is just one small part of a large orchestra, Ray can pick it out and identify the instrument which is making the error.

When *Playboy* magazine awarded Ray a gift of a motor scooter—Ray drove . . . *unaided* . . . around a quarter-mile track several times with only the sound of the exhaust from a scooter driven in front of him as his guide.

An exceptional man, Ray's talent and humility shine brightly like beacons in the vast and darkened ocean of many other over-rated performers. When Ray speaks of his music and of the success which he has enjoyed with it, he speaks with the voice of sincerity—and close introspection: "Too many artists, after reaching a point of success, just record anything, getting by on their past performances. I want my current record, and the record after that, to be better than anything I've done before. You have to improve and keep improving to stay on top. You can't fool the public."

And Ray makes no attempts to fool his public; he works ceaselessly toward presenting them with a sound which he can feel proud of, and which they can be proud to listen to. Over ninety percent of the songs which Ray records and plays for his audiences are his own compositions—and that includes the writing and arranging of the material. Ray is a perfectionist, and he will spend weeks—or even *months*—just *thinking* about the sound he hopes to achieve on record before he ever walks into a recording studio.

Recently, Ray was selected as the star of a new motion picture—"Ballad in Blue"—his first motion picture, which will have its United States premiere April 11, 1966 in New York City. The story is an emotional, heart-warming depiction of the world of a young blind boy; and the performance given by Ray is one of inspiration and sensitivity. The film is not biographical, and yet—it almost could be; there are many elements of fact within it which still apply to Ray.

He says of his own performance: "I play myself. I'm not really an actor and probably couldn't play the role of anyone else." And yet his director, Paul Henreid, found himself amazed at the sensitivity and depth which Ray poured into his performance before the cameras. Ray also collaborated with Rick Ward to write the title theme for the movie, "Light Out of Darkness;" a movie-theme which could well become a *life*-theme for Ray.

During his career, Ray has recorded some 13 albums, and over 25 single records; he has written countless scores of tunes now standard in the fields of rhythm and blues, jazz and pop.

His colleagues in the world of entertainment hold him in the highest esteem; to them, he is The Genius. His friends hold only the deepest affection and most sincere admiration and respect for Ray—a man of deep and enduring loyalty.

And we who must stand on the side lines and watch him—although we are often unable to see—must still ask, what is the "soul" of this man; what is it that Ray Charles *is*?

He is the *soul of a genius*. The Genius of a remarkable man; the man they call . . . *The Genius of Ray Charles.*

KRLA ARCHIVES

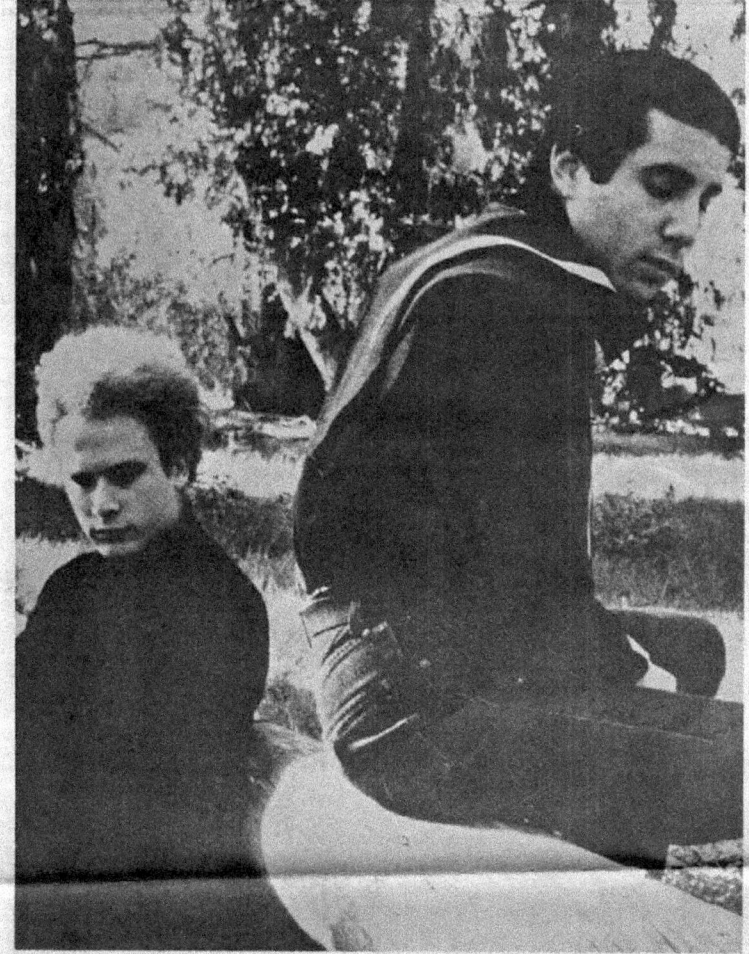

GOOD THINGS COME IN TWOS — Paul Simon and Art Garfunkel, two New York City folk singers, now have out their **second** hit single — "Homeward Bound" — and their **second** great album — "Sounds of Silence."

Paul And The Raiders Getting Their 'Kicks'

(Continued From Page 1)

"It was really quite an experience for us to see a country in the state of war," said Mike.

Besides visiting Santo Domingo the Raiders are also getting a considerable kick over their latest record, "Kicks." "I'm sure 'Kicks' is going to be a top five record," predicts Mike. "We had a little trouble at the start of it. Acid tapes got on the major markets before the record was released. So, Columbia had to work 24 hours straight to get it out to the rest of the markets."

Despite all of the volunteer work for the government, Drake is leaving the group to go into active duty in the National Guard. And no one is more surprised about this development than Drake himself!

"It was his local board," explained Mike. "He said he was supporting his mother, brother and sister plus we're doing all these USO shows but his local board had a quota to meet so they took him anyway.

"He'll be gone for four months and we're looking for a replacement right now. So far, there are about five people who we've heard."

The Raiders head out on a Dick Clark tour in April for five weeks and apparently Mike is viewing the up-coming tour with mixed feelings. "The Dick Clark Caravan is a rough tour. You don't eat regularly and it's really rough."

Mike says that television shows are much easier than a tour and, of course, you are seen by more people. However, he admits that the Raiders make much firmer and more devoted fans on a tour where the fans can see them "live."

Movies are possibly in the offing for the Raiders. "We're holding out to try and get a really good script," revealed Mike, "because we don't want to do a second-rate pop film."

And the future for the Raiders? "We have tours set up for all summer. We'll be going to Europe and England," said Mike.

There is a new album in the works and, naturally, they have to think about a follow-up to "Kicks." Busy but satisfying is the way the Raider's future lines up right now — and that isn't bad!

Adventures of Robin Boyd

(Continued From Page 4)

An odd, frightening smile. "Oh, yes," he said strangely. "Appointment. Head examined. I remember."

He then proceeded to stand up dizzily. Robin then proceeded to turn white as seventy-seven sheets.

First it had been the Beatles. She'd had them thinking they were balmy, had them going around swallowing guitar picks. Then the Stones. They had come unglued when she had flown out of their concert while in the pocket of Mick Jagger's jacket.

Had she done it *again*?

She feared so when the doctor handed her a notebook and a pencil and then stretched out on a nearby couch.

She *knew* so when he closed his eyes and began to tell her the story of his life.

She also knew that this time, she had *REALLY* done it. Because the story of his life began with these words . . . "My name is Robin Boyd, I am sixteen years old, and my mother thinks I'm off my nut."

(To Be Continued Next Week)

'Noted In The United Kingdom'
By Gil

IN MY OPINION . . . Allow me to nominate comedian PHIL FOSTER as public enemy number one for all young people in the world — no matter what their age. Dear PHIL FOSTER is seemingly only happy when knocking younger people. On a recent MERV GRIFFIN show Mr. Foster was giving his usual monologue on the "rotten kids" of today, when PHIL SPECTOR walked on the stage. PHIL SPECTOR didn't stay very long, but before he left he advised comedian FOSTER to listen to the BEATLE record "Nowhere Man" as he felt that it must have been dedicated to FOSTER. I think that PHIL SPECTOR made his point very well . . .

Much amusement is to be found in reading the various fan magazines to see what they think the term "Daytripper" means. Some of their ideas are really ludicrous. The BEATLES do use it in a slightly different context, but the traditional meaning of the word refers to a person who makes a trip to France from England and then returns home the same day. If the traveller returns within twenty-four hours then he has no need for a passport. Hence the term daytripper. The last few years, however, the daytrippers to France have carved out for themselves something of a wild reputation. Many Mods and Rockers go over for the day and really live it up. The French, of late, have started complaining that they are being terrorized by the visiting English.

* * *

STEVE WINWOOD, lead singer for the SPENCER DAVIS group, is one of the greatest soul singers that the U.K. has yet produced. The seventeen-year-old STEVE styles his vocalizing on such greats as RAY CHARLES . . . The new SPENCER DAVIS release will probably be a composition by STEVE entitled "Steve's Blues." Watch for this young man — he is really going places . . . ROLLING STONE BILL WYMAN thinks that OSCAR PETERSON is "brilliant." Even so BILL doesn't buy any of his records . . . KINK PETER QUAIFE horrified a BBC disc jockey by displaying a fake severed thumb.

* * *

American televison's spectacular "Anatomy Of Pop" was a real drag. As an 'analysis of Rock 'n' Roll it was a complete dud. I gave up on it after the commentator described CHUCK BERRY's song "Maybelline" as Country and Western music . . . Now that the BIRDS of London have decided not to sue the BYRDS of Los Angeles, their popularity seems to be soaring. Currently at London's swinging club the Carnaby Hive, the BIRDS are attracting large audiences . . . London's new underground city for teenagers has inspired other cities to do the same thing. Both Manchester and Birmingham have announced plans for the future development of underground teen centers . . . I wonder if this new trend of developing separate "underground teenage cities" is a good idea. As it is, teenagers and adults are on different frequencies, with this new development they may drift even farther apart. Like, maybe the kids will be bouncing messages off the moon, and adults will go back to using crystals.

* * *

Are the ROLLING STONES out to do a DYLAN? Their hit "19th Nervous Breakdown" sounded like something that DYLAN would dream up — the title I mean, not the song. On top of this, one of the tracks on their new album will reportedly last twelve minutes! This, I can't wait to hear. Imagine the STONES "do'in their nuts" for twelve straight minutes . . . It looks as if PETER & GORDON'S "Women" will only be a minor hit. Not really surprising, the arrangement is fair but the song is not very strong.

* * *

KINK RAY DAVIES should turn himself into a public corporation — he's already something of a factory. DAVIES turns out songs at a fantastic rate. Many stars have recorded songs by him, and there are plenty more who would like to do the same . . . CHRIS FARLOWE has a hit with his "Think." With KEITH RICHARD and MICK JAGGER producing his first album, that ought to stand a fair old chance also . . . TOMMY STEELE, who used to be a British Rock 'n' Roll star many years ago, will do a film for WALT DISNEY in May. STEELE has recently been in the New York smash "Half A Sixpence." . . .

* * *

On the subject of being outspoken, MICK JAGGER spoke up: "Anyone can turn around and say that the BEATLES are bad entertainers for effect. We don't need that kind of publicity. We just say what we feel." . . . DONOVAN'S impression of dogs: "Not as intelligent as cats, but nice people." . . . HERMAN'S HERMITS have the edge over everybody else, when it comes to making rubbishy records (that's if you don't count the BEACH BOYS and BARRY McGUIRE).

* * *

KEITH RICHARD and MICK JAGGER have proved that LENNON and McCARTNEY are not the only two Englishmen around who can write great Rock 'n' Roll. The appearance of a ROLLING STONE record is always a change from some of the drab stuff that has been hitting the charts of late.

KRLA ARCHIVES

'Would You Believe' Jerry Naylor Has A Hit

Jerry Naylor stopped by *The BEAT* this afternoon to play us his new Tower single, "Would You Believe," and to use a very "in" phrase made popular by TV's "Get Smart" we at *The BEAT* feel it's a "good" waxing for Jerry — "Would You Believe" GREAT!

Many questions came to us as we sat listening to Jerry's new record, like who wrote it? "Terry Stafford," answered Jerry, "who had a great successful hit record, 'Suspicion,' just a while back."

An "off the cuff" remark from the boss, "I'll bet the country and western stations will really like it." "Funny," laughed Jerry, "but some of them feel it's too bluesy for country and western air play!"

All in all, in it's early days of release it looks as though "Would You Believe" will be Jerry's first national hit. But it's been a long time coming. We remembered Jerry's first break with the Crickets and we wondered how he felt stepping into the shoes of Buddy Holly as lead singer of the Crickets at the peak of their popularity after Buddy's tragic death.

Pop Talk

My, my — how that boy does get around! I'm speaking about Paul McCartney, of course. If you've got a couple lines you can spare — I'd like to tell you how the Cuddly Beatle has been spending some of his not-so-spare moments of late. Just the other eve he joined Animal Chas. Chandler at the Scotch Club in London to observe Stevie Wonder, Georgie Fame, Charlie Foxx, and Chris Farlowe swinging with a groovy ad-lib jam session.

Then, of course, there is the exclusive info which Jonathon King slipped me when last he was in Our Town. Said that just the week before he had run into Pauly in a London Club (quite the little club-crawler, isn't he though?!) and after they had spoken for a few minutes — said good-bye and parted ways. Jonathan returned to his home and went to sleep — until about 4:00 that morning when his phone rang. It was Paul McCartney on the other end urgently pleading with Jonathan to allow him to use the large tape machine in John's office.

It seems as how Paul had been suddenly stricken by a thunderbolt of musical inspiration — in other words, he had a fab new idea for a song and since he can't read or write music, he needed a tape recorder in order to work out and preserve his little early-morning brain-child. Ah me! — the trials of an artist!!!

But the best news is yet to come. We all know of the fantastic, phenomenal world-wide success of Paul's beautiful "Yesterday." It was the song of the year which had about the most wide-spread effects on the pop music industry of any song ever recorded. As a further result of that hit disc, Paul has been commissioned by the London Philharmonic to compose a symphony. Now, are you ready for that???

Once again, *BEAT* readers, we take you to the Mighty Mouth of Mick. Sounds like The Jagger has been sounding-off once again, so — as a public service (for any serviceable publics who might be reading in this evening) we proudly present Keith's friend, Mick.

Talking 'bout a little *food*: "Oh, I love food. I hate bad food and food in America. I like interesting food and in America you only get one sort — steaks, which get a bit boring night after night. I prefer steak and kidney pudding."

To each his own, Michael!!! How about children? "A necessity. I like them, but I'm not a childomaniac. Some I can't stand. I hate precocious children and all American children seem to be precocious. They all want to say long words they don't understand. Gee, what a groovy scene!"

Well, at least now we know who to ask. But then, I certainly hope this doesn't place an indelible spot on America's spotless reputation for children and food! How about if we try once more? Got anything to say about a fella named Brian Jones, Mick? "He's the blond one on the right, and a very good friend." You really have a way with words, Mick. Would'ja like to write for *The BEAT?* We could use a few more of your probing, in-depth descriptions. Well, all right — one more once Michael-luv. Have you considered your rapidly approaching (it *is* the jet-age, you know!) old age? "I'm dreading it. There are only very few old people who are happy. When their minds stop thinking about the present and the future and stay wrapped up in the past, they are awfully dull. I mean, I don't want old dears saying: "How old do you think I am? 48? No, I'm 78 and I watch all the pop shows, and I've got all your records!! Then I think it's time they should grow up!"

Well, that's what happens when *The BEAT* gets *Jaggered.* (I would have said "Stoned" except that I just heard the Boss roar up in her Stingray!)

of Buddy Holly as lead singer of the Crickets at the peak of their popularity after Buddy's tragic death.

"No one will ever take the place of Buddy Holly," stated Jerry. "He was his own stylest and has been a giant influence on many of our current popular entertainers including the Beatles."

"I was chosen to carry on as lead singer which was a great break for me but I never tried to be, for I could never have been, able to fill the shoes of Buddy Holly.

"Yes, we had hit records after Buddy's death and traveled in most every state in this country, every province of Canada and repeated trips to England and Europe doing television shows, movies and personal appearances.

"Yes, we have a letter from the Beatles thanking us for our support and influence in their early days which came as a result of us hearing them and their first record while in England in 1962. We were, and still are, honored that they admittedly used the name 'Beatles' because of a closeness with the Crickets."

But before any of that, didn't we remember Jerry being a disc jockey? "Yes, starting when I was fourteen in my hometown in Texas and working finally on Los Angeles' KRLA in the spring and summer of 1960.

Some Failures

"I always sang during these years and cut some unsuccessful records and did shows and tours with Glen Campbell, Roger Miller, Billy Vaughn and others. This working as a DJ and a single artist ended when I joined the Crickets in late 1960," said Jerry.

How and why, then, did Jerry decide to leave his position with the world famous Crickets for the uncertainty of being a single artist? "I met a young, independent record producer, Mike Curb," revealed Jerry, "who thought I should be a single artist again and was willing to gamble the cost of a recording session to prove it.

"Shortly after the session was done, and with Mike's influence, Tower Records made me a seven year contract offer which I accepted. I had also about this time, been signed to a multiple performance contract with ABC-TV's 'Shindig.' These activities took up pretty much all of my time so I had to drop out of the Crickets."

Jerry's first big break, of course, was his chance to sing lead with the Crickets but what about lately — what was the turning point in his career as a single artist?

BEAT Awards

"Two things," Jerry promptly replied. "In early December I got the chance to perform at *The BEAT's* First Annual International Pop Music Awards. With the house filled with fellow members of the entertainment business and especially with the presence of one of my best friends, Roger Miller, (with his wife and parents who happened to be celebrating their 50th wedding anniversary) I sang Roger's giant hit, 'King Of The Road.' This to me was not only a break toward bettering my career but was an evening I will never forget.

"The other break, of course, was finding the song, 'Would You Believe,' again with the help of Mike Curb."

Now that the record is well on it's way to the top of the charts, what's in the future for Jerry? "With much depending on the success of the new single, plans are already being made for an album release, tours are planned, television shows are being booked and some have already been taped for airing in the next few weeks and even a movie deal in in the works!"

Jerry has been working on a book for about the last two years and he has finally taken his notes off of the scraps of paper and backs of envelopes and paper sacks and put them all down on typed sheets. So, it looks as if the book will be published in the very near future and to give you an idea of what Jerry's book will consist of and what he feels about himself, he has allowed us to use the following poem, "That Little Boy."

That Little Boy

When I was just a little boy
   Everyone around me was so tall
And . . . why . . . they'd pay little attention to me
   Or, most time, none at all
I used to go on big, long trips
   A mile . . . or maybe two
And I'd sit on top of that hill
   And plan all the things I'd someday do
I'd build a railroad for trains to ride
   Fight a war . . . and win a medal of honor to wear
     with pride
And from way up there I could touch the wind
   And almost outstare the sun
It's good to remember those carefree days
   And how simple it seemed to have great fun
But as days went by and summer's past
   And winters turned the year
I realized a boy must have a direction
   A goal to achieve, somewhere to go from here
I don't know what set me to thinking . . .
   About where I'd go and the future I had planned
But it must have had to do with that music hall
   And the sound that came from that old band
The place was not too far from home
   And sometimes, through a window I'd take a peek
I'd stand outside listening hard
   And trying not to miss a beat
I watched him closely . . .
   That man that made them laugh, or cry, and then
     they'd cheer
I wanted to be that man so bad
   My heart would thump with fear . . .
That maybe I'd never make it
   And all my wanting would be in vain
But something stronger inside me squelched that fear
   And I started building . . . not a railroad, but a road
     to an entertainers fame
Now the years have past . . .
   I've known the down, the up, the "comeback" and
     try once more
I've been schooled in disappointments . . .
   And graduated to learn the score
I was taught to give, and sell, and take
   And build a dream on promise and hope
And I guess it's funny . . . but here I am . . .
   Playing the same childish game I used to play on my
     hometown hillside slope
Wish, want, hope . . . pray for the things someday I'll do
   And you know . . . I'm still kind of that little boy too
     . . . And all of you still look so tall
As you stand there, sit there, looking straight at me
   I can only do my best to look up and give to you
     my all

Copyright 1966 Penfield Publishing

KRLA ARCHIVES

STAMP OUT STIFF HAIR.

Caryl Richards

CLIP ON DOTTED LINE

Student Discount Exchange Coupon
WORTH 50¢

EASTER VACATION FUN

TEEN-AGE FAIR
THE WORLD'S FAIR FOR TEEN-AGERS
HOLLYWOOD PALLADIUM
APRIL 1 thru 10, 1966
Doors Open Daily: Noon to Midnight

CLIP ON DOTTED LINE

SEE... IN PERSON... SONNY & CHER
• The REGENTS • The CHALLENGERS • JOEY PAIGE
• SAM RIDDLE'S TV SPECIALS • TOP TV, RECORD & MOVIE STARS

OVER $3,000,000 WORTH OF FABULOUS EXHIBITS & ATTRACTIONS

Fender Battle of the Beat — Model Car Drag Strip Racing — Dance Contests — Custom Car Caravan — Surfing Movies — Miss Teen International Pageant — Harmony Folk Festival — Guest stars in Person from Movies, T.V., Records and Radio (Top D.J.'s) — Beauty Clinics — Judo — Karate Thrill Shows — Photography and Home Movie Exposition — Fabulous Fashion Shows — Dream Cars of the Future — Bands and Drill Teams — Free Prizes and Gifts — Nonstop Record Hop

All above events and attractions included in admission price

VISIT CARYL RICHARDS' BOOTH AT THE FAIR
WIN HUNDREDS OF DOLLARS WORTH OF PRIZES

KRLA Tunedex

This Week	Last Week	Title	Artist
1	1	CALIFORNIA DREAMIN'	The Mama's & Papa's
2	5	BANG BANG	Cher
3	4	DAYDREAM	The Lovin' Spoonful
4	2	NOWHERE MAN	The Beatles
5	3	THESE BOOTS ARE MADE FOR WALKIN'	Nancy Sinatra
6	14	SOUL AND INSPIRATION	The Righteous Bros.
7	6	19TH NERVOUS BREAKDOWN	The Rolling Stones
8	8	THE BALLAD OF THE GREEN BERET	S/Sgt. Barry Sadler
9	9	I'M SO LONESOME I COULD CRY	B.J. Thomas & Triumphs
10	12	WOMAN	Peter & Gordon
11	19	CALL ME	Chris Montez
12	16	DARLING BABY	The Elgins
13	7	LISTEN PEOPLE	Herman's Hermits
14	10	HOMEWARD BOUND	Simon & Garfunkel
15	13	WALKIN' MY CAT NAMED DOG	Norma Tanega
16	20	BABY SCRATCH MY BACK	Slim Harpo
17	21	LOVE MAKES THE WORLD GO ROUND	Deon Jackson
18	11	I AIN'T GONNA EAT OUT MY HEART ANYMORE	Young Rascals
19	30	KICKS	Paul Revere & The Raiders
20	23	THIS OLD HEART OF MINE	The Isley Bros.
21	18	THE CHEATER	Bob Kuban
22	22	FOLLOW ME	Lyme & Cybelle
23	17	WORKIN' MY WAY BACK TO YOU	The Four Seasons
24	33	SHAPES OF THINGS	The Yardbirds
25	28	IT'S TOO LATE	Bobby Goldsboro
26	29	SURE GONNA MISS HER	Gary Lewis & The Playboys
27	32	SPANISH FLEA/WHAT NOW MY LOVE	Herb Alpert
28	31	ONE TRACK MIND	The Knickerbockers
29	25	INSIDE — LOOKING OUT	The Animals
30	36	SECRET AGENT MAN	Johnny Rivers
31	35	YOUNG LOVE	Lesley Gore
32	—	THE RAINS CAME	Sir Douglas Quintet
33	37	LULLABY OF LOVE	The Poppies
34	—	TIME WON'T LET ME	The Outsiders
35	—	634-5789	Wilson Pickett
36	39	MAGIC TOWN	The Vogues
37	38	YOUR PERSONALITY	Jackie Lee
38	—	SOMEWHERE	Len Barry
39	—	RHAPSODY IN THE RAIN	Lou Christie
40	40	WOULD YOU BELIEVE	Jerry Naylor

DAVE HULL • BOB EUBANKS • DICK BIONDI • JOHNNY HAYES
EMPEROR HUDSON • CASEY KASEM • CHARLIE O'DONNELL • BILL SLATER

English Pen Friends

Margaret Titterton
37 Enfield Road
Mackworth Estate
Derby, England

Anne Parker (15)
43, Joslin Rd.
Purfleet, Essex, England

Kathleen Wilson (15)
4, The Quadrant
Uplands Estate
Purfleet,
Essex, England

Pauline Groves (14)
3, Kent View
Aveley
South Ockendon
Essex, England

Rosemary Lay (15)
26, Joslin Rd.
Purfleet
Essex, England

Lesley Allat (14)
3, Shannon Way
Aveley
South Ockendon
Essex, England

Kay Hayden (14)
High Mouse Farm Cottage
Purfleet
Essex, England

Susan Brown (15)
8, Church View
Aveley
Essex, England

Ann Davies (15)
3, Central Ave.
Aveley
St. Ockendon
Essex, England

Janet Dowsing (15)
29, Hall Crescent
Aveley
South Ockendon
Essex, England

Anne Tyler (14)
41, Manor Close
Aveley
South Ockendon
Essex, England

KRLA BEAT Subscription
SAVE 33% OF REGULAR PRICE

☐ 1 YEAR — 52 Issues — $5.00 ☐ 2 YEARS — $8.00 ☐ 6 MONTHS — $3.00
Enclosed is _____ ☐ CASH ☐ CHECK

PLEASE PRINT — Include Your Zip Code
Send to: .... Age ....
Address: .... City ....
State: .... Zip: ....

Foreign Rate: $9.00 — 52 Issues

MAIL YOUR ORDER TO: KRLA BEAT
6290 Sunset, Suite 504
Hollywood, Calif. 90028

KRLA ARCHIVES

Inside KRLA

KRLA BEAT'S OWN JAMIE McCLUSKEY PROPOSES TO DJ BILL SLATER ON THE AIR!!!

Yes, friends—it's true; the shocking, heart-stopping headlines (quoted above) are absolutely true. For days now we have been receiving cards, letters, telegrams, and phone calls from all over Southern California. Everyone wants to know if it was really *our* Jamie McCluskey who brazenly called KRLA DJ Bill Slater—while he was actually in the middle of a broadcast!—and proposed to him, in front of 17,000,000 blushing ears!!!

Hard though it may be to believe, this actually happened. But you can't really get the full story from just a headline. So we went right to the people involved—Jamie and Bill—to get the real Bat low-down on just exactly what happened.

Jamie, herself, has already confessed to having given in to her heartfelt whims by having called Bill on the air to propose. As Jamie is a fellow *BEAT* reporter and a friend of mine, she confided to me that she simply couldn't control herself any longer.

Omelet Vision

"Then, when I heard Bob Eubanks propose to Nancy Sinatra on the air one night, I knew suddenly what I had to do. It came to me—like a vision on a frozen omelet—that my only course of action was to call Bill and just lay the big question right on him! So I did!"

After speaking with Jamie (who at that time *still* hadn't recovered!) I spoke with the man in question, Bill Slater. His immediate comments—in an *exclusive* interview with *The BEAT*, were: "I still can't believe it!! She called *right on the air*, and she said, 'Bill, I just think you're terrific, and I'd like to marry you!' And, y'know, she went *on and on!* Jamie McCluskey the Third—I mean, I had read her columns in *The BEAT* many times, but I *never* expected anything like *this!* I'd only seen her one time before, and she called up and . . . it was just terrific! I appreciated the compliment, and I just don't know what to say after that!

"My wife called immediately after I had the phone call on the air and she wanted to know what was going on! I didn't know, but it was *groovy!*"

Baby-Sitter Maybe?

Of course, it would have been impossible for Bill to have accepted—being basically married already, as he is—however, Mr. and Mrs. Slater did extend an invitation to Jamie to come and work for them. However, Jamie refused on the grounds that they had offered her only fifty cents an hour

. . . JAMIE McCLUSKEY III

to baby-sit with the Slater's two children.

At present, Jamie and Bob Eubanks are planning the beginnings of an international club to be known as "The Rejected Ones, Inc." Just looking at their initial plans—the club looks as though it will be a tremendous success.

The old Hullabalooer stopped by the other day with a few good words for all of his Hullabalooers, which he asked me to pass along: "My fan club had a meeting for all of the chapter heads of all the different fan clubs all over, and they met at Linda Thor's house on March 23. They all sat in to see how a fan club runs. By the way—our fan club is the largest one for any disc jockey with the exception of Soupy Sales, who is no longer a disc jockey. I was present at that to meet all the chapter heads, and this is the first time that any disc jockey has ever done that."

Also falling by our column this week is none other than the infamous Super Sissy, himself. As you all know, we have been following the trail of clues concerning the mysterious BatManager sign on John-John Barrett's door for some weeks now, and we have good reason to believe that Super Sissy is at least directly—or indirectly, as the sign may be—

Battle Of Beat, Cars And Girls Featured At Teen Fair

Dazzling spy-spoof cars and motorcycles, dramatic demonstrations of extra sensory perception and a laser beam in action top a list of new attractions planned for the fifth annual Teen-Age Fair.

The youth extravaganza makes the scene at the Hollywood Palladium beginning Friday night, April 1, and continues through April 10.

The go-go-go set will get their first look at the going-est collection of spy rods and cycles, built by George Barris, designer of the Batmobile and Munster Koach. Barris will unveil such spoofers as the ZZR, Silencer Wagon, the Chaser cycle, 003 Mustang, Apartment Station Wagon and a dozen other "way-out" creations.

High point of interest will be the ZZR, which was built for the spy sleuth movie, "Out Of Sight." Barris calls the twin-engine 25th Century agent hot rod his "wildest creation." It's an arsenal on wheels that can kill you, engulf you in connected with this baffling mystery.

At any rate, he has stopped by to give us a little description of his costume and equipment. Super Sis . . . take it away!

"My Super Sissy outfit consists of red tights, yellow trunks, black Beatle boots, white spats with Bats—those are Bat Spats!—a blue velour, and a flowing green cape with a green mask, *under* the glasses. Also, a large, black Bat on my forehead.

"My personal appearances in the last week have included outstanding places in Pasadena, South Pasadena, and Anaheim, and the KRLApes basketball games."

I then asked Super Sissy if he actually played with the Apes, to which he indignantly replied: "Of course not! It's not in my contract to touch the basketball—I can only use the rose and bat down evil with it! The rose is stronger than a utility belt—it serves all purposes, and can do anything I want it to!"

There is also a secondary sort of rumor going around that Super Sissy is just a secret identity for Tad—the Teen Age Dictator, very also known as Vaughn Filkins.

Hmmmmm—do you suppose that they are *all* in reality . . . John-John????

sleeping gas, hit you in the chin, blow tar and feathers at pursuing opposition and it has a skid juice spreader that shoots liquid on the ground to spin out eluding vehicles.

Screen Coverage

To top it all, a complete screen extends around the spy rod to make it a sign board along the side of the highway so as to be camouflaged from other agents. What ever happened to the Pierce Arrow?

Fairgoers are in for the thrill of a lifetime when they see French para-psychologist Paul Goldin demonstrate his power of extra sensory perception four times daily. It will be the first appearance in the U.S. for the internationally renowned exponent of E.S.P. Goldin has thrilled audiences around the world with his demonstrations of telepathic communication.

Proving that science truth is stranger than fiction, there will be a demonstration of the use of a laser beam for outer-space communication. The super-power laser will be in action throughout each day with technicians from North American Aviation in control.

Above all activity, of course, there will be the wild sound of teen music. The continuous "Battle of the Beat" event will pit teen-age folk-rock groups against each other in a torrid competition to determine the outstanding combo in the area.

Folk singing groups will enjoy their own event. Additionally, a three-hour musical show and dance session will be staged each afternoon and evening, featuring the nation's top instrumental groups.

Fashion Preview

For the girls, a preview of spring and summer fashions will be presented eight times daily by The Broadway. In a colorful fashion area, which will cover the main floor of the Palladium, The Broadway will present "The Mobile California Look" spotlighting the latest in teen togs amidst boldly colored custom cars and cycles.

Adding glamour to the Fair will be the "Miss Teen International Pageant." For the first time, teen beauties from foreign lands will be flown to Hollywood to compete against the best of American teen-agers.

While major Southland resort areas carry on a campaign to discourage teenagers from visiting during Easter vacation, the Hollywood Palladium will welcome the arrival of an expected two-hundred thousand teen-agers from throughout Southern Calif.

Eve's APPAREL
See if you can BEAT our prices on our new Jr. and missy lines. Samples at wholesale or less.
NO 3-4456
1800 N. Vermont
Hollywood, Calif.

Join The International Fan Club
Send $1.00 for one year to:
Dave Hull Fan Club
634 Sefton,
Monterey Park, Calif.
Monthly Bulletins, Photos, The Works!

Paul Newman is 'Harper'
...a different kind of cat!
BACALL · HARRIS · HILL · LEIGH · TIFFIN · WAGNER · WINTERS
PACIFIC'S PANTAGES THEATRE HOLLYWOOD
HOLLYWOOD BLVD. near VINE · HO. 9-2211
EXCLUSIVE ENGAGEMENT NOW!
CALL THEATRE FOR SHOW TIMES

Little Women
Casual to Cotillion
OUR CAPEZZIO'S HAVE ARRIVED!!!
Swing into Spring where Fashion's a FUN thing!
GASSY GARB FOR GROOVY GIRLS
Pre-teen Sizes 6-14
Jr. Petite Sizes 3-13
Junior Sizes 3-15
Open Mondays to 9:30 beginning March 21
136 SOUTH BEVERLY DRIVE
BEVERLY HILLS, CALIFORNIA
Validated Parking in Crest & Triangle Lots

UNLIKE ANYTHING YOU'VE EVER SEEN!
WARNER BROS. SUPER CINERAMA PRODUCTION
BATTLE OF THE BULGE
PACIFIC'S CINERAMA DOME Theatre Magnificent
SUNSET AT VINE · HOLLYWOOD
NOW PLAYING!

KRLA ARCHIVES

Who Are The Pop Critics?

By Eden

How often do you pick up a magazine or a newspaper to discover still another "critic"—well, that's what *they* call themselves!—panning all of today's contemporary music?

It happens nearly every day, yet I still can't quite believe that it's for real. These individuals set themselves up as critics, then immediately proceed to take the easiest way out.

Rather than offering some sort of valid criticism on various records by different artists, they simply lump the entire field of popular music together and proclaim it *all* to be positively worthless!

Some criticism! It seems doubtful that any of these self-styled critics have even heard any of the music which they are so vehemently condeming.

They say that popular music offers no variety—but I beg to differ with these people. In what other field of music can you find songs such as "Yesterday," "The In Crowd," "Like A Rolling Stone," "It Was A Very Good Year," "Satisfaction" and "Michelle" all going to the Number One spot on charts across the nation?

The answer is in *no* other field. The songs just mentioned were recorded by artists such as The Beatles, The Rolling Stones, Bob Dylan, Frank Sinatra, and the Ramsey Lewis Trio, and cover a vast number of musical fields, including folk, pop, "standard" and just plain beautiful.

I challenge anyone to find one of the so-called "good music" radio stations playing all of these different elements of contemporary music. It simply isn't done.

Nor is credit being given where it is long over-due. All of these songs just mentioned—and many, many others—have been made popular by the youthful buying public; the people under 25 years of age.

I might remind you that this is the same element in our population which is supposed not to have any taste! Well, they quite obviously *do* have some taste buds, and some mighty good ones at that!

Not so for our friends the "Critics." They have tongues, all right—tongues which frequently wag way over time!—but they seem to be completely devoid of any taste buds whatsoever. They just accept the traditional taste buds handed down from generation to generation, and use them as their own.

Oh well—maybe they are right after all. I mean, who knows—Bach and all his friends may just stage a little revival yet!!

...THE LETTERMEN

The Lettermen—Just Plain Good Singers

From coast to coast young adults flock to nightclubs and college campuses to hear the Lettermen and teens constantly keep their albums among the top sellers. Yet these three guys, Bob Engemann, Jim Pike and Tony Butala, are not British, have short hair, don't use electric guitars, dress sharp and look like average American college boys.

The Lettermen are sort of in a category all by themselves. They aren't a hard rock or folk-rock group and yet they're not out there with Jack Jones and Robert Goulet either, and neither are they a folk act like Peter, Paul and Mary.

Yet they sell records to the same people that buy hard rock, folk-rock, folk or what is called "good music."

And they do so on the basis of just plain good singing.

A Little Faith

They also have something else that is rather uncommon among groups today and that is faith—faith in God as well as in themselves.

All three are very religious and consider their faith and trust in one another a major reason for their success.

Bob, a devout Mormon, remembers well when the Lettermen were literally "lettermen" in college. "We were frequently told to forget a singing career. At first, we did feel like we were wasting our efforts. We didn't believe in ourselves and no one else did."

It wasn't until after college that they and other people began to have faith in them and they started up the ladder of success.

Public Opinion

Tony, the only Catholic in the group, remembers that even after they became popular public opinion was often against them. They received many letters asking them to sing faster songs.

They did work a few faster numbers and the result of that change is now evident in the over 200,000 miles they travel a year and the $500,000 they made last year off of concerts.

It also shows in their current schedule. They'll be in New York March 1-6 to tape the Sammy Davis Jr. Show for airing March 25.

Then they resume their college tour with dates at New Mexico University, Trinity College, Baylor University, Univ. of Missouri, Valpariso Univ., Oshkosh Univ., Franklin College, Univ. of Louisville, Carson-Newman College and Austin-Peay State College.

And one other little sign of success is the new Ghia 450 SS each one of the Lettermen is now sporting, a gift from Columbia Records for their appearances on tv this past season.

And somewhere along the line they must have found some time to record for now they have out a new single. It's called "You'll Be Needin' Me" backed with "Run To My Lovin' Arms."

COUNTRY & WESTERN WINNERS (l. to r.) Roger Miller, Bonnie Owens and Buck Owens with awards.
BEAT Photo: Chuck Boyd

C & W Music Awards Names Miller 'Man Of The Year'

HOLLYWOOD—Roger Miller was voted "Man of the Year" and Buck Owens "Best Male Vocalist" at last night's first Annual Country & Western Music Academy Awards Show held before a sellout crowd at the Hollywood Palladium.

Between them, Owens and Miller took four of the 21 awards. Miller also won in the "Best Songwriting" category and Owens took another as the "Best Bandleader."

	CATEGORY:
ROGER MILLER	"Man of the Year"
	"Best Songwriter"
BUCK OWENS	"Top Male Vocalist"
	"Best Bandleader"
BONNIE OWENS	"Top Female Vocalist"
	"Best Vocal Group" (with Merle Haggard)
MERLE HAGGARD	"Most Promising Male Vocalist"
	"Best Vocal Group" (with Bonnie Owens)
KAYE ADAMS	"Most Promising Female Vocalist"

KRLA ARCHIVES

Fashionable Turtles

When the Turtles first hit the pop scene with "It Ain't Me Babe" and the public got their first glimpse of the group, groans and moans of "they'll never have another hit—they couldn't possibly because they're so homely" were heard everywhere.

But the Turtles had other ideas—they were not about to be a one-hit group, not if they could help it. In the first place they had definite ideas about one-hit groups. They felt that if a group acquired one hit it wasn't some kind of a sign to never change their sound, to come out with changed lyrics but the same melody time after time.

So, they set out to prove that they could sing all kinds of songs—they weren't limited to "It Ain't Me Babe." Still, the critics insisted that with their looks they were just a passing fancy. The very least they could do would be to put on some suits and cut their hair.

But the Turtles held fast to their beliefs. They look the same today as they did then and, apparently, they were right for they have come up with hit after hit and their current smash, "You Baby," is their biggest one yet.

"Hullabaloo"

The really huge feather in the Turtles' cap, however, is the fact that "Hullabaloo" finally asked them to appear on the show. They had held out for quite awhile and with "You Baby" smashing up the national charts, "Hullabaloo" bowed to the Turtles—on *their* terms.

They are currently in New York at the Phone Booth playing to houses packed with the cream of New York society because, you see, the Booth has become the "in" place for all socialites.

And if you think it's ironic that the group who was tagged "extremely homely, not to mention sloppy," from the outset of their career is now playing to the social set, you haven't heard anything yet!

While in New York the Turtles will do a *fashion* lay-out for *Glamor Magazine!!!* They'll be modeling the very latest in men's fashions and, believe me, that *is* ironic because the Turtles pay little, if any, attention to clothes. They wear what they feel like wearing whether it's fashionable or not—and most times it definitely is not.

Chuck once told me that the only thing he does for a stage appearance is "to make sure that the hole in my jacket is in the back!" So, the fact that the Turtles are going to model men's fashions in *Glamor* has got to be one of the funniest things to happen in a long time.

Unchanged

Luckily their record success has not gone to the Turtles' heads. They still walk around minus guards and aids and all that goes with that bag. Their fans ask for autographs whenever they spot the boys but there are no hysterical mobbings and, in fact, many times the group members are not even recognized.

They go to clubs and shop in record stores just like everyone else, so if they're ever in your town keep your eyes peeled because most probably you'll find the six Turtles wandering around.

Most things have been rosy for the Turtles so far, but they still feel that it can all be ended if the draft board catches up with them—and they're afraid that it will.

The one big disappointment encountered by the group was their rejection by adult audiences in Las Vegas. They bombed. Literally. And they're the first to admit it, but they aim to see that it doesn't ever happen again.

The Turtles will shortly be coming out with a new album which besides being a fantastic LP also has one of the wildest covers you've ever seen! Yes, the Turtles are going places—despite everything—and they're not going slow either.

KRLA ARCHIVES

Brenda Lee: A Little Girl With A Big Voice

Brenda Lee rhymes with tenderly; and that's not a rhyme without reason. A balladeer who, in the face of somersaulting trends, sticks with what she does best, it's not just coincidence that every record she has cut since 1959 has made the charts—all but two of them with both sides. You might call it long-playing talent.

Her manager, Dub Allbritten, analyzes the Lee appeal in this way: "Brenda has always had three separate audiences. The kids liked her from the beginning, because she was one of them. Adults like her because she has the appeal of a little girl, with the aplomb of a woman; and ever since her records began hitting the charts, the teen-agers have gone for her. Since she appeals to all of those markets, she and her audiences can't outgrow each other."

Brenda started out on the kiddie contest circuit, but went professional at the age of six. She signed her first Decca recording contract when she was eleven, back in 1957, but it was two years before Decca began to draw any dividends on their investment. The record that set her career spinning was "Sweet Nothing's," a slow-starting, long-lasting hit that took a good six months to make the charts.

An "Enigma"

It may seem pretentious to apply the word enigma to anyone as uncomplicated and forthright as Brenda, but it seems to fit. Certainly it is hard to explain the riddle of her consistent success, year after year, when admittedly she has had very few number one records. Recently, in spite of the fact that she had not had a smash hit since 1965, she won out on one national poll over those two notables, Petula Clark and Marianne Faithfull for the title of "World's No. 1 Female Vocalist."

At twenty one, the little girl with the big voice is a veteran of fifteen years in show business, she has appeared on every major television show, and her nightclub and concert tours have taken her to every state in the Union, and to thirty-two foreign countries. In the States she tries to keep to a schedule of two weeks on tour, two weeks at home, in order to have some time with husband Ronnie Shacklett and their year-old daughter.

She has played a command performance for the Queen of England, Brazil's president has called her "America's finest good will ambassador," and in another South American city she generated so much excitement that six national police were assigned to 24 hour duty, to protect her from her admirers.

On Tour

On tour she is backed by The Casuals, six young bachelors who, with two exceptions, have been with her for nine years.

Because Dub Allbritten recognized her foreign potential early in her career, she was one of the first major record artists to re-record in foreign languages. As a happy consequence, the diminutive singer is a giant in the foreign market. Last year she cut eight sides in Hamburg for release in Germany and the United States, and has recently recorded in Japanese and English, for Japanese release.

"I don't think much about recording or singing when I'm at home in Nashville," says Brenda, "but Dub gave me all my old recordings in leather-bound volumes for Christmas, and I've had fun and some laughs, listening to those early records. My voice sounded very high, to me. It's changed a lot since 'Sweet Nothin's,' but a good deal of my phrasing is the same."

Perhaps that's the secret of her success—the basic changlessness, the consistent integrity, which keeps her on the charts year after year.

The Cats and Cars Of Jerry Van Dyke

By Carol Deck

Speaking of interviews, to steal a line from Shirley Poston (sorry 'bout that, Shirl), I've done some interesting ones but this latest one may never leave my mind. I think it has something to do with that pregnant cat.

I mean I've done interviews with seven guys in The BEAT's smallest office which only holds three people safely and I've done interviews in other people's offices or restaurants and cold dressing rooms (there seems to be a universal rule about banning heaters in dressing rooms).

But there I sat, in this very comfortable chair in the living room of Jerry Van Dyke's attractive home.

In my lap was one very pregnant cat named Tinkerbell. Sitting beside the chair with his head dropped over the arm trying to get me to pet him was one rather large red and white dog named Ike.

In the background I could hear children's counting records being played in the bedroom by Jerri Lynn Van Dyke, age three.

Leaning against another chair in the room watching me was Kelly Jean, seven, a budding young actress who's been on her father's show five times.

And in the midst of it all, directly across from me casually sat Jerry, star of "My Mother the Car."

Do-Nothing Car

"The trouble with the show is that the car can't do anything. I have to do all the reactions for two people, myself and 'mother.' The car doesn't do anything."

And this car that doesn't do anything is a bit interesting too. "It is supposed to be a 1928 Porter, but it's actually a remade model T," Jerry explained.

"There actually was a Porter made in 1921 but we didn't know that until after the show started. Our production manager is named Porter and we just named the car after him."

Jerry's known as many things in show business—a night club performer, an expert banjo player, the star of his own TV show and Dick Van Dyke's younger brother.

Both Jerry and Dick entered show business while they were in high school in Danville, Ill. Dick was a radio announcer and Jerry had a comedy act with a partner.

After four years in the service Jerry started his night club act which still is a major part of his life.

He had a daily one hour television variety show in Indiana for a while too.

Then he did a couple of top nation-wide shows like the Ed Sullivan Show and the Andy Williams Show as a comedienne and banjo player.

Sleepwalking

He came across great on Johnny Carson's Tonight Show and then really showed his talent in a two part series on his brother's show, The Dick Van Dyke Show, where he played a sleepwalker.

He considers himself mainly a comedienne but his act also includes some pretty sharp singing and banjo playing.

He also plays drums, but not in the act. "I was in a group once as a drummer," he recalls, "for one month."

But the banjo is really a part of him. He started playing shortly after he married his high school sweetheart.

"Carol's father was a banjo player and they had one around the house. I like the sound of it and picked it up."

He also noted that the banjo is the only really American instrument. It was created here and is strictly an American sound.

Being the younger brother of a very famous comedienne, might be difficult for any comedienne, perhaps not as difficult as being the son of someone famous, but Jerry doesn't seem to spend a great deal of time worrying about it.

"It isn't how I feel, it's how the public feels. If the public thinks I'm in Dick's shadow, then I am. I'm making a better living than Pinky Lee but not as well as my brother. Some people do better than me, some worse."

Murderous Work

To Jerry his TV show is real work because he has to work without a live audience. "It's almost murder to work without an audience. You just have to go with what you're doing and hope."

He can try out new things for his club act and discard or change them according to the audience's reaction, but not so on TV.

"When I get a script I have to do it and there's no trying it out on an audience."

He writes most of his own material for his club act using "what ever's current." Even "mother" sometimes works into the act. He has a line about mother being replaced by the Batmobile.

Jerry's not too sure his show will be renewed next fall but he's got several other things lined up anyway.

He'll do 12 weeks of "How To Succeed In Business Without Really Trying" this summer and will also play Las Vegas for awhile.

If "My Mother the Car" does go off he'd like to do another TV series.

"I might do a show where I play a minister. There's a lot of comedy in a minister's life. Ministers go places and do more things than anyone. They see a lot of comedy. Every one's got 40,000 funny stories."

Unfortunately neither Jerry nor I had the time to go into these 40,000 stories. So I removed the purring pregnant cat from my lap, gave Ike one last affectionate pat and bid farewell to Jerry Van Dyke, a casual young man with a contagious smile and laugh that should keep him in the spotlight for many years to come—with or without his mother the car and his brother the star.

...JERRY VAN DYKE

KRLA ARCHIVES

The Yardbirds Speak Out

By Eden

Some call it "pop art," some call it "English R 'n' B," some call it pop music gone electronic. At The BEAT — we just call it **Yardbirds**. They are a thoroughly unique and talented group, creating a sound that is specifically their own. It is a new sound, a sound of today — but also, a sound quite difficult to describe.

And so, it suits the Yardbirds — for they are **also** difficult to describe to someone else. Oh, we could tell you of the exceptional talents of lead guitarist Jeff Beck — said to be the finest guitarist in Britain today; or we could tell you of the feeling which lead singer Keith Relf pours into each song he sings. Or the good looks of Jim McCarty, or the quiet, intense determination of bass guitarist "Sam" and the almost-shy humor of rhythm guitarist Chris Dreja.

But, we won't. 'Cause that really wouldn't tell you much of anything. Instead, we will let the Yardbirds tell you about themselves. Recently, when the Yardbirds paid a brief visit to this country, we spent a few moments one evening speaking with them, and we played a sort of word-association game.

I gave them each a word and they, in turn, would give me the first word off the tops of their heads as their immediate reactions to my word. The results provide an interesting insight into the minds of three fascinating — and fantastic — Yardbirds.

Keith

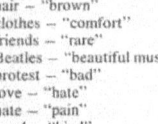

KEITH:
Keith — "me."
soul — "deep feeling"
R 'n' B — "something we used to play in the early days."
red — "angry"
Bach — "angry"
guitar — "Jeff"
instrument — "sounds"
flowers — "beauty, color"
nature — "beauty"
freedom — "beauty"
beauty — "a wonderful thing"
love — "a wonderful thing, beautiful"
Dylan — "genuine"
protest — "not usually genuine"
hobby — "fishing, shooting, open air"
unique — "I hope we are"
hair — "long — I wear mine long"
author — "Steinbeck"
trouble — "it's everywhere; I don't like trouble"
ambition — "for more and more people to hear what we're doing."

Sam

Jim

JIM:
soul — "blues"
R 'n' B — "blues"
Keith — "harmonica"
flowers — "roses"
red — "bull fighting"
Bach — "Handel"
guitar — "Jeff"
parents — "Mum"
Mother — "alone, loneliness"
man — "girls"
music — "Yardbirds"
hobbies — "sports"
pet peeves — "ignorant-type people that don't know what they're talking about, and think they do"
cold — "you have to put up with it! And getting up in the morning."
England — "home"
piano — "Rachmaninoff"
books — "Steinbeck"
Rave up — "album"
labor unions — "immigration"
clothes — "casual jacket"
Dylan — "folk"

SAM:
R 'n' B — "tired"
Keith — "friend"
Bach — "grand — preferably majestic"
drum — "beat"
Dylan — "love"
hair — "brown"
clothes — "comfort"
friends — "rare"
Beatles — "beautiful music"
protest — "bad"
love — "hate"
hate — "pain"
good — "kind"
people — "too many"
Americans — "fast"

KRLA ARCHIVES

Tone Up For Summer

Summer's on its way and it's time to get back into swim suit shape for the sunny days ahead.

Anne-Marie Bennstrom Prescott, internationally famous health expert and director of the co-educational health program at the Palm Springs Spa where people such as Frankie Avalon, James Garner and Ricky Nelson attend, offers the following exercises to tone those stud-weary muscles into beach party condition.

STRETCH YOUR HANDS as far as possible, holding a ball with one hand, swing your other arm around in a complete circle. Flex your right knee while holding the ball with your left hand and extend your left leg behind you to stretch entire body.

SWING YOUR HANDS as a windmill as you move your weight from right to left leg. Slightly flex your right leg, extending your left leg while touching your toes with your left hand and your right arm reaches for the sky. Good for the waist and it feels good.

FOR BALANCE, squat down as far as possible then extend one leg out as toes are pointed. Stretch, arms extended for balance. Alternate positions. Wonderful exercise for firming thighs.

ARCH YOUR BACK and flex your knees until they touch the floor while keeping your broomstick above your body. When your knees can touch the floor, you're ready for a size 8.

WHILE IN A SEATED POSITION, legs together, toes pointed, raise your legs slowly as far as possible stretching your toes outward and waving goodbye. Hold legs up while counting your shopping list, relax, and start all over again. Very good for firming your tummy and leg muscles.

Pop News From The London Scene

By Tony Barrow

NEWS BRIEFS . . . Drummer BARRY JENKINS, formerly with THE NASHVILLE TEENS, has replaced JOHN STEEL who has just quit THE ANIMALS. THE ANIMALS start a three-week American tour in the second week of April with an Ed Sullivan TV appearance fixed for Sunday, April 17 . . . The Musicians' Union seems to be standing firm in their shock decision to ban all lip-sync work on British television after the end of March. The new live-only rule will drastically affect top-rated small-screen pop programmes like "Thank Your Lucky Stars" and "Top Of The Pops" . . . Colour television will come to BBC's Channel Two towards the end of next year with no more than four hours of colour programmes each week for the first few months . . . Short April concert tour of U.K. packages THE SMALL FACES, LOU CHRISTIE, THE OVERLANDERS, MARTHA AND THE VANDELLAS plus CRISPIAN ST. PETERS and THE TRUTH . . . Electronovision's "T.A.M.I. Award Show," re-titled "Command Performance," is likely to be seen in British cinemas this Spring. Filmed a year ago last October in Santa Monica's Civic Auditorium, it is likely to have another title switch before it's shown here. Probable new name is "Gather No Moss." Stars featured include THE STONES, THE BEACH BOYS, THE SUPREMES, GERRY AND THE PACEMAKERS, BILLY J. KRAMER WITH THE DAKOTAS, JAMES BROWN and CHUCK BERRY. I was present at the filming but I never did see the finished product. I would have thought it had enormous commercial potential over here and I'm surprised it wasn't screened a year ago! . . . When "Top Of The Pops" featured "19th Nervous Breakdown" as our current Number One, televiewers watched THE STONES in a special movie sequence showing them swimming and fooling about on a beach outside Sydney, Australia. It was a knockout! . . . THE DAVE CLARK FIVE have notched up more Ed Sullivan appearances than any other British group. Yet another Sullivan date—Sunday, June 12—has just been set . . . Freshly released and rising in our charts—"The Sun Ain't Gonna Shine Any More" by THE WALKER BROTHERS, "Shapes Of Things" by THE YARDBIRDS, "Dedicated Follower Of Fashion" by THE KINKS and "Baby Never Say Goodbye" by THE UNIT 4 PLUS 2 . . . Hottest and most exciting single I've heard this month is "Blue Turns To Grey," penned by Stones Mick and Keith, recorded by CLIFF RICHARD AND THE SHADOWS . . . TOM JONES, his wife Linda and 8-year-old son, Mark, own 25,000 dollar home at Shepperton, just outside London.

HERMAN AND THE HERMIT'S, MGM Records hot British Recording Group, arrive from a successful tour of Japan. The group arrived with the good news that their group has outdistanced the Beatles in worldwide popularity polls. The Hermits recently completed their first motion picture musical entitled "Hold On" which is being readied for Easter release. They are in Southern California for a round of Press Conferences and recording sessions. (Left to Right, Front—Barry Whitwam, Derrick Leckenby. Rear—Karl Green, Keith Hopwood and Peter Noone.)

KRLA ARCHIVES

Cash On The Right

By Ollie Tooms

"The One On The Left Is On The Right;" that is the title of his new record, currently climbing up the pop charts of the nation. And it would certainly seem that Johnny Cash is "in the right" in the world of music and recording.

Born on a farm near Kingsland, Arkansas—which he has described as "just a wide place in the road"—Johnny has been composing songs since he was 12 years old, singing all his life, and one of the most successful recording artists in the country and western field in the last two decades.

Although Johnny had been singing with his family at home for years, he had never even given a thought to playing the guitar—for it was a luxury that his family just couldn't afford. It wasn't until Johnny—at 22 years of age—enlisted in the Air Force, and was stationed in Germany discovered that for the first time he had enough money to buy an old, used German guitar, and teach himself to play.

After Service

After his discharge from the Service, Johnny became an appliance salesman—a profession of which he wasn't especially fond—and in the evenings spent diligent hours of rehearsal with friends Luther Perkins—who played guitar, and Marshall Grant—who played bass. This, even though there was no possibility of a professional career anywhere in sight for the three.

But, regardless of the apparent hopelessness of the situation, Johnny and his "Tennessee Two" had faith in their ability, even if it *was* a rather shaky one!

Although none of the boys had any real connections with the recording industry, Luther did know Elvis Presley's guitar player, Scotty Moore. Elvis Presley—at that time—was a young man just beginning his recording career on a company called "Sun," and it looked as though he might someday be very big! It was Scotty who told Luther that Johnny ought to go to Sun and see a Mr. Phillips for an audition.

Case Of Nerves

Frightened half to death and in a voice quivering with nerves, Johnny presented himself to Mr. Phillips, introducing himself: My name is Johnny Cash. I write songs, sing and play the guitar and I wonder if you'd listen to me?"

Still playing the old, German guitar and standing uneasily with Luther and Marshall in the middle of one of Sun's studios, Johnny sang nearly a dozen of his own compositions. Then, after a short pause, Mr. Phillips—very uninterestedly—asked, "What else have you got?" "What else" turned out to be another one of Johnny's compositions, entitled "Hey, Porter."

Mr. Phillips showed his first sign of real interest as he listened to Johnny singing that song with all his heart, and when he had finished the number—the Sun recording executive stood up, turned on the recording machine nearby, and asked Johnny to sing that song once more.

The tape made by that recording became one side of Johnny's first record. The other side was a tear-jerker entitled "Cry, Cry, Cry"—a tune which Johnny had penned especially for that first disc.

Immediately after that successful audition at Sun, Johnny was signed to a contract with the company. As he was leaving the office, he walked out onto the street outside with only 15 cents in his pocket—which he promptly gave to a beggar, conveniently located around the corner.

He arrived home a few minutes later—just in time to run out of gas as he pulled into the driveway!

Johnny has since sold several million dollars of single records, his hits including "I Walk the Line," "Folsom Prison Blues," "Ballad of a Teen Age Queen," and his own personal favorite, "Pickin' Time."

His albums, also, have been tremendous successes on the Country and Western charts in this country and in others all over the world. Now on Columbia Records, Johnny is crossing over from a previously restricted residence of only Country and Western charts, to a broader range on pop charts all over.

World Favorite

Johnny has become a worldwide favorite through his personal appearances in many nations the world over, and through his occasional appearances on various television shows.

Johnny Cash—singer, actor, good friend and family man, talented musician—has *cashed in* on a good thing . . ., a thing called *talent!*

...JOHNNY CASH

KRLA ARCHIVES

Dave Hull's HULLABALOO
The Rock & Roll Showplace of the World
6230 SUNSET (AT VINE) HOLLYWOOD, CALIF.

Big EASTER WEEK EXTRAVAGANZA
ACROSS THE STREET FROM THE TEENAGE FAIR

SPECIAL MYSTERY STAR — one of the world's top rock 'n' roll entertainers
(Watch The BEAT For Details)

April 1-5
TURTLES
plus
DICK DALE
also
PALACE GUARD

April 6-10
Mama's & Papa's
plus
JOEY PAIGE
also
PALACE GUARD

Another Mystery Star Will Be Appearing

Coming May 1 in Concert — Peter and Gordon

MAKE RESERVATIONS – HO. 6-8281

KRLA BEAT

Volume 2, Number 4 — April 9, 1966

Wilson, Relf To Split For Solos

Keith Relf of the Yardbirds and Brian Wilson of the Beach Boys have split from their respective groups. Don't get all excited, though, because Keith and Brian will continue to record with their groups but will also go solo.

Keith revealed, "I'm going to record a Bob Lind composition, 'Mr. Zero,' as a solo record. It will be done without the Yardbirds and given an orchestrated backing."

But Keith hastened to add that, "this does not mean I'm leaving the group—just that I want to develop my singing in other fields."

They are still not sure which record label Keith will record for as he is under contract to EMI only as a member of the Yardbirds.

It is not at all surprising that Keith chose a Bob Lind composition for his first single as a solo artist. During their last Stateside visit both Keith and Sam became great fans of Lind's songwriting ability, so it is quite natural that Keith finally came up with "Mr. Zero," a song which many consider to be Lind's best composition thus far.

On the Beach Boys' side of the picture, Brian Wilson has formally broken with the group to record "Caroline, No." Brian actually wrote the song for the Beach Boys next album but for some reason decided to record the song himself.

"Caroline, No." is starting to happen in certain parts of the country but in California, Beach Boys' home state, the disc is not being played much.

He confided to The BEAT that he is very upset that the Beach Boys' "Sloop John B" is being played but not his "Caroline, No."

Of course, you know that the Beach Boys had some difficulty with their previous single, "Barbara Ann," in Southern California. Ron Tepper of Capitol Records differed with The BEAT on the point that the disc did not sell well in the Los Angeles area although it did receive large sales in San Francisco as well as in all other areas of the country. But then Ron turns around and says: "It is true that the single didn't get very high locally." So, maybe it sold well but didn't get on the charts?

Anyway, time is obviously going to play a very important role in determining whether Keith and Brian will be successful as single artists. It will also tell us if they *are* successful whether or not they will abandon the group scene altogether. Whichever way they decide to go, it's *got* to at least be interesting.

Kiss From A Teen Fan Endangers UNCLE Star

LONDON—David McCallum, the cool co-star of "Man From U.N.C.L.E.," has finally been forced to panic.

But it wasn't THRUSH agents who forced McCallum—alias Illya Kuryakin—to lose his "cool." It was a throng of screaming teenagers who mobbed the British actor at a news conference.

McCallum was in London for five days on his way to Rome where he is starring in "Three Bites Of The Apple."

His shirt was torn open and his black tie almost pulled from his neck.

McCallum yelled, "Cut out the violence," after being enveloped by a mob of screaming girls.

Shorn of much of the aplomb he brings to countless living rooms with spy partner Robert Vaughn, he finally had to be rushed from the Empire Theater, where the news conference was held.

It turned into chaos when David stepped down from the microphone to receive a kiss from a teenage girl. A dozen other girls surged forward and began tearing at his clothes.

While trying to give reporters serious answers to questions about his future acting career, he shook his fist at the teenagers and told them to shut up.

It did no good. David finally had to yell "Uncle."

Inside the BEAT

Baez To Do Rock & Roll? 2
Mitch Loses His Head 4
News On The Beatles 5
Hotline London 11
One Day On The Beat 13
Adventures of Robin Boyd 14
The Beat Goes To The Movies 15

The BEAT is published weekly by BEAT Publications, Inc., editorial and advertising offices at 6290 Sunset Blvd., Suite 504, Hollywood, California 90028. U.S. bureaus in Hollywood, San Francisco, New York, Chicago and Nashville, overseas correspondents in London, Liverpool and Manchester, England. Sale price, 15 cents. Subscription price, U.S. and possessions, $5 per year, Canada and foreign rates, $9 per year. Second class postage prepaid at Los Angeles, California.

No Tux For Sonny

Herb Alpert, dressed in a tuxedo, looked as handsome as ever, and won three Grammys—the top awards given out by the music industry.

Sonny and Cher, dressed in their usual attire, won none.

Sonny, being a good sport as always, congratulated Herb on his awards.

And people talked—not so much about Sonny and Cher not winning but about what they were wearing at the all formal affair.

They arrived in matching outfits of navy blue polka dot cotton. Cher's bell bottoms were fringed around the top and bottom with white cotton lace and Sonny's sleeves were trimmed in the same.

Sonny appeared to have had a recent hair cut and Cher wore part of hers up on top of her head.

Sonny has said, "Cher would wear a dress if there was really a good reason for it. If the occasion called for it, I might even put on a tux."

But apparently this occasion didn't call for it. Their contrasting (to everyone else there) attire caused some commotion, sure, but they were received better than they have been in the past when they attended formal affairs.

They were seated at a front row table, not like the back of the room nook they were banished to at the premiere of Richard Burton's "The Spy Who Came In From The Cold."

And they didn't have to put up with the rude booing they received at the WAIF Ball attended by England's Princess Margaret.

Sonny and Cher stuck to their guns and wore what is not only considered a part of them, but *them.*

They applauded the winners and joined in the standing ovation for Herb Alpert just like everyone else.

They were among their own crowd—musicians and singers—none of this high society movie crowd or the formal ball group and they were treated as fellow entertainers.

Among people in the music industry, there is enough respect to allow a man and woman to wear what they want without treating them like some sort of freaks.

Supremes Honored By Army

The Supremes are in the Army! As strange as that may sound, it's true. Mary, Diana and Florence have been made honorary members of the First Cavalry Division, United States Army which is currently deployed in An Khe, Vietnam.

The Supremes, America's top female vocal group recieved three insignia patches attesting to their membership in the Division in recognition of their two recent successful Motown albums, "Where Did Our Love Go" and "I Hear A Symphony."

Notice of the honor was accompanied by a letter from Captain Robert D. Taylor, who said, in part: "Keep up the good work and remember it's people like all of you and the entire free world that make our intolerable tour over here bearable."

Naturally, the Supremes were thrilled and extremely honored to be chosen by the First Cavalry Division. They've certainly come a long way from that backyard in Detroit and in the process have won more awards and honors than practically any other pop group in the world.

KRLA ARCHIVES

Baez Says: "Green Berets'—Revolting

Are you ready for this? In a recent television interview, Joan Baez announced she would like to make a rock and roll album!

"I won't read the mail that comes in after," she added, smiling.

Joan also had a few words to say on the subject of protest songs. When asked her opinion of the fact that many people feel protest songs are "sowing seeds of discontent among our young people," she made this comment.

"I say that's fine—there's plenty to be discontent about." But, she went on to say, "actually I'm not very keen on protest songs—they're usually badly done."

When asked who does them well, she replied: "Dylan did them well—the best was probably 'The Times Are Changin'."

Other comments of interest were on Teenage Music: "Good rock and roll is fading right now, getting watered down." The Beatles: "They're still doing good things." Future Plans: "I would like to do a Christmas album with ancient instruments."

Joan pulled no punches when expressing herself about the country's current top disc. "The number one song in the nation is 'Green Beret,' which I think is absolutely revolting."

She was equally frank about her hopes for the future. "I would like to grow up spiritually . . . I would also like to see an end to war."

'Noted In The United Kingdom'
By Gib

How often have you heard older people ridicule the lyrics and titles of the popular songs of today? Too many? If you, like me, get a bit tired of this standard criticism, then you will be just as interested in finding out what the kids of twenty years ago danced to. Your parents bought records with such titles as: "Frim Fram Sauce," and "Shoe Fly Pie." Other popular tunes of twenty years ago were: "When It's Toothpicking Time In False Tooth Valley," and "Apple Pan Dowdy." Then there was that great song, "E Bop A Lee, Hey Bob A Lee."

Many of the dances of twenty years ago were even wilder than the ones that we have today, and take a look at the short skirts that your mom used to wear. So the next time that your parents laugh at the BEATLES and "yeah, yeah, yeah," refer them to this column and ask for a couple of songs from their past such as: "E Bop A Lee, Hey Bop A Lee."

PETER and GORDON are thinking of waxing an album of compositions by the late country and western star, HANK WILLIAMS . . . BRIAN EPSTEIN has denied that the BEATLES have any investments in the Bahamas . . . Remember the hard rock days of LITTLE RICHARD, well RICHARD is trying to make a comeback. The "wild one" is still singing the same great kind of Rock 'n' Roll, but his hair style has changed considerably. He now has fantastically long hair. Personally, I don't care what he looks like, just as long as he starts making those great sounds again. The BEATLES, especially PAUL, were very much influenced by LITTLE RICHARD—although their sound has progressed since those days.

A record fan in England suggests that LENNON and McCARTNEY'S song "Help" was stolen from a 1958 GENE VINCENT record entitled, "Somebody Help Me." Listen to GENE'S record and see what you think . . . SPENCER DAVIS looks like a combination of GEORGE HARRISON and PAUL McCARTNEY . . . On the subject of PAUL McCARTNEY doubles, I just can not understand why so many people think that KEITH ALLISON looks like PAUL. The only resemblance that I can observe is the hair . . . The BEATLES are presently at work trying to top themselves. If they can top "Rubber Soul," I will buy ten or eleven copies . . . The WHO love to insult their fans, they call them morons and idiots. Maybe they have something there.

Listen to that final B-flat that TOM JONES hits at the end of "Thunderball." Having to hold the note for four bars at full volume was almost too much for TOM. He had no trouble reaching the note, but the strain of holding it for that length of time almost made him faint in the studio . . . TOM seems to be making a career out of recording movie-title songs. And very nice too . . . BEATLES record "Help" is still the top in Spain . . . WAYNE FONTANA and the MINDBENDERS remind me of DEAN MARTIN and JERRY LEWIS. When they split up, oblivion was predicted for the MINDBENDERS and success for WAYNE. Yet the MINDBENDERS have the first hit in England—and WAYNE is nowhere in sight.

FREDDIE LENNON (He's the father of "the man") will make several television appearances in the United States in order to promote his record, "That's My Life." . . . BEATLES American single "Nowhere Man" had to be released early due to premature exposure . . . Now that I think of it, HILTON VALENTINE is a pretty weird name for an ANIMAL . . . In celebration of FRANK SINATRA'S fifty years many record dealers in England published congratulations in various newspapers. The result: Sinatra called many of them from Hollywood and personally said thanks. That's just one of the reasons that he is where he is—he also sings . . . And how! . . . All the American girls in London are being married off. We shall soon have to send back to the States for a new supply . . . Now that British actor RICHARD BURTON wants one million dollars for doing, "Goodbye Mister Chips" will it be goodbye Mister Burton?

How many Americans know that before his recording career, HERMAN was an actor in English television's serial "Coronation Street?" The serial is Britain's answer to "Peyton Place." . . . DAVID and JONATHAN may be recording many more LENNON and McCARTNEY songs. With GEORGE MARTIN as their manager they really have an inside connection to JOHN and PAUL . . . If "Sunday Night At The London Palladium" does become the summer replacement for "Hollywood Palace," the United States will have more opportunity than ever to see British artists. This idea of different nations exchanging variety shows is a great new trend. Why not develop it even more and exchange popular music shows such as "Ready Steady Go" for "Hullabaloo." Now that really would be swinging.

Ten years ago BILL HALEY COMETS and LONNIE DONEGAN dominated the British Hit Parade . . . Promoters are beginning to publicize Indian music as the next thing after the "English Sound." . . . Maybe next year we will all be wearing Turbans instead of John Lennon hats . . . The KINKS say that American blues singer SPIDER KORNER is the greatest musical influence on them at the present time. SPIDER's specialty is a seven string guitar. According to DAVE DAVIES he produces "some fantastically weird chords by having the extra chords on his guitar." . . . Still talking about the KINKS, PETE QUAIFE is on a JOHN LENNON kick. He is attempting to write a book in the LENNON style (or James Joyce style if you prefer).

 ## Gold Record For 'Sounds'

Simon and Garfunkle are now numbered among the elite individuals who have won the record industry's coveted Gold Record for their million selling single, "Sounds Of Silence."

It was "Sounds," of course, which won the duo international fame. Before the record broke they were known in select folk circles but that was the extent of their popularity.

Besides "Sounds" Simon and Garfunkel are well on their way to a second Gold Record wih their follow-up disc, "Homeward Bound," which is currenly ascending the national charts with an amazing amount of speed.

Their record success has enabled the duo to be in constant booking demand—something an artist is continually striving towards. They recently played Hartford, Detroit, Chicago, St. Louis, Toronto, Cleveland and the famed Gaslight Club in Miami.

They're now on the college circuit playing colleges and universities across the nation. When the tour winds up Simon and Garfunkel are planning to tour Europe and the Far East, however, these plans are still in the negotiating stage.

KRLA ARCHIVES

...THE KINKS (l. to r. Ray Davies, Dave Davies, Pete Quaife and Mick Avory).

Ray Davies Admits

"I Don't Want To Be A Pop Star"

In England, where the vocal groups come from, there is an elite of three groups—the Beatles, the Rolling Stones and the Kinks. This triumverate has earned its eminence strictly on the basis of popularity and an unbroken string of hits.

Both the Stones and Beatles are well known to Stateside fans as individual personalities. And now it is high time that the Kinks receive the same recognition for they too are talented musicians as well as zany people.

Ray Davies is the King Kink. He composed all of their hits and although there is no official leader in the group Ray is the driving force behind their success.

As a person Ray is a highly sensitive composition of nervous energy and disciplined emotion. He talks very softly and earnestly. About himself he says: "I'm a collection of loose ends. I don't want to be a pop star. I think that this is just a part of my life which will come to an end.

Movie Producer

"I feel there are other developments taking place in my life. For example, I should very much like to produce a film. Something artistic that would convey emotion and reaction. I'm a great admirer of Ingmar Bergmann and films like 'The Face.'"

Upon leaving school Ray decided to become a draughtsman but it was something of a disastrous decision for him. "The job lasted about six weeks," said Ray. "I gave it up because I didn't like drawing straight lines.

"After that I tried commercial art. The first day of my new job my employer gave me some toilet paper to do a design on. Really now! I explained that with a job of this kind I would need two afternoons a week off to practice amateur soccer. I thought it was important to have a hobby—the boss did not!"

Ray is the married Kink and father of a small daughter and, of course, being the sensitive type is very conscious of the time he has to spend working away from home. "I feel very sorry for Rasa," Ray admits.

"I'm hopeless around the house, I'm afraid. I put a plug in an amplifier once and it blew up. My hand was all black. I put a bulb in a socket at home the other night. Same thing — a black hand," laughed Ray.

Dave Davies, Ray's younger brother, is the Joker Kink. "When Mick Avory came to audition for the Kinks and saw me he couldn't believe it," smiled Dave. "I was wearing a plastic raincoat buttoned to the neck, moccasins and I had shoulder-length hair. When he asked me what I was drinking I said 'pineapple juice' and he practically passed out!"

At school Dave wavered between being brilliant and idiotic and he became expert at forging dentists' cards and medical certificates. "Once I wrote a letter explaining that because of the mastoid in my ear I would have to go to the hospital every Friday for a check up," recalled Dave.

The school officials had had enough of the Davies' humor by the time Dave had reached 15. They decided that he spent more time out of school than in it anyway so they made it permanent.

Dave declares that as individuals the group is very mixed. He gets along best with drummer Mick Avory and they have just rented a house in the London area. "The only thing about Mick is that he insists on being last," complained Dave. "We have a great competition in the morning to see who is last dressed. It's generally afternoon before I give up."

Gene Pitney once told Mick Avory: "You're the quietest spoken illiterate I have ever met." Mick was delighted. Lanky, laconic and likes people to think he is thick—that's the Avory way!

Mick has never suffered fools gladly and has worked out a perfect defense when it comes to dealing with those insufferable questions—"Why are you called a Kink?" or "Are you a boy or a girl?"

He drops his jaw, rolls his eyes and drones in a Marlon Brando tone: "It's ... a ... pretty ... good ... scene ... man."

When a row breaks out or someone is pestering the group over some petty formality Mick sits there wearing his "nut of the week" face and the antagonists pass on. "How can you argue with an idiot?" Mick says happily.

Mick is probably the great undiscovered Kink for while Pete, Ray and Dave share the spotlight up front Mick sits back and beats a rear-guard action on the skins. But Mick's drumming actually began by accident while he was still in the Boy Scouts.

"I was a terrible Boy Scout," confessed Mick, "I used to go down to the hut to play snooker. They had a skiffle group there and one evening the drummer was sick and they asked me to play. Tapping away on that old snare drum balanced on a chair was the beginning."

"Not The Way"

"There was also a character who would keep repeating, 'That's not the way to carry on, Avory,' and clumped me round the ear to each syllable. Worst of all was the giant Welsh gym master who jumped off the top of wall bars and endangered your limbs. He threw medicine balls at me," recalled Mick.

Upon leaving school Mick became proficient in a number of trades. "I started as a trainee draughtsman," he revealed. "Then I became a snow clearer (in season) and gulley pot hole digger. I was never a garbage man—too proud!"

And last but not least is Pete Quaife, the Paul McCartney of the Kinks. Like Paul he plays bass and like Paul he is the finest public relations man in the group.

Pete comes from the tough side of Muswell Hill. "As a teenager, I was part of a gang called 'the Mussies,'" declared Pete. "We had a feud with the Finchley boys which developed into a grand-scale punch-up one evening at their local dance hall.

"I was posted as a look-out at the door and when the Law arrived I disappeared under a parked car. I was lucky. I got away but many of the gang were sent to approved schools. That cured me of being a delinquent," sighed Pete.

"Scientist" Kink

Pete has never had much time for anything but his music although at school he did consider becoming a scientist. "We found an old oxygen cylinder on a bombed site by my house," remembered Pete. "I suppose I was only about 13 and it seemed like a good idea to the gang when we lit a fire under it and left it.

"The explosion blew out windows in the flats for miles around. I was about five miles away at the time and shook like a leaf when I heard the bang. The neighbors thought it was an unexploded bomb. I decided not to be a scientist," said Pete.

And so Pete became a Kink instead of a scientist and "it's nice to be really appreciated at last." To be a sort of a "Well Respected Man" maybe!

KRLA ARCHIVES

Mitch Loses His Head

By Anna Maria Alonzo

Their first record was a smash hit all across the nation, and they called it "Jenny Take A Ride." Well, that disc certainly did succeed in taking Mitch Ryder and the Detroit Wheels for a ride—straight to the top. And from the looks of things, their second release—"Little Latin Lupe Lu"—is out to try for a return trip.

Besides Mitch, there are four "Wheels:" John Badanjek, James McCarty, James McCallister, and Mark Manke. They are a wild and soulful group, and a lot of fun to be around.

There are those who might think the boys are impulsive. For example, when they came to our offices a couple of months ago for an interview, Mitch introduced himself to me and asked me my age. I told him, and then he asked if I ever dated entertainers; I replied that I did, on occasion. Then he asked if I would go out with him that evening! Needless to say, I am definitely in love with him for eternity!!

Mitch has a large family, seven brothers and sisters in all. In speaking of them, he lists each one and his/her occupation, including students, reporters, singers and finally Robin, who is a professional "child!" He also boasts that, "I once had a dog that talked, but nobody believed what it had to say."

John Badanjek, the group's drummer, is also an interesting sort of fellow who is a sort of rebel-poet. He lists as his prime hobby the ever-popular sport of "building toothpick houses," and hopes someday to be able to accomplish his supreme ambition in life and "live on the moon!" He claims that he especially dislikes planes without wings, although he finds difficulty in explaining just why.

James McCarty is the tall, dark, quiet member of this talented group from the Motor City. He plays lead guitar and hopes to someday become a "first rate musician." He is, like his fellow group members, a very "soulful" sort of musician, and yet his favorite singer is Frank Sinatra. While John is a poet, and Mitch is the artist of the group, Jim upholds the electronics end of things, having once studied it for awhile. He has worked briefly in drafting ad major engineering.

Soulful Bassist

Jim McAllister is the bass guitarist for the group who has the distinction of having once studied basic musical theory. He hopes to someday be able to learn the string bass and to further study music. He prefers "soul" music and dislikes "being alone, with nothing to do."

Blue-eyed Mark Manke takes care of the rhythm guitar section of the group and is very adamant in his claim to disliking "people who stare at long hair." Although he has never had a formal music education of any sort, he hopes to someday become a professional guitarist.

The group has been described as being the most soulful white group around, and that comment seems quite valid. If you ever have the opportunity to see these boys perform in person, seize it, 'cause they're great.

Now, then — about that date, Mitch...

...MITCH PERFORMING

On the BEAT

By Louise Criscione

Suppose by now you've seen the great two-page article about the Supremes in the March 4 edition of *Time*. It traces the three girls' career from the time they began singing in a Detroit backyard up until today when they've sent six singles in a row skyrocketing to the top of the nation's charts.

Wouldn't mind being in Lake Tahoe at Harrah's for the Righteous Brothers' engagement beginning April 7 and continuing for three weeks. They'll be appearing with Jack Benny and the highlight of the show has got to be when Bill and Bobby sing "My Kind Of Town (Waukegan Is)" with Benny. The famed songwriting team of Sammy Cahn and Jimmy Van Heusen have re-written the words to "My Kind Of Town (Chicago Is)" for Bill, Bobby and Jack. Should be wild!

The only night club played by the Yardbirds here in the U.S. was the Hullabaloo Club in Hollywood. The boys did fantastically well, making a tremendous number of new fans for themselves. The Yardbirds were very well pleased with their engagement. Sam says: "The sound there was immaculate—the best sound we've ever had, except for the Marquee Club in London."

Sam also revealed that "Shapes Of Things" was recorded at the RCA studios in Hollywood during the group's visit. This, of course, is where the Stones record all of their singles and perhaps the Yardbirds will now follow suit (if they can get into the country, that is) as Sam declares it "a very good studio."

I forgot to tell you that a hilarious letter arrived from Jim McCarty, Yardbird's drummer. In part, Jim wrote: "So, they didn't deport us (it must have been that ten dollar bill I slipped in the post, with a free copy of *The BEAT*. Ho! Ho!) The latest we hear is that we've had it as far as coming into the country again is concerned."

I was naturally glad to hear from Jim as he admits that he "only writes letters every blue moon" but it makes me furious to think that the Yardbirds might not get to come Stateside again. Why, I'd like to ask our glorious Musicians' Union and our equally ridiculous work permit issuers?

It looks as if Petula Clark and Tony Hatch have done it again with "Sign Of The Times". It's too much of a record and the Clark-Hatch team has certainly proved itself to be a profitable one, hasn't it? Funny, but Pet admits that she didn't like Tony much at all when she first met him. In fact, she thought he was a "smart alec." But now that she's gotten to know him better she pronounces him a "good friend."

Frank Sinatra's film company has offered to back Dave Clark's next movie venture. Sinatra is vying with Paramount for the honors and the amount mentioned is allegedly one million dollars. A few other people are interested too so we'll see who wins out in the end. I don't know about Dave, but I'd take Sinatra any day!

John Lennon reveals that he and Paul are about to write the songs for their next album. Anyway, John states that their next L.P. "is going is going to be very different," and he strongly hints that it will contain all sorts of electronic music. They even wanted to put the LP out with just continuous songs and no break in between but the record company wouldn't hear of it.

About the future, John says that "we're obviously not going to work harder than we want to now but you get a bit fed up of doing nothing." Don't expect John's next book for awhile because he admits to having written only one page so far.

Get ready for another Herman invasion. He and the Hermits will jet in immediately following their Easter tour of Britain. Promotional appearances in connection with their movie, "Hold On," is the reason for their visit. They'll also make their fourth appearance on Ed "Pop" Sullivan's Show April 24.

I don't know how the movie is but the title song, "Hold On," is a gas, isn't it? Can't say as much for "Leaning On A Lamp Post," though. Incidentally, "Lamp Post" was scheduled to be released months and months ago but for some reason was held up until now.

...BILL MEDLEY

...HERMAN

KRLA ARCHIVES

Beatles No. 1 – Again!

The Beatles have again proved that their vast audience is definitely not limited to teenagers only.

Students from forty-four American colleges named the foursome the "Top Group On Campus" in a recent music poll. Runners-up to the title included the Stones, Supremes, Beach Boys, Lettermen, Righteous Brothers, Four Seasons, Dave Clark Five, Chad & Jeremy, Lovin' Spoonful, Herman's Hermits and the Miracles.

"Best In-Person Show" honors went to Peter, Paul & Mary, who also won the title of "Favorite Folk Group."

Bob Dylan and Joan Baez were crowned king and queen of folk, with Andy Williams and Barbra Streisand reigning as top pop artists.

Among the others who registered on the pop portion of the poll were Elvis, James Brown, Pet Clark, Bobby Vinton, Roger Miller, Cher Bono, Mick Jagger, Paul McCartney and Len Barry.

Other recent surveys have proved that many of the record buyers who purchase "teenage music" are past college level and well into the 25-30 age bracket.

Our music just isn't "teenage" any more. If anything, it's "ageless." But whatever you choose to call it, it's certainly here to stay.

THE BEATLES

Welcome back, Beatles!

After too long a time of reading about what the "fab foursome" *wasn't* doing, their hard-earned holiday is over and they're back in the headlines.

Biggest news of all was their tour announcement. The Beatles will definitely return to the States next August for a three-week, 14-city personal appearance trek.

Meanwhile, back at the record rack, the Beatles continue to rule. Their "Nowhere Man" came on the national charts like gangbusters, at #24 the first week. Destined to be the next Beatle goldie, this disc sold 744,000 during its first eight days of release!

Ringo Scores

And, just as there are two sides to every story, there are two sides to every Beatle 45. Ringo's "What Goes On Here" was a slow starter, hitting the charts a week later than the flip and coming on then at #89. But it's moving hard and fast now, so chalk up another double-barrelled Beatle bulls-eye.

The long arm of Liverpool has finally touched the contemporary folk fan. The Kingston Trio's "Norwegian Wood" single is a national pick to click and it's quite possible that this segment of the market may also find itself held gently but firmly in the palm of the powerful Beatle hand.

Album-wise, "Rubber Soul" has dropped out of the number one slot, but is still in the top five. This LP is well past the two-million-copies-sold mark and is expected to remain on the charts indefinitely.

Three other Beatle albums are still best-sellers. Namely, "Help" (#30 after 29 weeks on the charts), "Beatles VI" (#62 after 104 weeks) and "Beatles 65" (#104 after 62 weeks).

Three albums headlining Beatle compositions are also listed. Bud Shank's "Michelle" rates at #71, Billy Vaughn's "Michelle" at #84 and "The Baroque Beatles Book" at #93.

Coming up fast is the Hollyridge Strings new longie titled "The New Beatles Songbook."

Stereo Business

Additionally, the Beatles have now gone into the stereo tape business. All the songs from "Rubber Soul" and "The Beatles Second Album" will be featured on a package containing eight other reels.

Elsewhere in the world, the Beatles have once again cracked the hard-shelled record market in France. "Michelle" (released there as an EP) has parlayed to the number one spot and "Rubber Soul" is number two on the French LP charts.

Beatle discs (singles, EPs and albums) are also top-tenning it in thirteen other countries.

Since there doesn't seem to be anything the Beatles can't accomplish, perhaps they can do something about the fact that August is almost six whole months away!

Let's hope so.

...JOHN AND RINGO COMIN' BACK.

The Beatles are definitely coming! Brian Epstein has announced that the Beatles will make their third tour of America in late August or early September.

Tony Barrow sent a telegram to *The BEAT* saying, "Beatles playing 14 cities including New York, Chicago and San Francisco plus probably Washington. No other cities and no venues named at this time."

The Beatles' New York appearance will be at Shea Stadium which was the scene of last year's Beatle triumph. It was also at Shea that their entire concert was filmed and shown throughout England where it met with rave reviews from everyone.

Announcement of the Beatles' forthcoming American tour came as a slight surprise to people in the business because of the trouble the Beatles seem to be having getting started on their third movie. Beatle spokesmen hinted at the possibility of keeping the Beatles out of the U.S. until their movie is completed. There was even talk making the rounds that their movie would not even *begin* filming until late summer which would have, of course, kept the Beatles from an extensive U.S. tour before, at least, October or possibly November.

The fact that the Beatles have not firmed contracts to appear in Los Angeles is rather upsetting to all Beatle fans living in Southern California. On their previous tours the Beatles have played the Hollywood Bowl selling out within 24 hours after tickets went on sale.

It is highly conceivable that John, Paul, George and Ringo will skip San Diego this time around because last August when they played San Diego's Balboa Stadium they only managed to half fill the stadium.

San Francisco was the scene of the wildest Beatle audience ever. The Beatles' appearance at the Cow Palace was the most riotous performance by an audience that the Beatles ever witnessed in America. When it was over Brian Epstein stated that the Beatles would *never* play San Francisco again.

And yet San Francisco was one of the first cities the Beatles agreed to play on their third tour! Fans in Los Angeles are furious over the fact that they have faithfully supported the Beatles in record sales and especially in personal appearances and instead of showing their gratitude to L.A. they have decided to play San Francisco first!

The BEAT would like to caution Southern California Beatle fans not to panic just yet. The Beatles are negotiating at this very moment for a return to L.A. so it is more than likely that they *will* be playing the Hollywood Bowl once again.

Beatles Order Lookalikes

George Harrison's special custom-built "Millionaire's Mini" is ready for delivery. The tiny but powerful little car has a Mini-Cooper tuned engine, seats which are in the Rolls Royce class, power-operated windows which have dark-tinted glass, luxurious lambswool carpets and a load of other plushy extras. Cost of the finished product is in excess of 4,000 dollars and three other similar vehicles are being prepared for the other Beatles.

The boys were very specific about their requirements for the fleet of Beatle-Minis. They gave exact details of what they wanted in the way of special fittings and the cars were ordered late last year. Each one will have minor differences inside, according to individual requests from the boys.

It goes without saying that the outsides will be painted black, the all-time favorite color of The Beatles.

KRLA ARCHIVES

...LAINIE KAZAN.

...MRS. HERB ALPERT, JERRY LEWIS, JODY MILLER, HERB ALPERT, BILL DANA.

...FRANKIE RANDALL.

...LOUIS ARMSTRONG, MORT SAHL.

Stars Turn Out For Grammys: Standing Ovation For Herb Alpert

...HERB ALPERT, LOUIS ARMSTRONG.

...MOLLY BEE, BILL DANA.

By Louise and Carol

HOLLYWOOD:—In the finest tradition of glittering Hollywood premieres and openings, the Eighth Annual Grammy Awards were presented in the International Ballroom of the Beverly Hilton Hotel with Roger Miller, Herbie Alpert and Frank Sinatra emerging as top winners.

We *could* make it a straight news story and simply list the winners but we thought that you might like to know exactly what went on that night as a sort of behind the scenes look at the Grammy Award presentations.

First off, the affair was stricly formal which meant that we had to pay a visit to our hairdresser, Robert, to get our long hair piled high so as to look at least *slightly* sophisticated. Our floor-length gowns had to be pulled out of the mothballs and readied for our big evening. And, believe us, it *was* a big evening!

You see, *The BEAT* was the only teen paper properly represented by reporters and photographers. Anyway, when we were appropriately dressed and made up we set out for the Beverly Hilton. The scene in the lobby set the pace for what was to occur inside the Ballroom. Elegantly attired ladies and tuxedo-clad men mingled about everywhere talking and laughing and generally having quite a time.

Four At Once

The big stars and Grammy nominees begin wandering in around seven o'clock and most of the guests moved inside the Ballroom where the mingling continued. Since similar dinners were being held in New York, Nashville and Chicago, not all of the nominees were in Hollywood. But plenty of them were!

Strolling into the Hilton were Herbie Alpert and his beautiful wife, Sharon, Lorne Greene, Jerry Lewis, Louis Armstrong, Jackie DeShannon, Phyllis Diller (in a floor-length France original which she said was actually "DeGaulle's nightgown!"), Shelly Manne, Mort Sahl, Jerry Naylor, Molly Bee, Joanie Sommers, Connie Stevens (stunning in a yellow gown), John Gary, Anita Kerr, Lainie Kazan, the King Sisters, Tommy Leonetti, Sandy Nelson, Frankie Randall, Sonny & Cher (who, unfortunately, looked totally out of place in bell bottoms and furry jackets. We don't say that maliciously but Cher's bell bottoms looked about as chic as dirty jeans at a high school prom), and the list went on and on.

A prime rib dinner was next on the agenda. It was served by red-jacketed waiters with the know-how of years of experience behind them which made us happy because it meant that we probably wouldn't have gravy spilled accidentally down our backs!

Although everyone spread smiles across their faces, the anxiety and nervous feeling which naturally accompanies a Grammy nomination was present in all of the nominees. You could tell they wished desperately that the presentations would get underway so that they could at least be ecstatic if they won or miserable if they didn't.

Jerry "Proud"

At ten o'clock (an hour behind time) they got what they wished for—the awards program began as Jerry Lewis, master of ceremonies, leaped (literally) upon the stage and announced: "I'm proud to be Gary's dad." Jerry ran through a short monologue; he was his usual self but perhaps not as funny as he has been known to be.

The first presenters, Jackie DeShannon and Johnny Mercer, were introduced and the moment of truth finally arrived. Since there were some 47 categories we are naturally not going to list them all, however, we *are* going to let you in on all the big ones.

The biggest shock of the evening probably came when the Beatles, although up for nine awards, failed to bag even one! Another surprise occurred in the

JOHN GARY, JOANIE SOMMERS.

KRLA ARCHIVES

...HERBIE AND HIS GRAMMYS.

...SONNY & CHER

Best New Artist category. Nominees were the Byrds, Herman's Hermits, Horst Jankowski, Tom Jones, Marilyn Maye, Sonny & Cher and Glen Yarbrough. With Sonny & Cher seated at one of the front tables, Tom Jones was named the winner! Sonny & Cher both looked shocked at the announcement but after a split second they joined in the thunderous applause for Tom who picked up his award in New York.

Roger Miller repeated his last year's success by walking away with the most Grammys, six to be exact. Roger picked up four of them in the country and western field, one for Best Contemporary Rock 'n' Roll Vocal Performance by a male and another for Best Contemporary Rock 'n' Roll single which, of course, was "King Of The Road."

But the biggest winner as far as the Hollywood crowd was concerned was the man with the horn—Herbie Alpert. Fittingly enough, Herb's first award was presented to him by the great Louis Armstrong for the Best Instrumental Arrangement won by "A Taste Of Honey."

It was really the most dramatic presentation of the evening because there was a mix-up and just as Louis said, "the winner is," the band began playing "A Taste Of Honey" and the entire audience rose to give Herb a standing ovation!

Alpert then went on to win Grammys for Best Instrumental Performance, Non-Jazz, Record Of The Year and Larry Levine picked up an award for engineering Herb's recording of "A Taste Of Honey."

Levine gave the funniest acceptance speech of the evening when he announced: "I'd like to thank Gold Star for giving me a job, Phil Spector for making me an engineer and Herbie Alpert for being Mexican!" The audience doubled over with laughter because, as you no doubt know, Herbie is Jewish—not Mexican.

Everyone was amazed that with three Sinatras now in the music business, not one of them was present to accept Frank Sr.'s awards. Sinatra's LP, "September Of My Years," won an award for Stan Cornyn for writing the Best Album Notes as well as a Grammy for Sinatra as Album Of The Year. "It Was A Very Good Year" picked up an award as Best Arrangement Accompanying A Vocalist which went to Gordon Jenkins as the arranger. Best Vocal Performance by a male also went to Sinatra for "It Was A Very Good Year."

"The Shadow Of Your Smile" was named the Song Of The Year, winning out over "Yesterday," "King Of The Road," "September Of My Years" and "I Will Wait For You."

James Brown captured an award for Best Rhythm & Blues Recording with his "Papa's Got A Brand New Bag" and darling Jody Miller was on hand to accept her award for "Queen Of The House" as Best C&W Vocal Performance by a female. Pet Clark beat out Barbara Lewis, Fontella Bass, Lesley Gore and Jackie DeShannon to win the Best Contemporary Rock 'n' Roll Vocal Performance by a female for her "I Know A Place."

And thus the awards went on and on until after midnight. The winners were naturally thrilled and honored to be chosen by the National Academy Of Recording Arts and Sciences and the losers smiled bravely as they were assured that to even be *nominated* was an honor in itself. And it is an honor when you consider that there are thousands of records released annually.

The presentation of the last award was not a signal for the audience to leave—as it turned out, it was the signal for a mass exodus to Herbie Alpert's table! Photographers converged upon the smiling Herbie with just about everyone else in the Ballroom rushing over to congratulate him.

Pictures taken and congratulations conferred the guests slowly began to file out of the hotel. And the Eighth Annual Grammy Awards were officially over. It had been quite an experience for everyone involved—including us!

BEAT REPORTERS, LOUISE CRISCIONE & CAROL DECK, POSE HAPPILY WITH HERB.

...CHER, SONNY AND JACKIE DESHANNON.

...THE PARIS SISTERS.

...JERRY NAYLOR, CAROL AND LOUISE SMILE INTO THE CAMERA.

KRLA ARCHIVES

STAMP OUT STIFF HAIR.

Caryl Richards

★ CLIP ON DOTTED LINE ★

Student Discount Exchange Coupon
Exchange this coupon and $1.25 (tax incl.) at Box Office. Save 50¢ on $1.75 admission (one admission with each coupon)

WORTH 50¢

EASTER VACATION FUN

★ **TEEN-AGE FAIR** ★
THE WORLD'S FAIR FOR TEEN-AGERS
HOLLYWOOD PALLADIUM
APRIL 1 thru 10, 1966
Doors Open Daily: Noon to Midnight

★ CLIP ON DOTTED LINE ★

SEE... IN PERSON ... SONNY & CHER
• The REGENTS • The CHALLENGERS • SAM RIDDLE'S
TV SPECIALS • TOP TV, RECORD & MOVIE STARS

OVER $3,000,000 WORTH OF FABULOUS EXHIBITS & ATTRACTIONS
Fender Battle of the Beat — Model Car Drag Strip Racing — Dance Contests — Custom Car Caravan — Surfing Movies — Miss Teen International Pageant — Harmony Folk Festival — Guest stars in Person from Movies, T.V., Records and Radio (Top D.J.'s) — Beauty Clinics — Judo — Karate Thrill Shows — Photography and Home Movie Exposition — Fabulous Fashion Shows — Dream Cars of the Future — Bands and Drill Teams — Free Prizes and Gifts — Nonstop Record Hop
All above events and attractions included in admission price

★ VISIT CARYL RICHARDS' BOOTH AT THE FAIR
WIN HUNDREDS OF DOLLARS WORTH OF PRIZES ★

KRLA Tunedex

This Week	Last Week	Title	Artist
1	6	SOUL AND INSPIRATION	The Righteous Bros.
2	1	CALIFORNIA DREAMIN'	The Mama's & Papa's
3	2	BANG, BANG	Cher
4	3	DAYDREAM	The Lovin' Spoonful
5	4	NOWHERE MAN	The Beatles
6	8	THE BALLAD OF THE GREEN BERET	S/Sgt. Barry Sadler
7	5	THESE BOOTS ARE MADE FOR WALKIN'	Nancy Sinatra
8	10	WOMAN	Peter & Gordon
9	9	I'M SO LONESOME I COULD CRY	B. J. Thomas & The Triumphs
10	19	KICKS	Paul Revere & The Raiders
11	11	CALL ME	Chris Montez
12	7	19TH NERVOUS BREAKDOWN	The Rolling Stones
13	30	SECRET AGENT MAN	Johnny Rivers
14	24	SHAPES OF THINGS	The Yardbirds
15	12	DARLING BABY	The Elgins
16	16	BABY SCRATCH MY BACK	Slim Harpo
17	20	THIS OLD HEART OF MINE	The Isley Bros.
18	17	LOVE MAKES THE WORLD GO 'ROUND	Deon Jackson
19	15	WALKIN' MY CAT NAMED DOG	Norma Tanega
20	25	IT'S TOO LATE	Bobby Goldsboro
21	27	SPANISH FLEA/WHAT NOW MY LOVE	Herb Alpert
22	26	SURE GONNA MISS HER	Gary Lewis & The Playboys
23	22	FOLLOW ME	Lyme & Cybelle
24	28	ONE TRACK MIND	The Knickerbockers
25	34	TIME WON'T LET ME	The Outsiders
26	32	THE RAINS CAME	Sir Douglas Quintet
27	33	LULLABY OF LOVE	The Poppies
28	36	MAGIC TOWN	The Vogues
29	35	634-5789	Wilson Pickett
30	—	SIGN OF THE TIMES	Petula Clark
31	39	RHAPSODY IN THE RAIN	Lou Christy
32	38	SOMEWHERE	Len Barry
33	—	I'VE BEEN A LONG TIME LEAVIN'	Roger Miller
34	—	SLOOP JOHN B.	The Beachboys
35	—	MESSAGE TO MICHAEL	Dionne Warwick
36	—	I HEAR THE TRUMPETS BLOW	The Tokens
37	40	WOULD YOU BELIEVE?	Jerry Naylor
38	—	PUBLIC EXECUTION	The Mouse
39	—	IF YOU LOVE ME	The Lazy Susans
40	—	EIGHT MILES HIGH/WHY	The Byrds

DAVE HULL

BOB EUBANKS

DICK BIONDI

JOHNNY HAYES

EMPEROR HUDSON

CASEY KASEM

CHARLIE O'DONNELL

BILL SLATER

BRIAN JONES: Two girls in every town, a riot with every concert and a copy of **The BEAT** every week.

April 9, 1966 — THE BEAT

Inside KRLA

As you are probably already well aware, KRLA has long been one of the foremost stations in the area of public service.

In this area, there are the very popular basketball games—featuring our own lovable losers, the KRLApes—and the phenomenally successful Dick Biondi road shows.

The shows are conducted at various high schools and junior high schools in the Southern California area and feature many top name performers as well as presenting many new and upcoming artists. Frequent members of the road show family are Joey Paige, Jerry Naylor, the Knickerbockers, and The Association.

Joey Paige has been appearing on these shows for some time now, and he describes the audiences as being "wild and great! Something happens to the kids when they get out of school and go to the show. They know that school is over and they get to see a show on top of that, and everyone has fun!"

Looking back over the many shows he has appeared on with Dick, he says earnestly, "The most rewarding thing is the way the kids receive the shows. They are always very responsive and enthusiastic. And the great thing is that all the money which is made is used for good things, such as additions to the buildings. One school used the money to bring an exchange student over to this country."

Joey is very proud of his association with the road shows, and says, "I think that the road shows are very good for exposing new talent and allowing new artists to be seen by the kids and to gain valuable experience."

The only unhappy incident which Joey can recall in connection with the road shows, is one which left a rather sour taste in the mouths of just about everyone concerned. It involved a high school which is very well known for its dislike of long-haired performers.

The incident in question occurred when the school arranged to present one of Dick's road shows, during the early morning hours, as a special assembly for the students. The entire show was arranged and approved by those in charge at the school, and so, on the appropriate day, the entire road show cast and crew got up quite early and drove all the way out to the school, only to be told at the last moment that they would have to cancel their show because some of the performers involved had long hair!

Joey explains that shortly after the majority of the show's members had arrived, the vice principal of the school came out and informed them that they would not be allowed to present their entertainment, because "we just don't like people with long hair."

Of course, the gentleman gave absolutely no consideration whatsoever to the performers involved—all of whom had very busy schedules of their own, and were giving their time and efforts *without any sort of financial consideration in return.*

There had been no mention of a ban being imposed on long-haired singers before the entertainers arrived at the school; the vice principal had never explained this "regulation" or asked if there was any possibility that there would be any performers present who wore their hair in this manner.

Joey admits that it was a great disappointment to him and to all of the members of the road show, and says that "it made all of us feel just terrible."

Fortunately, mostly everyone else has been extremely cooperative and understanding, and the members of the various faculties all seem to agree that these shows—presented as good, clean, fun entertainment—have done only good at all of the schools where they have appeared.

The Dick Biondi road shows are absolutely free of charge to the schools, and will be presented in order to raise funds for any worthy cause which the school approves. If you would like to have Dick and his gang at your school in the future, you can do so by calling or writing to Dick at the KRLA studios, or by getting in touch with Dick Moreland.

SONNY AND CHER TO HEADLINE THE 1966 TEEN-AGE FAIR.

It's Teen-Age Fair Time

The 1966 Teen-Age Fair will be held April 1 through 10 at the Hollywood Palladium.

Continuous daily action will include games, contests, dance competitions and the "Battle of the Beat."

Among artists scheduled to appear for autograph parties and performances are Sonny and Cher, Sally Field, Bob Denver, Paul Peterson, Jackie and Gayle, Tony Dow, The Regents, The Challengers, Eddie Hodges, The Bees, The Spats and Joyce Hoffman, international women's surfing champion and L.A. Times Woman of the Year.

Following is a partial schedule of special events scheduled.

Friday, April 1	PREMIERE telecast from the TEEN-AGE FAIR.
Saturday, April 2	MISS TEEN WESTERN STATES competition.
Sunday, April 3	"California Wheels" Fashion Show.
Monday, April 4	Songleader Competition; MISS TEEN Western States SEMI-FINALS.
Tuesday, April 5	MISS TEEN U.S.A. FINALS.
Wednesday, April 6	MISS TEEN INTERNATIONAL PAGEANT. Harmony Folk Festival
Thursday, April 7	Harmony Folk Festival
Friday, April 8	Harmony Folk Festival
Saturday, April 9	"BATTLE OF THE BEAT" Semi-Finals.
Sunday, April 10	BATTLE OF THE BEAT FINALS. Fair closes at 10:00 P.M. Harmony Folk Festival Finals

Temptation Walk Hits Los Angeles

In case you are wondering what is going to happen next, the answer is coming out of Motown where the Temptations have inspired a new dance which is taking over in Southern California. The dance, which is called "The Temptation Walk," is basically the kind of cool soft shoe which the group does on stage. In their first stint at the Trip in Hollywood, these boys had crowds lined up around the block to see them, and the enthusiasm reached such a pitch that the customers began imitating the boys. The result is, a book of instructions is scheduled for publication and the dance will spread.

SPECIAL BONUS—SUBSCRIBE NOW and receive a free copy of The Bobby Fuller Four's best selling album, "I Fought The Law."

KRLA BEAT Subscription
SAVE 33% Of Regular Price

☐ 1 YEAR – 52 Issues – $5.00   ☐ 2 YEARS – $8.00
☐ 6 MONTHS – $3.00

Enclosed is_____   ☐ CASH   ☐ CHECK
PLEASE PRINT—Include Your Zip Code

Send to:..Age:........
Address:..............................City:..............
State:..........................Zip:..............

MAIL YOUR ORDER TO: KRLA BEAT
6290 Sunset, Suite 504
Hollywood, Calif. 90028

Foreign Rate: $9.00 – 52 Issues

WANT TO PLAY GUITAR?

We help you organize and promote your own group.

Call 793-6862 RIGHT AWAY! We have a few guitars to lend to beginning students to play at home.

Our pro teachers will show you how easy it is to play the top tunes now on KRLA.

COMPLETE RECORDING FACILITIES
We sell all types of guitars and amplifiers. You can take three years to pay!

THE FLAHERTY SCHOOL OF MUSIC
129 N. Hill Avenue — Pasadena

Paul Newman is 'Harper' ...a different kind of cat!

A GERSHWIN-KASTNER Production

LAUREN BACALL · JULIE HARRIS · ARTHUR HILL · JANET LEIGH · PAMELA TIFFIN · ROBERT WAGNER · SHELLEY WINTERS

PACIFIC'S PANTAGES THEATRE HOLLYWOOD
HOLLYWOOD BLVD. near VINE · HO. 9-2211

EXCLUSIVE ENGAGEMENT NOW!
CALL THEATRE FOR SHOW TIMES

APRIL 1-10
THE ONE AND ONLY
MUDDY WATERS
AND HIS ORIGINAL CHICAGO BLUES BAND

APRIL 12-26 — MORT SAHL

AT DOUG WESTON'S

Troubadour
9083 SANTA MONICA BLVD.
L.A. NEAR DOHENY

RESERVATIONS CR 6-6168

CLOSING MAR. 27—BROTHER DAVE GARDNER

KRLA ARCHIVES

CADET PRESENTS
The Top Selling Instrumental Group in the Country!

The Ramsey Lewis Trio

BEAT AWARD WINNER

THE IN CROWD
Recorded live at the Bohemian Caverns in Washington, D.C. 1965 best selling instrumental, "The In Crowd," and many more!

HANG ON RAMSEY!
Contains the hit songs, "Hang On Sloopy" and "A Hard Day's Night." Recorded live at the Lighthouse in Hermosa Beach, California.

THE BEST OF THE RAMSEY LEWIS TRIO
Choice! All the best and biggest hits in one great album! "Something You Got," "Lonely Avenue," "Look-A-Here," and many more!

BAREFOOT SUNDAY BLUES
Your favorites — "Lonely Avenue," "Don't Kick It Around," "Barefoot Sunday Blues," "Act Like You Mean It," "Island Blues."

THE RAMSEY LEWIS TRIO
Recorded live at the Bohemian Caverns in Washington, D.C. "West Side Story Medley," "Mario," "Something You Got," "The Shelter Of Your Arms."

BACH TO THE BLUES
Includes: "For The Love Of A Princess," "Why Don't You Do Right," "Misty Days — Lonely Nights," "You'll Love Me Yet," "Travel On."

MONO or STEREO
Mfr. List Price ~~$4.79~~

$3.74
AND YOU GET BLUE CHIP STAMPS, TOO!

We Give BLUE CHIP STAMPS on 25,000 items

Thrifty CUT RATE DRUG STORES

KRLA ARCHIVES

HOTLINE LONDON
Hermits Hurt

Tony Barrow

By Tony Barrow

Two of HERMAN'S HERMITS were sent to the hospital with minor injuries after a road crash. They were released after treatment and continued their journey to television studios in Bristol.

Herman's Hermits will be back in America directly after their upcoming U.K. concert tour. Their fourth Ed Sullivan Show appearance is scheduled for April 24, around the time the "Hold On" movie is released. In Britain "Listen People" has just been issued AS THE 'B' SIDE OF HERMAN'S NEW SINGLE! On the top deck is "You Won't Be Leaving."

In my HOTLINE LONDON column, issue of BEAT dated March 5, I gave you the exclusive tip that our London Palladium TV shows would be on your screens this summer. In fact you will see at least six of the Palladium spectaculars, filmed in colour, and they will be networked via NBC starting early July. Reports here suggest that NBC will pay well over 300,000 dollars for the six shows.

In Britain, we will not see the series until later in the year. The first program, starring Joanthan Winters, is to be filmed at the Palladium on April 24.

Yeah, well I guess TAMMY HITCHCOCK got around to believing that MICK JAGGER really DID write something called "Blue Turns To Grey." The title, recorded by CLIFF RICHARD AND THE SHADOWS, is well up in the current U.K. charts.

Fascinating feature on MITCH RYDER appeared in London's *Record Mirror*. It was written by MAUREEN PAYNE who used to be a telephone/receptionist at Brian Epstein's London headquarters before she settled in L.A. and took a job with the Dick Clark organization. (Dear Maureen, If I say "Hi!" to you here in HOTLINE LONDON will you say "Hi!" to me in *Record Mirror*? Luv, Tony.) Mitch told Maureen he was looking forward to coming to England and "seeing JOHN LENNON'S house and the bicycle MICK JAGGER had when he was younger."

London journalist Maureen Cleave, one of the first press people to write about THE BEATLES, has now done a brilliant in-depth series of articles called "How Does A Beatle Live?" for the *London Evening Standard*. She sums up JOHN LENNON like this: "He looks more like Henry VIII than ever now that his face has filled out—he is just as unpredictable, indolent, disorganized, childish, vague, charming and quickwitted. He is still easy-going, still tough as hell. He is very keen on books. He can sleep almost indefinitely. He has a morbid horror of stupid people."

Of RINGO she writes: "Though the smallest, the cutest and the favourite of tiny children, he seems less complicated and more mature than the others. Indeed, he gives the impression of being utterly contented. This makes him a charming host and restful company. He takes lots of pictures of Zak."

DAVE, DEE, DOZY, BEAKY, MICK AND TICH—in our current Top Twenty with "Hold Tight"—will make their first visit to America for TV and concert at Easter. Another best-selling U.K. outfit who have yet to make themselves known on your side of the Atlantic will visit you by a sort of remote control method. They're THE SMALL FACES who have just been to the top of our charts with "Sha-La-La-Lee" are to telerecord appearances for "The Dick Clark Show" in London.

NEWS BRIEFS... The LENNONS, STARKEYS and HARRISONS plus CILLA BLACK attended Brian Epstein's party in honour of HERB ALPERT AND THE TIJUANA BRASS. PAUL McCARTNEY was out of town on vacation. Alpert aggregation made much impact in London during their lightning three-day visit... Liner note on my copy of Scepter's DIONNE WARWICK "Here I Am" album repeats BURT BACHARACH'S name three times as Bachrach. Liner is signed by KAL RUDMAN, R & B editor of *Record World*...

GRAHAM NASH of THE HOLLIES, troubled by a stomach ulcer, is under doctor's orders to diet very strictly and go to bed early... KEITH RELF of THE YARDBIRDS making his own solo recording of BOB LIND composition "Mr. Zero" with massive orchestral backing... HERMAN says he'd never live in America permanently despite his great popularity on your side of the Atlantic... HOLLIES hope to record album tracks in America during their tour... Sorry to hear Byrd GENE CLARK is unwell.

BEATLES, GERRY AND THE PACEMAKERS, CILLA, FOURMOST, BILLY J. KRAMER and BRIAN EPSTEIN sent sympathy telegram to owner Ray McFall in Liverpool when Cavern was shut down... BILLY J. KRAMER WITH THE DAKOTAS now undertaking cabaret dates... When HERMAN agreed to pay them 60 dollars, the customs authorities at Manchester Airport handed over his Gold Disc Award. They confiscated it when Herman flew in with the American trophy.

HERB ALPERT AND THE TIJUANA BRASS hope to be back in Britain around July. They'd have loved to spend a few days sightseeing in London during their brief visit but TV taping and one concert at Britain's largest theatre filled all their time. Instead they detoured on their limousine drive into London from the airport so that they could take a quick glimpse at Buckingham Palace and Chelsea!... How about that fabulous album cover for NANCY SINATRA'S "Boots?" Looks to me like the best visual audio product in disc industry history!

...THE POPPIES

Hurry And Vote!

Wow! We have a feeling that the postman will never speak to us again. And we can't say we blame him. Ever since we printed the Beat's version of the Academy Awards and asked you to vote for the film and TV bests of the year, the ballots have been coming in by the bushel!

Your votes are now being tabulated, and although we probably shouldn't, we just can't resist letting you in on a few of the early reports.

We have several zillion more ballots to count, but at this stage of the game, "Help" is leading as the best film of 1965.

Patty Duke heads the race for favorite female TV personality, and a tie rages between Robert Vaughn and David McCallum in the fave male department.

It's too soon to say which TV show is at the top of the list. Many programs are running neck and neck at this point.

Paul McCartney and Elvis Presley are both hot contenders for the best actor throne, and Hayley Mills may just claim the best actress award.

In case someone "borrowed" your copy of *The BEAT* before you had a chance to vote, we've reprinted the ballot in this issue. If you've already sent in your choices, help your faves along by voting all over again.

Whatever the case, get your ballots in the mail today. The voting ends on April 21, so hurry faster! And watch coming issues for more news on the *BEAT* Awards!

OFFICIAL BEAT BALLOT

BEST MOVIE OF 1965: Vote for one nominated film or write in your fave.
- ☐ "Help"
- ☐ "Billie"
- ☐ "Goldfinger"
- ☐ "Ski Party"
- ☐ "That Darn Cat"
- ☐ "Where The Boys Meet The Girls"
- ☐ "Ferry Across The Mersey"
- ☐ "Catch Us If You Can"
- ☐ "Beach Blanket Bingo"
- ☐ "Harum-Scarum"
- ☐ _____

BEST ACTOR AND ACTRESS OF 1965: Vote for one film star in each of these two categories. Choose from those nominated or write in your candidate
- ☐ Paul McCartney
- ☐ Elvis Presley
- ☐ Peter (Herman) Noone
- ☐ Ringo Starr
- ☐ Sean Connery
- ☐ _____
- ☐ Patty Duke
- ☐ Annette Funicello
- ☐ Connie Francis
- ☐ Deborah Walley
- ☐ Hayley Mills
- ☐ _____

BEST TV SHOW OF 1965: Vote for one nominated show or write in your fave.
- ☐ "The Man From U.N.C.L.E."
- ☐ "Shindig"
- ☐ "Hullabaloo"
- ☐ "Where The Action Is"
- ☐ "Gidget"
- ☐ "I Spy"
- ☐ "Bonanza"
- ☐ "Peyton Place"
- ☐ "Tammy"
- ☐ "Get Smart"

BEST TV ACTOR AND ACTRESS OF 1965: Vote for one TV star in each of these two categories. Choose from those nominated or write in your candidate.
- ☐ David McCallum
- ☐ Robert Vaughn
- ☐ Michael Landon
- ☐ Bill Cosby
- ☐ Don Adams
- ☐ _____
- ☐ Patty Duke
- ☐ Mia Farrow
- ☐ Sally Field
- ☐ Debbie Watson
- ☐ Pat Morrow
- ☐ _____

The Poppies Popping In

A short time ago three very young and very unknown girls managed to get booked into a recording studio to cut their first record.

In one night they recorded their first single. They called it "Lullaby of Love" and themselves The Poppies and started on their way up the national charts.

The song is based on the familiar Brahms Lullaby and has opened up the door to allow these three Jackson, Miss. girls into a field topped by The Supremes and including Martha and the Vandellas and, more recently, The Toys and The Lazy Susans.

Lead singer of The Poppies is Dorothy Moore, a music major at Jackson State College where all three girls now attend.

Dorothy enjoys both classical and pop music and plays and composes both on the piano. She's a great fan of Al Hirt, The Supremes and The Vibrations.

The flip side of "Lullaby of Love" is called "I Wonder Why" and was written by Poppy Petsye McCune.

Petsy's not exactly the type you expect to find in a singing group. She's a botany major and hopes to get her Ph.D. in science. It's going to seem strange to call a Poppy Dr. McCune.

She was offered a scholarship to five different colleges before before choosing Jackson State.

When not buried in the books, Petsye can be found either writing more songs or taking part in her rather unusual hobby—she races snakes.

Third Poppy is Rosemary Taylor, one of six children and daughter of a gospel singer. Rosemary's a French major and is tremendously interested in literature.

She also plays piano and longs to travel.

Their song is just one more of the never ending hits from Nashville, Tenn. where it was recorded.

They really know how to produce them down there.

KRLA ARCHIVES

Happy 1st Anniversary Shebang

JOINING IN with congratulations to Casey Kasem on the first anniversary of "Shebang" are, from left, Johnny Hayes, one of the Paris Sisters, Bobby Sherman, Hullabalooer Dave Hull and pretty Donna Loren.

One year ago in a small Bakersfield television studio an afternoon show of popular music and dance geared for the modern set was about to kick off its premiere show.

The theme music began and a personable, handsome young man stood center stage, raised the mike and said: "Hi. Welcome to 'Shebang.' I'm your host, Casey Kasem."

That was the start of "Shebang." During the first few months of production the entire week's shows were taped on Saturday afternoon in Bakersfield and then flown to Channel 5 in Hollywood for programming.

Casey, who had and still has a daily radio show, had to dash up north for the tapings and make it back down here in time for his Monday morning show.

Then the show's popularity rose so much it was necessary for it to be moved to the Hollywood studios where "live" daily shows could originate, also saving Casey weekly trips to Bakersfield.

Now one year later, after some 300 successful productions, "Shebang" is observing its first anniversary and what could be more proper than to have many of the recording stars who helped make the show a success join in making the anniversary show a real occasion.

The KRLA disc jockeys joined many of the top name "alumni" artists who had appeared throughout the year to convey their congratulations to Casey and wish him the best for the coming years.

Also present was the original creator of the show, Dick Clark, along with the hosts of several other Los Angeles teen shows.

UNCLE DM—Dick Moreland also dropped by with anniversary greetings.

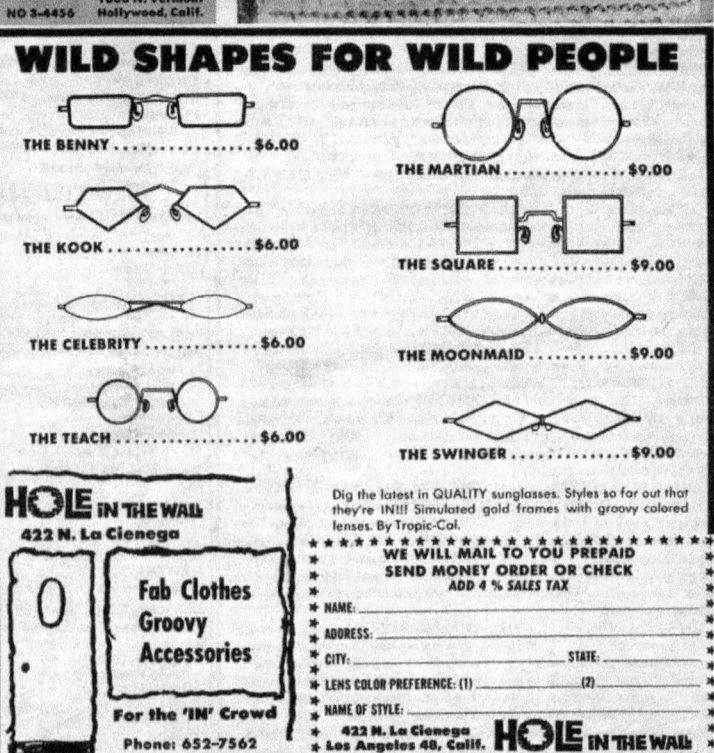

One Day On The Beat

By Carol Deck

So you'd like to be a *BEAT* reporter, huh? So you think we lead an interesting exciting life full of nothing but fun and games and meeting important and fascinating people.

Well, let me tell you about just one day in my life as a hard working *BEAT* reporter. I won't say it was a typical day—'cause there's no such thing—but it was the sort of day that happens every now and then in this business.

Let me start the day before—on Monday. Before leaving the office I checked my schedule for the next day and found that all I had for Tuesday (did I say *all?*) was a fashion show in the morning, an interview on a TV set in the afternoon and an interview at a recording session that night.

So, at 7 a.m. Tuesday I dragged myself out of bed somehow and tip toed around trying not to wake anyone else (in my household you get *killed* if you wake anyone before noon!)

ROBIN—On a cold golf course.

I then proceeded to get dressed for this fashion show—gloves, heels, hat, the whole bit.

However, when I got downstairs to my car, I got clever and read the invitation whereupon I discovered that the show was *Thursday,* and not Tuesday—great start for the day I thought.

Now I had two choices—I could go back to bed or go to work. Being a true-blue *BEAT* type people I naturally went to work (besides, I know me too well—if I'd gone back to bed no one would have been able to get me up before noon, and I had an 11 a.m. interview.)

I took off at 11 a.m. with a publicity man from ABC to hunt down the "Batman" crew.

We found them out in the middle of a very cold and windy public golf course (they'd been at a private course the day before but got kicked out—something about "how can you play a good game of golf with grown men running around in tights and capes?")

When I arrived back at the office another faithful reporter, Eden, came in and asked me if I wanted to go with her while she caught up on some errands she had to run. I had nothing scheduled 'till the interview late that night, so I said "sure"—I never was too bright.

We proceeded to go to a recording studio down the way where Eden had to ask Brian Wilson of the Beach Boys about something.

There we saw not only the Beach Boys, who were finishing up an album they're cutting, but a slew of other people as well.

We first saw Bobby Hatfield of the Righteous Brothers, with a new and very short hair cut. Bobby and Bill Righteous were cutting something with this huge mass of people they casually refer to as a band (it's actually more the size of an orchestra.)

BOBBY HATFIELD—Short hair and an extremely large band.

Danny Hutton and one of the "Hollywood A Go-Go" dancers wandered in for a short time.

After what seemed like hours Eden found out whatever it was she wanted from Brian and I clued her in that I was going to collapse from pure unadulterated hunger any minute.

Well, Eden's not too bright at times either and she ignored me. However, Beach Boy Carl Wilson finally took pity on me and took both unsympathetic Eden and starving me out to dinner (never let it be said that these Wilsons aren't generous people—that was

CARL WILSON—Thanks for the very delicious steak dinners.

one of the best steaks I've ever tasted.)

After bidding farewell to Carl, my faithful companion and I trooped over to a local folk type night club where Eden had to set up an interview with Eddie Brown, of Joe and Eddie.

After a brief talk with Eddie we fled the scene and dashed over to another recording studio where I had an interview with The Astronauts while they were recording.

There was only one minor problem—the studio that The Astronauts were supposed to be using is the one that The Rolling Stones do the majority of their recording in. And guess who just happened to be in town and had just happened to decide to record that night?

Would you believe The Beatles? No, well, how about The Stones—OK?

Anyway, The Astronauts got moved to another studio, but that wasn't the problem—it was a small matter of the fans camped outside the door and one uniformed guard (well, actually there were more like six but I don't want to sound too hysterical.)

Being naturally brilliant, I had forgotten to bring any kind of identification with me. Besides, The Stones weren't scheduled to record that night and I hadn't really figured on running into trouble with any guard type people.

However, there are some smart people in the world and one very clever manager of The Astronauts and one also very clever publicity

DANNY HUTTON—Wandering in and out, around and about.

man had already sent down clearance for me and my good buddy Eden.

And you should have seen the looks we got as we merrily trounced through the middle of all those Stone fans and walked through the door.

That was like around 8 p.m. and we didn't successfully get out of that building until after midnight—in fact we didn't even unsuccessfully get out.

I sat in the smaller studio with The Astronauts for a while watching them record and then I fired a few questions at them between takes.

Then I'd wander out in the lobby for awhile and kind of do nothing for a while—which I realize is sort of ridiculous when THE ROLLING STONES are in the next room.

I watched everyone wander about the building during their various breaks. It was quite an odd assortment of people that night—The Astronauts, all college guys with short hair dressed in sporty suits, Andrew Oldham, arranger Jack Nitzche, Mick, Keith, Brian, Charlie and Charlie's wife who was accompanied by Nitzche's wife and Green-Stone's secretary.

Joining me in the sitting, watching and generally staying out of the way category were two Stone-struck fan types.

This little circus went on until midnight during which time some gargantuan amount of cokes, candy bars, pizzas and other lovely fattening things were consumed by everyone concerned, including the six guards.

Anyway, around about midnight I completed my interview and

EDDIE BROWN—A brief chat.

discovered to my amazement that I was dead tired—and I do mean dead type.

So I collected all my various belongings which by now were scattered all over the building, thanked all the guards for their co-operation (one thing you learn early in this business is to always be nice to guards—it ain't practical to get a guard upset at you) put away all my empty coke bottles (I think I'm becoming a coke addict again), threw away all the candy wrappers (also empty) (this is one *BEAT* reporter who's going on a diet, *tomorrow*) and wearily trudged back out through the Stone fans (they're loyal, I'll say that much for them) and retrieved my car from under the building.

After returning Eden to her car, which was still parked at the office, I went home and got about eight of what I thought were well earned hours of sleep before starting all over again when Wednesday rolled around.

You still think we lead an exciting life? Well, actually some of it is, but the hours can get a bit ridiculous, and we do like to eat and even sleep sometimes.

But if you think any of us would trade places with you, we may threaten it now and then, but when you come right down to it, we love it or we wouldn't be doing it.

THE ROLLING STONES—Recording late into the night.

KRLA ARCHIVES

Adventures of Robin Boyd
By Shirley Poston

CHAPTER TWENTY-TWO

Robin Boyd is one of those rare kooks who always comes up with the greatest ideas at the worst possible moments.

For example, she once wrote an A-Minus (no one is perfect) English theme while her sister Ringo was burning her at the stake. (Actually, it wasn't a stake. It was the clothesline pole in the back yard, but at a moment like *that*, who bothers about *details?*)

However, she topped her past record the Saturday she arrived at the zingwhammer of all time while psychoanalying a psychiatrist.

Where the brainstorm came from, she hadn't the foggiest. It just occurred to her out of nowhere. And it was a WINNER!

Being the conservative sort (oh, *sure*), Robin did not leap wildly from her chair. She simply (and, she hoped, gracefully) fell out of it.

But, she soon scrambled back to a sitting position. There was a large problem to be solved before she would be able to carry *out* the aforementioned zingwhammer. A large problem which was at that moment lying on a nearby couch, blithering.

Chain Of Events

Taking a deep breath, Robin reviewed her notes, which she had organized in an organized manner (actually, that sort of went without saying, don't you think?), relating the chain of events thus far.

(1) Doctor scares holy heck out of Robin Boyd.

(2) Not to be outdone, Robin Boyd then scares holier heck out of doctor.

(3) Doctor loses memory (not to mention marbles) and now thinks that *he* is Robin Boyd, that *he* is 16, and that *his* mother thinks *he* is off his nut.

(4) Robin Boyd is inclined to agree with his mother.

Robin then closed the notebook quietly (what she *really* did was bang it shut frantically, but we wouldn't want to shatter her calm, cool image.)

It was an obvious case of amnesia, Robin reasoned reasonably. All she had to do was tell him who he really was and the problem would be solved.

But wait! She couldn't do that. Amnesia victims sometimes went berserk (a fancy word for ape) when confronted with their true identity. Or was that what happened whan a sonambulist was awakened in the middle of a pleasant sleep-stroll? Or was a sonambulist a stamp collector?

"Ratzafratz," Robin snarled under her breath, getting nowhere faster than usual.

The doctor giggled. "What does that mean?"

Robin gave *him* a look! "It means *nuts*," she answered impatiently (because she was starting to grow impatient, one would imagine.)

The doctor re-giggled. "That's what *I* am," he announced happily. "N-u-t-z, nutz!"

Robin stopped growing impatient and reached her full height. "So *what?*" she bellowed, before she could stuff the notebook into her big fat mouth. "*Everyone's* nuts! The only problem is, they won't *accept* it!"

"They should . . . it's fun," she added knowingly (and *she* should know.)

At this point, the doctor giggled so hard he almost fell off the couch. But he seemed calmer in a hysterical sort of way. Maybe she was on the right track!!

Dearly hoping so, Robin took another hurried glance at her notes. It was then that she noticed the name engraved atop each page.

Where his cards had read Dr. A. G. Andersrag, the notebook was less impersonal. It read, instead, Alex Andersrag.

Robin's ears stood straight up (which, in itself, is quite the accomplishment.) *Alex Andersrag??* Why did that sound so strangely familiar?

Suddenly, it hit her. Of course!! And it was then that Robin knew what she must do.

She couldn't take the chance of coming right out and blabbing what his real name was (see notes if you've forgotten why) (no, on second thought, consider yourself fortunate and leave well enough alone), but one could always flail about in the underbrush (or, if you prefer, beat around the bush a bit), couldn't one?

One could sure try!

Getting to her feet, Robin stalked to the center of the room. Then she turned to face the doctor, who was staring inquisitively.

"We're going to play a little game," she explained. "It's called *Guess That Nut* . . . I mean, *Name That Tune!*"

And, on that note she burst into song.

Ragtime Band

"Come on and hear," she warbled, "come on and hear, ALEX ANDERSRAG time band!!"

Prepared to go through the entire number several times, and to add a bit of the olde soft shoe if necessary, Robin got no farther than the first line. Because this time the doctor giggled so hard he *did* fall off the couch.

Robin rushed to his side (not to mention the rest of him), but he was already standing by the time she reached him. And he wasn't giggling. He was *roaring* with laughter.

"Alex Andersrag time band," he howled again and again. And he didn't stop until Robin kicked him right square in the left shin.

"You *rat* fink," she cried, seeing the light. "You were putting me on all the time!"

Gasping for breath (not to mention from pain), the doctor staggered to his $2,000 desk and sank into his chair. (Fortunately, he was a good swimmer.)

"I always do that with new victims . . . er . . . patients," he re-roared, wiping his eyes. "It's my bag!"

At this point, *Robin* giggled so hard she almost fell *under* the couch. But she suddenly ceased her cackling.

"What are you going to tell my mother?" she quaked.

"That you're the smartest, sanest, most fascinating psycho in the world," the doctor further howled. "We nuts have to stick together!"

Moments later, Robin raced madly out of the elevator and scurried to a secluded phone booth. She'd really wanted to stay awhile and chat with Super-Cool Andersrag. But she'd be seeing him again soon, seeing as how he'd threatened to tell her mother all *sorts* of things if she didn't stop by for a few larfs every so often.

But, at this particular moment, there were more important things to do. *So* important they couldn't even wait until she got home and could drag George out of his nice warm tea pot.

Putting a dime into the telephone, Robin crossed her fingers and toes (and, for good measure, her eyes) and dialed her home number.

Mind Reader

George had read her mind plenty of times when she didn't *want* it read. Which meant he could work the same magic when she *did* want a thought transferred.

After all, he was a *genie*, wasn't he? He could answer that phone without anyone else hearing it ring, and without anyone seeing him. And, if he *didn't*, she'd never *speak* to him again.

"I should be so looky," said a sleepy Liverpudlian voice on the other end of the wire.

"*George!*" she shrieked. "Get down here immediately!"

Just then she felt a good, swift yank being delivered to her right (or was it her wrong) arm.

"Don't you go orderin' *me* about," George warned, appearing out of thin air. He then took the receiver out of her remaining hand and hung it up with an angry thud.

Robin smiled meekly. (George was not like American boys, and when a good, swift yank didn't work, he had been known to shake her until her teeth rattled.)

"I'm sorry," she apologized, and she meant it. One look at George's dark handsome face and she was, and always would be, a goner. "It's just that I have this MAGNIFICENT idea!"

She then proceeded to tell him what it was. When she had finished, George stared at her aghast (for those interested, the aghast is located just to the right of the clavicle.)

"Who do you think I *AM?*" he bellered. "*The Wizard of Oz?*"

Robin shrugged. So what if she *had* been watching too many old movies on the telly. It still was a magnificent idea and he *could* manage it. All he needed was a little coaxing. (Which just had to be the second-best idea she'd had all day.)

"*Luv,*" she said coaxingly, advancing toward him (which is not the *slightest* bit difficult in a phone booth.) "Please, George?"

George tried to step aside (which is *impossible* in a phone booth.) "Why the Beatles" he snapped jealously. "Why do your *magnificent* ideas always concern the *Beatles?*"

"Because they remind me so much of you," she cooed, further advancing. Then she took aim and fired a persuasive smooch.

"*Robin Boyd!*" George said (when he was able) in shocked amazement, but Robin only chortled and re-aimed.

Seconds later, she was huggging her tall genie furiously. She hadn't won yet, but she was going to! She could just *tell* he was going to give in and grant her magnificent (not to mention outrageously difficult) wish.

How could she tell? Well, she began to get the general idea when George threw back his dark head and *whispered* for help.

(To Be Continued Next Week)

MEL CARTER AND STEVE ALAIMO sure lead an easy life, don't they? They pretend to be working feverishly on "Action" but The BEAT has found them out! They're not working at all—just loafing around on the beach. And to think they would try to put us on like that!!

'Gold' Guy Hits Gold

If there were a special group of Very Nice People in the Entertainment Industry Club, Bobby Goldsboro would probably be found holding a high executive position. He would at least be a charter member.

Bobby is not only one of the nicest young men in the pop field, he is also one of the most talented.

Bobby was born in Maryanm, Florida, on January 15, 1941, and after graduating from high school in Alabama, spent two years studying at Auburn University. He quit school at this point and spent a short time doing some free lance work as a musician, then joined Roy Orbison as a guitarist in January of 1962.

After spending two years with Roy—during which time he gained some invaluable experience—Bobby signed a recording contract with United Artists records and released his first record, "See The Funny Little Clown." It was a hit on charts all over the nation and Bobby was well on his way.

1964 was a very good year for Bobby; it marked the successful beginning of his career as a solo artist and it was also the year in which he married his childhood sweetheart, Mary Alice.

Both Bobby and his wife love to swim, and are confirmed baseball nuts. So "nutty" in fact, that when Bobby signed his recording contract he insisted that they include in it the stipulation that he would not have to record while the World Series was being played!

Aside from being a talented singer, Bobby is also a very accomplished songwriter, having written several of his own hits as well as penning tunes for other artists. He has often collaborated on his songwriting ventures with his good friend Roy Orbison, or with sidekick, Buddy Buie.

Currently riding high—and set to climb even higher—on the charts is Bobby's latest release, "It's Too Late." It is still very early in the career of this talented young man, and it is very nice to know that he'll be around long enough to watch it getting late . . . successfully.

KRLA ARCHIVES

The BEAT Goes To The Movies
"Frankie and Johnny"

By Carol Deck

Frankie and Johnny were lovers—that's the way the song goes. And that's the way the movie goes too, but in this case Johnny is Elvis Presley and Frankie is Donna Douglas.

The story is that Johnny loves gambling almost as much as Frankie and Frankie refuses to marry him until he stops gambling.

But a fortune teller steps in and tells Johnny that his luck will change with a new redhead who's coming into his life.

The redhead turns out to be the old flame of Johnny's boss, the owner of a Mississippi gambling-showboat where Johnny bets and sings.

Frankie gets jealous of the redhead who tries to use the boss to try to get Johnny to marry her but the boss is jealous of Johnny.

Johnny's piano-playing sidekick, Cully, takes the whole deal and writes a song—"Frankie and Johnny"—which is introduced on the boat. And everything looks great as Frankie and Johnny get a chance to go on Broadway after the Mardi Gras is over.

But that redhead louses things up again when Johnny wins a fortune with her by his side, just as the fortune teller had predicted, and Frankie, in a fit of jealousy, throws it all away.

The boss's bodyguard, in an effort to help the boss get Johnny out of the redhead's life, puts a real bullet in the gun that Frankie uses to "kill" Johnny with while they're singing the title song.

The song ends with Johnny's death—but this time Johnny is The King himself—will El die for the second time in a film?

As someone once said—see the movie and find out!

FRANKIE (DONNA DOUGLAS) and redhead (Nancy Kovak) get catty over who's Johnny's (Elvis) girl.

IN THE SONG Frankie shoots and kills Johnny in the end—and in the movie?—well, go see it and find out.

ONE THING CAN BE SAID FOR ELVIS—his gorgeous leading ladies. **IT'S ALL THIS** Gypsy's fault Johnny tells his sidekick, Cully. She told me the redhead would bring me luck.

KRLA ARCHIVES

Dave Hull's HULLABALOO
ROCK & ROLL SHOWPLACE OF THE WORLD
presents
EASTER WEEK EXTRAVAGANZA

APRIL 2-5
12 — 2 & 4 P.M.
THE TURTLES

plus
DICK DALE

APRIL 1-5
6 — 8 & 10 P.M.
P.J. PROBY
IN HIS FIRST RETURN U.S. APPEARANCE

plus
The PALACE GUARD

APRIL 6-10
12 — 2 & 4 P.M.
MAMA'S & PAPA'S

plus
M.F.Q.

APRIL 6-10
FANTASTIC SURPRISE—GUEST FROM EUROPE

also
THE PALACE GUARD
plus
JOEY PAIGE
& A HOST OF OTHER GREAT STARS

also
SPECIAL MIDNIGHT SHOW NIGHTLY

Coming May 1 in Concert — Peter and Gordon

MAKE RESERVATIONS — HO. 6-8281

KRLA ARCHIVES

America's Largest Teen NEWSpaper

KRLA BEAT

APRIL 16, 1966

Righteous Brothers Lash Out At Spector

KRLA BEAT

Volume 2, Number 5 — April 16, 1966

'Uncle' Floored By Adoring Fans

LONDON: Robert Vaughn, televisions' Napoleon Solo, the "Man From U.N.C.L.E.," was the victim of a mobbing by 200 screaming, hysterical fans at London's Airport. As his fans surged through police barricades to reach him, Vaughn was forced to take refuge in the airport's men's room.

The girls ran after him shouting, "Solo, Solo." When the police felt it was safe for Bob to emerge from the men's room they beckoned him forward with a circle of police around to guard him. But as so very often happpens in situations such as these, the police underestimated Vaughn's fans. Unfortunately, they didn't realize their mistake until Bob was dragged to the floor by young girls attempting to kiss him.

Many anxious minutes passed before Vaughn was escorted out of the airport by row upon row of policemen. Making his exit, Bob looked like anything but a movie star. What he actually resembled was a poor soul who had just received a liberal dose of "Thrush" meanness!

Bob's airport arrival certainly equalled that of his television pal, David McCallum, when he made the mistake of landing in London last week. David was in England for a press conference at the Empire Theater. His shirt was torn open and his black tie was tugged so hard that David almost choked to death.

David finally yelled, "Cut out the violence," but it did no good. At one point David was quite obvisouly fed up with the girls' behavior. He was trying to answer serious questions while the girls screamed, "He's sexy, sexy." His temperature hit the boiling mark about that time and he shook his fist at the teenagers telling them to shut up. They didn't.

The moral of the story is that from now on both David and Bob will consider the "Thrush" agents mere child's play when compared to a mob of screaming, teenage girls! And they're probably right!

'Shebang'—From Bakersfield To Hollywood To Number 1

It's taken just one year for Casey Kasem's "Shebang" to get from its humble beginnings in a small Bakersfield studio to the top rated young adult daily dance party.

Now, celebrating their first anniversary and looking ahead to the coming year, the host and stuff of the show are also looking back at what they've accomplished.

The show boasts many "firsts." It was the first young adult show to be broadcast live and in color on a daily basis, the first to present invited guest artists in production settings on a regular basis, the first to feature not only the current best selling records but the oldies as well, the first to offer daily viewer participation contests that test knowledge of pop music and the first to feature 'special' days such as Western Day, Surfers Day, Hot-Rod Day and the very popular 13-year-old-days.

Among the stars who've headlined "Shebang" are Sonny and Cher, the Byrds, Ian Whitcomb, the Lovin' Spoonful, Simon and Garfunkel, Chad and Jeremy, the Temptations, Martha and the Vandellas, Peter and Gordon, Donovan and the Sunrays.

There are many reasons for the show's success but paramount among them is the show's host—KRLA disc jockey Casey Kasem, a very handsome, personable, young man.

One of Casey's high points on the show was the initial reading on the show of a letter he got from a Beatle fan who'd hugged her favorite Beatle. The result was Casey's first venture on records, "A Letter From Elaina."

And with the show's high standards of dress and conduct "Shebang" has managed to survive in a market where many shows like "Shindig" have died.

They managed not only to survive but to keep growing and growing. Look for even better things from "Shebang" this year.

Inside the BEAT

Dancin' In The Streets	3
Norma Has A Real 'Dog'	4
Music And Motorcycles	6
Backstage With Chad & Jeremy	7
Hotline London	9
The Legend Of Lennon	11
At A Stone's Session	12-13
Dionne's Smash 'Message' Song	14
The Beat Goes To The Movies	15

Paul Exposed

By Tony Barrow

Here's what I consider to be the best "now-it-can-be-told" pop story of 1966!

Where shall I begin? Well, for a start, let me put it this way—there *is* a fifth Beatle and his name is Bernard Webb. I'd love to send you his photograph but it can't be done. Bernard Webb is a faceless Beatle.

Look closely at the record label on your copy of "Woman," the current chart-climber by Peter and Gordon. You'll see that Webb gets a composer credit and that the song is published through The Beatles' own music company.

In London pop press circles there have been rumors that Webb is connected very directly with The Beatles. Eventually one particularly enterprising journalist did some concentrated investigation at the headquarters of the Performing Rights Society and came up with the mysterious fact that composer royalties for "Woman" were pouring into Northern Songs Limited, the London publishing company which has never handled anything but Beatle compositions! This raised the question of why Bernard Webb should be handing over all his hard-earned cash to John and Paul.

'Woman' Mystery

Apparently, Bernard Webb was a young university student whose hometown was Leeds, Yorkshire. He had sent in "Woman" to Northern Songs as a possible number for The Beatles to record. The song had been passed on to Peter and Gordon. Apparently Bernard Webb had a current Paris address but had left it and disappeared on some kind of extended skiing trip in the Swiss Alps.

On the face of it, the talented young Bernard might have met up with PAUL McCARTNEY who has just returned to London after vacationing at a secluded ski center hideaway in the Swiss Alps!

Now the secret behind the "Woman" rumors can be told—in one way McCartney and Webb *did* meet for Paul has admitted he is the composer of "Woman!" Bernard Webb was born in the fertile McCartney mind and exists only there and on the label of the Peter and Gordon "Woman" disc!

Behind this deception are perfectly good reasons for cloaking the true identity of Bernard Webb. Paul wanted to put out one of his songs anonymously to see if it could hit the Top Twenty without carrying the usual much-publicized Lennon/McCartney tag. On the other hand Peter and Gordon were anxious to record "Woman" without being accused of riding on a Beatle bandwagon.

I'd say these were two pretty good motives for what turned out to be a totally successful project.

Not Fair

Says Paul: "I knew someone would find out the truth sooner or later, but I'm glad the story didn't leak out until after "Woman" had become a hit in Britain and America. I hate to read record reviews which say that so-and-so will have a hit just because a Beatle number is involved. It's not fair on the artists concerned. Anyway my idea worked. Incidentally, this is the only song I've published under a pen-name. I don't plan to repeat the idea . . . well, not at the moment anyway!"

Who created all the background *(Turn to Page 2)*

Haircuts And A Hit For The Righteous Brothers

The Righteous Brothers have shorter hair, a number one record (which Bill produced to get back at Phil Spector) and are continuing their record breaking precedent by smashing all standing records at Harrah's Club in Lake Tahoe.

The shorter hair bit came about because Bobby simply got tired of his old hair style so he had it chopped off. Bill left his the same for awhile but then gave in to the barber's shears as well. Some people dig it, some don't but the Brothers Righteous like it and that's all that matters.

When Bobby and Bill released "You've Lost That Lovin' Feeling" many thought they could never equal it—either in sales *or* in sound.

But Bobby and Bill fooled them with "Soul And Inspiration" which shot to the top of the nation's charts despite heavy competition.

"Soul And Inspiration" sounds like Phil Spector, the man who really started the ball rolling for the Righteous Brothers by producing most of their big hits. But not too awfully long ago trouble brewed between the forces of Spector and the forces of Bobby and Bill. So, the boys left Spector's label, Phillies Records, but not without plenty of hard feelings on both sides. *(Turn To Page 4)*

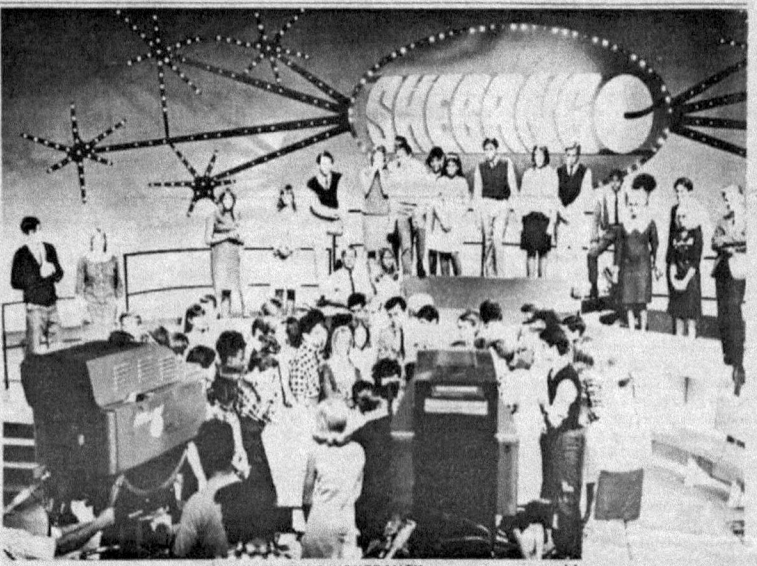

. . . CASEY KASEM'S "SHEBANG" — now one year old.

KRLA ARCHIVES

WAR

By Louise Criscione

There is a war going on in Vietnam and whether the United States has officially declared war or not—it is there, it's happening. And because it *is* the draft has been stepped up.

The war and the draft are two problems which face young adults more than any other segment of our population because it is they who must fight the war—it is they who are drafted.

Some of them go willingly—some do not. Some protest, burn their draft cards and flee the country to escape the draft. Others feel that since they share all of the profits of living in America they must also shoulder some of the responsibility. And that responsibility today, right now, is to serve the U.S. by bearing weapons and wearing a U.S. uniform, by fighting in jungles and, unfortunately, by killing—if asked. Like it or not, agree with it or not; but that's the way it is.

Are They?

The young entertainers in the pop field are no exception. They are just like the rest of us—almost. *The BEAT* called countless publicity offices and spoke to a great many draft-age performers. Time and time again the answer was the same: "We'd be happy to go if we were called." But would they?

It is common knowledge that a certain percentage of these "happy to go" performers are trying everyway possible to get *out* of being called. Take for instance Chad and Jeremy. They maintain permanent residency here in America. They live here, they work here, they haul in money here. They are eligible for the draft *unless* they go back to England during a certain time period.

You may remember that recent trip they paid to Britain supposedly for recording sessions? Recording was only an excuse—they fled to escape the draft.

Chad and his wife, Jill, have just recorded a protest song. "The Cruel War." "For me," admits Chad, "making 'The Cruel War' was the only way I could say anything in public about the Vietnam war or any other war for that matter. I don't go for those sick patriotic songs glorifying death. This story constitutes an objection to war which is universal because it is concerned with the human misery (or one aspect of it at least) which results from it."

America has always been an open country, one which welcomes (or at least tolerates) immigration. But it does ask one thing—if you reap the harvest, baby, you have to help sow the crops.

A radio station in Los Angeles hired a foreign disc jockey. He too was a permanent resident. But when he learned that the draft board was hot on his heels he ran, or rather flew, back to his native country. He was in such a hurry that he even left his wife here until he could scrounge up enough money to pay her way back.

But please don't get the impression that *all* immigrants are like that—they're not. Take John English. He's a young Englishman whose career was just beginning to happen when he was drafted. But instead of running scared he willingly went into the Army. Why? "I could have beaten it. I could have just gone back to England and laughed at them. But if I'm living here and taking advantage of what this country has to offer, I guess I have to pay like everyone else."

Enough about immigrants, what about our native Americans? Brian Wilson speaking for the Beach Boys says: "Those in our group who have been eligible were found not acceptable."

Drake Levin, of Paul Revere and the Raiders, is about to go into the National Guard for 4½ months of active duty. He probably could have gotten out of it but he didn't. "I'm looking forward to getting some exercise and sleep," grins Drake. "But I'm going to miss the fun, excitement and money," he admits.

Elvis The First

Elvis Presley served his full time in the service, so did Bobby Rydell and so did many others. Whether it hurt their careers or not is debatable but they seem to have no regrets about going. Others, if they can help it, join the reserves. Of course, they take the chance of being called up but more times than not they win the gamble and for them it seems to be worthwhile.

As was mentioned before, practically every single artist we spoke to was more than reluctant to discuss either the war in Vietnam or the draft. It's too controversial—they'd rather play the dumb guy and have no opinions, at least, none which they feel like making public.

The Association and the Sunrays were two pleasant exceptions. Just like everyone else they have their opinions and beliefs but unlike the sickly, smiling "yes" boys they were willing to talk.

"I agree with the war in Vietnam," states Russ of the Association. "I believe it's a necessary thing. I believe what is being done there is right. I'm in complete agreement on how the President is handling it."

But Russ is opposed to the draft. "I don't believe that anyone has the right to tell me what to do, especially to kill another human being. It's a loss of individual rights." So, Russ believes in the war but, personally, he'd rather not be the one to fight it. He'd most likely go on his own but he doesn't want to be *told* to go.

The Sunrays are all in college and maintaining a B average, therefore, they're deferred from the draft.

"I don't believe the war in Vietnam is a true war," says Eddie. "I think it's a great way for the big organizations to make a haul and they're the kind of people who don't want to see the war end."

"It's a good way to help the population explosion," reasons Rick. "It keeps the American economy the way that it is."

"I personally wouldn't mind going in and serving my time as far as the draft is concerned," admitted Byron. "We're very patriotic."

Mark believes in the war in Vietnam. "It's not a question of who belongs there. It's a question of communism. It's a question of stopping them there before they get to Australia. I hate draft card burners. It's for a good cause but they started too late and now they're making a big thing about it.

"The most pathetic part about it are the guys who don't know the first thing about it. It's like anything else, you've got to know what you're doing. The other thing is they have guerrilla warfare over there. The first thing I'd do would be to burn down the whole jungle and make them come out into the open and fight," said Marty.

Protesters

The protesters are protesting all across the nation and the draft card burners continue to send their draft cards up in smoke. But the war goes on anyway. Do the protesters do any good at all? Bob Dylan, who many label a protester himself, doesn't think so.

"Burning draft cards isn't going to end any war. It's not even going to save any lives. If someone can feel more honest with himself by burning his draft card, then that's great," says Dylan, "but if he's just going to feel more important because he does it, then that's a drag."

What about the marchers? They certainly get enough publicity by marching about with signs and so forth. "People that march with slogans and things tend to take themselves a little too holy," believes Dylan. "It would be a drag if they, too, started using God as a weapon."

The war in Vietnam and the draft laws of the U.S. are controversial, yes. And whether or not you support or defy them you *should* at least have some sort of an opinion. Forcing yourself to think these problems out is good and it's healthy. It makes for maturity.

The BEAT would very much like to hear what your opinions are, be they pro or con. Don't be like the vast majority of entertainers—afraid to express their opinions, afraid that they'll lose popularity, afraid that they'll bring the draft board down on them, afraid that they'll have to fight. It's a shame because *The BEAT* admires those who are strong enough to stand up for what they personally believe in, don't you?

This *is* your newspaper, we're here to print what you feel—what you believe—what you want. All you have to do is let us know.

A BEAT EDITORIAL
Insurance Soars... Teen Drivers Sore

The BEAT wonders why the insurance rate for teenagers who drive are so high. Drivers between the ages of 16 and 25 must pay higher insurance premiums than any other age group, in spite of the fact that they have faster reflexes, better eyesight and hearing, and smoother coordination.

To find an answer, *The BEAT* spoke with representatives of several large insurance companies, and learned that there are many factors involved in the formulating of insurance rates and responsible for the increased rates for young drivers.

Less Careful Drivers

Primarily, insurance rates for drivers are based upon the driver's past record and the accident rates of each age group. According to current statistics, the 16-25 age group has more accidents and receives more tickets for careless driving than any other age group. One insurance agent explained that this is due to several factors, beginning with the inexperience of these drivers. He explained, "A driver of 15½ lacks the experience of an older driver, and although his reflexes are superior to those of an older person—he still misjudges things and gets careless in his driving habits. Also, youngsters do tend to show off. Teenagers are generally less cautious than a man of 35 with a wife and family who won't risk his life to cross a railroad track in the path of an oncoming train!"

It Gets Worse

This is certainly a pessimistic viewpoint, but what follows is even worse. Because of the higher accident rates of young drivers, the insurance companies are forced to raise the premiums to insure that group in order to compensate for the losses they must take. One insurance agent indignantly claimed that "*all* insurance companies have lost money with these drivers! If I insured 1,000 boys at the present rate for older drivers—I'd lose my shirt!!"

Not all insurance agents are quite as dismal-sounding as this one, however. There are many who have a much more practical attitude toward the situation. One such agent explained to *The BEAT* that there are several areas in which young drivers can obtain reductions on their insurance rates.

Drivers between 16 and 25—who are single—are classified 2C by the insurance companies, and members of this classification must face a price tag of at least $300 as the lowest possible liability rate. For those over 25 and married, the comparable policy would run about $125.

Possible Discounts

For a person 18 and married, a lower rate is possible. Also, a student with a B-average or better is eligible for a 20 percent discount. Discounts are given if there is only one car in the family—"because then he can't be doing too much driving if a husband or father is using it during the day, and he has it only part-time." — or if the young applicant has taken the Driver's Training course while in high school, he will generally be able to receive a 10 to 15 percent discount.

One insurance agent insisted that "people who think that the insurance companies are getting rich off of young drivers are wrong; these companies aren't making money off of youthful drivers—and these drivers have brought these higher rates on themselves! Their accident rates are higher, and the insurance companies can't be blamed for this!"

Perhaps not, but *The BEAT* joins the Federal Government in the feeling that these rates should be lowered. It is true that drivers in this age group have the *potential* to be the best drivers on the road—but it is still up to them to exercise their superior capabilities in driving a little more carefully in order to *be* the best. And for the most part, it is up to these drivers to lower the insurance rates themselves—by lowering their own accident rates. A little courtesy on the road can be very important—and economical!

'Woman' By Paul

(Continued from Page 1)

biographical data for an invisible Bernard Webb? The details were worked out by Paul himself—with helpful suggestions from Dick James who runs the Northern Songs organization.

"Naturally other people in the business wanted to get Bernard Webb" reports Dick. "They recognized 'Woman' as a terrific song and wanted him to write more material for them. For very fair reasons Paul wanted to use another name and I was happy to go along with him on this. Everyone at Northern Songs stuck to the fictitious Webb story until the true story broke and Paul made up his mind that the time had come to tell all!"

Paul is to be congratulated on his elaborate scheme to let "Woman" stand or fall on its own merits. High placings for "Woman" in the charts of so many different countries prove that Paul has made his point. And nobody can claim that Peter and Gordon took their latest winner into the Top Ten on the strength of The Beatles' popularity. Two important points have been proven, nobody has been hurt and the mystery-sheathed secret of an elusive Fifth Beatle has been solved!

Say you read it in The BEAT

KRLA ARCHIVES

Martha And The Vandellas

By George L. Culver

"*DANCIN' IN THE STREETS*" that's what Martha and the Vandellas are doing, 'cause they've got a whole lot to dance about. A double-sided hit record on the charts, following three hit singles before it. Not bad for three young girls from Detroit.

The organization at Tamla-Motown has given the world a wealth of talent and entertainment over the last few years, and the latest edition to their hall of fame is Martha and the Vandellas. The lead singer—Martha Reeves—is a beautiful, talented girl who used to be a secretary for one of the top A&R men at Motown, and though she has every reason to dance through the streets with pride over the group's success, she is content to say:

"I was *so* excited and *so* shook! My whole life changed! Can you imagine what it's like to go from a secretary to a singer, with people suddenly asking you for your autograph?!"

It *was* quite a change, and one which Martha has accepted and handled very well. It is unusual to find a singing star who has retainer her "down-to-earthness," but Martha has accomplished this very well. Perhaps it has to do with her philosophy on living; she spent several years working toward her goal of being a singer, and then—as now—she maintained that, "If you want anything out of life—you have to stick to it! You have to work for what you want!"

... MARTHA AND THE VANDELLAS on stage at The Trip.

DANCIN' in the streets!

"Soul Sound"

The sound which Martha and the Vandellas produces has been described as a "soul" sound—a term which is as indefinable as "folk music." It seems quite certain that these three talented girls have a lot of soul—but just what does that mean?

Martha explained: "This way of singing is a *feeling*; it's a way of getting a message to the people with feeling. You kind of open up a little more with it. It's always *pop* music when the public *buys* it; but "soul" music is the way you deliver the song and what you want to get across to the people.

"We're trying to open ourselves up to the public and give them more than we really have to offer. That's soul. It's soul if you have to get involved in the music."

Martha admits that "I enjoy people and I love kids; I think that any adult should take a real interest in his child. If he has a friend at home, then he doesn't have to go out in the streets looking for one."

Martha has succeeded in making a lot of friends through her records and personal appearances, but she remains a perfectionist in her work. Always very concerned about the audience's reaction to the group, she still finds that you can't always please *every*one:

"Sometimes I just can't satisfy them, and I'll *never* be satisfied! If it didn't click with me, than it was *terrible*—no matter what *any*one says!"

The group *has* clicked with a good many people, and the future is looking very bright for Martha and the Vandellas. Outside of the records and personal appearances in which they are involved, many of their fans are wondering about the possibility of a motion picture. Martha laughs and says: "I'm a little leery about acting—'cause everytime I see an actor I still go to pieces! I'd like to be in a movie where I could say something that had meaning—not just to sing. I want to do my very best in anything I do."

Martha feels that the lyrics of a song are one of the most important elements, and insists that, "I couldn't sing a song if the lyrics didn't mean anything to me; they're *so* important." She wrote the lyrics to the flip side of the group's first disc, and right now she is devoting as much of her spare time as possible to learning how to write music. She plays "a little piano and a little guitar," and hopes to greatly increase her talents in that area.

First Book

Martha is also involved in writing her first book—a project which is very close to her heart. It will be about many of her experiences in show business, and if it is anything at all like its author—it will undoubtedly be a warmly-human—sometimes funny, sometimes sad—story.

Martha is something like that; she is a bubbly person because she likes to be happy and to make others happy. She is also prone to nervous stomachs because she worries about her work and how it will be accepted. She is one of the kindest, most generous people in existence, and that demands that "I still read all of my fan mail, and try to answer a lot of it. You can't forget the people who helped you on the way up!"

Talks To Fans

Not only does she answer as much of her mail as she can, but whenever possible—she tries to make herself available to her fans. When the group is traveling and staying in a hotel, her phone rings constantly—and she accepts *all* calls and speaks to all the people who call to talk to her. There aren't many people who would allow a fan to call and wake them up after having performed all night, and then sit and speak with them for several minutes and even invite them over to meet the other members of the group; but Martha does.

Currently on an extensive cross-country tour, Martha and the Vandellas will soon be making their *third* trip in the last two years to England, for a 17 day tour in that country. After that, there will be more records and appearances back home in Uncle Samland. And then? Well, considering the enormous talent and success of these three girls from Detroit... Martha and the Vandellas will probably be doing a whole lotta *dancin'* in *the streets* in the future!

... BACKSTAGE after a successful show.

KRLA ARCHIVES

...NORMA TANEGA

Norma Wants Music For Herself And Dog

She considers herself "sort of but not really" a folk singer. She doesn't like "any kind of war between people" and she "only wants to make music." She's Norma Tanega and she owns a cat named dog whom she likes to take walking.

Norma admits that "I can only tell the truth" but the truth she tells is wild almost beyond belief and yet she is certainly believable.

One year ago found Norma in Europe. "Somebody said 'why don't you go to Europe' and wrote me a check. I said, 'I couldn't take that,' but three days later I left!

"In Europe I sang on the road and in youth hostels. Most of the American folk singers go for the lines outside of the theaters but I didn't do that. I just sang for people wherever they were. It was great! One suitcase and one guitar – I learned how to hitchhike!"

Truck Driver

But before Europe and hostels there were trips across the U.S. for Norma–flying, driving with other people and driving herself... in a catering truck no less!

Norma really does own a cat named Dog. "I decided to write a song. I've only been writing for a year now. Most of the songs I've written are not really protest songs–they're bent on commentary. So, I decided to write a song just about me – and Dog."

And what a hit that song turned out to be. Even Norma bought it! "Well, if I was running for President I'd vote for me," laughed Norma and then seriously added, "I like my record but I don't like my voice."

Norma doesn't consider herself a performer and has never worked with any other performers. "I never really perform–I just sing."

Further wild truth was brought to life when Norma revealed how "Walking My Cat Named Dog" came to be recorded. "Some high school student heard me sing, came up and told me that Herb Bernstein used to teach there. Anyway, they made an appointment for me to see him. I sang 'Jubilation' and he said, 'Come in tomorrow,' and within three days the song was recorded."

Being a composer as well as a painter, Norma is naturally a creative person. Therefore, creating her own sound in a recording studio for the first time did not put her uptight as it does so many singers cutting their first record. Rather, she "loved it."

Since finding the right material is the biggest problem faced by a singer, Norma decided to get around that hang up by simply writing her own songs. Before jetting to the West Coast for seven television shows, Norma put the finishing touches to her first album–penning all of the songs herself.

Prior to her writing and singing there were years and years of schooling for Norma–high school, college, graduate school. "I never thought about going to school; I just got scholarships. I really do miss it and I would like to get my Ph.D. in Art History. I've almost got enough units now.

"I studied painting, art history and humanities. I'm really a print maker but I don't try to explain it to anyone!

"I started singing in graduate school. I was singing in some hootenanies. It's really a drag to arrive at nine and around one thirty or two you finally get to sing a set and by then you're so tired."

More than anything else Norma enjoys performing before teenagers. "Teenagers will either boo you or yea you. I had one job at a night club. It was awful–the people go there to drink. But kids go to listen."

Made It

Norma has faced a bad audience only once and "I lived through it." Perhaps it made her more determined to get through to them? "I'm pretty determined as it is. I'm sort of a sky, tree, ocean way. If I can walk along the beach everything is all right. I mean that."

Norma is near-sighted so she wears a pair of prescription sunglasses that would knock your eyes out. She shows her sense of humor by admitting that "If I don't like someone I take my glasses off and turn them off completely!"

To say that Norma's musical tastes run the gamut would be a gross understatement. Her two favorite groups are, for example, the Beatles and the Andrew Sisters! "It's true–I love them. Wow! They're a gas!"

Norma lists Dylan as a personal friend but proclaims Mitch Ryder "beautiful." She was once a secretary on Madison Avenue but left after nine months, "I figured that was a school year."

She's about to head out as the only female performer on the six week Gene Pitney cross-country tour. She's Norma Tanega and "it should be interesting." She is!

On the BEAT

By Louise Criscione

Had to laugh at Brian Wilson's statements on pop marriages: "Marriage has no bearing on a girl fan's adoration for an artist anymore. Two or our guys, Mike Love and Al Jardine are already married."

Well, all that's fine and dandy but if marriage has "no bearing" then I'd like to ask Brian why the rest of the Beach Boys (including Brian) keep *their* marriages a secret?

Dick Clark's "Action" crew just returned from London where they taped 63 segments including such entertainers as the Yardbirds, Spencer Davis Group, the Small Faces, the Fortunes, Them, the Mindbenders, Billy J. Kramer, Wayne Fontana, Paul and Barry Ryan, the Moody Blues, Marianne Faithfull, and about 50 other artists!

Stones Off

Stones are off on a short tour which will take them to Amsterdam, Brussels, Paris, Marseilles, Stockholm and Copenhagen. Then it's back to London for the filming of "Back, Behind and In Front." Sometime during autumn the Stones will be touring England again which makes their British fans happy but Stateside fans should be even happier because Mick says the boys will tour the U.S. in late summer. It would be too much if both the Stones and The Beatles appeared Stateside at the same time, wouldn't it? Too much for security officers, I mean–not the fans.

...KEITH RICHARD

The Dave Clark Five's new one, "Try Too Hard," is definitely their best yet. Even those who dislike the Five dig this one!

Watch for Dylan's next album. You'll have to because the LP will have neither Dylan's name nor Columbia's anywhere on it! Only Bob would come up with something as wild as that!

News Notes

QUICK ONES: Herman is now the proud owner of a brand new Cadillac. Peter also owns a Jag . . . Ramsey Lewis Trio has been set for a six day engagement at the Royal Tahitian, Ontario, California from August 2-7. Marks the group's first stand in Southern California . . . Lou Christie wins a Gold Record for "Lightnin' Strikes." Lou is also set to headline a show at Madison Square Garden in New York and the Astrodome in Houston before heading off on a three week English tour . . . Funny line from Herb Alpert describing the Tijuana Brass: "We're a sextet plus one, or an oversext-et." . . . Bob Dylan clinging to his British popularity by selling out his Royal Albert Hall concert . . . Paul McCartney holidaying in Switzerland . . . Johnny Tillotson headed for a July date at the Copa . . . If you dig real blues don't miss the "Sonny Boy Williamson and the Yardbirds" LP. Fantastic!

Keep a lookout for Sonny & Cher's next LP, "The Wondrous World Of Sonny & Cher." It's a great album featuring such songs as "Summertime," "I'm Leaving It All Up To You," "Bring It On Home To Me," "Leave Me Be," "Set Me Free," "Turn Around," "So Fine" and three of their big singles – "But You're Mine," "What Now My Love" and "Laugh At Me." The cover shot is out of sight!

A Sick Davies

Ray Davies is sick again–this time the flu bug bit him. Anyway, the other Kinks are touring without Ray. Dave reveals that they were going to cancel the tour altogether but Ray talked them out of it by finding a replacement for himself–an old friend of his, Mick Grace. Dave says that Mick is okay but that no one could ever *really* replace Ray. Agreed.

Spoke to Dave Levin of the Raiders yesterday and he sent along a message for all you Raider fans. Drake says: "Hi, fans." Logical. As you already know, Drake is headed for a 4-1/2 month stint in the National Guard. Paul and his Raiders just spent a wild weekend in Atlanta and Drake admits that there is a definite difference between West Coast and Southern audiences: "Everybody there screams with a drawl!"

...RAY DAVIES

Righteous Bros. Even Score

(Continued from Page 1)

A spokesman close to Bobby and Bill revealed to THE BEAT that just to get back at Phil, the Brothers cut "Soul And Inspiration," cut it in such a way that it sounded like something which Spector would have produced– *if* he had the Righteous Brothers to work with.

Anyway, for whatever reason, the disc was released and it's a smash. The record company is clapping its hands in monetary glee for it looks as if "Soul" will sell a neat two million records!

The Righteous Brothers have broken away from their strictly teen oriented appeal to hit the supper club audiences. And in making the switch they've set up a string of broken gross and attendance records in every one of the major clubs which they've played. And, believe us, they've played *every* major club in the country!

Following their stint at Harrah's they move on to New York's Basin Street East in May and then to the Cocoanut Grove in Los Angeles for a three week stint beginning June 7. And then it's back to Vegas for their second three-week appearance there this year (the first was with Frank Sinatra) at the Sands on July 20.

One thing about the Brothers– you can't say they're just loafing around.

KRLA ARCHIVES

THE WONDROUS WORLD OF SONNY & CHER

SIDE 1
- Summertime
- Tell Him
- I'm Leaving It All Up To You
- But Your Mine
- Bring It On Home To Me
- Set Me Free

SIDE 2
- What Now My Love
- Leave Me Be
- I Look For You
- Laugh At Me
- Turn Around
- So Fine

And Don't Forget The One That Started It All
INCLUDES
I Got You Babe – Sing C'est La Vie
It's Gonna Rain – And Nine More Big Hits

And You Get Them At Fabulous Discount Prices At Your Nearby

 Record Dept.

KRLA ARCHIVES

The Adventures of Robin Boyd
By Shirley Poston

Chapter Twenty-Three

It wasn't that George gave up easily. It was just that he was no match for Robin Boyd. (Join the crowd, George.)

"All *right!*" he said at last, untangling himself from her clutches.

Robin jumped up and down hysterically. "You mean you'll *do* it?" she blithered.

Removing her right foot from his left toe, George sighed. "Well, let's put it this way. I'll *try.*"

Robin jumped down and up hysterically. "Oh, *George,*" she blathered. But she suddenly ceased blathering. "What do you mean *try??*"

George patiently removed her left foot from his right toe (actually, he yanked her arm clean out of the socket and flung her against the side of the phone booth, but we wouldn't want to shatter George's calm, cool image.)

"I mean that I cannot *possibly* grant *this* wish on me own," he growled. "*No* one has *that* much magic power. Well, *hardly* anyone," he rephrased as a bolt of lightning grazed his eyebrow.

Robin resumed jumping on what was left of George's winklepickers, realizing, of course, that if she didn't stop soon, he'd have nothing left to wear when he went out to pick winkles (and nothing to wear them *on*) (the winklepickers, not the winkles) (is this getting ridiculous or is this getting ridiculous?) "*How* are you going to try?" she raved joyously.

Tooth Rattler

George, who had been known to shake her until her teeth rattled when and if a good, swift yank failed to work, shook her until her teeth rattled.

"That'll do for a start," he hissed. "Now *shurrup!*" He then proceeded to pick up the receiver and dial thirty-seven numbers.

"Hullo?" he said finally, flexing his remaining nine fingers. "This is George. I'd like to apply for a power loan."

Robin would have tittered a bit at that one, but she was far too impressed. Thirty-seven *numbers,* yet! And, you should pardon the pun (and will if you know what's good for you), Heaven only *knew* who was on the other end of that wire.

After that, George could say no more. He just listened. And although Robin's ears vibrated nosily, she failed to pick up so much as a word of the one-way conversation.

"Did you get the power loan?" she screeched quietly (let's face it, sixteen *is* a little young for dentures) when he'd hung up. "What's a power loan?" she added.

George gave her a withering look, looking so much like George Harrison it was almost against the law (and is, we hear, in several states.)

"It's a loan of extra magic powers. I'm going to need help to pull *this* bit of nonsense off."

"Well, did you get it?" Robin re-jumped.

"I don't know," George admitted. "But I'll soon find out. We're to report to my immediate supervisor in five minutes."

Robin paled. "*We??*"

George gave her a withering-er look. "Yes, *we.* Did you think I'd go making a moronic request like this one all by meself?"

Robin gulped. "*Where* do we report?" she quaked, raising her eyes skyward.

George laughed. (You mustn't let George's occasional—hah!—gruffness fool you. He gets the world's largest charge out of Robin Irene Boyd.) (Who would give him another large charge if she knew that he knew her vile middle name.) (Right between the eyes, for instance.)

"We're going to Liverpool," he answered. "Now call your mum and tell her you'll be a couple of hours late coming home."

"My mum?" Robin echoed nervously.

Safe Again

George patted her reassuringly. (For those interested, the reassuringly is located just slightly above the elbow.) "You're safe again," he soothed. "Your mad psychiatrist has just telephoned your mum and given you a clean bill of health."

Despite the fact that George said this in a manner which indicated that he definitely did not agree with the findings of good Doctor Alex Andersrag (of time band fame), Robin obediently fished for a dime.

"This one's on us," George chortled, handing her the receiver.

"Who's this?" inquired Mrs. Boyd, who was suddenly and mysteriously on the other end of the wire.

Robin, who had a tendency to become compleely unnerved, became completely unnerved. "Is Robin there?" she rattled.

"Just a moment, I'll ask her," her mother replied sourly. "I'm talking to her on the phone now," she added.

Robin giggled. "I was only kidding, mum . . . I mean, mom."

Mrs. Boyd failed to respond by falling into gales of hopeless laughter, but she did meet her daughter half way. "What *now?*" she asked hopelessly.

"I've just bumped into a friend," Robin explained (Who now has the scars to prove it, she added mentally.) "Is it okay if I don't come right home?"

"Where are you going?"

Robin re-fainted. "Oh, just flyin' about," she hurried when George glared at her through the glass door.

Sighing one of her oh-well-it-could-be-worse-and-come-to-think-of-it-has-been-worse-ers, Mrs. Boyd agreed and Robin emerged triumphantly from the phone booth.

"Let's be off to Liverpool," she chirped.

Fortunately, George was a fast thinker, and managed to cram her into his pocket before *too* many innocent bystanders ran screaming into the sunset.

That Word

"You bloomin' nit," he bellered, leaping back into the phone booth and cramming her *out* of his pocket. "Don't you *know* what happens when you say *Liverpool?*"

Robin, who had turned into a *real* Robin at the mention of the abovementioned word, nodded apologetically and gave him a loving tweak of the olde beak.

"Gerron," George said, but he couldn't help grinning, a bit of flirting having done the olde trick. (When if if it ever *stops* doing the olde trick, this world is going to be in a whole peck of trouble.)

Then he mumbled something under his breath and they vanished.

The next thing Robin knew, they were seated at a table in a secluded corner of an unfamiliar restaurant.

"Are we in Liver . . . I mean are we in that place that starts with L, that I'm not supposed to say already?" Robin gasped incredulously (not to mention ungrammatically.)

"That we are."

As a waiter approached them, Robin gave George a look that said now-I've-seen-everything. But the effect was purely transitory (it didn't last long, either.)

In fact, it faded the moment Robin saw that the waiter was Paul McCartney.

(To Be Continued Next Week)

Fan Club For Smothers Bros.

The demand for a Smothers Brothers Fan Club has been so heavy since the brother team began their television series that Kragen/Fritz, the brothers' personal management office has organized a national fan club for the comedy duo.

Further information regarding the fan club can be obtained from Jackie Burrud, 451 North Canon Drive, Beverly Hills, California.

...THE MOUSE

Music And Motorcycles

Bob Dylan is *not* Mouse despite the fact that the two sound exactly alike on record. Mouse's "A Public Execution" has caused all kinds of comment because people find it hard to believe that someone else can actually sound so similar to Bob Dylan. In fact, one of Columbia Records' public relations men got the fright of his life when he went to a radio station (which shall remain nameless, but you know which one!) and the playful jocks covered the label of Mouse's disc and told the unfortunate P.R. man that it was a Dylan record.

He listened to the whole record and as it spinned around the turn table, his face became redder and redder. He couldn't understand how a Dylan dub had gotten out and he feared that his job would be no longer. Even he couldn't tell the difference!

Actually, Mouse is a 23 year old from Dallas, Texas. His real name is Ronny Weiss but he received the nickname, Mouse, from a high school pal of his and the moniker just stuck.

Mouse has thus far remained mum on the subject of his Dylan sound but he did reveal that "A Public Execution" was written and composed to a letter he had received from an admirer.

Mouse has lived in Tyler, Texas for the past few years. He has a boyish, pleasant manner which people find most likable. Sincerity counts a great deal with him and those who know him well speak fondly of him. Mouse has a keen sense of humor and a quick smile. He has little use for intolerance and what he considers "willful prejudice." Motorcycling, next to music, seems to be Mouse's favorite occupation.

His manner is easy going, yet he seems to always be going someplace in a hurry. He considers time too valuable to waste but at the same time he remains casual. Mouse speaks warmly of the established artists whose style has affected his own. That, of course, means that Dylan surely comes at the top of his list.

When asked what he would buy if his record sold a million, Mouse replied: "A hundred-fifty gallon water heater and an electric overcoat!"

Do you think he's trying to tell us something?

STAMP OUT STIFF HAIR.

Caryl Richards *just wonderful* PROFESSIONAL HAIR SPRAY

HOLDS AND HOLDS...

DO IT NOW! AT All Toiletries Counters

KRLA ARCHIVES

For Girls only
by shirley poston

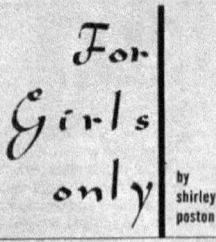

I've been thinking. And, I must say, it was a refreshing change of pace.

No, seriously (would you believe *semi*-seriously?), I may have come up with a real zingwhammer.

But, before I tell you what it is, I'll keep you in suspense for a few paragraphs. (In other words, I'm about to bore you senseless with the endless details of how I arrived at said brainstorm.)

Well, it all started when it suddenly occurred to me that at least half of the people who ready my column think I'm totally out of my tree. Right then, I started wishing there were some way of writing just for the other half (those of you who *know* I'm totally out of my tree.)

That way I wouldn't have to go around pretending that I have a few (very) sensible and rational moments every now and again. That way I would also get to write about things that *some* people just wouldn't *understand*.

It dawned on me this morning, which is a poetic statement if I've ever heard one (obviously, I never have). And it did so while I was trying to think of a way to tell you about the grooviest idea in the world. You know, in a way that wouldn't have the sane set bursting into low moans.

Tass Bracks?

Have I kept you in suspense long enough? Okay, have a friend wake you and let's get down to tass bracks.

From now on, when I have something really secretive to tell you, I'm going to write it in code! Morse, for instance. No, really! I've devised this special kind of language where all the letters stand for other letters.

How are you going to decipher (try decipher if that doesn't work) it? Simple (and how!) You're going to send for your de-coder! All you have to do is mail me the top from a box of Soggies, and you'll receive a Roy Rogers whistle ring as a special bonus.

Cease, Shirl. They'll think you're kidding. Which I don't happen to be, except about the box top and whistle ring. (We'll get around to that later when I've *completely* flipped.)

What you do is mail me a stamped, self-addressed envelope. Write the word "code" on the outside of the envelope you mail the envelope in.) I *am* making myself clear, I presume? (if so, that's another refreshing change of pace.) Then I'll send you a copy of the code, and when I write something unreadable in my column, you'll be able to translate it!

How is this going to separate the men from the boys (that lacks a certain something, but I couldn't think of any other way to put it)? Well, the people who couldn't care less *what* I have to say, in code or otherwise, won't bother sending in. And those of you who *do* understand me will! (You realize of course that if *no* one send in, I am going to kill myself deader than a door-nail) (whatever that is.)

I'll start the messages two weeks from now, so hurry up to the post office. The first will be about that idea I mentioned a few million paragraphs back. If you really dig a special star, and if you have a tendency to be even the slightest bit balmy on occasion, you'll luv this one!

Speaking of George, (didn't last long, did it?) (I, for one, hate pretense, but I have nothing against her sister priscilla) (what, I ask you, did I just *say*?) . . . anyway, speaking of George, I keep getting letters from girls who are falling for Robin's George of genie fame.

Need I tell you that I feel somewhat the same, and have been writing about him? I particularly liked the part where he was hiding behind the palm tree. (I *would*.)

Crash! I just knocked 11,431½ letters off my desk, and what to my wondering eyes should appear (no, I'm not going to say a miniature sleigh and eight tiny reindeer) but something I've been trying to find for months.

You guessed it, my marbles! No, really, I've just found the letter from the boy I mentioned a few weeks back. The one who made *me* look *co-ordinated* (in case you don't recall, I do things like shutting my ear in the car door, etc.).

Neck By Head

He says, and I quote: "I just read about you breaking your ear. I didn't think anyone else did things like that. Have you ever tried explaining that you broke your neck falling on your head? Well, I have. The looks you get you wouldn't believe.

"The worst part of it is that they don't believe me, because I'm still alive and can walk, run, ride a skateboard and everything. I'm so clumsy they won't let me in a regular P.E. class. Really! In the past three years, I've had two broken fingers, a football knee (still have it), a broken neck and a broken ankle. Try that. Hope your ear's okay."

Isn't that a panic? I'd print his name, but he'd probably see to it that *I* soon had a few broken bones of my own. However, if any kind soul would like to send him a get well card, I'd be happy to forward it. He isn't "sick," but with his luck, he probably will be any minute.

The more I think about him, the more I begin to wonder if the two of us weren't meant for each other. Well, if so, I hope George will be able to bear up under the strain of losing me. (Which is something he's been trying to do for years!)

Nuts. I've used up all my space and now I can't tell you about something really wild. I went to this slumber (ho) (and not as in hum) party and all we did was sit around and think up ways to make other people think you're crazy. You know, ways to send strangers shrieking into the sunrise.

Well, if they haven't come for me by next week, I'll tell you then. Providing, of course, that they haven't come for you.

Wait! I just remembered a joke. Why can't Batman find anyone to go out with him? Because he has bat breath!

Give Your Friends The BEAT For Graduation

BEAT Art: Jon Wolker

backstage with Chad and Jeremy

By A *BEAT* Reader

It was about 8:30 when the lights were dimmed at the Valley Music Centre. When they were on again Chad and Jeremy were on stage. In between songs and screams fan's learned Chad's secret identity – as told by Jeremy – which is no less BATMAN!!!!!

During one portion of the show they made up a song, on the spur of the moment, when something went wrong with their instruments. These two fantastic performers sang their way into everyone's heart in only an hour-and-a-half.

After the show my friend and I somehow got into their dressing room. Although they were very tired both Chad and Jeremy were very nice to us. When I got in I *had* to brag that I was a British citizen, so I did. They both congratulated (?) me!

The first real question we asked them was– What's the difference between American and English fans? Chad said we are more enthusiastic and that was great in his opinion. Then, to our surprise, he started singing "California Girls!" Sorry Beach Boys, but I liked that version better. Next we asked if Chad and Jill found a house yet. When Chad said no we gave him some helpful suggestions! (Hey, Chad there's a house for sale 2 blocks away from me. It's really very nice!)

Both Chad and Jeremy agreed that their fans were fab, but they hate for someone to scream out their name during a song. (Jeremy, sorry I screamed your name during that song, I'll never do it again!!!) (Jeremy, I wouldn't count on that!!!)

Then their manager came in and I could see they had to go, so my friend took one more picture and I asked them if they are going to make a television series. Jeremy said they would really like to and Chad said they wanted someting to the effect of LAREDO.

After they left I couldn't believe that Chad and Jeremy were so nice. They were really great!!!

Beatles Bag Their Tenth Gold Disc

The phenomenal Beatles have won their tenth Gold Record for singles for "Nowhere Man/What Goes On." At least, Capitol Records has asked the RIAA for a Gold Record certification for the disc.

"Nowhere Man," undisputedly the "A" side of the record, was released on February 15 and according to sales figures it sold nearly 750,000 in the first eight days of sales and topped the one million mark on February 28. Since that time sales on the single have continued to soar with an average of 75,000 records moved each week since March 1. Naturally, the disc's sales are slipping now but it is definitely a million seller anyway.

Just as '64 and '65 were the years of the Beatles it looks as if '66 will be no exception. "Nowhere Man" has been their only single released thus far in the new year and being awarded a gold record for it certainly seems to indicate that the Beatles have not lost their tremendous popularity.

And now that they've announced their summer tour of the U. S., *real* Beatlemania will assuredly start up in full force again – as always.

KRLA ARCHIVES

Now you can see a once-in-a-lifetime Broadway show at your own movie theatre!

STOP THE WORLD I WANT TO GET OFF

Warner Bros.' out-of-this-world entertainment innovation where the songs and fun never stop!

HEAR "WHAT KIND OF FOOL AM I," "ONCE IN A LIFETIME," "GONNA BUILD A MOUNTAIN" AND ALL THE OTHERS. GET THE ORIGINAL SOUND TRACK ALBUM AVAILABLE NOW ON WARNER BROS. RECORDS!

INTRODUCING **TONY TANNER** STARRING **MILLICENT MARTIN**
Original Book, Music and Lyrics ANTHONY NEWLEY and LESLIE BRICUSSE
Directed by PHILIP SAVILLE · Produced by BILL SARGENT
Music Supervisor AL HAM · MITCHELL SYSTEM 35

TECHNICOLOR® FROM WARNER BROS.

EXCLUSIVE ENGAGEMENT **STARTS FRIDAY, APRIL 15th**
PACIFIC'S **PANTAGES** THEATRE · HOLLYWOOD

Inside KRLA
By Eden

KRLA has gone SUPER RADIO now, and they've done it by adding the magic ingredient . . . *you!!* For two weeks in a row, KRLA offered its listeners the opportunity of choosing all of the songs which were played on *their* radio station by having an all request week-end.

The request week-ends began at 6:00 Friday evening and continued straight through Sunday. During the first three-day request program, KRLA logged over 100,000 calls from KRLA listeners all over the Southland.

Due to the huge, overwhelming success of the new request week-ends, KRLA decided to give more and more listeners the opportunity to select the music they listen to and to take a personal part in their radio programming. During Easter vacation, every record played on the air will be a request record from a KRLA listener. The lines will be open 24 hours a day throughout the entire Spring vacation, and the calls will be answered by a crew of KRLA listeners who were hired especially to handle the flooded phones at the station.

Phone Crew

The phone crew will be under the supervision of the KRLA DJ's, who will also be answering the phones themselves occasionally. Who knows, if you're lucky you may get to request your favorite songs from your favorite DJ. And maybe, if you are really *Super* lucky, you may even get an opportunity to *propose* to your favorite DJ (if you're a girl, that is!) as Jamie McCluskey of *The BEAT* staff did just recently.

Speaking of the Easter vacation, there will be a whole lot going on that week and *The BEAT* reminds you not to miss out on any of the fun.

KRLA will have their own booth once again at the Teenage Fair, to be held again this year in the Palladium in Hollywood. All of the DJ's will be down there as much as their schedules will allow, so when you get to the Fair, be sure to stop by and say hello.

Dick Biondi will once again be taking the brunt of things at the Fair, as he will be suspended this year above a tank of freezing water. The visitors to the KRLA booth will have an opportunity to play the baseball-throw game and try to dunk Biondi in the drink.

Dunk Biondi

By the way, all of the rest of the great KRLA DJ's will be turning out at the booth to try their hands right along with the kids to dunk Biondi. So, with the combined valiant efforts of the DJ's and the KRLA listeners—we should have one disc jockey feeling kind of wet behind the ears by the time the Fair is over!

The BEAT will have its own booth for the first time this year, and of course we are all looking forward to meeting all of you, so be sure to stop by. We are also planning on entering an alliance with the other DJ's to drop Biondi in the drink as often as possible, and since he will be suspended in position for most of the day each day—it promises to be a very funny *and* very *moist* situation!!!

Our Groovy Leader held a small press conference for various members of the *Batty BEAT* staff recently, and raised some very pertinent and baffling questions. He wondered—aloud, as he went—just why doesn't Nancy Sinatra ever visit KRLA during the daytime. And—what about that very mysterious telegram which Bob Eubanks received from Nancy Sinatra? Was it, by any chance, an invitation of some sort?

Cool Bat Cave

John-John also dropped the clue that all is "cool" upstairs in the Bat Cave at KRLA. He mentioned this in answer to some of our questions, but we weren't the only curious ones this week. Quite on the contrary—some of the visitors to the station this week have also experienced some doubts as to the contents of that mysterious vestibule.

Among those stopping by KRLA in the last week or so have been Brian Wilson of the Beach Boys and Johnny Rivers, who just returned from Viet Nam and currently has a smash hit on the KRLA tunedex . . . "Secret Agent Man."

We don't have too many new clues in our BatManager mystery this week, but there is one question which should be raised at this point. And that is . . . John-John: just what about the telegram which *you* received from one Miss Nancy Sinatra, hmmmmmmm???????

She wouldn't by any chance be an accomplice in the BatManager Sign Crime, would she?

KRLA BEAT Subscription
SAVE 33% Of Regular Price
☐ 1 YEAR — 52 Issues — $5.00   ☐ 2 YEARS — $8.00
☐ 6 MONTHS — $3.00

Enclosed is _____ ☐ CASH   ☐ CHECK
PLEASE PRINT—Include Your Zip Code

Send to: .... Age: ....
Address: .... City: ....
State: .... Zip: ....

MAIL YOUR ORDER TO: KRLA BEAT
6290 Sunset, Suite 504
Foreign Rate: $9.00—52 Issues   Hollywood, Calif. 90028

KRLA ARCHIVES

...DUKE KAHANAMOKU AND MIKE DOYLE

Surfer Mike Doyle Will Highlight First Surfari

The first Surfari with Mike Doyle will be held this Easter vacation south of Rosarito Beach in Mexico.

Two Surfaris will be held to include students whose vacations fall before and after Easter Sunday.

Mike Doyle, winner of nearly one hundred surfing awards, will be surfing at these Surfaries, along with several life guards and qualified girl advisors.

Mike has been named Number One Surfer in the World in a national poll by Surfer Magazine and was recently presented with the coveted Duke Kahanamoku Trophy for Best Sportsmanship in surfing at the Makaha International Surfing Championships at Oahu, Hawaii. (He's shown above accepting the trophy from the Duke.)

Director of the Surfari activities is Sharidan Byerly, L.A. County lifeguard, jr. lifeguard instructor, all American college swim team member, La Jolla Paddleboard champion in 1956, Dory Rescue champion in 1964 and a member of the Surf Lifesaving Team representing the United States in International Surf Lifesaving competition in Australia.

The Surfari will also include professional instruction in surfing and water safety, surf films, guitar hoots, dancing, sports and food.

Further information may be obtained by writing to Surfari, 9000 Sunset Blvd., Los Angeles.

...MIKE DOYLE

KRLA Tunedex

 DAVE HULL

 BOB EUBANKS

 DICK BIONDI

 JOHNNY HAYES

 EMPEROR HUDSON

 CASEY KASEM

 CHARLIE O'DONNELL

 BILL SLATER

This Week	Last Week	Title	Artist
1	1	SOUL AND INSPIRATION	The Righteous Bros.
2	—	MONDAY, MONDAY	Mama's And Papa's
3	2	CALIFORNIA DREAMIN'	The Mama's And Papa's
4	3	BANG, BANG	Cher
5	13	SECRET AGENT MAN	Johnny Rivers
6	10	KICKS	Paul Revere & The Raiders
7	6	THE BALLAD OF THE GREEN BERET	S/Sgt. Barry Sadler
8	14	SHAPES OF THINGS	The Yardbirds
9	4	DAYDREAM	The Lovin' Spoonful
10	5	NOWHERE MAN	The Beatles
11	9	I'M SO LONESOME I COULD CRY	B.J. Thomas & The Triumphs
12	8	WOMAN	Peter & Gordon
13	11	CALL ME	Chris Montez
14	7	THESE BOOTS ARE MADE FOR WALKIN'	Nancy Sinatra
15	17	THIS OLD HEART OF MINE	The Isley Brothers
16	15	DARLING BABY	The Elgins
17	18	LOVE MAKES THE WORLD GO 'ROUND	Deon Jackson
18	12	19TH NERVOUS BREAKDOWN	The Rolling Stones
19	20	IT'S TOO LATE	Bobby Goldsboro
20	30	SIGN OF THE TIMES	Petula Clark
21	25	TIME WON'T LET ME	The Outsiders
22	26	THE RAINS CAME	Sir Douglas Quintet
23	21	SPANISH FLEA/WHAT NOW MY LOVE	Herb Alpert
24	24	ONE TRACK MIND	The Knickerbockers
25	—	GOOD LOVIN'	The Young Rascals
26	22	SURE GONNA MISS HER	Gary Lewis & The Playboys
27	40	EIGHT MILES HIGH	The Byrds
28	28	MAGIC TOWN	The Vogues
29	—	GET READY	The Temptations
30	34	SLOOP JOHN B.	The Beach Boys
31	27	LULLABY OF LOVE	The Poppies
32	31	RHAPSODY IN THE RAIN	Lou Christie
33	35	MESSAGE TO MICHAEL	Dionne Warwick
34	—	TEENAGE FAILURE	Chad & Jeremy
35	29	634-5789	Wilson Pickett
36	36	I HEAR TRUMPETS BLOW	The Tokens
37	—	TRY TOO HARD	Dave Clark Five
38	—	LOVE MADE A FOOL OF YOU	Bobby Fuller Four
39	—	FALLING SUGAR	The Palace Guard
40	39	IF YOU LOVE ME	The Lazy Susans

COME ON OVER AND VISIT

Lou Lewin's Famous English RECORD PARADISE

★ Featuring ALL Your Favorite Recordings
★ English Imports Our Specialty

All Stones — Beatles — Yardbirds
Who — Leaves — Seeds — Them
Love — Etc.
Singles, Albums and Glossy Pictures In Stock

Phone: HO 4-8088
Address: 6507 Hollywood Blvd.

"We Dig The Most"

UNLIKE ANYTHING YOU'VE EVER SEEN!
WARNER BROS. SUPER CINERAMA PRODUCTION
BATTLE OF THE BULGE
PACIFIC'S CINERAMA DOME Theatre — NOW PLAYING!

NOW PLAYING IN THEATRES and DRIVE-INS EVERYWHERE!
DIRECT FROM ITS PREMIERE SHOWINGS.
SPECIAL ENGAGEMENT AT POPULAR PRICES. NO RESERVED SEATS.
NOW EVERYONE CAN SEE THE MOST LOVELY MOTION PICTURE OF ALL TIME!
My Fair Lady
Winner of 8 Academy Awards including Best Picture.
AUDREY HEPBURN · REX HARRISON
TECHNICOLOR® SUPER PANAVISION® 70 FROM WARNER BROS.

Join the Dave Hull International Fan Club
Send $1.00 for one year to:
DAVE HULL FAN CLUB
634 sefton, monterey park, calif.
Monthly Bulletins, Photos, The Works!

Little Women
Casual to Cotillion

OUR CAPEZIO SHOES ARE HERE!
Swing into Spring where Fashion's a FUN thing!
EASTER COAT SALE NOW IN PROGRESS
Pre-teen Sizes 6-14
Jr. Petite Sizes 3-13
Junior Sizes 3-15

Open Monday Evenings
136 SOUTH BEVERLY DRIVE
BEVERLY HILLS, CALIFORNIA

Validated Parking in Crest & Triangle Lots

KRLA ARCHIVES

HOTLINE LONDON
CYRKULAR BALL!
Tony Barrow

What do you think of THE CYRKLE and the first Columbia recording, "Red Rubber Ball?" To me it sounds as though this fresh-voiced young threesome might have a major hit on their hands.

They're managed by Nat Weiss, New York attorney and close personal friend of Brian Epstein. I first heard "Red Rubber Ball"—penned jointly by Bruce Woodley of THE SEEKERS and PAUL SIMON—a few weeks ago when Brian played me his special advance copy. In fact it was Brian who gave the group its new name.

It seems they were The Rhondells when Nat Weiss invited Brian to hear them at the Downtown Club in New York City. THE MOODY BLUES went along too and they were all equally impressed with the act.

Since this is Nat's first excursion into Artists' Management it's natural he should have sought Brian Epstein's advice on handling his potentially hot pop property. Brian suggested that The Rhondells should become THE CYRKLE. And he went along to watch them record "Red Rubber Ball" for Columbia—his first visit to an American studio session.

The CBS label—the U.K. outlet for Columbia's product—will release "Red Rubber Ball" on our side of the Atlantic at the end of April. If all goes well, there's a strong possibility of a European tour for The Cyrkle later this year.

Walkers Not Coming

The projected June tour of America for THE WALKER BROTHERS is unlikely to happen even if their chart-topping U.K. success "The Sun Ain't Gonna Shine Any More" climbs high in the U.S. best-sellers. Reason for the change of plan is a just-negotiated trip to Australia, scheduled for June, with extra concerts in the Far East on the way home. In July, The Walkers have a string of dates set in various parts of Europe.

In June another of our 1966 chart-toppers, THE SPENCER DAVIS GROUP, expect to undertake an Australian concert tour. Their U.S. visit, pencilled in for that month, will now be re-scheduled for later in the summer. Right now the Davis aggregation is having its second consecutive U.K. hit with "Somebody Help Me."

Balladeer MATT MONRO will arrive in Hollywood on Wednesday, April 20—to record his first Capitol album plus material for future singles. Producer DAVE CAVANAUGH will handle the sessions.

Matt tells me he is both nervous and excited about his huge deal with Capitol. "Of course it's a terrific new step in my career and one which any artist would be proud of," he says. "On the other hand it gives me a great deal to live up to and my first sessions in Hollywood will be the most important experience of my life."

Matt has no intention of making his home in California although he's likely to visit your part of the world for frequent extended periods not only for recording sessions but live appearances.

Work Permit Problems

A week or two ago SIMON AND GARFUNKEL should have been with us in London. I understand that their failure to arrive was caused by a refusal by our Ministry Of Labour to issue Paul Simon with a suitable work permit.

Because U.K. work permits were not forthcoming for a Swedish group, the Scandanavian authorities are threatened to refuse entry to British touring stars including groups of the calibre of THE ROLLING STONES and THE KINKS.

Don't you think this work permit bit is getting out of control? I know for a fact it is preventing many of our most talented British pop favourites undertaking tours of America. It's time all these entry restrictions were ripped away. Surely pop music is one of the few international forms of entertainment which need not be limited by political or other barriers. If exchanges of talent and a universal appreciation of top performers are to continue, the appropriate public servants of Britain, America, Sweden and anywhere else involved ought to get together and work out ways of destroying the existing work permit problems once and for all!

NEWS BRIEFS . . . Deejay TOMMY VANCE who has worked in Los Angeles, Seattle and Detroit has now left the pop pirate station Radio Caroline to join Radio Luxembourg...Sorry, but I found BRIAN WILSON'S solo disc "Caroline, No." (just issued in the U.K.) a great disappointment . . . New 5,000 dollar Marcus sports cars for WALKER BROTHERS John and Gary . . . Latest album from THE ROLLING STONES now has the programme title "Aftermath." British release is schedule for late April after The Stones finish their European concert tour . . . Tours of U.S. with JAMES BROWN and GENE PITNEY turned down by THE KINKS but they might accept another offer to appear in a package with ROY ORBISON in July . . . Rumour has it that TOM JONES plans to have nose operation when he returns home after April Hollywood visit. Tom smashed his nose playing rugby football. His next U.K. single features the movie title ballad "Promise Her Anything" . . . FREDDIE AND THE DREAMERS making album entitled "In Disneyland" . . . ANDREW OLDHAM took advertising space in all the major U.K. music paper to express his considerable personal admiration for "California Dreamin'" but the record by THE MAMA'S AND THE PAPA'S has yet to click in this country despite fair deejay play. Andy's ad said the record was "more relative to today than the general election" . . . THE ANIMALS plan to record their next single in The Bahamas which is almost as surprising as the Oh-so-secret plans for April location recording sessions by THE BEATLES!

...SIGNE, JACK, MARTY, SKIP, PAUL AND JORMA
BEAT Photo: Chuck Boyd

Jefferson Airplane Taking Off...Fast

By Carol Deck

Interviewing an airplane is kind of an absurd idea but interviewing the Jefferson Airplane, a fast rising group from San Francisco, verges on ridiculous. It's kind of like trying to talk to six John Lennon's at the same time. Getting a straight answer from any of them is totally out of the question.

Example—a simple question like, how'd you get the name Jefferson Airplane brings the following answers:

Marty Balin, 22, lead singer: "We were all working for the Jefferson Airplane Line. I was the pilot, Paul was my co-pilot, Jack was the purser and Signe was the stewardess. So when we decided to form a group we used their name."

Paul Kantner, 24, "driving lead rhythm guitar": "A dog came along and led us into this church and behind this pew was a large bag of 'Jefferson Airplane Loves You' buttons, so we figured we'd better make good use of them."

Signe Anderson, 24, second lead singer: "The Spirit of St. Louis flew over and dropped a lot of 'Jefferson Loves You' buttons."

One thing they *do* agree is that their name is Jefferson Airplane and not *The* Jefferson Airplane. They don't want to claim to be the only one—there might be another.

Ask them about long hair and they tell you about moustaches. "I had a moustache and they made me shave it off," notes Jack Casady, 21, bass guitar. "They said I couldn't be a rock and roll star with a moustache."

Ask for a description of their sound and you get: "We all play our own thing. We play our own thing together and it turns out to be one *thing*," from Skip Spence, 21, drummer.

And if you think the group's name is unusual try and remember the lead guitar player's full name —Jorma Ludwik Kaukonen Jr.

Then try asking what they like in the way of music and groups. "I really love Marcel Marceau recording," replys Paul. "They're so peaceful." (Marcel Marceau is Frances' greatest pantomine artist)

And why does Marty wear sunglasses when he's inside an already dark recording studio? "I'm one of the X-Ray men. If I take them off, you die," he whispers.

"Tell them about our friendly dog dance," reminds Paul. Okay, here it is. The Jefferson Airplane is going to throw a "friendly dog dance" and wants to invite everyone everywhere. A "friendly dog dance," by the way, is a huge bash with huge numbers of unknown groups. They want to bring all the unknown San Francisco groups down to Los Angeles and then bring all the unknown Los Angeles groups up to San Francisco —sort of an exchange program for nobodys.

At that point you feel you don't even want to know about the three foot high yellow and brown desert type flower sitting in the middle of their equipment in the studio.

This group has been very big in San Francisco, particuarly in The Matrix, and now they're taking off for wider horizons.

But never fear. Paul assures us, "We're very conservative people actually."

Sure fellows.

Hideaways' Fight Is Now On To Re-Open The Famed Cavern Club

A company, The New Cavern Ltd., is being formed to re-open the world famous, Cavern Club in Liverpool. The idea was started by the Hideaways, a local Pool group which hold the record for performing at the Cavern more than any other group in the world and for being the last group on stage before it closed.

As you know, Liverpool teens are especially close to the Cavern, the club where they first met the Beatles. They've done all sorts of things to keep the club from closing, including a giant nine hour marathon. The Hideaways' bass guitarist, John Shell told *The BEAT* all about it: "When we came off we were told that the Cavern (God rest its soul) was closing and the marathon was going on all night and as long as it could stay open with the groups playing for nothing and the staff stayed on as well.

"We went on about 10 o'clock the next morning and played till one o'clock. Meanwhile, at eleven o'clock the police and bailiffs came to close it down but were locked out for two hours. But they finally got in at one o'clock. While we were on we played lots of old Liverpool standards such as 'Roll Over Beethoven,' 'Love Me Do,' etc."

But despite their efforts the Cavern was officially closed. Now the Hideaways have come up with a bigger and what they hope will be a more successful plan. They're forming a company to which the public will be invited to take up shares in denominations of one pound ($2.80) each.

The Hideaways are appealing to everyone interested—not only those in Liverpool but people everywhere—to send in money to save the club.

"We are getting in touch with the official Receiver to ascertain the possibility of acquiring leases of the Cavern and to acquire fixtures and fittings," explained Alderman Livermore, legal adviser to the Hideaways.

Livermore added that if it is not possible to get leases etc. the money would be refunded minus a modest sum for bank charges.

If you wish to contribute to the campaign to save the Cavern you may do so by sending your donation in the form of a check or money order (not cash) to New Cavern, District Bank Ltd., 51 Dale Street, Liverpool 2, England. But please be sure to include your name and address along with your money.

KRLA ARCHIVES

BEHIND THE SCENES

With Sonny Bono

By Eden

As we promised a few issues back in *The BEAT*, in this next-to-last article in our series on record producers, we are going to speak with two of the most successful producers in town, Sonny Bono and Steve Barri.

Sonny has confined himself lately to producing only those records which he and Cher are cutting, and he explained that the most important element in record production—for him—is the "personality in the record."

He continued, "I have to find something to *make* it have a personality; it can be in the music *or* in the vocal—usually in both. You develop a sound after so long, and that basic sound is actually *you*; it's really the producer. After that, it's just a matter of *varying* the personality with each new record."

Obviously, Sonny and Cher do have a distinct personality, which is readily indentifiable, in all of their efforts. But Sonny goes much deeper into the qualities of the producer himself: "In my mind, I think there's only about four or five *good* record producers in the country; *real* record producers. It's their life, their motivation—they are *creators*. And you must be a creator, you must *live* that particular record that you're creating."

Of course, Sonny writes much of the material which he and his wife record himself. Of these songs he says, "When I write a song, and I know it's right—I'm happy. It's just a *feeling* you get within yourself."

Does he walk into the studio with a complete sound already formulated in his head? "Sometimes—not always. When I do go in with a sound in my mind, I feel much better. After it's recorded; I study it and listen to it for its hooks, and I study it more than the average person."

Sonny admits that, "It's easy fro me to keep *my sound* in a record now, because I've been using the same musicians and engineer for over a year now." But he goes on to explain, "Yes, we *do* like to have a big record and a different sound, but I don't care about starting any new trends." In this line, I asked about Cher's latest record—"Bang, Bang," —and Sonny said that he did have the entire sound in mind the night he wrote the song.

He explained that the song sounds somewhat Russian with strains of gypsy music in it to him, and admitted to having been just a little bit afraid when he had originally gone in to cut it. "The Beatles used Indian music and used it very well. They pioneered the use of foreign instruments and gave me the courage to use them on this record. Somebody's gotta do something different, and I decided that I'm not gonna back down."

As for any new trends which might be approaching the pop scene now, Sonny said, "Oh no! The only trend I see is everyone trying to be different now. Some people are different *right*, and some people are different *wrong*. But there has been a much stronger concentration on production in the last year or so . . . and I think it's great!"

Steve Barri

Steve Barri is one half of a very successful songwriting team—Sloan-Barri—and is also one of the most talented young producers in the pop field right now. With his partner, singer-composer P.F. Sloan, he has written many of the top chart hits of recent months, including "A Must To Avoid," "You, Baby," "I Found A Girl," "Secret Agent Man," and "Hold On" which will be the next single and title tune from the new movie by Herman's Hermits.

Steve explained that he considers the most difficult aspect of record production to be "picking the right material for your artists." On the other hand, he explains that the most important aspect of record production is "mostly having a good ear for the type of thing that's happening. But there are so many things which are important—it's a combination of nearly *everything*, and it all begins with the selection of the material."

I asked if there were any special techniques which he used in record production, but he shook his head, saying, "Not really, unless we're going for a certain kind of sound. We have learned a great deal from Lou Adler, though."

As far as any new trends in the music business are concerned, Steve looks for at least one new influence. "I think the Spanish influence is going to be big, and people are going to be doing vocals with a Tijuana Brass type of background."

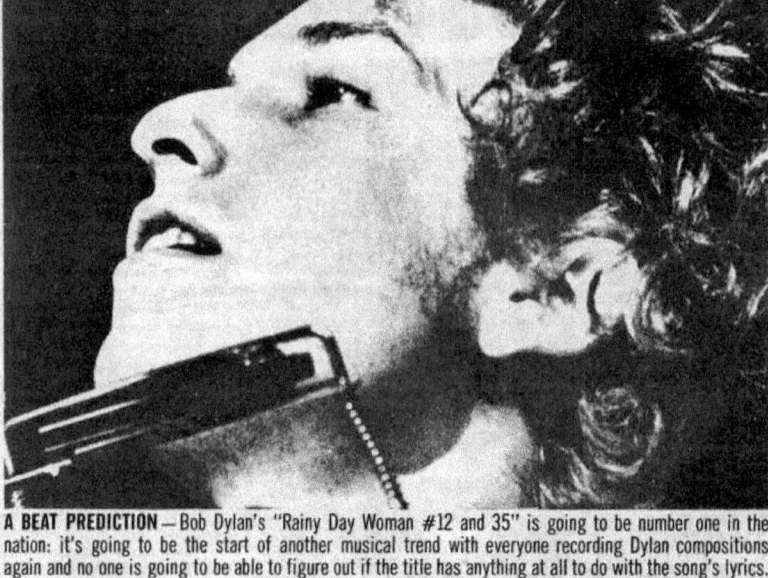

A BEAT PREDICTION—Bob Dylan's "Rainy Day Woman #12 and 35" is going to be number one in the nation; it's going to be the start of another musical trend with everyone recording Dylan compositions again and no one is going to be able to figure out if the title has anything at all to do with the song's lyrics.

Lennon's Legend

By Gil McDougall

The perpetuation of Lennon's legend has begun. The legend has begun to spread. It is being spread by the people who know John; by the people who wish they knew him; and by the people who couldn't care less. All are in awe of such an obvious abundance of talent, but it is his attitude to life and the people he meets that confounds critics and friends alike.

When a performer attains stardom he sometimes gets that well-known illness commonly known as being big-headed. John doesn't act this way, and because of this he expects the people that he meets to have regular size heads as well.

To Lennon a rude or snobbish attitude is completely unacceptable, not only in himself but in others as well. Meeting a person with an arrogant fault such as this will provoke insults from John in return.

It has been suggested many times that some promoters, and theatre managers, are actually afraid of John and the other Beatles. Afraid, that is, of the possibility of being humiliated by the boys. It is all part of the myth, but any intelligent person would never allow such thoughts to enter his head. True, John and the others have a bit of a sarcastic way with themselves, but they usually refrain from insulting anyone who hasn't provoked it.

Softy?

Aggressive, intelligent, belligerent, witty, intolerant (with idiots) and irreverent as he is, there is the possibility that Lennon is a lot softer than he likes to let on. He might even be the most vunerable Beatle of all.

Since the loss of his mother Lennon had developed a tough

Of course Lennon's legend is not completely inaccessible. Since achieving his present standing he has developed, perhaps faster than he would have normally, into a mature human being who is capable of great understanding. He has also developed musically at a fantastic rate.

Lennon simply refuses to put on any airs, and acts the same way in public as he does in private. Perhaps this kind of honesty is a little too much for some. After all, though many people surely need it, few of them actually enjoy being told "Where it's at."

Annoying

Lennon often annoys people but he never fails to impress them. A British reporter described his opinion of John: "His face has the fear-neither-God-nor-man-quality of a Renaissance painter's aristocrat." Brian Epstein maintains that John has "a controlled aggression that demands respect." To all of this Lennon would almost certainly say "they must be soft or something."

Interviewers are often shaken, and sometimes amazed by the total impression that they get of John. Like most of us he is a mass of contradictions, but unlike the majority, his talents are very bright indeed.

One of Lennon's greatest qualities is his ability to make friends. Like the time that the Beatles met Elvis Presley during their 1965 tour of the United States. John immediately broke the ice as he said in his best Peter Sellers accent: "Zis is ze way it should be. Ze small homely gathering with ze few friends and a little music." Elvis grinned and Lennon was immediately in.

John and the Beatles don't forget old friends either. They have often gone out of their way to do shows etc., when they are asked by someone who has helped them in their climb to the top.

John and Paul compose at a pretty fantastic rate, and their compositions are recorded by singers and stars from almost all spheres of popular music. While appreciating the compliment John is not always happy about some of the versions of their songs. According to John: "The reason that so many people use our numbers and add nothing to them is that they do not understand the music. Consequently they make a mess of the music."

Lennon himself enjoys running over their first compositions and trying to find some sort of progression in their music. John revealed: "Sometimes, when I am at home, I sit down and put all of our albums on the phonograph. I hardly ever manage to hear them all. I get to the stage where I'm beginning to realize that we have progressed musically and then somebody will start knocking on the door. I feel like an idiot sitting there listening to my own music."

"Coming Home"

John doesn't exactly need the money, but he is doing very nicely as a writer at this particular moment. More important, is the fact that both of his books were received very well critically. Much of his work was compared to that of author James Joyce, who in his day was something of a celebrity. At first Lennon was surprised by the comparison, but he picked up Joyce's "Finnigans Wake," and after reading it reported that "it was like coming home."

It is impossible to say that Lennon is the literary Beatle, or the married Beatle because John simply does not fit into a neat slot like that. John and the other Beatles are different things to different people. The important thing is, however, that Lennon knows exactly what he is and exactly what he wants out of life. He simply wants to enjoy it. And the best of British luck, mate!

KRLA ARCHIVES

Exclusive: BEAT Attends

By Eden

ED. NOTE: Once again The BEAT has captured an exclusive story, as we spent three days with The Stones on their recent visit to Hollywood. The Stones were in town for a week-long recording session which was conducted behind closed doors; closed to just about everyone except The BEAT! When our reporters, accompanied by our photographer, asked permission to attend the session and take pictures of the boys, Brian Jones inquired, "Are you with The BEAT?" When they replied that they were, Brian nodded and agreed, "It's okay then." So come with us now as The BEAT takes you behind closed doors—exclusively—and spend three days with the Stones.

STONES AT RCA! The news spread like wild fire throughout Hollywood recently, causing hundreds of teenage fans to rush out in search of their long-haired idols. While the fans were combing the streets in search of The Stones, the Stones were busily engaged in recording 12 tracks for the sound track album for their upcoming movie, "Back, Behind, and In Front." It required a week of intensive work—recording sessions of 17 and 18 hours, stretching into the wee small hours of the morning.

At RCA, large groups of fans remained camped outside the glass doors—in the company of several armed guards who remained on duty around the clock—throughout the week, while inside—the lobby outside the Stones' studio remained fairly calm. The relative quiet was broken only when one or more of the Stones emerged briefly and walked into the lobby.

Mick came out once to walk across the room and peek in on another recording session which was going on. Later, Charlie came out to make a phone call and then he sat down in a corner and chatted quietly with a friend, arranger-composer Jack Nitzche.

Quiet Fatigue

All of the Stones were tired from the intensive work, but they said very little of their fatigue. Only once, when The BEAT mentioned to Charlie that he looked somewhat exhausted, he just looked up and nodded: "Yes, I am."

Bill Wyman slipped out briefly to one of the famous night club-discotheques on the Sunset Strip in Hollywood, and when he returned, he looked much more like a Bill Wyman Doll, than like Bill Wyman! In person, he is much shorter than he appears on the screen—although he is just as quiet and pensive in person.

Very few people were allowed to enter the Stones session—it was strictly a closed affair. One of the few people who was able to gain admittance to the Stones' studio was a young man who brought over a variety of guitar strings which the Stones had requested.

The Stones use a large number of instruments on this new album, many of which were rather unusual. Exclusively in The BEAT, we have a partial list of some of the instruments which you will be hearing. Among them, listen for a dulcimer, a sitar—there will be a heavy Indian accent on this album; seems to be the thing to do these days, some vibes, piano, an organ, a harpsichord, a fuzz organ, and the oddest-looking collection of guitars ever seen. The boys seem to have been very definitely affected by the current Indian trend in music, inspired by the work of Ravi Shankar and encouraged by the great songs of the Beatles.

One constant interruption of the almost-quiet of the lobby was the never-ending stream of people bearing packages of food for the hard-working Stones. Cans and cans of soft drinks found their way into the studio. Also, Mick was to be found in the almost constant companionship of some very strong-smelling pizzas which he ate with great relish. The rest of the Stones seemed content to stick with the old American standby—the hamburger.

Have A Coke

Charlie decided to get creative, and invited Jack Nitzche to join him for a coke—in the restaurant near the corner of Sunset and Vine!!

Probably the funniest sight of the year was seeing Charlie Watts sitting right next to a huge glass window, enjoying his coke and chatting quietly with his friend, as groups of nearly hysterical fans searched frantically for him and his four companions right down the street.

Tuesday had been the second day of recording for the Stones, and although it had been hectic—

...BILL WYMAN — A LIFE SIZE DOLL?

...KEITH RICHARDS AND MICK JAGGER ARRIVE FOR A LATE SESSION WITH CHARLIE WATTS CLOSE BEHIND.

KRLA ARCHIVES

Closed Stones' Session

it was nothing compared to the days which followed.

On Wednesday evening, the Stones were still hard at work in their recording studio, as their many fans were hard at work trying to get into that studio just outside the door.

One of those fans was a very excitable young lady, who, in her frustration at being unable to catch a glimpse of her favorite Stone, Mick, kicked angrily at the metal edging at the bottom of the huge glass doors outside. But she missed, and wound up putting her foot right *through* the heavy glass barrier instead!

No Pain

Fortunately, her foot was not seriously injured, although the door was thoroughly destroyed. Within moments, Mick was in the lobby, comforting the girl and telling the guards that he would be glad to accept all financial responsibility for the accident. Somehow that girl didn't seem to be feeling too much pain just then. The reason *could* have been her extreme euphoria at finding herself suddenly *Jaggered!*

Friday evening was the next to last day of recording for the Stones, and they all seemed thoroughly exhausted. Charlie was finished quite early and wanted very much to go back to his hotel. He asked the chauffer if he would drive him, but unfortunately—the limousine was located just outside the door... in plain reach of all the fans. Also, the chauffer had to leave shortly to retrieve Brian—whom he had delivered to one of the popular jazz clubs in town earlier that evening.

Finally, one of the guards on duty volunteered to rescue Charlie and he delivered him safely to his hotel. In the meantime, Brian was returned by the chauffer, in one of the most unusual outfits ever seen —even in *Hollywood!!!* It consisted of a polka-dotted western shirt, a white leather vest, tight western jeans, black silk kerchief —knotted western-style—a wide leather belt... and a green felt bowler-style cowboy hat! His attire was completed by the golden-tinted "shades" he sported underneath his "leprachaun hat."

Another outstanding dresser that evening was one Mr. Michael Philip Jagger, who emerged only twice—dressed entirely in the most dazzling white outfit ever. He was so bright, that it almost hurt to look at him! He came out of the studio once to get a cup of coffee, and the other time to stand in the middle of the lobby area... reading *The BEAT!* But even that wasn't very easy; poor Mick was so exhausted after a week of recording almost around the clock, that he could barely focus his eyes on the print!

Glaring Mick

Keith, too, was dressed appropriately for the occasion, in an outfit which featured some super-sized sunglasses. Probably to keep out the extreme glare of Mick's outfit!

Singer-guitarist Glen Campbell came over to the studio to say hello to the Stones, and chatted briefly with Keith in the lobby. Just before he left he asked if the Stones planned on recording all night, to which Keith cheerfully chirped, "Yep!" and promptly disappeared into the studio once again.

He was probably the *only* cheerful Stone in the studio at that point—the rest were just too tired to be overly happy about anything. With the exception of one track, they became extremely ecstatic and proclaimed themselves to be thoroughly "gassed" over the cut.

9 A.M. Finish

At the end of the long week of recording—a week which found its finish at 9:00 *Saturday morning!*—the Stones raced back to their hotel just long enough to wash and hastily pack their belongings. Then they were rushed to the airport for a flight directly to London—where they would immediately begin work on their picture, now in the final stages of production.

A Stones' work is never done, but they love it and put so much of their time and energy into their work only because they are perfectionists and really care about the finished product which they eventually present to the public.

We've taken you behind the scenes at the Stones' recording session now and given you a little idea of all that went on for that one, short hectic week. Soon enough you will be able to hear the finished results for yourselves, but if you were to ask the members of *The BEAT* staff who were there whether or not this album will be great—about all we could do would be to quote Keith Richard, in his immortal statement: "Yep!!"

Exclusive BEAT Photos: Chuck Boyd

... BRIAN JONES — STICK 'EM UP PARTNER!

... CHARLIE WATTS — A COKE AT THE CORNER.

... SOME OF THE FANS DISCOVERED THE STONE'S SESSIONS AND CAMPED OUTSIDE.

KRLA ARCHIVES

In Memory of

Jim Washburne

EARN LEARN and TRAVEL IN EUROPE

Grand Duchy of Luxembourg — Every student in America can get a summer job in Europe and a travel grant by applying directly to the European headquarters of the American Student Information Service in Luxembourg. Jobs are much the same as student summer work in the U.S. with employers offering work periods ranging from three weeks to permanent employment.

Lifeguarding, office work, resort-hotel jobs, factory, construction camp counseling and farm work are only a few categories to be found among the 15,000 jobs ASIS still has on file. An interesting summer pastime not found in America is tutoring. Numerous well-to-do European families are inviting American college students to spend the summer with them and teach their children English.

Wages range to $400 a month, and in most cases neither previous experience nor knowledge of a foreign language is required. ASIS, in its ninth year of operation, will place more American students in summer jobs in Europe this summer than ever before.

Students interested in working in Europe next summer may write directly to Dept. VII, ASIS, 22 Ave. de la Liberté, Luxembourg, enclosing $2 for the ASIS 36 page booklet which contains all jobs, wages, working conditions, etc., job and travel grant applications, and to cover the cost of handling and overseas air mail postage.

AMERICAN STUDENT INFORMATION SERVICE

A PRIVATE, NON-PROFIT, NON-POLITICAL, NON-SECTARIAN, GOVERNMENT APPROVED ORGANIZATION FOUNDED IN 1958

HEADQUARTERS: 22 AVENUE DE LA LIBERTÉ, LUXEMBOURG CITY, GRAND DUCHY OF LUXEMBOURG

CABLE: ASISLUX . TELEPHONES: 45425, 45426 · BANK: KREDIETBANK

EDUCATION THROUGH PRACTICAL APPLICATION

KRLA ARCHIVES

The BEAT Goes To The Movies

Dr. Zhivago

JULIE CHRISTIE, Omar Sharif share tender moment in "Dr. Zhivago."

By Lyle W. Nash

Behind the conflict in "Doctor Zhivago" is the greatest living drama of the 20th century—the Russian Revolution. The flashing pageantry of 150 million people fighting and dying for human dignity offers a background almost greater than the Civil War tableau of "Gone With The Wind."

"Doctor Zhivago" spans the period from about 1900 to 1935 when violence and death was the constant companion of Czarist Russia. The dramatic clash has the harsh cruel state seeking to crush the individual. How the force of the individual triumphs makes for dynamic cinema entertainment.

Julie Christie, as a pawn of life's endless tragedies, is superb. This MGM production will establish her as a world-wide motion picture star. Fans of another generation will recall that GWTW accomplished the same result for an English actress—Vivian Leigh.

Omar Shaif, as the doctor and poet, offers a magnificent performance. Zhivago is the focal point of the production: through his eyes unfolds the stark story of 197 minutes. He observes the downfall of the decaying Romanov Russia with a doctor's compassion for people and a poets sympathy. The magnetic charm of Sharif projects with devastating appeal. The Egyptian born actor has the most appealing brown eyes in the world of motion pictures. Their mysterious power work overtime in "Doctor Zhivago."

It requires a film of great magnitude to enable an in-experienced actress to play a role with conviction. Newcomer Geraldine Chaplin is most winsome in her part. There is a striking resemblance to her famed father.

The entire cast is worthy of mention but Alex Guinness, Tom Courtenay, Rod Steiger, Ralph Richardson and Rita Tushingham give outstanding performances in demanding roles.

The haunting, desolate and cold vastness of Russia is captured with stunning sharpness in the magnificent color photography. The snow-covered Ural mountains, the lonely lakes, the snow drenched forests and the golden wheat fields of mother Russia flow across the screen with radiant and wondrous beauty.

Director David Lean, the creator of "Bridge on the River Kwai," and "Lawrence of Arabia," has another Oscar contender in "Doctor Zhivago." His excellent direction might well reward him with his third Oscar in nine years at the Academy Awards this month.

Enchanting is the best word to describe the musical score of Maurice Jarre. The repeated lyrical theme will linger long after you've seen the film.

Unless your motion picture needs are no deeper than kiddie cartoons or monster-bikini-beach quickies, "Doctor Zhivago" should be one of the most memorable films you'll see in this decade.

The Group

THE GROUP'S Lakey (Candice Bergen), right, talks with Baroness friend.

By Carol Deck

Anyone who read Mary McCarthy's book "The Group" and enjoyed it should definitely see the movie.

The movie sticks surprisingly close to the book, adding very little, and leaving out only what can't be put on the screen.

What really makes the movie is the great job of casting. Good performances are given by all eight members of The Group, a clique of girls from the class of '33 of an unidentified swank eastern school (Vassar in the book.)

Joanna Pettet plays the bride Kay who dominates most of the movie, which begins with her marriage and ends with her funeral.

As the literary snob, Libby, Jessica Walter comes through as a real cat. Joan Hackett's sensitive portrayal of the staid Bostonian Dottie never wavers.

The other members, Shirley Knight as Polly, Candice Bergen as Lakey, Kathleen Widdoes as Helena, and Mary Robin Redd as good ole Pokey, all bring very much to life Mary McCarthy's eight little kittens who took their diplomas and went out into the cold cruel world to *really* begin to learn things.

In order to pull together the eight separate yet connected dramas, Director Sidney Lumet has created a ticker tape type chatty alumni news letter which ticks across the bottom of the screen like foreign subtitles but does serve to keep things running.

The only fault with the movie seems to be that it runs a little long and at first it's hard to adjust to the 1930's costumes when the action seems so up to date.

It's hard to imagine a movie with eight practically even female leads that doesn't degenerate to a mass attempt to upstage everyone else. But these girls work together to produce a memorable movie from one of last years' best selling novels.

KRLA ARCHIVES

Dave Hull's HULLABALOO

ROCK & ROLL SHOWPLACE OF THE WORLD

presents

FANTASTIC EASTER WEEK EXTRAVAGANZA

APRIL 6-10
12 - 2 - 4 - 6 P.M.

THE MAMA'S & PAPA'S

plus

M.F.Q. & P.F. SLOANE

APRIL 6-10
8 - 10 - 12 P.M.

THEM
(SINGING "GLORIA")
"BABY PLEASE DON'T GO"
"MYSTIC EYES"
& ALL OF THEIR GREAT HITS)

JOEY PAIGE *plus* THE PALACE GUARD

★ **ATTENTION BEAT READERS**

GIANT DANCE CONTEST DAILY
REGISTER NOW — ANY AGE — PRIZES — CELEBRITY JUDGES

SPECIAL MIDNIGHT SHOW NIGHTLY

COMING MAY 1
TWO SHOWS ONLY — 2 AND 4 P.M.

Peter & Gordon

MAKE RESERVATIONS — HO. 6-8281

KRLA ARCHIVES

America's Largest Teen NEWSpaper

KRLA Edition BEAT
APRIL 23, 1966

15¢

KRLA BEAT

Volume 2, Number 6 — April 23, 1966

Vice President Latest To Enter The 'Wondrous World' Of Sonny & Cher

The world of Sonny and Cher is truly becoming more "wondrous."

The latest tidbit involving the darling duo is a special government performance in which they will "co-star" with Vice President Hubert Humphrey.

At the request of the Office of Economic Opportunity in Washington, Sonny and Cher will compose and record a song urging students not to drop out of school. It will be distributed with a special message from the Vice President.

Filming continues on their first movie, "Good Times," after a brief halt caused when Sonny sprained his back during shooting at Africa, U.S.A. It occurred during a scene in which he hoisted actor Hank Worden and did several rope-swinging drops.

Aside from the obvious appeal of Sonny and Cher starring in a full-length film—particularly one in which they cavort through the jungle with all sorts of wild animals—the Steve Brody Motion Pictures International production will offer an added treat.

When not riding elephants they'll spend part of the time driving two of the most glamorous cars in the world—matching custom cars designed especially for them by the fabulous George Barris.

Sonny and Cher fans are eagerly awaiting release of the soundtrack album from the movie. If it goes anything like their other records it will be another smash.

Their two latest albums, "The Wondrous World of Sonny and Cher," and "The Sonny Side of Cher," are threatening new sales records throughout the country. And their last single, Cher's "Bang, Bang," was one of their biggest yet.

And as their popularity continues mounting to even greater heights, the once-untalkative Cher is becoming noted as much for her wit as for her vocal talents.

The most recent example occurred at a West Coast concert in which they faced the usual frantic rush from screaming fans. Turning toward a shrieking girl trying to push through policemen guarding the stage, Cher announced with a twinkle:

"If you like us that much, enough to jump on the stage, please don't do it—it scares me to death." And she added, in her relaxed drawl, "If you frighten me, I'm goin' home."

It brought a laugh from the audience, but the rush continued.

Stars Fall In England
Orbison and Walkers Injured While Touring

By Tony Barrow

The current ROY ORBISON/WALKER BROTHERS U.K. concert tour, playing nearly 70 shows in more than 30 cities throughout the country and finishing in the first week of May, was hit by a shoal of misfortunes in its opening week.

Orbison was rushed to hospital with a fractured foot after accepting an invitation from the winners of a motor cycle scramble to ride around the course at Hawkstone Park circuit in a special lap of honour. On a borrowed bike, Orbison misjudged a particularly tricky corner and rode into a sandpit.

The smashed foot-bone has forced the star to perform with his leg heavily covered in plaster and, at the last count, he was appearing on stage seated on a stool for the whole of his act. Despite the pain and inconvenience — he's using crutches and sticks to help him walk around off stage — it is to Orbison's considerable credit that he refused to miss a single sell-out concert. Apparently exaggerated reports of the bike crash reached his wife, Claudette, who flew into London and joined up with Roy at his show in Chester, near Liverpool.

Walkers Out, Too

The Walker Brothers were out of the show after the Chester performances. A mob of over-enthusiastic Walker fans rushed the three boys at their Chester hotel and John had to be treated for head injuries involving a concussion. The same day Walker Scott, under doctor's orders with a severe attack of flu, was sent to bed and forbidden to travel from Chester to the next venue, Wigan.

Meanwhile, as if these bill-top problems were not enough, supporting songstress with the package, diminutive Scottish girl LULU was off the tour for three days with laryngitis. She stayed in London and rejoined the tour in Scotland. Newcomer PERPETUAL LANGLEY, a youthful but promising Belfast girl, deputised for Lulu on the three dates.

Stone News

THE ROLLING STONES made a fantastic impact upon European pop fans during their lightning concert tour. In Paris CHARLIE WATTS was suffering from some sort of blood poisoning but he went on as scheduled at the Olympia, ignoring doctor's advice to rest in bed. On the credit side in Paris there was a wildly successful post-performance party at the plushy George V Hotel with BRIGITTE BARDOT, MARIANNE FAITHFUL and FRANCOISE HARDY amongst the starry array of guests.

Help Save 'Them'

Is Them, or ain't Them?

That's the question the U.S. Government is asking—while trying to untangle the grammatical problems—and it appears they're looking to YOU for the answer.

Before getting any deeper involved let's explain that THEM is the Irish singing group which has recorded a string of worldwide hits. They've requested permission to enter the U.S. and perform here, but have been denied entry by the U.S. immigration authorities.

Immigration officials say they don't think Them is a big group in this country or that the fans really want to see them. Although uncertain grammatically, they state positively, "Them are (is?) not artists of distinguished merit and ability."

So far the immigration authorities have been shown favorable statements from two U.S. Senators and several recording companies. And they've been shown commitments for more than $100,000 in bookings scheduled for Them in this country.

But in addition to this they demand actual material evidence that Them is (are?) popular over here. That's where you come in.

The BEAT has been contacted by Them's American managers, Buddy Resnick and Larry Goldblatt, on behalf of their British manager, Philip Solomon, to enlist its readers in the fight to get Them into the country.

They asked our help and we're asking yours. You are the only ones who can save Them. The authorities will listen to you, because you are the ones who determine an artist's true popularity.

Remember Them are the ones who brought you "Gloria," "Baby Please Don't Go," "Here Comes the Night" and "Mystic Eyes." They also have a new single titled "Call My Name" which they hope to come and perform for you live.

Them is also the only big foreign group to ever have a number of smash hits over here without coming over in person. This is to

(Turn to Page 11)

Americans Again Leading British Record Charts

LONDON — American record artists are sweeping the British charts again! A neat 50 per cent of the British hit parade is owned by American singers, half of which are new names to English record buyers.

What accounts for this surge of American popularity? Naturally, you can't credit it to one reason alone, but a big piece of the chart pie can be had by practically any American artist who stops off in England to make personal appearances and television dates.

Although the plugging of discs by pirate radio stations is all important in making a hit record, it is still television which carries the most weight with the record buyers and is instrumental in breaking a record.

Herb Alpert made a lightning three day visit to England for one concert and some TV appearances. The man's talented, sure, and his records were selling all right before. But now he is one of the most popular entertainers in England.

Bob Lind, just returned from his first trip to Britain, succeeded in sending his "Ellusive Butterfly" flying up the charts leaving the local version by Val Doonican far behind.

And so it goes. The American artists come, the British teens see and another hit record is born. Don't fret if you haven't the money to fly to England, though, because Britain's top pop show, "Top Of The Pops," is getting all the film clips they can to use with records played on the show.

Inside the BEAT
Hair — Long and Short Of It	4
A Visit with The Beau Brummels	6-7
For Girls Only	10
Spring Fashions	11
Batman	12-13

The BEAT is published weekly by BEAT Publications, Inc., editorial and advertising offices at 6290 Sunset Blvd., Suite 504, Hollywood, California 90028. U.S. bureaus in Hollywood, San Francisco, New York, Chicago and Nashville, overseas correspondents in London, Liverpool and Manchester, England. Sale price, 15 cents. Subscription price, U.S. and possessions, $5 per year; Canada and foreign rates, $9 per year. Second class postage prepaid at Los Angeles, California.

KRLA ARCHIVES

Yeah, Well Young Rascals...
Some More Help Please

By Tammy Hitchcock

Yeah, well guess who I've managed to drag onto our "Yeah, Well Hot Seat" this week? Give up?

All right I'll stop beating around the bush and tell you ('course, if you were smart enough to look at the picture you already know, but then if you were *that* smart you probably wouldn't be reading this "thing.") The Young Rascals are currently smoldering on the "Hot Seat." And rascals that they are it's taken me *three* weeks to get all four of them to sit still up there!

I have to admit that the Rascals (despite their tendency to be late) are *BEAT* favorites. When they were in town they kept dropping by to visit us. We won't long forget the day that we were swamped (literally and if you've ever been to our office you *know* we ain't kiddin'!) with work (it was Friday – deadline day – the day *everyone* insists on coming up to visit.) By the way, if you made it through that mess of a sentence (at least, I think it was a sentence!) you'll be glad to know that you'll have absolutely no trouble getting through the rest of this "article." I hope.

Cowboys

Anyway, there we were working, or pretending to work, depending on which staff member you're thinking of, when who should stride serenely (?) through our door but Eddie and Gene – wearing 20 gallon cowboy hats – I swear.

Yeah, well they immediately saw our state of business (not to mention mind) and so they gallantly offered to help. And being somewhat lazy we *never* refuse an offer to help – even if it means just making some coffee. But I guess we should have this time – we'll learn yet!

Gene and Eddie poured themselves some coffee, lit some cigarettes, sat their hats on Louise's head and then proceeded to "help" by spilling their coffee on our dummy sheets, practically setting fire to our carefully laid out pictures, knocking over chairs and in general just being one great, big, wonderful help!

Yeah, well they meant well – I *think*. Actually, things are a lot quieter, less exciting and not nearly so funny now that the Rascals have gone back to New York. When they were around you just never knew what was going to happen next and practically everything that could did.

Susie, our receptionist, is really having a difficult time trying to get used to answering the phones without Eddie around. You see, he would sneak into the office behind her back, get on one of our phones (well out of her hearing) and dial our number. Poor Susie would pick up the phone and Eddie would get her so flustered that she didn't even know which end was up – never mind which end was down!

...THE YOUNG RASCALS (l. to r. Felix, Gene, Dino and Eddie.)

Yeah, well the first time he pulled that trick was really the best. She answered the phone and he said, "Hi. This is Eddie of the Young Rascals. We're sorry we're late and we'll be right up."

Susie said okay and hung up the phone. Then it hit her. The Young Rascals were already here, weren't they? And if they *were* how could he call her and why would he say they'd be right up? And if it wasn't the Rascals here being interviewed then *who was it?* And dare she ask?

Naturally, she daren't! After all, one just can't come in and ask one of the top groups around who they were. So, she sat there with her mind all messed up until Eddie walked out to her desk and said, "Hi, I'm Eddie. Are you Susie?"

Very reluctantly she admitted that she was indeed Susie and Eddie said: "Good, then you're the one who I'm supposed to ask to show me where I can get a drink of water." Pointed in the right direction, Eddie disappeared through the door without another word.

Ignorant

Yeah, well Susie was really confused then so she came flying back to demand that we tell her what was going on. Was everybody crazy – or was she the only one? The rest of the Rascals and the entire staff pleaded total ignorance to the whole thing and suggested that perhaps Susie should get more rest so that she wouldn't go off imagining things like Young Rascals calling to say that they'd be right up when they were already up and had been for the last hour.

So, you see, things really are dull now but we're all glad to see that "Good Lovin'" is doing so well. We knew that it would be an altogether different sounding record than "I Ain't Gonna Eat Out My Heart Anymore." Because they told us so.

Cheap

"If you put out a second record which sounds exactly like the first why should the kids buy it?" asked Gene. Yeah, well I wouldn't know, Gene – I didn't even buy the first one! It's not that I'm cheap (really I am) but we had a copy of "I Ain't Gonna Eat Out My Heart Anymore" (you'll excuse me – I love to write the whole title; it has to be the wildest one ever!) right here in the office so *I* claimed it.

However, I made the slight mistake of leaving it here overnight and somebody made off with it. I like to pretend that's what happened – actually I put it in my purse and lost it forever. So, instead of doing the logical thing and merely going out and buying another copy I asked everyone who came in (even if they'd never been here before – and if so they're lucky) if they had seen a record with a red label on it and a hole in the middle.

(Turn to Page 10)

On the BEAT

By Louise Criscione

Sam The Sham is leaving the Pharaohs! *The BEAT* learned of the split exclusively, it comes from the group's publicity office and, unfortunately, it is true. Parting was said to have been friendly. No reasons were given for the break and Sam has not revealed if he plans to form another group or go solo or what.

Sam's family never did want him to go into music – they wanted him to be a lawyer. In fact, Sam's brother even offered to pay his way through law school but Sam would not have it. He told *The BEAT* that his main ambition was to sing in the Met – will he?

Tide Not Water

With "19th Nervous Breakdown" currently topping the nation's charts, the Rolling Stones have come out with an album titled, "Big Hits (High Tide And Green Grass)," which features all of their smash singles and as a special bonus contains a flyer full of Stone photos.

This is not the album which the Stones (or rather Andy Oldham) have been bickering with their record company over. You remember, that's the one they wanted dubbed, "Could You Walk On The Water?" The record company nixed the idea so it's still up in the air at the moment with neither side budging.

...SAM THE SHAM

Herman will be billed in all of his movies as Peter Blair Noone. Herman, or Peter if you wish, says: "I'll have two separate names as I'll still be Herman for pop purposes." Fair enough.

WHERE THEY ARE: Dick Clark is presenting Herman and the Animals at L.A.'s Sports Arena on July 3 . . . Herman is due in Hollywood April 16 . . . Mitch Ryder to New York for Murray the K show . . . Since James Brown's appearance at Madison Square Garden was such a smash (he is the only single artist to ever sell-out there), promoter Sid Bernstein is scheduling a similar show for his top group, the Young Rascals, at the Garden sometime in September. Meanwhile, "Good Lovin'" continues climbing up the nation's charts looking very much like it will make it to number one . . . Animals at Fordham on April 15, Georgetown on April 22 . . .

Spoonful To England

The Lovin' Spoonful are set to visit England during April for TV, concerts and club dates and then they tour Ireland beginning April 23. Their newest album is a gas, pick it up if you haven't already.

Speaking of too much albums, have you heard "The Sonny Side Of Cher" yet? It's a fantastic LP in which Cher sings two Bob Lind compositions, "Elusive Butterfly" and "Come To Your Window." Cover has a wild shot of Cher and the back photography may look familiar to you as it's the picture which appeared on our cover on the January 29 issue of *The BEAT*!

Since the Stones overtook the Beatles in the national charts reporters have been plaguing them with questions concerning who is more popular Stateside – Stones or Beatles. To which Brian Jones answers: "You understand that the Beatles are a phenomenon. We've probably overtaken their record in the charts because we're doing more personal exposure at the moment.

"You can't be as big as the Beatles until you've done something like Shea Stadium and I doubt whether even they could do that so successfully again."

QUICK ONES: Marianne Faithfull took a screen test for a role in the Liz Taylor – Richard Burton movie, "Taming Of The Shrew" but lost out . . . Peter & Gordon not at all happy over Paul's announcement that he wrote "Woman." Fans are blaming P&G for keeping the whole thing a secret so as not to get shoved further into the Lennon-McCartney bag . . . Bob Lind has "a lot of respect" for the Yardbirds. It works the other way too as Keith Relf has chosen a Lind song, "Mr. Zero," for his first solo.

...PAUL McCARTNEY

QUESTION OF THE WEEK: Are the Beatles or are they not flying Stateside in the very near future to record their next album and possibly their next single?

KRLA ARCHIVES

Dionne Has A Smash With 'Message' Song

A little over two years ago the name Dionne Warwick was virtually unknown to the public. Then she recorded "Don't Make Me Over" and everything changed with Dionne becoming an internationally recognized and extremely gifted artist.

Dionne has studied music since the age of six which is natural since she comes from a family of Gospel singers. As a young girl she did a great deal of singing in choirs for different organizations. Dionne went to the Hart College of Music of the University of Hartford where, in time, she became an accomplished singer and pianist.

Dionne's next step forward took her to the recording studios in New York where she sang in the background chorus on numerous recording sessions. It was there that her unique song styling attracted two of the top songwriters and record producers, Burt Bacharach and Hal David. Bacharach and David thought so much of the talented Dionne that they brought her to Scepter Records which in turn lead to "Don't Make Me Over."

Second Smash

Dionne's next disc, "Anyone Who Had A Heart," was one of the most successful ballads in many years and it established Dionne as an entertainer of great magnitude. Such stars as Marlene Dietrich and Petula Clark have included "Anyone Who Had A Heart" in their repertoires and, as a matter of fact, Miss Dietrich was so impressed with Dionne's recording that she personally introduced her at the Olympia Theater in Paris where Dionne received fantastic critical acclaim.

Next came "Walk On By" which became a top five record throughout the entire world. Dionne returned triumphantly to France in April as the star of the 1964 Cannes Television and Film Festival which was shown throughout the continent.

In May Dionne appeared on all of the major television shows in England where her recording of "Walk On By" reached the select top ten in an era of chart domination by such groups as the Beatles, Stones, Searchers, etc.

August of 1964 found Dionne on a four month personal appearance tour of Europe. It was an extensive tour which covered every major country this side of the Iron Curtain and which included a return to the Olympia Theater in Paris as co-star of the show and also a guest appearance on the world famous "Sunday At The Palladium" TV show in London.

Double Market

And so Dionne's career has gone—onward and certainly upward. Her latest release, "Message To Michael," promises to be as big if not bigger than her previous smash singles. With her talent and originality there is no way Dionne can miss. If she chooses to stay in the teenage market, she has it made as her appearances on "Hullabaloo" can attest to her popularity with teens. She has guested on the show three times this year and each appearance has been followed by a tremendous volume of mail.

But if Dionne decides to hit the adult market she will face no obstacle there either. Dionne has played the top clubs all over the world and has yet to bomb at any

Joe Tex: Successful Singer Texas-Style

Joe Tex started his career on a gamble with a flourish when he left Texas, after graduating from high school, to try for an audition and a spot on the Arthur Godfrey TV show in New York. He was successful in making the show and won wide plaudits. His next stop in the big city was the amateur night at the Apollo Theatre in Harlem. He was the winner for four weeks in a row and was signed on the spot to a recording contract with King Records. His first effort with King, "Come In This House," and on flip side, "Baby You Upset My Home" were instantenous hits and small wonder, with his talents and the recording genius of Henry Glover.

Since then, Joe has appeared in innumerable theatres and night clubs throughout the country. He is particularly proud of the fact that he has been invited to play return engagements in every place he worked. Joe is also an accomplished song writer. In addition to writing songs for himself, Joe has penned tunes for James Brown, Jerry Butler, Ernie-K-Doe, and others. James Brown's 1961 hit, "Baby You're Right,"

is one of Joes' compositions. Joe has written hundreds of songs and finds that his best moments of inspiration come between two and three o'clock in the morning after completing a hard night's work.

If anyone hadn't already been aware of Joe Tex's immense talents, then certainly his recording of "Hold On To What You Got" straightened out the situation pretty well. When this single started getting air play on the radio stations, it literally caused a traffic jam in many record stores. Record buyers had to stand in long lines to buy the disc. The reaction to his follow-up record entitled "You Got What It Takes" seems to duplicate the response to "Hold On To What You Got." And this is not all. Joe's latest release, "A Woman Can Change A Man," is also a nation-wide smash. Between recording sessions and night club work, Joe Tex found time to record a best selling album entitled "Hold What You've Got."

Joe Tex isn't just another singer, but is endowed with a flare and flavor which gives him a feeling that generates and stimulates an audience to no extent.

The Supreme Supremes

What's in a name? Success, that's what.

Three young girls from Detroit call themselves the Supremes and that's exactly what they are, supreme.

They stand at the top of their field. They are the top female vocal group in the United States, probably in the world. No one even comes near to the record these girls have set.

They started in the early sixties with four singles that were good, but not great. They were "I Want A Guy," "Buttered Popcorn," "Breathtaking Guy" and "Lovelight In His Eyes."

But then it happened. Their fifth single, "Where Did Our Love Go," smashed straight to the number one position in the nation.

They didn't stop there. They followed that with five more consecutive number ones nationwide – "Baby Love," "Come See About Me," "Stop! In The Name Of Love," "Back In My Arms Again," and "I Hear A Symphony."

In doing so, they became the only American group, male or female, to ever have six consecutive number one records in the nation. The only other group of any kind that has ever topped that record is The Beatles.

They've put out seven albums, all of them top sellers, including "A Little Bit of Liverpool" and "We Remember Sam Cooke." One of their albums, "Where Did Our Love Go," stayed in the top 40 best sellers in the country for over a year, a feat comparable to a human being living to be well over 100.

And the honors they've stacked up along the way are unbelievable for anybody short of Frank Sinatra.

They were designated as the official United States Representatives at Holland's Annual Popular Song Festival, recently held in Amsterdam.

But the one honor they recall the most occurred during the eight day Gemini Five Flight of Astronauts Charles Conrad Jr. and L. Gordon Cooper. Among the songs played to the Astronauts while they were orbiting the earth was "Where Did Our Love Go."

Among The Supremes credits are a highly successful tour of Europe and England, a record breaking engagement at New York's famed Copacabana, a concert at New York's Lincoln Center and two movies, "Dr. Goldfoot and the Bikini Machine" and "Beach Party."

Their television credits include "Shindig," "Hullabaloo," "Hollywood Palace," and the Ed Sullivan, Red Skelton and Dean Martin Shows.

Even more amazing than the mere list of accomplishments of this group is the amount of pure class they've carried with them all the way to the top.

You never hear any slander, scandal or dirt about Diana Ross, Mary Wilson or Florence Ballard.

These girls are the epitome of class, personality, talent and originality.

They have the kind of healthy image that America likes to send abroad. You always know that no matter where they are appearing they will be great and they will bring honor not only to themselves but to their race, their country and the entire entertainment industry.

Greene And Stone Bag The Toggs

Sonny and Cher's former managers, Charlie Greene and Brian Stone, have discovered a new British vocal group, the Toggs, and have set a recording session for them at the Pye Studios in London.

Actually, Larry Page, the London head of Greene-Stone Productions, found the Toggs and immediately brought them to the attention of Charlie and Brian.

Their record will be produced by Greene and Stone who will then bring the Toggs' master back to the U.S. where the "new sound" will be heavily promoted and debuted at a New York press conference. Even Sonny and Cher don't go that far with a new release!

KRLA ARCHIVES

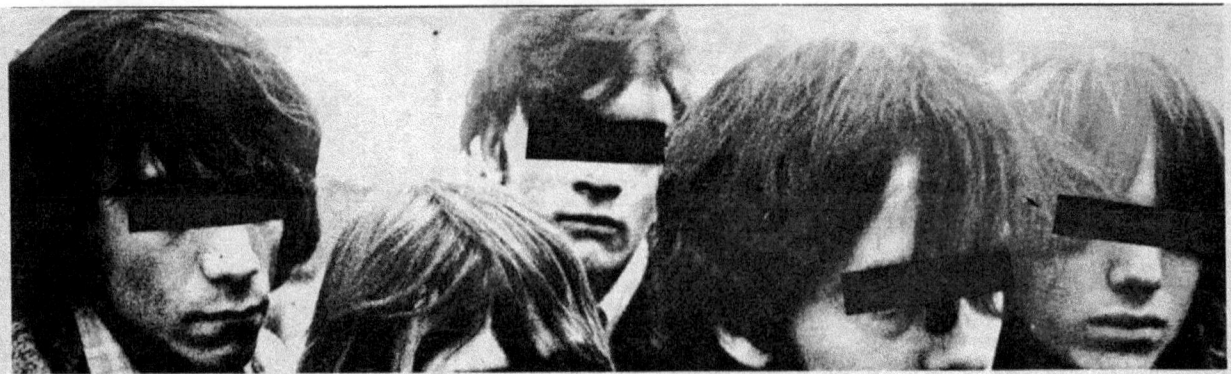

A GROWING CONTROVERSY
Hair—The Long and Short Of It

By Carol Deck

The growing controversy over long hair on guys has passed the stage of mere parental complaint and gone on to involve public school officials and even the courts.

In many public high schools in California, male students have been suspended or threatened with suspension unless they cut their hair to conform with school regulations.

By placing these regulations, although often very vague regulations, on the students, the schools have brought over to the side of the so called long haired rebels many people who don't actually like the long hair but feel the schools have no right to place restrictions on something like hair styles.

Personal Right

In schools across the state, students and parents alike have protested the restricting of what they consider a basic personal right.

One San Diego high school faces a $28,000 legal suit from an incident where a 15-year-old boy was forcibly held down while a teacher sheared his hair with sheep shears.

Another California high school saw a week of near riots when 50 male students were handed suspension notices due to long hair. Students picketed in front of the school for several days carrying signs reading "Lice are Nice — Support Long Hair." The school also received notice of legal action from one irate parent and the American Civil Liberties Union.

In still another school, the school board adopted regulations regarding the length of hair stating that it should be no more than three inches long and "from a reasonable length at the top of the ears to no hair at all at the bottom of the ear."

Shaved Heads

The immediate reaction was that several students shaved their heads completely in protest and several others were suspended for refusing to comply with the regulation.

One student, 15 year old Terry M., was suspended, shaved his head, was allowed back in school for a week and then was suspended again after being quoted in a local newspaper saying that students have the right to wear their hair any way they wish.

Things like this are going on in many public schools right now and the students and the parents are getting tired of the whole thing.

The controversy is not so much over the actual length of hair but how far a public institution can go in regulating students appearance and behavior.

Greg W., a long haired California high school student, sums up the overall general feelings of the guys who do let their hair get long as follows:

At another Southern California high school students rallied to the cause of Dale B., a popular and long haired student who was elected cheerleader.

No Previous Mention

During the election there was no mention of any regulations regarding hair length but after he was elected Dale was told by the vice principal that he would have to cut his hair or he could not represent the school as a cheerleader.

Dale, feeling that the school has no right to regulate hair length any way and in protest to the fact that nothing was said before or during the election, resigned the position which he had worked very hard for and actually wanted very badly.

Dale is still the major topic of discussion at the school. Although many of the students think his hair, which is just below his ears, is too long, they definitely admire him for standing up to the administration for his rights.

Dale says the school officials have actually been very nice to him and he's gotten no more static from them but he is slightly worried about graduation. He fears they may threaten to keep him out of the graduation ceremonies unless he cuts his hair.

The entire incident prompted the school's editor, Linda Kaplan, to write an editorial on her opinion of the matter — "I think people should consider not what's on the head but what's in it."

Another Side

And of course, as in any controversy, there's the other side. School officials feel that the California Education Code gives them the right to regulate student's appearance according to a vague clause in the code stating that pupils must "comply with the regulations, pursue the required course of study and submit to the authority of the teachers of the school."

And there are students who agree that the schools *have* the right to set regulations.

Steve L. says he thinks "sloppy appearance makes for sloppy behavior."

Another high school student, Richard E., feels that unless regulations are made things will get out of hand. "School is supposed to be a business-like place and if they didn't make a restriction on hair, soon there wouldn't be a restriction on clothes. Girls would come to school in shorts and things. You have to draw the line. It's a thin line, but you have to draw it."

And so it goes on — the long hairs versus the short hairs, the rule passing school officials against the supporters of basic personal rights.

Many people feel the long hair phase is beginning to fade out, but it hasn't actually reached its peak yet, at least not in the public schools, not until the school officials either set arbitrary regulations on every facet of human appearance or until they stop worrying about appearances all together and get back to the business of educating America's youth.

"Long hair is a very controversial subject. Anyone who takes a view on it believes he's right, and anyone who differs is out of his mind.

"I'm like that myself. I try and keep my hair long because; one, I think it improves my appearance, and, two, you're different with long hair.

"You're a leader, not a follower. Not many kids wear their hair long, but enough for it to cause some teachers and school officials to take action.

"A teacher, principal, or any school official wouldn't penalize a student for wearing a new style of clothing, or walking different. Then why do we get penalized for wearing our hair in a new style?

"It causes no harm, and 95% of the kids keep it neatly combed. If we thought it made us look silly, we'd be the first to do something about it."

On the other side of the fence are the short haired guys who actually don't go for long hair yet feel forced to defend it on the principle of the whole matter.

"The way you look is your own personal business," says Don B. "I don't like long hair. I think it looks cruddy, but I think it's each person's own business how they look.

"People are going to do what they're going to do — they're going to get straight A's or flunk out — whether they have long hair or are bald."

How The Stars Feel About It

What about the people who are supposedly responsible for this whole long hair kick? How do the pop singers feel about the controversy?

The BEAT asked many of them if they felt the public schools had the right to require guys to cut their hair on threat of suspension if they didn't.

Here are some of their replies:

CHAD STUART:
"We're living in the twentieth century,
Let's talk about you and me.
I don't bug you about your crewcut,
You're a girl with a mind of her own.
Why don't you keep your crewcut,
And leave my long hair alone."*
*From "Hair" by Rod McKuen, copyright 1966

JEREMY CLYDE: "If they don't require you to wear a uniform, why should they be able to dictate any other part of the anatomy."

BRIAN WILSON: "They don't have the right to tell you when to polish your shoes or brush your teeth, so they shouldn't have the right to tell you when to cut your hair. That's up to the parents and the kids."

AL JARDINE: "As a guy I instinctively say no, but there's got to be a reason for it. They feel if they keep all the hair a uniform length, the guys will be less hippy and arrogant."

(Al also added that he doesn't like himself in long hair because he doesn't think he looks good in it.)

(Turn to Page 14)

KRLA ARCHIVES

ELVIS PRESLEY IN "FRANKIE AND JOHNNY"

ELVIS – NEWEST – BIGGEST – BEST FROM RCA VICTOR

Special bonus for a limited time only. Full color portrait of Elvis in the new Frankie & Johnny album.

This brand new original soundtrack from RCA Victor brings you Elvis at his all time best. Frankie & Johnny, Come Along, Beginner's Luck, Shout It Out, Hard Luck and all the rest of the great music from his newest film. If you like this album don't forget the two below – they're great too.

Original Soundtrack Album includes Hey, Little Girl Harem Holiday and nine more Soundtrack favorites.

A collection of all time favorites Your Cheatin' Heart, Memphis Tennessee, Finders Keepers; Losers Weeper's and nine more Elvis hits.

NOW AVAILABLE AT YOUR NEARBY
ZODY'S DISCOUNT RECORD DEPT.
At Regular Low, Low Discount Prices!

KRLA ARCHIVES

BEAU BRUMMELS
"that's the way we want it"

HOLLYWOOD: Unlike last summer there are no female hikers along Benedict Canyon Drive. No long bangs—no bell bottoms—no police cars. You see, the Beatles aren't there now and as far as the girls know there's no action, no popular group, staying up in Benedict. All's quiet—they *think*. But they're wrong. The Beau Brummels are there.

Halfway up the Canyon, on one of the small sidestreets paving its way into Benedict the Beau Brummels have been spending the last two weeks amid relative calm.

In the circular driveway a taxi waits. The door is opened by Ron Elliott. He smiles, "Come on in." He yells: "Anybody send for a cab; it's here."

You sit down on one of the five sofas and as you wait for the other Brummels your eyes roam around the spacious living room and out through the sliding glass doors to the huge swimming pool. The house drapes itself around the pool, Oriental features stare down from a painting on the wall opposite you and slowly the other Brummels file in... Ron Meagher, John Peterson, Sal Valentino bringing up the rear.

New Brummel

All here? Yes. No, there's one more you remember, a new Brummel. A thin, fair-haired, young looking Brummel. Don Irving. They're hiding him maybe—keeping him out of sight when Ron Elliott is around? In the back of your mind you remember how Don Irving came about. Ron Elliott was not in the best of health, he could make the long engagements but the one-nighters hurt.

So, the Brummels were faced with a problem, a big one. What do they do? Get rid of Elliott altogether? No, he was an integral part of the group. They could make it without him, maybe—but they could make it much better with him.

In the end they resolved the problem by hiring Don to hit the road with them while Ron stayed in San Francisco writing more Brummel hits. Then when they appeared on television or played a week's stand somewhere Ron returned and Don exited.

You're thinking it's not fair to keep Don hidden from you now. But you're afraid to ask. It might be touchy. They might clam up because they're tired and it shows by the way they're sitting—all around you but hardly moving.

The chiming doorbell breaks through your thoughts and you discover (happily) that you were dead wrong. Don Irving (smiling broadly) strides in, is introduced and plops himself down next to Sal. You're curious about this Brummel. Being a new member in an established group is a difficult adjustment to make. You wonder if it was hard for Don.

"It was at first. It was a complete change. But it's great," Don says and you know he means it.

Sal is a little wider awake now. He glances around and notices that practically everyone else is smoking. He's been trying to give it up and he's down to two cigarettes a day but he decides to give in to temptation. "Anyone have a cigarette?" A Kool and a Marlboro are quickly extended. Sal stares at the outstretched cigarettes for a second and then slowly reaches for a Kool.

They all start talking about old times—the broken guitar string, *The BEAT* award as the Best New Group of 1965. The broken string incident is funny now—it was embarrassing then. The Brummels were on *The BEAT* Pop Award Show. They flew down especially to sing one of the nominated songs, "Mr. Tambourine Man." They also came just in case they won an award. They really didn't think they would, "but we were hoping," says Ron Elliott.

Anyway, during the guitar intro the string broke. It was probably one of the most embarrassing moments of their lives—standing in front of their fellow entertainers with a broken guitar string! But a quick exchange of guitars was made and the Brummels plunged into the song again.

Whether they realized it or not the whole incident was beneficial to them because it separated the Brummels from the amateurs. Only a professional group could make a comeback like that. And when the Brummels were named Best New Group over the Byrds, Dino, Desi & Billy, Gary Lewis and the Playboys and the Lovin' Spoonful the audience thundered its approval. You had made a wise decision — you had chosen the best.

Fresh coffee arrives and the talk continues, only now they speak of the new instead of the old. The new recording contract, the new record, the new experience of playing one of Hollywood's top clubs, the Whiskey.

They're reluctant to reveal too much about the contract with Warner Brothers. But you know a little about it anyway—enough to allow you to speculate. Although Reprise has several young and upcoming artists, Warner Brothers itself has none. So, it stands to reason that the Brummels will be on the receiving end of a big promotional campaign.

You've heard that Warner Brothers is planning a television spectacular to showcase their artists. It means that the Brummels will be seen by millions of viewers across the nation. And you think, "it's about time," but you say nothing.

A Groove

They play what they're pretty sure will be their next single—a Bob Dylan song, "One Too Many Mornings." As the record plays everyone listens and you notice that they've changed the lyrics slightly. When it's over no one speaks—they're waiting for your opinion. You honestly think it's great and you say so. Relieved smiles spread across their faces and you wonder why your opinion matters. Or if it does.

But why *did* they change the lyrics? "That's the way we wanted it, the way we arranged it," answers Sal. Fair enough. Ask a stupid question...

Their stand at the Whiskey on the Sunset Strip has been a profitable one—for the Brummels and for the club. It's been packed every night and it's proven that the San Francisco bred Beau Brummels can draw (and draw very well) in callus Hollywood, can hold their own in a city hardened by seeing too many top groups.

"It was kind of a challenge for us," John admits. "We've done some of the beach cities and we did a couple of Cinnamon Cinders but we've never played right here in Hollywood."

KRLA ARCHIVES

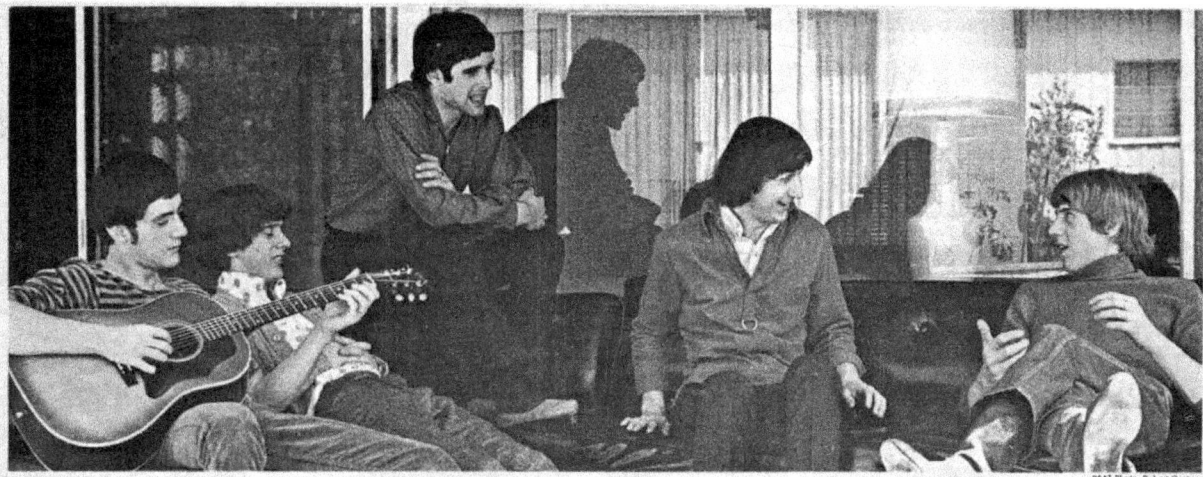

...THE BEAU BRUMMELS (l. to r. Ron Elliott, Don Irving, Sal Valentino, Ron Meagher, John Peterson)

...MR. & MRS. RON ELLIOTT.

...REMEMBER WHEN THERE WERE ONLY FOUR AND THEY SHOPPED AT SY DEVORE'S?

AND NOW THEY'RE FIVE AND THEY WEAR WHAT THEY WANT TO.

Not only did their stint at the Whiskey draw fans but other performers flocked to see the Brummels as well. People such as Bob Dylan, Gene Clark, Johnny Rivers, Barry McGuire, Donovan (who himself was playing down the street), Peter of Peter, Paul and Mary, Barry Sadler and Phil Spector came night after night.

You wonder if it makes them nervous having people like that in their audience but in unison they assure you that it doesn't. "We like it," says Ron Meagher. "It's a compliment," believes Sal. "We know how busy they are so it makes us feel good just to see that they're interested in us."

Speaking of clubs, they reveal that this is only the second club they've played in a year. "It's nice though," says Ron Elliott, "because in a concert everything is so huge."

You drop your pen and as Sal retrieves it you notice how much better he looks with his hair cut, how much better they all look now. Sal and John with their noticeably shorter locks ("a lot more comfortable," John tells you), Ron Meagher with his brilliant red sweatshirt and Ron Elliott — you can't quite place what it is about him except maybe the extra rest he's been getting lately. Anyway, whatever it is it definitely agrees with him.

You were in San Francisco last week, you realize that they probably couldn't care less but you tell them anyway and to your surprise they all begin talking at once. "Where'd you go?" "What did you see?" "Did you find the street made out of bricks," Ron Meagher inquires. "How was the weather?" Sal wants to know.

You mention the cable cars and admit that you got on the wrong one. They laugh and you laugh with them. Cable cars bring memories cascading down on them as they sit in a $75,000 home remembering when they took the cable cars everywhere for 15 cents. "As soon as I get back," Sal vows, "I'm going to ride one of them. I haven't been on a cable car for years."

Mid-April will find a new Beau Brummel album on the market. It sounds as if it will be the grooviest LP they've ever cut. They tell you some of the songs which will be on it: "Mr. Tambourine Man," "Hang On Sloopy," "Yesterday," "Play With Fire" and "Zorba The Greek."

It's typical Beau Brummels—a cross section, a touch of everything which makes up the crazy world of pop. Hard rock, country and western, rhythm 'n' blues—the Brummels mix it up, add their own special ingredients and emerge with a clean, fresh sound. One which belongs to them.

It's past time for you to leave. You know it but you hate to go. You've been invited to the Whiskey tonight and you're naturally looking forward to it. The Strip is packed and as you pull up in front of the Whiskey you note the line outside winding itself around the corner and down the block like a snake. Inside you find wall to wall people, the Grass Roots on stage and the Beau Brummels sitting in a booth saving it for you.

The Grass Roots finish up and the Brummels come on for their first set, Sal launches into the opening number and his mike goes dead. You're beginning to think you're some kind of a jinx. First the guitar string—now the mike.

Carl Scott, the Brummels' manager and probably one of the nicest men around, searches for someone to fix the mike but only one of the Grass Roots knows where the switches are hidden and he has disappeared.

The Brummels squeeze in on the good mikes and the show continues. They're great and you can't get over how much they've improved. Don Irving fits in so perfectly that you feel he's always been a Beau Brummel.

You're happy for them and after they finish but before they reach your table you leave. It's been a long, long road for them but they've finally made it. And you're very glad.

Louise Criscione

KRLA ARCHIVES

Inside KRLA
By Eden

We have done a lot of kidding around with our station's General Manager, John Barrett, but the last time we spoke with John, the mood was quite a bit more serious than usual.

Just a couple of weeks ago, a young man named Jim Washburne was killed in a tragic car accident in San Jose. Jim was a disc jockey on KRLA until about two years ago, and his passing came as a shock to everyone at the studio who had known and worked with him.

When we spoke with John, he expressed the feelings of everyone at KRLA as he said: "We were all saddened by the tragic death of Jim Washburne. Jim was one of the brightest young men in radio. Many of the innovations in radio and on KRLA can be traced to Jim's influence. We will all miss him very much."

Sort of sadly ironic was the power failure which occurred shortly after Jim's death. It seems that a construction truck cut off a coaxle cable when it knocked into a telephone pole just off the freeway. The result was that it temporarily disconnected the KRLA studios in Pasadena from its transmitter, briefly interrupting the station's programming.

John had been making a telephone call outside of the station, and when he turned on the radio, the first thing he heard was a taped voice announcing that the station's programming had been temporarily interrupted. The voice was that of Jim Washburne.

Playing Host

KRLA has been playing host to quite a number of celebrities recently, including Brian Wilson and Johnny Rivers this last week. Then of course, there are nine million, five hundred and thirty-one thousand KRLA listeners who have visited the studios during the Spring vacation. We love every one of them . . . honest! It's just that the lobby is beginning to look like Ringo's front lawn during the Christmas holidays, in the middle of the tourist season!!!

Incidentally, if you have been wondering just what has been happening with Jamie McCluskey and Bill Slater, you will probably be interested to learn that several love letters have been rather surreptitiously appearing up in Bill's Weather Room of late.

It seems that our Jamie just can't quite get over the shock of losing him . . . or at least, that's what *we* thought. *Until* we read some of the notes, that is. Jamie explained that she hated to sound unfaithful or anything, but she no longer wanted to propose to Bill. Jamie insisted that she had fallen in love all over again. Wonder with whom?

Great Feat

About the only other performers I can think of who have accomplished a feat of this sort are the Beatles. I'm talking 'bout the KRLA tunedex now; this week, "Monday, Monday" by the Mama's and Papa's debuted at *Number Two!* About the only other time something of this sort has occurred was when The Beatles came in first week on our charts right smack dab at the Number One position. Congratulations kids; you're in good company!

Nothing happening at the Bat Cave this week, and our Beloved Bat Manager, Our Groovy Leader, *John-John*, hasn't been doing too much on his own lately, but he promises to have some news for us next week, so tune in again then Batfans!

L.A. Welcomes Muddy Waters

Famed blues artist Muddy Waters is receiving enthusiastic reception in his West Coast debut at Doug Weston's Troubadour. The king of American blues has with him for this special engagement his original Chicago blues band.

Also appearing on the show are Dick Davy and folk singer Peter Tork.

SPECIAL BONUS—SUBSCRIBE NOW and receive a free copy of The Bobby Fuller Four's best selling album, "I Fought The Law."

KRLA BEAT Subscription

(COUPONS FROM THE TEEN FAIR MAY BE REDEEMED WITH THIS SUBSCRIPTION FORM)

☐ 1 YEAR — 52 Issues — $5.00   ☐ 2 YEARS — $8.00
☐ 6 MONTHS — $3.00

Enclosed is _____ ☐ CASH ☐ CHECK
PLEASE PRINT — Include Your Zip Code

Send to: .... Age: ....
Address: .... City: ....
State: .... Zip: ....

MAIL YOUR ORDER TO: KRLA BEAT
6290 Sunset, Suite 504
Hollywood, Calif. 90028

Foreign Rate: $9.00 — 52 Issues

KRLA ARCHIVES

Donovan Returns With 'Now' Music

By Carol Deck

HOLLYWOOD — Whatever happened to Donovan, the little boy who sang about colors and wars and things and was often compared to Bob Dylan?

No one seemed to know where he was or what he was doing until he recently showed up at The Trip for his first public appearance in quite a while.

Then everyone seemed to know where he was and everyone came to see him.

Opening night at the club was packed and in the midst of the full house could be seen many other celebrities who'd come to find out whatever happened to Donovan.

Among those who dropped in opening night were Barry McGuire, Chad and Jeremy, P.F. Sloan, Johnny Rivers, the Mamas and Papas, Tommy of the Smothers Brothers, Paul and Mary of Peter, Paul and Mary and British stage actor Anthony Newley.

They came and they saw. They saw Donovan start out as his usual self, just a single folk singer alone on the stage with only his guitar and his music.

Then he was joined by Shawn Phillips and one very large electrified sitar and later a three piece rock group called The Jagged Edge.

His ever present hat was gone, as was the sign on his guitar that used to say "This machine kills" and the harmonica holder. But his quiet, almost lisping voice was still the same.

The audience waited expectantly for some of Donovan's commercial hits. But they never came. He didn't sing his "Catch the Wind" or "Colours" or "Universal Soldier."

Instead he sang what the advertisements called "now" music and indeed some of it was so "now" it almost seemed as though he was making it up as he went along.

Although it was his first live appearance in a while he seemed relaxed and natural. When The Jagged Edge came on to back him up there was a pause as everyone got set up and Donovan filled in with "While we're setting up you can, uh, look at us."

And he admitted, "I haven't worked in so long, it's kind of weird."

And weird it was, looking as small and vulnerable as usual he handled himself quite well before a large crowd of mostly just curious people.

The curious came to see what Donovan was all about and if he'd changed and if he could still pull in an audience. And in doing so they helped him pull in that audience. And they came back as night after night he played to a packed club.

No, Donovan hasn't had a record on the charts for many months. But people still come to see and hear him and thus he's still alive as a singer and writer and an influence on the world of pop music.

KRLA Tunedex

DAVE HULL

BOB EUBANKS

DICK BIONDI

JOHNNY HAYES

EMPEROR HUDSON

CASEY KASEM

CHARLIE O'DONNELL

BILL SLATER

This Week	Last Week	Title	Artist
1	2	MONDAY, MONDAY	The Mama's & The Papa's
2	1	SOUL AND INSPIRATION	The Righteous Brothers
3	4	BANG, BANG	Cher
4	3	CALIFORNIA DREAMIN'	The Mama's & The Papa's
5	5	SECRET AGENT MAN	Johnny Rivers
6	6	KICKS	Paul Revere & The Raiders
7	8	SHAPE OF THINGS	The Yardbirds
8	21	TIME WON'T LET ME	The Outsiders
9	7	THE BALLAD OF THE GREEN BERET	S/Sgt. Barry Sadler
10	9	DAYDREAM	The Lovin' Spoonful
11	27	EIGHT MILES HIGH/WHY	The Byrds
12	10	NOWHERE MAN	The Beatles
13	12	WOMAN	Peter & Gordon
14	25	GOOD LOVIN'	The Young Rascals
15	13	CALL ME	Chris Montez
16	30	SLOOP JOHN B	The Beachboys
17	14	THESE BOOTS ARE MADE FOR WALKIN'	Nancy Sinatra
18	17	LOVE MAKES THE WORLD GO 'ROUND	Deon Jackson
19	20	A SIGN OF THE TIMES	Petula Clark
20	16	DARLING BABY	The Elgins
21	22	THE RAINS CAME	Sir Douglas Quintet
22	15	THIS OLD HEART OF MINE	The Isley Brothers
23	19	IT'S TOO LATE	Bobby Goldsboro
24	—	RAINY DAY WOMAN	Bob Dylan
25	23	WHAT NOW MY LOVE/SPANISH FLEA	Herb Alpert
26	28	MAGIC TOWN	The Vogues
27	29	GET READY	The Temptations
28	33	MESSAGE TO MICHAEL	Dionne Warwick
29	32	RHAPSODY IN THE RAIN	Lou Christie
30	37	TRY TOO HARD	The Dave Clark Five
31	36	I HEAR TRUMPETS BLOW	The Tokens
32	38	LOVE'S MADE A FOOL OF YOU	The Bobby Fuller Four
33	—	LEANIN' ON THE LAMP POST/HOLD ON	Herman's Hermits
34	34	TEEN-AGE FAILURE	Chad & Jeremy
35	39	FALLING SUGAR	The Palace Guard
36	—	PLEDGING MY TIME	Bob Dylan
37	—	I CAN'T GROW PEACHES ON A CHERRY TREE	Just Us
38	—	CAROLINE, NO	Brian Wilson
39	—	ALONG COMES MARY/YOUR OWN LOVE	The Association
40	—	NOTHING'S TOO GOOD FOR MY BABY	Stevie Wonder

Biondi Road Show A Hit

By Marlyn Sylva

The KRLA Road Show appeared at an assembly in the Duarte High School gym recently.

At 11:00 a.m. "The Band Without A Name" arrived with Dick Biondi, the Deuces Wild, Joey Paige, and The Bobby Fuller Four. Dick Biondi started off the show by appearing in a Duarte Varsity Jacket.

After calming the audience down, Biondi introduced the "Band Without A Name." The band then performed several numbers including the Four Seasons' new hit, "Working My Way Back To You."

The Deuces Wild then appeared and led a yell for the Duarte crowd. The real star of the show then appeared — Joey Paige. After being brought on stage, Joey brought down the house with his version of "Goodnight My Love."

After several other numbers including "Roll Over Beethoven," the Bobby Fuller Four then performed their popular hit "I Fought The Law" and their new record titled "Love's Made A Fool Of You."

The many antics of the Band Without A Name, Joey Paige, The Deuces Wild, The Bobby Fuller Four and the zany Master Of Ceremonies, Dick Biondi, will long be remembered by the Duarte Welcoming Committee made up of Marlyn Sylva, ASB Director Of Activities, Gail Heath, Senior Class Secretary, Chick Mangan ASB President, Alan Mack, Yell Leader and the Advisor, Mr. James B. Lockner.

The entire school is still talking about the show.

... BOBBY FULLER FOUR

Eve's APPAREL
See if you can BEAT our prices on our new Jr. and misey lines. Samples at wholesale or less.
1800 N. Vermont
NO 3-4456 Hollywood, Calif.

UNLIKE ANYTHING YOU'VE EVER SEEN!
WARNER BROS. SUPER CINERAMA PRODUCTION
BATTLE OF THE BULGE
PACIFIC'S CINERAMA DOME Theatre
NOW PLAYING!

NOW PLAYING IN THEATRES and DRIVE-INS EVERYWHERE!
DIRECT FROM ITS PREMIERE SHOWINGS. SPECIAL ENGAGEMENT AT POPULAR PRICES. NO RESERVED SEATS.
NOW EVERYONE CAN SEE THE MOST LOVELY MOTION PICTURE OF ALL TIME!
My Fair Lady
Winner of 8 Academy Awards including Best Picture.
AUDREY HEPBURN · REX HARRISON
TECHNICOLOR · SUPER PANAVISION 70 · FROM WARNER BROS.

KRLA ARCHIVES

For Girls only
by shirley poston

You'll be glad to hear that this isn't going to be one of those dull, boring columns where I rave on hysterically about one subject.

It is going to be one of those dull, boring columns where I rave on hysterically about *several* subjects.

You see, I've made this list of things I've been meaning to tell you about. (I just LUV to make lists.) (I even make lists of lists I'm going to make.) (Down, Shirl.)

Speaking of George . . . whoops . . . speaking of lists (and I list heavily to the right every time I say that *georgeous* name), onward.

John Dream
(1) JOHN DEERE: What??? Why did I write that? Isn't that a tractor or something? Or is it a cigar? Oh, who cares???

Anypath, what I meant to say was John *Dream*. Little slip of the lip—er—typewriter there. Care to analyze it, any of you experts?

About that John Dream. Will the person who did such a fantastic job of analyzing my Lennon-with-parachute dream please start over and send me another copy of your original letter? I can't find it anywhere and I want to print it in me column.

While I'm still on the subject, thanks to Marlene of Huntington Park for sending me a dream book called The Key To Your Secret Self. However, I'm about half afraid to discover my secret self. I'm having *enough* problems with my *un*-secret self.

Name Game
(2) NAME GAME: Let's once and for all establish some way of letting me know whether you'd like your names printed in this column. I never know whether to mention people by name, because about half of the letters I receive ask me not to (cowards). But now I'm nervous about mentioning anyone. Please always remember to TELL ME if you'd rather I didn't refer to you in "For Girls Only."

(3) This wasn't the real #3. I just feel like talking about GEORGE. So I promise to send a copy of the "Rubber Soul" album to the first two people who tell me what song he wrote on this LP!

I'm sitting here staring at a picture of him right now. (Isn't *that* interesting.) (It sure is.) Someday when I've been at the cooking sherry I'll try to explain something weird. One of the things about George that gets me all unhinged, I mean. But it's too silly to put into rational, sensible words. Hey, I'll wait until you all have your code goodies and tell you then!

Code Goodies
(4) CODE GOODIES: Yes, I realize I'm getting repetitious, but no one is perfect. Anyroad, don't forget to send for your code goodies so you'll be able to decipher our secret messages beginning next week. (You'll also receive a free Dick Tracy two-way wrist radio as a special bonus.) (I'm kidding, I'm kidding.) (Come to think of it, I'm *lying*.) Just don't forget. Ridiculous as it may sound, you'll soon find it to be *twice* as ridiculous as it may sound. (Did I write *that* mess? I dearly hope not.)

Write the word "Code" in the lower left-hand corner of the envelope, and enclose a stamped, self-addressed thingy inside.

(5) If any of you are wondering why it took so long for me to send your rawhide, here's why. I got a whole bunch of it, but I cut the pieces too short and had to start all over. Two hints for making star scares (especially Beatle scares). Soak the rawhide for a few moments before tying the knots. It's easier that way. Also, if you'd like to make a few thous-and scares as gifts, use the leather shoelaces you can buy in shoe repair shops. They cost about 60¢ a pair, and are quite long.

Can you believe how boring and sensible I'm being today? This has got to STOP!

George . . . George . . . some-where you're breathing.

There! That's more like it. You know, that always gives me the oddest feeling. You know, to suddenly realize that somewhere he *is* breathing. Alive, I mean. Not just a picture. Down, Shirl.

Robin Boyd
(6) ROBIN BOYD: For those of you who've written and asked how far in advance I write Robin's adventures, I write them each week. I suppose I should get all organized and compose several at a time, but that would spoil everything. Then I'd know what was going to happen next week!

(7) CRAZY: Do you like to drive other people crazy? By making them think *you're* crazy? (Which, of course, you are or you wouldn't be reading this retarded column.) Well, here's a really great way to get the point across (the one on the top of my 'ead, that is). Pick out several words and start saying them exactly the way they are spelled. You know, just sprinkle them around in your conversation and people will soon be snickering and pointing.

My especially fave word, which I've been saying wrong for years just to cut up a bit, is sword. (Sorry about that pun.) (Among other things.) I say it *with* a W, not without. Castle is another good one (as in cas-tel), and there are about a million more.

I suppose, if a person were *really* some kind of a nutto, you could say *every* word exactly as it's spelled. (And we could come round and see you every visiting day.)

George
(8) GEORGE: Speaking of, lots of my newer victims...er...readers have written and asked if I've ever met George. GASP! I did! Just to say hi, though. But he held my hand for thirty seconds. (I later had it cast in bronze.) You should have *seen* me! Standing there like a *human being*, when what I really wanted to do was fling myself at him and blither. And yes, yes, yes, (as in yeah, yeah, yeah) I have seen the Beatles in concert. Oh, George. Why aren't you *here* breathing?

(9) HELP: Someone write to me quick and tell me how to operate a ouija board. So many of you rave about them in your letters, I raced out to buy one, but I think the instructions are written in Chinese. HELP!

(10) A BRIBE: Mary Ann Geffrey of 1122 West Desford in Torrance, Calif., has promised to make me an honorary member of her branch of Louise's Beatles (George's sister's club for the fab-four) if I'll print her address in my column. Send her a stamped, self-addressed (addressened?) (once again, I hear the swish of nets) envelope for details if you'd like to join. Then send additional bribes to yours truly.

Discovery
(11) A DISCOVERY: Do you ever shriek and scream and fall out of the car when your favorite song plays on the radio? Have you ever wondered why you don't get as frothed-up when you play this same record on the phono? Me too. But I think I've finally figured it out. When the song plays on the radio, you know thousands of others are listening to the same disc. Which for some crazy reason seems to bring on the blithering.

Yipes. Outta room. More boring subjects next week!

Young Rascals
(Continued from Page 2)

Yeah, well no one had seen it but they had seen enough of me to realize that I was permanently off my nut (and they're probably right.) Then when they came out with "Good Lovin'" they sent Louise a copy of it. So, I planned to claim that one too on the grounds that Louise could buy her own record since she has more money than I have (when you come right down to it — everyone has more money than I have!) but I was fooled again. The record was broken in the mail!

Yeah, well I guess crime doesn't pay after all. But I really do wish the Young Rascals would come back — we haven't had coffee spilled, photos almost sent up in flames or chairs knocked over since they left. And they call that dull. So, come on back, boys, and spill all the coffee you wanta spill.

... MARCUS AND CARL

An Extraordinary Pair

By Carol Deck

Once in every musical era there comes along something that is so totally unique and so completely tuned to *that* era that it is destined to go straight to the top and stay there.

That is what the Pair Extraordinaire are — totally unique and completely tuned to *today*.

They are unique in so many ways it's almost unbelievable. The first and most obvious thing that strikes you about them is the act itself.

It's just one very good solo singer and one excellent bass player — no guitars, no drums, no nothing except two extremely talented men, each doing what he does best and nothing more.

There's nothing pretentious about the Pair. They'll come right out and tell an audience "We hope you like us" and then add their own brand of humor by adding "'cause we're awful good."

And good they are. Carl Craig has got more honest soul and true rhythm than you'll ever find in five men.

Simplicity
"We try to pick songs such that their structure lends itself to the way we like to operate. And I try to sing each individual note as simply as possible," Carl explains.

When people ask Carl how he has the nerve to come on with nothing but a bass as a back up he replys, "It's easy, when you have the best bassist in the solar system."

But Marcus Hemphill will just say, "We got a lot of nerve."

Marcus puts more into and gets more out of that bass than many groups can with any number of guitars and drums.

The Pair have gotten used to the reaction they get when just the two of them walk on a stage.

"When we first come on stage," Marcus says, "it's like, uh, 'they gotta be kidding.' But the audience draws in their own musical accompaniment — the violins and drums and things."

Another big part of their uniqueness is the tremendous amount of professional respect they have for each other. You won't find them putting each other down, except in pure jest. Just as Carl considers Marcus the solar system's top bassist, Marcus considers Carl a true genius.

And they both consider their own music as fun, because, Carl says, "fun sells fastest and it's one of the nicest things to be a part of."

Both of them are tremendous fans of the Beatles and consider them brilliant. They feel that the Beatles have always been great and probably always will be, that they've changed and matured a great deal but that that does not make their early material any less great.

"In order to be as successful as quickly as they were you had to have everything right then, nothing in waiting," Carl explains.

No Noise
"Their music never was just loud noise — it was loud music. They were selling hysteria — and that was the total movement then. They weren't ready for 'Rubber Soul' then.

"At first they didn't have the knowledge for a 'Rubber Soul.' They were doing what they could do best then and still are."

Carl and Marcus both feel "Rubber Soul" is a real work of art and that it's also one more major accomplishment of the Beatles — and for one very good reason.

"They had never written a song trying to tell people where it's at until 'Rubber Soul' — and then they did it with one word — LOVE."

The Pair Extraordinaire have a lot of respect for each other, for people who put out a good product and for life in general.

This respect combined with the unbelievable amount of talent these two possess has created an act that is unique and highly refreshing to watch and listen to.

The BEAT would like to make just one recommendation. If you get the chance, and they're currently appearing at San Francisco's Hungry i, see them live. After you've seen them live, to see or hear them in any other media — on records or television — is anticlimatic.

Say you read it in The BEAT

KRLA ARCHIVES

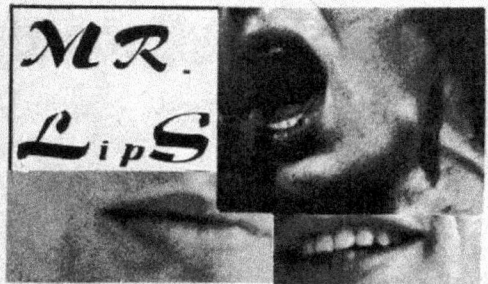

MR. LipS

By Bruce McDougall

At a Rolling Stone concert I overheard two teenagers talking before the show began: "Who is Mick Jagger then?" The other answered: "He's the one with the lips."

Mick's lips may be a prominent part of him, but they are not his only out-standing feature. Jagger, and indeed most of the Stones, speaks out when the occasion warrants — and sometimes when it doesn't. Naturally this helps to confirm the rebellious, non-conformitive tag that is always given to the Stones. Why are they given that tag? The Rolling Stones are not in the traditional clean-cut style that so many stars like to cultivate so naturally they get knocked by the people who are.

Of course the Stones are unconventional, but they are at least honest about it. Some performers come out with fantastic opinions simply for the publicity that they will gain because of it. Jagger, however, comes out with fantastic opinions purely because he believes what he says.

The international press is in the front when it comes to knocking the Rolling Stones. Mick therefore feels that he has a right to criticize the press: "We are the most pop conscious country in the world and yet most of what is reported in the national press is either nonsense or knocking popular music. They usually go after stories such as, 'who has knocked who from the number one position.' They build you up to destroy you. Reporters who do not take notes put the quotes in their own vocabulary and make us sound daft. They always ask us why we are so rude. We aren't! We just say things as honestly as possible."

All of the Stones admit to being influenced by Chuck Berry (wasn't everybody?) and Mick is no exception. On Chuck, Mick has this to say: "Everybody has been very much influenced by him. Not just the singing but the sound as well." The Stones have a real bluesy feeling but Mick confesses to a dislike for modern jazz: "Charlie plays me some things, but I don't like modern jazz. I just like sounds, I'm not a big critic. I like Charlie Mingus and Jimmy Smith. A lot of Jimmy Smith is a bit Rock and Rolly."

The Rolling Stones seem doomed to be a controversial subject for some time to come. This is pretty natural. The Beatles are now accepted, in fact they are practically idols. It is much easier for a young person to associate himself, or herself, with the wilder image of the Stones. After all, if the parents don't like them, they must be all right.

Why do so many young people dig the Stones? It isn't only because they have been rejected by the adult world. A sociologist could probably come up with a million reasons, but the truth is that they just happen to make a great sound when they pick up those instruments and play.

Have you ever wondered just where the fans get all of that stuff to throw at the Stones during a concert? I must admit that the subject has more than crossed my mind. One can imagine a sort of supply train from the entrance to the crowd at the foot of the stage. After all, many of the girls throw more than one set of unmenttionables. These objects hurled at the Stones can quite easily be injurious to them. Luckily the boys possess a sense of humour that would be a credit to Lennon. After a particularly heavy avalanche of clothes landed onto the stage during a concert, Mick was heard to say: "I feel like a laundromat."

Help Save Them

(Continued from Page 1)

be their first visit to America. It'll be their first visit *if* they can get in. They can only get in if *you* help them.

Here's how you can convince immigration authorities that Them is a popular group in the U.S.: Since they are seeking printed proof, collect anything you have from any U.S. publication regarding Them and send it to their American managers. Or just write a letter telling them how much you want Them in the country. They'll personally take all the material they receive and pile it all on the authorities' desk as material proof that you care.

Send your clippings and letters to: Help Them, 144 S. Beverly Drive, Beverly Hills, Calif.

It's Going To Be Bright And Casual This Spring

By Carol Deck

Are little girls getting older or are big girls getting younger?

Either way it seems, fashions are definitely emphasizing the young this spring.

Catalina Sportswear's spring line of fashions for girls shows that this season it's going to be simple, young and easy to care for in the fashion field.

Cotton velour is the big thing, especially in sleeveless pullovers with capris. Materials that are machine washable and take little or no ironing are going to comprise the majority of spring clothes.

Lines are getting simpler. Even the Cher look is becoming a little less extreme with the bell bottoms a little more subtle and less of the large lace around the bottoms.

The Paris Couture is bringing in the little girl look of provincial prints and short hemlines. And Correge boots are still very popular with the modern crowd.

Disappearing Sleeves

Necklines are getting simpler with little or no lace or decoration and sleeves are practically disappearing for the warm summer months ahead.

And with those warm summer months comes the swimming and surfing season. The trend towards two piece suits for girls continues each year.

This year there will be more and more of the not quite matching tops and bottoms in swim wear — the solid bottoms with print tops or pop art designs reversed in the top.

In capris, it's going to be the nylon and nylon stretch pants that are so popular and so easy to take care of. The miracle of the permanent press materials that has already taken over the men's wear field is beginning to show up in women's and girl's wear, particularly in capris.

To go with capris are the shells and poor boys that came in big last season along with the sharp looking velours, another material that's finally coming over from the men's wear to the women's.

Less Extremes

As for school wear, it's going to be much the same as last season but a little less extreme. The French look is being made even more popular by the movie "Viva Maria."

And a slight cowboy influence is beginning to show up in shades of brown and materials like imitation leather.

The A-line continues to be the most popular, comfortable and practical line for school clothes.

And colors this spring are going to be bright but not far out — the reds, blues and yellows are coming back with great force.

The English "Mod" look is going out and the French and American West look is coming in.

But no matter what you're wearing this spring, if you're with what's happening, it'll be bright, easy to care for, not as extreme as last year and very definitely young.

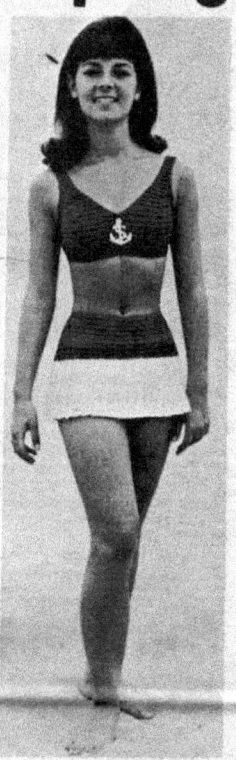

FASHIONS THIS SPRING are going young, with bright colors, casual lines and easy to care for materials.

KRLA ARCHIVES

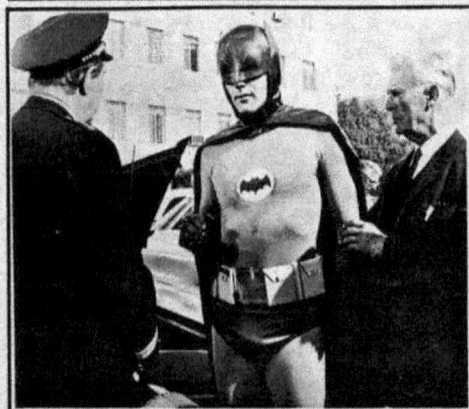

Batman's In Trouble!

BOSTON — Batman is in trouble with the Automobile Legal Association of Boston.

The Association has branded the caped crusader television's poorest driver and a "vicious example" for the nation's youth.

The automobile owners group says that in one program alone Batman was guilty of the following violations:
- U-turns in the middle of busy streets
- Crashing through safety barrier
- Crossing highway white line safety marker
- Parking illegally
- Speeding
- And failing to signal at a single turn

Holy stop sign — Batman may get a ticket!!

Bat Music, Bat Problems and Other Assorted Bat Babblings

Batman On Record

... THE PENGUIN

HOLY TOP 40! — Not only has Batman taken over road signs, bumper stickers and the latest slang, now he's breaking into records too.

Adam West, alias Bruce Wayne, alias Batman, has just released his first single record entitled "Miranda" with "You Only See Her" on the flip side.

Burt Ward, alias Bobby Wonder, is supposed to be working on his first record now but we haven't gotten any further word on titles or release date on that yet.

But now the villains that Batman and Robin work so hard to erradicate are getting back by releasing their own records — a sort of battle of the bat records.

Burgess Meredith, perhaps Batman's highest acclaimed guest villain, The Penguin, has just released a record he cut for 20th Century – Paramount Records.

The record's based on his experiences on the show and is titled "The Capture" with "The Escape" on the flip side. It's a narrative record.

And these records just add to the collection we've already got of Bat albums by such people as Jan and Dean, The Markettes and Neil Hefti, the original composer of the Batman Theme.

All we need now is a "Ballad of Batman" by The Crusaders?

The Story Behind The Real Batheme

One other man who's largely responsible for the smashing success of "Batman" is a man you won't find on the set. He's already done his part for the show and is now on to bigger and better things.

That man is Neil Hefti, the composer of the original Batman theme and much of the music used on the show.

His "Batman Theme" has been recorded by numerous artists including himself, the Markettes and Jan and Dean.

On his just released album of original Batman music Neil explains the situation when he was assigned the task of composing the music for the series that at time was still a well-kept secret.

The meeting took place in the offices of William Dozier, the producer of the show and a friend of Neils.

"When I arrived at his offices, instead of the usual greeting from a pretty receptionist, I was pinned to the wall by guards and frisked.

"Then mug shots were taken and I was fingerprinted. After pronouncing me clean, the guards whisked me into Mr. Dozier's office and quickly left the room.

"He swore me to secrecy and administered the loyalty oath, then came swiftly and precisely to the point. His eyes softened a little but he was no less stern as he said, 'Neil, I am going to commission you to compose the Batman Theme.'

"My mouth went dry and my skin became chilled as his words rang in my ears. I knew this would be hard, very hard, to keep to myself.

"Although I was unable to speak clearly, my friend knew that I was accepting this challenge by the humility in my eyes.

"I worked around the clock until my job was done. I planned carefully to take my batuscript to the studio when it would not be noticed. The guards were there to meet me, and I was congratulated on keeping the great secret. Batman Theme was now a reality."

And so Neil added another great score to his list of credits that include the scores of "Sex and the Single Girl," "Synanon," "How to Murder Your Wife," "Harlow," "Boeing-Boeing" and "Lord Love A Duck."

... NEIL HEFTI

... WHAT THE WELL DRESSED caped Crusader wears while his cape is at the cleaners.

KRLA ARCHIVES

BATMAN

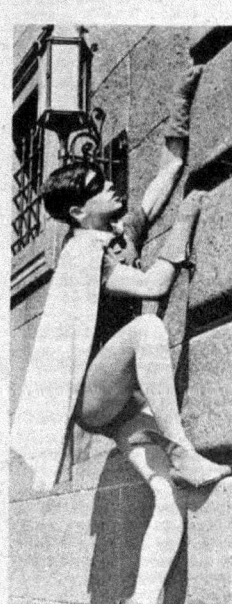

ROBIN — "It's so easy."

By Carol Deck

Put on your tights and capes kiddies, we're going to visit the "Batman" set.

We arrive on the set in the middle of this large public golf course just before noon and find all sorts of people milling around each trying to keep warm in the rather nippy breeze that's present.

Like that one woman over there. She's one of the extras. That's really a fetching outfit she has on — the black and white bell bottoms, red velour top with a large gold medallion around her neck — she's keeping warm by wearing that full length fur coat. To each his own, somebody once said.

As we trek across the parking lot we pass the Batmobile, a Gotham City Ambulance and Adam West's own personal car — a huge black vehicle complete with ski racks.

When we finally make it onto the actual set we find the stars, Adam West and Burt Ward, both huddled in faded yellow robes also trying to keep warm — those tights don't offer a whole lot of warmth.

As they bravely take off the robes and go back to shooting we notice this large yellow statue that the scene seems to center around. The statue looks a lot like the one in "Help" except it only has two arms.

Watch out! Don't step on that Gotham City Police Officer sprawled there on the grass. Let's go over and say hello to Alan Napier, who plays Bruce Wayne's faithful butler on the show.

Alan's the epitome of British gentlemen and sure looks it in that all light blue outfit he has on.

He wants to introduce us to a friend — it's his dog Tippy, another star of the show although no one seems to know it. If you watch the show carefully you may notice Tippy in several crowd scenes — quite an actor this dog.

Gee, I wonder whose phantom checker game this is laying here half finished in the middle of the set — looks like the blacks are winning.

Oh well, it's lunch time finally, and Burt Ward has asked us to join him and his cute little wife Bonnie for lunch.

Now if we can only get both of them to stop babbling about how overjoyed they are that Bonnie's pregnant, maybe we can learn something about what it's like to be a Boy Wonder.

"It's so easy. Really, you just gotta relax in front of the cameras. If anything goes wrong they'll re-shoot it. It's just so easy," says Burt.

Right there is the major difference between the two stars of the show that's captured the world.

Adam West is a veteran actor of many TV shows and movies and to him this is serious business — a job.

But to Burt this is his very first acting job of any type and nothing could be simpler to him. He's never spent hours in acting classes or playing other parts and the whole thing is almost a game to him.

Burt is not all hung up on the part either. "Robin ends at the studio gate," he states flatly. "On weekends I don't even shave. I just put on my riding clothes and ride my horses."

"Hey, you're just in time for some news," he interrupts himself. "I'm going to cut a record this weekend. I'm recording three songs in three different styles to see if I can find something I like."

And Burt's got a sharp songwriter behind him. Two of the songs were written by P.F. Sloan who's written many hits for Jan and Dean and many others but is probably best known for his "Eve of Destruction."

Let's get back to the show. Future plans for the show include the eventually 16th birthday of Robin (he can't stay 15½ forever you know.) There's talk of his getting to drive the Batmobile too, — can't you just see Batman giving Robin driving lessons in it?

Any chance of romance for either character? Burt sure hopes so.

"In terms of protection of Batman and Robin as men I think something should be done."

And Burt has a few complaints too. The hours do get a little rough at times. Their average working day is from 7:30 a.m. to 9 p.m. and they often stay much later.

Also, for those of you who wonder about such things, yes, those tights are uncomfortable.

And there is some danger involved in some of the stunts performed on the show. Adam and Burt do almost all of their own scenes except for a very few that entail some real danger of physical danger — then stunt men are used — but most of the time it's really them.

Burt had one close call when he was working a scene involving some gas. He fell, hit his head, started taking in great gulps of gas and had to be rushed to the hospital.

"That's what I like — excitement," Burt replies calmly.

And one last complaint from Burt is the lack of space in the Batmobile. The Batmobile is a completely custom made creation of George Barris that is equipped with everything from a cannon to a laser beam.

"It has everything but hot and cold running water and collapsible dishes," said one special effects man whose job it is to accomplish all the stunts the scripts call for.

It has everything all right, except space to move around in. "I wouldn't want to take it out on a date," Burt says.

But now it's time for everyone to get back to business. As we walk back to the set we pass about six stunt men rehearsing a fight scene. They're wearing kilt-like skirts and have grey droopy things on their heads and look like something from a biblical Salvation Army.

Once again the extras take off their fur coats and Batman and Robin take off their faded yellow robes and everyone tries not to shiver while delivering their lines.

And as we start back toward our car to leave we notice the labels on everything in sight. The technical crew all wear baseball caps labeled "Batcrew." The cars in the parking lot have bumper stickers that say "Eradicate Evil — Vote for Batman." And even the cameras have sticky type bat deelies on them.

Holy Insanity!

KRLA ARCHIVES

Adventures of Robin Boyd
By Shirley Poston

CHAPTER TWENTY-FOUR

Dizzily clutching George for support, Robin Boyd started to faint. Then she stopped and analyzed the situation carefully. A trick she'd recently picked up from the level-headed (amen) Dr. A.G. Andersrag.

Moments ago, George and Robin had been in California. Suddenly, they found themselves seated at a table in a Liverpool restaurant. Shortly thereafter, a waiter brought them a tray of tea thingys. Then the waiter had joined them at the table.

Now, was *this* reason enough to go round passing out? No! Was it, however, reason enough to *drop dead* of sheer shock? Yes! Because the waiter happened to be the famous (not to mention delicious) Paul McCartney.

Secretly spearing her knee with his fork, George gave her a be-cool-and-calm-or-I'll-katywinter-you-a-good-one look. "Say hullo to Paul," he re-speared.

"Hullo to Paul," Robin drooled obediently. Then she gasped. Not only from pain, having just coolly and calmly rested her elbow in a cup of tres torrid tea (it was hot, too). Also from concern.

"What if they recognize you?" she hissed, her eyes darting fearfully about the now-crowded room. "Won't you get mangled?"

"Cute"

Paul grinned that *grin* of his, and bounced a bit, causing Robin to drink the entire contents of the cream pitcher in a single gulp. "She thinks I'm him," he bounced. "She's cute," he added, giving her that *look* of his. "I always did go for the little-girl type."

"Don't ever let her get you alone in a phone booth," George muttered. "And don't get any ideas," he added, seeing that Paul was giving Robin a *double-look*. "She's mine . . . I mean, ours is not the ordinary genie-master . . . er . . . genie-*client* relationship," he continued, fishing for words.

"Oh," Paul said with a knowing look. "I catch." (Knowing, that is, that George was going to really *catch* it when Robin got him outside.)

But, in spite of the fact that Robin had turned as red as seven million cranberries and drank the entire contents of the sugar bowl in a single gulp, her mind was elsewhere. Because Paul's previous comment had started to sink in.

"What do you mean I *think* you're him?" she inquired sweetly (not to mention lumpily) (using both terms literally). "*Aren't you?*"

Paul chortled mysteriously. "He looks like George Harrison, right?"

"Right," agreed Robin. A little bit of *all* right, she added mentally, sneaking a side glance at her gorgeous (ahem) genie.

"Well, *I* look like Paul McCartney!"

A Genie!

"Hear, hear," Robin re-drooled. And just then it sank. "Wait!" she blithered. "Say no more! I get it now! You're a genie, too!! And you're not afraid of being recognized because everyone in this *place* is a genie! *Right*??" she concluded noisily.

Paul gave her a pat. "I can say no more."

But Robin, who had long ago discovered that George wasn't about to tell her a bloomin' thing, and who also did not give up easily, did not give up *that* easily.

"Why do you look like Beatles and how did you get to be genies and are you the immediate supervisor we were supposed to meet to talk about my wish and when *are* we going to talk about my wish, anyroad?" Robin rattled. (You have just visited the world's longest question.)

"Shur*up!*" George commanded. (You have just visited the world's shortest answer.)

"I know it must seem a puzzle to you," Paul soothed, "but you'll understand everything in good time. As for your wish, the supervisor has been detained, but I've been sent to loan George part of me own powers."

George groaned. "Would you believe *all* your powers and then some?"

"Jest South"

Paul punched George in jest. (For those interested, the jest is located jest south of the liver.) "Oh, come now, it couldn't be *that* bad."

George re-groaned. "Tell him, Robin."

Robin took a deep breath. "I want to see the Beatles," she began.

Paul gave a larf. "That's easy! All we have to do is . . . ."

"She's not quite *through*, Paul," George interrupted in a low moan. "*Are* you, Robin."

Robin took a deeper breath, hoping the restaurant had a large supply of alka-seltzer. "Not exactly. I want to see the Beatles at the *Cavern*. In *1961*."

Paul stared at George in utter disbelief. "My gawd," he breathed. "Did she just say what I *thought* she said? The Beatles at the *Cavern*??"

George stared back at Paul. "In *1961*," he reaffirmed. "Which shouldn't be *much* more difficult than re-creating the entire second world war."

Robin giggled. "I can see it all now," she raved dreamily. "A step into the past . . . into the wonderful days of olde when the Beatles were just four young musicians from . . . from that place I can't say that starts with an L. or I'll turn into a bird . . . huh? . . . anyroad, the crowds, the smoke, the cheers, the music, and the birth of the most beautiful malady in history . . . Beatlemania."

George gave Robin the all-time yank. "Are you quite *finished?*"

Drooms?

"Almost," Robin sighed happily. "Except for two things. I'd like Ringo on the drooms and . . ." She paused to dig into her purse, utilizing the shovel she always kept handy for just such occasions. "And I've made up a list of fifteen songs I'd like for them to perform."

With this, Paul's chair crashed over backwards, taking him along for the ride.

"*Robin Irene Boyd!*" George bellowed, rushing to Paul's side. (Yes, yes, he also rushed to Paul's back and front.) (Details, details.)

But his words fell on deaf ears. Robin Irene Boyd was suddenly too far gone to hear anything, including George's mention of her vile middle name. (Which she double-despised because it made her initials spell R.I.B.) (Something she didn't like being ribbed about one olde bit.)

Too far gone to hear anything but the hammering of her own heart, that is.

A condition which developed the very second she noticed that John Lennon was sitting across the room, beckoning to her.

(To Be Continued Next Week)

EXCLUSIVE BEAT INTERVIEW

Gerry Marsden Blasts Brown, Dylan, Byrds

By Michael G. Mitchell

Interviewing Gerry Marsden isn't exactly an easy task, putting a few bars of "I Like It", in every sentence is original to say the least, but doing it while plodding around the dressing room in his underwear can be very distracting. Fortunately he soon settled down and we began:

BEAT: *What is your opinion of the current Pop Scene in general?*
GERRY: As long as James Brown stays out, there are fantastic opportunities for American Groups in Britain, take the Walker Brothers for instance.
BEAT: *Don't you like James Brown, Gerry?*
GERRY: Terrible, absolutely terrible.
BEAT: *Any predictions for the Pop Scene in the near future?*
GERRY: Only one, I think the Spencer Davis Group will become tremendously popular and deservedly so.
BEAT: I asked Gerry to say the one word that the following subjects suggested to him.
GERRY:

Subject:	Word:
Bob Dylan	Rotten
Byrds	Fair
Hollies	Great
Beatles	Fantastic
Drugs	Rubbish
California	Love it
Music	Hymns
Favourite British Artist	Tom Jones
Segregation	Blown completely out of proportion by people who like to make mountains out of mole-hills.

BEAT: *Can you give us a particular reason why you haven't been releasing so many records lately?*
GERRY: Well actually I could give you a million reasons, but they all boil down to the fact that I'm too lazy.
BEAT: *Gerry and the Pacemakers latest release in the States is "La-La," when asked about it Gerry said.*
GERRY: Truthfully the record didn't do too much in Britain, so we're more or less pinning our hopes on the American Market for this one.
BEAT: *What are your plans for this year?*
GERRY: We're doing a night club act in Manilla soon, and then we do Summer Season at a British holiday resort.
BEAT: *Any plans for a visit to the States this year?*
GERRY: I wish there was but unfortunately no, I think we'll be there early next year though.
BEAT: *Gerry then went on to say that he thought American Kids were more with it than British Kids, and much more enthusiastic towards groups.*
GERRY: I just found out today that my wife is expecting, so stand by for a barrage of cigars in the near future.
BEAT: *Favourite American singers?*
GERRY: Definitely Sinatra, and Sammy Davis, Jr.
BEAT: *Any chance of another movie in the near future?*
GERRY: Not for a while I'm afraid.
BEAT: *What are you doing at the present time?*
GERRY: Mostly Night Club stuff and a weekly T.V. Show.
BEAT: *Gerry concluded by saying that if he had to live anywhere else rather than England it would definitely be California.*

He then slipped on his famous Hi-Heeled Boots and said Ta-Ra.

Stars' Comments on Hair

(Continued from Page 4)

MARK LINDSAY: "From my point of view I have a pretty unusual hair style. I'd call it early American. (Ed. note—Mark sports a fairly long but neat ponytail) I get a lot of comments from so called adults who take a dim view of unusual hairstyles like mine. Our forefathers wore their hair like this. However, I would draw the line at people who have long hair and don't wash it for three or four years at a time."

JOEY PAIGE: "I think there should be some kind of standard set as to how long hair can be. I think it's infringing on a person's personal rights to require him to cut his hair but I think it's the school's privilege to discourage long hair. I don't think they should be suspended for it though.

P.F. SLOAN: "On basic principle I have to say no. As long as it's not dirty. If it's clean I don't think they have the right. The next thing they'll do is tell you you can't have brown eyes or something."

EDDIE MEDORA of the Sunrays: "I'm with the kids. School is for learning and not for being told how to look. That's a personal thing."

RICK HANN of the Sunrays: "I think school is a place where you go to learn but you have to learn more than just education—you have to learn life. Long hair is a rebellion thing. In high school you can't get away with wearing your hair too long but in college you're supposed to be a man and do what you want to."

Then there is also **BOB DYLAN's** recent comments on hair: "The thing most people don't realize is that it's *warmer* to have long hair. Everybody wants to be warm. People with short hair freeze easily."

KRLA ARCHIVES

The BEAT Goes To The Movies
'Stop The World— I Want To Get Off'

...MILLICENT MARTIN

...AND MILLICENT MARTIN

...AND GUESS WHO?

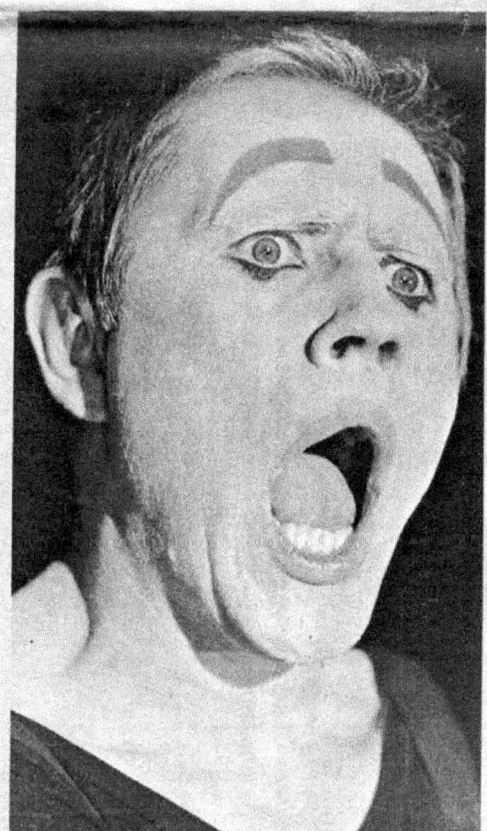

...TONY TANNER

...BEHIND THE SCENES

Critically acclaimed as a major breakthrough in the legitimate musical theater, "Stop The World—I Want To Get Off" has now been made into a giant Warner Brothers motion picture crammed with color, music and superb acting.

Anthony Newley and Leslie Bricusse created "Stop The World," writing the original book, music, and lyrics and making a star out of Newley. Universal in theme, the movie depicts the triumphs and tribulations of an amoral, though endearing, eternal opportunist called Littlechap.

The fantasy character is evoked by a mimicing clown in a deserted arena. Gradually, the rest of the troupe join in bringing Littlechap's world to life.

Newley both directed the show and starred as Littlechap on stage. Midway through the London run, a young performer (Tony Tanner) stepped into Newley's role when Newley went to New York to open the show on Broadway. Some felt that Tanner was even better than Newley in the part.

In the motion picture production, Tanner again plays Littlechap while Millicent Martin (a British actress who originally starred in the English version of "That Was The Week That Was") takes the multiple parts of his long-suffering wife, Evie, and his international girl friends.

For all of its intermittent seriousness, the show has some of the liveliest numbers ever written for a musical. Among the movie's 15 songs are "What Kind Of Fool Am I?," "Once In A Lifetime" and "Gonna Build A Mountain." These songs alone have been recorded by 98 American artists and in places as diverse as Australia and Israel where the show has also been staged with resounding success.

Except to say that "Stop The World—I Want To Get Off" is a symbolic morality-musical whose anti-hero, Littlechap, could be any man, it would be unfair of us to give you any more of the plot. But we do advise you not to miss what could very well be the best musical of 1966.

KRLA ARCHIVES

America's Largest Teen NEWSpaper — 15¢

KRLA BEAT
Edition
APRIL 30, 1966

be good to your **MAMA'S** and **PAPA'S**

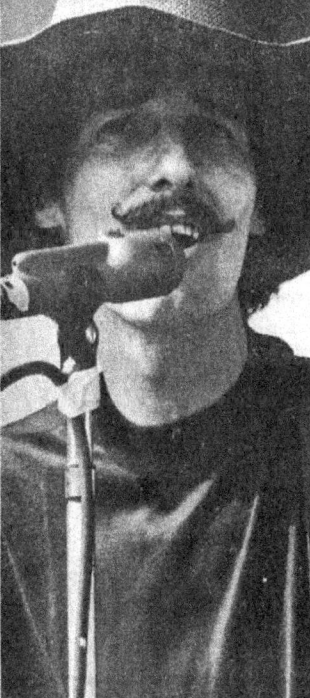

KRLA BEAT

Volume 2, Number 7 — April 30, 1966

Here They Come!

By Louise Criscione

The Beatles have announced the schedule for their August tour of America and Tony Barrow cabled *The BEAT* the information immediately so that you would be the first to know what dates and cities will be featuring Beatle concerts this year.

Fourteen cities are now certain for the Beatle tour which will open in Chicago on August 12 and then rapidly move on to Detroit (13), Louisville (14), Washington (15), Philadelphia (16), Toronto, Canada (17), Boston (18), Memphis (19), Cincinnati (20) and St. Louis on August 21.

The Beatles will then take a slight breathing spell before hitting New York City on August 23. The 24th of August will be a free traveling day and then John, Paul, George and Ringo appear in Seattle on the 25th.

Los Angeles will definitely be a Beatle stop this year despite some initial talk that the Beatles would by-pass the city this year. August 28 is the date firmly set for the Beatles appearance in L.A. which leaves them a full two days rest between Seattle and Los Angeles. On both of their former cross-country tours, the Beatles chose to spend time-off in L.A. just lazing about.

Seclusion?

In 1964 they spent their free time in supposed seclusion among the movie star colony in Bel Air. However, as always happens, their fans discovered their hideaway and the Bel Air Patrol was forced to work extra long shifts to keep fans from overrunning not only the Beatles' house but all homes in the vicinity.

August of '65 found the Beatles hoping for a little peace and quiet again up in the hills, but this time in Benedict Canyon. Once more their faithful and diligent fans discovered their house and camped out all up and down the street until police cleared them out. At which time the persistent fans found hiding places in trash cans, behind bushes and anything else that was handy.

And so it went in every single city where the Beatles spent more than a few hours. It bothered everyone but the Beatles. Paul once told *The BEAT* that the Beatles weren't at all disturbed because they saw what they wanted to see and went where they wanted to go. And they did too. They popped up at recording sessions, night clubs and Elvis Presley's house. The people who the Beatles wanted to meet or old friends who they wanted to see again were merely invited to wherever the Beatles were staying.

After Los Angeles the Beatles will make one more stop, closing their tour in San Francisco—where they chose to end their tour last year, too. The San Francisco Beatle appearance will be on August 29 and as of now it is not known whether the Beatles will immediately head back for England following their concert or if they will remain in San Francisco for a few days to rest, relax and see the famous San Francisco sights.

Speaking with the various promoters along the Beatle route, *The BEAT* has discovered that if at all possible, the Beatles would rather skip the prestige spots such as the Cow Palace and the Hollywood Bowl and instead play the bigger auditoriums where more of their fans will be able to see them.

Sullivan, Too?

It is highly probable that somewhere on their hectic tour, the Beatles will take time out to appear on "Ed Sullivan," the show which first introduced them to America in February of 1964. But as of yet their appearance is not definite.

If you are lucky enough to live in any of the 14 chosen cities you have only to save up your ticket money. However if you don't, *The BEAT* suggests that you really start penny-pinching in order to have enough money for not only your concert ticket but your plane fare as well!

And if you can't possibly come up with enough money to attend one of the 14 Beatle concerts yourself, don't fret. *The BEAT* will follow the tour along from the time it begins in Chicago until it winds up in San Francisco letting you in on all of the highlights of the entire tour.

HERB AND HUBERT—Tijuana Brass leader Herb Alpert and Hubert Humphrey, Vice President of the United States, chat briefly after the recent White House Press Correspondents Dinner in Washington D.C. where Herb and the Tijuana Brass performed. The group received the first standing ovation given to an artist in the history of the dinner.

...RINGO AND PAUL STEPPIN' DOWN STATESIDE

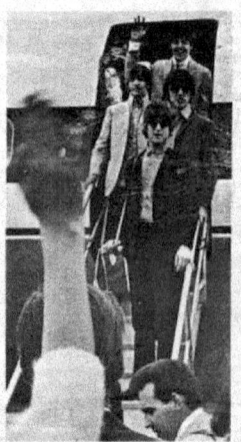

...ARRIVING AUGUST 12

Beatles Sell Out

Beatles, Paul McCartney and John Lennon, know as much about handling large amounts of money as they do about writing fantastic material, since they're experienced in both.

Quite some time ago, Brian Epstein formed Lenmac Enterprises, Ltd. with John and Paul holding 40 per cent each and Epstein holding the remaining 20 per cent. The company was formed to receive the composers' share of the royalties from the songs which Lennon and McCartney wrote which included "From Me To You," "She Loves You" and "All My Loving."

Since its formation the Lenmac company has been doing landslide business. Its income last year was more than a half million dollars and this year it will net well over one million dollars. Next year, unfortunately, it will drop to only about $200,000 as the royalties decrease.

Now, John and Paul as well as Epstein have sold their shares in Lenmac to its sister company, Northern Songs Limited. Each Beatle received a nice $408,000 and Epstein sold out for $204,000.

Lennon and McCartney will continue to derive a hefty profit from Northern Songs which collects royalties on their songs as publishers. They own about 30 per cent of Northern Songs — worth one and a half million dollars.

What the whole thing boils down to is the fact that it will be a long, long time (would you believe about a century and a half) before John and Paul will be forced to scrub floors for a living.

Inside the BEAT

On The Beat	3
The Mama's And Papa's	4-5
Proby — The Man And The Boy	7
Teen Panel Discussion	10
Adventures of Robin Boyd	12
Where The Real Action Is	13
For Girls Only	14
Winners of Beat Poll	15

KRLA ARCHIVES

... JEREMY AND CHAD

SETTING IT STRAIGHT

British Duo Against Draft, But Didn't Flee

The April 16th issue of *The BEAT* ("War" by Louise Criscione) inferred that Columbia recording artists CHAD and JEREMY were attempting to evade U.S. military service.

Miss Criscione stated that CHAD and JEREMY were among those entertainers who had suggested that they would be happy to serve, but who, in fact, were trying "every way possible" to avoid being called.

It was further alleged that CHAD and JEREMY's recent London trip was made to "escape the draft."

We hereby make an absolute retraction of the foregoing inferences and statements regarding CHAD and JEREMY, and extend our sincere apologies to them. We find the information upon which the article was based to be totally unsubstantiated.

We have invited CHAD and JEREMY to state their own position on the subject, and their reply is below.

The Editors

What really makes us angry about the article is that bland inaccuracies are stated with authority.

It is alleged that we returned to England to escape the U.S. draft. This is untrue on two counts:

(1) Jeremy had been in London since June of last year performing in a musical show called "Passion Flower Hotel" and I was required to join him in London as a matter of urgency because had I not done so, we should have had no records to release.

In fact, Columbia Records insisted that we record in London and it was for this reason that I returned home for a brief spell.

(2) As our status in America is that of "resident aliens," we do not have to resort to "draft-dodging" and there is no truth in Miss Criscione's suggestion that the draft can be evaded by returning to England "during a certain time period."

What happens is this: If, as and when an alien receives so-called "Call-up" papers, he has two alternatives. He can either stay in America and enlist or he may return to his native country.

If Jeremy and I received "Call-up" papers, we would most certainly return home and we see nothing to be ashamed of.

We are not Americans and do not owe any military obligation to the United States.

There is no question of "dodging" or trickery. We were also dismayed with the reference to us "hauling in money" over here. We cannot understand resentment of our earning-power.

In a free economy, it is one's entitlement to earn as much as possible and it should be remembered that in addition to making money over here, we also pay taxes over here.

We object very much to Miss Criscione associating us with entertainers who had given their views on the Vietnam war and the draft and who, Miss Criscione says, "were reluctant" to give their opinions.

In fact, neither of us was asked for our opinion. But we are taking this opportunity, now, to express some of our views.

We do not believe in the draft, which was abolished in England some time ago, and we believe that if the armed services were run in a more humane manner there would be sufficient voluntary enlistment from more natural-born fighters.

We would not fight in Vietnam for two reasons: Firstly, because we believe the war is immoral, and secondly, we don't need to fight there.

We haven't been associated with any of the anti-war movements because, chiefly, we are entertainers carving a career for ourselves.

But we do respect the protestors who expose themselves to the possibility of violent reprisals. We believe that minority groups who say "I will not fight" demonstrate more courage than those who go with the tide and do what they feel their neighbors would like them to do.

We wish every decent, ordinary person in the entire world would just sit down and say "This lunacy has got to stop. Let's stop killing each other."

Finally, we would suggest that if Louise Criscione feels impelled to crusade for the U.S. Government in a pop-music newspaper, she should select her targets with accuracy and with care.

We — on this occasion — don't answer the description of the wanted men.

CHAD STUART & JEREMY CLYDE

Donovan Says He's Not 'Folk Singer'

Many have tried to categorize Donovan, along with other poets and singers in contemporary music, but Donovan insists that "it's getting more difficult every day to do that." Does he agree with the label which has been tagged on him so often; that of "folk singer?"

"No. *Any* label which suffices to the person who's using it and helps them in thinking about me... well then, by all means *use* it, if you have to explain it. I don't think I'm a folk singer at all; I think I'm just a contemporary writer. It was okay three years ago to be called a folk singer, but in the new thinking... in the new explosion of intellect... I'd say you can't use the term any more. There are still some folk singers around, but it's just a name."

Very Aware

Though still very young, Donovan is already very aware of everything going on about him. Very much involved in "what's happening" in contemporary music, and in creating "what's *going* to happen," he speaks of the new trends now taking shape in pop music.

"The Indian classical sounds, Moroccan music, raga, the *exotic* sounds that the groups have been listening to in their leisure time while they played pop music influenced them; and now the pop music has become Indian. Like the Byrds, and the Beatles, and me. In a few months the sounds will all have Eastern flavors to them, probably in the pop music."

Donovan is also certain of the dominant influences on pop music of the last two years, and just what effects they have had. The most important of these influences have been "Bob Dylan and the Beatles. They have personalized it; made it one man's feelings which turned into the whole nation's feelings."

Has *he* had any influence on pop music? "Whether I *want* to or not, I'm *going* to. Whether Dylan or the Beatles, or *anybody* wants to, *they're going to* because we're writing things that the young are listening to."

He Colors

In the stories which he weaves with his words and music, what main themes is Donovan trying to communicate to his listeners — young *and* old? He is thoughtful of this when he explains, "I color in different ways, but the main things are touch and contact." He writes also of *love;* love between all mankind.

His songs contain much sun and color imagery, and frequently are written in the form of fairy tales. Of the colorful, sunny side of his work, Donovan admits: "The things that hit my eye the most in *any* situation: colors, the drama of it, and the *splendor,* maybe."

Too often Donovan has been crowded into the tiny vacuum which some critics reserve for those entertainers whom they have labeled "message singers." Donovan feels little antagonism toward these people, and explains: "Most entertainers don't use it to *be* message. The message is spoken by the *songs*. There isn't really a *message;* there's only a big story, told by one artist. A big, long story, and the story's in different sequences and different things happen; and out of that come a lot of songs, and in the end you get a whole story which influences and is a message, really.

"But the word 'message' is for the older generation to use; the young just nod their heads: 'I understand' inside themselves. Leave the 'message' to the older generation, 'cause the young are getting on pretty good, now.

"Music is being produced on a nice, beautiful level, and it's happy."

An innovator, rather than a follower, Donovan enjoys creative experimentations with his art. "I'm already writing for children — fairy tales in music; I'm writing classical, and jazz, pop blues or 'folk rock' — whatever you call it — I do all that; and Greek and Indian melodies.

A Visual Side

"Then there's a visual side of it which I'm going to do in films. I'm going to do some movies, but not the usual pop-style movies. They won't be accepted, maybe, at first — but they'll be *beautiful!*"

When *The BEAT* asked Don what other areas of show business he would like to get into, his face lit up and he enthusiastically replied, that "We're gonna do stage plays, and blow the theatrical minds! There might be a chance to do something on Broadway, but we'll probably do something in London first. But I'm afraid we won't be following the formula of audience looking at the stage; more the stage will engulf the audience, and the people won't know *what's happening!*"

Donovan seems to know "what's happening" in the world about him, and he is making a sincere attempt to communicate some of his impressions of his own experiences in that world and to share them with others. The songs he sings, the stories he tells — all are light and happy; pervaded with a sunny feeling of well-being and peace. Perhaps Donovan really is the Lyric Prince of Happy Songs in this sometimes dizzy world of pop music.

KRLA ARCHIVES

On the BEAT
By Louise Criscione

The Young Rascals are certainly keeping themselves busy enough by doing a photo layout for *Seventeen*, playing the Brooklyn Fox for eight days, doing a tour of one-nighters throughout the East, then a tour of the Mid-west and finally winding up in Hollywood during the later part of May.

They've also just released their first album, titled strangely enough "The Young Rascals." And by the way, although they appeared on "Hullabaloo" minus their knickers etc. this doesn't necessarily mean that they have abandoned their on-stage outfits. But on the other hand – it doesn't mean that they haven't. I kind of like them without the knickers – what do you think?

Controversy

Peter and Gordon are off on an eight week coast to coast tour to promote their newest LP appropriately titled after their smash single, "Woman." There has been quite a bit of pro and con press given to "Woman" now that Paul McCartney has officially admitted to penning it.

... YOUNG RASCALS

One British paper came right out and said they couldn't blame Paul for wanting his name on it. Others are 100% behind Paul and his Bernard Webb bit (or Ace Smith here in the States.)

Personally, I can see Paul's viewpoint very well. I can understand his wanting to see if one of his compositions could make it without his famous name anywhere on it. At least, now he knows that his work can stand on its own considerable musical merit.

The Shadows of Knight have done something which Them could never do. They've made "Gloria" a nationwide hit. More than a year ago, Them released "Gloria" and it immediately soared to the top of the Southern California charts and remained there for what seemed like months. But in the national charts it never went any higher than the low nineties.

Shadows of "Gloria"

Now, the Shadows of Knight (who have to be the wildest titled group to come along in ages) is sending "Gloria" bounding up the nation's charts. The five Shadows (or Knights if you prefer) – Warren, Jerry, Tom, Jim and Joe – begin their career in the summer of '65 by playing the Cellar in Arlington Heights, a suburb of Chicago.

"Gloria," their debut disc, broke in Chicago and has since spread throughout the nation. The record is really a groove and from the sound of it so are the Shadows of Knight. Their name *alone* is worth a mint!

QUICK ONES: Mick Jagger believes that the Beatles are the most creative song writers and performers going ... Rick of the DC5 is buying a stationery store in London and Mike Smith has just purchased a new, black, hard-top E-type Jag ... Is Scott Walker trying to cash in on some publicity by knocking Mick Jagger? ... While in Paris, Brigitte Bardot asked to meet the Stones and got her wish when the Stones threw a small party. Outcome was that Brigitte asked Stones Mick and Keith to write a song for her next movie and they agreed to "have a bash at it."

Guess I'm forced to eat my words. I once wrote that it was unlikely Bob Dylan would ever again have a great impact on the pop market. Would you believe that since "Rainy Day Woman #12 and 35" everyone and their brother will record with a dirge band backing them up?

Come On, El

One of my pop wishes for 1966 was that Elvis would come out with a fantastic single which was not a re-issued oldie or a song from one of his movies. So far, it hasn't happened. But I'm still hoping. After all, Elvis is the one who started this whole thing and it seems a shame to me that he insists on either releasing old records or else singles taken from his one-right-after-the-other movies. Come on, Elvis, show us that you can cut a brand new, fresh sounding hit.

... ELVIS PRESLEY

For those of you who don't think that Paul McCartney is still dating Jane Asher, you're wrong. They showed up together at the premiere of Jane's latest movie, "Alfie."

Yeah, Well ...
Johnny's Better Than Ann
By Tammy Hitchcock

Yeah, well if we don't have that Secret Agent Man himself, Johnny Rivers, strapped down to our "Hot Seat" this week. What do you know about that? To be completely honest, not much. But then I never *do* know much about anything!

However, prepare yourselves for a shock – I have gathered quite a bit of information on Johnny Rivers (being as he lives in the same city, drives down the same streets and frequents the same clubs as I and roughly eight million other people do.)

Anyway, I have discovered that Johnny is 22 years old (perfect) and was born in Baton Rouge, Lousiana (which means a lot if you happen to be from Baton Rouge, which I'm not.)

Wasted

Yeah, well now that I've wasted three paragraphs on absolutely nothing, suppose we get down to business. Like what's gonna happen on the pop scene, Johnny?

"New trends? No, I don't know." Yeah, well that's great, Johnny, you're doing just fine. Anything else you wanta say on the subject?

"I think rhythm and blues is just as strong as it ever was and the protest songs. I'm pretty sure, are on their way out. Folk tunes will always hit if they're a good one – ballads will always hit if they're good and country songs will hit if they're good."

Yeah, well can I get a word in here somewhere, Johnny? I can? Groovy. I'd just like to know how far you think I'd get if I wrote and produced and sang (since no one in their right mind would come near me) a song entitled, "Help Raise Tammy Hitchcock's Wages."

Not very far? Then would you like to donate to the cause? You wouldn't. Yeah, well then how about if we change the subject. Like to Johnny Rivers. That you like – I thought so.

Who Asked?

Did you all know that Johnny is in the National Guard? Yeah, well I didn't either until I spotted him one day all decked out in his uniform and since it wasn't Halloween or anything and since I hadn't heard of any masquerade balls being held anywhere, I figured it out for myself. That he was in the National Guard, I mean. Which is quite brilliant, don't you think? You don't. Well, who asked you anyway?

Despite all that drabble, Johnny told me later that he *is* in the Guard and that he had just been to Vietnam (as a civilian) to entertain the troups with Ann Margaret. Oops, I don't think I wrote that right! But you know what I mean and if you don't – forget it.

What Johnny didn't tell me but what I heard by having big ears, was that Johnny went over bigger with the servicemen than Ann did. Yeah, well those servicemen are pretty smart – I dig Johnny better than Ann too!

But I don't want all of you Ann Margaret fans down on me – I said I just *heard* that Johnny went over better. 'Course, I have to admit that I heard it from another girl. So, you can take it from there.

Back to Johnny. He was talking about something but I was so absorbed in looking at him that I don't have the foggiest idea what he was talking about, *however* I'm sure it was interesting and I wish

... JOHNNY RIVERS

he wasn't so cute (I don't really) so that I would pay less attention to what he looks like and more to what he's saying.

I did catch the last part, though. "It eliminates a lot of people that are making it who more-or-less just got lucky on a few songs." Yeah, well I agree with you Johnny. Fact of the matter is, you once told me that the moon was red and I believed *that*. Which goes to show what I think of Johnny Rivers ... Groovy!!!!!!

Say you saw it in The BEAT

KRLA ARCHIVES

A Tale of Mama's and Papa's

By Carol Deck

Once upon a time there were four people.

Actually there were more but you don't write fairy tales about the entire human race so let's just stick to these four.

One was named Denny and was a rather good looking young Canadian who could have possibly been another Marlon Brando or John Lennon if he'd really wanted to, but he didn't seem to, so he stayed a Denny. He was a member of a group called the Halifax Three.

Another was named Cass and was totally indescribable except in superlatives. She was a large, bubbly, broad minded soul who loved antiques, art and Bob Dylan. She had an obsession about John Lennon, so perhaps it was good that Denny wasn't another Lennon—Cass couldn't have taken another of her idol. She was a member of the Big Three, who ruled the New York folk scene for a time.

Another was named John and was of Greenwich Village vintage. He was a tall thin creative song writer who might have looked like any rising young executive except for his perpetual poverty stricken image.

A Lovely Lass

The fourth was a lovely lithesome blonde lass named Michelle whom every guy fell in love with at first sight. She was a model with a voice and a smile that could have conquered the world had she wanted to, but she didn't seem to.

All four seemed to have a total lack of a thing called ambition.

Denny and Cass played for a while in a rock and roll group known as the Mugwumps. Other fellow Mugwumps at the time included a couple of Lovin' Spoonful types by the names of John Sebastian and Zal Yanovsky.

Then for a while more John and Michelle and Denny were in a very big group called the Journeymen.

Finally, one day, John, Michelle and Denny made a decision—they decided they didn't want to work anymore. So they went to the Bahamas.

They took with them an itinerent guitar player they called The Doctor because he told science fiction stories. The Doctor had played with the Halifax Three and a folk duo called Ian and Sylvia.

In the Bahamas they spent their time doing exactly what they wanted to do—nothing. However, the governor of the islands decided one day that they were not contributing too greatly to the economy of the area and started hinting that they should perhaps either go to work or leave.

So they started singing again, this time in a little local club. It just so happened, as things often do in fairy tales, that Cass was working as a waitress in that very club.

Cass' Visions

Now Cass didn't exactly picture herself as the world's greatest waitress but she did have visions of herself as somewhat of a singer and started bugging the three beachcombing singers to let her join them.

They told her she didn't have the range they needed for a fourth voice and she was brokenhearted. Then her good fairy appeared and mysteriously gave her the range they wanted and she joined the group.

After a while they tired of the island life and moved on to other pastures—New York.

There John wrote a song called "California Dreamin'" that they liked so much they did what was to them the only natural thing—they stopped dreaming about California and moved out here.

Somewhere along the line down the folk family tree they had met a guy by the name of Barry McGuire who thought they had a lot of talent.

Barry took them to Lou Adler, head of Dunhill Records, who produces Barry's records, including one called "The Eve of Destruction" that caused a few ripples in everyone's cool.

Lou promptly put them to work (which was a major feat in itself) as the back-up group behind Barry.

They backed Barry on his second album and on a nationwide television special and they cut a single all by themselves called "Go Where You Want To" which John had written.

And then it happened—they went back and picked up the song that had brought them west and was to bring them into the hearts of the world.

Up The Ladder

They recorded "California Dreamin'" and started on their way up the express ladder to success.

They followed that with an album titled "If You Can Believe Your Eyes and Ears" and most people couldn't.

By popular demand they pulled from that album their single, "Monday Monday," written by John and Michelle. And they considered pulling a third single, "I Call Your Name," from it—an unprecedented move in the recording industry.

However, Lou seemed to feel maybe he could get them to start work on a new album.

However, Lou knew it wasn't easy to get *any* work out of them. "We hate to work you know," said John, "So we turn down everything that comes in."

THE MAMA'S AND PAPA'S — John, Michelle, Cass and Denny, reverting to their old Bahaman ways and partaking of their favorite past time — doing nothing. "We just hate to work."

KRLA ARCHIVES

Photo: Guy Webster

And Lou added, "I always have the feeling someday I'm going to wake up and they'll all be gone—back to the Bahamas or somewhere."

Meanwhile they're all living happily every after in newly purchased houses complete with swimming pools they keep warmed up to over 100 degrees so they can swim all night.

And they're all driving new cars or motorcycles they've bought since their first hit. That's a bit of a change from the rented car they drove to California and then had stolen along with everything they didn't have on them at the time.

Right now, and probably for years to come, they are one of America's most popular groups. England hasn't exactly caught on to them yet, but give 'em a chance.

The Rolling Stones' manager, Andrew Oldham, has recognized them as the talented lot they are and even took out a full page advertisement in every large British paper to tell people how great "California Dreamin'" is, but it still hasn't gone as well over there as it has here.

So Lou's getting even by not giving them "Monday Monday" until he's sure they're ready for it. He says if the record becomes number one nationwide over here maybe England will realize what they're missing.

But we know how great the Mama's and Papa's are—'cause we do believe our eyes and ears, and they're telling us that the Mama's and Papa's are on their way to becoming an American institution.

Be Good To Your Mama's And Papa's

Join Their International Fan Club   321 South Beverly Drive, Beverly Hills, California

KRLA ARCHIVES

The Mystic 'Them'

By Carol Deck

Them are truly a mystic group. They've had four huge hits in this country and yet they've never been seen live here.

Their "Gloria" is one of the all time top selling records both here and in England. It's a standard now. Every group plays it and it consistently comes back as a request number.

The Shadows of Knight have just released a new version of it and the reaction has caused Them's original version to creep back on the national charts.

And yet what do *you* know about Them?

Quick – can you rattle off their names and vital statistics?

You know their sound and their records – "Baby Please Don't Go," "Here Comes the Night" and "Mystic Eyes" – but what do you know about these five mysterious Irish lads?

Stateside

Hopefully they will be coming to the country soon, if the Immigration Authorities will recognize them as the great talent they are, and you'll be able to see and hear this wild, turbulent pop-jazz group live.

When they do come, be prepared to meet five highly individualistic creative young men.

You'll probably first become aware of Van Morrison, creator and leader of Them. Van's a moody, unpredictable but always creative young man who's written several hits not only for Them but for other groups as well.

People always seem to be asking Van how he writes which automatically sets him off. "How can you explain to someone in a half hour interview what images and emotions result in my writing a song?" he says.

Van Explains

But then sometimes he *can* explain how a certain song came about. Asked about their latest hit, "Mystic Eyes," he tells of being in Nottingham Park one day and seeing a graveyard beside one of the parks' boundary walls and children playing next to the wall.

"You know man, there was life and death beside one another . . . so close . . . yet so different . . . 'n then I thought of the bright lights in the children's eyes . . . and the cloudy lights in the eyes of the dead . . . 'n 'Mystic Eyes' happened."

And the other members of the group are equally as aware of things around them as Van. Due to numerous changes in the group, there are now only two of the original Them still in the group – Van and Alan Henderson.

Alan's the group's quiet member, with deep set eyes that many find almost violent in appearance. He plays bass guitar and is one of those guitarists who become totally engrossed in their playing.

Lead guitarist is Jim Armstrong, who looks like the boy next door, but is actually one of England's top session men. He's responsible for a lot of the group's jazz influence.

The one with the beard and leather coat who reminds you of Manfred Mann is Ray Elliott, organist and sax player. He was schooled in jazz along with Jim and feels Them have just the right combination of jazz and pop to create a new art form.

And newest member of the group is David Tufrey, drummer, who replaced John Wilson.

You may sometimes see pictures of Them where there are six. The extra one is their A&R man, Tommy Scott, who plays with them and wrote their newest single, "Call My Name."

Van's Group

They're a group, but they're Van's group. They're not an "in" group nor an "out" group. They often feel alone on the music scene because they're starting something new that's just beginning to catch on.

Meanwhile they walk alone, a mystic lot of individuals trying to unite the worlds of pop and jazz.

With a little cooperation from U.S. Immigration Authorities, Them will soon be bringing the original "Gloria" back to America and at the same time hit us with their new material – all totally original and totally Them.

Some Producers' Hints From Beach Boy Brian

For the last few weeks, we have been speaking with various record producers exclusively in *The BEAT* in an effort to take *The BEAT's* readers behind the radio dial to find out just how records are made.

In our concluding article of this series, we are speaking with Brian Wilson – a man who has succeeded in producing one of the most important sounds in pop music in the last five years.

Standing in the middle of today's contemporary music production and looking around us, we asked Brian to give us an idea of what was going on in production. "I think that record production has definitely improved. Several people have managed to raise the standards of the record business, and I feel that records are being made with much more care and there's much more *music* involved in the record industry.

"First of all, there's a consciousness of the value of a good bass line, and records are being made so that they sound as though they were thought out and the things in the records belong there for a reason; there aren't as many unnecessary elements in records."

No Traveling

Brian has produced the Beach Boys' many hit records with a great deal of care and skill for several years. Lately, he has discontinued his road traveling with the rest of the group in order to devote more and more time to his producing activities, experimenting with many new sounds of his own. "In record production, I'm trying to be as harmonic and as melodic as I can, and at the same time dynamic. I'm trying to use dynamics more effectively.

"I'm experimenting in sound combinations with combinations of instruments which aren't generally associated with the rock 'n' roll business.

"I think that the melody is a thought in itself, and it has body just like the words are in a good word-body. I think that a marriage of good lyrics and a good melody is a very powerful medium of expression.

"I try to be conscious of originality in melody. I think *harmonically*, to start with. Harmony inspires melody with me. I feel that there could definitely be more originality in melody writing in the business; melodically, I think this business is weak and there isn't enough emphasis placed on it."

As a record producer, Brian must constantly watch the rest of the record business, observing all new techniques which are being employed in producing as well as any elements which gain increased importance over a period of time.

"Other elements which have evolved are elements such as using voice a little more subtly – not quite as much of the stereotyped background sound. I think background music – especially in vocals – are using much more than just three notes now. I think that subtlety – thanks to Phil Spector – is in record making where you hear something as a total unit, and eventually discover things in the record, which is a beautiful contribution to the business. Also, subtlety in arrangement."

Brian has created, developed, and expanded his craft – and he has some very definite opinions about what is being done with it. "Popular music – in the form of Top 40 – has to expand and has to gain much more widespread respect as a result of someone making an art out of that kind of music. There are enough elements to work with now.

"There is now an acceptance of certain instrumentations. There is a widespread acceptance of new and unlimited instrumentation in this business, that we have reached the spot now where there is an infinite amount of things you can do; now it's really just up to the creative people."

Inspiration

Brian explains some of his efforts in this way: "I think *any* artistic endeavor – if it's really inspired – is something that only the person that's inspired knows, and to make that manifest – it's generally very individualistic how a person goes about making manifest what he conceives.

"So, when I conceive of something, generally it's a conception of harmony-melody-arrangement-song . . . it's all more or less *one* conception. I usually develop the song and the arrangement simultaneously, and the production ideas I build. I usually go in very prepared – before I ever get to the studio I have a general idea of how it's going to come out. But a lot of things develop *in* the studio out of enthusiasm about what's happening at the time. Usually, the record comes out a *little* bit differently than I originally conceived it, but only different because it's more *expanded*.

"I don't mean that the original conception was buried with all kinds of ideas that were generated in the studio; the original conception always shines right through. Things happen in the studio that don't happen at home – there's an *atmosphere* working in a studio, and only there can certain things be generated."

Other Producers

About record producers in general, Brian theorizes that: "I think it is essential to a producer's ability to generate an enthusiasm toward a product which he has, to other people. It's a *controlled* enthusiasm to those you're working with – that is what is really important."

As for himself, when asked where *he is going* as a record producer, he replies: "I want to *grow* – and I think that the only way to say where I'm going is to listen to the new sounds I have produced in 'Pet Sounds.' I think that is the only good, accurate indication of where I'm going."

Thank you, Brian – and thank you to all of the producers who given their time and shared some of their knowledge of record production and what it takes to produce a good record with *The BEAT* over the last few weeks. We hope that it has been as interesting and informative for you as it has been for us.

KRLA ARCHIVES

Proby—The Man and The Boy

By Eden

They call him a man, but in so many ways he is still a little boy. His outfits—always velvet, his high-buckle shoes, and the velvet bow which temporarily restrains his shoulder-length locks—always remind you of the attire of the mid-Victorian schoolboys.

But P.J.Proby isn't a schoolboy, and when he gets onstage, he teaches his audience the kind of excitement they would *never* learn in school! P.J.depends, in great part, upon his audience and their reactions for the success of his performance. He reacts to whatever emotion they display, and if they are wild and enthusiastic—so is he.

But if the audience is perhaps a little too young to understand his act, and if they don't respond, P.J. is likely to tell them to go right back home. He will even offer to refund the price of their admission!

Such was the case recently when P.J. appeared at the Hullabaloo club in Hollywood. He played a four-day engagement at the club which was eventually fairly successful. However, opening night was not quite what it might have been. In fact, it almost *wasn't* at all! It just happened to be the same night that the Teenage Fair opened across the street, and fifty thousand screaming teenagers had all come to give the Fair a rousing send-off.

But while they were sending *up* the Fair, they were sending *down* Mr. Proby. There were very few people in the audience, and what few there were obviously were not overly appreciative of P.J.'s talents. He poured his soul into his performance for them and knocked himself out onstage for his tiny audience . . . but they were just too young to care. So P.J. finally asked them, "Why don't you just go back to the Fair? I'll even *give* you the money!"

Boy and Man

He was at once a little boy having a tantrum, and a man doing his best for an audience and getting no thanks in return. And, though he did at times resort to slight sarcasm, for the most part P.J. Proby wore his widest grin . . . a very infectious, appealing sort of smile . . . and gave that audience his all.

He has been quoted as saying that he would someday be the "God of pop music" and he has been accused of an enormous conciet. But in person, P.J. is far more sincere and level-headed than others would have you believe. He is an exceedingly honest and straight-forward person, and when you ask him what ambitions he has for other areas of show business, he will reply that he wants to try his hand at "everything; everything that has to do with the entertainment business I'm interested in . . . as long as I can do it, and do it *well!*"

There is very little in the field of entertainment which *doesn't* interest P.J., and he is constantly trying to broaden his sphere of talents. Although he doesn't generally incorporate them in his stage performances (with the exception of the harmonica), P.J. is able to play the drums, guitar, and the harmonica.

Watching the pop scene in England where he has lived for the last two years, P.J. observes that "in England, it's going more towards the ballad stuff; the beat is slowing down, and it's going back to the old crooning." Will any one artists or group of artists set and build this trend? The man answers firmly, "Me!"

It may come as quite a shock to most of P.J.'s fans, but as of now—he definitely intends *not* to make another single record *for three years!* The reasons for this are many, primarily revolving around a serious disagreement with the record company for which P.J. has been recording, and as they have been thus far unsuccessful in ironing out the difficulty—P.J. staunchly refuses to do any further recordings until he is free of his present contractual commitments.

In the meantime, he will keep his voice in the public's ear by way of the concert and cabaret circuits—here and in England—and by singing the title tunes of various motion pictures. He has already recorded the title tune for Marlon Brando's film "The Chase," and says that there is the possibility that he will record the main theme for the next Sean Connery 007 flick.

P.J. has an enormous, overpowering, professional singing voice with a very wide range, and the songs which he includes in his repertoire of stage material are equally as broad in scope. However, here the conventionality ends. His chestnut brown hair falls softly below his shoulders, and his attire is quite *striking*, to say the least. Has this all been part of a master scheme, of sorts; part of an image which he originally set out to create?

Fast Happenings

"It happened so fast, I didn't have an initial idea. I was thrown into my first big show with Adam Faith after the Beatles' show so fast, that I just decided to do a big band act and see if I could get away with it; no beat group, no guitars, and if I couldn't—I hadn't lost anything. I'd just come back to Hollywood. But it worked!"

Frank and candid . . . that is P.J. Proby. He was banned from most theater and television performances in England recently, and P.J. very honestly explains the reason for his censure: "I was banned because I created a lot of enemies over there for telling the truth. I told the groups over there how they were being taken advantage of and cheated, so the promoters wanted me out of the country. So they were waiting for a chance, and when my pants split onstage, they made a big indecent-type thing out of it. But my pants only split below the knees!

"But this was their chance, so they banned me from all the theaters and from all television."

His own hair is often the point of concern and controversy, but how does P.J. feel about the school officials in this country who prevent their students from growing their own locks? "I don't think school officials have any right to do anything except *teach!* The guidance should be left to the parents, and the teaching should be left to the teachers." Incidentally, a product of military schools himself, P.J. admits that he would probably send his own son to a military academy now.

"I firmly believe in military training for a boy from the very beginning. It gives him a sense of discipline."

Unpredictable in his actions, impulsive and straight-forward in his nature; certain of his talents, and convinced of his own success, past, present, and future. Very much a little boy in moments, on and off stage, yet still a man wrapped up in living his life the way he sees fit. All these are parts of P.J. Proby. For the complete picture of this self-assured, talented, contradictory human being . . . well, you'll have to see him for yourself.

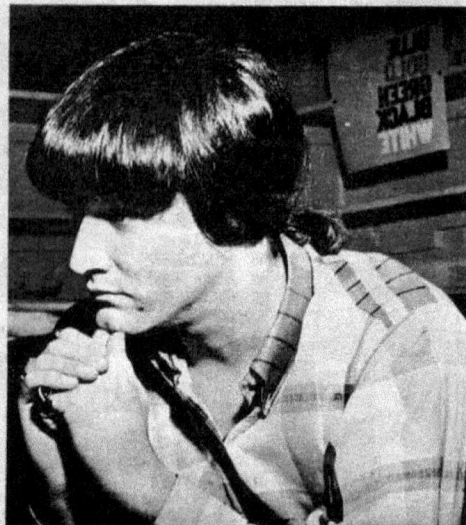

. . . PROBY THINKIN'
BEAT Photo: Chuck Boyd

. . . PROBY IN ACTION

Hawaii-a-go-go Don Ho Style

By Pam Fourzon

You might have seen him on *"Shindig"* (rest its soul), you may have seen him on *"Where The Action Is,"* or, if you were really lucky, you've had the opportunity to go to Hawaii and see in person, the "wild, unpredictable Don Ho and the Swinging Alii's."

Don performs fifty weeks a year at Duke Kahanamoku's in Waikiki.

Have you ever seen a performer in person that you just wanted to drag all your friends to see? Someone that you just want to shout out their greatness from the rooftops?

If so, you know how I feel, and can catch some of this wild excitement about this wild performer! In fact, how popular Don Ho and the Alii's get is going to be up to you, and it is going to be really fascinating to watch, 'cause we, the public, have never made a star out of any pop artists out of our tropical 50th state.

Would you believe that Don Ho got booked over here at one of the most important nightclubs we have . . . simply on word of mouth alone?

Would you believe entertainers like Sonny & Cher, The T. J. Brass, Frankie Avalon, The Righteous Brothers, and the entire SHINDIG cast have all been on his stage in Hawaii and come back shouting his praises?

Don Ho (who introduces his brother, tongue in cheek, as Gung Ho), records on the Reprise label.

He has two ablums out of his own and one of the Alii's, and has sold hundreds of thousands already without even really trying . . . just by one person playing them for another!

Keep your eyes open and tune in your ears and just listen, 'cause once you do you'll probably be a fan. Also, if you listen now, you'll be able to say, "I knew he'd make it."

. . . DON HO

KRLA ARCHIVES

KRLA Tunedex

This Week	Last Week	Title	Artist
1	1	MONDAY, MONDAY	The Mama's & The Papa's
2	24	RAINY DAY WOMEN #12 & 35	Bob Dylan
3	2	SOUL AND INSPIRATION	The Righteous Bros.
4	8	TIME WON'T LET ME	The Outsiders
5	5	SECRET AGENT MAN	Johnny Rivers
6	4	CALIFORNIA DREAMIN'	The Mama's & The Papa's
7	7	SHAPES OF THINGS	The Yardbirds
8	6	KICKS	Paul Revere & The Raiders
9	3	BANG, BANG	Cher
10	11	EIGHT MILES HIGH/WHY	The Byrds
11	16	SLOOP JOHN B	The Beachboys
12	21	THE RAINS CAME	Sir Douglas Quintet
13	14	GOOD LOVIN'	The Young Rascals
14	10	DAYDREAM	The Lovin' Spoonful
15	19	A SIGN OF THE TIMES	Petula Clark
16	12	NOWHERE MAN	The Beatles
17	13	WOMAN	Peter & Gordon
18	9	THE BALLAD OF THE GREEN BERET	S/Sgt. Barry Sadler
19	22	THIS OLD HEART OF MINE	The Isley Bros.
20	30	TRY TOO HARD	The Dave Clark Five
21	29	RHAPSODY IN THE RAIN	Lou Christie
22	28	MESSAGE TO MICHAEL	Dionne Warwick
23	26	MAGIC TOWN	The Vogues
24	23	IT'S TOO LATE	Bobby Goldsboro
25	25	WHAT NOW MY LOVE/SPANISH FLEA	Herb Alpert
26	27	GET READY	The Temptations
27	33	LEANIN' ON THE LAMP POST/HOLD ON	Herman's Hermits
28	31	I HEAR TRUMPETS BLOW	The Tokens
29	—	PLEASE DON'T STOP LOVING ME/FRANKIE & JOHNNY	Elvis Presley
30	34	TEEN-AGE FAILURE	Chad & Jeremy
31	37	I CAN'T GROW PEACHES ON A CHERRY TREE	Just Us
32	39	ALONG COMES MARY/YOUR OWN LOVE	The Association
33	35	FALLING SUGAR	The Palace Guard
34	—	THE SUN AIN'T GONNA SHINE ANYMORE	The Walker Bros.
35	38	CAROLINE, NO	Brian Wilson
36	—	I GOT MY MOJO WORKIN'	Jimmy Smith
37	—	IN MY LITTLE RED BOOK	Love
38	40	NOTHING'S TOO GOOD FOR MY BABY	Stevie Wonder
39	—	HOW DOES THAT GRAB YOU DARLIN'/LAST OF THE SECRET AGENTS	Nancy Sinatra
40	—	HISTORY REPEATS ITSELF	Buddy Starcher

DAVE HULL

BOB EUBANKS

DICK BIONDI

JOHNNY HAYES

EMPEROR HUDSON

CASEY KASEM

CHARLIE O'DONNELL

BILL SLATER

Inside KRLA
By Eden

Everybody's talking about the all-request radio at KRLA this week. Yep, our fave station has done it again, and it looks as though we're starting trends already. The switchboard has been lit up 24 hours a day with listeners' requests from the very beginning of this brand new program, so it looks as though everyone out in radio-land is pleased with it as well.

Of course, this brand new system has brought about many

...DICK BIONDI

changes in the programming on KRLA, and now we are able to offer you a wider selection of the music that *you* want to hear. All you have to do to make your request is to dial one of the two numbers now servicing the request lines. In Los Angeles County, the number is 681-3601, and in Orange County the number is 523-4330.

Be sure to phone in your request today, 'cause it's your turn now to have a voice in the music we play for your listening pleasure.

Scuzz Speaks

The Scuzzy One himself decided to fall by our column this week and swears that he has a couple of things to tell us. First off, he informs us that George Harrison — you remember him; he's the one who wears a Beatle wig — bought and completely furnished a bungalow for his parents at Christmas time last year.

Mr. and Mrs. Harrison moved into their brand new home in February, but they have requested that we not give out the new address. There are several good reasons for this and I'm sure that the Beatle fans here in California will be able to understand.

There are many Beatle fans here in Southern California who have also become *Mrs.* Louise Harrison fans as well because of George's mother's graciousness. Mrs. Harrison has been really wonderful in trying to answer all of the letters which she received for George — and for herself and her husband — in the last two years, and the Beatlemaniacs of Southern California are very grateful.

But, you must understand that she and her husband have had very little privacy in the last couple of years, and it can get somewhat irritating to have your phone constantly ringing, your front door always knocked upon, and bags and bags of mail constantly crowding up your living room.

So as a favor to them we have agreed not to print the new address; but we have been asked to assure all Beatlemaniacs still writing to George and his family that all mail received at the old address will be forwarded to their new home for the period of one year. So fear not — your mail *will* get through!

Hang-Ups, Dick?

As we go to press, poor Dick Biondi is trying to solve his latest hang-up. It seems that he now has developed permanently wrinkled fingers!!! Well, what can you expect from a man who has been dunked in the Bat Tub about 9,372½ times? Ah well, those were the good old days of the Teenage Fair!

And speaking of *Bats* — the mysterious Bat Manager sign has somehow reappeared on John-John's door. Not only that, but the Amazing Pancake Man has been seen entering the upstairs Bat Cave... and he never came out again!!! Uh oh! — looks like trouble in the Bat-Kave-RLA!!!

UNLIKE ANYTHING YOU'VE EVER SEEN!

BATTLE OF THE BULGE

WARNER BROS. PICTURES PRESENTS A CINERAMA, INC. PRODUCTION "BATTLE OF THE BULGE" Starring HENRY FONDA · ROBERT SHAW · ROBERT RYAN · DANA ANDREWS · PIER ANGELI · BARBARA WERLE · GEORGE MONTGOMERY · TY HARDIN · CHARLES BRONSON · HANS CHRISTIAN BLECH · WERNER PETERS · JAMES MacARTHUR and TELLY SAVALAS · Written by Philip Yordan, Milton Sperling, John Melson · Produced by MILTON SPERLING, PHILIP YORDAN · Directed by KEN ANNAKIN · A SIDNEY HARMON IN ASSOCIATION WITH UNITED STATES PICTURES, INC. PRODUCTION · TECHNICOLOR® · ULTRA-PANAVISION®

PACIFIC'S **CINERAMA DOME** Theatre
Magnificent
SUNSET AT VINE · HOLLYWOOD **NOW PLAYING!**

NOW PLAYING IN THEATRES and DRIVE-INS EVERYWHERE!

DIRECT FROM ITS PREMIERE SHOWINGS.
SPECIAL ENGAGEMENT AT POPULAR PRICES. NO RESERVED SEATS.

NOW EVERYONE CAN SEE THE MOST LOVELY MOTION PICTURE OF ALL TIME!

my Fair Lady

Winner of 8 Academy Awards including Best Picture.
AUDREY HEPBURN · REX HARRISON
TECHNICOLOR® · SUPER PANAVISION®70 · FROM WARNER BROS.

DURING the past three years, Stan Major has reported on more than two hundred important news events and now he has been dispatched to Viet Nam and will be reporting back to all of KRLA's listeners all of the latest news.

Great Western Battle of The Bands
JUNE 1 THRU JUNE 5
General Public Will Attend Competition
Send Your Entry Blank Now
GREAT WESTERN EXHIBIT CENTER
P.O. BOX 22108   LOS ANGELES 22
PHONE RA3-3678

SPECIAL BONUS — SUBSCRIBE NOW and receive a free copy of The Bobby Fuller Four's best selling album, "I Fought The Law."

KRLA BEAT Subscription

SAVE 33% Of Regular Price

☐ 1 YEAR — 52 Issues — $5.00   ☐ 2 YEARS — $8.00
☐ 6 MONTHS — $3.00

Enclosed is _____ ☐ CASH ☐ CHECK
PLEASE PRINT — Include Your Zip Code

Send to: .... Age: ......
Address: .... City: ....
State: .... Zip: ....

MAIL YOUR ORDER TO: **KRLA BEAT**
6290 Sunset, Suite 504
Hollywood, Calif. 90028

Foreign Rate: $9.00 — 52 Issues

KRLA ARCHIVES

Teens Study Better With Loud Music!

The next time your parents hit you with "Can't you turn that music down?" you can hit them right back with this. Dr. John Hoffman, currently earning his Ph.D in Education at the University of Southern California, has made experiments and proudly announces that studying with loud music works for teenagers!

Dr. Hoffman tested 281 eleventh grade students while recorded music blared at them with a force of 85 decibels for 30 minutes, which is about as loud as a pneumatic drill.

The good students scored as well or better on the tests than they did when tested in a quiet room. However, students of average and below-average intelligence seemed to be bothered more by the sound.

Dr. Hoffman admits, however, that there is no wonder why parents can't understand their teenagers' tendency to really dig studying with the radio or record player full blast because apparently only teenagers can study that way.

It doesn't work for pre-high school students nor for college students. And it certainly doesn't work for adults, as Dr. Hoffman found out the hard way. He spent eight hours a day for four days giving those tests in all that noise and he says: "It almost drove me nuts!"

THE BEAU BRUMMELS are definitely a very "happening" group, and they manage to keep on top of all the very latest "happenings" by always reading The BEAT. And that goes for catching up on any back reading they may have missed while they were out on tour, as well.

Don Adams To Sue Over 'Detective'

Would you believe that Don Adams, television's "Get Smart" guy, is bringing action against Roulette Records seeking damages and an injunction over their unauthorized release of an album titled, "The Detective." Would you believe the suit has already been filed?

In the complaint, Adams alleges that he made the recording in question in 1960 for the now defunct Hanover-Signature label. Since signing with Hanover-Signature at that time, he has never been paid nor received a statement of any kind.

When Hanover-Signature went bankrupt, masters were acquired by Roulette with whom Adams has never had any correspondence. He was not aware of the Roulette attempt to cash in on the success of his "Get Smart" series until several weeks ago when the album was reviewed in music trade journals. The album cover pictures the back view of a man's head, presumably a detective, but not Don Adams.

Adams' suit seeks to enjoin Roulette and all distributors carrying their product from further issuance of the album, seeks damages and a complete accounting of royalties due.

What makes it even worse is that Adams is currently under contract to United Artists Records and is currently preparing to cut his first album since his emergence as the star of "Get Smart."

The Mama's And Papa's Cancel At Hullabaloo

By Carol Deck

If you were among those who bought tickets to see the Mama's and Papa's at Dave Hull's Hullabaloo over Easter vacation and didn't see them, don't blame the group.

The group did want to appear but were cancelled out by their manager, Bobby Roberts.

Roberts said he pulled the group out for two reasons.

The first was that the club's owner, Gary Bookasta, has distributed hundreds of 50c discount tickets without his permission thereby cutting down on the percentage the group was to have been paid.

The other had to do with the appearance earlier in the week by P.J. Proby.

Lou Adler, head of Dunhill Records which the Mama's and Papa's record for, explained that he had spoken to Proby's manager, Terence Hillman, and was informed that Proby and his musicians had not been paid in full for the first three days of his four day stint and therefore did not go on the last night.

Adler noted that the Mama's and Papa's respect Proby as an artist and therefore would not go on themselves for the five day stint they had booked.

Adler also mentioned that he was promised $11,000 in advertising that he never received and that there had been a possibility that the musician's union would not allow any musicians to go on the night the Mama's and Papa's were set to open until Proby was paid in full.

Bookasta admitted that Proby had not been paid in full but added that he had been contracted to do three shows nightly, 15 in all, and had actually only done eight.

GAC representative Terry Dene said that Proby was booked for $6500 against 50% of the gate, with the band getting $2000.

He charged that the club owes Proby $450 for the third night's shows and the full $1300 for the last night, which never came off.

Bookasta alleged that in view of the fact that the club paid the $1700 plane fare to get Proby to Los Angeles from London as well as the $2000 for the band that Proby actually owes the club money.

Bookasta added that the cancelling of the Mama's and Papa's had only to do with the discount tickets and that the union was not involved at all.

Meanwhile, with the Mama's and Papa's cancelled, as well as the MFQ, another Dunhill group that had been scheduled, the club opened with Joey Paige headlining with the Band Without A Name and the Palace Guard.

Join The DAVE HULL International Fan Club
Send $1.00 for one year to:
Dave Hull Fan Club
634 Sefton,
Monterey Park, Calif.
Monthly Bulletins, Photos, The Works!

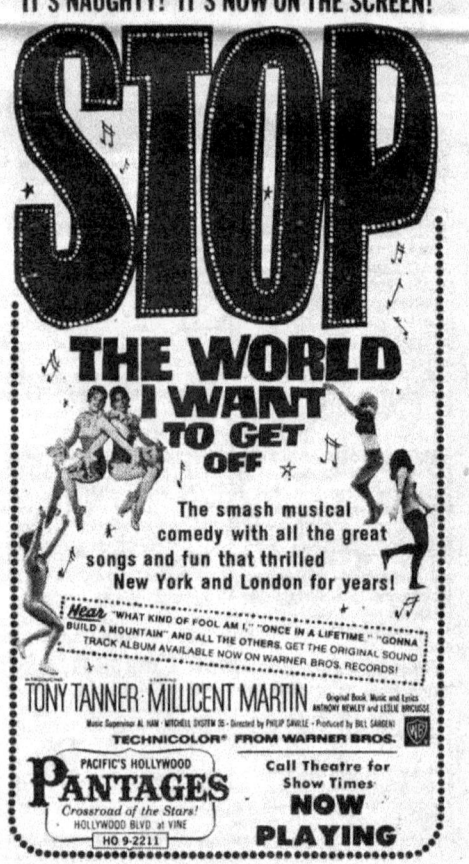

KRLA ARCHIVES

TEEN PANEL DISCUSSION

Green Berets and Barry McGuire

The article you're about to read is the first in a series of teen discussions which will be sponsored and published in The BEAT.

In one respect, the series isn't a new idea. It's been done before, many times.

In another respect, it's brand new. Because The BEAT is going to do it differently.

The teen panel discussion angle has always been too "public" to be of much value. There are some things you just don't care to discuss that openly. There are others you don't dare.

As a result, true feelings aren't always expressed, and the real issues at hand are often bypassed and replaced by less touchy subjects.

The way we're going to go about conducting The BEAT discussions may sound like a "Man From U.N.C.L.E." script, but there's a reason for the cloak and dagger tactics.

To insure complete freedom of speech, we must also insure complete privacy.

Only the five participants will be present during any given discussion. Participants will be chosen from five different areas, and will identify themselves by a first name only. (Their own or a "pen name.")

No adults will be present to moderate the discussion, nor will any representative of The BEAT. The only "outsider" will be a tape recorder. And once the taped material has been transcribed for use in The BEAT, the tapes will be destroyed.

See what we mean about sounding a bit like "U.N.C.L.E.?" But, unfortunately, the element of secrecy is necessary.

We want you to feel free to speak your minds without having to worry about what could happen as a result of making your private opinions public. Such as conflict at home, at school, etc.

We want to hear what *you* have to say, about the subjects that *really* matter to young people.

We won't always agree with your feelings, but we will respect your right to feel them. What's more, we'll listen carefully when you express them, and hope that everyone else will do you the same courtesy.

The exchange of ideas built a world. Perhaps more communication between individuals will help make it a better place to live in.

The topic of this first teen analysis is a hot one.

A few months ago, protest songs were the order of the day. Songs which painted a grim portrait of war, and lashed out at man's inhumanity to his fellow man.

Then a young soldier started a new trend. S/Sgt. Barry Sadler, a member of the U.S. Special Forces, wrote and recorded "The Ballad of The Green Beret." A song that marched right to the number one spot on the charts.

There has been a lot of talk about both trends. Pro and con. The following is more of the same, only this time the talking is being done by the people whose record-buying powers made both trends possible. Today's teenagers.

Participating are Sharon (15), Paul (18), Joanne (16), Bill (17) and Mari (15).

Our transcript of the discussion begins about a half-hour after the participants met in the conference room. After the usual icebreaking, the conversation began to turn toward the subject at hand.

As we begin, Bill is recalling the first time he heard the first "pop" protest song, "Eve Of Destruction."

* * *

BILL—"I wasn't very impressed the first time I heard it. I'd already heard too much about it. The way people were talking, I expected the song to be really radical."

MARI—"It was radical enough for me. All that blood and coagulation stuff. They shouldn't have that in songs. Who wants to think about dying?"

SHARON—"That's what it made me think about too, but I'm glad it did. To me, the word *war* meant H-bombs and X-Y-Z-bombs, and I never really thought much about it besides hoping it would never happen. That song and others like it made me realize that war is *people*. Human beings slaughtering each other. I think about war now, a lot. I even think about me dying, and that's another first."

PAUL—"Has any of this thinking made one bit of difference in your life?"

SHARON—"Yes! I used to feel like my life was...permanent, and that nothing could change it. I know better than that now, and it's made me more conscious of the people around me, and more considerate of them. And I'm not so hung up on my own problems since I realized there is so much injustice in this world."

BILL—"How do you personally define the word injustice?"

SHARON—"Well, injustice is some people starting wars that others have to fight, and some people starving when others have millions. That sort of thing. And anyone being stupid enough to think he's automatically better than someone else because of the color of the other person's skin."

JOANNE—"Remember the line in 'Eve Of Destruction' about the hate in Selma, Alabama? There's a lot of this kind of truth in protest music. Not sugar-coated truth. Facts...what's actually happening. I really wonder about adults who are so against protest music. Maybe they're afraid teenagers might learn how things really are and start wanting to change the world. It could sure use a few changes."

SHARON—"That just made me think of something I was never able to put into words before. If I'm smart enough to know that violence never really solves anything, why doesn't *everyone* know it? Everyone *must* be aware of this. I'm just not that smart or unique. So why don't they *do* something about it?"

PAUL—"That's exactly *why* some people protested against protest songs. They're afraid of change. They don't really like the way the world is, but it's less effort for them as individuals if life follows an established pattern. That way they won't have to go to the trouble of waking up from the great American dream."

MARI—"I'm almost afraid to ask what you mean by that. I suppose you're referring to our way of life. There's nothing wrong with living well. People shouldn't have to feel ashamed of having two cars, or nice clothes. They wouldn't have these things if they hadn't earned them."

PAUL—"That isn't the dream I mean. I refer to the fallacy that everything America does is *right!* We've made many mistakes, internationally and internally, but people still won't wake up and face the fact that we aren't perfect or infallible. We are, at best, human. And how can we make a national effort to correct our mistakes if we won't even admit making them?"

JOANNE—"Protest songs pointed out a lot of human errors. Not just America's, every country's. That's probably why the trend died so quickly."

BILL—"I doubt it. The kids who bought protest records aren't afraid of facing facts. I think the trend died because the songs themselves weren't very good. As music, I mean. Songs have to be more than just speeches to stay popular."

JOANNE—"What I can't understand is how the patriotism trend became such a big deal so fast. It seems like we jumped right from one extreme to another."

BILL—"We did, because one trend creates the next. After all that 'down with war' stuff, the time was perfect for songs like 'Green Beret.' We were just ready to be exposed to the other side of the story. Ready psychologically. I think a lot of teenagers bought 'Green Beret' because they felt guilty about going along with the protest idea. After all, there is a war going on."

PAUL—"Although we won't admit it."

BILL—"*Some* of us won't, you mean. But young people *know* we're at war, because a lot of us know guys who are getting killed in Viet Nam. And we also know we could be next. Whatever you choose to call it, it's still a war."

JOANNE—"I'd like to retract what I said about the patriotism trend. I don't think 'Green Beret' is nearly as patriotic as a lot of the protest songs. Those songs were against destruction. 'Green Beret' almost sounded like it was *for* it. In my opinion, it's far more patriotic to want to learn how to live than it is to want to learn how to destroy life."

MARI—"That's ridiculous! 'Green Beret' was a hundred times better than any protest song could ever be, and I'm really proud of kids for coming to their senses. How can you say that song was *for destruction?* It encouraged people to stand behind their fighting men, and it encouraged those men to be better soldiers."

PAUL—"You've got to be kidding. That song sounded like a Madison Avenue advertising campaign to promote war. It made being 'trained in combat hand to hand' sound *glamorous!* And that part about pinning wings on his son's chest. If it hadn't been for that, I wouldn't have been offended by the song. But that did it. No responsible parent would wish that kind of future on a child. I don't blame the Special Forces for being proud. They worked hard for those berets. But every member should be hoping to God there won't *be* any future need for specially trained combat troops. That's what they're fighting for. The safety of their homes and families. Sometimes I wonder if they aren't fighting because they enjoy it. Some people thrive on violence, you know. It's possible that this type is just naturally attracted to an organization like the Special Forces."

SHARON—"I don't know enough about any part of the Armed Forces to pass judgment, so I can't agree or disagree with you. But you have made a very good point. A person who is mentally and emotionally healthy will turn to violence only as a last resort, and then only to protect himself and what he believes in. But there is something wrong with *any* individual who fights because he *wants* to, whether it's on a battlefield or in a back alley."

MARI—"It looks like I get the last word—we're running out of tape. I just want to say that I haven't changed my mind about any of my views, but I have realized something from just talking about all this. I never stopped to think that it really *is* the same kids. The ones who bought protest songs are buying things like 'Green Beret' now. I don't think it's because they feel guilty. I think it's just because they're willing to listen to both sides. Adults could learn a few lessons from teenagers."

* * *

This series will be continued in a near future issue. If you would like to participate in one of the forthcoming discussions, send your name and address to Teen Panel c/o The BEAT.

KRLA ARCHIVES

BOB AND BILL
THE RIGHTEOUS BROTHERS

YOU'VE LOST THAT LOVIN' FEELIN'
OLD MAN RIVER
LOOK AT ME
WHAT'D I SAY
HUNG ON YOU
<u>MANY</u>
  <u>MANY</u>
    <u>MORE</u>

JUST ONCE IN MY LIFE
UNCHAINED MELODY
THE BLUES
GUESS WHO
EBBTIDE
<u>MANY</u>
  <u>MANY</u>
    <u>MORE</u>

A TRIO OF THE RIGHTEOUS BROTHERS' ALL TIME BEST SELLING ALBUMS. THIS DYNAMIC DUO IS CURRENTLY THE HOTTEST GROUP IN THE COUNTRY AND THESE ARE MUST ALBUMS FOR YOUR COLLECTION. BOTH MONO & STEREO AT BIG SAVINGS AT ALL THE STORES LISTED BELOW. HURRY!

AVAILABLE NOW AT YOUR LOCAL
F.W. WOOLWORTH STORE

KRLA ARCHIVES

Lennon And The Yardbirds –'Bob Lind Is The Greatest'

By Carol Deck

Bob Lind's back from England and from the looks of things we should be glad he came back at all.

Britain discovered Bob so fast and furiously he could have stayed over there and made a mint, but he decided to come home.

He was only there three and a half weeks and just to promote one single, his first, "Ellusive Butterfly."

In just those few short weeks, he filmed every British pop television show, and "Tops In Pops" were so impressed with him they asked him to film four more so they'd have them on tape to show at later dates.

They were that sure that "Ellusive Butterfly" is not a one shot thing and that Bob Lind is going to be one of the major influences on the pop scene.

And his album which is already on the nationwide charts here hasn't even been released there yet, so all they've officially gotten released over there is the one single.

And Bob made some impressive friends while he was in England.

John Lennon's absolutely mad about his writing and says "Ellusive Butterfly" is one of his favorite songs.

The Yardbirds threw one of their famous parties for Bob and then took out ads in the British papers saying, "We think Bob Lind is the greatest."

The Yardbirds are also recording some of Bob's things, as are the Animals and Manfred Mann. And the Four Pennies are recording a "Tribute to Bob Lind."

And America didn't exactly forget him while he was abroad either.

Cher's recorded two of Bob's songs on her new album and the Turtles and the Cascades are all currently cutting Bob's stuff.

Bob worked a tremendous amount while he was in England, but it all payed off. He caught on faster than anything they've seen in a long time.

He also managed to write three songs while he was there.

And if he thought he was getting a vacation when he returned, he was sadly mistaken.

After a quick stopover in California to tell us how it went, he's gone home to Miami for a short visit and then he'll be back to film several television shows here before taking off for London again.

His bookings for the next couple of months include a concert at Lincoln Center with arranger Jack Nitzcher conducting a string section behind him, another tour of England and appearances at the Hollywood Bowl and the Cow Palace with the Beach Boys.

He's also received a movie offer from England.

That's nice work for someone who was making $30 a week two months ago. He now makes $3,000 a night.

With just one record Bob Lind has crashed on the scene and appears destined to become one of the greatest songwriters of the decade.

And now he's released his second single. It's called "Remember the Rain" and if it hits with the impact of "Ellusive Butterfly," there'll be no forgetting it.

The Adventures of Robin Boyd

By Shirley Poston

CHAPTER TWENTY-FIVE

Robin Boyd was not a partial bird, but should she ever be forced to make a choice, George The Genie's chances were excellent.

So, however, were John Lennon's. Therefore, when she saw a reasonable facsimile thereof beckoning to her from a nearby table, Robin gracefully galloped to his side, not to mention the rest of him (and she's been known to) (often.)

"Hullo," she said cleverly. (Robin Boyd has often been called a real wit, you know) (Half, that is.) "What can I do for you?" she asked hopefully, having several possible answers in mind should he find himself stuck for a reply.

John grimaced, pointing to his outstretched foot. "That'll do for openers."

Blushing prettily (actually, she turned a rather malignant shade of magenta, but this is no time to be blowing Robin's cool) (calm image), she removed her boot from what remained of his.

"Sorry about that," she muttered, taking the chair he offered (which she, being the basically honest sort, intended to give back later.) Then she aimed a deep and soulful gaze into his deep and soulful eyes.

He was just a genie, of course (just?????), and looked like John the way George looked like George and Paul looked like Paul (tell that to someone who doesn't drink), but Robin never was one to concern herself with details.

John gave her one of his famous snarls. "Aren't you going to tell me I look just like him?"

Robin giggled. "You don't look a thing like him," she soothed, willing to play that game if he was (willing, if the truth were known, to play any game he was.)

John lifted an eyebrow (fortunately, it wasn't all that heavy.) "Oh," he quipped. "Well, then ask me why I called you over here."

"Okay," Robin said obediently. "Why I called you over here?"

John ignored her sally (who, by the way, still hasn't been heard from.) "It's about your mates. Those two," he gestured.

Robin glanced across the room where George was fanning the prostrate Paul with a menu. "Don't mind them," she chortled. "I've just given them a bit of a shock. My wish, you know."

John stared at her blankly. (For those interested, the blankly is located just to the right of the ratzafratz.)

"My wish," she repeated. "Haven't they told you? It wasn't bad enough when I said I wanted to see the Beatles in person, but when I gave them a list of songs I wanted them to perform, well, that really set them off."

"I can't imagine why," John replied, drinking the entire contents of the fingerbowl.

Robin shrugged. "Neither can I. They can do it. I mean, after all, are they genies or aren't they?"

"You might well arsk," John replied, drinking the fingerbowl. "In any carton, they definitely look just like him . . . er . . . them," he added, picking his teeth (up, that is) (those which he felt would bring the highest price when he placed them under his pillow later that night, that is.) "And what's more, you even look familiar." (And probably would be if I gave you 'alf a chance, he added mentally as Robin leered openly.)

Robin gave him a bat of the olde eyelashe. "I do?" she simpered. "Well, you've probably seen me in London, or with George somewhere."

"Speaking of George," John said (not to mention swiped) (well, it's certainly his turn.) "I believe someone who bears him a resemblance that defies description is endeavoring to attract your attention."

"Hah?" Robin asked politely.

"I believe George is trying to tell you something," John translated.

Robin re-glanced across the room, at which time her georgeous genie gave her a murderous stare and a cantankerous crook of the olde forefinger.

Re-shrugging she turned back to John.

"I KNOW George is trying to tell me something," she bellowed a second later as her arm was yanked clean out of the socket.

"I am that," George said grimly, sitting down. "And I won't want to be telling you again," he re-yanked. "You either," he shot in John's direction.

"I beg your problem?"

A sudden grin lit George's dark handsome face. "It is good to see you," he said, leveling a good-natured punch at John's shoulder.

"And Lord knows I need you. But none of your larkin' about with this one. She's taken. Taken seriously ill above the eyebrows," he added, longing to level a less good-natured punch at Robin's nose.

John nodded fervently.

"She'd told you about her wish, then" George laughed.

John nodded nervously.

"You will lend me a hand, won't you?" George continued. "Paul's going to. I could manage the Beatles on me own, but not the way she wants to see them." George paused to moan a lot. "No one is this world but Robin Irene Boyd would insist on seeing the Beatles at the Cavern. In 1961, yet! Which explains why we need help."

John nodded hysterically.

"I'll say you do," he yelped. "LemmeOUTTAhere!"

"Gerroff it," George chided. "The three of us can do it, and if we get boggled, we can always send for Ringo."

John vaulted out of his chair. "I think you'd best send for the men with the nets!"

It was then that Robin Boyd felt a cold twinge of panic, and knew what she must do.

"How did you happen to stop in here?" she asked, suddenly fearing the worst.

John trembled. "That sign out front caught me eye. Jeweller's Cafe, it said. We Never Fail, it added. Had a nice ring to it, I thought."

Robin's dizzy head spun dizzily. Oh, no!! No wonder he was carrying on so. He didn't just look like him. He was him! They had the wrong John (a trying experience by anyone's standards!)

"George," she wailed. "It's the real one! John Lennon in the flesh! Right here in Liverpool!"

DOUBLE OH NO, she thought hysterically. She'd said the magic word again!

George tried to cram Robin into his pocket before John got a look at the real robin which had just replaced the long-haired bird sitting next to him. But it was too late.

"Now I remember," John whispered in stark terror. "The concert in London. I did see a real bird waring Byrd glasses. I saw that!" he pointed. "No wonder I swallowed a guitar pick. I'm surprised I didn't swallow the guitar as well."

"I can explain, I can explain," George raved, trying to catch Robin, who was flapping frantically overhead.

"That would be nice," John replied, Complete Control Lennon having regained complete control. "You come around and tell me all about it just as soon as they'll let me have visitors."

And, with this, he lurched listlessly toward the nearest exit.

And, with that, Robin Boyd poised momentarily on the chandelier, chirped a tearful "goodbye forever" and dived into the nearest tea pot.

(To Be Continued Next Week)

KRLA ARCHIVES

The Orbiting Astronauts

... THE ASTRONAUTS

By Carol Deck

Let me introduce you to five guys you already know.

That's not really as dumb as it sounds. You see, these guys are one of America's top selling singing groups, yet they've managed to stay away from becoming instantly recognizable.

If you see them walking down the street, you may just think, "there go five sharp looking guys."

Those five sharp looking guys are the Astronauts. They don't exactly look like most rock singers today. They all have short college style hair cuts and dress very collegiate.

And they *are* very collegiate. They're all college educated guys from Boulder, Colorado.

The outstanding thing about these guys is that they made a million dollars in the last 2-1/2 years from their albums. They've never been too strong in the singles field but they're going to attempt to change that now.

After returning from their third annual Japanese tour, they spent a few days in California recording both a single and part of their next album. Now they've gone home for a short rest before beginning a college tour of the Mid-West.

Two Movies

And somewhere along the way they found time to film two movies just recently released — "Out of Sight" and "Wild, Wild Winter."

Individually the Astronauts are Richard Otis Fifield, James Richard Gallagher, Dennis Lindsey, Jon Storm Patterson, and Bob Demmon.

Bob, who graduated from the University of Colorado with a degree in music, likes to listen to just about anything in the way of music. His favorite singer is Elvis but he's currently on a Sonny and Cher "jag."

"I can associate with them," he explains. "Their music does for me what music used to do for me when I was a kid."

When asked about the group's short hair, Bob merely replys, "We did let it grow once, and it didn't help our music a bit."

Jon, or Stormy as he prefers to be called, was quite the prize student in high school — class president, member of the student council, state champion in wrestling and holder of state and national honors for football.

Stormy seems to have enjoyed this latest Japanese tour more than any other member of the group. While Bob was out looking for hamburgers, Stormy was perfectly happy to partake of his favorite food, oysters, which are very common in Japan.

Richard is the reader of the group, finding time to read on busses, trains, planes, anywhere.

He sums up the group's concern over getting a hit single. "The sound that a group adapts depends on the sound of their first hit single. Who knows what the Stones or the Supremes did before their first hit?"

Dennis is the wanderer of the group. He ran away from home a number of times — once he came to California to become a star and ended up a fry cook so he finally went back to Colorado and enrolled at the University of Colorado.

He's held numerous jobs from caddie to truck driver but now feels he found what he wants in music.

Drummer of the Astronauts is James, who's also known as Jim, The Kid, Hey You, and anything else the group feels like addressing him as.

He's a jazz buff who also digs Errol Gardner, "Ho-Dad" Mancini and Stan Kenton.

"I think my early style development was through old Kenton records my folks played the grooves off of, that also featured Shelly Manne in his early days," Jim says.

And that's the Astronauts. They've been orbiting together for seven years and seem to be destined for a permanent place in the music industry.

'Action' Is Where The Real Action Is

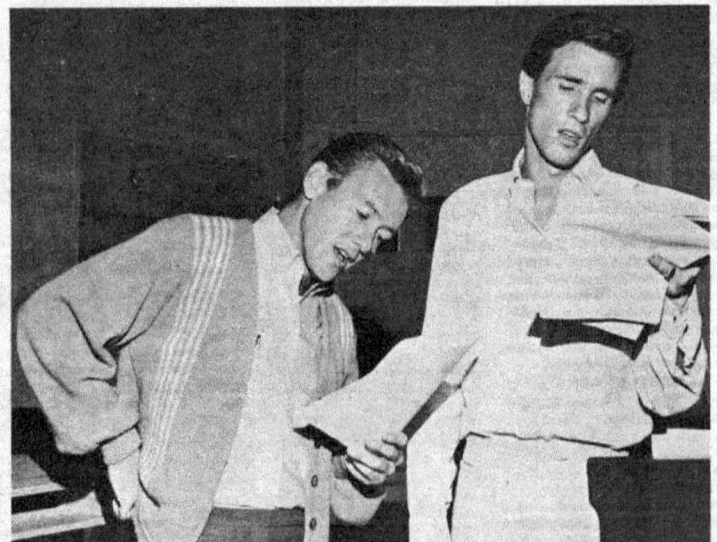

... BOBBY AND BILLY getting ready for 'Action.'

With pop shows dying almost as fast as they're born, it's nice to see that "Where The Action Is," Dick Clark's brainchild, continues to really be where the action is.

While Ed Sullivan and "Hollywood Palace" are booking all the big names in the pop world, Clark is grabbing practically the same artists for his "Action" show.

The entire "Action" crew has just returned from London where they filmed 63 sequences to be interspersed throughout the upcoming weeks. The first of these London-based inserts was shown last week when the Yardbirds sang their international hit, "For Your Love."

The Righteous Brothers, making their debut on "Action," belted out the cross-country smash, "Soul and Inspiration," with the Mama's & Papa's, Martha and the Vandellas, Bobby Freeman, Randy Boone, Jimmy Rogers, the Kingsmen and the "Action" cast on hand to cheer them on.

It was quite a week for Clark's popular daytime show and from the list of performers scheduled for "Action" shots it looks as if this is the place where the action will continue to be.

KRLA ARCHIVES

HEADLINERS' HAIR BEAT

'Cool It' If You Iron Your Hair

By Robert Esserman and Frank DeSanctis

HOLLYWOOD—Hot irons—hot irons everywhere! What are all the girls doing to their hair?

"I wish my hair looked like hers, it's so shiny and straight." Sound familiar?

The BEAT has been asked by many of our readers to solve this problem and many other questions concerning girls and their hair. Providing the answers are Robert Esserman and Frank DeSanctis, who operate the famed "Headliners" in Beverly Hills, where many of the top movie and television stars are regular patrons.

To begin with, girls, ironing your hair can be done successfully providing you don't make the mistake of using a *hot* iron. So cool it!

Any hot metal object put to your hair can result in breaking it and may frizz it or dry it out. Through our experience we have found the best way to achieve the straight look is to use an electric air comb, a fairly simple process.

First we wash your hair, then towel dry it. Third, comb out the tangles. After this we take the electric air comb, start from the top of the head and comb the hair straight to the ends.

While we comb through your hair the hot air blows the hair dry and the comb straightens it. This method can be used as often as necessary. Unfortunately, you cannot use the hot iron method so often without severely damaging the hair.

Shiny and Healthy

We feel straight hair is attractive but you've got to remember your hair must always be conditioned. The most beautiful thing about long, straight hair is having it shiny and healthy looking.

Face it, girls, no matter how long the hair, split ends, dryness and stringiness *won't* make the guys' heads turn your way!

We find that the best method of conditioning hair is to apply a liquid conditioner to the hair with cotton. This is followed by wrapping the head in a towel, causing the heat from the scalp to drive the conditioner into the interior of the hair.

The process takes only 20 minutes for all the magic ingredients in the conditioner to really sink in—magic because after rinsing and drying the results can be really beautiful.

Quickie Method

For girls who are late for their dates, we have a quicker method, a conditioner that can be just poured over the head then set immediately. The results of both are "Like, Wow!" But, of course, the conditioner washes out with the next shampoo.

Long hair is groovy all right, but it requires constant trimming. The hair splits from excessive brushing, combing and weather conditions. Always try to keep the ends of your hair even and trimmed, trimming about once every four weeks.

The latest cut that requires little attention is the Headliners' popular "Guy Cut." The "Guy" is a short cut that needs little setting during the week because the line of the hair cut is trimmed around the contours of your head. We can honestly claim we haven't sheared one girl yet who didn't dig her new "Guy Cut."

Short hair *is* very feminine, if any of you gals have any doubts. Short hair can be styled in many different ways, each cut individualized to accent your best features.

Many girls are more conscious than ever before of short Do's, since there are so many extremes today in haircuts. Ma.. new styles have come about as imitations of the Beatles' haircuts and those of Sonny & Cher.

ROBERT IS PUTTING THE FINISHING TOUCHES to Pat Priest's hair. Pat, of course, is seen regularly on "The Munsters" television show.

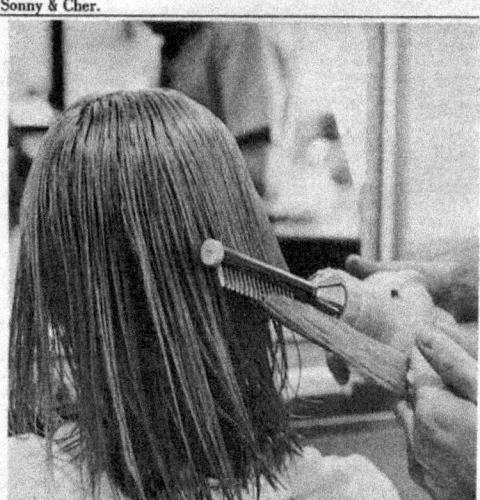

HERE IT IS — the electric air comb in action.

FRANK IS PICTURED HERE busily working on one of the Headliners' regular customers.

KRLA ARCHIVES

BEST TV SHOW: "MAN FROM U.N.C.L.E."
BEST TV ACTOR: DAVID McCALLUM
BEST ACTRESS: HAYLEY MILLS

BEST FILM OF 1965: "HELP!"
BEST ACTOR: PAUL McCARTNEY
BEST TV ACTRESS: SALLY FIELD

Here's the news you've been waiting to hear!

A few BEATS ago, we said it was time teenagers had their say about the Academy Awards, and then we gave you a place to say it. We sponsored our own awards race for the movie and television's bests of the year, provided a ballot and left the choice up to you!

Our thanks to the thousands of BEAT readers who voted, and our congratulations to the winners!

Now, are we going to play the award game according to the established rules and not reveal the runners-up? Not on your life! Read on!

In the Best Film division, "Help" won by an absolute landslide. The Beatle starrer received over ninety percent of the votes cast. Elvis Presley's "Harum-Scarum" came in second, followed by "Goldfinger," "Billie" and "That Darn Cat."

The Best Film Actor was another landslide (to put it mildly) Elvis again came in second, Sean Connery next, followed by Ringo Starr and Peter (Herman) Noone. There was a smattering of write-in candidates in all categories listed on the ballot, but none of the "favorite sons" received enough votes to register in the top five.

John Lennon, however, came close! He took sixth place in the Best Actor race without having been nominated.

"Man From U.N.C.L.E." literally walked away with Best TV Show honors. Runners-up were "Gidget," "Where The Action Is," in that order.

At first, it appeared that David McCallum and Robert Vaughn would tie for Best TV Actor, but as more and more ballots were tabulated, McCallum took the lead. Vaughn came in second, with Bill Cosby, Mike Landon and Don Adams right on his heels.

The Best Actress race was a tight one. Patty Duke lost to Hayley Mills by a rather slim margin. Then along came Annette Funicello, Connie Francis and Deborah Walley.

Voting in the Best TV Actress category was even closer! Patty Duke just barely lost again, this time by an even slimmer margin. Runners-up were Pat Morrow, Mia Farrow and Debbie Watson, respectively.

Here's hoping we'll be able to find our way out from under the mountain of ballots in time to do it all over again next year!

Hit Bound Sounds of Your Choice

Mirwood Records presents / **Mira Records presents**

HEY JOE!! - THE LEAVES
MY BABY LOOKS BUT HE DON'T TOUCH - CAROL CONNORS
SWEET SHERRY - RENE BLOCH
TEMPTATION WALK - JACKIE LEE
MINE EXCLUSIVELY - THE OLYMPICS
HIDE OUT - THE HIDEAWAYS
I'VE JUST SEEN A FACE - DON RANDI & THE MUSIC CO.
BIG BROTHER - BOBBY GARRETT

=== Plus Four Of The Most Exciting Albums Ever To Hit The West Coast ===

THE DUCK ALBUM - JACKIE LEE

RUBBER SOUL JAZZ - DON RANDI & THE MUSIC CO.

THE AFRO BLUES QUINTET PLUS ONE

THE HAWK & THE HUNTER - COLEMAN HAWKINS, FRANK HUNTER

MIRA PRODUCTIONS INC. / 9028 SUNSET BLVD., LOS ANGELES CALIF. 90069 / (213) 278-1125

KRLA ARCHIVES

America's Largest Teen NEWSpaper 15¢

KRLA Edition BEAT
MAY 7, 1966

'Mother's Little Helper'

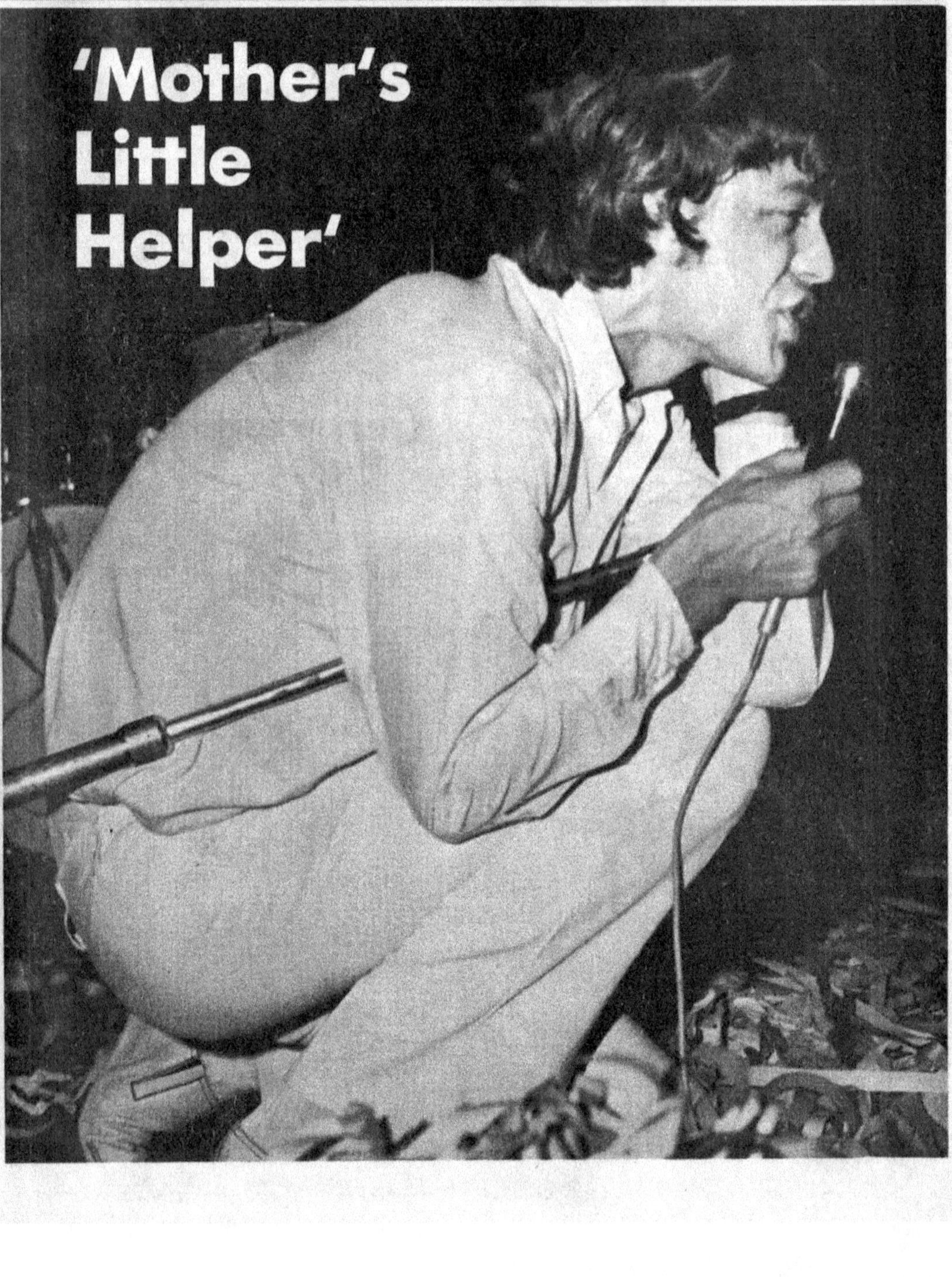

KRLA BEAT

Volume 2, Number 8 — May 7, 1966

BEAT 'HUNG UP' BY THE RASCALS

The BEAT is hanging proudly on a building being constructed on Broadway, the Young Rascals have broken all attendance records at the famous Palisades Park in New Jersey and a New York City record store owner is mad about the whole thing!

You remember that "Yeah, Well Young Rascals," The BEAT printed in our April 23 issue? Well, the Rascals read the story and decided on the spot that it should be hung up somewhere so that everyone could see it.

With that decided the next problem was to find a place to put it. However, being extremely talented in such things, the Rascals promptly found a suitable place to hang The BEAT where everyone in New York (practically) could see it – a building on Broadway which construction workers are slaving to get finished.

BEAT and nails in hand, the ceremony was properly and stylishly (we might add hurriedly so as not to get caught doing the "hanging") completed. So, thanks to the Rascals everyone passing the spot can now read The BEAT.

The Young Rascals themselves are the hottest group on the East Coast with their "Good Lovin'" currently topping the charts of both New York City pop stations and finding itself at number four in the nation.

They proved their drawing appeal last week by breaking attendance records at Palisades Park where they brought 269,000 fans into the showplace on Saturday and Sunday!

In fact, many people are predicting that the Young Rascals will very shortly be the top American group around. And The BEAT is one of those people. It has to happen. Look at the facts – less than six months ago the country had never even heard of the Young Rascals. Then they opened at the Phone Booth in New York, packing the place every night and drawing not only fans, but such notables as the Rolling Stones, Bob Dylan and Herman.

After the Phone Booth, "I Ain't Gonna Eat Out My Heart Anymore" was released and proceeded to smash its way up toward the top of the charts. Then along came "Good Lovin'" and you know what happened to that one! So, without sticking our necks out at all we can safely say that the Young Rascals will soon be the top group in the country.

There is, however, one record store owner in New York who is not anxiously awaiting the day. You see, the Rascals have their first album out and this particular store owner was busily putting up a display of the album jacket in his window when along came some Rascal fans and the next thing he knew all of his Rascal jackets as well as all of his Rascal photos were making their way out the door via the eager hands of Rascal fans!

It was actually a rather funny sight except to the record store owner, but it does show what New York City fans think of the Rascals – they dig 'em! And they're not alone – everyone else does too.

...NEW SOUNDS IN A NEW STUDIO?

HOTLINE LONDON SPECIAL
Beatle Rumor Half True

By Tony Barrow

Just about half of those widespread rumours about THE BEATLES' plans for a U.S. recording session were true. What I mean is that John, Paul, George and Ringo would like to go into an American recording studio although there are no concrete plans in hand for them to do so at this time.

The rumours started when Brian Epstein visited Memphis after bringing Cilla Black to New York for your Ed Sullivan and Johnny Carson TV shows. In fact, the main purpose of Brian's trip to Memphis was to make various routine checks in connection with The Beatles' August concert at the Memphis Coliseum. While he was in the area, he looked into one or two aspects of the local recording situation and, immediately, a lot of people decided that The Beatles would be traveling to Memphis very soon.

There would be no possibility of The Beatles recording in Memphis during their 1966 concert tour. The night before they're scheduled to play in Boston and the night afterwards they'll be in Cincinnati.

I talked to George about the general idea of having some recording sessions in America. He told me: "If we ever did I'd like us to go to a good place – not just any American recording studio. People like Otis Redding, Wilson Pickett and a lot of others who are amongst our personal fave-rave artists make their records in Memphis. The recording engineers there are specialists. It's not just a job to them. They love our kind of music. There'd be this great atmosphere."

Paul added: "It would be interesting to discover what new sounds we could get by using a different studio."

Recording manager George Martin would go along with the boys wherever they planned to have sessions. "If we ever do go out of London for sessions," George Martin told me, "it would be experimental. It's true that different local musical environments could have a strong affect on The Beatles. We wouldn't know what to expect in the way of results but it would be a new experience for all of us."

Meantime, The Beatles are right in the middle of an extended series of sessions with George Martin at the EMI studios, St. John's Wood, London. Sessions will continue until nearly twenty new numbers are on tape – enough material for a fresh album plus a single.

The complete list of August U.S. concert dates for The Beatles has now been announced. The series will kick off with two performances at the mighty International Amphitheatre in Chicago on Friday, August 12. All told, fourteen cities are included with a grand total of something like twenty concerts.

Last year there was a week-long stop-over in L.A. when The Beatles lazed in the sun beside their inviting pool up in Benedict Canyon. This time they won't be in California for quite so long. After playing New York City's Shea Stadium (August 23), they move to Seattle (August 25) before coming into Los Angeles for their Dodger Stadium date on August 28. The tour finishes on August 29 in San Francisco.

The 1965 tour took in 10 cities. Places like Washington, Philadelphia, Boston, Memphis, St. Louis and Seattle appear in the '66 schedule and did not show on last year's list. The idea is to take in new cities which were missed last time. The Beatles return to New York, Los Angeles, San Francisco and Toronto but a number of '65 cities like Atlanta, Houston, Minneapolis, Portland and San Diego are not lined up for repeat visits this summer.

In 1965, the group's charter aircraft covered something like 10,000 miles during the tour and the boys played to 350,000 Beatle People. This year's audience total is estimated at over 400,000.

★ ★ ★

THE YARDBIRDS, on their way up your charts with their U.K. best-seller, "Shapes Of Things," recorded the instrumental backing for their current money-spinner before the lyrics were even written! *(Turn to Page 5)*

Spector's Side Of The Brothers Story

In the April 16 issue of The BEAT we let you in on the Righteous Brothers side of the supposed "feud" between the Brothers and Phil Spector. Now, we feel that it is only fair to give you Phil's side of the story which was revealed to us by Philles Records' employee, Danny Davis.

"First of all, let me say that I like the boys and I respect their talent, but it was Phil Spector who built them into what they are today. When he found them in Orange Country earning $15 a night they had no idea of their potential," said Danny.

"We have no big beef with them. They are not fighting Philles, but they have a contract with Moonglow Records which still has two and a half years to run. But the Righteous Brothers declared their contract void all by themselves and if they get away with what they've done then no contract is worth anything.

"The case may very well go to trial. MGM knows that they're playing with fire and the courts of New York have already said that in any event, damages are due us.

"The Righteous Brothers are misguided gentlemen and Phil Spector has only the greatest regard for them and is happy for their success with 'Soul and Inspiration.'

"Anyone can tell by listening to the record that they've taken a page from the Spector book and they've learned their lesson well. They have no reason to get back at him. In fact, they should pay him back money for what they learned from him free," finished Danny.

Inside the BEAT

Beatles London Fan Club 2
Pet Clark Wants To Stay 3
Adventures of Robin Boyd 4
Here Comes Dylan 5
Stones & Walkers Speak Out 6-7
Shadows Win 'Gloria' Race 11
The Everly's On Tour 12-13
For Girls Only 14
Beat Goes To The Movies 15

The BEAT is published weekly by BEAT Publications, Inc., editorial and advertising offices at 6290 Sunset Blvd., Suite 504, Hollywood, California 90028. U.S. bureaus in Hollywood, San Francisco, New York, Chicago and Nashville, overseas correspondents in London, Liverpool and Manchester, England. Sale price, 15 cents. Subscription price: U.S. and possessions, $5 per year. Canada and foreign rates, $9 per year. Second class postage prepaid at Los Angeles, California.

KRLA ARCHIVES

Behind Closed Doors At The Fab Four's London Fan Club

By Carol Gold

Fan club presidents—you think you've got headaches! How would you like to answer sacks of mail a day, have your phone never stop ringing, and spend $3,000 on postage alone every time you send a newsletter to your members? Well, there's one fan club in the world that does just that—and more.

You turn from one tiny London street into equally narrow Monmouth Street, with aged buildings high on either side. If you're watching, you can't help noticing the almost hidden door beside the bookshop, because it's covered with writing. "I love Ringo." "Paul, my phone number is TAT 4307." "Beatles, your fans from New Zealand were here" and so on into the hall and up the narrow stairway to the door on the second floor (what they call here the first floor) which bears a plate reading "NEMS Enterprises Ltd."

Fabled Club

You knock, the door opens and you're in the fabled headquarters of the Beatles Fan Club.

It's not very big, very glamorous or very covered with Beatle pictures. There are two small rooms with two desks each on that second floor and two more one winding flight up. You'd never guess—except for the two large framed pictures of the fab four—that you were in the offices of the Beatles' massive fan club organization, which takes care of 75,000 British fans! I was surprised to see no sign of the sacks of mail I had expected to find standing about. "You've caught us on one of our rare days when we're organized," explained Michael Crowther-Smith, the young, good-looking NEMS officer in charge of the fan club office.

A staff of three boys and four girls man (and woman) the Beatles' fan club and answer their fan mail. Pretty Anne Collingham is Beatles' Fan Club Secretary. She didn't start out that way—she was working for NEMS as a sort of Girl Friday when she was asked to navigate the club with Bettina Rose, its founder, who has since left to get married.

There have been times when the staff has practically had to set up housekeeping in the office, they were there so much. When the club exploded as the Beatles skyrocketed in 1963, a full-time staff of eight worked 12 hours a day just to keep from being drowned in the mail. Some people had to wait four months to get their membership, the flood was so overwhelming.

When the staff of the club talk about their job, it often sounds as if they were discussing great battles. "Valentine's Day is the worst," said Dennis Scott, about the flow of mail. "Christmas is bad, too, but the mail builds up gradually over a couple of weeks. Valentine's Day, it comes all at once."

Even the Government is involved with the Beatles' fan club, because the post office must be notified whenever one of the Beatles is about to have a birthday. When a Beatle has a birthday, the postman gets overtime! The most hectic Beatle birthday was George's 21st, when the post office delivered 64 overflowing sacks of mail!

As one who has had the experience of running a national fan club, I was properly sceptical about what I'd heard of the Beatles' interest in their fan organization. But, as it turns out, they really *do* care! During that membership crisis I mentioned, Paul came in to help address envelopes—so some fans got truly personal service!

Paul also drops in every now and then and takes all the girls in the office out to lunch. And, says Michael, "If any one of the Beatles should get the slightest criticism of the club, they're down on our heads like a shot!" All four visit the club, although less regularly than they used to when there were three bachelor Beatles, instead of just one. But whenever they do, no matter how unannounced the visit, or how unassuming the car they come in or empty the street when they arrive, within minutes the road is jammed with people! Uncanny, but it happens wherever the Beatles are.

In recalling their experiences with the club, the inventiveness of the fans sparks admiration from the staff. And the fans are especially ingenious with gifts. Like the two girls from Brighton who talked their father into driving all the way to London to deliver their birthday present for George—not content with sending him the key to their door, they brought the door!!

Then there was the old-fashioned bicycle sent by students at a posh boys' school in London. There have been cards as high as the ceiling, complete movie scripts, and one American girl even sent them a heart—not a valentine, but a real animal's heart! They discovered it by the smell—I guess the donor hadn't thought what a few weeks in the mail would do to her heart.

Livestock is no novelty, either. When John's birthday came round in 1964, parcels and mail poured in. Imagine the surprise of the fan club people when one of the parcels meowed! Upon investigation, they found a lovely ginger kitten who was of course subsequently named Cynthia.

Just recently, a girl delivered two goldfish named Paul and McCartney. The human Paul was telephoned and told of the new arrivals. Soon after, a chauffeur in full livery appeared to fetch the finny ones and carried them off to be fitted for a bowl in Paul's home, where they're swimming still.

When you think of the amount of mail that the club answers, the staff that runs it, and the special newsletters, souvenirs, magazines, photos and gifts sent out to British members, you realize that the cost of maintaining the service is staggering. And as you fan-club-running readers know, membership dues of 75c a year (which is what they are for British fans) wouldn't nearly cover the cost of it all. But the Beatles happily support their fan club operation because they really enjoy having it. Might I point out here that all this concerns just the British and main branch of the club. Only residents of the United Kingdom can join it. Americans must join their own branch, as must residents of every country where there is an official club.

Mail, however, is answered from all over the world at the office in Monmouth St.

Beatles Do Write

Do the Beatles ever answer any of their fan mail themselves? The fan club staff are pretty sure they do. From the stacks of mail, many letters are passed on to the Beatles—letters that are especially interesting or that ask questions only the Beatles can answer.

I was told, "Often we'll get a letter saying, 'Dear John, Thank you for your letter.'" so they suppose he must have written one.

The Beatles' fan club people are in the ideal position to judge the often heard cries that the Beatles are slipping. "Ah," sighed Michael, "we're about due for another siege of knocking. But they always come back even stronger afterwards."

Beatlemania is not gone, it's just "sorted itself out."

Sorted itself out so that the jelly babies that once nearly filled a room have stopped pouring in—though Anne points out that pillowcases are the thing now, since it was publicized that Paul autographed one recently.

Sorted itself out so that the phone counts to ten before ringing again after the receiver is replaced instead of ringing right away. (Though let something unusual—if that word can be applied to the Beatles—occur and watch it jangle its head off!)

But not sorted itself out enough to keep two boys hitchhiking from Tokyo from placing a visit to the club headquarters first on their list.

What's it like working for the Beatles, working at what is regarded by many people as as close to them as possible, in a sort of shrine? In the words of the staff—Super!

KING OF THE BEAT VS. KING OF THE BEASTS — Sonny fights with a lion in a scene from his and Cher's first movie, "Good Times," now being filmed. See next week's **BEAT** for behind the scenes report.

Chad & Jeremy State Their Views On Draft

Last week *The BEAT* apologized for erroneous inferences which appeared in the April 16th issue regarding Chad and Jeremy. Based upon unsubstantiated evidence, *The BEAT* had stated that they were attempting to evade U.S. military service and that their recent trip to London was made to "escape the draft." This week, at our invitation, Chad and Jeremy re-state their own position on the subject.

■ What really makes us angry about the article is that bland inaccuracies are stated with authority.

It is alleged that we returned to England to escape the U.S. draft. This is untrue on two counts:

(1) Jeremy had been in London since June of last year performing in a musical show called "Passion Flower Hotel" and I was required to join him in London as a matter of urgency because had I not done so, we should have had no records to release.

In fact, Columbia Records insisted that we record in London and it was for this reason that I returned home for a brief spell.

(2) As our status in America is that of "resident aliens," we do not have to resort to "draft-dodging" and there is no truth in Miss Criscione's suggestion that the draft can be evaded by returning to England "during a certain time period."

What happens is this: If, as and when an alien receives so-called "Call-up" papers, he has two alternatives. He can either stay in America and enlist or he may return to his native country.

If Jeremy and I received "Call-up" papers, we would most certainly return home and we see nothing to be ashamed of.

We are not Americans and do not owe any military obligation to the United States.

There is no question of "dodging" or trickery.

We were also dismayed with the reference to us "hauling in money" over here. We cannot understand resentment of our earning-power.

In a free economy, it is one's entitlement to earn as much as possible and it should be remembered that in addition to making money over here, we also pay taxes over here.

We object very much to Miss Criscione associating us with entertainers who had given their views on the Vietnam war and the draft and who, Miss Criscione says, "were reluctant" to give their opinions.

In fact, neither of us was asked for our opinion. But we are taking this opportunity, now, to express some of our views.

We do not believe in the draft, which was abolished in England some time ago, and we believe that if the armed services were run in a more humane manner there would be sufficient voluntary enlistment for more natural-born fighters.

We would not fight in Vietnam for two reasons: Firstly, because we believe the war is immoral, and secondly, we don't need to fight there.

We haven't been associated with any of the anti-war movements because, chiefly, we are entertainers carving a career for ourselves.

But we do respect the protestors who expose themselves to the possibility of violent reprisals. We believe that the minority groups who say "I will not fight" demonstrate more courage than those who go with the tide and do what they feel their neighbors would like them to do.

We wish every decent, ordinary person in the entire world would just sit down and say "This lunacy has got to stop. Let's stop killing each other."

Finally, we would suggest that if Louise Criscione feels impelled to crusade for the U.S. Government in a pop-music newspaper, she should select her targets with accuracy and with care.

We—on this occasion—don't answer the description of the wanted men.

CHAD STUART & JEREMY CLYDE

KRLA ARCHIVES

BEAT Exclusive
Petula Clark Wants To Stay

By Louise Criscione

Petula Clark has been called The First Lady of Pop and she must be because ever since "Downtown" she has had only hit after hit, and yet she has never done a concert appearance in the United States!

She has played the top night clubs Stateside but, of course, the teenage record buyers don't get to frequent those spots much.

"Really, it's marvellous playing the Cocoanut Grove," Petula told *The BEAT* as we sat beside her hotel swimming pool watching her two young daughters splash around in the water.

"I've done Harrah's in Reno, but kids weren't allowed in there at all. Next time I go to Reno, I'm going to do a concert because I haven't done anything in the States for the teenagers."

Following her stint at the Grove Pet heads back to Chicago for a concert with Count Basie. "I hope I'll be singing to a mixed audience. It's a funny thing how I've only worked in night clubs to adult audiences in the U.S. and yet the teenagers buy my records.

"People like Sinatra, Bennett and Lee are not in the big record selling thing, therefore, they're not relying on records. But if I hadn't made hit records no one would come to see me in night clubs. Strange."

We wondered if Pet found that adults were more musically fickle than teenagers or vice versa. "I think teenagers are more "fickle," answered Petula, "because there is so much being thrown at them, so much happening and there are so many groups. It's not really their fault and it's very difficult to stay fidel.

"Adult audiences seem to be more fidel, possibly because they choose an artist when he's young and they sort of grow up with him.

"What I want to prove to the teenagers is that besides singing I can do other things as well and that I want to stay. I think a lot of teenage artists when they go out to do an act, tend to rely on their popularity and don't work as hard as they should.

"There's a lot of difference when you're on stage. You have to prove to your audience that you're worthwhile. It means showing another side of your talents, if you have another side," laughed Pet, "so that people get to like you and maybe then they'll like you better than when they came in.

"It's often the fault of a manager who hasn't advised his young artists properly. Being in a theater is a different experience and when you go and pay I think the performer should give you more than your money's worth."

Petula has been the recipient of numerous awards from all over the world and Stateside she has been awarded two Grammies. But do these awards have any tangible results?

"It's marvelous," said Pet. "It's not the sort of thing you go out and show everyone. I mean, I don't bring mine with me but I'm very honored and thrilled. Apart from that I don't think it means very much more."

Pet began her career when she was nine years old, and soon after she became known as the Shirley Temple of England. It's been a long time since Pet has made a movie, does she want to act again?

"The thing that frightens me is the offers I've had so far. I'm a very whole-hearted person and I'd rather do a small role in a good film than a big role in a bad film. I would work very hard at it.

"Another problem is that there are a lot of producers who are inclined to think that since I'm a singer they'd just give me a little part and pay me well and I'd sing a couple of songs and that would be all. I really don't want to do that.

"I think the Beatles are being very clever about not doing tatty films to prove that they can make money. I think it should be worthwhile artistically," stated the pert Petula.

She is due back in London in June for a month where she will make personal appearances and record. She does all of her recording in London except, "My Love" which was cut right here. And oddly enough, Pet hated the record!

She spoke with Warner Brothers for a day and a half but they released the disc anyway and it immediately became a smash. "Which just goes to show that you never know what's going to sell," grinned Pet.

Off stage Pet is the epitome of casual dress (the day we spoke to her she was wearing a simple shift) but on stage she has great style and is most often seen wearing floor length gowns which she designs herself.

"Yes, I design my own clothes because I can never get anything to fit me being so small and I don't like my clothes to be too way out. Then they're made up in Paris in a boutique in the sort of Greenwich Village of Paris."

Pet was a smash at the Copa but she revealed that she had had only a day and a half to rehearse before her opening. "I went out there really not knowing what I was going to do. I worked the whole act out myself which is not the way to do it!

"There is a certain excitement about going on stage and not really knowing what you're doing. It gives you an extra shot of adrenalin so that you can really come across. I think it's never good to be completely sure of what you're going to do," Pet declared.

And without even being asked, Pet suddenly spurted out: "I love what I'm doing now—I really do." And you don't have to be with her very long before you realize that she really does!

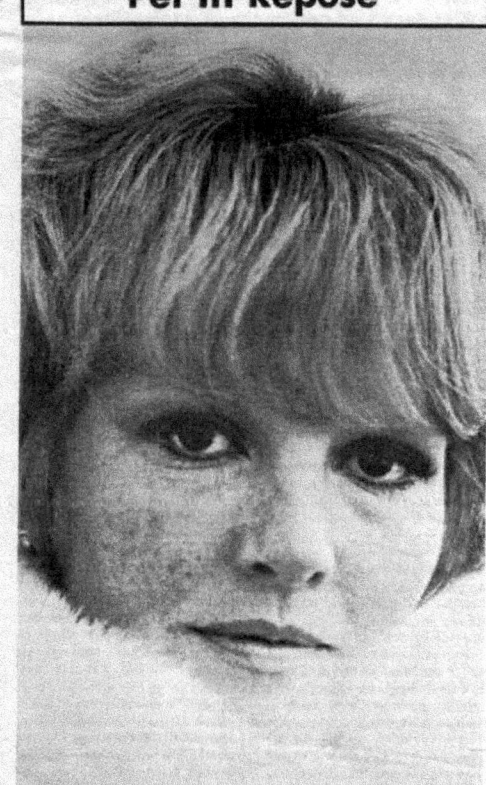

... PET POSES WITH HER GIRLS (l. to r.) Catherine and Barbara.

Pet In Repose

And Pet In Action

BEAT Photos: Chuck Boyd

KRLA ARCHIVES

No Movie For The Brass, They Want Their Rights

By Carol Deck

The pop world is going movie mad.

The Beatles started it with "Hard Day's Night" and "Help."

The Dave Clark Five followed quickly with "Having a Wild Weekend" and Herman's Hermits have just jumped in with "Hold On."

And we're still waiting for the completion and release of flicks by the Rolling Stones and Sonny and Cher.

But there's one group that's not so anxious to jump into the movie bag, and that's Herb Alpert and the Tijuana Brass.

They've received and turned down numerous offers from almost every major movie company.

They've turned them all down for the same reason — they want to keep the rights to music recording and publishing.

Offers of over $250,000 have been discussed but always turned down because the movie companies wanted to keep the music rights.

There are current negotiations going on for a film bow for the group in a Joseph E. Levine film and a possible movie of their own, but all hinges on who gets the music rights.

All of the Brass's recordings have been produced and released through A&M Records, owned jointly by Herb Alpert and Jerry Moss, and they plan to stay with A&M in all fields.

Meanwhile, the group is cutting down their television appearances to allow for more live shows.

After taping a 'Hollywood Palace' segment to be aired April 30, they plan only one TV special for next season and then are saying 'no' to other guestings.

They are currently completing a 14 city tour which started April 9 in Detroit and ends April 23 in Chicago. The entire tour was a complete sellout including a two day stint in Carnegie Hall.

Although a TJB movie doesn't seem evident right away, the group has made a 12 minute film for use as a promotion aid for an upcoming European tour. The group made the film at a cost of $10,000 to themselves, but you can bet *they* have the music rights to it.

By the way, for those of you who haven't quite gotten past the handsome Mr. Alpert, his six sidemen, the Tijuana Brass, are Lou Pagani, Tawny Kalash, Bob Edmundwon, Pat Senatore, Nick Cerolli and John Paisano.

The Adventures of Robin Boyd

By Shirley Poston

CHAPTER TWENTY-SIX

Ask anyone who knew her. They'll tell you what she was like. "Robin Boyd," they'd undoubtedly muse, their faces brightening with remembrance. "That girl had so much *life*. In fact, she was absolutely full of it."

And the fact that her sixteen short years had been so lively sort of made up for the fact that they hadn't exactly been graceful.

However, *nothing* would ever make up for the clumsy way she had ended her stay on earth. She had *really* outdone her ex-self *that* time.

It had been a dramatic moment of sheer poetry. Poised there on that chandelier, Robin had come to grips with herself. She had just re-committed the unpardonable sin and sent John Lennon shrieking into the streets, again fearing for his alleged sanity.

There was nothing left for her. Except martyrdom.

When she had swan-dived into the nearest tea pot, she had only meant to drown bravely and with quiet dignity. But, true to form, she'd blown the whole bit.

Instead of heroically sinking for the third and final time, she had chosen a *covered* tea pot as her target and smashed herself to smithereens (not to mention several million feathers) on the *lid*.

And it is no small wonder that the first thing she did when she began to regain consciousness was blush furiously. It had been, to put it mildly, a rather *unromantic* way to go.

Uncertain Future

It is also no small wonder that the second thing she did was stop worrying about the first thing. That was all in the past. What she *really* had to worry about now was the future. Or rather, *where* she would be spending same.

Being careful not to flicker so much as an eyelash, Robin sniffed soundlessly.

No . . . there was no tell-tale scent of sulphur. But, as she vibrated one of her remaining ears, she didn't exactly hear any harps, either.

But she did hear voices.

Ordinarily, this wouldn't have bothered her one whit. (She'd been hearing voices for years.) (Even Joan of Arc heard voices, you know.) (Which even further substantiates the theory that no one is perfect.) However, one of those voices was unmistakably John Lennon's.

Praying that the poor dear soul hadn't come to an equally messy demise (after what she'd done to him, it wouldn't surprise her a bit if he'd stumbled into a thoroughfare and been mashed by a Mr. Whippy truck), Robin's ear re-vibrated just in time to hear him say: "She really thought I was Lennon!" At which time she was surrounded by peals of larfter.

"Man, did you see that *dive?*" gasped another voice which was unmistakably Paul's. "I wouldn't have missed that for the world!"

Hmmmm, thought Robin, snarling inwardly. There was more here than met the eye (which wasn't much, seeing as how her remaining one was swollen shut at the time.)

Then her suspicions were confirmed by still another voice.

A Rare Bird

"I told you she'd do something moronic," chortled George The Genie. "She's a rare bird, that one."

Then he stopped chortling. "She will be okay, won't she?" he asked worriedly.

Robin re-snarled, seeing the light (not to mention red.) Yes, she *will* be okay, she thought furiously. But *you* won't. Why, it had been John (The Genie) all along! It had also been a rat-finky plot to see if she could top the time she had flapped out of a Rolling Stones' concert while in the pocket of Mick Jagger's jacket.

She wasn't dead at all! (Which was somewhat of a disappointment as she'd been planning a rather elaborate funeral.)

But she knew of three genies who would soon be wishing they *were*.

Raising an eyelash just a hair (which was about all there was left of it), Robin sneakily surveyed the scene.

What she had imagined (no, make that *hoped*) was a fast-moving cloud was actually a careening Rolls Royce. John was driving. That is to say he was behind the wheel giving it the olde college (Liverpool Art) try.

Paul was in front with John, and she was sprawled gracefully (oh, *sure*) in back, covered warmly (not to mention originally) by an orange blanket. George was in back with her, cradling the remains of her head in his lap.

It was then that Robin Boyd knew what she must do. And if you've seen "Help" 7954½ times (the ½ accounted for the time your parents didn't just *threaten* to burn the theater down), so do you.

Handy Spoon

First she stirred under the blanket (using the spoon she always kept handy for just such occasions.) Then when she had gained the attention of the three wretches, she opened her eyes.

"Hel-lo," she said wryly, famous-Ringo-style.

"*Beautiful!*" chorused the aforementioned three wretches, bursting into uproarious laughter.

Robin sat up, shaking off George who was hugging her hysterically. (When she wanted her hysterically hugged, she'd let him know.) (The utter wretch.)

Then she calmly rolled down the car window, took a deep breath of Liverpudlian air and shrieked at the top of her very lungs.

What she shrieked is of no importance. Let it suffice to say that it would have attracted the attention of the constable on the corner even if John *hadn't* chosen this particular moment to mesmerize a parked motor bike.

But Robin's sadistic guffawing (gsuendheit) (thank you) (you're welcome) stilled when the policeman walked over to the car.

Instead of rushing to her rescue, he shined his torch mercilessly in their faces.

"*YOU!*" he thundered in an unmistakably German accent. "I've been waiting for this moment for five years!"

"Huh?" chorused three wretches plus one.

"Think you can make your own rules because you're Beatles, right?" he re-thundered. "*You*," he quivered, pointing at Paul. "You're the one who set the fire!"

Fire?

"What fire?" Paul gulped. Then he remembered his namesake's adventures in Hamburg (not to mention the Maine) and disappeared into thin air.

"And *you*," he shouted at John. "Hand over your driver's license!"

"What driver?" John inquired politely just before they vanished.

Turning a most unattractive shade of tangerine, the policeman yanked the car door clean out of its socket - er - clean off the hinges. "Come out of that Rolls Royce," he ordered. "All of you!"

"What Rolls Royce?" inquired the Rolls Royce politely just before it vanished.

Seconds later, the policeman vanished. Not into thin air. Up the street. And he was last seen walking at a brisk pace in the general direction of Germany. (Actually, he was trotting in a terrified manner, but we wouldn't want to shatter his cool, calm image.)

Half an hour later, the four of them were still sitting on the curb, roaring. Suddenly, Robin stopped giggling and took a firmer grip on George's hand.

His eyes glinted at her in the misting darkness, wordlessly asking if something were wrong.

Robin shook her head. Nothing was wrong. It was just that everything was so right.

Today had been an all-time rave-up. And next Saturday would be even more so, thanks to George and John and Paul, who had arranged for the Beatle performance at the Cavern.

They were being so wonderful to her, she felt a bit unworthy and ashamed.

What more could I possibly ask for, she thought tenderly, resting her head on George's shoulder.

But, as he read her thoughts, George grinned to himself. If he knew Robin Irene Boyd (and, he did), she'd think of *something*.

(*To Be Continued Next Week*)

A Bus For The Christys

The New Christy Minstrels are on the move again — this time in a bus.

In an attempt to cut down the growing travel costs of the large group, their managers, George Greif and Sid Garris, have bought a specially equipped bus to carry the group and their managers to college campuses that are too close together to warrant flying.

The group already leases a jet plane for all long distance traveling.

The bus is equipped with a complete kitchen, refrigerator, dictaphone equipment, typewriters, television, upper and lower berths for the male Christys and a roomette for the two female Christys.

Beach Boys' Summer Tour

The Beach Boys, currently riding the charts with two singles, "Sloop John B" and Brian Wilson's solo "Caroline, No," are set for three major concerts this summer.

They'll appear in New York's Yankee Stadium on June 10 then return to the West Coast for appearances at San Francisco's Cow Palace on June 24 and Los Angeles' Hollywood Bowl on June 25.

KRLA ARCHIVES

On the BEAT
By Louise Criscione

Good news for you Beatle fans. The Beatle concert filmed at Shea Stadium last year will most probably be shown to American audiences right before the Beatles arrive Stateside in August.

John says the Beatles think it's "a fabulous film. In color it's great because all our faces look blue and brown under the flood lighting. It starts with Paul doing 'I'm Down' and we all look very sweaty because it's hot in New York in August and, in any case, 'I'm Down' was at the very end of our act and we'd been on stage over half an hour by the time that bit was filmed."

Of course, the film was shown in England not too long ago and everyone flipped out over it. The reviews were very favorable and Ringo would just like you all to know that those badges the Beatles were wearing at Shea are genuine Wells Fargo Agent badges which were given to them while riding in a Fargo van on the way to the concert.

Wrote For Cher

Looks as if Bob Lind is getting to be one of the most popular song writers around. In fact, Lind compositions are popping up on all sorts of new albums put out by other artists. However, the only song Bob ever wrote especially for another performer was "Come To Your Window" which he wrote for Cher.

...JOHN LENNON

For those of you who can't seem to pass your driving test, here's a little bit of consolation for you—Keith Richard can't pass his either! Both Keith and Bill took their tests recently and while Bill managed to successfully pass, Keith successfully failed! So, poor Keith just has to go on using his chauffeur, Patrick, to drive his Bentley Continental.

There is a reason for Bill Wyman nearly always wearing dark clothes on stage—he doesn't get hit by flying objects that way! "I always wear dark clothes, my hair is dark and perhaps they can't see me well enough to hit me," he laughs.

By the way, Keith would like you all to know that it's the music that makes Mick move on stage—not itching powder!

Bobby And Bill Sellin'

The Righteous Brothers are certainly doing business. Their single, "Soul And Inspiration" has now passed the one million mark and is heading for two. And their latest album, titled after "Soul," achieved an advance sale of over 268,000 copies in the first three days of release. Off hand, I'd say they're going to have a million selling album despite their new hair cuts which most people seem to dislike.

Tom Jones did not attend the Academy Awards in Hollywood after all. He's in the hospital to have his tonsils removed and his nose fixed via plastic surgery. It also means that Tom missed out on singing before the Duke of Edinburgh.

Ray Davies (King Kink) has now fully recovered from his illness and the Kinks are resuming bookings. Their manager, Robert Wace, stated that the nine dates lost as a result of Ray being unable to appear will be made up by the Kinks as soon as possible.

Kinks Coming?

There is a definite possibility that the Kinks will be touring the U.S. with Roy Orbison for six weeks beginning June 22 and winding up on July 31. However, negotiations are still being made and then, of course, there's the slight problem of obtaining an American work permit *if* they do decide to come.

The Walker Brothers are now all

...GARY WALKER

wearing crash helmets as they enter and leave their concerts! Ever since the Walkers became so popular in England, every single one of their personal appearances has ended in mobbings with the Walkers as the victims.

The fans really blew their cool a couple of weeks ago when John received a concussion and Scott was knocked unconcious. That did it and from now on, not only will they wear crash helmets, but they will be met by police as they enter each city and personally escorted under heavy guard to and from the theater.

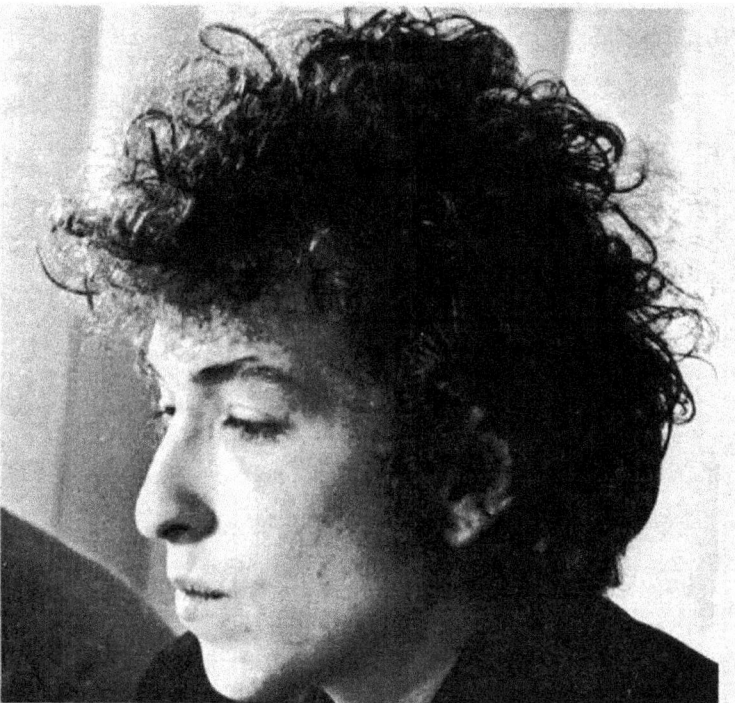

LOOK OUT WORLD
Here Comes Dylan

The elusive Bob Dylan, recognized as one of the world's most influential song writers and singers, has set off to bring his music to the world through an extensive two-month 'round the world concert tour.

Dylan started the tour, his first around the world tour, with an appearance before a very enthusiastic audience at the H.I.C. Arena in Honolulu on April 9.

He followed that with a trip over to Australia for concerts at the Sydney Stadium, Brisbane Festival Hall, Melbourne Festival Hall, Adelaide Palais Royal and the Perth Capitol Theater.

From Australia he travels to Scandinavia this week for concerts in Stockholm, Sweden April 30 and in Copenhagen, Denmark, May 1.

On May 5 he begins an extensive round of appearances in Ireland, England, Wales and Scotland with a concert in Dublin, Ireland.

He'll appear in Belfast, Ireland on May 6 and at Colston Hall in Bristol, England on May 10.

On May 11 he'll visit Wales for a concert at Sophia Gardens in Cardiff.

Then he'll continue his English tour with concerts at Town Hall in Birmingham on May 12, Philharmonic Hall in Liverpool on May 14, DeMontford Hall in Leicester on May 15, the TBA in Sheffield on May 16, and the Free Trades Hall in Manchester on May 17.

During his first visit to Scotland, Dylan will appear at Glasgow's Concert Hall on May 19 and Usher Hall in Edinburgh on May 20 before returning to England for a concert at City Hall in Newcastle on May 21.

Then he's scheduled for a brief trip to the continent on May 24 for a performance at the Salle Pleyel in Paris.

Dylan will conclude the exhausting tour at the Royal Albert Hall in London on May 26 and 27. This hall is the same one that Dyland scored a major triumph in last year.

He's in the middle of this long hard tour now but he left us here in America with a goody to play with while he's gone—his latest single, "Rainy Day Woman #12 & 35."

Yardbirds Record In Strange Way

(Continued From Page 1)

Drummer Jim McCarty came up with the march-beat and guitarist Paul Samwell-Smith added a bass riff. Then Jeff Beck thought of the wild guitar sequence to go with the background rhythm. Singer Keith Relf says that Jeff's guitar playing has "a sort of Arabic sound about it" on this deck. "He really produced a weird, vicious sound and we managed to use feedback effects very successfully" adds Keith.

The Yardbirds often put the finishing touches to their new numbers during actual studio sessions. In this instance they made a finished recording of the backing before the combo's built-in songwriting team of Relf and Samwell-Smith went away to write the lyrics. When the words were ready, the boys returned to the studio and dubbed in the vocal while they listened to a playback of the backing!

NEWS BRIEFS... RADIO LONDON became Britain's first 24-hour station when they broadcast non-stop night and day throughout the Easter weekend... Rediffusion's TV show "Ready, Steady Go!" was screened live from The Locomotive in Paris a couple of weeks ago but the sound quality was disastrous!... Liberty re-issued. EDDIE COCHRAN'S "Come On Everybody" here April 22, six years after the artists' tragic death... Since my report last week about fans injuring THE WALKER BROTHERS on their current U.K. tour, the chart-topping trio have taken to wearing crash helmets... My personal tip for the top is "Pretty Flamingo" the latest from MANFRED MANN. Incidentally, Manfred vocalist, PAUL JONES is writing a musical based on the book, "Just Me And Nobody Else." Meanwhile, Paul's solo single "She Needs Company" will only be released in Britain via an EP disc...

DAVID AND JONATHAN suffered from severe attack of tonsilitis but refused to miss concert engagements... SOUNDS INCORPORATED making a fantastic instrumental album in stereo. Aimed at the U.S. market...

PETER AND GORDON do not plan to record any more Lennon/McCartney songs...

The Stones
'I'm Not That Sort Of Bloke'

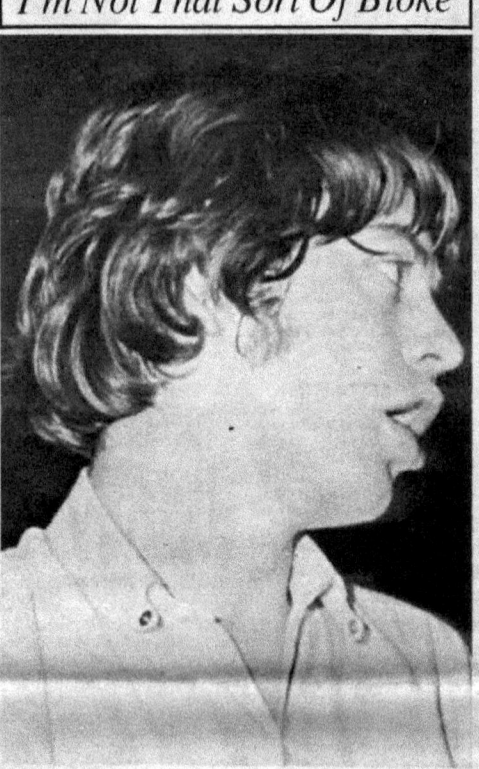

Mick could have been killed, the Walker Brothers now wear crash helmets to their concerts and everyone's mad.

Fate seems to be drawing the Rolling Stones and the Walker Brothers together in injuries and publicity and neither group is very happy about it.

In exclusive information from Tony Barrow in London, *The BEAT* learned that Mick Jagger had to be rushed to the hospital during a concert in the Olympia Theater in Paris that turned into a riot.

Mick was hit in the head by a flying seat and had to have six stitches taken near his right eye.

And after the group was safely out of the theater, the fans proceeded to tear apart the building.

The Walker Brothers, after receiving injuries including a concussion, from fans who got out of control on the Roy Orbison tour, have announced that they will now wear crash helmets to all their performances.

A Feud?

On top of both groups receiving injuries from brawling fans, now the Stones and Walkers have been tied together in a so-called feud that British papers have been building up.

Some time ago Scott Walker was quoted as saying, "Who is Jagger anyway? He flung cigarette ends at me in a London club one night," and since then the papers have been full of this so-called feud between Mick and Scott.

Mick stood by silently and took it as long as he could, but now he's had it. He's mad and he's fed up with all the publicity.

"The Walkers for some inconceivable reason have been pushing these stories around for months. It's not a new story, this cigarette end things. But I'll tell you this—it's not true. I believe it's been made up just for publicity.

"Look, I'm not the sort of bloke to deny things. If I'd chucked something at them I'd admit it. I'd say I'd done it and I'd say why. If I thought they were a right load of rubbish I'd own up.

"But I don't even *know* the Walker Brothers, never met them. I remember seeing them in the booth at a recording session in Hollywood a long time ago, long before they meant anything here. I just saw them—nothing social about it."

Mick's really fed up with the whole thing. "It's got so ruddy ridiculous that they'll soon be bringing everybody into it... my dog, my mother, or Chrissie or anybody. It's been blown up so high that I just felt I had to get this bit off my chest.

"Once and for all, I've never thrown anything at the Walkers."

Although Mick hasn't met the Walkers he does have some opinions on their music. "They're certainly not the sort of records I'd go out and buy, but they probably wouldn't buy ours."

U.S. Stunt

And Mick also feels the whole publicity thing is a typical *American* stunt.

"I'm not saying it's deliberate here, but it's true of the way American performers get publicity going for them. I don't like this American trick, but until now I've refused to get involved with it."

And Mick had a few comments for John Walker too. "And then there's John saying our last record didn't get to the number one spot in ALL the charts last time," Mick says.

"Well OK. He says ALL theirs have sold 250,000 copies, so what's this guy Jagger beefing about? ALL their records? They've only had three!"

"But I'm not beefing. I'm not in a hate campaign. I just felt I had to speak out after having ignored these stories for so long."

Two New Ones From The Stones

Stone things are happening again.

We haven't quite gotten over our "19th Nervous Breakdown" yet and we're being hit on all sides by new things from the Stones.

Their "Nervous Breakdown" turned into quite a smash. It went to number one in the nation and the West Coast followed suit.

In Los Angeles it went straight to number one, stayed a few weeks and then gradually fell off. In San Francisco it took a little longer to get to the top but it's staying longer too. And now, as a result of Otis Redding releasing "Satisfaction," the Stones' original version has joined "Nervous Breakdown" high on the charts.

But that's not all folks, they've just hit us with another single, "Mother's Little Helper," a hard driving number with sudden breaks and another one of those peculiar guitar sounds the guys are known for.

And that still ain't all, folks, 'cause they've just released a new album in England that we should be getting pretty soon.

It's the one they recorded during their last stay in Hollywood, the one they wanted to call, "Could You Walk on the Water?"

But they couldn't get away with that title so they settled for "Aftermath" and if you take the picture above and expose it three times you have the album cover.

Just released last week in England, the album seems destined to be the smash LP of the year—a "Rubber Soul" for the Stones.

The titles on the British version are, "Mother's Little Helper," "Stupid Girl," "Lady Jane," "Under My Thumb," "Doncha Bother Me," "Think," "Flight 505," "High and Dry," "Out of Time," "It's Not Easy," "What To Do," "I Am Waiting," "Take It or Leave It" and an eleven and a half minute track called, "Goin' Home."

All numbers on the album were written by Mick and Keith and the entire album runs over 50 minutes long.

We can't guarantee that all 14 numbers will be on the American version as there are usually some differences between the American and British versions of albums.

Stones Buy Rights Back

The Rolling Stones and their manager, Andrew Loog Oldham, have bought back an American publishing firm that holds the rights to several of the Stones' records.

They reacquired Immediate Music, Inc. from Dan and Bob Crewe for an undisclosed amount of money.

Immediate Music owns the copyrights to such Jagger-Richard compositions as "Satisfaction," "The Last Time," "Play With Fire" and "Heart of Stone."

"Satisfaction" alone has resulted in almost 4,000,000 sales world-wide and is now making a comeback as a result of Otis Redding releasing his version of the song.

The corporation will be run by Allen Klein and Co. who also run Gideon Music Inc., another Stones-Oldham company which holds the rights to "Get Off Of My Cloud" and "19th Nervous Breakdown."

Klein is co-manager of the Stones.

MICK, injured by a flying seat, had to have six stitches over his eye.

KRLA ARCHIVES

And The Walkers Feuding And Hurting

'He Flung Cigarettes At Me'

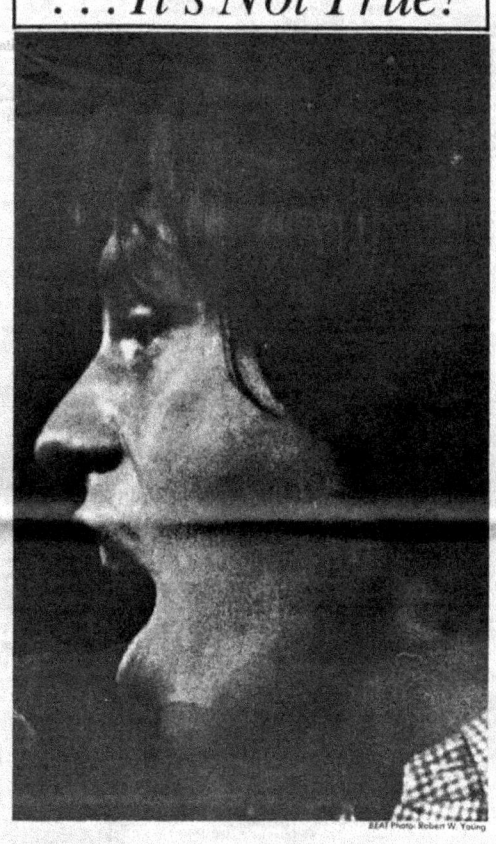

'...It's Not True!'

'I've Never Thrown Anything'

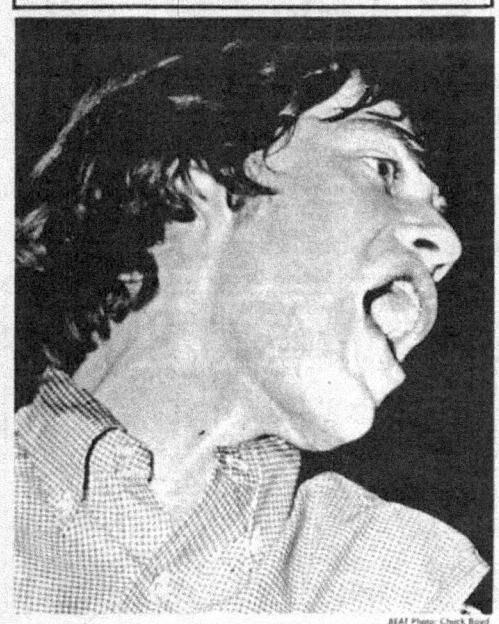

'Who's This Jagger?'

KRLA ARCHIVES

KRLA Tunedex

This Week	Last Week	Title	Artist
1	1	MONDAY, MONDAY	The Mama's & The Papa's
2	2	RAINY DAY WOMEN #12 & 35	Bob Dylan
3	4	TIME WON'T LET ME	The Outsiders
4	3	SOUL AND INSPIRATION	The Righteous Bros.
5	12	THE RAINS CAME	Sir Douglas Quintet
6	5	SECRET AGENT MAN	Johnny Rivers
7	6	CALIFORNIA DREAMIN'	The Mama's & The Papa's
8	7	SHAPES OF THINGS	The Yardbirds
9	10	EIGHT MILES HIGH/WHY	The Byrds
10	11	SLOOP JOHN B.	The Beachboys
11	—	WHEN A MAN LOVES A WOMAN	Percy Sledge
12	13	GOOD LOVIN'	The Young Rascals
13	8	KICKS	Paul Revere & The Raiders
14	23	MAGIC TOWN	The Vogues
15	9	BANG, BANG	Cher
16	22	MESSAGE TO MICHAEL	Dionne Warwick
17	15	A SIGN OF THE TIMES	Petula Clark
18	17	WOMAN	Peter & Gordon
19	27	LEANIN' ON THE LAMP POST/HOLD ON	Herman's Hermits
20	—	HEY JOE	The Leaves
21	19	THIS OLD HEART OF MINE	The Isley Bros.
22	20	TRY TOO HARD	The Dave Clark Five
23	21	RHAPSODY IN THE RAIN	Lou Christie
24	26	GET READY	The Temptations
25	25	WHAT NOW MY LOVE/SPANISH FLEA	Herb Alpert
26	33	FALLING SUGAR	The Palace Guard
27	30	TEEN-AGE FAILURE	Chad & Jeremy
28	29	PLEASE DON'T STOP LOVING ME/FRANKIE & JOHNNY	Elvis Presley
29	34	THE SUN AIN'T GONNA SHINE ANYMORE	The Walker Bros.
30	31	I CAN'T GROW PEACHES ON A CHERRY TREE	Just Us
31	39	HOW DOES THAT GRAB YOU DARLIN'/LAST OF THE SECRET AGENTS	Nancy Sinatra
32	28	I HEAR TRUMPETS BLOW	The Tokens
33	32	ALONG COMES MARY/YOUR OWN LOVE	The Association
34	37	IN MY LITTLE RED BOOK	Love
35	40	HISTORY REPEATS ITSELF	Buddy Starcher
36	36	I GOT MY MOJO WORKIN'	Jimmy Smith
37	38	NOTHING'S TOO GOOD FOR MY BABY	Stevie Wonder
38	35	CAROLINE, NO	Brian Wilson
39	—	CRUEL WAR	Peter, Paul & Mary
40	—	LOVE IS LIKE AN ITCHING IN MY HEART	The Supremes

 DAVE HULL
 BOB EUBANKS
 DICK BIONDI
 JOHNNY HAYES
 EMPEROR HUDSON
 CASEY KASEM
 CHARLIE O'DONNELL
 BILL SLATER

Inside KRLA

The big news 'round KRLA this week is the fab job which our own Dick Biondi did for the American Cancer Society at the Teenage Fair in Hollywood. At the KRLA booth at the Fair, Dick sat bravely in his cage while his "fans" tried to dunk him.

When the whole thing was over, soaking Dick had been dunked 18,000 times and had brought in $974.50! The dunking bit was Dick's own idea and after the Fair had closed KRLA attempted to get Biondi to take a week's rest and dry off. But it was all in vain, for our brave and fearless (not to mention extremely wet) nine to midnight man refused to take even one day off.

The rest of the news this week concerns that great innovation of Request Radio. Uncle Dick Moreland would like you all to know that a San Fernando Valley line has been installed as well as the Los Angeles and Orange county numbers.

Each day a different guest seems to appear from nowhere to help answer all your calls. Last week Pet Clark and Joey Paige took their turns as receptionists. Who knows who will pop up next week?

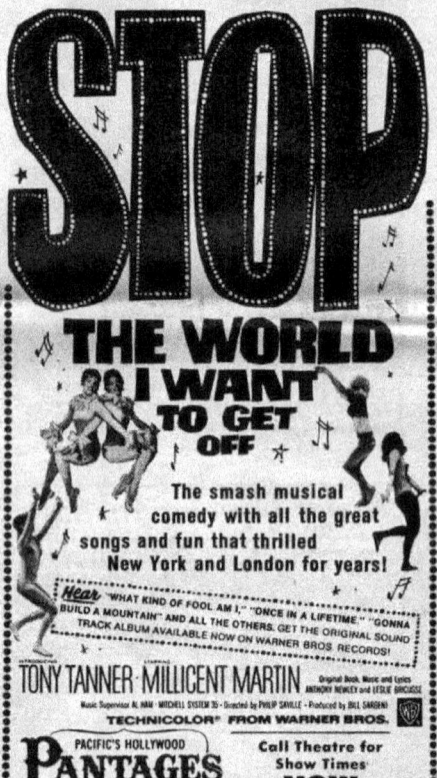

They Forgot An Academy Award

They left out an Academy Award this year.

Maybe they thought it was so obvious it wasn't needed.

But the most recorded motion picture song of the year has got to be the Paul Webster-Johnny Mandel composition "The Shadow of Your Smile" from the movie "The Sandpiper."

The song's been recorded by no less than 70 different artists, including Herb Alpert and the Tijuana Brass, Chris Montez, David McCallum, Trini Lopez, Bobby Darin, Frank Sinatra and Barbra Streisand.

Raise Money For Your Club

Want to raise extra money for your club treasury? You could easily make several hundred dollars. For information write Fan Club Funds, KRLA BEAT, Sunset-Vine Tower, Suite 504, Hollywood, Calif. — 90028

KRLA BEAT Subscription

SPECIAL BONUS — SUBSCRIBE NOW and receive a free copy of The Bobby Fuller Four's best selling album, "I Fought The Law."

☐ 1 YEAR - 52 Issues — $5.00 ☐ 2 YEARS — $8.00
☐ 6 MONTHS — $3.00
Enclosed is ☐ CASH ☐ CHECK
PLEASE PRINT — Include Your Zip Code

Send to: .... Age: ....
Address: .... City: ....
State: .... Zip: ....

MAIL YOUR ORDER TO: KRLA BEAT
6290 Sunset, Suite 504
Hollywood, Calif. 90028

Foreign Rate: $9.00 - 52 Issues

KRLA ARCHIVES

Dunkin' Biondi At The Fair

  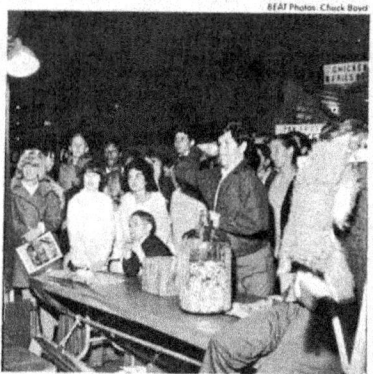

Singers Sign In At The Hullabaloo Club

...PALACE GUARD

...JERRY NAYLOR

...PAUL PETERSON

A whole new era was ushered in recently when the Hullabaloo Club in Hollywood invited recording artists to come by the club and sign their names to the front of the world famous Moulin Rouge building.

The plaques on the Hullabaloo front (facing Sunset Blvd.) formerly held the autographs of such great movie stars as Clark Gable, Gary Cooper and John Wayne.

In order to make room for the new signatures several of the "oldies" had to be taken down causing the elderly citizens of Hollywood as well as the former owner of the building to protest violently.

But it was all to no avail as such popular artists as the Palace Guard, Jerry Naylor an Paul Peterson were on hand to sign the plaques and watch their names rise high on the Hullabaloo wall.

The young are takin' over where the old used to rule.

ONE WEEK ONLY!
APRIL 26 – MAY 1
THE BIRTH OF THE BLUES

Sonny Terry
AND
Brownie McGee

AT DOUG WESTON'S
Troubadour
RESERVATIONS
CR 6-6168
9083 SANTA MONICA BLVD.
L.A. NEAR DOHENY

KRLA ARCHIVES

THREE GREAT GROUPS
FROM MGM–VERVE
THE ANIMALS—HERMAN'S HERMITS—RIGHTEOUS BROS.

3 Must Albums for all and we have them and all the rest of your favorites in our Big Record Dept.

Soul And Inspiration
- Stand By
- He
- He Will Break Your Heart
- In The Midnight Hour
- I'm Leaving It Up To You

Mine All Mine
- Rat Race
- Hey, Girl
- Turn On Your Lovelights
- Change Is Going To Come
- Bring It All Home

House of The Rising Sun
- I'm Crying
- Boom, Boom
- Don't Let Me Be Misunderstood
- We Gotta Get Out Of This Place

Bring It On Home To Me
- It's My Life
- Roberta
- I'm Mad
- Gonna Send You Back To Walker
- I'm In Love Again

I'm Henry VIII, I Am
- Mrs. Brown You've Got A Lovely Daughter
- Mother-In-Law
- I'm Into Something Good
- Can't You Hear My Heartbeat

Just A Little Bit Better
- Silhouettes
- The End Of The World
- Sea Cruise
- I Gotta Dream On
- Wonderful World

We Give BLUE CHIP STAMPS on 25,000 items

Mono or Stereo At Fantastic Savings at Your Friendly

Thrifty CUT RATE DRUG STORES

KRLA ARCHIVES

Three Irish Lads Coming Our Way

Move over England, Ireland's movin' in.

England's sent us hit group after hit group but now we're beginning to hear from Ireland. They sent us Them and now they're releasing three of their most incredibly handsome Dubliners on us.

Their names are John Stokes, Con Cluskey and Dec Cluskey and they call themselves The Bachelors.

They've got a style as strong and sweet as Irish coffee and they can sing. They've been dusting off some old Tin Pan Alley favorites they found in a bottom drawer somewhere, applying their own Bachelor sound and coming up with million selling chart toppers all over Britain and Europe.

They've had a couple of successful records over here but America hasn't fully caught onto their Irish charm yet.

So they're trying again with their new release, the old beautiful standard, "Love Me With All Your Heart."

No Gimmicks

There's no gimmicks or fads to the Bachelors. They're all very handsome talented young singers who just sing well.

"It's just the basic Irish style," says Dec, who is so Celtic even his eyes are green. "We don't compete with the rock-and-rollers. We prefer folk and country and western. It's *singing*."

Dec's the youngest (22) and the shortest (5 ft. 10 in.) of the group. He and his brother Con were both educated at O'Connells Schools, the Dublin school which is renowned for turning out doctors, lawyers, engineers and sportsmen. Show business people are still rather rare there and Dec and Con confused them all by becoming fine musicians.

Con got his start in show business at the tender age of four when he won an Irish dancing contest. "My father immediately booked me, at enormous expense to appear in a concert he was running," he remembers. "I got half-a-crown for the date."

Con plays a number of instruments including piano and harmonica and is quite a sports nut. He's taken up rowing, road racing and flying at various times.

A Floating Club

He was the one who came up with the idea that the Bachelors buy their own flying boat and turn it into a floating night club.

Oldest member of the group is John, 26. He was a reluctant Bachelor who thought he'd never measure up to the group's standards.

"Con and Dec had studied piano for years before me," he says. "When I first joined them I was afraid I might hinder them with my own lack of musical knowledge."

John's now rated as one of the best harmony singers in the world.

But if it hadn't been for an injury he might never have been a singer at all. He started out as an athlete of great potential. The day he was supposed to have been given a trial for the Irish soccer team against Germany he hurt himself and couldn't turn out for the game.

He lost the chance for his cap and after that soccer took a back seat to singing.

All three of the Bachelors are crazy about drumming—the drumming of hoofbeats that is. With their manager, advisor and discoverer, Philip Solomon, they own shares in five thoroughbred mares who've produced many top Irish race horses.

Those mares graze peacefully on an emerald green pasture somewhere while their owners rush about in the frantic star spangled show business world.

The Bachelors don't have extra long hair and they dress in suits when they perform and they all have excellently trained voices. They just plain sing well that's all, all.

The Bachelors are arriving on the West Coast May 17 to bring us some of that good Irish charm.

Say you read it in The BEAT

... THE BACHELORS

THE SHADOWS OF KNIGHT have not only won the battle of the "Gloria" singles but they've also released their first album on Atco, titled after their smash hit single, "Gloria." This group's definitely a winner!

Shadows Of Knight Win 'Gloria' Race

By Louise Criscione

They have shut down Them with their recording of "Gloria." They're the first rock group to come out of Chicago and really make a sizable impact on the pop world and they kicked their career off by being the resident group at a teen club in Chicago called The Cellar. Put all of the facts together and you come up with the Shadows of Knight.

The five Shadows of Knight—Jerry, Warren, Joe, Jim and Tom—were recently in town to do several television shows promoting their smash, "Gloria," which has now climbed all the way up to the Top Ten in the national charts while "Gloria" by Them can't even make it into the Top 100!

While they were here they all dropped by *The BEAT* to sort of get acquainted and let us know exactly where they're at. And where they're at right now is the swingin' Phone Booth in New York, but where they come from is Chicago's "in" spot, the Cellar.

Hard Climb

Since there are literally thousands of young amateur groups in the U.S., but there is only room for a hundred artists on the nation's charts, it's not easy to fight your way up in the pop world.

And, unfortunately, talent isn't enough—you've got to have someone behind you and in the case of the Shadows of Knight it was their manager, Paul Sampson who helped them rise from the ranks of the amateurs to that of one of the hottest new groups in the country.

"Jimmy, Warren, Tom and two other guys were in the group the first time I spotted them at a VFW hall," recalled Paul. "I didn't think they were stars but they looked different—they had something which other groups didn't.

"The very first one I noticed was Tom. He's a very showy drummer and impressive to watch. He caught my eye so I began talking to them and about this time we put them into a dance called The Blast," continued Paul.

"They were called the Shadows then and on a night when all kinds of other things were going on, 800 kids showed up to see them. At Blast #2 they pulled in a 1,000 kids and they were on their way."

Superman

At this point Jim, wearing a Superman tee shirt (guess he doesn't know Superman is out and Batman is in) took up the story. "We went into Paul's teenage night club, the Cellar, as the resident group and it turned into one of the biggest places in the Midwest," said Jim.

Although they were packing the Cellar so well that the crowds had to be cleared out after every show to make room for those waiting outside, the Shadows of Knight were still not as professional musically as they would liked to have been.

"We played junk," admitted Tom frankly. "That's how a group starts out by copying everything until they come up with a sound of their own."

And a distinctive sound of their own is what the Shadows of Knight eventually came up with, a sound which they call the "Chicago Sound" but what really boils down to commercial blues.

Minus

So, now they were Chicago's most popular group—a group which specialized in commercial blues but they were still minus a recording contract. They did, however, have five permanent Shadows as two of the original group vanished and Joe and Jerry had arrived.

Paul had been in the record business for six years—he knew lots of different record company personnel and he brought them around to hear his Shadows. Atco became very interested in the boys but they had one small problem.

Atco had the English group, the Shadows, and naturally they were not about to put out records by two different groups with the same name. So, the American Shadows became The Time, but when "Gloria" was relased the name on the label read the Shadows of Knight.

"The disc jockeys were so confused," laughed Jim, "that everytime they played our record they'd call us by a different name. We were the Shadows, the Time, the Shadows of Knight, the Shadows of Time, the Time Shadows and the Knight Time. It was really funny, but I think all the confusion helped because it generated a lot of interest in this group with all the names."

Brown Sound

While all of the boys dig hardcore rhythm 'n' blues they don't think that as such it will ever become very popular in the pop market. "A lot of groups have a brown sound but not real hardcore R&B," said Jim. "The black sound doesn't have good set arrangements. They know where they're going but they don't work it all out."

Although Chicago's their hometown they all agree that there is really no action there. "The radio stations would never push a record," revealed Tom, "there's no scene there, no pop shows. The kids are all right but there's just nothing there."

Brown sound, black sound, Chicago sound, commercial blues—no matter what you choose to call it, the Shadows of Knight definitely have it and they're not about to let it go. Except on stage, that is. There they let *everything* go and as Joe said: "It's really exciting."

KRLA ARCHIVES

The Everlys In Action

Bob Hope's getting some stiff competition for the title of America's number one Ambassador of Goodwill.

The Everly Brothers, Don and Phil, have just completed a tour of Vietnam, the Phillipines and Hong Kong that broke records and brought up morale faster than anything short of an end to the war.

These two Tennessee lads charmed everybody—from hoards of screaming teens to hospitals of wounded veterans—with their casual and refreshing brand of humor and talented singing.

In Manila, they broke all existing records for any type of performance. The previous record, set by the late Nat "King" Cole, fell by the side-line quickly.

The brothers were booked for five nights. After all five nights were sold out and the crowds still clamoured for more, they were held over for another night, another complete sell out, and finally ended up staying an extra *three* days just to answer the demand for tickets to see them.

Great Press

There had been a big build up in the Phillipine press before their arrival but it never matched the reviews *after* their eight days of performances in the Araneta Coliseum in Quezon City.

Several pop acts had appeared there before and been panned badly but the brothers really came through.

One local paper reported, "Phil and Don, aside from giving superb performances were also gentlemen. This is a refreshing departure from the boorish example of The Searchers, those mop-haired Beatles imitators."

Another said "Even the parents of the bop set would have approved of the two singers—no wild gyrations, no riots among the girls. The mild hysteria of the fans turned into universal suffering when the Everlys wailed, "I'll Do My Crying in the Rain" with many in the audience recalling old hurts and broken hearts."

It was like that everywhere they went—great reviews of the show and marvelous comments on what gentlemen they were. The boys really did America proud.

In Hong Kong they appeared in the Kingsland Night Club and at Clark Air Force Base they played right in the hospital where so many of the wounded from Vietnam are taken.

DON AND PHIL get off the plane in Manila to start their five day stand that was held over for eight.

In Vietnam itself they did another sell out show for the 4,000 members of the Airmen's Open Mess at Tan Son Nhut Air Base and then donated all the proceeds to the Go-Vat Orphanage, which cares for over 900 children left homeless by the war.

They received a touching letter from the custodian of the orphanage thanking them for their generosity and saying, "It is impossible to describe in words what this means to me, my members and most of all, the unfortunate children of the orphanage."

Everywhere they went, whether in the sunny Phillipines or the war-torn Vietnamese towns, they were met with wild enthusiasm and in return they gave their usual great show.

The only complaint they received during the entire tour was that the show was too short. They sang at least 15 numbers each show but the crowds still wanted more. They just can't get enough of the Everlys over there.

And did they rest after returning to America? Nope, they're off on another English tour right this minute.

Hey fellas, when are you going to come back and spread some more of that Everly magic around America a bit? We love you too, you know, and we're mighty proud of the way you're representing America around the world.

A TRIUMPHANT RIDE through the streets for the popular American duo.

200,000 FANS jammed the Araneta Coliseum in Quezon, the Philipines every night for eight days to see the Everly Bros. and to break all existing attendance records there.

KRLA ARCHIVES

THE EVERLY BROTHERS met an enthusiastic press everywhere they went on this tour.

A QUICK STOP to pose with two lovely girls who appeared on the tour with them.

HOW'S THAT AGAIN? — The boys and manager Don Wayne, left, hold an informal press conference in Manila.

DON AND PHIL IN ACTION — Great as usual.

KRLA ARCHIVES

For Girls Only
By Shirley Poston

I'm a nervous wreck, I tell you! The next time I start thinking up brilliant ideas like "codes," I hope someone beans me with a large jagged rock.

I'm kidding really. The whole thing has been a ball, and now that I'm finally ready to present the first coded message, I think I'll present the first coded message. (No wonder my guidance counselor kept encouraging me to give up my dream of becoming a writer and take up plumbing.)

Anypath, only those of you who have a copy of the S.P. (as in Silly Poston) code will be able to decipher the scrambled (try scrambled if that doesn't work) words. If you don't have a copy, I suggest you just leave well enough alone and realize how fortunate you really are.

Coded Messages

Now, remember, I warned you that this was an absolutely ridiculous idea. But, are you the sort of person who goes around *wzbbzar ezyixvnb* of your fave, when no one is looking, of course? Well, if you do, you're a perfect victim - er candidate for a new thought transference game called, "*Wzbbzn.*"

How to play? First of all, find just the right *epkik* (if you know what I mean) (and, you do). Then designate a certain time a day for *rzlzar zig jgvrn bukkyp*. Don't forget, or get carried away, because the game can only be played once a day.

If you think extra hard, your fave is supposed to be able to actually *cnnj hkxv ikwnake gccnyizka*. And, so the story goes, if you continue your plan for exactly 365 days (without missing even one) at the same exact time of day, he will someday return the favor.

Wild, huh? Even if it doesn't work, what do you have to lose? Besides several marbles, that is, but your supply was dwindling anyway.

Speaking of George (well, I was thinking about him, which is almost as good) (which, come to think of it, is a whole lot better), have you seen all the wedding type pictures plastered all over the newsstands? Magazines work so far in advance, the pix are just coming out now. Course, *The BEAT* had them months ago, but to say that would be bragging, so I won't say it.

I, however, will say that Pattie looks like a very agreeable sort. Wonder if she'd be agreeable to my borrowing George on occasion? No, I doubt if anyone is *that* agreeable. (Would you believe renting him for a reasonable price?)

I am now going to try to explain something, so prepare yourselves. Remember when I was raving about how much fun it is to pronounce words the way they're spelled? Well, I just got a letter from a girl who used this idea for a school report.

Her subject was pronunciation, and when she got up in front of the class, she said every single *word* the way it was spelled. Everyone about flipped. And the teacher went right along with the gag.

Teacher's Trouble

But, you know what? The teacher was later called on the carpet by the principal, which makes me LIVID! They're always screaming for teachers, but just let one of them display a sense of humor and they're in trouble.

Sorry about getting on my soap box. I know this isn't a very *fascinating* subject, but it really makes me burn.

Not long ago, I got the greatest letter from a teacher who reads my column. She even sent me a present! But she made me promise NEVER to mention her name. Honestly, she sounded like she'd be burned at the stake if I did.

I won't, of course, but I still think it's a shame.

Down, Shirl. Get back in de box. Or at least get off it! I know what I'll do! I'll submit the teacher topic to the boss and see if it can't be used for a future panel discussion. (Providing of course, that I get to participate.)

Speaking of letters (fooldya again), some of the envelopes I've been receiving are almost as great as what's inside. What I mean is, you've been writing and drawing groovy things on the envelopes (like big hearts saying Shirley + George), and I've starting putting some of them up on my wall!

Ho, ho! Just had another zing-whammer. Let's have an envelope contest! Lemme see, what can I scrounge up to give away? Ahah! I have it! That jerk of a brother of mine owes me ten whole dollars! Which means I can give a whole dollar to each of the ten people who send in the wildest envelopes!

This contest, as you may have guessed, serves two purposes. One, I'll have more goodies for my wall. Two, I will have the supreme pleasure of throttling the mon out of you-know-who(m).

Just thought of something else. You know how I am about explaining stuff. Well, I've just figured out a way to put an end to war! All I have to do is get a job writing the instructions they have on bombs and guns and all that. Why, it would be a hundred years before they'd be able to understand what I was raving about! (A problem which has already confused the lives of my readers.) (Both of them.)

Whether you know it or not, you have just been treated to a ten minute intermission. My mind went absolutely blank! And I've just been sitting here staring at some of the notes that are scattered all over my "desk." I always write down fragments of sentences to remind me of things I don't want to forget, but when I try to translate them, I'm sadly out of luck.

Here's one of my reminders as a for instance - "Three weeks from Keith." Now, I ask you. What is *that* supposed to mean? And why am I telling *you* about it? (Well, at least it's more interesting than orange popsickles and feet.) (Or is it?) (Never answer that question.)

New Tag

Oh, here's one I do understand! Several of you have suggested that "For Girls Only" be re-titled something like "For Retards Only." I think it's a good idea, because "F.G.O." gives the impression that this is a helpful, rational, sensible column which occasionally contains bits of useful information. Well, as everyone knows, that's hardly the case.

Tell you what. You be thinking of possible re-titles, and just as soon as I can scrounge up still another fantastic (as in you've got to be kidding, kiddo) prize, we'll have another of our ridiculous contests and pick a new tag!

Well, now that I've rambled and raved for several million paragraphs, and sid (remember him?) . . . er . . . *said* so many vastly interesting (as in snore) things, it's time to close (my mouth.)

But, would you believe that I'll be back next week with more of the same inane blithering?

Thousands wouldn't. Millions sure hope not.

KRLA ARCHIVES

The BEAT Goes To The Movies

The Silencers

By Jim Hamblin
(The BEAT Movie Editor)

The United States is in trouble. The "Big O" organization of enemy spies is about to take over one of our most important missile firing projects. How can they be stopped? There is only one man for the job— Matt Helm!

His name alone strikes fear in the hearts of evil-doers and spies. His assignment by I.C.E. (our guys) thwarts the plans of the enemy for an easy takeover.

But where is Matt Helm? Well, right now he's home on his portable circular bed. Soon he's taking an automatic bubble-bath, with full-time lady attendant. Ah, such is the life.

And, ah, such is this wildly funny film that takes Dean Martin through some of his finest tongue-in-cheek adventures.

We can't really call this movie a spoof, because it's too funny for that. But it is about spies *a la James Bond*, and it has come out for public view at least slightly ahead of the rash of horrible reproductions of the variations on a theme of *Thunderball*.

Like many of the screen's best comedies, you get nothing out of just reading about it, you must see it. And that we recommend with clear conscience.

Besides, I'm in love with The World's Most Beautiful Woman, Stella Stevens.

300-LB. VICTOR BUONO — enemy operations head.

STELLA STEVENS in one of her less glamorous moments in the movie.

SOME FOUL fellow put *COFFEE* in Dino's cup.

DINO was enjoying the sun until the enemy's most effective weapon stopped that.

CLAUDIA MARTIN, one of Dino's seven children, visited for a few moments on the set.

KRLA ARCHIVES

America's Largest Teen NEWSpaper

KRLA Edition **BEAT**

15¢

MAY 14, 1966

'GOOD TIMES'

KRLA BEAT

Volume 2, Number 9   May 14, 1966

JEFF BECK COLLAPSES TAKEN SERIOUSLY ILL

Jeff Beck, lead guitarist for the Yardbirds, collapsed after the group's concert in Marseilles, France and was immediately rushed seriously ill to the hospital with suspected meningitis.

Shortly afterwards, Jeff was flown back to a London hospital while the rest of the group continued on to Copenhagen. The Yardbirds have not yet decided whether to get a temporary replacement for Jeff or not.

An interesting question has been posed in the English trades concerning Jeff. They wonder if Jeff isn't looking for a way out of the Yardbirds. The BEAT sincerely hopes not for the Yardbirds would never be the same group without him. However, it has been reported ever since the Yardbirds were Stateside in January that Jeff was unhappy with the group, with the record scene, with everything.

Rumor True

We'd like to point out that neither Jeff nor the Yardbirds have commented on Jeff's supposed desire to leave the group. We'll all just have to patiently wait and see what happens. However, one rumor concerning the group and their manager, Giorgio Gomelsky, has come true.

They've split. Trouble has been brewing between the two forces for quite some time now and the Yardbirds apparently admitted that when Giorgio's five year contract ran out they would find themselves another manager. It did—and they did. Yardbirds' new manager is Simon Napier-Bell, former jazz musician and producer of documentary films.

Since The BEAT is friends with both Giorgio and the Yardbirds, we prefer not to take any sides in the split but just to wish the best

BEAT Photo: Chuck Boyd

of luck to all concerned and a speedy recovery to Jeff Beck.

Jeff's sudden illness is probably the biggest blow to hit the Yardbirds yet for, quite frankly, he is their sound. The weird guitar and the heavy use of the reverb which have become the Yardbird trademark were Jeff's idea. And he is the only one who has been able to master the guitar in just that style. He is widely copied but so far never imitated.

Chris Dreja, who formerly played rhythm guitar for the group, is now attempting to take over Jeff's spot until he is able to return or until they can find a replacement for him.

HOTLINE LONDON SPECIAL
Mime Ban In Britain?
By Tony Barrow

In England we call it MIME. In America you call it LIP-SYNC. Either way, it means the much-used idea of having singers move their mouths in time with their own records while gazing into the lenses of the television cameras.

Inside the BEAT

Sonny and Cher's 'Good Times'	2-3
For Girls Only	4
On The Beat	5
Mindbenders Bend Your Mind	7
Hotline London	11
Adventures of Robin Boyd	12
Oscar Awards	15

The BEAT is published weekly by BEAT Publications, Inc., editorial and advertising offices at 6290 Sunset Blvd., Suite 504, Hollywood, California 90028. U.S. bureaus in Hollywood, San Francisco, New York, Chicago and Nashville; overseas correspondents in London, Liverpool and Manchester, England. Sale price, 15 cents. Subscription price U.S. and possessions, $5 per year, Canada and foreign rates, $9 per year. Second class postage prepaid at Los Angeles, California.

Most major stars have mastered the knack of miming even if more than a few instrumentalists make a poor job of flicking their fingers across silent guitar strings or letting their drumsticks just miss cymbals and skins with an obvious and intentional lack of good marksmanship!

Miming has become an important point of pop controversy in London since the opening of the year. Stars, producers, journalists and fans have spoken out for or against the mime game. Some said it was just as acceptable as a five in-person TV performance. Others argued that the whole concept of miming was phony and undesirable.

Now, with the flow of printed and spoken words on the subject reaching some kind of climax, our

(Turn To Page 12)

Shadow Follows Bob Lind Correspondent Flys Over

Bob Lind has been compared to Bob Dylan by many people but now he appears to be falling into a category with the Beatles.

Bob's managers, Charlie Greene and Brian Stone, have been notified by cable from London that the London Daily Express is flying a special correspondent to America this week to do a full page layout on Bob and his writing.

The only other time the Express has flown anyone anywhere to do a full page layout on anyone was for The Beatles. This is the first time they've ever done it for just one person.

That makes Bob equal to the Beatles as far as the Express is concerned.

The apparent reason for this is Bob's recent three week smash tour of Britain.

In just the short amount of time that Bob was over there promoting his first single, "Elusive Butterfly," he became one of the most talked about personalities over there.

Also as an apparent result of his visit, the record shot to number two on the British charts although there was another version out at the same time by Val Doonican.

And the same song is now number one on the British sheet music charts, a series of charts that America doesn't even keep.

And all of this was the result of just one record. At the time he was over there neither his album or his second single, "Remember The Rain" and "Truly Julie Blues," had been released there.

As far as most people can remember there was never as big a reaction as fast as there was to Bob Lind in England. Even the Beatles came up slower than Bob.

And yet during this dizzying flight to the top, Bob has remained totally unchanged and unimpressed. He doesn't seem to yet comprehend his full popularity.

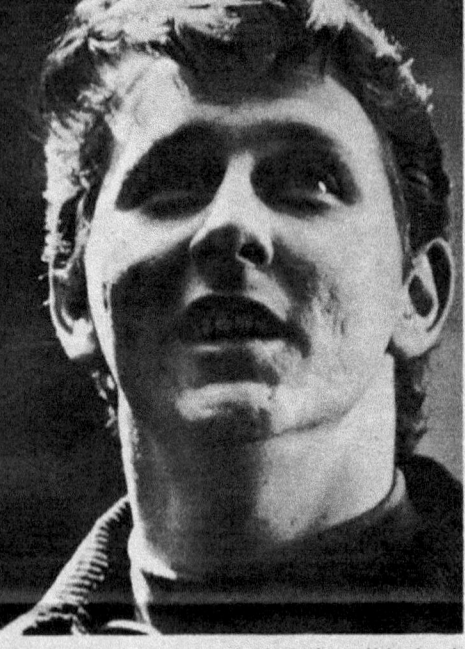

You can still find him wandering around alone with just his guitar, looking lost and unconcerned. The only time he becomes difficult is when you try to interview him—he doesn't think he's interesting or important.

He's been compared to another Bob—Dylan—but most people find his writings much more refreshing and optimistic than Dylan's.

It's even been said that the only real difference between Lind and Dylan as far as writing influence is that Lind writes in English.

If you run into Bob in the next couple of weeks, he won't be alone. That shadow following him everywhere is a British reporter who thinks Bob is as important and influential as the Beatles and is trying to find out what makes him tick.

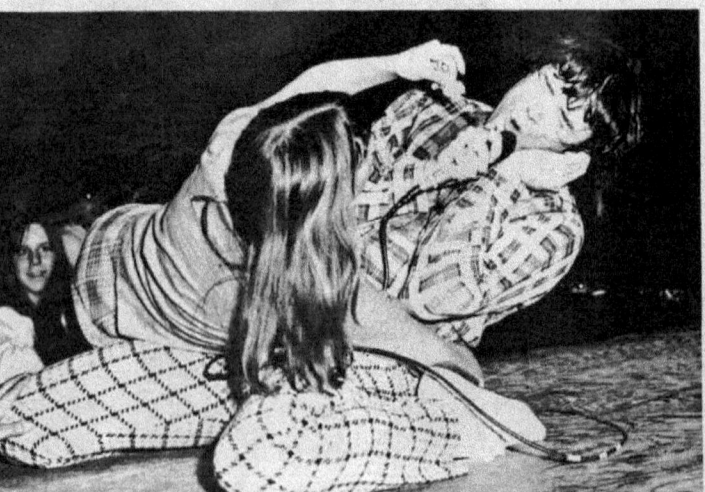

P.J. PROBY is back in the United States and it may be for good this time. Not only has he purchased a new home for himself (in California) but he bought one for his manager, too. He is currently negotiating several movie offers and getting his cabaret act back together for American audiences to enjoy.

BEAT Photo: Chuck Boyd

KRLA ARCHIVES

'Good Times' With

By Carol Deck

You expect the set of a movie about America's number one pop couple to be enveloped in excitement, to have fans milling about, and to have a general air of tension just because it's Sonny and Cher and it's their first movie.

The BEAT, recalling some interesting moments on the sets of the Beatles' movies, visited the Paramount lots in Hollywood to view the filming of the movie tentatively titled "Good Times."

We found Sonny sitting alone in the middle of an old time western town scene early one morning. Cher wasn't around as they were just shooting exterior shots with Sonny that day so he told Cher she could have a day off.

Sonny, dressed in buckskin pants with fringe around the bottom, a bright red print shirt, boots with huge oversized spurs, a rather large battered brown hat with a feather and numerous bullet holes in the rim and covered with about a dozen tin deputy badges, gave us some insight to the movie.

Basically, it's about Sonny and Cher. It starts with them, as they are now, young married singing stars with millions of fans 'round the world.

Cher's pretty content with things as they are, but Sonny isn't. He thinks they should branch out into movies. A powerful film tycoon makes Sonny a screen offer that Cher argues against but that starts Sonny to daydreaming.

He imagines himself out West. He's Sheriff Irving Ringo, the only man who can keep peace in this big land. He also has a way with Nelle Belle, the dance hall queen, and Irene Goodnight, the school marm, both of whom are dead ringers for Cher (funny thing about that.)

Things get a little out of hand before Sonny wakes up and realizes that with his hat too big, his pants too long, bullets constantly falling out of his gun because of the angle he keeps the holster at, and the fact that even his sheriff's badge is bent, he makes a pretty silly cowboy.

Morry And Zora

But he still can't get the idea of a movie out of his head. Next he dreams he's Jungle Morry, raised by apes. He and his mate Zora (another amazing Cher look alike) live in a tree complete with elevator and two elephants in the elephant port.

Again things get out of hand—it could have something to do with Sonny's 85 year old son—and he wakes up just in time.

Soon Sonny's drifting off again. This time he's Bogie Mann, private eye, with a sultry singer named Samantha, who looks enough like Cher to be her twin, as a sidekick.

Funny how those Cher lookalikes keep popping into Sonny's dreams.

As Bogie Mann he's out to capture the local crime lord who ends up capturing him, hypnotizing him

"COME ON BILLY, YOU CAN DO IT" — Sonny and Cher take a break during filming and work things out with their director, William Friedkin, whom Sonny has great respect for.

KRLA ARCHIVES

Sonny And Cher

A Funny Thing

By Louise Criscione

and setting him loose to blow up the police headquarters and himself.

This time when he wakes up, he finally gets the message and refuses the whole picture deal and goes back to just being one of America's favorite singers.

This movie means a lot to Sonny, who wrote a good deal of the script and the entire music score.

"It's a definite story," he says, "with a beginning, an end and a reason. It's beyond just a rock and roll movie. The songs are a vehicle for the story situation."

As for the writing, Sonny explains, "I wrote a great deal of it out of desperation. When it got down to where we had to shoot it, it wasn't there."

The original script was written by a professional script writer. Then Sonny took it for two weeks and did most of the Sonny and Cher dialogue. And then a comedy writer was hired to polish up some of the jokes.

But the songs are all Sonny's. On the day we visited him on the set he had written one the night before and had three more to do.

Title Problems

One of those songs is "Good Times," the title tentatively set for the movie. When the idea of the movie first came up, it was to be titled "I Got You Babe," after their first and biggest hit.

Then "Bang Bang" jumped on the charts and became their biggest hit next to "I Got You Babe" and they decided to change the title to their latest hit.

However there's an Ian Fleming movie in England called "Kiss, Kiss, Bang, Bang" and they could not get the rights to use "Bang Bang."

The title had been copyrighted as a song title and not a movie title so they lost it. They're now calling the movie "Good Times," but Sonny warns they might change it again.

As we sat on the set we watched Sonny shoot a scene for the cowboy sequence where he had just been deserted by all his deputies.

Sonny's in a saloon and one by one the deputies come up and hang their badges on him until he looks like a walking invitation to a magnet.

The final scene they have to shoot is where Sonny walks out of the saloon and sees his mule sitting down outside. This sit down strike by his faithful companion is the last straw and he shakes his fist in disgust and walks off.

Mean Sonny

One of the funniest sights of the year has to be Sonny Bono standing in the middle of this old western town in that get-up of his trying to look mean. He stood there for a few minutes making faces, but without much luck. Sonny's just too cute to look mean.

The mood on the set is relaxed and friendly with a lot of joking about hair and things. Everyone kids Sonny, good naturedly, about his hair and even the extras on the project say, "This is a funny picture."

During a break in the filming someone asks what the delay is and someone else replies, "The mule wants more money."

Sonny's working hard on this movie but he's also managing to keep up a few other projects at the same time.

He and Cher are working on the sound-track of the movie which should be released about the same time as the movie, either in June or July.

And they're looking for another single. Sonny said he cut one the other night called "Have I Done Something Wrong?" that could be their next single but, "I have to listen to it a few thousand times more."

Just before leaving the set we posed one last question to Sonny. "Aren't you a little afraid, working on your first movie?"

"Yeah, I'm scared. I think you are about anything that's important."

Any movie that's put together with as much sincere care and effort as this one is can't be anything but great.

It's funny how fame affects some people and fails to affect others. Strange how some remain relatively the same despite their sudden popularity and how others become so swell-headed that it's really unbelievable.

I'm glad Sonny & Cher haven't changed much at all since the first time I visited them. It seems like years ago but was actually about eleven months ago. I remember it very well because it was one of the first interviews I had ever done and it was one of the first interviews that they had ever given.

"Just You" had broken locally but outside of Los Angeles no one had ever even heard of Sonny and Cher. They lived in a rather small hillside home which they were in the midst of furnishing.

Cher liked it because it had a magnificent view of the city and Sonny liked it because it had a garage with a piano in it. He could write songs down there where it was quiet and he could work without interruptions.

They were playing the local clubs then and were so proud that they had become popular enough to draw several hundred into a small night spot. Cher told me about a beach club they'd just played and had somehow managed to pull in a neat 500. They felt it was the greatest accomplishment they had made.

They probably dreamed of having a smash single in the national top ten and drawing sell-out crowds into the huge auditoriums throughout the country but it was so far off (if it ever did happen) that they were afraid to even talk about it.

Their clothes weren't so far out then. Cher wore rather conservative bell bottoms with a poor boy shirt and Sonny wore striped shirts above hip-hugging plain colored pants.

As their cleaning lady attempted to make a path through their black and white tiled kitchen, Sonny sipped coffee from an enormous mug and answered the phone while Cher sat Indian style on the sofa talking about how someday she hoped they would be able to visit London so that she could replenish her clothes closet.

Cher admitted to being scared on stage if Sonny wasn't up there with her and one got the distinct impression that that was the only reason Sonny *was* singing with Cher. He probably would have preferred to let Cher be the star while he concentrated on song writing and record producing.

They were thrilled at the prospect of having an entire article devoted to them in The BEAT because then, no one was writing about them at all. They weren't news and if they faded from the scene, probably no one would even notice that they were gone.

They had just finished a walk-on for one of the Beach Party type movies which they were enthusiastic about because they never thought they'd be the stars of their own movie only months later.

Yes, it's funny how fame doesn't affect some people much at all. Sonny and Cher have had more than one top ten single, they've produced hit albums, they've drawn thousands to their concerts, they've evoked a clothes revolution in the teenage world, they've moved into a huge new home and they've had pages and pages written about them.

But they've remained basically the same two people who once lived in a small house, drew several hundred into tiny clubs and dreamed big dreams.

Funny, isn't it? But a nice sort of funny.

CHER has some pretty wild outfits but we never expected this.

CHER AND A FRIEND — Sonny had to wrestle with a lion but Cher only got to pet one.

"I'M MEAN, MISTER" — Sonny plays Sheriff Irving Ringo, the bumbling hero of the West

KRLA ARCHIVES

For Girls only
by shirley poston

Narcissa Nash has struck again. If you're a long-time reader of this (excuse for a) column (haven't they come for you *yet*?), that name should ring a bell.

N.N. is the pen name (I hope) (so does she) of the girl who composed the greatest Beatle dream of all time some months back, which I stole - er - printed word for word. Now N.N. has analyzed one of my Beatle dreams! For the second time, I might add (and, if you'll notice, just did). I lost her first letter (which figures) and had to hint around (as in beg openly) for a copy. And you're about to read same, re-stolen . . . er . . . printed word for word. Take it way, Nar (as in cissa!)

Preface:

!!!#?%¢%#%!!$#✓•*!!!

Pardon my Scouse, but I'm in a bit of a twitter, having read that you've lost me previous letter about the "Lennon-with-parachute" dream. Being as I can't find the original writty, I'll have to improvise. (They're putting me to sleep at three of the clock.)

The Lettuce:

Dear Shirley: Go lie down on a couch . . . I'll wait . . . comfy? All right then, I'll begin. I am going to analyze your dream about the Beatles, and, as any twit knows, the analyzee (?) must be lying on a couch while being analyzed by the analyzer (?) (perhaps we'd better switch places.) Anyroad, I shall proceed.

The airplane symbolizes the Beatles popularity as a group, which will eventually go down. You represent the loyal fan, and you are afraid that the plane will crash (i.e. that the Beatles' popularity will die.) But the Beatles themselves are not afraid, because they are prepared; they have parachutes.

The parachutes symbolize the Beatles' individual talents which will "rescue" them after their popularity as a group dies. The reason you hang onto John and his parachute is because John has a greater variety of talents, and he will undoubtedly remain more popular than the others after the group splits. (Spoken as only a true Lennon fan may speak.)

John's comment when you hit the ground ("how can you laugh when you know I'm down") signifies that John's parachute will eventually fold and he will retire from the public eye. You, the loyal fan will become mature (?) adult who will look back on Beatlemania with a larf. But to John and the other Beatles, it will not have been a larf; Beatlemania will have been their lives.

Ya dig?

Well, I must be off now, being as my analyzer is gonna analyze my dream where John and I were locked in a coffin together. Sound cozy? Actually it was a grave undertaking. (Forgive me.)

Narcissa Nash

Absolute Gem

P.S. You may get off the couch now if you're still awake.

Well, I can't say I agree with all of N.N.'s analysis, but isn't it an absolute gem? If this girl ever finds out how talented she is, I may be out of a job instead of just out of my gourd. Anypath, let's just hope N.N. strikes again, and soon!

Speaking of George . . . whoops . . . I really wasn't going to say that at all. But now that I'm on the subject (I have never, to me recollection, been *off* it), here's something I've been meaning to tell you.

Remember the girl whose toenails curl every time Paul looks like he needs a shave? Well, here's what gives me goosebumps (make that moose mumps) about George. His gqgubgeejn! Sorry I had to use the code, but some people just wouldn't understand.

Speaking of . . . down, girl . . . codes, was that something else! First I lost the original code and had to look through everything (and, considering that mess, *everyone*) in my room to find it. The funniest thing happened though! I was writing codes everywhere I went, trying to fill all the "orders" and one time I had a bunch of them with me at lunch. I was busy writing "hi-S.P." on the envelopes, when I noticed this boy kept walking past and staring at me incredulously (for those interested, me incredulously is located . . . whoops, sorry about that Robin.) Finally he tapped me on the shoulder.

Hisp!!

"Yesssss?" I simpered.

He sort of groaned. "Would you mind telling me what h-i-s-p means?" he asked.

I smiled calmly. "It means hisp," I confessed.

"Thank you," he said calmly as he ran hysterically out of the restaurant!

Well, *I* thought it was funny. Speaking of . . . oh no you don't . . . funny (as in rubber crutch) things, my strange little brother has finally made his second reasonably humorous remark.

The other Saturday morning we were at home alone, and before I got up he ate practically everything in the house. I couldn't find a single thing to have for breakfast, so I just sat at the table and shrieked at him, hoping to ruin his digestion (an impossibility.)

Finally, he got up, went into the kitchen, came back and slammed a box of cereal down on the table with these words: "Kix just keep gettin' harder to find."

Honestly, I laughed so hard I fell off the chair I was lying on (my posture leaves something to be desired.)

Marone!

Marone! (That's Italian for golly.) I'm forgetting a most important thingy. Remember that rawhide bit with the bracelet and all? Well, I've had another of my irrational ideas.

You know those safety belts you wear on flaps . . . they're coming for me . . . I mean that you wear on planes? Well, now I'm wearing one on earth! (If you understand that last sentence, please see a doctor.) (Before *he* sees *you*.)

What I am trying to say is that I bought a rawhide shoelace, tied a whole bunch of knots for the safety of all me faves, and now I wear it as a belt! It really looks gab (not to mention fear.) (Anser: This is getting riduculous.)

The only problem is, now *my mother is searching frantically through the yellow pages.*

Golly! (That's English for Marone.) Why is someone banging loudly at our frong door? (I ask you.)

Oh, oh. You know how I always keep saying they're coming for me? Well, guess what?

They're *here*!

Will I or won't I see you next week? Only my keeper knows for sure.

Revlon creates the perfect makeup for imperfect skin...
Medicated 'Natural Wonder'

Something fabulous has happened to this year's faces: Revlon's 'Natural Wonder' makeup. There's never been such a clear case of complexion flattery! 'Natural Wonder' goes on misty-sheer (but covers like crazy). Doesn't smell antiseptic (just acts that way). The more you use 'Natural Wonder' the less you need it... because it doesn't just hide; it helps! Comes in all the this-minute shades... and looks so Revlon-y even your cattiest friends won't know it's medicated.

KRLA ARCHIVES

On the BEAT
By Louise Criscione

Last week you read in *The BEAT* about the "feud" between Mick Jagger and the Walker Brothers. Now Gary Leeds says: "Don't ask me any more about Mick Jagger. I don't want to talk about him or any of those incidents. I just want to forget about it. In fact, I don't even know Mick Jagger and I am not concerned with replying to any of the allegations he makes. Incidentally, I like the Rolling Stones in as much as I can like anything of that type of music."

I hope the Walkers do forget it. Since I wasn't there I can't say for sure if the cigarette throwing incident was true or not but I tend to believe that it never happened at all. Not that Mick Jagger is above throwing cigarettes at anyone—he isn't. However, if he did he would admit it. He's sort of like that—impulsive but honest.

Private to the Beau Brummels: Love you all. Glad you dug it.

Knockin' 'Em Out

Herman and the Mindbenders are knocking them out on their current tour of England. The Mindbenders are a possibility for a Stateside tour now that "Groovy Kind of Love" has finally made it.

Herman and his everlovin' Hermits are coming for sure. They'll be touring with the Animals beginning July 3 in L.A. Sports Arena and then quickly moving onto Seattle, Denver, Tulsa, Little Rock, Detroit, Boston, Toronto and Pittsburgh ending the tour on August 7. I'm afraid it won't do you any good to write to me for further information this early because I don't have either the concert times nor the ticket prices.

...MICK JAGGER
BEAT Photo: Chuck Boyd

Meanwhile, the Animals are currently touring Stateside and have been for the last couple of weeks. Dates left to play include Harvard on May 6, Amherst College on May 7, Trinity College on May 14 and the University of Massachusetts on May 15.

John Lennon's father made a remark recently which really put John's fans up tight. Said the elder Lennon: "John might have a million but it would cost him more than a million to live the kind of life I've led." To which John's fans answered: "So, who'd want to?"

And Another

Here's some really hot news for you—Elvis is going to make another movie!!! Sorry about that. Anyway, he *is* going to make "Too Big For Texas" which is a story about cattle barons and will be set against the background of a huge Texas ranch. Film's producer will be Pandro S. Berman who produced Elvis' 1957 effort, "Jailhouse Rock." That one eventually grossed $9,000,000 which is enough to make a cattle baron out of anyone!

Congrats to the Young Rascals. They did it this week—made it to Number One in the nation with "Good Lovin'."

I'm still wondering if the Beatles are coming, have come or are not going to come Stateside to record. Tony Barrow doesn't exactly say "yes" but then he doesn't exactly say "no" either. Reports out of New York say that they were due in last week and had already booked time in a New York and Memphis recording studio, while reports in the trades say the Beatles will record here sometime during their up-coming tour. So, who's right? Tell you one thing for sure—I haven't seen any Beatles wandering around here!

New In May

The Beach Boys and the Outsiders are both scheduled for new album releases in May. The Outsiders' LP is already completed and will most probably be titled after their first hit single, "Time Won't Let Me." Brian Wilson is currently putting the finishing touches to the Beach Boys' album which will be titled, "Pet Sounds."

I heard a Bobby Rydell oldie on

...BOBBY RYDELL

the radio the other day and it occurred to me that we haven't heard from him in ages. I have to admit that I once considered Bobby *the* absolute groove, so I checked into it and discovered that Bobby is still very much on the scene. He just closed a most successful engagement at The Top Hat in Windsor, Ontario and is currently on the road hitting the Eastern colleges.

...THE LEAVES

No Fall In Sight For These Leaves

One windy afternoon amateur singer and song writer Bill Rinehart was lounging around in his back yard with three of his fraternity brothers from college.

The four had formed a combo to play at college dances and local community affairs and were looking for a name.

The breeze whipped some loose leaves off the trees. Someone asked, "What's happening?"

Another answered, "The leaves are happening."

"Hey!" exclaimed a third, "That's what we ought to call ourselves—the Leaves."

And, so the story goes, the Leaves were born.

They played at many local happenings and finally got their big break when they were booked into a Hollywood night club. There they were seen and heard and liked by Pat Boone's manager who promptly signed them to a recording contract.

A few weeks later they released their first single, "Too Many People," written by Bill. The song had only mild local success, but it got them appearances on many top TV shows including "The Lloyd Thaxton Show," "Hollywood Discotheque," "9th Street West," and "Shivaree."

And now The Leaves have followed that first release with a second that just may be their first big hit. It's called, "Hey Joe" and it's happening all over Southern California and should start breaking nationwide soon.

However, Bill has since left the group to spend more time on his studies.

New lead guitar player for the group is Bobby Arlin who also writes songs.

Collaborating with Bobby in the song writing business is Jim Pones. He's the athletic one of the group. He keeps in shape by playing football, basketball or swimming.

When it comes to clothes, Jim digs long sleeve, high collar shirts and vests.

Bob Reiner, rhythm guitar player, is a muscular six footer who can't remember ever wanting to be anything but a singer. He was an anthropology major in college before joining the group. He's a great blues fan and particularly likes the Stones, James Brown and Chuck Berry.

John Beck is probably the group's most versatile musician. He's accomplished on the harmonica, tambourine, saxaphone, bass, maracas, guitar, organ and piano.

To relax he listens to Manfred Mann or hits the ski slopes or motorcycle trails. His clothing trade mark is the colorful silk scarfs he usually wears around his neck, especially when performing. "It gets awfully hot under the lights," he says.

The group's drummer is Tom "Ambrose" Ray, a Hollywood product who wanted to be a veterinarian before the Leaves happened.

His wardrobe is very casual and dapper—including long sleeve shirts with lace cuffs.

It seems certain, as certain as spring follows winter, that these leaves won't be falling for a long time. They're working on an album now so you know there's more to come.

KRLA ARCHIVES

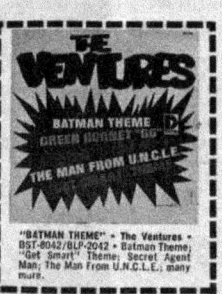

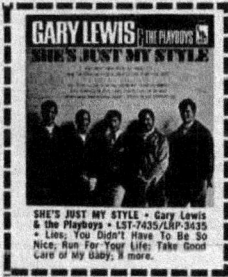

KRLA ARCHIVES

Long Play Action

By Tracy Allen

Hi! Did you think I'd forgotten all about you? Never, it's just that I was waiting until we had some really groovy new albums to tell you about—and we finally have.

The first, and probably best, is "The Young Rascals" by guess who? It's the group's first LP and, believe me, it's out of sight! Side one opens with a fantastic version of "Slow Down" and then cools down for a semi-slow R&B packed cut, "Baby Let's Wait," wailed in a too-much way by Eddie Brigati.

Gene Cornish next takes the lead for the Brummels' old hit, "Just A Little," and then it's Eddie's turn again with a version of the standard, "I Believe" which makes him sound the least bit like Bobby Hatfield, and is the grooviest arrangement of the song *ever* heard by *anyone* in *The BEAT* office! "Soul" is the word.

Side one ends with an up-tempo original, "Do You Feel It," sung by Felix Cavaliere and jointly composed by Felix and Gene. Side two opens with their current chart-topping single, "Good Lovin'," and moves on to a six minute, nine second Dylan favorite, "Like A Rolling Stone."

Cut three on the second side is an R&B flavored number, "Mustang Sally," which lasts 3 minutes and 59 seconds and is worth every second—it's great! "Sally" leads into the song which first introduced the Young Rascals to the nation. "I Ain't Gonna Eat Out My Heart Anymore."

The organ is predominate throughout the entire album and some fancy guitar work is also employed, especially effective on "I Believe." The LP is out on Atlantic and we advise you not to miss it—it's fantastic!

Shadows of Knight

For those of you who like heavy R&B, the Shadows of Knight's first LP, titled "Gloria," is perfect for you. This group's new to the nation, but they wail those R&B songs like they've been doing it for 20 years.

Such great cuts as "I Got My Mojo Working," "Dark Side," "Boom, Boom," "You Can't Judge A Book By The Cover," "I'm Your Hoochie Coochie Man" and "I Just Want To Make Love To You," are all featured on this Dunwich LP.

Sonny Side Up

The last album on this week's list is Cher's latest effort, "The Sonny Side of Cher." It's received all sorts of criticism by so-called (and probably so-named) "critics" but I think it's by far her best LP yet.

It contains several of her big hits, such as "Bang, Bang" and "Where Do You Go." It also features Cher's version of some of the big singles by other artists—"Elusive Butterfly," "Like A Rolling Stone," "The Girl From Ipanema," "It's Not Unusual," "Old Man River," "Time" and "A Young Girl."

Bob Lind thought enough of Cher to pen a song especially for her, something which he had never done before. It's "Come To Your Window" and it's great! It has that Lind touch to it and without even looking at the composer's credit you know he wrote it.

...THE MINDBENDERS (l. to r.) Bob Lang, Ric Rothwell and Eric Stewart

MINDBENDERS
Bending Your Mind

By Louise Criscione

A split in a group usually results in pop disaster for someone. Wayne Fontana and the Mindbenders had one of the biggest smashes in the U.S. with "Game Of Love" but they couldn't seem to follow it up Stateside.

Wayne and the Mindbenders come from Manchester and for months they were what is known as a "group's group." In other words, their fellow performers recognized their talent and potential but the record buyers couldn't seem to see it.

Mick Jagger used to always say: "It's about time Wayne Fontana and the Mindbenders had a hit." But for quite sometime no one listened to Mr. Jagger because the Mindbenders made five attempts at chart success and all of them failed.

They were extremely popular in their home territory but that was all. And then it finally happened for them—they got that hit record in the form of "Um, Um, Um, Um, Um." It was an embarrassing hit for the group. They couldn't imagine how anyone could go into a record shop and actually ask for "Um, Um, Um, Um, Um," so they had cards printed up which read: "I want 'Um, Um, Um, Um, Um' by Wayne Fontana and the Mindbenders."

Worrying

But after all of the cards had been distributed, the group began worrying that perhaps the recipients of the cards would think that if they presented the card to their local record store they would get a free record.

Apparently, they were worried about nothing because if they did misunderstand the meaning of the cards when they discovered that they had to *pay* for the record, they went ahead and put down their money. In any case, it was a smash on the British charts.

Wayne and the Mindbenders followed it up with a bigger record yet and one which made them one of the best-selling groups Stateside. That record was, of course, "Game Of Love."

With two hits in a row, the Mindbenders with Wayne always out in front as the lead singer, began really moving. They appeared on television, performed at concerts, made tours and visited America. "Game Of Love" flew up to number one in the nation and most people just naturally assumed that Wayne Fontana and the Mindbenders would continue putting out great sounding records and eventually would become one of the most popular British groups in America.

One Hit

But, unfortunately, most people were wrong. They couldn't seem to follow up "Game Of Love" and eventually they found themselves categorized Stateside as another of the one-hit wonders who had an initial hit during the take-over of our charts by the Beatles et al. and then had simply vanished from the scene.

Several months ago their name again cropped up when the rumors hit that Wayne was unhappy and was considering leaving the group. Wayne denied all of the rumors, declaring that he and the Mindbenders had their disagreements, sure, but then so did every other group. He was not leaving the Mindbenders—he wasn't even *thinking* about it.

Shortly after that, Wayne collapsed from nervous exhaustion. He went home to his parents' house in Manchester to recuperate and a couple of weeks later Wayne issued a public apology saying, in part: "I'm sorry I let you down. Now I hope I'm over my nervous complaint and can get back to work properly."

He did go back to work with the Mindbenders but the splitting rumors continued and finally Wayne could deny the obvious no longer. He wasn't happy being a member of the group and he wanted out.

Wayne Happy

Many reasons were given for Wayne's split with the Mindbenders, but no one really knew what had happened—they only knew that Wayne was gone. He appeared to be happy and relieved to be out on his own and said so. For their part, the Mindbenders remained silent except to say that they would continue recording.

The three Mindbenders—Eric Stewart, Bob Lang and Ric Rothwell—did continue recording and finally came up with a hit which literally ran up the English charts.

And it didn't take Stateside teens long to catch on to "Groovy Kind Of Love" either! It put Wayne in a rather embarrassing position because he had always been the group's focal point, the one member who received the most press and the most recognition. Yet, when he split it was his back-up group and not Wayne who first produced a successful disc while Wayne still hasn't been able to comeback in the U.S.

The Mindbenders originally got their name from a horror movie and perhaps that's what the whole thing has turned out to be for Wayne Fontana—a little bit of horrible.

KRLA ARCHIVES

KRLA Tunedex

This Week	Last Week	Title	Artist
1	1	MONDAY, MONDAY	The Mama's & Papa's
2	11	WHEN A MAN LOVES A WOMAN	Percy Sledge
3	2	RAINY DAY WOMAN #12 & 35	Bob Dylan
4	3	TIME WON'T LET ME	The Outsiders
5	5	THE RAINS CAME	Sir Douglas Quintet
6	20	HEY JOE	The Leaves
7	4	SOUL AND INSPIRATION	The Righteous Brothers
8	9	EIGHT MILES HIGH/WHY	The Byrds
9	10	SLOOP JOHN B	The Beach Boys
10	12	GOOD LOVIN'	The Young Rascals
11	14	MAGIC TOWN	The Vogues
12	6	SECRET AGENT MAN	Johnny Rivers
12	29	THE SUN AIN'T GONNA SHINE ANYMORE	Walker Bros.
13	19	LEANIN' ON THE LAMP POST/HOLD ON	Herman's Hermits
14	16	MESSAGE TO MICHAEL	Dionne Warwick
15	8	SHAPES OF THINGS	The Yardbirds
16	7	CALIFORNIA DREAMIN'	The Mama's & Papa's
17	13	KICKS	Paul Revere & The Raiders
18	17	A SIGN OF THE TIMES	Petula Clark
19	26	FALLING SUGAR	Palace Guard
20	33	ALONG COMES MARY/YOUR OWN LOVE	The Association
21	23	RHAPSODY IN THE RAIN	Lou Christie
22	47	A GROOVY KIND OF LOVE	The Mindbenders
23	22	TRY TOO HARD	The Dave Clark Five
24	27	TEEN AGE FAILURE	Chad and Jeremy
25	34	IN MY LITTLE RED BOOK	Love
26	40	LOVE IS LIKE AN ITCHING IN MY HEART	The Supremes
27	28	PLEASE DON'T STOP LOVING ME/FRANKIE AND JOHNNY	Elvis Presley
28	30	I CAN'T GROW PEACHES ON A CHERRY TREE	Just Us
29	35	HISTORY REPEATS ITSELF	Buddy Starcher
30	38	CAROLINE NO	Brian Wilson
31	32	I HEAR TRUMPETS BLOW	The Tokens
32	31	HOW DOES THAT GRAB YOU DARLIN'/LAST OF THE SECRET AGENTS	Nancy Sinatra
33	37	NOTHING'S TOO GOOD FOR MY BABY	Stevie Wonder
34	36	I GOT MY MOJO WORKING	Jimmy Smith
35	39	CRUEL WAR	Peter, Paul and Mary
36	—	FUNNY HOW LOVE CAN BE	Danny Hutton
37	—	I WOULD NEVER DO THAT	Jimmy Boyd
38	—	DADDY YOU JUST GOTTA LET HIM IN	The Satisfactions
39	—	TOGETHER AGAIN	Ray Charles
40	—	RIVER DEEP, MOUNTAIN HIGH	Ike and Tina Turner

DAVE HULL

BOB EUBANKS

DICK BIONDI

JOHNNY HAYES

EMPEROR HUDSON

CASEY KASEM

CHARLIE O'DONNELL

BILL SLATER

IT'S PRETTY CASUAL around KRLA most of the time, but our best dressed DJ, Dave Hull, always spruces up when anyone drops by out of the blue, particularly when it's beautiful and talented Maxine Brown.

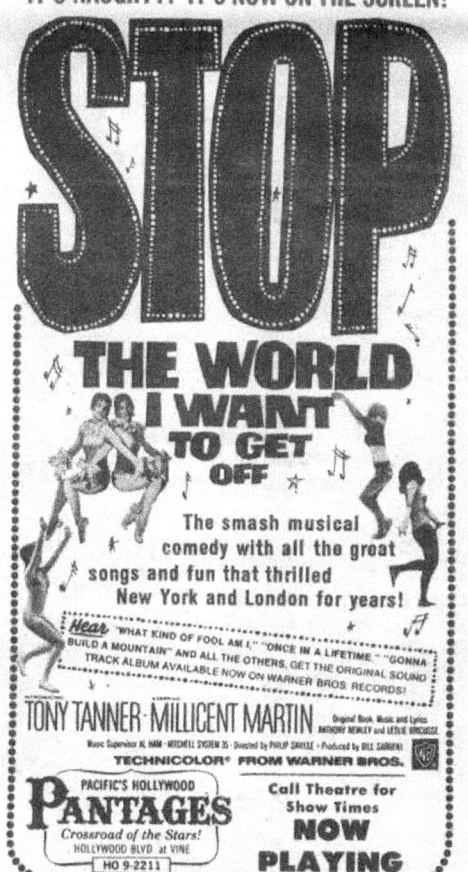

IT'S UNUSUAL! IT'S DIFFERENT! IT'S NICE!
IT'S NAUGHTY! IT'S NOW ON THE SCREEN!

STOP THE WORLD I WANT TO GET OFF

The smash musical comedy with all the great songs and fun that thrilled New York and London for years!

Hear "WHAT KIND OF FOOL AM I," "ONCE IN A LIFETIME," "GONNA BUILD A MOUNTAIN" AND ALL THE OTHERS. GET THE ORIGINAL SOUND TRACK ALBUM AVAILABLE NOW ON WARNER BROS. RECORDS!

TONY TANNER • MILLICENT MARTIN
Original Book, Music and Lyrics ANTHONY NEWLEY and LESLIE BRICUSSE
Music Supervisor AL HAM • MITCHELL SYSTEM 35 • Directed by PHILIP SAVILLE • Produced by BILL SARGENT
TECHNICOLOR® FROM WARNER BROS.

PACIFIC'S HOLLYWOOD **Pantages**
Crossroad of the Stars!
HOLLYWOOD BLVD at VINE
HO 9-2211

Call Theatre for Show Times
NOW PLAYING

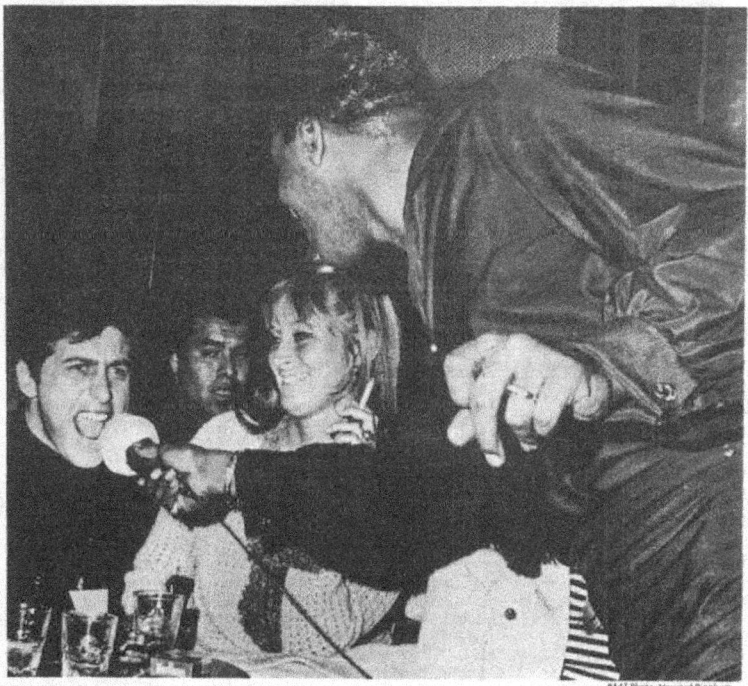

JOHNNY RIVERS is never going to make a good Secret Agent unless he learns to keep his mouth shut and he just couldn't seem to keep quiet at all when he dropped by The Trip to see the fabulous Four Tops.

KRLA ARCHIVES

Inside KRLA

In case you haven't noticed yet, KRLA is now being run by some new people — YOU.

A few weeks ago the station went all-request for one weekend just to give you a chance to tell the DJ's what *you* wanted to hear.

Well, you came through and thoroughly tied up the phone lines all weekend. So they decided to give you another chance to do the same.

They repeated the all-request thing the next weekend and once again you flooded the phone lines. For once you had the chance to dictate what your favorite radio station played and you took advantage of the situation.

Well, after the second time the station began to get the idea that all request was what you wanted and since station policy is to give you just that — what *you* want — they decided to go all-request for a week during the Easter vacation.

But you didn't let them stop then and now they have gone all-request indefinitely.

And on top of going all-request, something that has been tried sparingly in other parts of the country, they've also been giving dedications with the requests, something that no other all-request station has ever done.

The entire change in format is costing the station hundreds of dollars for additional phone lines and additional people to man them, but KRLA's been the number one AM station in Los Angeles for many years and they don't intend to change.

Whatever you want to hear is what they are going to play so give them a call and clue them in to your latest fave.

Here's your chance to run your own radio station.

GUITAR & AMP

Luster finished electric guitar plus big power amp for that Boss Surf Sound — Usually priced at $39.50 each. Now $29.95 each.

Combination Guitar and Amp.

$57.50*

*Surfboard not included, but service always is at the G&D specialists

ALSO — FENDER... GIBSON... VOX, etc.

Eve's APPAREL — See if you can BEAT our prices on our new Jr. and missy lines. Samples at wholesale or less. 1800 N. Vermont, Hollywood, Calif. NO 3-4456

JOIN NOW
The American Society for the prevention of the extinction of **"THE YARDBIRDS"**
Dues $1.00 plus four 5c stamps
3023 Leeward Ave. - Apt. 7
Los Angeles, California 90005

Great Western Battle of The Bands
JUNE 1 THRU JUNE 5
General Public Will Attend Competition
Send Your Entry Blank Now
GREAT WESTERN EXHIBIT CENTER
P.O. BOX 22108 LOS ANGELES 22
PHONE RA3-3678

THE ICE HOUSE
The Travellers Three
through May 1st

Tim Morgon
April 26 — May 29

The ICE HOUSE GLENDALE
folk music in concert
phone 245-5043 for reservations

DRUM SET

Your choice of Blue, Red, or Gold Sparkle — This beautiful 4-piece drum set has chrome plated rims on six ply hardwood shells with durable mylar heads to give many years of keeping neighbors awake.

$189.50*

*Belly dancer not included, but drum lessons, guitar lessons, and a lightning course in belly dancing are available at the G&D specialists.

ALSO — LUDWIG... ROGERS... GRETSCH... SLINGERLAND

UNLIKE ANYTHING YOU'VE EVER SEEN!
WARNER BROS. SUPER CINERAMA PRODUCTION
BATTLE OF THE BULGE
WARNER BROS. PICTURES PRESENTS A CINERAMA, INC. PRODUCTION "BATTLE OF THE BULGE" Starring HENRY FONDA · ROBERT SHAW · ROBERT RYAN · DANA ANDREWS · PIER ANGELI · BARBARA WERLE · GEORGE MONTGOMERY · TY HARDIN · CHARLES BRONSON · HANS CHRISTIAN BLECH · WERNER PETERS · JAMES MacARTHUR and TELLY SAVALAS · Written by Philip Yordan, Milton Sperling, John Melson · Produced by Milton Sperling, Philip Yordan · Directed by Ken Annakin · A Sidney Harmon in Association with United States Pictures, Inc. Production · TECHNICOLOR · ULTRA PANAVISION

PACIFIC'S CINERAMA DOME Theatre
Magnificent SUNSET AT VINE · HOLLYWOOD
NOW PLAYING!

FOLK GUITAR

Fastest guitar in the West!!! See it at the G&D specialists. Top Quality at Unbelievable prices — Great Folk Guitars from...

$13.95*

*Honda not included, but wheel in anytime for after sale service, free tuning, or free advice on how to get your girlfriend to stop playing your guitar and start paying more attention to you.

YOUR LOCAL G&D SPECIALIST IS...

IN BUENA PARK	IN HUNTINGTON BEACH	IN VAN NUYS
Kay Kalie Music	**Manolios Music**	**Adler Music Co.**
805 ON THE MALL	18547 MAIN STREET (5 POINTS SHOPPING CENTER)	14115 VICTORY BLVD. (AT HAZELTON)
IN SANTA FE SPRINGS	IN TUSTIN	IN SIMI
Kay Kalie Music	**Winn's Music**	**Adler Music Co.**
11504 TELEGRAPH RD. (THE SHOPPING CENTER)	540 E. 1st STREET (IN LARWIN SQUARE)	1792 ERRINGER ROAD (NEXT TO SAFEWAY)

SPECIAL BONUS — SUBSCRIBE NOW and receive a free copy of The Bobby Fuller Four's best selling album, "I Fought The Law."

KRLA BEAT Subscription

SAVE 33% Off Regular Price

☐ 1 YEAR - 52 Issues - $5.00   ☐ 2 YEARS - $8.00
☐ 6 MONTHS - $3.00

Enclosed is ☐ CASH ☐ CHECK
PLEASE PRINT — Include Your Zip Code

Send to:.. Age:........

Address:.................. City:.................

State:.................. Zip:.................

MAIL YOUR ORDER TO: KRLA BEAT
6290 Sunset, Suite 504
Hollywood, Calif. 90028

Foreign Rate: $9.00 — 52 Issues

KRLA ARCHIVES

TEEN PANEL
Are Songs Unhealthy?

ACNE and ACNE PIMPLES CONTROLLED IN 7 to 14 DAYS or you'll get your money back!*

ALPHACENE. Really Works!
This two-step cleanser and treatment is a thoroughly tested and proven prescription, developed by a group of noted dermatological MDs. You'll get startlingly happy results with Alphacene. No prescription needed.

1. **CLEANSER** and
2. **TREATMENT**
BOTH FOR **$3.98**

Buy Alphacene® at Your Nearby Thrifty Drug Store or use the Mail Order

---- MAIL ORDER ----
Thrifty Drug Store Co. Inc., Dept. M
Box 2063 Terminal Annex, L.A. 54, Calif.
Please send me _____ Alphacene® Cleanser and Treatment at $3.98. Enclose check or money order.

Name _____
Address _____
City _____ State ____ Zip ____
Add 4% Sales Tax

*If not completely satisfied, return unused portion to manufacturer for full refund.

Editor's Note: Welcome to the second installment of *The BEAT's* new Teen Panel series.

These discussions are being sponsored and published by *The BEAT* in an effort to find out how the younger generation *really* feels about the world around them.

Because many teenagers are wary of broadcasting their opinions, the conversations are held in complete privacy. Only the members of the panel are present, and their opinions are recorded on tape which is later destroyed.

Participants are asked to identify themselves only by the first name of their choice and their age.

Each panel is composed of five teenagers. If you would like to express your views in a future discussion, you can volunteer by filling out the application blank which appears with each installment.

* * *

In the first segment of this series, a particular phase of music (protest vs. patriotism) was discussed by The BEAT panel. Today's topic is still another phase of that same subject.

The pop world has undergone many changes this past year, but one of the most important has been the trend toward song lyrics which can not only be heard, but which also have something to say.

Our question is, are some of today's lyrics saying too much? Here to answer and explore that question are Jerry (18), Pattie (14), Barbara (18), Brian (16) and Scott (17). Jerry volunteered to open the discussion.

JERRY—"No, I don't think they're saying too *much*. But most of them are saying it too crudely."
BARBARA—"Amen to that. It's come to the point where I have to listen to a record three or four times—listen closely, I mean—before I dare buy it and take it home."
PATTIE—"I do the same thing. I have to. My folks really flipped about some of the records I've bought recently. They even made me take one of them back to the shop!"
BRIAN—"What reason did they give?"
PATTIE—"They didn't. They just said I'd better never buy anything like that again if I knew what was good for me. Oh — they did give one reason. They said such songs were an unhealthy influence on young people."
SCOTT—"I think they're more of an unhealthy influence on adults than they are on kids. They make parents realize that their teenagers aren't children any more, and this realization scares them. It's just natural to worry about your kids. And the more they know *we* know, the more they worry."
JERRY—"You said *more* of an unhealthy influence. Does that mean you think earthy lyrics do have *some* influence on kids?"
SCOTT—"I suppose they do, but only on *some* kids. You can always find people—teenagers and adults—who make no effort to develop a mind of their own. This sort of person is easily swayed. Take most TV commercials as an example. They insult the intelligence of anyone over the age of three, but some people believe every word and go ripping down to the nearest store."
BARBARA—"I agree, but I think a shocking line in a song could very easily have an adverse effect on the judgement of a younger, more inexperienced teenager."
PATTIE—"Thanks a lot! I've heard so many people say stuff like that and it really burns me up. If something as unimportant as a song affects the judgment of a fourteen-year-old, it isn't because she's a fourteen-year-old. It's because she's stupid! Age has nothing to do with good judgment. Some individuals are responsible at thirteen. Others are still simps when they're sixty."
BARBARA—"I wasn't directing that at you. And, now that I think about it, age probably isn't that much of a factor. But who needs this type of song at *any* age? Even if they didn't do one bit of harm, they sure don't do anyone any good. Except the people who get rich writing and singing them."
BRIAN—"In my opinion, even a *really* rank song serves a purpose. It proves that free speech actually does exist, for one thing. It's the writer's privilege to express himself, just the same as it's your privilege not to listen to what he has to say."
BARBARA—"I don't think this kind of song falls into the self-expression category. I'd classify it as more of a deliberate attempt to grab the teenage dollar. There's a song that's popular right now that's a perfect example. I'd rather not mention it by name, but it's so gross I'd rather not even call it a song. It's more a *pitch*. I can't believe that someone sat down and actually *composed* it. They *concoted* it, using every tired junior-high-school phrase in the books, hoping it would get everyone all fired up. I think that shows a lack of talent and imagination on the part of the writer, and a lack of consideration for others. People like this just want money and don't care how they get it."
BRIAN—"I don't know what record you mean, so I can't argue that point, but as I was going to say before, you have to admit that earthy songs are a lot more realistic than some of this frilly junk that makes teenagers sound like first-graders in pinafores. At least these songs talk about things that really exist, and I'm all for that. It's about time people stopped being ashamed of being human, and I think these songs are helping people—teenagers especially—to understand that sex isn't a dirty word, or something to giggle and whisper about. I don't see how a song that's at least honest could possibly hurt anyone."
JERRY—"I'm with you, but only up to a point. A song with down-to-earth lyrics does help in ways. If nothing else, it *confronts* people with taboo subjects. This can't help but make them think, and maybe accept life as it *is* instead of what someone else says it *should* be. This also helps people accept themselves, and understand themselves. But, personally, I don't dig many of the songs that have touched on this type of subject. Some of them are obvious put-ons, like Barbara said. Others try too hard and end up sounding coarse instead of frank. On the other hand, a few of them have been great."
PATTIE—"I'll bet I can guess who wrote some of the songs you did like."
JERRY—"So, go ahead."
PATTIE—"The Beatles, right?"
JERRY—"Right. I probably won't be able to explain this, but there's been a little bit of everything in their songs. But they're cool about it. Take "Norwegian Wood"—that says a lot but it couldn't possibly offend anyone. Their music has kind of a natural flavor to it, if you know what I mean."
PATTIE—"I know exactly what you mean. I get the same type of feeling about their songs. They don't make a big deal out of anything. Some of their music is very direct, but in a *gentle* way that you can understand and accept."
BARBARA—"I don't think Beatle music really belongs in this conversation. We're talking about songs that go too far out, and that's something Beatle songs just don't do. As writers, the Beatles have *talent* and *class*. They don't have to resort to being obvious or crude to get a point across, which is a lot more than I can say for most pop music composers. Well, not *most*, but too many."
BRIAN—"There is something that does belong in this conversation though. We haven't even mentioned songs that sound like singing commercials for L.S.D., Inc. and I think we should. Personally, I'm all for the blunt lyric bit, but that's going overboard."
SCOTT—"I thought you were an advocate of free speech."
BRIAN—"I am, but this is one area where I exercise my right not to listen."
PATTIE—"I don't really know much about this subject."
BARBARA—"Neither do I, and I plan to keep it that way. But I do think this kind of song is extremely harmful."
SCOTT—"I don't."
BRIAN—"Are you saying you approve of drugs?"
SCOTT—"No, but I am saying that this kind of song is mostly a matter of personal interpretation. If you aren't familiar with certain terms or phrases, you'd never know what the song was implying. If you are hip to what the song suggests, you've probably already had the opportunity to—shall we say imbibe. If this is the case, you've either declined or accepted the offer, and it's too late for a song to affect your decision. Not that it would have anyway. And, if you don't even know what the song's about, which the average teenager wouldn't, it couldn't possibly have the slightest bit of influence on you."
JERRY—"One last thing. Are you referring to the average teenager in this area?"
SCOTT—"I didn't know there were any."

(Stay tuned to The BEAT for more teen panel discussions soon.)

Hollies' Trouble

The Hollies are certainly having their share of problems here in the U.S. They've been unable to appear on any television shows so far and no satisfactory explanation has been given to the Hollies.

The Musician's Union stopped the Hollies from appearing on "Hullabaloo" as originally scheduled and at the last minute the Young Rascals were asked to step in for the Hollies.

Tony Hicks revealed that the Hollies had been told something about keeping "Hullabaloo" an all-American show and since they are British they could not appear on it.

What's going on???? An all-American show, are they kidding?

British Top 10

1. YOU DON'T HAVE TO SAY YOU LOVE ME ..... Dusty Springfield
2. SOMEBODY HELP ME . Spencer Davis
3. HOLD TIGHT .... Dave Dee etc.
4. BANG, BANG .... Cher
5. SOUNDS OF SILENCE ... Bachelors
6. SUN AIN'T GONNA SHINE ANYMORE ...... Walker Brothers
7. ALFIE .... Cilla Black
8. SUBSTITUTE .... The Who
9. ELUSIVE BUTTERFLY ... Val Doonican
10. PIED PIPER ... Crispian St. Peters

KRLA ARCHIVES

HOTLINE LONDON
FALL FOR FILM

Tony Barrow

By Tony Barrow

One by one Brian Epstein's 1966 diary dates for THE BEATLES are being inked-in and officially announced. Latest news brings details of the group's upcoming trips to Germany and Japan. On Friday, June 24 they'll play two evening shows in Munich at the Circus Krone. The following night there'll be two more performances in Essen at the Grugahalle which has a capacity in excess of seven thousand seats. Final shows in Germany will be on Sunday, June 26 at the Ernst Merck Halle in Hamburg. From that city The Beatles fly directly to Tokyo on June 27. On June 30, July 1 and July 2 they will appear for one performance each day at Tokyo's 12,000-seater Budo Kan hall.

Unless a further Far East date is confirmed for July 4, the group will fly back to Britain directly after the three Tokyo shows.

Script Search

Movie producer WALTER SHENSON continues in his exhaustive search for a suitable script and there's no possibility of The Beatles going before the cameras to make their third motion picture prior to September or early October.

Meantime their marathon series of recording sessions at EMI's North London studios will continue for at least another two weeks.

A month ago it may have looked to Los Angeles Beatle People as though John, Paul, George and Ringo would not be playing the Southern part of the state. In fact there was never any question of missing out the Los Angeles/Hollywood area. By chance as much as anything else, contractual formalities for a performance in San Francisco on August 29 were far enough advanced to allow for a formal announcement regarding the date. In due course, the same behind-scenes paper work was completed for the Dodger Stadium date.

Candlestick

Brian Epstein emphatically denies that he ever made any statement to the effect that The Beatles would not be playing any further San Francisco dates following last year's riotous Cow Palace performance. Indeed, neither Brian nor anyone else with us backstage at the Cow Palace showed any great alarm at what amounted to little more than a tempetuously enthusiastic Beatle welcome given to the boys by their spirited San Francsico fans. The 1966 concert in San Francisco will not be at the Cow Palace. At the time of this story, the most likely venue seems to be Candlestick Park. What a picturesque name!

When the enormous stadium at Philadelphia was named for an August 16 concert appearance by THE BEATLES, it looked as though last year's all-time attendance record for a Beatles show—60,000 at New York City's Shea Stadium—would be shattered. Now it seems that the Shea record will stand. Only 40,000 tickets will be made available for the Philadelphia date although the venue is capable of seating more than twice this number of Beatle People. Reason for the restriction on numbers? Rear-of-stage seats which would not afford a fair view of the show will not be put on sale.

One of our top female singing stars, SHIRLEY BASSEY, will be a regular visitor to the U.S. over the next few years. She has signed contracts for extensive cabaret work which will take her to New York, Las Vegas and the Sahara Hotel at Lake Tahoe. She'll be at the Vegas Sahara for two weeks from May 24 and a further four weeks over Christmas and New Year. In addition, Shirley hopes to do a great deal of recording in New York and elsewhere during her U.S. trips.

NEWS BRIEFS . . . Union bans have prevented THE HOLLIES appearing on TV shows including "The Dick Clark Show" and "The Clay Cole Show" during their current U.S. tour. But the Manchester fivesome are still hopeful about projected recording sessions to take place in Chicago before they return home. Next dates for the group take them to Germany and Sweden . . . ROY ORBISON and DIXIE CUP songstress Barbara Hawkins joined British deejay JIMMY SAVILE on BBC Television's "Juke Box Jury" panel . . . April U.K. dates for BETTY EVERETT cancelled because of work permit problems experienced by her accompanying musicians . . . Tonsil removal operation on TOM JONES at The London Clinic last week a total success . . . DAVE CLARK FIVE have stockpiled no fewer than 60 recordings . . . If stories in British trade papers are not exaggerated the feud between MICK JAGGER and WALKER BROTHER SCOTT still at flashpoint! . . . Every member of Official Beatles Fan Club in the U.K. receiving exact replica of Shea Stadium 1965 concert ticket together with booklet of color pix taken at the same venue . . . NANCY SINATRA made LP album in London between April 27 and 29 during her two-week visit . . . HERMAN'S HERMITS now extending summer U.S. trip to take in total of 32 towns and cities during July and August . . . For CBS-TV series "Hippodrome," now filming in London, lengthy list of big names includes DAVE CLARK FIVE, NANCY SINATRA, EVERLY BROTHERS, GERRY AND THE PACEMAKERS, FREDDIE AND THE DREAMERS, JOHNNY MATHIS, THE SEARCHERS, THE ZOMBIES, THE ANIMALS, LISA MINNELLI, ALLAN SHERMAN, DUSTY SPRINGFIELD and BILL DANA. . . . THE MOODY BLUES and THE ANIMALS attended JAMES BROWN'S Paris concert . . . . . What's this about DAVID McCALLUM learning to play the oboe????

Blue-eyed, Green-eyed Tommy Reveals Smothers' Secrets

By Eden

Tommy Smothers is officially recorded as the owner of one blue eye and one green eye. Now, right away you've gotta kinda wonder about someone like that, right?

Well, I wondered—and my wondering led me in search of two folks, collectively known as The Smothers Brothers. I *think* I found them—but they succeeded in so thoroughly confusing me, that who knows? I may have spent an hour and a half talking to two reasonable facsimiles!

Born February 2, 1937, Tommy is just one year older than Dick. But it is very possible that the 12 months have made all the difference in the world. For example, Tommy's description of the duo: "If I were to describe us, I could not help but mention ears, being as they are a great part of us. I have very nice blond hair, while my brother Dick has rather ratty black hair."

"We are both tall enough to see over counters and strong enough to . . . to . . . well, you just better believe we're *STRONG!!!*"

Who's Protesting?

The boys explained that they were originally regarded as folk singers, and that it has taken seven years for them to be accepted as comedians. They admit to having done a small amount of "protest-type" material in the beginning, but they laugh when they recall the experience.

Tommy tells us: "When we started in North Beach in San Francisco, the beatniks really thought that Dickie and I were *message singers*; and he went right along with it and said, 'yeah, man!' We didn't have any message! I was talking *nonsense*, and these guys were going, 'yeah, yeah!!'"

So many singers have protested the label "folk singer," and all the different variations which go along with it. But Tommy freely admits to being quite ethnic!

"We are, as you know, ever so ethnic. But ethnicity does not come easily to one who has known only health and wealth all of one's lives. So we became ethnic the hard way. We had to fight and struggle to make our way down the ladder of success so that we could have something to protest about.

"But let me tell you, there were a lot of hard feelings from my brother and myself towards our parents because we hadn't been born in a slum or on a chain gang. Parents just don't go out of their way to make life easy for a guy these days."

Poor Baby!

Your heart just has to go out to him, doesn't it?! Wait, there's more. Dick explained to us that he and Tommy weren't necessarily "buddy-buddy" when they were growing up, "but if anybody put one of us down we'd stick up for each other."

Then Tommy added, "Yeah, and invariably it was *me* that was in the fights—protecting *him!* He was *always* antagonizing someone to the breaking point, and then *I'd* get hit in the mouth!"

"And *he* was real cool: he'd just sit there and say, 'Gee, that's a *shame!!*'"

Both boys hope to be able to do a film someday soon, but they want it to be something special. They feel that the first Beatles' film was especially well done, and have a great deal of admiration for the director, Richard Lester.

Tommy says, "That's the kind of a guy we want. A bright, aggressive, new person who's not hung up with old techniques. It's gonna be hard to find, because we're not in a position to get a hold of them. They've already made their mark."

Although their television show never ranked high on the national ratings, they did exceedingly well in many regional surveys. Dickie explained briefly just why they had originally gone into TV—something which was totally unrelated to their act at the time.

"The reason we went into the TV situation was that we had gone as far as we could as night club and concert performers and there was no way we could go up; we had started to get stale. We felt that television, with acting, would be a new challenge."

It was that, and both boys feel that they have learned a great deal from the experience. They feel ready now to participate more actively in the actual scripts; Tommy says they don't really enjoy writing, but they would both like to have more to say on the *premise* of each script.

At present, both boys agree that their live performances and their guest spots on various other TV shows are the best and most exciting elements of their career for them.

They have just recently released a brand new LP—"The Smothers Brothers Play It Straight (Almost!!)"—on which they tried a few new forms of music . . . including rock and roll.

Future plans? Probably more touring during the summer months, and Tommy is thinking about pursuing one of his oldest ambitions in the line of dramatic acting. He's always harbored a not-so-secret desire to be a *weirdo killer!*

He's also interested in directing. *Ahem* . . . hope he decides to stick to *that!* I mean, what with that grudge he holds against his mother for always having liked his brother Dickie best, and all!!!

KRLA ARCHIVES

The Adventures of Robin Boyd

By Shirley Poston

CHAPTER TWENTY-SEVEN

Robin Boyd held George's hand very hard as they walked down the steep stairway.

"You aren't frightened, are you?" he asked when they had hit bottom and were standing in a dark room that seemed to be more a collection of tunnels.

"I'm petrified," she answered, trying to smile. But she wasn't. She did have a strange feeling, but it wasn't fear. Fear was cold. This was a numbness, but even in this chill damp cellar, it was warm.

"This is the Cavern now . . . what's left of it," she said, making a statement but really asking a question.

George nodded grimly, freeing a table from the pile of furniture scattered against a wall. "But it won't be for long," he said, brightening as he placed the table near the stage and found chairs.

Robin took a deep breath of the staleness and savored it. "When will . . . " she began, stopping in mid-sentence because it didn't need finishing.

George moved his chair closer. "Whenever you say."

Seven million butterflies took wing and soared in Robin's stomach. It sounded so simple. *Whenever she said*, time would be turned back nearly five years. Outside it would be a spring day in Liverpool, vintage 1966. Inside it would be autumn of 1961. Another kind of spring. The early days when something new was beginning to bud and grow. Something that would later ripen and burst and change the world.

"It's all arranged?" she asked at last. "The technicalities, I mean?"

"All arranged," George answered.

Not Cold

Robin shivered, but not from the cold. That meant that Ringo would be on the drums. That they would sing her list of songs (which had been cut to ten out of necessity) although most of them hadn't even been thought of in 1961. That it was really going to come true, her impossible dream. And suddenly she couldn't wait another second for it to start.

"Now," she said solemnly, settling her vile glasses on her nose. "I'm ready now." She wasn't really. There was still that inexplicable numbness. But she had no sooner said it than it began to happen.

The room came to life. Tables and people were crammed everywhere. And there was a breathlessness to the noise and clatter as all eyes stared in one direction. A darkened stage.

Then the lights dimmed on and four shadows became four Beatles. And with a casually waved acknowledgement of the cheering welcome, they launched into the first number on Robin's list. Which was, of course, the song that had somehow started it all. "My Bonnie."

They were half-way through the song before Robin could believe her eyes. She had known what to expect. She had even seen photos of them in the early days, but she was still amazed.

They seemed so small. Almost frail. No, they were too alive for that. Lean was a better word.

They were dressed just alike in boots and jeans topped with leather jackets. Their hair was neither long nor short, but there was a lot of it. They were pale, but not drab, and they looked marvelously exhausted. And they were so young. So unbelievably young.

Sheer Magic

Still, they were very much the Beatles she now knew, in many ways. They were the same strange mixture of gentleness and tough-as-hell. And their music was sheer magic.

When the song was over, John stepped up to the mike. As Robin took a considerable gulp of damp air, he took a huge swallow from a nearby cup and addressed a remark to Paul. Something about things going better with coke. And it was several minutes before the Beatles could stop laughing at their private joke long enough to forge ahead. The audience twittered along, not knowing what was funny and not really caring as long as their Beatles thought something was.

Then John began "You've Really Got A Hold On Me." From the way he sang it, one would never have suspected that he would one day consider this his all-time worst solo.

He looked very certain of himself, but he grinned teasingly all the way through the song. And, knowing that George was watching her, Robin made every effort to look at John's face often.

Then it was George's turn to stop being so intent on playing the guitar that was almost bigger than he was. He seemed a little frightened for a moment, but with the first strains of "You Like Me Too Much," he relaxed.

Robin stared at him lovingly, feeling the sting of tears somewhere behind her eyes. He looked even younger than the rest. Like her own George (of Genie fame) must have looked five years ago. And she suddenly wished that she had known both of them then.

Ringo was next on the bill, and in spite of the numbness that was still very much there, Robin had to kick herself under the table to keep from rushing up on the stage and hugging him furiously.

A Cool Beard

For one thing, her feeling for Ringo was the most comfortable of all her Beatle emotions. After hearing her sister (Ringo Boyd) (of 12-year-old sturdy fame and frame) rave about him 24-hours-a-day, Robin had come to utterly worship Ringo (as in Starr) in a brother-in-law-ish sort of way. Besides, he was wearing the world's coolest beard.

Before Ringo had finished warbling "I Wanna Be Your Man," she'd had to kick herself twice more.

It wasn't until Paul, with his velvet eyes and dark tousled hair, had finished "Yesterday," that the numbness began to fade. And when it did, an ache took its place.

Robin continued to ache while the Beatles, between jokes to the audience and bites of sandwiches, went on to perform "Kansas City." But, as always, the yeah-yeah-yeah parts didn't fail to make her knees knock noisily.

Although she applauded wildly, Robin ached even worse during "No Reply" and "I Feel Fine." But it was that first crashing chord of "Hard Day's Night" that brought the tears. They slid quietly down her cheeks throughout the song. And when the Beatles went into their final number, they streamed.

"Help" was the name of it. And for the first time, Robin knew why she had ached. It was also the name of the game. The Beatles had helped. Helped her and everyone else who had been touched by their magic. People were different because of them, so was the world. People were bigger and the world was smaller.

But that wasn't why she was crying. She was crying because although the Beatles were close enough to reach out and touch, there was still a wall. And there was sacrifice on both sides of it.

That Wall

The Beatles, these carefree boys larking about on a clumsy stage, had grown up and given most of themselves to millions of teenagers who were ready and waiting for something worth caring about. And those teenagers had given a part of themselves in return. But the wall remained.

The Beatles needed their fans as people, but they saw them only as faces on the other side of footlights or shrieks in an auditorium or tear-stained letters. Their fans needed the Beatles as people, but they were able to see them only as miniature figures on a miles-away stage or voices on a record or pictures on a paper.

They had given each other so much. And in spite of this exchange of self, they would always be strangers.

"They should all be here," Robin said aloud, holding George's hand so hard she completely shut off the circulation. "Not just me. It would help them so much."

Then, as George gave her an odd look, the Beatles and the excitement around them faded and they were again alone in a dusty cellar.

Robin sat terribly still for a long time. Finally George spoke.

"Robin," he said gently, not sounding at all like the sort of person who had been known to yank her arm clean out of the socket. "They *can't* all be here. It isn't humanly possible." He made a helpless gesture. "*This* wasn't humanly possible."

Robin looked away. "Why not?" she said. "Why does it have to be this way?"

George touched her bright red hair. "You know why," he answered. "Because that's life. You can't always have the person who teaches you how much love you have to give. You have to look for someone who can give it back."

Robin swallowed hard as the truth of these words almost jolted her right out of her chair. And she started to say she'd stopped looking, but she never quite got around to it as it was rather difficult to talk while he was kissing her.

Robin was blithering again in a moment, but it was a different kind of crying. And there was no better place for her to have done a bit of growing up herself than in this, the shabby but beautiful birthplace of a new way of life.

British Mime Out?

(Continued from Page 1)

Musician's Union has stepped in with a surprise demand for a total ban of TV mime work.

One of our top small-screen pop productions, "Thank Your Lucky Stars" is to be pulled off in the final week of June after a 5-year 260-program run. During this period more than 500 solo artists and groups — including THE BEATLES and THE ROLLING STONES—mimed to 2,500 different records on TYLS. The TV company concerned has announced that the series will be replaced by a new show which will not involve miming.

There is much to be said in favour of miming. It allows a complete program to be rehearsed and screened in one day's work. Producer and camera crew can concentrate full attention on visual detail without having to match good camera work with faithful sound reproduction. A mimed program can afford far more big names for each show because of the hard cash saved in production overheads and appearance fees.

Exact Sound

Artists who say they're perfectly happy with the miming idea justify their opinion by reminding us that viewers are sure to hear an exact version of the recorded sound. Artists worry just as much as producers about the sound quality on TV shows.

The anti-mime spokesmen say that only inferior performers prefer to let a recording do their work for them. They say that any group of reasonable calibre should be willing and able to produce in the TV studio a sound which is just as good as they achieved in the recording studio. They argue that the viewers are cheated by the mechanical duplication of the exact same audio performance on an endless number of different mime shows.

In the end, of course, it's all down to the TV production people. Faced with adding live sound to every pop program, most producers would have to double or triple their preparatory pre-screening work. They'd have to work out intricate plans for positioning microphones—and re-positioning them for each individual act on any given show.

To be truthful, one has to agree that the majority of television shows appear incapable of producing an entirely satisfactory balance of sounds even when a beat group gives out with a great performance in the studio.

Difficult

Even top-rated network shows like Ed Sullivan's program experienced a lot of difficulty in capturing and putting out to home viewers a good sound in the earlier days of the group boom. They were used to handling the problems of balancing a single voice against an orchestral backdrop but the arrival of so many guitars, organs, pianos and so forth seemed to baffle their audio experts.

On our side of the Atlantic it's no secret that several top groups will not undertake live TV appearances because they have gone through the misery of hearing their sound go out to the public in a distorted or badly balanced way. These are the groups who go along with the idea that miming is O.K. and always will be until every TV studio is geared to give hi-fi sound along with hi-fi vision.

So far the BBC in London, traditionally opposed to all things revolutionary, have remained quiet throughout all the mime argument. They may plan to dig in their heels and refuse to obey the edict of the M.U.—certainly they have given no indication of a change of format for their top mime show "Top Of The Pops" which has enjoyed a viewer audience of up to ten million people.

The whole situation is an interesting one. We await the outcome of all the talking and all the writing. Meanwhile the drummers keep on just missing their drums and the singers part their lips in silence and let their recorded voices sound out for them.

KRLA ARCHIVES

Oscar Night In Santa Monica

BEST ACTOR — Lee Marvin, presented by Julie Andrews.

The women snuggled into their mink coats and crossed the wind swept entrance area of the Santa Monica Civic Auditorium.

They came to see and be seen, hopefully to accept an award or watch a friend accept one and to gaze at show business' greats, from Bob Hope to Rex Harrison.

But best of all, they came. For the first time in many years the majority of the winners of the annual Academy Awards were there to pick up their awards in person and those who weren't had valid reasons — illness or filming problems.

Aside from the top awards shown here, the other top winners included Best Motion Picture and Best Direction—"Sound of Music." "Dr. Zhivago" led the field with 'Oscars,' followed by "Sound Of Music" with five and "Ship of Fools" and "Darling" each with three.

And once again they tried to express the unexpressable thanks due to America's number one entertainer, Bob Hope. But they had to make up a new award just for him—he became the Academy's first Gold Medal winner.

BEST ACTRESS — Julie Christie, presented by popular Rex Harrison.

BEST SUPPORTING ACTOR — Martin Balsam, Lila Kedrova presenting.

1ST GOLD MEDAL — Bob Hope.

BEST SUPPORTING ACTRESS — Shelley Winters, by Peter Ustinov.

THE SCENE — A cold and windy night at the Santa Monica Civic Auditorium in California.

SCENE STEALERS — Lynda Bird Johnson and George Hamilton.

KRLA ARCHIVES

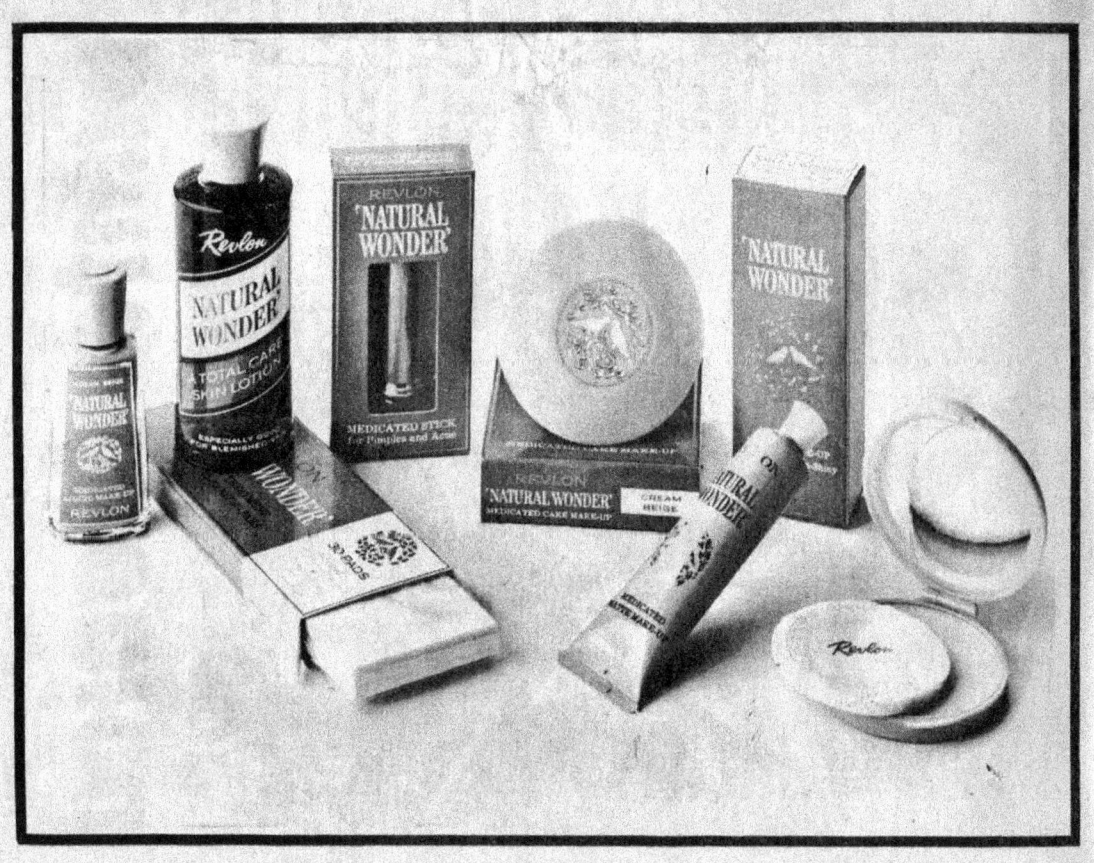

KRLA ARCHIVES

KRLA BEAT

America's Largest Teen NEWSpaper — 15¢

KRLA Edition

MAY 21, 1966

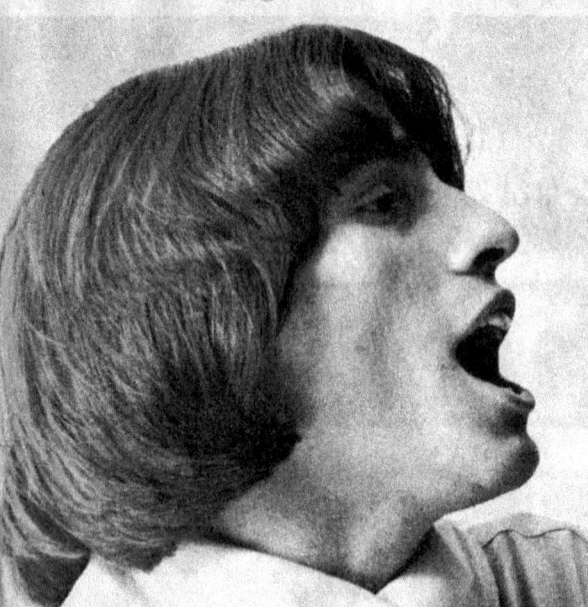

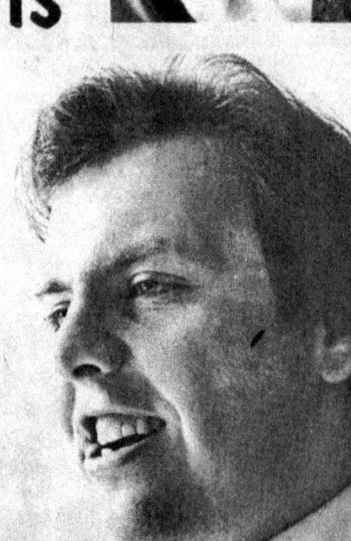

rascals every last one of 'em

KRLA BEAT

Volume 2, Number 10 May 21, 1966

Rascals Invade The World!!!

The Young Rascals are set to headline their own show at the Madison Square Garden in September. They tour Europe in August, there's a possible movie starring the Rascals to be filmed within the next eight or nine months, they've acquired a long-haired mascot, they have an up-coming schedule of appearances which just won't stop, they have a new single due out within the next three weeks, they're having problems deciding what to wear on stage. And six months ago the nation didn't even know if the Young Rascals were a group, a gang or a disease!

The Rascals' co-manager, Sid Bernstein, is the huge New York promoter who was responsible for the Beatles' mammoth show last August at Shea Stadium. He's the man behind this year's Beatle encore at Shea and booking James Brown into the Garden was also Bernstein's brainchild, one which paid off handsomely as Brown succeeded in selling-out, the first time a single artist had ever achieved such a feat in the New York showplace.

In other words, Bernstein never misses. He's a winner and now he feels that his Young Rascals (the only group Bernstein has seen fit to manage so far) are ready for the Garden and, consequently, he has booked them into the auditorium for a gigantic September concert.

The Madison Square Garden date will follow on the heels of the Rascals' first visit to Europe which they will undertake in August, the month the Beatles will be cooling it in America. Countries bracing themselves for a Rascal invasion are England, Italy, France and possibly Germany.

Meanwhile, the Rascals are fill-

(Turn to Page 6)

What Do You Really Want From Your Favorite Group

By Tony Barrow

JUST WHAT DO YOU WANT FROM YOUR FAVOURITE RECORDING GROUP? I ask the question as bluntly and as briefly as that because I get the impression that American fans are more easily satisfied than Britan's disc-buying public. If an American artist or group comes up with a jackpot-winning formula, the same money-spinning style is clung to through thick and thin. There seem to be very few American stars who would look back on a smash-hit record and say to themselves "O.K., now let's try something different. Let's be original. Let's not repeat any of the same ideas. Let's think new and be creative all over again." Instead your biggest names are content to be "type-cast" in their own particular style.

MAYBE THAT'S THE WAY YOU WANT IT.

Take Len Barry for instance. His "Somewhere" is more or less identical to "One-Two-Three" in everything except the basic tune and lyrics. In America he's taken "Somewhere" into the Top Twenty. In Britain it isn't showing at all on our charts although "One-Two-Three" was a best-seller.

Look at Nancy Sinatra. She's repeated everything we heard on "Boots"—with just minor modifications—on her new one "How Does That (etc.)". What's more she's grabbed hold of all the "Boots" gimmicks so firmly that they show up most of the way through her album tracks, too!

Don't get me wrong. I'm not belittling the major talents of Mr. Barry or Miss Sinatra. I'm just throwing out for discussion the suggestion that maybe you'd prefer to have these people come up with something entirely fresh each time they go into the recording studios.

Perhaps you'll accuse me of taking an extreme example if I bring The Beatles into the argument. But just look at the progression

(Turn to Page 5)

BEAT EXCLUSIVE

Beatle's New Single

The BEAT has learned some exclusive news from Tony Barrow which will probably be met with mixed reactions from Beatle fans. The Beatles follow-up to "Nowhere Man" will be "Paperback Writer" sung by Paul with John and George on chorus, backed with "Rain" sung by John with Paul and George supplying the falsetto chorus.

What's bad about that? Not a thing except that you will have to wait practically a whole month before the record is released! Due date is June 6, which means that May will have to roll by without a new Beatle record and "Nowhere Man" has already fallen off most of the charts.

Meanwhile, the Beatles are working on their next album which really should have been released long ago as "Rubber Soul" has been out for months although it still finds itself nestled securely in the nation's top twenty best-selling albums.

The June 6 release date for "Paperback Writer" will be met with approval by most pop groups as it means that they have a whole month to release *their* new singles. It's gotten to the point now that no one in their right mind will release a new record the same time as the Beatles. Even the Rolling Stones and the Yardbirds have admitted to cooling it with new releases until the Beatles have had time to hit.

The Stones' new one, "Paint It Black," will have no trouble in racing up the charts to number one and will, undoubtedly, be coming down as the Beatles' next single is coming up—therefore, avoiding collision at the top.

Inside the BEAT

Association Talk 2
Ike and Tina Turner 4
Knickerbockers' Soul 5
New Image For Rascals 6
The Animals Are Dead 11
For Girls Only 12
Adventures of Robin Boyd 14
BEAT Goes To The Movies 15

The BEAT is published weekly by BEAT Publications, Inc., editorial and advertising offices at 6290 Sunset Blvd., Suite 504, Hollywood, California 90028. U. S. bureaus in Hollywood, San Francisco, New York, Chicago and Nashville; overseas correspondents in London, Liverpool and Manchester, England. Sale price, 15 cents. Subscription price: U.S. and possessions, $5 per year; Canada and foreign rates, $9 per year. Second class postage prepaid at Los Angeles, California.

KRLA ARCHIVES

The Association Talk About The Association

By Jamie McCluskey III

There are some people in this universe whom you just don't interview—at any time, for any reason, anywhere. There can be a variety of reasons for this, but they all amount to just about the same thing: don't bother!

Such is the case with the Association. It is simply a physical impossibility to interview this group of gentlemen. There are six of them—all highly intelligent, all highly talented—and all highly *interviewable.*

Well, you *could* interview them, if you really tried, but it probably wouldn't make much sense to anyone but them. That's just the point: they're about the *only* ones who *really* understand what they're saying, and actually—they are the only ones really capable of interviewing them!

And that's exactly what they've gone and done; yep—interviewed themselves. On an evening just recently, I turned over my magical *BEAT* Notetaking Pen-and-combination-zap-gun (protected by Batman!) to all six of the Association, and what you see below is the result.

P.S. Good luck!!!

TED BLUECHEL JR.:

Well, here at the introspective interview of the self I feel I should tell a few of my beliefs to anyone who wants to live a life of experience.

That means to do as many things as you want or to encounter as many different situations for the sake of learning or experiencing.

One of them is to accept and love everything your understanding can allow. And, second, logically, learn to understand everything you encounter! Those are just a couple of my philosophical viewpoints which help my life become groovier.

Other than that, other things I do are that I really love music and the outdoors. I try to incorporate my beliefs into my music and freak out. I dig sincerity and honesty in people. I want to live at the beach when I am able to afford to.

I love money and its security but I like to live in a moderate, comfortable environment. I like the mystical scene, and think my parents and friends are all groovy people. Until then, if I don't see you in the future, I'll see you in the pasture!

RUSS GIGUERE:

What is your name? Russ Giguere.

What does the H. stand for? I don't know.

Is Bob Dylan? Yes, and a fine one.

Where is *it* at? I always keep it in my "potatoe."

Are a comedian? No.

Would you say something funny? Glad to meet you.

Is it true that you are foul? No, it's Ted that's foul.

Is it true that the ever all encompassing good irridescent effervesces constantly as a guiding substance heretofore unknown in the physical world? Well, I really couldn't say, but I have always been beneath the exterior.

GARY ALEXANDER: (Ed. note: No, your stereophonic, wide-screen, ultra-groovy *BEAT* column *isn't* out of focus. This next "interview" is *for real . . . we think!!!*)

BRIAN COLE:

Are you Brian L. Cole? No.

Do you pretend? Yes, why? No.

Are you really a bad guy? Yes. If you had it to do all over again would, etc. you do it all over everything? Yes.

Do you have talent? No, I'm riding on all the other guys.

Do you? Yes.

What is your Social Security Number? 541-46-4013.

Do you have columnist friends? Sure.

Russell (Rustte) says I shouldn't.

Are you a hippie? No, are the other guys? Yes.

Good nite Chet—cheerio Dave.
BRANK

JIM YESTER:

As long as you're not going to ask questions, I'll just rap for a while. I was born in Birmingham, Alabama, and spent my formative years there. At the ripe old age of three, I moved to Burbank, California, where I grew up slowly and in lots of sunshine. Father is a musician (piano player.) I attended Notre Dame High School, one year at Valley College, and three years in Germany with U.S. Army Special Services as a singer and banjo player.

After a few months in Greenwich Village, and Joshua Tree, California, I wound up here (Los Angeles).

On the BEAT
By Louise Criscione

Jeff Beck has recovered from his illness (reportedly meningitis) and has rejoined the Yardbirds. However, while he was in the hospital they discovered the sad state of Jeff's tonsils and the verdict was "out." Means that Jeff will head back into the hospital as soon as possible.

The Shadows of Knight are receiving all sorts of rave reviews for their stand at the Phone Booth. Their album, "Gloria," is pretty wild, too, pick it up if you haven't already.

Both Sam the Sham and his beard are back with the Pharoahs! Don't know what happened to change his mind about leaving but he's with the group now playing the Gay Haven Club in Dearborn, Michigan.

On Tape

John and Paul were recently talking about how they write songs. As soon as either one of them gets an idea for a possible Beatle song, they put it on tape. John admits that Paul's tapes are suprior to his as they contain dubbing and everything while John's have only his voice and a single guitar. Both reveal that this taping of their ideas is extremely important. Otherwise, they tend to forget them before they ever reach the recording studio.

...JEFF BECK

Wonder what happened to Lou Christie? He returned Stateside a week early from his English tour and promoter, Mervyn Conn, is reportedly considering legal action against Lou for breach of contract. While in London, Lou announced his engagement to U.S. singer, Timi Yuro. At least, that's what the papers said.

WHAT'S HAPPENING: The Young Rascals set for "Murray The K's Special For The Year 2000" which will be aired in New York on May 19 and possibly across the country at a later date. Hollywood expects the Rascals in July and England, France and Italy are preparing for an August Rascal invasion . . . Lovin' Spoonful wowing 'em in England. John says the Spoonful's sound is "happy time music with roots in Chicago blues" but Zal says they play "jug band music without the jugs" . . . Fans in England attempting to get Hal Wallis to re-release Elvis' "King Creole" again . . . Mick Jagger says the Beach Boys make "music to wake up by" . . . Pete Quaife of the Kinks is currently writing a book a'la John Lennon . . . John and George turned up at the Marquee to see the Spoonful . . . Beau Brummels in New York cutting a new LP, "Beau Brummels—66" . . . Remember that "Little Red Riding Hood" television special the Animals were on sometime ago? Well, it will be the American entry for the world's top TV award, The Golden Rose of Montreux . . . Dick Clark producing a country and western TV show for the fall season.

S & C For Europe

Sonny and Cher's movie is supposed to wind up shooting sometime in May and then the duo is set for a European tour but you know how movie schedules are! Anyway, the movie execs are certainly impressed with Sonny & Cher and have picked up two more options on them.

Johnny Tillotson heading for Tokyo to appear in a Japanese made film, "Goodbye Mr. Tears." Johnny will have a cameo role in the movie, titled after Johnny's record of the same name which became number one in Japan. Funny how some American artists have to go to a foreign country to make it. I can think of quite a few who have had to do it that way, can't you?

Dave Clark Five's next Stateside tour scheduled to kick off on June 12 with the group's twelfth appearance on "Ed Sullivan." They're the house group, I think.

Nancy Sinatra is in England for ten days. The dual purpose of her visit is to cut an album at the Pye Studios in London and to make promotional appearances on two major television shows.

Mitch Ryder and the Detroit Wheels are doing all right on their current tour of the East and Midwest. Fact is, they're doing "ripping" well. So far, they've lost $3,000 worth of custom made clothes which were torn, stolen and destroyed by eager fans. "Sometimes I feel like an ad for underwear," sighs Mitch who has come to the conclusion that he will spend considerably less on his clothes in the future!

...MITCH RYDER

Righteous Brothers: 'Don't Ignore Us'

By Louise Criscione

The Righteous Brothers. The Brothers Righteous. Bobby and Bill. It doesn't really matter what you call them. People know who you're talking about anyway. Two years ago you could have called them anything and no one with the possible exception of the Orange County hippies would have had any idea in the world who you were talking about.

But today the whole bag is different. The Righteous Brothers are solidly "in." Hollywood, New York, London and everywhere in between. They're "in."

A long time ago you could have knocked them over, pushed them aside or sat next to them in a drab classroom but today you can't touch them. They're the biggest duo in the entertainment field, second to absolutely no one. How did it happen? How did these two Orange County amateurs who are so alike and yet so different come to join the ranks of the highest paid and most in demand performers in the country?

Hazy

Even they're not sure how it all happened. They distinctly remember how it started. They know where they are right now. It's just that part in the middle they're a bit hazy about.

The whole thing had its beginning in Southern California's Orange County, the part of the state which used to be known for housing Disneyland but which is now being referred to as Righteous Brothers' country. Anyway, it sits outside of Los Angeles and is where Bobby and Bill each headed up their own combo in the early 60's.

They played in small clubs and tiny coffee houses and very slowly they managed to build up a following in Orange County, a following which was fiercely loyal and which if they liked Bill's group didn't particularly dig Bobby's. Naturally, Bobby had heard of Bill and Bill had heard of Bobby. So, on their nights off they took to catching each other's shows, as small and insignificant as they were.

Then in 1962, they were hit with the idea of merging, certain that this step would further their careers along. Merger completed, they were booked into the Charter House in Anaheim for a high school prom. They went over well and decided on the spot to add song writing to their list of achievements.

Lupe, Baby

Their first joint attempt at composing ended in the now famous "Little Latin Lupe Lu," a song that was later to become their first hit single.

From the clubs of Anaheim and Santa Ana, Billy and Bobby moved on to the Rendezvous Ballroom in Balboa, California, the scene of what was to become surfers' haven, the place where Dick Dale later held court for surfers, gremmies and ho dads from all over Southern California.

Their opening at the Rendezvous was disappointing. It was their first really professional date and the small crowds which greeted the boys those opening nights sort of made them wonder if they should have ever bothered leaving Anaheim at all. But word of their unique style spread quickly and before long crowds of 2,000 were lining up nightly to see them.

The song which seemed to go over best was "Little Latin Lupe Lu" and, in fact, local record shops were flooded with requests for the record but Bobby and Bill weren't even the Righteous Brothers yet! That came shortly after the Rendezvous when they were playing the Black Derby in Santa Ana.

The Black Derby crowd dug the rhythm and blues wailing of the guys so much that after each song they would scream out: "That's righteous, brother!" And the name simply stuck. They were all at once the Righteous Brothers.

From the Black Derby the newly dubbed Righteous Brothers moved from club to club but they never ventured far out of the Southern California area. They did make it to a club on the Sunset Strip and it was there that they were spotted by ABC-TV producer, Jack Good, the man who eventually sold an idea to the network – an idea which finally crossed your television sets for a few triumphant months as "Shindig."

The Righteous Brothers' popularity continued to spread and when Good finally produced "Shindig" he remembered Bobby and Bill and lost no time in securing their signatures to contracts which made them semi-regulars on the show. It also made them two of the most popular entertainers in the nation – pronto.

As the show grew older, Bobby and Bill were seen on "Shindig" less and less. Not because they weren't in demand – but because they were. Promoters were begging for Righteous Brothers' bookings and one by one the Brothers were knocking down every top club in the country and smashing attendance and gross records everywhere they went.

Hit After Hit

They've had only hit after hit – "Koko Joe," "Fanny Mae," "Try And Find Yourself Another Man," "You've Lost That Lovin' Feeling," "Just Once In My Life," "Hung On You," "Unchained Melody," "Ebb Tide" and "Soul And Inspiration." Their albums – "Righteous Brothers Right Now," "Some Blue-Eyed Soul," "Lovin' Feeling," "This Is New," "Just Once In My Life" and "Soul And Inspiration" – linger in the LP charts so long that people begin to wonder if they'll ever leave!

They travel around so much now that they spend more time in planes than they do in their Hollywood homes. They're popular but they're not exactly sure why.

"We don't have any gimmicks. Our approach is with one specific quality in mind – the heart of the song. We stick to our bag, one type of song. We don't do surf or hot rod or skate board," says Bobby. "People who hear us may like us or they may hate us, and that's all right as long as they don't ignore us, as long as they remember us. We have to grow. We're always choreographing and working on special material."

What's Right

"The secret is to create a mood rather than articulate words. When the lyric is good, then you hear the words. One of the advantages of making money is the freedom to do what's right and what you want to do," continued Bill.

Because they both believe in progressing, in always moving forward, they have definite ideas of what they'd like to do next. "After the national concert tours we want to do college tours," says Bill, "for there is a special kind of communication that we get with the students.

"Because of the difficulty we had in getting started we'd like to open a club that features nothing but new, young talent, a place to give them an opportunity to break in material.

So, the Righteous Brothers have moved from Orange County to the Strip, to "Shindig," to Las Vegas, to the world. They know they've moved – they're just not sure why. I wonder if they ever thought of narrowing it down to "talent"????

... BILL AND BOBBY GATHERING SOUL AND INSPIRATION.

... "WHAT'S THAT YOU SAID, BILL?"

KRLA ARCHIVES

Ike And Tina Deep And High

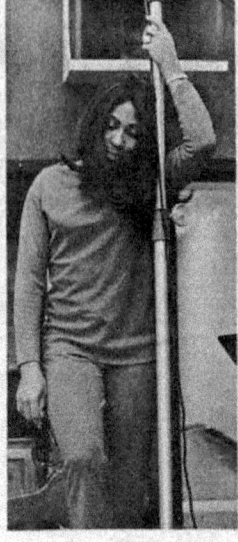

... IKE AND TINA TURNER TALKING IT OVER.

"River Deep, Mountain High," Ike and Tina Turner have signed with Phil Spector and there's no telling what fantastic sounds they'll come out with now! The whole Ike and Tina Turner Review which features their band, The Kings of Rhythm, and the soulful wailing of the Ikettes is currently out on a 90-day one-nighter tour which will take them through July.

Ike was born in Clarksdale, Mississippi where he was a disc jockey as a young boy but even then he was sitting in with different bands, playing the piano and writing. He soon tired of Mississippi and moved on to St. Louis. As it turns out it was a smart move for Ike because it was in St. Louis that he met Tina.

Tina was born in Tennessee but then traveled on to St. Louis where she took dramatics in high school, participated in all the singing and acting events at school and sang in the choir at the Baptist church.

After high school she worked as a nurses aid in a St. Louis hospital, often singing for the patients. During this time Tina obtained her first professional experience standing in for part time gigs with some of the local dance bands in St. Louis.

And then she met Ike. "It all happened by accident," recalled Tina. "While watching Ike on stage in St. Louis one night (he played the organ during intermission) I asked to do a number. The drummer handed me a mike and that was it! Ike liked my voice and I started out as an Ikette."

Their first hit single together sort of came about by accident as well. "Ike was about to record 'Fool In Love' but the lead singer didn't show up for the session," says Tina. "I knew the song, so I sang it. As Ike predicted it skyrocketed to popularity, quickly becoming on the top ten charts across the nation."

One marriage and four sons later, Ike and Tina Turner now have a happy home life as well as a successful show business career together. The duo first went out on tour as a duet in 1960. The tour carried them across the country to California and they both dug it so much that they decided to make it their permanent home.

Tina, often referred to as the "Bronze Bombshell," literally explodes the moment she rears back and belts out that first note. She has one of the most unusual voices in show business. It's hoarsy and throaty but she can also reach the very high notes with a clear brilliant tone.

Tina experiences all the emotions of her songs as she performs. None of those emotions she displays during a performance are contrived. They're real because Tina pours every ounce of her strength into every note. And such an effort is a strain on her 5'4" frame. "That's why I stand pidgeon-toed when I sing," she explains. "It helps me keep my balance as I strain to reach the notes and to react to all the various emotions in each song."

Tina digs performing with the Revue best of all. "In a big show with numerous artists you are limited and can't really show the audience what you have to offer. I enjoy my work and I like to feel close to the audience. I look into their faces as individuals, not just as a crowd. Because of this I always laugh when I sing."

Besides being recognized as one of the most talented female performers around, Tina is also rated one of the best dressed women in the business. She frankly states that Ike selects most of her clothes and admits: "He's very good at it and I like his taste."

Lately Tina has taken to making television appearances minus Ike because, "we have no duet numbers together." Ike heads the band and plays the guitar on stage and ocassionally shares the mike with his out of sight Tina.

Tina has appeared on all the television shows originating from Los Angeles. Sometimes the Ikettes are on with Tina to back her up, other times she faces the cameras alone.

Ike and Tina recently signed with Phil Spector's Philles Records and they're debut release on the label is, of course, the fantastic "River Deep, Mountain High." They've cut a new album which is scheduled for release within the next three weeks. They're really moving now and no one knows where they'll stop — or if they ever will.

... TINA, IKE AND "RIVER DEEP, MOUNTAIN HIGH" PRODUCER, PHIL SPECTOR.

KRLA ARCHIVES

Searching For Soul

By Eden

Most people don't think of the Knickerbockers as a "soulful" group, although certainly the boys have soul. They also have a large quantity of talent distributed generously throughout their four musical personalities.

Probably the most "soulful" member of the group is Jimmy Walker—the man behind the skins. He's the one who does the wailing "soul" songs for the group, and when we asked him to give us his impressions of soul, he contributed the following:

"It's just about the *vaguest* thing you can define! A lot of people say it's rhythm and blues, which is probably the closest thing to it. It comes out of gospel music, which is probably why they call it 'soul' music, because at the revival meetings—they used music to pray, and they probably figured that way it gets to your *soul* better, and that's where the term came from.

"But, it's been over used—as everything else has—it has been used as a product to sell; and now, anybody who imitates the Negro sound has, quote 'soul' unquote.

"But, I think Frank Sinatra's got 'soul' in a way, and the Mama's and the Papa's, and the Beatles, and anybody who sings with *feeling*. In the over used term – soul is *feeling*: just because you scream, doesn't mean you've got *soul!!*"

Buddy Rendell agrees that the rhythm and blues music does represent an important influence on our pop music: "R&B is, even now, a dominant influence—it always has been, ever since the advent of early rock and roll.

"It was based on a combination of some of the country and western things along with the rhythm and blues things, and it kind of weaved itself into American music, where it's there now to stay for quite some time, and I don't think it's going to go away now, unless some completely brand new thing comes and takes everything by surprise and makes it obsolete."

Although all four of the boys have a great admiration for the work and the musical experimentation being done by other groups, they feel that most of their own experiments in pop music lie in the vocal aspects of their music, rather than the instrumental.

Beau Charles explained this for *The BEAT:* "Luckily enough, we have a good blend of voices; all our voices kind of make it together for some reason—don't ask me why! We all have a different sound, but together we can get it to sound almost like one—which is good.

"Some of our songs—well, if *I* write, I put them through vocal calisthenics!! We just did a thing I wrote and they were all dying through the whole thing!

"We work more vocally on good songs—I think people still like to hear a nice, simple song with a good lyric and an easy thing that they can sing along with. I think they'll always be hits."

Brother John

Beau's brother John joined him then to explain: "We're pretty normal guys and we dig normal records, but we also look for things rather than different, and odd, and far out just because it will sell a record—we like to look for tasty things that are in context either with the music, or the song, or the lyric and have a universal appeal but still are listenable to the point that you don't have to think, 'what's that in the background?' and 'what are they doing there?'"

Jimmy made the discussion a threesome, agreeing: "When you get too far out, people just don't accept it."

Although the Knickerbockers have been rewarded with success and popularity throughout the pop world in the last year, there are still many things which they hope to do. Jimmy spoke for all of the boys:

Headline Wish

"Each of us has desires of our own, but as a group—I know that we would love to do concerts . . . and *headline.* This would be the greatest thing, as a group. And maybe later to go into colleges. Individually, Buddy wanted to go into arranging, Beau wanted to go into writing, I want to go into producing, John digs movies and acting. As a group we just want to cut records, and get the respect that we feel we've earned in the last couple of years."

Just a few short months ago, the Knickerbockers visited the offices of *The BEAT* for the first time. Four boys who had been building a fine reputation for themselves in a popular Hollywood nightclub for several months, with their first record just about to be released.

The record was "Lies," and it was one of the biggest hits of 1965. When I met the boys for the first time, they were just four talented, fun-loving, warm human beings waiting for their big break.

Nearly half a year later they are still the same four people with just a little change—they have had that break, and now they aren't just four talented musicians . . . they're just *great.*

What Do You Want From Your Favorite?

(Continued from Page 1)

there's been between "Please, Please Me" or "She Loves You" and "Nowhere Man" or "We Can Work It Out." Listen to "Help!" and then "Yesterday" or "Day Tripper" and then "Michelle." Musically The Beatles are on the move all the time.

Maybe you wish they'd stayed static with the simple but exciting beat format of their early discs? No, surely you don't because if that's all you're after you can hear the '64 sound of The Beatles re-created without too many problems by The Knickerbockers!

If The Beatles had decided to stay with their first successful style, their recording sessions would take about one tenth of the time. As you know, they've spent three weeks working in the studio on their next album and single. In fact the material is still incomplete. The reason is not that songwriting comes harder to The Beatles today than it did in '63 or '64. The words and tune don't take long.

But it's after those have been written that The Beatles really get down to work these days. They try different instruments, various vocal ideas. They record and re-record. They listen to play-backs and then add more new ideas. That's where the hours and days are consumed. That's why they average less than one track per day during their lengthy '66 sessions!

In fact they're taking all this extra trouble to satisfy themselves as much as anything else. Whether you would be just as keen to hear carbon copies of "She Loves You" or not, they're out to find new ways of presenting their material. It's a slow but thoroughly rewarding process.

Like John, Paul, George and Ringo, I believe all that extra thinking, all those extra session hours, are well worthwhile. But I often wonder if American Beatle People feel the same way about it.

KRLA ARCHIVES

...THE YOUNG RASCALS (l. to r. Felix Cavaliere, Gene Cornish, Eddie Brigati and Dino Danelli).

With Or Without?

(Continued from Page 1)

ing dates which will take them to Connecticut, New Hampshire, Massachusetts, Rhode Island and back again to Southampton, New York where it really all began for the Rascals at The Barge in the summer of '65.

June hopefully promises a breathing spell for the group before they again head out in July on a 30 day tour which will carry them through the Mid-West and into Southern California for a stand at either the Strip's Whiskey or Trip.

A New One

"Good Lovin'" topped the nation's charts and their first album, "The Young Rascals," is reported in the trades as being the fastest selling LP in the country but now it's time for a new single. Three weeks is the deadline because in order to make it to number one, they've got to hit after "Paint It Black" but before the next Beatle release. They've got 'em in the can but the hang-up is in trying to decide which two sides will go.

They've been booked for their second guest shot on "Ed Sullivan" and they've adopted a long-haired dog named Cuff acquired while the boys were on the West Coast. Cuff travels with them everywhere and was nationally introduced on "Hullabaloo" several weeks back.

Put-On

The Rascals currently have their minds messed up over a problem which you can help them solve. As you know, the Rascals appear on stage in knickers, Lord Fauntleroy shirts, etc. They wear these outfits for one reason only — they want to.

When *The BEAT* questioned them about it, we received three different answers. "We don't want to wear suits," replied Gene. "It's easy to play in," answered Dino. And the last and probably most logical reason came from Eddie: "We do it just to be different. It's really a put-on but we think our sound is much more important than the way we dress."

However, now they're having second thoughts about the whole thing. They're not quite sure if their outfits are dug, hated or simply ignored. The question is very much open for discussion — so what do you think?

Should they continue wearing the knickers? Should they discard them? Or do you even care? The Rascals will go whichever way you want them to, but you'll have to let them know and until you do the knickers are "in."

Mrs. Miller At Her Best

Batman may have met his match. It's not the Joker or the Riddler, but Mrs. Elva Miller, the little lady from Claremont, Calif, who's taking the country by storm with her first album, titled "Mrs. Miller's Greatest Hits."

In just the first week the record was released the reaction to it included:

A special election in Kalamazoo, Mich. where she was elected Honorary Mayor of the City.

She was greeted in Hawaii with the wildest celebration since Hawaii obtained statehood.

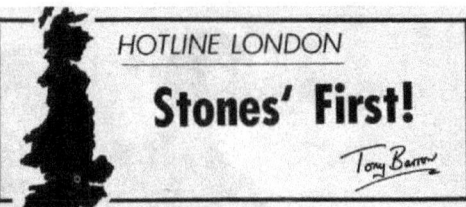

HOTLINE LONDON
Stones' First!
Tony Barrow

By the time you read this I expect THE ROLLING STONES will be heading for the top of the U.S. charts with "Paint It Black," the Mick Jagger/Keith Richard composition recorded in Hollywood on March 3.

In fact, American fans of The Stones have heard this new single before their U.K. counterparts — Decca will not issue "Paint It Black" in Britain until May 6.

A week later The Stones will showcase the single plus one or two tracks from their "Aftermath" album on one of the last programs in our "Thank Your Lucky Stars" series.

With new records and American concerts it looks as if The Stones are getting in just ahead of THE BEATLES. A new U.K. single from John, Paul, George and Ringo is expected in the third or fourth week of May. Latest summertime plans for The Stones mean that they're likely to undertake a short series of major concert appearances in America just a few weeks before The Beatles begin their August tour at Chicago.

The "Aftermath" album, on sale in Britain just two weeks, has moved into the Number One spot on our album charts — displacing the "Sound Of Music" movietrack from the top position.

* * *

Looks like there will be a rush to record "Aftermath" material for upcoming singles. Jagger and Richard are to personally produce a CHRIS FARLOWE recording of "Out Of Time" and THE ZOMBIES will make the "Aftermath" ballad "Lady Jane" the top deck of their next single.

* * *

MICK JAGGER, BOB LIND and JACK NITZSCHE attended a recording session together — but as spectators and not performers. They watched newcomer Reg Presley and THE TROGGS make their first single called "Wild Thing." And the finished product was just that!

* * *

NEWS BRIEFS... Stars flocked to watch THE LOVIN' SPOONFUL in action at London club date. Audience included BEATLES, JOHN & GEORGE, chart-topper SPENCER DAVIS and writer/singer JONATHAN KING... "Sadness" by ORNETTE COLEMAN (no less!) recorded by MARIANNE FAITHFULL... BESS COLEMAN, once 'our girl in New York' when she worked as a PR assistant with the Brian Epstein organization, has left the London HQ of Island Records to take up New York editorial executive position with *Teen Life* magazine... Liverpool group THE KOOBAS who toured Britain with The Beatles last December planning late-May promo trip to America... THE BACHELORS will be in New York for three weeks in May for Carson and Sullivan programs prior to Las Vegas appearance... Since STONES are known to love California so sincerely, BRIAN JONES' quote that Hollywood is "just like a big, horrible movie set" quite surprising!... 250 dollar portable TV set was BRIAN EPSTEIN's gift to CILLA BLACK when she opened a three-week cabaret season at London's classy Savoy Hotel... RINGO proving the superior chess player in 'tween-takes matches with road manager NEIL ASPINALL during current Beatles recording sessions... THEM considering Simon & Garfunkel title "Richard Cory" for U.K. single... Pity that her infanticipation will shorten London "Funny Girl" starring run for BARBRA STREISAND... Having announced August 4 as their scheduled Los Angeles marriage date, LOU CHRISTIE and TIMI YURO posed beside "Do Not Disturb" sign for photographers at London's Savoy Hotel... 18-year-old JOHNNY BLUNT replaced founder-member, leader and drummer CHRIS CURTIS who quit THE SEARCHERS immediately before the group left for America... Pozo Seco hit "Time" recorded for U.K. single by CRISPIAN ST. PETERS... For May TV series songstress DUSTY SPRINGFIELD paid dress and gown bill of over 7,000 dollars!... Under-deck title for latest PRETTY THINGS single is "L.S.D."... LOU 'n' TIMI promise they'll honeymoon in London... Complains Beatle John, sightseers keep organizing picnics on the Lennon lawns at Webridge!... MICK JAGGER searching Chelsea stores for furniture... HOLLIES bought great loads of cowboy gear in South Dakota... Watch out for striking record called "That's Nice," current fast-riser in U.K. charts for newcomer NEIL CHRISTIAN... GERRY (Pacemaker) MARSDEN to be a dad before September... Every batch of words exchanged during the BEATLES Tokyo Press Conference on June 29 will be relayed via an interpreter!... Celebrity audience of 200 at Savoy Hotel on Sunday, May 1 for colour TV filming of "Cilla At The Savoy"... Star-stacked invitation list for ROY ORBISON birthday party in London last week... PHIL UPCHURCH is latest new name in U.K. Top Thirty with "You Can't Sit Down"... GERRY & THE PACEMAKERS a smash-hit in cabaret at the Stockton Fiesta.

One More Down

Another teen-type television show has joined the list of shows that won't be back next fall.

ABC-TV's daytime soap opera, "Never Too Young," has been axed and will be aired for the last time in mid-June.

It will be replaced by "Dark Shadow," a mystery program produced in New York by Bob Costello.

"Never Too Young" has only been on the air since last summer.

Ringo: 'John's Personality Made Us'

By Gil McDougall

Whenever I sit down to write about Ringo Starr I suddenly have an immense feeling of happiness. The same kind of feeling that one would get when meeting Ringo for the first, or the one hundreth time. The little man from Dingle has been described by many, as the Beatle who is the swingingest in private. But in private, or in public, Ringo exhibits a tremendous feeling of good will to all men.

During his life Ringo has perhaps been cursed with a fair amount of illness and misfortune, but parallel to this is the luck and good fortune that he has experienced in his professional career. The Beatles together are a fantastic show business combination, but had they never joined together in one group, who know's what their fortunes might have been. Brian Epstein puts it this way: "Ringo was the catalyst for the others. He suddenly completed the jigsaw."

Ringo's Luck

In a way it was pure luck that Ringo ever joined the Beatles. But for his friendship with Paul and George he might still be playing the drums at Bulins holiday camp in Skegness. Of course, he would be playing them just as well, and probably having as big a ball as he is today, but the Beatles and the world just wouldn't be the same without Richie.

The Beatles are lucky in that they are all friends. As John has said: "Members of a group like this are usually not friends. I mean that they are friends but they don't necessarily hang around together on their days off. Sometimes a couple of them might go off and be friends, but usually they get enough of each other while they're working."

Though the Beatles popularity shows no sign of dying down, at one time or another they have all voiced the opinion that it must sooner or later. Ringo and John have both said: "We don't want it to go on forever you know."

One day the Beatles may dissolve their partnership and concentrate on quieter things. After all, it is a bit wearing to tour the world all the time. It is doubtful that they will ever stop recording as a group, but there is a possibility of each Beatle doing single records.

Comedy Role

If John and Paul decide to take some time out and try to write that musical that they have been discussing for some time, George might go solo and Ringo might decide to try a film comedy on his own. As a comedian he certainly has the potential.

Having been born in Dingle, which is one of the toughest parts of Liverpool, Ringo was more than ready for any obstacles that life might present. His series of illness' more than primed him for the hard aspects of life. Ringo was five years old when he was sent to St. Silas school. He started out well, but soon was stricken with appendicitis. Unfortunately, complications set in and for some time Ringo was expected to die. He didn't, of course, but nevertheless he had to spend some four years in that hospital. Anyone who has ever been in the hospital just a couple of weeks will know how very long that four years must have seemed to Mr. Starkey.

Ringo doesn't confine his activities to drumming and singing however. He would very much like to write some country music. He has actually done this. Together with John and Paul he helped to write "What Goes On," which appeared on the flipside of the Beatle hit, "Nowhere Man."

Ringo has said: "It was John's personality that made us." Though there is plenty of truth in this, it is not the entire story. They all participated, and Ringo no less than the rest. To George's next-door-boyness; to Paul's charming ways; and to John's irreverence, Ringo added the quaintness of the little man. The Beatles are superstars, but they are not super-humans. That is why we find it so easy to identify ourselves with them.

More To Come

Before the Beatles became famous, Brian Epstein made this claim: "They will be bigger than Presley." They may well turn out to be even bigger than Sinatra—and that's really going some. Despite all that they have achieved, despite all of the records that they continue to break, I can not help but feel that the Beatles haven't even begun to show the actual extent of their talents yet.

Ringo is a very fortunate man indeed. Not only is he a fantastic success, but he also has a wonderful wife and some of the most respected friends in the world. He also lives in a very pretty part of England. He lives in the country and yet is only minutes from the second biggest city in the world.

It has been suggested that the Beatles actually changed the face of London. This may be stretching it a bit, but they have had a tremendous effect on the city and its inhabitants. They have changed the lives of many people.

Ringo and the other Beatles get a big kick out of hobnobbing with other groups. At the premiere of "A Hard Days Night," Mick Jagger and Keith Richard turned up unexpectedly and Ringo and John demanded that they be invited in. At the 1965 Beatle concert in New York the Rolling Stones again turned up, and were greeted with great enthusiasm by the Beatles. As the Stones approached John was heard to exclaim: "It's the famous Rolling Stones!"

Ringo enjoys his fame, but he gets annoyed when he is singled out from the other Beatles for any particular honor. After all they are a team, and anything that they do, they do together. During the Beatles first tour he was very embarrassed by the "Ringo for President" campaign. It was only a joke, of course, but he still did not enjoy becoming the sole Beatle in the spotlight.

Whatever is to become of Ringo, the fact remains that he has already secured most of the things that man struggles to gain through out his life. He has made an excellent marriage; he has achieved fame and fortune; and he has obtained the friendship of half the population of the earth. That isn't too bad for a little man from Dingle.

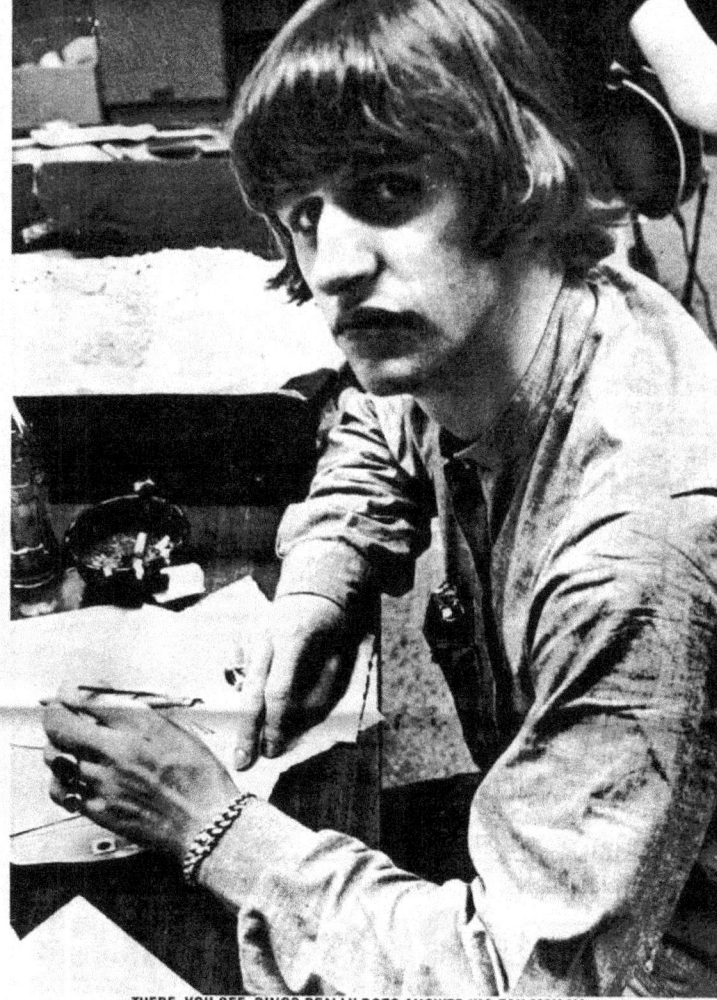

...THERE, YOU SEE, RINGO REALLY DOES ANSWER HIS FAN MAIL!!!

BEAT Photos: Robert Young

KRLA ARCHIVES

KRLA Tunedex

DAVE HULL

BOB EUBANKS

DICK BIONDI

JOHNNY HAYES

EMPEROR HUDSON

CASEY KASEM

CHARLIE O'DONNELL

BILL SLATER

This Week	Last Week	Title	Artist
1	2	WHEN A MAN LOVES A WOMAN	Percy Sledge
2	1	MONDAY, MONDAY	The Mama's & Papa's
3	6	HEY JOE	The Leaves
4	3	RAINY DAY WOMEN #12 & 35	Bob Dylan
5	22	A GROOVY KIND OF LOVE	The Mindbenders
6	4	TIME WON'T LET ME	The Outsiders
7	20	ALONG COMES MARY/YOUR OWN LOVE	The Association
8	7	SOUL AND INSPIRATION	The Righteous Bros.
9	12	THE SUN AIN'T GONNA SHINE ANYMORE	The Walker Bros.
10	5	THE RAINS CAME	Sir Douglas Quintet
11	9	SLOOP JOHN B.	The Beach Boys
12	11	MAGIC TOWN	The Vogues
13	13	LEANIN' ON THE LAMP POST/HOLD ON	Herman's Hermits
14	8	EIGHT MILES HIGH/WHY	The Byrds
15	10	GOOD LOVIN'	The Young Rascals
16	14	MESSAGE TO MICHAEL	Dionne Warwick
17	25	IN MY LITTLE RED BOOK	Love
18	24	TEEN-AGE FAILURE	Chad & Jeremy
19	19	FALLING SUGAR	Palace Guard
20	26	LOVE IS LIKE AN ITCHING IN MY HEART	The Supremes
21	18	A SIGN OF THE TIMES	Petula Clark
22	27	PLEASE DON'T STOP LOVING ME/ FRANKIE AND JOHNNY	Elvis Presley
23	21	RHAPSODY IN THE RAIN	Lou Christie
24	23	TRY TOO HARD	The Dave Clark Five
25	36	FUNNY HOW LOVE CAN BE	Danny Hutton
26	32	HOW DOES THAT GRAB YOU DARLIN'/LAST OF THE SECRET AGENTS	Nancy Sinatra
27	40	RIVER DEEP, MOUNTAIN HIGH	Ike & Tina Turner
28	33	NOTHING'S TOO GOOD FOR MY BABY	Stevie Wonder
29	30	CAROLINE, NO	Brian Wilson
30	—	YOUNGER GIRL	The Hondells
31	38	DADDY YOU JUST GOTTA LET HIM IN	The Satisfactions
32	34	I GOT MY MOJO WORKING PT. 1	Jimmy Smith
33	—	DID YOU EVER HAVE TO MAKE UP YOUR MIND	The Lovin' Spoonful
34	35	CRUEL WAR	Peter, Paul & Mary
35	—	THERE'S NO LIVING, WITHOUT YOUR LOVIN'	Peter & Gordon
36	—	COME AND GET ME	Jackie DeShannon
37	—	I'M A ROCK	Simon & Garfunkel
38	—	IT'S A MAN'S, MAN'S, MAN'S WORLD	James Brown
39	—	GREEN GRASS	Gary Lewis & The Playboys
40	—	I'D NEVER DO THAT	Jimmy Boyd

Beatles Coming, $100,000 Going

The Beatles are coming to Los Angeles again this August and they're planning to take a good deal of money with them when they leave.

They've been set for one evening performance in Dodger Stadium Aug. 28. Tickets will be the same as last year, $3 to $7, but the when, where and how they may be purchased, has not been announced yet.

The Beatles themselves have been guaranteed $100,000 against 65% of the gate. The $100,000 guarantee is a record for any entertainment act here in Southern California.

It's nothing for the Beatles though, who are sort of used to breaking records. They received the same amount last year from appearances in New York's Shea Stadium and the Kansas City Athletic's ball park.

Last year the Beatles received $45,000 a night for their two performances in the Hollywood Bowl.

Although they'll only do one show this year, more fans will actually be able to see them since Dodger Stadium holds over twice as many people as the Hollywood Bowl. The Bowl holds just under 20,000 while the Stadium holds 50,000.

This is actually a feather in Dodger Stadium's cap. They've been trying to lure in more entertainment acts since the L.A. Angels moved to Anaheim.

Tim Morgan At The Ice House

Tim Morgan, legendary folk hero of Fink Records, is currently appearing at the Ice House in Glendale.

This is Tim's first night club date outside of the beach area, where he tends his flock of legion fans.

He will be at the Ice House for a total of five weeks. The Travelers 3 appeared with him the first week.

The Deep Six, known for their first hit single, "The Rising Sun," will share the bill with Tim the last two weeks of the engagement, which ends May 29.

Petula Clark— 'Most Popular'

Pert Petula Clark, currently on the charts with "A Sign of the Times," has been named "Most Popular Television Performer" by Eurovision, the television system which telecasts in France, Holland, Belgium, Italy and Germany.

Petula will accept the award May 28 in Venice, Italy, during the taping of a one-woman television special she's doing for Italy's RAI network.

Eve's APPAREL
See if you can BEAT our prices on our new Jr. and missy lines. Samples at wholesale or less.
1800 N. Vermont
NO 3-4456 Hollywood, Calif.

Travelers 3 & Tim Morgon
Now Through May 29
The ICE HOUSE GLENDALE
folk music in concert
phone 245-5043 for reservations

SPECIAL BONUS — SUBSCRIBE NOW and receive a free copy of The Bobby Fuller Four's best selling album, "I Fought The Law."

KRLA BEAT Subscription

SAVE 33% Of Regular Price

☐ 1 YEAR — 52 Issues — $5.00   ☐ 2 YEARS — $8.00
☐ 6 MONTHS — $3.00
Enclosed is _____   ☐ CASH   ☐ CHECK
PLEASE PRINT — Include Your Zip Code

Send to: .... Age: ....
Address: .... City: ....
State: .... Zip: ....
MAIL YOUR ORDER TO: **KRLA BEAT**
Foreign Rate: $9.00 — 52 Issues 6290 Sunset, Suite 504
Hollywood, Calif. 90028

CARROUSEL THEATRE, Opposite Eastland Center, W. Covina
IN PERSON DIRECT FROM ENGLAND
DAVE CLARK FIVE
Exclusively on EPIC RECORDS
LATEST ALBUMS
"THE DAVE CLARK FIVE'S GREATEST HITS"
"I LIKE IT LIKE THAT"
"GLAD ALL OVER"
Plus A Great Supporting Cast
1 Perf. Only—Mon. June 27, 8 pm.
Seats at Box Office and by Mail Only
PRICES $7.50, $3.50, $4.50, $5.50
CALL (213) 966-4571

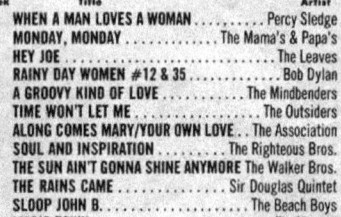
UNLIKE ANYTHING YOU'VE EVER SEEN!
WARNER BROS. SUPER CINERAMA PRODUCTION
BATTLE OF THE BULGE
Starring HENRY FONDA • ROBERT SHAW
ROBERT RYAN • DANA ANDREWS • PIER ANGELI • BARBARA WERLE • GEORGE MONTGOMERY • TY HARDIN • CHARLES BRONSON
HANS CHRISTIAN BLECH • WERNER PETERS • JAMES MacARTHUR and TELLY SAVALAS
Written by Philip Yordan, Milton Sperling • JOHN MELSON • Produced by Milton Sperling, Philip Yordan • Directed by Ken Annakin • A SIDNEY HARMON IN ASSOCIATION WITH UNITED STATES PICTURES, INC. PRODUCTION • TECHNICOLOR® • ULTRA PANAVISION®
PACIFIC'S CINERAMA DOME Theatre
SUNSET AT VINE • HOLLYWOOD
NOW PLAYING!
For Reserved Seats Information Please Call HO 6-3401 • For Theatre Parties & Group Sales Call PR 8-2519

MAY 10-15 ONE WEEK ONLY!
THE MITCHELL TRIO
Plus
LARRY HANKIN — COMEDIAN
AT DOUG WESTON'S
Troubadour
RESERVATIONS CR 6-6168
9083 SANTA MONICA BLVD.
L.A. NEAR DOHENY
MAY 19, 20, 21 — THREE DAYS ONLY — GLENN YARBROUGH

KRLA ARCHIVES

Inside KRLA

Whewwwwwww! What a week this has been! The KRLA studios will very probably never be quite the same again after the past few days.

It's been a hectic week around here with everybody and their brother-in-law's pet turtle dropping in to say hello. The Hollies — one really fab group from across the faom in Blightyland — passed through... sort of like a hurricane!

These talented boys who look so nice and quiet and normal at first glance are actually about the most exuberant, spirited, and *noisy* young men in the entire pop world! But that's okay, 'cause we luv 'em, and besides — they make very good records!

It was also birthday week in Hollywood for an old friend of everyone here at KRLA and at *The BEAT* as well. Joey Paige celebrated his 24th birthday, and several of his good buddies decided to help the festivities along by throwing Mr. P. a surprise party.

Believe it or not, somebody actually got word to Dick Biondi that there was a Fiendish Birthday Thingie afoot, and in a twinkling of a "Ditty Wah Ditty" Dick had the birthday boy himself on the air talking to his may fans in Southern California.

Happy Birthday, Joey!

It was really a very happy birthday for Joey, and he has asked us to thank all of his fans who wished him well; he really did appreciate your thoughts.

Jim Steck has returned from his European vacation (the dirty, well-rested rat!) and since he had the wonderfulness of his own kind-hearted, remembering self *not* to bother writing us... perhaps we can convince him to drop by the column for a few lines next week and tell us about all of his adventures.

I know one thing for certain now, though — I asked him to bring me a souvenir from Merrie Olde England; just one little, old remembrance from the Mother Country... but I certainly didn't see any Beatles hanging from his trunks when he fell off the airplane!! You really know how to hurt a girl, Jim!

Fiendish Plot

Our Bat Manager has been very quiet and very secretive lately, but I think perhaps it is only because he has been occupied dreaming up another fiendish plot to spring on his poor unsuspecting Bat Employees at the station.

Special note to Bill McMillon: with the warm weather returning, have you checked your air conditioner to be sure it's in perfect working order?

7 From Sonny

Sonny's been a bit busy lately. While filming his and Cher's first movie, "Good Times," he has also found time to complete seven songs for the movie.

With two numbers still untitled, he has complete "Good Times," "Just a Name," "Don't Talk to Strangers," "Trust Me" and a new arrangement of their hit, "I Got You Babe."

The movie is currently being filmed in Hollywood and is due for release in either June or July.

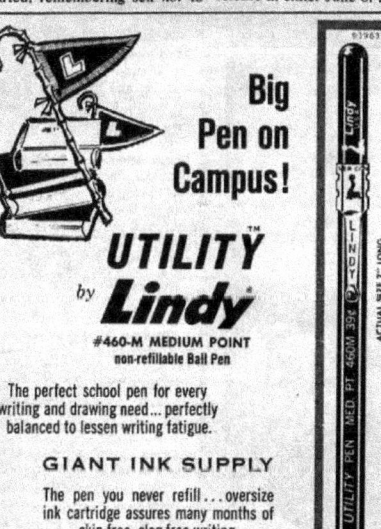

Big Pen on Campus!

UTILITY™ by Lindy®

#460-M MEDIUM POINT
non-refillable Ball Pen

The perfect school pen for every writing and drawing need... perfectly balanced to lessen writing fatigue.

GIANT INK SUPPLY

The pen you never refill... oversize ink cartridge assures many months of skip-free, clog-free writing.

39¢

12 BRILLIANT INK COLORS

Manufactured by LINDY PEN CO. INC., North Hollywood, Calif. 91605, U.S.A.

Guitar & Drum SPECIALISTS

GUITAR & AMP

Luster finished electric guitar plus big power amp for that Boss Surf Sound — Usually priced at $39.50 each. Now $29.95 each.

Combination Guitar and Amp.

$57.50* Complete

*Surfboard not included, but service always is at the G&D specialists
ALSO — FENDER... GIBSON... VOX, etc.

DRUM SET

Your choice of Blue, Red, or Gold Sparkle — This beautiful 4-piece drum set has chrome plated rims on six ply hardwood shells with durable mylar heads to give many years of keeping neighbors awake.

$189.50*

*Belly dancer not included, but drum lessons, guitar lessons, and a lightning course in belly dancing are available at the G&D specialists.
ALSO — LUDWIG... ROGERS... GRETSCH... SLINGERLAND

FOLK GUITAR

Fastest guitar in the West!!! See it at the G&D specialists. Top Quality at Unbelievable prices — Great Folk Guitars from...

$13.95*

*Honda not included, but wheel in anytime for after sale service, free tuning, or free advice on how to get your girlfriend to stop playing your guitar and start paying more attention to you.

YOUR LOCAL G&D SPECIALIST IS...

IN BUENA PARK	IN HUNTINGTON BEACH	IN VAN NUYS
Kay Kalie Music	**Manolios Music**	**Adler Music Co.**
805 ON THE MALL	18547 MAIN STREET (5 POINTS SHOPPING CENTER)	14115 VICTORY BLVD. (AT HAZELTON)
IN SANTA FE SPRINGS	IN TUSTIN	IN SIMI
Kay Kalie Music	**Winn's Music**	**Adler Music Co.**
11504 TELEGRAPH RD. (THE SHOPPING CENTER)	540 E. 1st STREET (IN LARWIN SQUARE)	1792 ERRINGER ROAD (NEXT TO SAFEWAY)

KRLA ARCHIVES

Norma Tanega's World Of Beautiful Music

By Barri

A young woman raised in an atmosphere of art and music, she loves "beautiful things," and says "I always wanted to make music."

That young woman—who studied classical piano for 12 years, obtained a B.A. in Art History and Painting, and a Master's Degree in Painting and Graphics—is making a lot of music these days. And very beautiful music it is, too.

Her name, Norma Tanega. Her first record, her first hit, "Walkin' My Cat Named Dog." Her first home, Mare Island in the San Francisco Bay where she was born during World War II, in January of 1943.

Her father was a Band Master in the Navy for 30 years, and her mother was a student of painting and sculpture. Shortly before the war in the Pacific broke out, the small family moved to the United States.

Norma first began to show her love for music when she was just four years old and she began to play the piano. By the time she reached the end of her teen years she was an accomplished pianist, painter, poet, and singer.

Musical Student

After high school, Norma went on to Scripps College to obtain her B.A. degree, and upon graduation, entered Claremont Graduate School. While there, she was able to utilize her many years of musical training to teach herself to play the autoharp, banjo and the harmonica.

There was a brief period of time after Norma completed her graduate studies, spent in New York for the purpose of simply "absorbing life." Then, she went on to Europe "to see what I had studied during my college years."

Although she sang in youth hostels in France and Spain on her tour of Europe, Norma had never performed professionally until after she had returned to the States and was discovered by Herb Bernstein, who is her present producer and arranger.

She names the Beatles and the Andrew Sisters as her two favorite groups, and claims favorites in other fields of artistic endeavor to include Vincent Van Gogh, Maximilien Robbespierre, Franz Kafka, Dostoyefsky, Isadora Duncan, Carl Millis, Barlach, and Garbo.

Many Facets

Truly a talented young woman of many facets, Norma wields her musical pen in as many areas as her interests. She writes about the beauty of the ordinary things in life—and raises them to a level of importance seldom seen by the average person.

Somehow, Norma seems to have captured the child's innocent wonder at the glories of the world and nature all around us and she has put them into the music she sings and shares with everyone.

To follow up her first nationwide hit record, Norma will soon release another of her own compositions, "A Street That Rhymes At 6 a.m."

It may not rhyme with very many things, but the name "Norma Tanega" is rapidly becoming synonomous with sensitivity, beauty, and rare talent in the world of contemporary music. It is becoming a very integral part of a world of very "beautiful music."

DISCussion
By Eden

First bit o' wax set to spin around our column this week is a little further info on some of last week's waxations. I mentioned that Peter and Gordon had a new record out that was probably going to be a hit, entitled "Stranger With A Black Dove."

Also mentioned that there wouldn't be any composer hang-ups this time around (you all remember our friend Bernard Webb of "Woman" fame?) as the tune was penned by a non-Beatle type. Just one thing I forgot to tell you: Peter and Gordon have finally gone "deep" on us, and *they* are responsible for the penning of this new platter.

* * *

The Outsiders are currently occupying hit positions on charts across the nation with their first successful disc, "Time Won't Let Me." In hopes of providing the platter with a companion smash, the boys have released a new record: "Girl In Love," b/w "What Makes You So Bad, You Weren't Brought Up That Way."

The latter (you didn't really think I would say it *twice*, did you?!) is an uptempo tune and *might* have a possibility of someday becoming a moderate follow-up chart success for the boys. But it's only an *outside* chance!

* * *

If you've all been watching the telly lately, and maybe boning up on your Lebanese a little, you are probably familiar with Danny Thomas. Well, Danny decided that he wasn't about to let Jerry Lewis and clan get ahead of him in the pop world. No siree! So Danny's son—Tony Thomas—went out and formed his own group.

They chose—originally enough—the Thomas Group as their official name, and they have a brand new record out on the Dunhill label. Another Sloan-Barri tune—"Penny Arcade."

It's a strong song once it gets going, and the beginning is just a little reminiscent of "You Baby." There are five boys in the group—all between the ages of 18 and 20—and this new disc could be an important beginning for them. Lay an earlobe on it and see what you think.

* * *

I am very happy to report to you at this time that contrary to some popular opinion, Barry McGuire did *not* get destroyed. Now he is back again with a brand new record you really won't believe.

At first listen, you might be inclined to think that the blond bombshell who sang about the "Eve" has suddenly gone Lovin' Spoonful on us, but he hasn't. He's simply come up with a brand new sound that can only be described as "Rag 'n' Roll!"

Or as Mama Cass puts it—"Rag Rock." Barry has recorded the old Bud and Travis tune, "On A Cloudy Summer Afternoon," with a ragtime, Dixie-land influence stamped all over it.

And it's great! Yep—this one's gonna blow some minds. Could be his biggest since "Destruction," and if it is—it should put him right back on the "Eve" of Success!

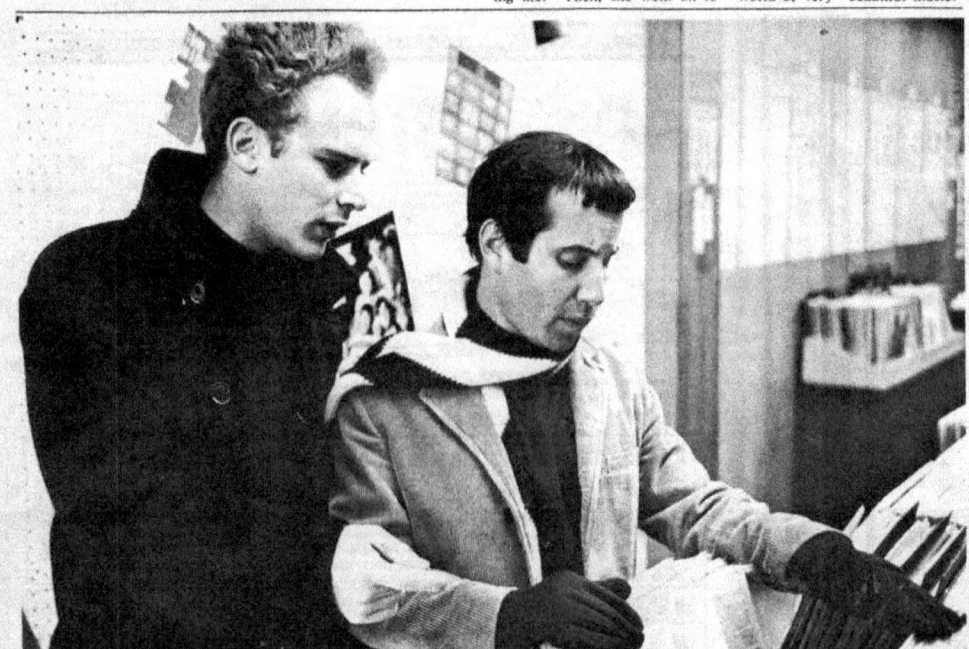

STEADY AS ROCKS—Simon and Garfunkel broke onto the scene with "Sounds of Silence" and people talked about their funny names. Then came "Homeward Bound" and people began to realize that something was happening. Not it's "I Am A Rock" and the realization that Paul Simon and Art Garfunkel, the two New York singers who are just outside the "message bag," are here, not only to stay, but to be a major influence as well.

KRLA ARCHIVES

'The Animals Are Dead'

I submit to you this obituary. An open letter, if you wish, to The Animals and all their fans. Whether you print this is a matter of your own integrity; it is in the minds of many and I believe it needs to be heard.
— B.A. Tremayne, a BEAT Reader

The Animals were five extraordinarily talented men. The adhesive which creates groups is unique and indefinable; in their case almost unbelievably superb. When I met them in 1964 they were happy, determined and optimistic. I respected them for their personal as well as professional integrity.

As a writer I met quite a few groups, and each time I went away respecting The Animals a little more. I didn't respect them solely because they were five intelligent, decent human beings; I respected them as a whole. Their collective personality was indeed one of many contradictions, but it was one of hard-core honesty and sincerity. Not everyone who has met The Animals liked them, but they respected them, and perhaps were even a bit in awe of them.

The Animals were great. I say "were" because The Animals now exist in name only. A sound, an image, an identity — who can say surely what creates it; but when it exists you can feel it. Somehow five specific individual sounds, images and identities came together with an unknown adhesive producing something memorable.

Alan Price, whose name the group carried in its earliest beginnings, is a gifted musician. His inimitable style and perceptive instincts provided the perfect catalyst for Eric Burdon's sensitive lyric style and impelling dynasm. Johnny Steel's subtle jazz born drumming complimented Chas Chandler's fine bass within the most demanding definition of perfection. Hilton Valentine's very personal technique rounded out this unbeatable team.

The Animals were irrevocably resolved to set the world on its ear. I believe they would have. It is maddening as well as saddening to realize how demanding today's public is of its artists. How sad it is that a person must sacrifice his private life to the god of commercialism to gain professional recognition.

Alan Price, fatigued and driven to his limit of endurance left The Animals abruptly. Today he says: "I wandered out of the house to get a coffee and think things out, then the next thing I knew, I was sitting on a train bound for Newcastle. I was so exhausted, I must have been in a daze."

Alan Price went out for a cup of coffee and The Animals lost a link in their chain of perfect reaction. They were never quite the same. Dave Rowberry is a fine musician, but he's also a distinct individual. Things didn't jive like they used to; the chemistry had changed.

John Steel has a responsibility to his family, and he feels he can't fulfill these important responsibilities and maintain his career at the same time. The person who replaces John will undoubtedly be a good drummer. But then it won't be the same, will it?

How long before Eric decides to go it alone? Eric, unchallenged as the greatest white soul singer in the world, can only follow the path he has already laid. The public will accept him as a single because that's the image he has projected; Eric talks more of *his* career, than the group's career. This is good, this is the essence of Eric's uniquely individual approach to everything.

When will Chas conclude he's too old to bang on a bass guitar at all corners of the world, before a horde of screeching girls? He'll be 28 this year. Chas will make a good manager, he's already voiced his intention to go into the agency side of the business. Only Hilton knows which way his life is going. Perhaps he too will turn to the lucrative agency business.

What I'm saying is that The Animals, the magnificent artists who soared to fame with "House of the Rising Sun," and made such memorable musical statements in their L.P.s, are dead. The Animals still exist technically, but the once in a lifetime combination of Alan, John, Chas, Hilton, and Eric is dead.

This is not so much an obituary as it is a eulogy. When I stood offstage watching The Animals in 1964, I never imagined I would be writing of their death. As I thrilled to their brilliance and admired their rugged individuality, I allowed myself the luxury of detaching myself from journalistic objectivity, liking them as people, and becoming a fan. From that time of my first encounter, my admiration and respect for them has only grown.

I have detached myself once again to write this, my own very personal statement of regret and sadness. I'm sure I'm not alone in my feelings. I hope you will print this, if only in respect to the memory of what they once were. Because no matter how hard they work, they can never reachieve that instantaneous combusion created when they knocked them out in the Tyneside clubs that inspired them, and brought them together.

A Lucky Mistake For The Outsiders

By Carol Deck

Far from being "outside," the five young Cleveland lads who call themselves The Outsiders are fast becoming the "in" group of 1966.

Their first record, "Time Won't Let Me," was released early in January, didn't do much for about six weeks, then suddenly took off and sold over half a million copies in just three weeks.

Leader of the quintet is Tom King, although there are actually only four regular members of the group. The fifth, a drummer, has always been temporary.

King wrote "Time Won't Let Me" and credits his brother for helping him get started in music.

"He taught me to play," Tom says. "We liked the 'Third Man Theme' when it first came out and thought it had a great sound. We duplicated it on guitar. Of course we didn't find out until later that the song had been recorded on a zither!"

That lucky mistake proved to be the start of Tom's career and The Outsiders.

While playing in clubs around Cleveland Tom met Mert Madsen, a native of Denmark who became interested in pop music through the U.S. armed services.

"One day on the Armed Forces radio I picked up a broadcast from Germany that featured Elvis Presley and 'Heartbreak Hotel.' That sold me."

By the time he came to America he had learned to play several instruments including accordian, harmonica, guitar and bass.

Lead vocalist for the group, Sonny Geraci, had sort of lost interest in music until the Beatles came along. He was stirred by the sound the Beatles could produce and started singing locally. After several years on the local spots, he met Tom and became an Outsider.

While these three were deciding how to get their group started, a student at the University of Pittsburgh had formed his own group

and was playing college dances. Bill Bruno found out about the Outsiders at a party. The group needed a lead guitar player and Bill was the man.

After adding a drummer, they played around the Cleveland area some more until the first recording happened.

Sonny kept prodding them to try recording but Tom had cut several discs before, without much luck, and was discouraged.

He didn't want another bomb and he didn't want to cut something that any other group had done.

"Okay," Sonny said, "So write us a new song."

Tom did and after a mere four hours recording they took it to a Capitol Records executive and were signed to their first contract.

With the success of "Time Won't Let Me," they've gotten a little less leary of recording and have an album due for release this month.

English Long-hair Joins U.S. Army

John English is British.

Less than a year ago he had shoulder length hair and was a member of The Preachers.

Now he has a standard U.S. Army hair cut and proudly wears the uniform of this country's army although he's still a British subject.

And he doesn't regret for one moment cutting his hair or going in the army.

John more or less went into the army voluntarily. He was drafted on December 13 and the same day he enlisted in order to get more of a choice of what he did in the service.

He could have easily gotten out of it. He's a British subject living here on a permanent visa and all he had to do was go back to England and they couldn't have touched him.

But he feels that if he lives in this country and takes advantage of everything it has to offer then he has to pay for it just like everyone else.

An Extra Year

Because he enlisted he'll have to spend three years instead of two in the service but he's doing what he wants to. He's in weapons training at Fort Ord now and he's continuing his career as a singer but as a solo singer now.

"The Army's not as bad as I thought it would be," he says. "It's good experience, as long as they don't send me to Vietnam."

As it stands now the only way he'll go to Vietnam is as a performer to entertain the troops.

As for his hair, he had a Beatle cut for quite a while then he really let it grow, down to 12 to 14 inches long.

"I liked it when I had it," he says. "But I did want to cut it."

John cut his hair before he actually went into the army.

"I wouldn't have ridden down there on that bus with my hair long for all the money in the world."

And now he's glad that he did cut it. "After you cut it off it feels real good."

From Preachers To?

The Preachers, who have since disbanded, were a very long haired and very wild act. Where did they go? Well, John's in the army, three other members of the original group are in The Vejtables, one is in The Bees and one is a physicist for Lockheed Air Corps!

John's starting out on his career as a solo singer and he has his first single release out now. It's called "Moanin'" and it's an old jazz number that's pretty wild.

There's another member of the U.S. Armed Services who's made a lot of noise on the pop scene and that's S/Sgt. Barry Sadler.

Commenting on Sadler's "Ballad of the Green Berets," John says, "We used to hate it in basic training."

About Barry Sadler John says, "I think he was lucky, but I admire him — he's making a name for himself."

John's somewhat unique in the pop world. He's one singer who deliberately and voluntarily cut his hair and went into the armed service.

It isn't so bad after all according to this one exception.

...JOHN ENGLISH

More Awards For Motown

The Motown dynasty has proven once more that they're tops by walking off with the greatest share of the BMI (Broadcast Music Inc.) Awards for 1965.

Jobete Music Company, Motown's publishing company, won 12 of the awards which are presented annually based on trade paper polls of national popularity acceptance, reflecting record and sheet music sales as well as radio and television performances.

The writing team of Brian Holland, Lamont Dozier and Eddie Holland won eight of the awards while William "Smokey" Robinson, lead singer of the Miracles, won three.

Jobete was cited for the following songs:

"Back In My Arms Again," "I Hear A Symphony," "Nothing But Heartaches," and "Stop In The Name of Love," all recorded by The Supremes and written by Holland-Dozier-Holland.

Singles Hitting

(Continued from Page 1)

However, the Yardbirds are going to have to rush out another single or else wait until after June 6 to release a follow-up to "Shapes Of Things." The time is perfect now, so you can expect a rash of new singles within the next month. Recording artists aren't stupid, you know, so they'll be attempting to hit somewhere in between "Paint It Black" and "Paperback Writer."

So, watch out 'cause here they come!

 # For Girls Only
By Shirley Poston

Well, I'm back!

How did I manage to escape from those men in the white coats when they came for me with a net (and I don't mean Funicello?) Easy! Only next time they come for me, I'm going to be better prepared. It took me *hours* to cut through all that mesh with those little manicure scissors.

Now, in an effort to keep from blithering incessantly about one senseless topic, I will resort to my list of tactics and blither incessantly about several senseless topics.

1 — FOREHEADS

First it was orange popsickles, then it was feet. Now it's foreheads. And something tells me it's going to get worse. However, before it does, I've got to tell you about this really retarded idea I've come up with.

Have you seen the banana (banana?) (details, details) commercial where the girl pastes the Chiquita sticker on her forehead? (If you haven't, I have the feeling *you* may be coming for me, too.)

Well, I think it looks rather cool, and I'll bet *anything* it becomes a huge giant fad to go around with goodies glued slightly above the eyebrows!

Gasp! That reminds me of something I did one time! My mother literally *forced* me to go out with this real snurd who was visiting one of her friends named Fred. No, I don't believe that will do at all, Shirl. The snurd's name was Fred, not the friend's. Oh good grief, what *difference* does it make??

Anyroad, I did something really snaky (I meant to say sneaky but I do believe I have a point there) (and, if I wear a hat, no one will even notice it.)

What I did was cut out a small square of paper. Then I wrote something about Fred on it (let it suffice to say that the something was rather *unkind*) and pasted same on my forehead under my bangs.

He couldn't see it, of course, but it gave me the most *fiendish* feeling. Everytime he said something really moronic, I'd think of what was written there and what he'd do if he *did* see it and about fall out of my tulip laughing.

Okay, okay, so I'm not well. Okay, okay, so I also forgot all about the list thingy.

2 — ROBIN WAS HERE!

I want to thank Georgia (luv that name) Fraser of Los Angeles for the grooviest present I've ever received in my entire life (this is living?) Also for the most fantarvelous (parddon?) idea in the entire world.

Georgia sent me a bunch of little stickers that say *Robin Boyd Was Here!* What you're supposed to do with them is paste them in the world's most unlikely places. Like on the inside of a gas cap (which, as anyone knows, is a cap you wear when you get gassed) and that kind of thingy. Or inside the principal's desk drawer. It's more fun to watch people's reactions when they see the dealies.

When my ship comes in, I'm going to have a whole bunch of them printed and send them out to whoever (as in whomever) wants some. (Wants some *what*? How should I know?)

3 — ILL, ILL, ILL

I just thought it was time to remind you that I have spent several million paragraphs raving about stickers. Which reminds me (of something totally unrelated, of course.) I'd also like to thank all of you who've been sending me letters on *that paper* again. What I mean is, I'll thank you to stop sending them!

And I also do not think it is funny that several of you have suggested that my column be re-titled "For Gawd's Sake." (I think it's *hilarious!*)

Well, I can't stand it another minute, so here goes. SPEAKING OF GEORGE!

Oh, pain. Somewhere at this very moment he is actually inhaling and exhaling. (Well, I certainly *hope* he is!)

4 — GREAT DREAM!

Want to hear another whopper? Too bad, you're going to anyway. It was sent to me by a fellow coward who asked that her name not be printed, and her name is... oh relax, would I do anything that vile? (Never answer that question.)

Anyroad, here's her masterpiece!

"I live in England in a quaint little village somewhere. My father is a horrible ogre. He makes me work for him so I decide to run away from home.

"I do this by hopping into an open trunk (as in car), and pretty soon some unobservant chauffeur slams the lid down.

"When I regain consciousness, I crawl into a big basket and close it's lid (this is an *awfully* big trunk.) Finally, the automobile stops. The trunk opens and the basket is lifted up and carried up some stairs into a room where some rather familiar voices are heard.

"One of the voices (called Ringo) asks the other three voices (called John, George and Paul) why the empty laundry basket weighs a ton. I, of course, choose this choice moment to jump out and yell *surprise!*

"Fortunately, the engine is missing from under the hood of the car at this secret hideaway which is hundreds of miles from civilization. And we've been having a jolly time for the past three years. (The engine, hallelujah, has never been found!)

5 — GOODBYE FOREVER

(Don't you wish.) Cute dreamo, what? I sure hope she's keeping her hands off my George though.

And I sure hope I'll be able to do the same when August rolls around (*Sure* I do.)

Speaking of rolling, a large truck just rolled up in front of the house and if I know what's good for me I think I'd better start searching for a larger pair of scissors!

Oh, before I go (which will take some doing because I've been gone for years), I'm curious as to how many of you noticed my gross goof in the Beatles at the Cavern chapter of R.I.B. More about that next week. More gross goofs, too.

Sunrays: 'It Takes A Lot Of Capital'

The Sunrays are not the Beach Boys. They are not related to the Beach Boys and they don't intentionally mean to sound like them. It *is* true, however, that the Sunrays once wore the same striped shirts which have become the Beach Boys' trademark, and it's also true that Murray Wilson (Beach Boys Carl, Brian and Dennis' father) is their manager.

Whether their association with the Beach Boys has been a help or a hinderance to the Sunrays depends on which side of the fence you're peering over. From what they themselves say, one gets the definite impression that the Sunrays are not the least bit worried about it and rather tend to think that it has helped their career along.

However, they become quite up tight if confronted by publicity claiming that they are a mere imitation of the Beach Boys. "We didn't try to follow them," admitted Eddie, "it's just natural. When you sing five part harmony it always comes out that way."

They joke and kid around about Murray Wilson but they really think the world of him and state frankly that if it wasn't for him they would probably still be playing local clubs and school dances.

"He's the greatest man in the whole world and if he told me to jump out of the window – I wouldn't," laughed Rick.

"The thing that nobody realizes is that it takes a lot of capital to get a group started," said Marty. "Our manager is interested in us not only as dollar signs but he's like a father to us and he took a great risk in us."

That risk has apparently paid off as the Sunrays have had two giant smashes—"I Live For The Sun" and "Andrea." And "Still," their latest release, is making noise in certain parts of the country and from the way it's selling, looks as if it will break out all over the nation.

The Sunrays are all in college and find that mixing school with a career is "very hard." They manage by appearing on weekends, touring during vacations and studying in between.

For instance, Easter vacation found them in such places as Portland, Salt Lake City, Vancouver and Toronto, and this summer the Sunrays head out on a 60 day cross country tour which will hit practically every major city in the nation.

Switching the talk from strictly Sunrays to general competition in the pop field today we wondered if the Sunrays found themselves faced with more competition than when they began playing five years ago.

"It's always been competitive," answered Rick. "The span of a hit record now is so short, which is why there are more groups around today."

The Sunrays are probably one of the most outspoken groups on the scene – they know what they like, dislike and feel strongly about. "We don't dig people who come on too strong," declared Rick, "you know, people who've had one hit record and come on strong. We're the humbliest guys in the world!"

They also don't like artists who come out with the same sounding records time after time. "We don't like that at all," said Byron. "It's bad and in poor taste."

"It's like saying to the kids that they're a bunch of idiots. A bad record will never make it," finished up Vince.

"It's like Motown," said Marty re-opening the closed subject. "I'm really getting sick of Motown, every record sounds the same. But they keep selling – wow!"

It's been quite a while since I've heard an artist say that they really dug Elvis but that's exactly what Byron told me. In fact, he even has a horse named Elvis. "Elvis has always been one of my biggest fans," said Byron howling when he discovered that he had just said it backwards. "Seriously, I've always dug that cat. This horse reminded me of him."

And with that the Sunrays proceeded to sing "Still" at the top of their five ample voices, devour all *The BEAT's* in the office and then proceed merrily down the hall and out of the building. Too much – that's all we can say!

...THE SUNRAYS IN THEIR OLD STRIPED SHIRTS AND WHITE PANTS.

THE MODERN SUNRAYS (top to bottom, Marty DiGiovanni, Eddie Medora, Rick Henn, Byron Case and Vince Hozier) in their up-dated, modern velours.

Junior Success—Dino, Desi And Billy Style

Dino, Desi, and Billy... a modern success story, junior style. Although the boys are just fourteen years old, they have already managed to come up with two hit records — with their first two releases.

The boys are currently concentrating on their educations, which is of the utmost importance to all three. For this reason, it is very difficult for them to make many personal appearances or to make any plans for extended personal appearance tours around the country. Their personal manager, Mac Gray, explains that "school keeps them all very busy, and everything else is secondary to them right now."

It may be secondary, but that doesn't prevent them from receiving several large mailbags of fan letters daily from their many fans —both young and not-so-young— for which they must have two girls who do nothing but handle their mail.

In just a short time, the boys will again go into a recording studio to produce their next single, and working as producer on the session will be a man named Lee Hazelwood, who was also responsible for Nancy Sinatra's record, "These Boots Are Made For Walkin'." Also, there is a very strong possibility that the boys may make a motion picture—the first for all three—for Paramount in the near future.

... DINO, DESI AND BILLY

The Adventures of Robin Boyd

By Shirley Poston

CHAPTER TWENTY-EIGHT

When Robin Boyd's alarm clock rang at promptly seven a.m. that Saturday morning, she did the only sensible thing.

She staggered sleepily to the dresser, silenced the jangling with a murderous left hook, stumbled back to her trundle bed and crawled under it.

As you know, there are several (thousand) people who already strongly suspect that Robin has dropped one or two. And only their absence from the scene of *this* smooth move prevented the organization of a mass marble hunt.

Which is just as well. Although one of her favorite aggies was missing, Robin hadn't quite lost *all* her marbles (yet). She was simply trying to escape from someone whose steelie bag had been empty for years.

Namely, her sister Ringo. (Think that sounds far-fetched?) (Stick around, it gets worse.)

Changed

Things had changed in the Boyd household during the past couple of weeks. For one, since the good Dr. Andersrag (as in nut) had given her daughter a clean bill of mental health (an act he will refer to in later years as his *first* mistake), Robin's mother had stopped knitting a colorful collection of straight jackets. She had even stopped thumbing hysterically through the yellow pages, now content to wait until they made it into a movie.

What's more, Ringo Boyd's attitude toward her older (not to mention beloved) (not unless you're a pathological liar) sister had shifted gears and gone into reverse.

In the past, their relationship had consisted of a series of right-to-the-point-not-to-mention-the bone droomstick thrusts. But, due to Robin's recent and mysterious disappearances and her strange attachment to the olde English tea pot that resided on the living room mantle, some of the spearing had been replaced by *peering*.

In other words (English, preferably), Robin Boyd was up to something, and if it was the last thing Ringo Boyd did (promises, promises), she was going to find out *what*.

Hence, Robin's down-under tactics. When Ringo sneaked noiselessly (as in herd of herds) into her sister's room, she would discover still *another* mysterious disappearance. And Robin was in for a few more hours of peaceful repose while the sturdy secret agent looked *that* one up in her U.N.C.L.E. handbook.

Although she had furnished her hide-out with all the comforts of home (a blanket recently put out of its misery by the Boyd dog, who had never liked it much anyway because wool gave her hives), it was awhile before Robin could go back to sleep.

And it was no small wonder. There was so much to think about and remember. Seeing the Beatles at the Cavern (in 1961) (told you it gets worse) . . . and, of course, her own dear George Genie. (A name she was going to have to do something about before she marched him off to the altar.) (*Robin Irene Boyd* was quite bad enough, thank you.) (You're welcome.)

Off To Sleep

And, with this thought in mind, Robin instructed an all too chummy flea to stay on her *own* side of the blanket (or was it *his* own side) (where some things in this world are only impossible, others have got to be kidding), and wafted gently to dreamland.

Precisely one-half hour later, she was rudely removed from same by the insistent prodding of a strategically aimed droomstick.

"How did you find me?" she groaned as her sister's twelve-year-old face (the rest of her was twelve-and-a-half to hear *her* tell it) came into view.

"It was easy. You snore like a mack truck," Ringo replied tactfully.

Forgetting where she was, Robin sat up. "*Ratzafratz*," she soon bellowed (among other things), closing her remaining eye in agony. (She had *hoped* for a *spring* day, but hadn't meant to be taken quite so *literally*.)

Re-groaning, Robin rolled out from under the bed gracefully (as in kick over the nightstand, stupid, and smash the all-day sucker that had two perfectly good hours left to live.)

Not Sister's Keeper

"Whaddyahwant?" she snarled in a tone which subtly implied that although she was not her *sister's* keeper either, someone had best apply for the position swiftly.

Ringo twirled her droomstick. "There's a John D. Winston on the phone," she said. "D. as in dolt," she added.

Robin re-re-groaned. (Where some people are only losers, others are *losers*, and John D. Winston was a perfect candidate for the latter category.) (She would have never bothered with him in the first place if his name hadn't been the same as Lennon's first two.) (A comment only Lennon himself could possibly hope to follow.)

"What does that creep want?" she asked finally, knowing that being on a phone was a position to be reckoned with and wanting to make his discomfort last as long as possible.

Ringo shrugged, jamming her mouth full of the linty remains of Robin's late sucker. "I think he wants to know what time he's supposed to pick you up."

Robin glowered. "Pick me *up*?? What does he think I am, a *pick-up*?" (Robin, as you know, has a tendency to become repetitious shortly before becoming violent.) (No one is perfect.)

Never Faints

Ringo re-shrugged and re-stuffed. "Of course he does," she soothed. "He also thinks he's taking you to the prom tonight because you promised six months ago that you'd go with him."

If there was one thing Robin Boyd did *not* do when faced with shocking news, it was faint. But that was the *only* thing she didn't do. Included in her ladylike reaction were four hysterical yelps, three moments of advanced heel-kicking, and two attempts at flinging herself out the window (a death-defying three foot drop.) One giant bang of the olde head against the olde closet door served as a finale.

When she was quite finished (using the term literally) (no, make that loosely, as in teeth), Ringo gurst into wild applause. "I take it you forgot," she chortled.

Darting a daggerish look which subtly implied that her sister not only took it correctly but knew what she could do with it, Robin limped in the direction of the telephone.

At the close of the lengthy conversation (3½ seconds approximately, or however long it takes to shriek *why-was-I-born*) which followed, Robin looked to make sure that Ringo was still munching contentedly (as in cow.) Then, grabbing a coat, she lifted the lid of the tea pot and implored George to meet her on the corner.

On her weary way to same, Robin blithered inwardly. She was *trapped*. She'd promised and now there was *no way out*. She was going to have to go to the prom with that *microbe!* Not even George could help her out of this pickle (not as in dill).

But at least he could comfort her sympathetically. And since her sympathetically could sure *use* a little comforting, she started running the moment he came into view. Off at the mouth, that is.

George didn't say a word until she'd finished her sad story. And, for a moment, she was almost afraid he might be mad or something. Then she immediately put such thoughts out of her head. Sure George was a little on the jealous side and sure he had a temper and sure he'd been known to shake her until her teeth rattled on occasion (not to mention the floor.)

Wanna Bet

But he wouldn't get livid over something like *this*. Not when she *already* had *more* than enough problems, thank you. (You're welcome.) (Stop that!) (Anything you say.) George was too *understanding* for that, and really very *gentle* in his own Liverpudlian way.

"Okay," he said when she'd ceased raving, his eyes growing deeper and darker as he stared down at her. "You can go out with another guy on one condition."

Robin gave him a lower of the olde eyelash. "Whatever you say, George," she simpered.

George narrowed those aforementioned deep-darks. "Good! Because I say *over me dead bod!*" he hissed *understandingly*, as he delivered two *gentle* yanks which forever spared her the expense of having her ears pierced by a professional.

(To Be Continued Next Week)

Workin' That Mojo

The King of the funky organ has taken up singing.

You've learned to expect the unexpected and the unusual from Jimmy Smith, the world's number one jazz and blues organist, but are you ready for his singing?

He's just released a new album, cut last December, that features a full seven and a half minutes of "Got My Mojo Workin'" that's guaranteed to upset your soul.

Jimmy brings to his usual hypnotic organ playing a voice that reminds you of the best of the best.

He's a restless, probing artist with deep convictions and a great awareness of his responsibilities as a serious artist. He knows the importance of communicating to his audience and he rarely fails.

Born in Norristown, Penn., back in the 20's, Jimmy began his music training on the piano under the attention of his mother and father, who both played.

As a pianist, he played with a number of groups around his home town and soon became known as one of the leading Bud Powell disciples. Even today, it's amazing that the brilliant technique Jimmy displays on organ is equalled on piano.

By 1955 he had mastered the organ and was ready to go try it in the jazz market.

He was booked into the Cafe Bohemia in New York along with his two close friends, Thornel Schwartz and Donald Bailey. They were to be an intermission group.

It didn't take long, though, for people to discover that something was happening with Jimmy Smith and his organ.

Other musicians began to come down to see Jimmy. They'd bring their instruments and play far into the morning, much to the distress of the club's owner.

And Jimmy Smith became a full fledged artist with something important to say – and that was that the organ was a legitimate instrument in any field.

Jimmy's not afraid to try anything. He's played many of the major jazz and blues spots around the world and he's chalked up a collection of 21 albums featuring some of the top names in his field.

His recording of "Midnight Special" was the first to make the national charts but that soon disappeared under the avalanche of requests and sales of his swinging "Walk on the Wild Side."

In his willingness and desire to communicate his music to the people he's toured the South while many of his peers refused to take *their* message south of Washington D.C.

In 1962 he made his first trip to Europe to appear at the Antibes Jazz Festival and discovered he was already a star over there. The Europeans had never seen Jimmy live before, but they'd bought his records and they'd heard him over Voice of America and they made him the real star of the Festival.

In his restless drive to challenge the ability of the cumbersome organ to produce the sounds he hears and to reproduce the feeling of his Music, Jimmy Smith remains uncompromising.

He's added his voice to his message now but he knows that the number of ways of expressing his jazz soul are unlimited and you can be assured he won't stop finding new ones.

The BEAT Goes To The Movies
Promise Her Anything

By Jim Hamblin
(The BEAT Movie Editor)

If nothing else, this picture will be the biggest publicity windfall in years for the perfume manufacturer who uses the title as a selling slogan. As a matter of fact, those in the movie trade were given a sample bottle of the stuff when they attended private screenings.

It seems that nothing ever makes sense in this world of make-believe ... and this picture is a classic example. The story and plot all are placed in New York's Greenwich Village, which is sort of a campground for kooks. So, where's the logical place to film the story? *London, England, of course.* At Shepperton Studios they carefully constructed an exact replica of Greenwich Village for the occasion.

But however complicated the producers want to make life, they seem to have themselves a rather well done movie in the process.

The cinema screen lost a great and talented dancer when Leslie Caron decided to move into dramatic acting, and so far her *new* career has yet to make up for the loss of the *old* one.

But Miss Caron does wear a terrific two-piece outfit that nobody should miss!

Her male co-star, Warren Beatty, has had more space in gossip columns than theatre marquees, but unexpectedly turns in one of his better performances in this sort-of domestic comedy.

Portraying an amateur photographer who makes nudie-cutie films, he runs afoul as a babysitter and even winds up getting married.

There is a steady flow of laughs, and starlet Asa Maynor provides some sumptuous legs to look at.

THE REAL STAR OF THE SHOW turns out to be baby Michael Bradley in the movie filmed in England.

SOME HIGH LEVEL CULTURE with sign repairman Lionel Standler.

KEENAN WYNN, seen without his motorcycle on.

BOB CUMMINGS—the untroubled baby doctor.

KRLA ARCHIVES

ANDY WARHOL'S smash scene from N.Y.

THE PLASTIC INEVITABLE SHOW

THE VELVET UNDERGROUND AND NICO

AND THE M.F.Q.

THE TRIP
8572 SUNSET STRIP
PHONE 652-4600

FLIP OUT! SKIP OUT! TRIP OUT!

you have to see it to believe it
happening 'til May 18th — fall by

OPEN 2 A.M.–4 A.M.   HIGH FLYING FOOD
Warhol's Underground Movie

Food & Fun 'til 2 A.M. — Age 18 & over with I.D.

WHISKY A' GO-GO

Don't miss it!

May 11th to May 22nd

Everybody's talking 'bout the return of

Johnny Rivers
King of The Go-Go '60's

8901 Sunset Strip
652-4202